THE FundLine Advisor

1999 Edition

Also by the Authors

The Beginner's Guide to Investing:
A Practical Guide to Putting Your Money to Work for You

THE FundLine Advisor
1999 Edition

The Essential Mutual Funds Handbook for Canadian Investors

Richard Croft & Eric Kirzner

HarperBusiness
HarperCollins*PublishersLtd*

For information address HarperCollins Publishers Ltd,
Suite 2900, Hazelton Lanes, 55 Avenue Road,
Toronto, Canada M5R 3L2.

http://www.harpercollins.com/canada

First edition

Cover photograph: Russell Monk

Canadian Cataloguing in Publication Data

Croft, Richard, 1952–
The fundline advisor

1999 ed.
ISBN 0-00-638657-1

1. Mutual funds - Canada. 2. Mutual funds - Canada - Rankings. 3. Registered Retirement Savings Plans.
I. Kirzner, Eric, 1945– . II. Title.

HG5154.5.C765 1998 332.63'27 C98-931393-X

The material in this publication is provided for information purposes only. Laws, regulations, and procedures are constantly changing, and the examples given are intended to be general guidelines only. This book is sold with the understanding that neither the authors nor the publisher is engaged in rendering professional advice. It is recommended that legal, accounting and other advice or assistance be obtained before acting on any information contained in this book. Personal services of a competent professional should be sought. The authors, publisher, and all others directly or indirectly involved with this publication do not assume any responsibility or liability, direct or indirect, to any party for any loss or damage by errors or omissions, regardless of the cause, as a consequence of using this publication, nor accept any contractual, tortious, or other form of liability for its contents or any consequences arising from its use.

98 99 00 01 02 03 04 WEB 10 9 8 7 6 5 4 3 2 1

Printed and bound in Canada by Webcom

To my wife, Barbara,
and my children
Christopher, Loa and Machaela
—R.C.

To Helen, Diana, Jennifer and Jordan
—E.K.

The publisher wishes to thank the Royal Bank of Canada for providing its trading floor at *The Royal Bank Plaza*, Toronto, as the backdrop for the cover photograph of this edition of *The FundLine Advisor*.

Contents

List of Figures

List Of Tables

New for 1999

The first edition of *The FundLine Advisor*, published in October 1996, was a success in a couple of ways. The book obviously filled a need because it sold well, which is very gratifying for us. But also, the critics gave the book mostly positive reviews, although they did point out some things that needed our attention. So we made some changes to make future editions better value for our readers.

We have created a benchmark index to help investors assess the value the fund manager is bringing to their portfolio. Like everything else in life, the person running the show has to be held accountable. So many variables affect the performance of a mutual funds portfolio, that creating a benchmark for a manager was difficult to do—but very necessary.

Also, we needed to talk about how to invest in mutual funds inside an RRSP. It is imperative that no matter what our age, we need to look at retirement planning, and the RRSP is the most pervasive—yet underutilized—vehicle available to Canadians.

We added the category of "Dividend" funds to the FundLine as a significant component of mutual funds investment. In addition, the term "momentum" replaced "market timing" at the recommendation of the financial community.

For the 1999 edition of *The FundLine Advisor* we added some exciting elements, again because of the acceptance of the book in the financial community. We created the Financial Post Indexes, or the FPX as they are called, that are updated weekly, and we will talk about their purpose and benefit for the investor. Also new for the 1999 edition are discussions of segregated funds, a much-overlooked investment tool; bank packaged products and whether they are intelligent investment choices, especially now that, apparently, size does matter; and our take on ethical investing, currently a hot topic.

The Best Bet funds are all new for this edition, and our regular entertaining (and we hope on-the-money) feature, our economic forecast, is our look at the year ahead in terms of money and markets.

Why We Wrote This Book

We cannot escape the fact that our financial well-being is critical to our overall well-being. People in a strong financial position are more confident, make clearer decisions and, although we have no ready statistics to make the point, probably live longer. A weak financial position, on the other hand, can strain your family life, cause anxiety at work and force you to make decisions that are not always in your—or your family's—best interests. So, like it or not, we need some level of financial independence.

Most Canadians understand this. A study conducted by Decima Research showed that "87% of Canadians agree that saving for retirement is very important." Talk to most baby boomers and they will take that position one step further. They simply don't believe the government, principally through Canada Pension and Old Age Security, will be able to provide any measure of support in their retirement years. The more skeptical baby boomers believe that the Canada Pension Plan will be empty of funds by the time they retire.

The point is, we understand the importance of establishing a set of objectives, putting in place a long-term plan and periodically re-examining our position with so-called financial checkups. *Unfortunately, many don't do it!*

Statistics from that same Decima study showed that 50% of Canadians make only a token effort to review their finances, and those who do, do so less than once a year. Even more startling was the fact that only 25% of Canadians regularly contribute to a Registered Retirement Savings Plan. So, what's the problem? We understand what is needed, yet many of us fail to act.

We think there are a couple of reasons for this. Issue number one for most individuals is not knowing where and how to start. And often, when seeking advice from those in the financial services industry, individual investors end up with more questions than answers. You may find, for example, that a stockbroker will tell you why this stock or that bond is a good investment, but not be specific on how it fits within your long-term financial objectives and risk tolerances. A financial planner, on the other hand, might provide excellent tax advice and a reasonable financial blueprint, yet not be able to recommend the right investments to get you to where you want to go.

For individuals who fall into this camp, we have some straightforward advice. This book is geared to you, because it will provide the foundation on which to build a long-term investment plan. It will do so within the context of your sensitivity to risk and your personal financial circumstances.

Issue number two, and a difficult one, concerns the investor who distinguishes *investing* from *investment planning*. These individuals have a more sophisticated knowledge, or think they do, about the financial markets. For them, investing is as simple as Will Rogers once advised: "Buy a stock that goes up. If it doesn't go up, don't buy it."

These individuals invest to earn a profit. Fair enough! But making an investment with little or no thought as to how it fits within your personal financial circumstances is akin to setting out on a cross-country trip without a road map. When you get lost, it is critical you get off this road and back onto a proper investment planning path. Establish some goals, construct a balanced portfolio to meet your personal circumstances, and then, when you are well on your way, go ahead and make some of those short-term investments with confidence.

What *The FundLine Advisor* Is About

The FundLine Advisor is more than just a book about mutual funds. Think of it as your one-stop shopping guide to investment management. Updated every year, this book will provide you with an annual financial checkup and, more than that, will act as your guide every step along the way. We will show you how to get ahead with your money and provide you with the tools to help you get your money working for you, rather than you working for it.

We will help you to see the big investment picture and not get caught up in the emotions of the moment; to buy when everyone is standing on the sidelines; to know how to invest for the long term and what to invest in. In short, we will take you step-by-step through the world of investing with a long-term investment plan that will meet your objectives and let you sleep at night.

These are the principles on which this book is built. You will, in the chapters that follow, learn all you need to know about personal investing and portfolio construction. And you won't have to predict changes in the business cycle, the direction of interest rates, the outlook for inflation or whether or not a particular stock will rise or fall.

We'll help you establish long-term goals, walk you through a lesson in risk management and examine the need for self-discipline. And having developed a reasonable long-range investment plan, we'll construct a portfolio to get you from here to there, using a top-down approach that focuses on you, rather than on your investments.

The Croft-Kirzner Approach

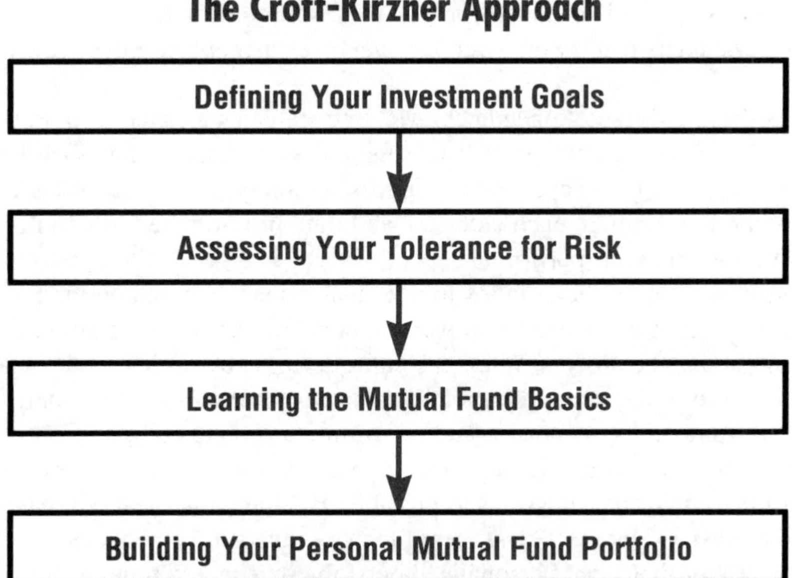

When it comes to selecting specific investments, you can pick and choose from our list of **Best Bet** funds in each category, judged not solely on the basis of past performance but in terms of risk-adjusted performance. The funds were chosen using two criteria:

1. The proprietary Manager Value Added (MVA) index that evaluates funds on the basis of risk-adjusted performance and consistency. To be included in this category, the funds must have at least a three-year track record, although we occasionally provide honorable mentions—without providing a score—for funds with specific objectives that we think will pay off in the year ahead.
2. An examination of each fund in terms of investment style and the approach of the fund's management, as defined by our exclusive FundLine. In other words, the FundLine provides the basis to mix and match funds within your portfolio, providing solid returns with the least amount of risk.

As for the ongoing management of your portfolio, you need to simply purchase the yearly updates to this book. In these updates, we will provide our ideal asset mix in terms of what percentage you should commit to each asset class for the year ahead, and update the Best Bet funds in each category.

You Be the Guide

You may choose to read each chapter in sequence, to make sure you understand the fundamentals that support our approach to investment planning. For example, Chapter 2, "Your Risk Profile," provides an in-depth discussion of risk. Chapter 3, "Mutual Fund Categories," looks at the essentials of mutual fund investing and discusses the merits of load versus no-load funds.

If you are a fairly sophisticated investor, you may want to skip the fundamentals and move right through the chapters that lay out your personal investment plan. Either way, we'll be there by your side.

For our Best Bet funds (see Appendices), we used statistics gleaned from Pal-Trak's database of funds. Of course, we cut the potential candidates down from more than 1,800 to fewer than 100, all having—with rare exceptions—at least a three-year track record. We want to recommend only the top funds in each category and then provide the tools to mix and match investment styles within your portfolio.

As mentioned, we use the MVA index to rate fund managers based on the fund manager's risk-adjusted performance numbers relative to a benchmark. But we caution that the MVA index is but one step in the process. While the index defines how well a fund manager has balanced risk and return in the past, it offers no guarantees for the future and, more importantly, it examines each fund on its own merit, and not within the context of a portfolio.

To properly construct a portfolio of funds, you want to mix and match Best Bet funds that fill as many of the FundLine categories as possible. By doing that, you will have a personalized portfolio diversified by asset class, geographic region, fund objectives and management style—in short, a well-balanced personalized portfolio that should remain strong through all the different phases of a business cycle. And just for good measure, we'll also give you some advice on how to fine-tune your portfolio using our economic outlook in the FundLine forecast (see Chapter 13).

For even a casual observer, the results of not planning for the future and investing wisely should be obvious. Looking for government handouts during your retirement years is not a very appealing alternative—especially when you can create your own situation with some judicious planning now.

The issue is not whether to invest; it is how to overcome the real or imagined hazards of investing. Don't walk away from the capital markets because the game is too complex. It needn't be!

Acknowledgments

Writing a book of this nature is a daunting task. The objective was to write a book that is different—a one-stop top-down guide to investment planning that takes you from the asset mix decision all the way to the FundLine—an understandable approach for mixing and matching mutual funds within a portfolio. At the end of the day, you end up with a well-balanced portfolio that does not sacrifice performance.

A successful book requires a great deal of support. A special thanks to Toronto-based Portfolio Analytics who supplied much of the data in the appendices, and who worked closely with us providing the number crunching for our MVA index, and to the entire staff at HarperCollins.

Also, a special thanks to Manulife Securities, who have supported me in my work as a consultant and mutual fund analyst, and to the mutual fund companies for their support and input in the development of the FundLine.

—R.C.

PART I

Your Investment Personality

CHAPTER ONE

Personal Investing: Pillars and Perils

Investor Personalities

We believe the first step in any sensible investment program, and, we might add, one of the more difficult aspects of investment management, is gaining some understanding of your investment personality. *Your investment personality dictates how well you can tolerate risk and, more important, lays the foundation for you to quantify the trade-off between risk and return.*

For example, conservative investors are more interested in not losing money than in earning big returns. Aggressive investors, on the other hand, are willing to forego safety of principal and income in search of greater profits. Seems simple enough, but in reality most investors fall somewhere between these polarities. Even conservative investors have to be willing to assume some risk, and some aggressive investors may not have the financial wherewithal to handle the roller coaster action of the stock market. There are, as you might expect, trade-offs. Our approach is to look at investment management the same way a professional money manager looks at it. And to that end, we present four personal investment cornerstones as seen in Figure 1.1.

Figure 1.1: PERSONAL INVESTMENT CORNERSTONES

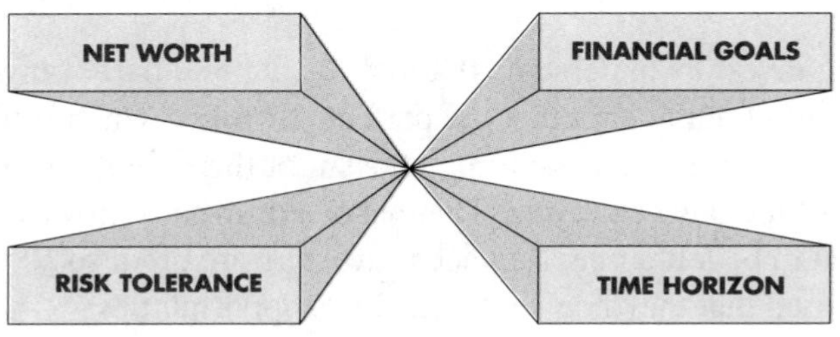

(Note: Pension fund managers think of "Net Worth" as "Assets under Administration." "Financial Goals" becomes the "Required Rate of Return." "Risk Tolerance" for the professional pension fund manager is evaluated using actuarial studies to determine cash inflows and outflows, year over year. The final issue is "Time Horizon," which for a pension fund manager is unlimited. As individual investors, we have a more defined time horizon.)

We offer six distinct investment personality categories and present at the end of Chapter 2 an optimum asset mix for each. (See Figure 2.3.) The asset mix is the second step down the road to independent financial freedom.

1. ***Safety*** investors are uncomfortable with risk. They lean toward investments that provide regular returns, even if these returns are low. Their attitude toward financial planning is apprehensive and, at times, pessimistic. Whereas others dream of wealth when they invest, safety investors are motivated by the dread of poverty.

2. ***Safety/Income*** investors are concerned about safety but often require a specific income stream to meet their financial obligations. They recognize the need for a trade-off. Safety/Income investors want to make certain their principal investment is secure but share a keen interest in the income that can be generated by that principal investment. We find many retirees who may be living off a fixed income and require the receipts from their portfolio to supplement their living standards in this investment category.

3. ***Income/Growth*** investors focus their attention primarily on the income side of the investment equation. However, unlike Safety/Income investors, the portfolio's income stream is not usually considered a critical supplement to their standard of living. At least not yet! Often we find that Income/Growth investors will reinvest the income stream into more securities within the portfolio, effectively dollar-cost averaging their investment program. Income/Growth investors understand that financial security depends on some growth being attained within the portfolio and, to that end, will spend a great deal of time understanding just how much return is required to meet their long-range financial objectives. They often set more reasonable goals that, for the most part, can be attained with their investment style.

4. ***Growth/Income*** investors understand that risk is a natural part of investing. With this in mind, they set out to structure the perfect portfolio, which is usually a balanced investment scheme. The assets are chosen for their ability to survive the ups and downs of the business cycle. There is one drawback, however: the portfolio is designed to be left alone. Balanced investors are often so absorbed with day-to-day survival that they neglect tomorrow's opportunities.

5. ***Growth*** investors are not at all concerned about income. Usually, this group of investors has a long time horizon and often a sizable net worth. The objective here is to maximize the potential growth within the portfolio, with reasonable risks. Growth investors have an appreciation about the trade-off between risk and return, and are willing to assume higher levels of risk as long as they are rewarded with greater returns.

6. ***Aggressive/Growth*** investors are the quick-draw artists of the investment world, fingers often poised to move from one opportunity to another. They switch from asset to asset, thriving on risk, seeking the thrills that accompany a profitable trade, and are willing to accept, or some would say, *ignore,* the risks associated with that type of investment philosophy. Aggressive/Growth investors are often young, have a reasonable income base and, although they tend to look for results over the short term, are seeking some long-term guidance.

These classifications provide us with a general overview of an investor's ability to tolerate risk. However, knowing how much risk individual investors can tolerate is only part of the task. Equally important is the need to outline specific investment goals and objectives and to examine your current net worth and income stream in order to define your goals within the context of your current financial position and time horizon. Only by understanding these four factors can you lay the foundation on which to build a long-term investment plan.

The Personality of Investing

Successful long-term investing requires a balancing act between risk and return, something we'll spend more time on in Chapter 2. For now, it's important to understand that every step up the performance ladder requires the investor to take on more risk. The goal is to (1) decide how far up the performance ladder we need to go, and (2) make sure that each step taken requires as little risk as possible.

Start this process by examining your current financial objectives. The question, of course, is where do you see yourself in 10 years? Retired and enjoying the finer things in life? Nestled in the home of your dreams? Content and pleased with the accomplishments of the past and your aspirations for the future? Or maybe you'll be climbing the career ladder and developing a successful foundation in the vocation of your choice.

Financial security is obviously important, but you may not feel qualified to properly manage your affairs. You've watched helplessly as inflation eats away at your savings and gotten angered as the tax man nickel-and-dimes away chunks of your earnings, so that for every step forward, you seem to be taking two steps back. But you can take some decisive steps toward financial independence. The first step is to assess your current financial condition to determine your current net worth. But before firing up the calculator, you should decide whether or not to include your principal residence. The bottom line is that you need now and always will need a place to live. Of course, you may decide to rent at some point in the future. In that case, you may want to sell your principal residence and invest the tax-free profits into upgrading your lifestyle. Or, you may prefer to retain your residence and simply utilize other forms of disposable income to meet your financial requirements. If you fall into the former camp, and are clear about your long-term plans, then by all means, include the principal residence as part of your net worth. For those of you who fall into the latter camp, or simply have no plans to sell the family homestead, we suggest you do not include the family home as part of your net worth. Write down your net worth score on the chart below.

Rating Your Net Worth	**Points**
Your net worth is $5,000 or above, but less than $25,000	1
Your net worth is $25,000 or above, but less than $50,000	3
Your net worth is $50,000 or above, but less than $100,000	5
Your net worth is $100,000 or above, but less than $250,000	7
Your net worth is $250,000 or more	10
Net Worth Score	____

Note: Ratings and scores are tabulated in Chapter 2.

Setting Your Financial Objectives

Many factors affect not only the way we view money, but the way we invest. At the outset, many of us are unclear about our financial goals, because most of us have never been taught just how important goals are in the context of investment management. We think goals are critical, because they define for us the required performance objectives.

As you might expect, there is a wide range of investment objectives. They include such things as growth of capital, protection of principal, levels of income and tax considerations. There are also short- and long-term goals, such as the future education needs of our children, retirement planning, saving for a house or simply improving our lifestyle. Take a few minutes with the family and think about some of the financial objectives you want to accomplish. Everything is on the table at this point, from a vacation in Hawaii or a new car to a cabin cruiser—name your own dream! Of course, aside from your financial objectives, there are issues you need to address, including retirement and, if you have children, some commitment for their university tuition. So write down your goals in order of importance and in terms of timing. For example, a trip to Hawaii may be a short-term goal, especially if you hope to take the trip within say the next five years. In fact, any goal that is to be reached within the next five years should be included on your short-term list; goals with a longer horizon should be included on the long-term list. Your children's education is a longer-term goal, and obviously retirement planning deserves some special attention.

Short-Term Goals (five years or less)

Short-Term Goals	Years to Goal	Goal Amount	Current Net Worth	Amount Required

Long-Term Goals (more than five years)

Long-Term Goals	Years to Goal	Goal Amount	Current Net Worth	Amount Required

Having put together a list of potential goals, try to rank them in terms of importance and then put some realistic costs on them. For example, your retirement income should be at least 70% of your current income and, to be safe, you should adjust that number to reflect the impact of inflation.

Fixing your rate of return assumes that you never need to review your investment objectives and goals. But the fact is that, over time, they change. A regular annual review is in order and, of course, if personal circumstances change—like a death in the family, marriage, divorce, the birth of a child—you will need to take a few moments to re-think your priorities. Finally, it is always important to keep some funds set aside for emergencies. A good rule of thumb is to have enough savings to meet three to six months' worth of expenses. With that in mind, below is a goal calculation worksheet which can help you determine how much you need to set aside for specific goals. You will need to use some of the numbers from the tables at the end of this chapter to help you complete the worksheet.

GOAL CALCULATION WORKSHEET #1

1.	Name your goal	________	
2.	How much money does this goal require?	________	(in today's dollars)
3.	How much have you already saved for this goal?	________	
4.	How long do you have to meet this goal?	________	(in years)
5.	Projected value of current investments	________	(enter factor from Table 1.1)
6.	Future value of current savings	________	(multiply line 3 by line 5)
7.	How much additional capital is required?	________	(subtract line 6 from line 2)
8.	Calculate annual savings required	________	(enter factor from Table 1.2)
9.	Annual savings required to meet goal	________	(multiply line 7 by line 8)
10.	Monthly savings required to reach your goal	________	(divide line 9 by the number 12)

GOAL CALCULATION WORKSHEET #2

1.	Name your goal	Buy a car	
2.	How much money does this goal require?	$27,000	(in today's dollars)
3.	How much have you already saved for this goal?	$10,000	
4.	How long do you have to meet this goal?	5	(in years)
5.	Projected value of current investments	1.13	(enter factor from Table 1.1)
6.	Future value of current savings	$11,300	(multiply line 3 by line 5)
7.	How much additional capital is required?	$15,700	(subtract line 6 from line 2)
8.	Calculate annual savings required	0.20	(enter factor from Table 1.2)
9.	Annual savings required to meet goal	$3,140	(multiply line 7 by line 8)
10.	Monthly savings required to reach your goal	$261.67	(divide line 9 by the number 12)

(Source: Adapted from *Worth Magazine*)

The Magic of Compounding

Having established some financial goals and assessing their costs, we need to look more closely at rates of return, because how much you need to earn on your investments, and over what period of time, dictates how far up the performance ladder we need to go.

And that also plays a role in helping to establish financial goals that are reasonable. We can't say, for example, that we want to be a millionaire someday. It may be possible to reach that goal, but how much do we need to set aside, over what period of time and at what rate of return? Having figured that out, is it realistic? Having sustainable expectations is important, because we need to establish some successes in order to maintain a solid footing on our way to financial independence. Failing to meet unrealistic expectations can be discouraging, and that can have a negative impact on your long-range plans.

Realities and Expectations of Compounding

One of the world's wealthiest bankers, Baron Rothschild, was once asked if he could name the Seven Wonders of the World. As was his style, the answer was brief and to the point: "I cannot recall all the world's Seven Wonders, but let me suggest to you the eighth wonder of the world. It can be utilized by each and every one of us to get what we want. It is compound interest."

The concept of compound interest is not that difficult. Suppose you place money in an investment that pays interest compounded annually. During the first year, you would earn interest on the principal. However, in subsequent years, you would earn interest not only on the original principal, but also on the interest earned in the first year. For example: Assume that you invested $1,000 today, at 10% interest, compounded annually. At the end of the first year, your investment would have grown to $1,100. This represents the original investment of $1,000 plus $100 in interest earned on the principal. Assume you reinvested the entire amount for another year; the investment would appreciate to $1,210 ($1,100 x 1.10). During the second year, you earned $100 interest on the original investment, plus $10 interest on the interest earned in the first year. The amount at the end of two years can be broken down as follows:

Original investment	$1,000
First year's interest	100
Second year's interest on original investment	100
Second year's interest on interest	10
Total Return	**$1,210**

Reinvestment for the third year would produce $1,331 ($1,210 x 1.10). The third year's interest of $121 accounts for $100 on the original principal, plus $21 on the interest earned during the first two years. The interest-on-interest component of the investment is what causes the snowballing effect on the growth of money.

To underscore the importance of this, assume the original $1,000 investment was left to compound for 50 years at 10% per annum. The investment would have grown to $117,390.85.

The interest payable in the 50th year would be made up of $100 on the original principal, plus $10,671.89 on the $105,781.96 interest earned during the first 49 years.

The Million-Dollar Goal

Suppose you had set aside an extra $1,000 five years ago. Now suppose you left it in a savings account earning, say, 6% interest, compounded annually. That money would be worth $1,338.23 today. By placing it in a term deposit earning 10% interest, compounded annually, that $1,000 would have grown to $1,610.51 today.

Forget about finding an extra $1,000, and instead commit to saving, say, $100 a month at 8% interest. In five years, that $100 per month will be worth $7,347.68. Shop around at a few more financial institutions, and you might get 10% interest on $100 per month. At that rate, your savings program would net you $7,743.71 after five years. The longer that money is left to compound, the more dramatic the effect on the value of your portfolio. Setting aside $100 per month for 10 years at 8% interest leaves you with a nest egg of $18,294.60; at 10% interest, you would have $20,484.50. Once you start saving, the condition becomes contagious, which is why we suggest you set up a regular savings plan and stick to it. And it's important that your savings do not force you to change your lifestyle. Save an amount that you can live with, and over time it will become second nature.

Now, let's see what is required for our millionaire status. Let's begin with a savings program of $200 per month, at an interest rate of 10% per year. At that rate, it will take you 37.75 years to reach your million-dollar goal. Earn 12% on your $200 per month, and it takes just under 33 years to reach that goal. If you can save $400 per month and earn 12% per year, it will take you just over 27 years to reach $1 million; at 10%, it will take just under 31 years.

The Rule of 72

We trust you get the picture. It is one thing to plan for the future, but it is quite another to understand what it will take to meet those goals. Needless to say, there are a number of formulas that can be used to calculate the future value of a lump sum of money put aside today.

But while formulas can be useful in determining the value of an investment at some point in the future, they are not a tool that you carry with you to the local bank or trust company. As you probably guessed, then, there is an easier way to calculate the future value of a fixed investment today. It is known as the "Rule of 72." Simply stated, if you divide the number 72 by the return on a particular investment, it will tell you how many years it will take for your money to double. For example, if the current rate of return was 9%, your funds would double in 8 years (72 divided by 9 = 8). If the interest rate is 12%, your original investment would double every 6 years (72 divided by 12 = 6). Now, assuming you invested $10,000 in a bond fund that, historically, has been compounding at 10% a year; how soon will your money double? The answer is 7.2 years (72 divided by 10). How about this? Suppose you have $10,000, and you want to double this amount in 10 years to fund your retirement nest egg.

What compound rate of return must you earn? Divide 72 by the number of years, and you get 7.2%. To double it in 5 years, you'll have to earn an annual return of 14.4% on your investment (72 divided by 5). Simplicity at work, yet the Rule of 72 illustrates some powerful investment principles, most notably the magic of compounding. It also drives home the advantages of mutual funds, where dividends and interest can be automatically reinvested into additional shares. Interest makes your investments grow; compound interest makes them grow faster. And how about the role 72 plays in assessing the impact of changes in the level of your potential return? Money compounding at 6% annually will take 12 years to double; compounding at 12% it will double in half the time.The flip side of this compounding debate is the impact inflation can have on your investments. And there, too, the Rule of 72 plays a role. An inflation rate of 3% means that a dollar today will be worth roughly 50 cents in 24 years. A 5% inflation rate means that your cost of living will double every 14.4 years. Tell that to a 40-year-old who is just beginning to establish a retirement fund.

Rating Your Financial Objectives

Retirement planning is a bit more complex in that the goal is usually a longer-term issue. Then there is the question of whether your investment portfolio is compounding inside or outside an RRSP or some other tax-sheltered investment vehicle. Moreover, the accumulation of wealth is but the first step in the investment process. Once you have accumulated enough wealth to retire, you need to maintain an investment portfolio in order to generate sufficient income so as to protect your principal while also providing a certain level of income.

RETIREMENT PLANNER

1.	Current annual income	_______	
2.	Annual retirement income goal	_______	(in today's dollars)
3.	How many years to retirement?	_______	
4.	Inflation factor	_______	(factor from Table 1.4)
5.	Annual retirement income goal (inflation adjusted)	_______	(multiply line 2 by line 4)
6.	Amount required to support retirement income	_______	(multiply line 5 by 10)
7.	How much have you currently set aside for this goal?	_______	
8.	Projected value of current investments	_______	(enter factor from Table 1.1 or Table 1.3)
9.	Future value of current savings	_______	(multiply line 7 by line 8)
10.	How much additional capital is required?	_______	(subtract line 9 from line 6)

11.	Calculate annual savings required	______	(enter factor from Table 1.2)
12.	Annual savings required to meet goal	______	(multiply line 10 by line 11)
13.	Monthly savings required to reach your goal	______	(divide line 12 by 12)

SAMPLE RETIREMENT PLANNER (assumes 2% inflation factor)

1.	Current annual income	$50,000	
2.	Annual retirement income goal	$40,000	(in today's dollars)
3.	How many years to retirement?	20	
4.	Inflation factor	1.49	(factor from Table 1.4)
5.	Annual retirement income goal (inflation adjusted)	$59,600	(multiply line 2 by line 4)
6.	Amount required to support retirement income	$596,000	(multiply line 5 by 10)
7.	How much have you currently set aside for this goal?	$200,000	
8.	Projected value of current investments	2.41	(enter factor from Table 1.1)
9.	Future value of current savings	$482,000	(multiply line 7 by line 8)
10.	How much additional capital is required?	$114,000	(subtract line 9 from line 6)
11.	Calculate annual savings required	0.04	(enter factor from Table 1.2)
12.	Annual savings required to meet goal	$4,560	(multiply line 10 by line 11)
13.	Monthly savings required to reach your goal	$380.33	(divide line 12 by 12)

(Source: Adapted from *Worth Magazine*)

For most of us, the longest-term financial goal is our retirement. And, in all likelihood, we will be drawing on our retirement income long after having met our shorter-term goals. The point being, our retirement goal will be financed with income left over after meeting our shorter-term goals.

With that in mind, we need to determine the compound annual rate of return you require to meet your retirement objective (refer back to the last line on your retirement planner).

Required Rate of Return	**Score**
If required compound return is 6% or less	1
If required compound return is more than 6%, but less than or equal to 8%	5
If required compound return is more than 8%, but less than or equal to 10%	10
If required compound return is more than 10%, but less than or equal to 11%	15
If required compound return is greater than 11%	20
Financial Objectives Score	____

Note: Ratings and scores are tabulated in Chapter 2.

Summary

Defining your goals is an important part of investment planning. Armed with this information, you have an understanding of where you want to get to. Chapter 2 will help you to evaluate how much risk you are willing to assume in order to attain your stated goals.

As long as you are willing to move forward with an understanding that risk and return are two sides of the same investment coin, then you will become a successful long-term investor—perhaps even in spite of yourself!

TABLE 1.1: COMPOUNDING FACTORS FOR CURRENT SAVINGS (NOT TAX SHELTERED)

Year	4%	5%	6%	7%	8%	9%	10%	11%
1	1.02	1.03	1.03	1.04	1.04	1.05	1.05	1.06
2	1.04	1.05	1.06	1.07	1.08	1.09	1.10	1.11
3	1.06	1.08	1.09	1.11	1.12	1.14	1.16	1.17
4	1.08	1.10	1.13	1.15	1.17	1.19	1.22	1.24
5	1.10	1.13	1.16	1.19	1.22	1.25	1.28	1.31
6	1.13	1.16	1.19	1.23	1.27	1.30	1.34	1.38
7	1.15	1.19	1.23	1.27	1.32	1.36	1.41	1.45
8	1.17	1.22	1.27	1.32	1.37	1.42	1.48	1.53
9	1.20	1.25	1.30	1.36	1.42	1.49	1.55	1.62
10	1.22	1.28	1.34	1.41	1.48	1.55	1.63	1.71
15	1.35	1.45	1.56	1.68	1.80	1.94	2.08	2.23
20	1.49	1.64	1.81	1.99	2.19	2.41	2.65	2.92

Table 1.2: FACTORS TO DETERMINE HOW MUCH ADDITIONAL CAPITAL IS REQUIRED

Year	4%	5%	6%	7%	8%	9%	10%	11%
1	1.00	1.00	1.00	1.00	1.00	1.00	1.00	1.00
2	0.50	0.50	0.50	0.49	0.49	0.49	0.49	0.48
3	0.33	0.33	0.33	0.32	0.32	0.32	0.31	0.31
4	0.25	0.25	0.24	0.24	0.24	0.23	0.23	0.23
5	0.20	0.20	0.19	0.19	0.19	0.18	0.18	0.17
6	0.17	0.16	0.16	0.16	0.15	0.15	0.14	0.14
7	0.14	0.14	0.14	0.13	0.13	0.12	0.12	0.12
8	0.13	0.12	0.12	0.11	0.11	0.11	0.10	0.10
9	0.11	0.11	0.10	0.10	0.09	0.09	0.09	0.08
10	0.10	0.10	0.09	0.09	0.08	0.08	0.08	0.07
15	0.07	0.06	0.06	0.05	0.05	0.05	0.04	0.04
20	0.05	0.05	0.04	0.04	0.03	0.03	0.03	0.02
25	0.04	0.04	0.03	0.03	0.02	0.02	0.02	0.02
30	0.03	0.03	0.03	0.02	0.02	0.02	0.01	0.01
35	0.03	0.02	0.02	0.02	0.01	0.01	0.01	0.01
40	0.03	0.02	0.02	0.01	0.01	0.01	0.01	0.01

Table 1.3: RETIREMENT FACTORS FOR CURRENT SAVINGS (TAX SHELTERED)

Year	4%	5%	6%	7%	8%	9%	10%	11%
1	1.04	1.05	1.06	1.07	1.08	1.09	1.10	1.11
3	1.12	1.16	1.19	1.23	1.26	1.30	1.33	1.37
5	1.22	1.28	1.34	1.40	1.47	1.54	1.61	1.69
7	1.32	1.41	1.50	1.61	1.71	1.83	1.95	2.08
9	1.42	1.55	1.69	1.84	2.00	2.17	2.36	2.56
11	1.54	1.71	1.90	2.10	2.33	2.58	2.85	3.15
13	1.67	1.89	2.13	2.41	2.72	3.07	3.45	3.88
15	1.80	2.08	2.40	2.76	3.17	3.64	4.18	4.78
17	1.95	2.29	2.69	3.16	3.70	4.33	5.05	5.90
19	2.11	2.53	3.03	3.62	4.32	5.14	6.12	7.26
21	2.28	2.79	3.40	4.14	5.03	6.11	7.40	8.95
23	2.46	3.07	3.82	4.74	5.87	7.26	8.95	11.03
25	2.67	3.39	4.29	5.43	6.85	8.62	10.83	13.59
27	2.88	3.73	4.82	6.21	7.99	10.25	13.11	16.74
29	3.12	4.12	5.42	7.11	9.32	12.17	15.86	20.62
31	3.37	4.54	6.09	8.15	10.87	14.46	19.19	25.41
33	3.65	5.00	6.84	9.33	12.68	17.18	23.23	31.31
35	3.95	5.52	7.69	10.68	14.79	20.41	28.10	38.57

Table 1.4: INFLATION FACTORS

Year	1.00%	1.50%	2.00%	2.50%	3.00%	3.50%	4.00%
1	1.01	1.02	1.02	1.03	1.03	1.04	1.04
2	1.02	1.03	1.04	1.05	1.06	1.07	1.08
3	1.03	1.05	1.06	1.08	1.09	1.11	1.12
4	1.04	1.06	1.08	1.10	1.13	1.15	1.17
5	1.05	1.08	1.10	1.13	1.16	1.19	1.22
6	1.06	1.09	1.13	1.16	1.19	1.23	1.27
7	1.07	1.11	1.15	1.19	1.23	1.27	1.32
8	1.08	1.13	1.17	1.22	1.27	1.32	1.37
9	1.09	1.14	1.20	1.25	1.30	1.36	1.42
10	1.10	1.16	1.22	1.28	1.34	1.41	1.48
11	1.12	1.18	1.24	1.31	1.38	1.46	1.54
12	1.13	1.20	1.27	1.34	1.43	1.51	1.60
13	1.14	1.21	1.29	1.38	1.47	1.56	1.67
14	1.15	1.23	1.32	1.41	1.51	1.62	1.73
15	1.16	1.25	1.35	1.45	1.56	1.68	1.80
16	1.17	1.27	1.37	1.48	1.60	1.73	1.87
17	1.18	1.29	1.40	1.52	1.65	1.79	1.95
18	1.20	1.31	1.43	1.56	1.70	1.86	2.03
19	1.21	1.33	1.46	1.60	1.75	1.92	2.11
20	1.22	1.35	1.49	1.64	1.81	1.99	2.19
21	1.23	1.37	1.52	1.68	1.86	2.06	2.28
22	1.24	1.39	1.55	1.72	1.92	2.13	2.37
23	1.26	1.41	1.58	1.76	1.97	2.21	2.46
24	1.27	1.43	1.61	1.81	2.03	2.28	2.56
25	1.28	1.45	1.64	1.85	2.09	2.36	2.67
26	1.30	1.47	1.67	1.90	2.16	2.45	2.77
27	1.31	1.49	1.71	1.95	2.22	2.53	2.88
28	1.32	1.52	1.74	2.00	2.29	2.62	3.00
29	1.33	1.54	1.78	2.05	2.36	2.71	3.12
30	1.35	1.56	1.81	2.10	2.43	2.81	3.24

CHAPTER TWO

Your Risk Profile

Types of Risk

At the outset, we need to understand that there is no such thing as a "risk-free investment." When we think of risk-free investments, we think of the guarantee that the amount of your investment will be returned intact. Using that narrow definition, investments such as Government of Canada Treasury bills, bank accounts and/or money market mutual funds are considered risk free.

However, investments that guarantee the return of your principal still fall prey to other risks. Inflation, for example, can erode the purchasing power of that principal investment. Risk-free investments generally pay interest, and again, the purchasing power of your return is susceptible to the highest form of taxation.

Risk, then, is not just a question of how we view a particular investment, or whether that investment will return a set amount. Risk also takes into account such things as the business cycle, tax burdens and inflation. Indeed, there are a number of risk factors that can be quantified:

1. **Business risk** covers a number of issues but primarily means a decline in the earning power of the corporation. On a company-specific level, this risk could take the form of a strike, a rise in fuel costs (which would impact the airline industry) or perhaps, as was the case with Exxon, an oil spill. It also includes the risk that a business cannot meet its obligations and so defaults.

2. **Market risk** affects virtually all shares and any other investment asset that has an active secondary market. The events of October 27, 1997, illustrate a classic case of market risk. Because the market sold off sharply as the crisis in Asia began to surface, virtually all shares declined, whether or not there was any change in a company's long-term prospects. The bond market works much the same way.

When the level of interest rates changes, it affects the price of all bonds, whether they are issued by governments or corporations.

3. **Liquidity risk** is the risk of not being able to sell your investment quickly. A house is a good example of an asset that is not liquid, because there is no active secondary market in which to sell it. In other words, when selling your house, you need to find an agent—unless, of course, you are going it alone—and the agent needs to ferret out prospective buyers. That all takes time. So assets such as houses or collectibles, for which there is no secondary market, have poor liquidity.
   An active secondary market simply means that there are always investors willing to buy and sell your investment. With stocks and mutual funds, for example, there are always willing buyers and sellers, and the prices they are willing to pay are always posted. As such, you can instantly sell your stocks or mutual funds with a simple phone call and can receive cash for the sale usually within three business days.

4. **Inflation**, which, as we have already seen, affects the performance of nearly all investments.

5. **Interest rate risk** is the risk that the price of your security will fall as interest rates rise.

6. **Political risk** can come from the domestic side, with tax increases, changes in tariffs or subsidy policies. It can also come from other parts of the world if national security or world stability is threatened.

Table 2.1: TYPES OF RISK

Investments	Business Risk	Market Risk	Liquidity Risk	Inflation Risk	Interest Rate Risk	Political Risk
Stocks and Equity Funds	Yes	Yes	No	Yes	Yes	Yes
Government Bond Funds	No	Yes	No	Yes	Yes	No
Corporate Bond Funds	No	Yes	No	Yes	Yes	Yes
Treasury Bills/Money Market Funds	No	No	No	Maybe	Maybe	No
GICs	No	No	Maybe	Maybe	Maybe	No
Precious Metals Funds	No	Maybe	No	Maybe	Maybe	Yes

By using the broader definitions of risk, it is clear that T-bills and money market funds are not risk-free investments. How much importance you attach to "inflation risk" or "liquidity risk" will tell you how well these investments suit your needs. In many ways, while you are guaranteed your principal repayment and any interest along the way, you could still end up, after factoring inflation into the picture, with a negative real after-tax return.

Fortunately, because we can define risks, we can examine how each type of risk affects each asset class, and by how much. Depending on the particular security and the investor's time horizon, the impact can be quite different.

Prudent investors strive to reduce risk by extending their time horizon, by spreading their investment dollars across a number of asset classes and through other diversification techniques, including spreading their dollars across geographic regions and investing in different investment management styles. The easiest way to implement those risk-reduction techniques is through an investment in a portfolio of mutual funds.

Mutual funds are ideal for the investor who wants diversification and professional management, but who doesn't want to keep track of a whole bunch of different investments. But it's not as easy as it sounds, because you are still stuck with the problem of selecting the right funds. Just consider, for example, the following information that you could have gathered from data in *The Financial Post*'s "Mutual Funds Performance Survey":

Over the 10-year period from August 1, 1985, through July 31, 1995, the Altamira Capital Growth Fund, a Canadian RRSP-eligible equity mutual fund, earned an annual compounded rate of return for its holders of 9.6% before load fees. What that tells us is that a $10,000 investment made on August 1, 1985, would have grown to $25,009 by July 31, 1995, assuming, of course, you reinvested all of your dividend and capital gain distributions in the Altamira Capital Growth Fund.

Over this same period, Prudential Growth Fund of Canada, an equity fund with similar characteristics, earned 10.2% compounded annually; $10,000 grew to $26,413. Furthermore, a portfolio of Canadian stocks as measured by the Toronto Stock Exchange 300 Composite Total Return Index showed an 8.6% return; $10,000 would have grown to $22,819. An investment in three-month Canadian Treasury bills yielded 8.9%; $10,000 would have become $23,457.

There are some obvious conclusions. First, both of these equity mutual funds compensated investors for the time value of money—each outperformed an investment in Canadian Treasury bills. Second, the managers of both funds earned their management fees (at least partially) by outperforming a randomly selected portfolio of Canadian equities as measured by that TSE 300 Composite Index. The Prudential Growth Fund of Canada appeared to have been, in retrospect, the better investment for an investor who actually held the shares for those 10 years, as it yielded a higher return than the Altamira Capital Growth Fund.

Useful information to be sure, but if we are to look only at returns, then our analysis is incomplete. Looking to the future, do we conclude that Prudential Growth Fund of Canada is now a *better buy* than

Altamira Capital Growth Fund? Did its performance justify the risk inherent in the fund's portfolio over the previous 10 years? Were there, in fact, other mutual funds in the RRSP-eligible Canadian equity classification that dominated both? A deeper and more critical analysis would have been necessary before informed decisions could be made on which, if either, fund to invest in.

The objective in mutual fund analysis is to evaluate a fund's past performance and compare that performance with funds that have the same objective, then measure the performance of all funds with the same objective against an appropriate benchmark index. (See Chapter 15 on Manager Value Added.)

How do you select from among the long and growing list of available mutual funds? You need both information and a consistent way of analyzing what you get. Your two major sources of mutual fund information are the prospectuses of the funds and the published performance data as found in the various newspapers and periodicals as mentioned below.

The prospectus, which you can obtain from the mutual fund itself, will outline the general investment philosophy of the fund managers, the current structure of the investment portfolio, sometimes identified by industry (and for global and international funds, the geographic breakdown of its investments), the management fees and the names of the fund advisors.

The performance data, published in the financial press, provides for each of the thousand or so Canadian open-ended mutual funds descriptive and analytic data, including the initial launch date of the fund, RRSP eligibility, total assets, net asset value per share, maximum entry and/or exit load fees, the tenure of the fund manager, annual compounded rate of return over various time periods, some measure of volatility or standard deviation (remember, the higher the volatility the wider the swings in net asset values and returns) and other useful material. These data are essential to compare mutual funds for decision making.

The underlying data, and indeed most or all of the calculations, can be found in Canadian publications such as *The Financial Post*'s monthly "Mutual Funds Performance Survey," the quarterly "Survey of Funds" and *The Globe and Mail Report on Business* monthly "Report on Mutual Funds." Southam newspapers also produce monthly fund inserts for a number of their regional publications.

In the Mutual Fund Tables, funds are classified by objectives, as stated by the fund management or the prospectus. The Canadian performance-ranking publications normally list the surveyed funds by these stated investment objectives, allowing investors to conduct their analyses on a comparative basis within fund groupings.

Although there is some consistency among the services with respect to data supplied, none of the services provides everything. Generally, either *The National (Financial) Post, The Globe and Mail* or the Southam mutual fund inserts will provide enough for your needs. However, it may be necessary to utilize other services if you require some special analytic information.

The Return Side of the Investment Equation

The appropriate measure of return is straightforward; it is simply the annual compounded rate of return. Compounded annual rate of return includes the change in net asset value, plus dividend and capital gain distributions, which we assume the investor reinvests in additional units. The objective, then, is to determine the annual compounded rate of return over a specific time period.

For example, suppose that the initial net asset value of Fund A was $10, and you purchased 100 units. Your initial investment, then, is $1,000. Assume that over the next 10 years, the dividends and capital gain distributions allow you to purchase an additional 80 units, and at the end of that 10-year period, the net asset value per share is $28.00. Your investment is now worth $5,040, since you own 180 units of $28 per unit. For those who like mathematics, the annual compounded rate of return is calculated as:

$$\$1{,}000\ (1 + R)^{10} = \$5{,}040$$
$$R = .1756 \text{ or } 17.56\%$$

The annual compounded rate of return for this fund, which we denote as R, is then 17.56%.

No sales charges, commissions or loads are considered in the calculations that are presented in the published performance tables. However, if you are ambitious, you can translate the pre-load returns to an after-load basis by subtracting the load from the initial investment, compounding the remainder at the annual growth rate of the fund and then calculating the rate of return on the terminal value relative to the total initial investment.

For example, if Fund A had a 4% load and earned 17.56% compounded for 10 years, the after-load return is reduced to 17.10%. The impact a load has on the performance numbers is relevant, but all returns should be evaluated in light of the risk undertaken.

Measuring the Risk/Return Trade-off

You cannot avoid risk. Even a decision to do nothing has an impact on the performance of your portfolio. The choice is not to find risk-free investments, but rather to understand what types of risk you are willing to assume. But before you can do that, it is useful to gain some insight into the various measures of risk.

Beta

A number of definitions apply to the word "risk" when used by investors. The term most familiar to stock market investors is "beta." In nontechnical terms, beta is an indicator of how a fund's value has fluctuated relative to past changes in an appropriate benchmark. (An equity fund, for example, might be compared with the Toronto Stock Exchange 300 Composite Total Return Index.)

The higher the fund's beta, the greater the degree of fluctuation for a given change in the overall market. We assume, by definition, that the benchmark index (the TSE 300 Composite Total Return Index, in this example) has a beta of 1. A Canadian equity fund with a beta of 2 would be expected to advance twice as fast as the benchmark index in an uptrend and fall twice as fast in a downtrend.

A high beta equity fund, therefore, would be expected to realize high rates of returns when the stock market was strong but relatively large losses when the market was weak. A low beta fund would be expected to have relatively lower rates of returns when the market was strong but suffer smaller losses when the market was weak.

However, beta has some drawbacks, particularly when looking at a portfolio that includes a broad cross section of assets. And that is an issue with mutual funds. Canadian equity funds usually hold some cash in their portfolio. Indeed, some funds have a lot of cash. The Ivy Canadian Fund, for example, had about 32% of its assets in cash at the halfway mark in 1997. With mutual funds, we think more emphasis should be given to the degree of risk in each asset class (i.e., bonds, precious metals, real estate, etc.) rather than the risk of a particular fund relative to its benchmark index.

Standard Deviation

To measure the variability of returns for specific funds, we enter the realm of standard deviation. Simply stated, standard deviation is the amount that a fund's price has varied from its mean or average price over a given period of time. It differs from beta in that it measures the volatility of a specific investment, and not specifically how that investment performs relative to some benchmark index.

Standard deviation is a useful measure of risk for investors who hold small, nondiversified portfolios of investments, including mutual funds. It is simple to calculate and relatively easy to understand. The information is supplied by most financial newspapers, although, to be fair, the financial press usually provides only a broad measure of standard deviation by simply classifying funds as either average, above average or below average in this risk measure relative to all of the funds in the same objective category.

Finally, there is one other caveat; like all such measures, standard deviation is based on past results.

STANDARD DEVIATION OR BETA?

Conventional wisdom is that if the portfolio represents merely a part of the investor's total assets, then market risk or beta is appropriate. If the portfolio represents the client's sole asset, then total risk or standard deviation should be used.

Mathematical Mumbo Jumbo or Vital Statistics?

We think it is important to show you how standard deviation is calculated. And to do that, we need to look at a few statistical tools.

As an illustration, we will take the Trimark Canadian Fund as an example and do our own standard deviation calculation. The following percent changes in net asset values were recorded over a 36-month period ending July 1995.

Table 2.2: TRIMARK CANADIAN FUND MONTHLY RETURNS

Period	Monthly Return	Value of $10,000
Aug-92	2.71%	$10,271.10
Sep-92	1.25	10,399.80
Oct-92	2.51	10,660.62
Nov-92	-0.37	10,621.61
Dec-92	4.12	11,059.64
Jan-93	3.01	11,392.20
Feb-93	-4.67	10,859.85
Mar-93	1.66	11,040.55
Apr-93	-4.88	10,502.11
May-93	0.30	10,533.82
Jun-93	-0.36	10,495.80
Jul-93	2.66	10,774.56
Aug-93	6.23	11,446.25
Sep-93	-5.75	10,787.98
Oct-93	2.21	11,026.61
Nov-93	-0.06	11,019.66
Dec-93	-1.92	10,807.97
Jan-94	-2.06	10,585.00
Feb-94	5.17	11,132.14
Mar-94	3.39	11,509.97
Apr-94	1.49	11,681.47
May-94	5.71	12,348.36
Jun-94	-1.04	12,220.06
Jul-94	5.05	12,836.93
Aug-94	-1.28	12,672.75
Sep-94	1.50	12,863.34
Oct-94	3.17	13,271.50
Nov-94	3.43	13,726.44
Dec-94	5.46	14,476.18
Jan-95	5.52	15,275.12
Feb-95	0.41	15,337.29
Mar-95	2.06	15,653.86
Apr-95	1.43	15,878.18
May-95	-2.64	15,459.63
Jun-95	1.42	15,678.38
Jul-95	-1.09	15,507.64
Average Period Return	***1.27%***	

Having done those calculations, we then calculate an arithmetic mean or, as it is commonly referred to, an "average." An average is the sum of all the monthly returns divided by the number of observations, which in this case is 36. The average can be found at the bottom of Table 2.2.

Variance and Standard Deviation

Variance and standard deviation define how far the monthly returns for the Trimark Canadian Fund varied from the average monthly return, which we know to be 1.27%. For example, in July 1995, the fund returned -1.09%; or, put another way, Trimark deviated from its average return by -2.36%. Table 2.3 looks at the deviations from the average monthly return for the 36 periods.

Table 2.3: DEVIATIONS AND DEVIATIONS^2 FROM AVERAGE—TRIMARK CANADIAN FUND

Period	Monthly Return	Deviation	Deviation^2
Aug-92	2.71%	1.44%	0.02%
Sep-92	1.25	-0.02	0.00
Oct-92	2.51	1.24	0.02
Nov-92	-0.37	-1.64	0.03
Dec-92	4.12	2.85	0.08
Jan-93	3.01	1.74	0.03
Feb-93	-4.67	-5.94	0.35
Mar-93	1.66	0.39	0.00
Apr-93	-4.88	-6.15	0.38
May-93	0.30	-0.97	0.01
Jun-93	-0.36	-1.63	0.03
Jul-93	2.66	1.38	0.02
Aug-93	6.23	4.96	0.25
Sep-93	-5.75	-7.02	0.49
Oct-93	2.21	0.94	0.01
Nov-93	-0.06	-1.33	0.02
Dec-93	-1.92	-3.19	0.10
Jan-94	-2.06	-3.33	0.11
Feb-94	5.17	3.90	0.15
Mar-94	3.39	2.12	0.05
Apr-94	1.49	0.22	0.00
May-94	5.71	4.44	0.20
Jun-94	-1.04	-2.31	0.05
Jul-94	5.05	3.78	0.14
Aug-94	-1.28	-2.55	0.07
Sep-94	1.50	0.23	0.00
Oct-94	3.17	1.90	0.04
Nov-94	3.43	2.16	0.05
Dec-94	5.46	4.19	0.18

Jan-95	5.52	4.25	0.18
Feb-95	0.41	-0.86	0.01
Mar-95	2.06	0.79	0.01
Apr-95	1.43	0.16	0.00
May-95	-2.64	-3.91	0.15
Jun-95	1.42	0.14	0.00
Jul-95	-1.09	-2.36	0.06

Average Monthly Return ***1.27%***

Variance = (sum of deviations^2) / 36 ***0.09%***

Standard Deviation = square root of variance ***3.01%***

To compute the "average deviation" for each fund, our natural impulse is to add up the 36 deviations and divide by the number of observations. However, if we do that for the Trimark Canadian Fund, we end up with zero, suggesting that the fund never varied from its mean, which clearly is not the case. Of course, that the sum of the deviations equals zero defines the central tendency of an average. The sum of deviations around an arithmetic mean or average should always equal zero. The way around this problem is to square the deviations and then sum the resulting numbers. By doing that, we convert the negative deviations into positive numbers, and the larger the deviation, the larger will be the squared value of it. The squared deviations can also be found in Table 2.3.

With the squared deviations from Table 2.3, we can now calculate the variance for our Trimark Canadian Fund. Variance is simply the sum of the squared deviations divided by the number of observations:

Variance = 3.26%   36 observations = .091%

The standard deviation is simply the square root of the variance:

Standard Deviation = $\sqrt{.00091}$ = .0301 or 3.01%

Statistically, 68% of all observations in a normal distribution are expected to lie within one standard deviation of the mean. We would expect, given a normal distribution of returns, that in 68% of all observations, the monthly return of the Trimark Canadian Fund will fall between +4.28% (1.27% average plus 3.01% standard deviation = +4.28%), or -1.74% (1.27% average return minus 3.01% standard deviation = -1.74%).

The true test of how well the model works can be seen by looking at observations within two standard deviations of the average. We would expect that in 95% of all cases, the monthly performance of the Trimark Canadian Fund will fall within two standard deviations of the average. Using the Trimark Canadian Fund example, two standard deviations represent a monthly return that could be as high as 7.29% (6.02% *plus* 1.27% average) or as low as - 4.75% (1.27% average *less* 6.02%). Note that in Table 2.3, over the 36 monthly returns, Trimark Canadian Fund never exceeded either the upside or downside boundary as defined by our two standard deviations from the mean.

Understanding standard deviation gives us an idea how much the price of a fund might vary from one month to the next. We think that adds an important element to the discussion for investors who want to know not only what the performance numbers look like, but what the manager had to do to achieve those results. However, use care when looking at a fund's historical standard deviation, because like past performance numbers, historical measurements only tell you what did happen—not what may happen in the future.

Correlation

By now you've probably learned more than you ever wanted to know about statistics. And you're probably thinking, why? Are these stats really necessary?

If it helps, we understand your concerns and appreciate your indulgence. We also believe that it is useful that you become familiar with the fundamental concepts in this discussion, because these are the principles that underpin a number of our performance measurement systems—specifically, how we rank mutual fund performance on a risk-adjusted basis.

With that in mind, we ask you to consider one other concept: correlation. Simply stated, correlation defines how closely the performance of one fund tracks the performance of another. For example, suppose that we had two funds in our portfolio, and the performance of each fund was identical (see Table 2.4).

Table 2.4: PERFECT POSITIVE CORRELATION OF FUND A AND FUND B

Period	Fund A Monthly Return	Fund B Monthly Return	Value of $10,000.00
Aug-96	1.00%	1.00%	$10,100.00
Sep-96	0.50	0.50	10,150.50
Oct-96	0.00	0.00	10,150.50
Nov-96	-1.00	-1.00	10,049.00
Dec-96	2.00	2.00	10,249.97
Jan-97	1.50	1.50	10,403.72
Feb-97	1.00	1.00	10,507.76
Mar-97	0.50	0.50	10,560.30
Apr-97	0.00	0.00	10,560.30
May-97	-1.00	-1.00	10,454.70
Jun-97	2.00	2.00	10,663.79
Jul-97	1.50	1.50	10,823.75

	Fund A	**Fund B**	**Combined Fund A and Fund B**
Average Return	0.67%	0.67%	0.67%
Standard Deviation	1.03%	1.03%	1.03%

Every month, Fund A went up by a certain percentage; so did Fund B, and by the same percentage. At the end of this 12-month period, your portfolio generated an average monthly return of 0.67%, and over that period had an annual standard deviation of 1.03%.

If the goal of diversification is to reduce risk and enhance return, why own the second fund? Because both funds are generating exactly the same return at exactly the same time, we gain nothing in terms of risk reduction or performance enhancement. Obviously, there is more to diversification than blindly buying more than one fund.

That's where the final piece of statistical information comes into play—correlation. Simply stated, correlation mathematically defines how closely one fund tracks the performance of another fund. Correlation can vary between +1 (perfect positive correlation) and -1 (perfect negative correlation). Of course, while Table 2.4 shows two funds that have demonstrated perfect positive correlation, that is not something we would expect to see in the real world. Most often, two funds have a positive or negative correlation that falls somewhere between the +1 and -1 extremes.

With that in mind, we would like you to take a look at Table 2.5. In this table, we examine two funds, A and Z, that have demonstrated perfect negative correlation.

Table 2.5: PERFECT NEGATIVE CORRELATION OF FUND A AND FUND Z

Period	Fund A Monthly Return	Fund Z Monthly Return	Value of $10,000.00
Aug-96	1.00%	-1.00%	$10,000.00
Sep-96	0.50	-0.50	10,000.00
Oct-96	0.00	0.00	10,000.00
Nov-96	-1.00	1.00	10,000.00
Dec-96	2.00	-2.00	10,000.00
Jan-97	1.50	-1.50	10,000.00
Feb-97	1.00	-1.00	10,000.00
Mar-97	0.50	-0.50	10,000.00
Apr-97	0.00	0.00	10,000.00
May-97	-1.00	1.00	10,000.00
Jun-97	2.00	-2.00	10,000.00
Jul-97	1.50	-1.50	10,000.00

	Fund A	**Fund Z**	**Combined Fund A and Fund Z**
Average Return	0.67%	-0.067%	0.00%
Standard Deviation	1.03%	-1.03%	0.00%

By combining Funds A and Z in Table 2.5, we bring to light a good news/bad news scenario. The good news is that in terms of standard deviation (0.00%), you now own a riskless portfolio. The bad news is that your portfolio is going nowhere!

The idea, of course, is to find two real-world funds that are not perfectly correlated either positively or negatively, and more to the point, fine-tune that combination so that we (1) reduce risk, and (2) maintain an optimum level of performance.

With that in mind, we want to once again look at the monthly returns of the Trimark Canadian Fund. In this case, we've assumed that while the long-term returns from the Trimark Canadian Fund are attractive, the deviation in monthly returns is too high. In other words, we want to reduce the risk in the portfolio without losing all of the performance.

To accomplish this, we have decided to add another fund to the portfolio, which in this case is the Dynamic Income Fund. The Dynamic Income Fund carries substantially less risk than the Trimark Canadian Fund, and as might be expected, the returns are also not as stellar as the Trimark Canadian Fund.

Table 2.6: TRIMARK CANADIAN FUND AND DYNAMIC INCOME FUND

Period Return	Trimark Canadian Fund	Dynamic Income Fund	Value of $ 10,000.00
Aug-92	2.71%	-0.58%	$10,106.80
Sep-92	1.25	0.31	10,185.84
Oct-92	2.51	1.61	10,395.36
Nov-92	-0.37	-0.83	10,333.14
Dec-92	4.12	1.78	10,638.12
Jan-93	3.01	1.02	10,852.11
Feb-93	-4.67	0.66	10,634.25
Mar-93	1.66	1.40	10,797.38
Apr-93	-4.88	0.68	10,570.96
May-93	0.30	1.64	10,673.39
Jun-93	-0.36	-0.85	10,608.55
Jul-93	2.66	-0.53	10,721.48
Aug-93	6.23	1.39	11,129.92
Sep-93	-5.75	0.57	10,841.60
Oct-93	2.21	-0.32	10,944.10
Nov-93	-0.06	-0.28	10,925.28
Dec-93	-1.92	0.11	10,826.57
Jan-94	-2.06	0.28	10,730.05
Feb-94	5.17	2.42	11,137.20
Mar-94	3.39	0.86	11,374.31
Apr-94	1.49	1.49	11,543.62
May-94	5.71	-0.55	11,841.27
Jun-94	-1.04	1.44	11,864.78
Jul-94	5.05	2.45	12,309.77
Aug-94	-1.28	-0.19	12,219.47
Sep-94	1.50	-0.15	12,302.32
Oct-94	3.17	0.19	12,508.88

Nov-94	3.43	1.70	12,829.29
Dec-94	5.46	1.89	13,300.90
Jan-95	5.52	-0.38	13,642.86
Feb-95	0.41	-0.75	13,619.60
Mar-95	2.06	1.50	13,862.17
Apr-95	1.43	0.00	13,961.49
May-95	-2.64	0.84	13,836.05
Jun-95	1.42	1.25	14,020.27
Jul-95	-1.09	1.52	14,050.49

	Trimark	**Dynamic**	**Combined**
Average Return	1.27%	0.65%	0.96%
Standard Deviation	3.05%	0.97%	1.70%

Note from Table 2.6 that we have reduced the risk in this portfolio by 44.2% (standard deviation of 1.70% versus 3.05%), while reducing the average monthly performance by only 24.2% (average monthly return of 0.96% versus 1.27%). What this example demonstrates is the risk-reduction aspect of diversification across asset classes (i.e., a Canadian equity fund and a Canadian bond fund).

Investors can further reduce risk by diversifying not only across asset classes, but by geographic region and investment style (and that is the rationale behind the FundLine, which we discuss in Chapter 16.

The bottom line is this: with a well-diversified portfolio, you will end up meeting your financial goals with as little exposure to risk as possible.

The Power of Positive Investing

When it comes to buying mutual funds, performance is clearly one of the most important issues. It is, however, not the only issue. If it was, then we need only match your required rate of return (see Chapter 1) with a fund that has generated that rate compounded over, say, the past five or 10 years.

For example, suppose that the required compound annual rate of return over the next 20 years to meet, say, your retirement needs was 10%. With a scan of Pal-Trak, we would screen only those funds with at least a 10-year track record and then simply buy into a fund whose compound rate of return exceeds 10%. Mission accomplished!

Of course, as you might imagine, things are never really that simple. The problem is that our tolerance for risk defines for each of us how well we can adapt to the ebb and flow of our investment return, and how much of an impact those changes have will determine our ability to maintain investments for longer periods of time.

Consider, for a moment, the mountain charts that accompany mutual fund marketing literature—the ones that graphically display what a $10,000 investment made 10, 20 or 30 years ago would be worth today. If nothing else, they emphasize the "power of positive investing." Figure 2.1, for example, charts the growth of a $10,000 investment in the Marathon Equity Fund. If you had invested $10,000 in the Marathon Equity Fund on January 1, 1987, it would have grown to $50,280 by December 31, 1997. That translates into a 17.5% compound annual return.

Figure 2.1: MARATHON EQUITY FUND: THE POWER OF POSITIVE INVESTING

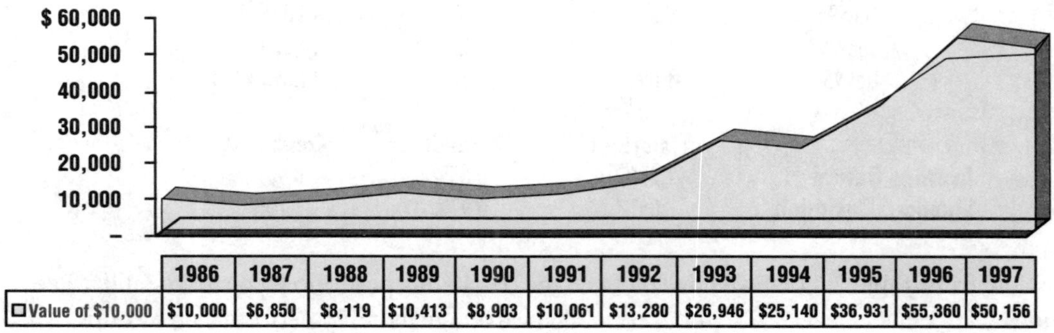

	1986	1987	1988	1989	1990	1991	1992	1993	1994	1995	1996	1997
Value of $10,000	$10,000	$6,850	$8,119	$10,413	$8,903	$10,061	$13,280	$26,946	$25,140	$36,931	$55,360	$50,156

1. Over the years January 1993 through December 1997 the fund returned 30.4% compounded annually. That was good enough to earn top marks in the performance parade of Canadian small-cap funds. More important, those returns were good enough to attract the attention of the financial press and excite more than a few investors looking to catch a ride on the next hot-performing fund.
2. It provides an insightful commentary on the importance of balancing risk and return.

Riding the Bumps along the Way

What we don't pick up from the long-term mountain charts is the wild roller coaster ride funds can take—something that can be seen in Figure 2.2. You can see how investors can get tripped up. There are advantages to having a competent financial advisor holding your hand through the rough stretches.

Figure 2.2: MARATHON EQUITY FUND: RIDING THE ROLLER COASTER

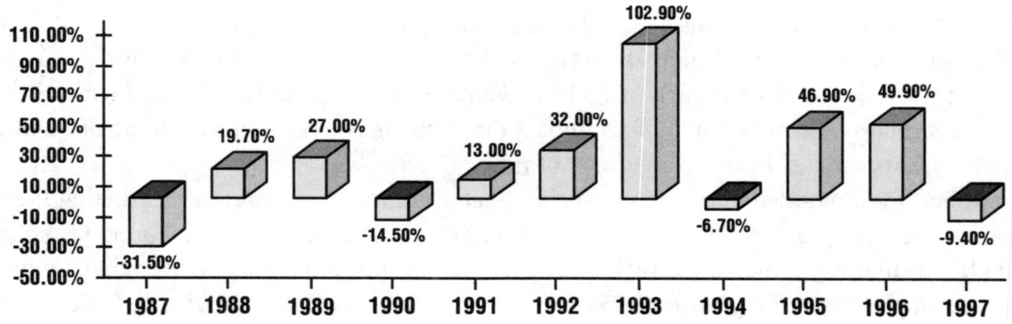

To make the point, allow us to draw your attention to the period beginning in January 1987 and ending in December 1991. Convincing an investor to put money into this fund at the beginning of 1987 should have been relatively easy. After all, stocks had been booming through most of the 1980s, and small-cap stocks were particularly hot. Small companies, which is what the Marathon Equity Fund invests in, were in the 1980s routinely being bought out by larger companies, and that was regularly providing shareholders with double-digit returns.

Given such a strong period of growth, a mountain chart depicting the returns for most equity funds would have looked like the side of Mount Everest at a time, we point out, when the attractiveness of Guaranteed Investment Certificates (GICs) was beginning to wear thin.

Investors who bought $10,000 worth of the Marathon Equity Fund in January 1987 and held the fund until the end of December 1991 (some five years later) saw the value of their investment rise to $10,075.50. (Assuming the investor had remained in the market after the 1987 stock market crash.)

We like to think that Figure 2.2 shows "real-world investing." And just to add some real-world grist to this mill, we would submit that after the October 27, 1997, collapse in stock prices, a lot of investors were rushing for the sidelines, asking themselves why they ever abandoned GICs.

In real-world terms, nothing is as frustrating for investors as watching the value of their portfolio stagnate. And as that frustration grows, investors begin to lay blame and tend to cast all mutual funds in the same light.

In this context, we would expect by the end of this five-year cycle that very few long-term investors would still be holding this fund, and more than likely most investors would have sold out at the worst possible moment.

Two Conflicting Points of View

What we have, then, are two conflicting points of view: our mountain charts that show, beyond the shadow of a doubt, the power of positive investing, and our annual return chart that sets out the real-world roller coaster experience.

In order to bridge these two conflicting points of view, we need to establish a balance between our long-term financial objectives and our ability to tolerate risk. And that requires a diversified investment strategy that (1) builds a reasonable mountain chart, and (2) helps smooth out the real-world highs and lows along the way.

In our view, strategic asset allocation fits the definition of just such a strategy. Asset allocation is to the 1990s what diversification was in the 1970s and 1980s. Diversification, as in owning a large portfolio of stocks, is the most significant aspect of buying mutual funds. The reason is simple, writes Sheldon Jacobs in his *Handbook for No-Load Fund Investors*: "There are two basic risks in owning stocks—(1) the risk the market will go down, and (2) the risk an individual company will do poorly. Diversification can eliminate the latter risk. And since the wise investor is risk averse, it makes sense to avoid taking any risk that is unnecessary."

In 1996 and 1997, the average Canadian and U.S. equity funds returned *18.5%* and *23.7%* (compounded annually) respectively. Far East funds collapsed, particularly in the emerging Asian markets. And today, Japan remains mired in a recession with no end in sight.

Your Risk Assessment Profile

Market conditions constantly change. Over time, securities will be affected by economic circumstances. These changes must be met with decisive action. Take the case where an investment performs poorly and its price drops sharply. You don't want to let your losses accumulate when you would have been in a better position by simply selling and looking elsewhere.

That decision, however, is also a matter of the investor's personality. Veteran money managers will tell you that many investors are reluctant to sell when faced with a loss. Many investors find it difficult to admit to a mistake or believe (falsely) that they do not incur a true loss until a security is sold.

On the other side of the risk/return coin, you have to be able to maintain your positions for the long term, being careful not to take profits quickly. Many of the same investors who will let their losses run will just as quickly take a profit. There is, of course, some psychological satisfaction in making money. But over the long term, this reduces your chances for gains. All too often it takes you out of a market that is performing well. In this case, a little patience is its own reward.

Our personal investment profile looks at risk and return as two sides of the same coin. We have established your return requirements, and with the Risk Assessment Profile we can gain some insight into your ability to tolerate risk.

By totaling your scores, we establish a kind of policy statement, which, for lack of a better term, is your benchmark asset mix. Indeed, we will use that to gauge the performance of our annual asset mix relative to your personal benchmark.

For now, take some time to read the questions in the Risk Assessment Profile. Answer each of them as honestly as you can and, where required, work together with your spouse. Investment planning should be a family affair.

Please indicate how much importance you attribute to each of the following considerations. Use the scorecard below each question to rate your response.

RISK ASSESSMENT PROFILE

1. Liquidity

How important is it that you have access to your investment capital in case of emergencies or other investment opportunities?

It is extremely important	1
It is important	2
It is slightly important	4
It is not important at all	5
Score:	

2. Safety

You have been an investor for a full year. Assume you are holding blue-chip investments. How much would the value of your long-term investment capital have to decline before you would sell it and take a loss?

I would sell if my investment declined by 5%	1
I would sell if my investment declined by 15%	2
I would sell if my investment declined by 25%	3
I would sell if my investment declined by 50%	4
I would not sell my investment	5
Score:	

3. Current Income

How important is it that you receive an income stream from your investments over the period of your investment horizon?

It is extremely important	1
It is important	2
It is slightly important	4
It is not important at all	5
Score:	

4. Future Gains

How would you describe your reaction to financial news that may have a detrimental effect on your investments?

I would likely sell my investments	1
I would be fearful and consider selling my investments	2
I would be uncomfortable, but would hold my investments	3
I would remain calm and definitely hold my investments	4
Score:	

5. Portfolio Variability

How important is it that you never experience a loss in your portfolio during any given time period?

It is extremely important	1
It is important	2
It is slightly important	4
It is not important at all	5
Score:	

6. Performance Reviews

What performance numbers are you most concerned about?

Monthly performance numbers	1
Quarterly performance numbers	3
Annual performance numbers	5
Score:	

7. Speculation

Within the past five years, how often have you invested money in speculative investments?

I have never invested speculatively	1
I have invested speculatively once	2
I have invested speculatively twice	3
I have invested speculatively three or more times	4
Score:	

Risk as a Function of Time

If you are like most investors, you want to see your capital grow. Of course, just how substantial your growth objectives are depends, to a large extent, on how well you tolerate the risk of owning stock.

What you may not sufficiently appreciate is that stocks are one of the few investment assets that can deliver growth over the long term. We trust you see the problem. Too many individual investors looking for growth are preoccupied with safety of principal and because of that are not willing to assume the risk that accompanies an investment in equities. They simply cannot afford, or are not willing to accept, the volatility associated with equity investments.

What we are really talking about when discussing risk is the potential of loss. And within that context, equity investments are risky, because over short periods of time there is a reasonable chance that you could lose money. However, if you are willing to take a longer-term view to investing, the risk of loss diminishes dramatically.

Robert S. Bell of BellCharts, a company that publishes data on mutual funds, in a recent study examined the monthly performance of two key North American stock market indexes from December 31, 1981, to September 30, 1995. The two indexes in question were the Toronto Stock Exchange (TSE) 300 Total Return Index (i.e., the TSE 300 Composite Index, assuming all dividends are reinvested) and the U.S.-based Standard & Poor's 500 Total Return Index, reflected in Canadian dollars.

This period comprising almost 14 years "provided us with statistics for 153 different annual time periods, 141 two-year periods, 129 three-year periods, 105 five-year periods and 45 ten-year periods," observed Bell.

What Bell discovered is very interesting. He concluded the following: "Looking at the action for the TSE over the 153 one-year time frames, we see that the index declined 22.9% of the time. The worst one-year decline was -18.5%. Conversely, the best 12-month period was +86.9%, and the average was +12.9%." What this tells us is that despite the high average annual return, there is a better than one-in-five chance of losing money over any given one-year time period.

If you look at the TSE Total Return Index over the two-year time periods, the results are dramatically different. There was less than a one-in-fifteen (6.4%) chance of losing money in any given two-year period, and the worst two-year loss for the TSE was only -3.7%.

Interestingly, over the five-year and 10-year time periods, the TSE never recorded a single losing period, even if you had bought at the peak during any given month. The worst 10-year period for the TSE 300 Total Return Index since December 1981, including 45 different 10-year time periods, was a +7.8% compounded annual return. Downside risk went from -18.5% (worst one-year time period) to +7.8% (worst 10-year time period) by simply extending the time frame of reference from one year to 10 years.

Of course, these performance numbers are for the benchmark TSE Total Return Index and do not take into account the performance of Canadian equity fund managers. Good managers add performance value, a factor that will further skew the time horizon statistics.

Tables 2.7 and 2.8 examine the statistics for the TSE Total Return Index and the S&P 500

Total Return Index. "In each case, notice how the risk of losing money declines sharply over time," says Bell.

Table 2.7: TSE TOTAL RETURN INDEX (SINCE DECEMBER 31, 1981)

	1 year	2 years	3 years	5 years	10 years
Best period (% return)	86.9	32.8	30.7	27.8	13.5
Worst period (% return)	-18.5	-3.7	-7.2	0.2	7.8
Average (% return)	12.9	10.9	10.2	9.4	9.7
Number of plus periods	118	132	118	105	45
Number of negative periods	35	9	11	0	0
% chance of losing money	22.9	6.4	8.5	0.0	0.0

Table 2.8: S&P 500 TOTAL RETURN INDEX (SINCE DECEMBER 31, 1981)

	1 year	2 years	3 years	5 years	10 years
Best period (% return)	55.7	38.1	33.4	30.8	18.3
Worst period (% return)	-22.8	-1.1	-2.3	6.2	14.4
Average (% return)	18.1	16.7	16.5	15.2	16.0
Number of plus periods	138	139	127	105	45
Number of negative periods	15	2	2	0	0
% chance of losing money	10.9	1.4	1.6	0.0	0.0

The upshot, says Bell, is to hold: "Too many investors sell after a period of weak performance and are not there when the fund or the markets recover. They have moved on to the hot performer of the previous year, only to participate in the ensuing correction. It is quite possible to own nothing but the best-performing funds in Canada and still lose money. The winners are the buy-and-hold investors."

We are not suggesting, then, that equity investments carry no risk. What we are suggesting is that your time horizon has a great deal to do with risk, and by extension how much equity you can tolerate in your investment program.

8. Your Time Horizon

How long do you plan to hold your investments? If you are planning to retire some 20 years down the road, then you would expect to hold your investments for 20 years. Similarly, if you are putting together a portfolio to save for a down payment on a house five years in the future, your time horizon is five years.

Less than 2 years	0
Between 2 and 5 years	3
Between 5 and 10 years	6
Between 10 and 20 years	10
More than 20 years	15
Score:	______

Risk Assessment Profile Total Score: __________ ***(Total of 1 through 8)***

YOUR PERSONAL INVESTOR PROFILE

Category	Total Score
A: Net Worth	______
B: Financial Objectives	______
C: Risk Assessment Profile	______
D: Time Horizon	______
Total Score (A + B + C + D)	______

What Does It All Mean?

The final tally is your "Personal Investor Profile." But remember, financial circumstances and goals change, so take the time to re-evaluate your situation periodically.

Your Personal Investment Profile is structured as an aggressiveness index, and provides the foundation on which to establish your personal asset mix. The higher the score, the more aggressive the asset mix. The first step when constructing a long-term portfolio is deciding how much emphasis should be given to each asset class.

With that in mind, we start the process by defining your "policy statement." That is simply the average weighting we would expect you to hold in each asset class. Your policy statement is defined as the midpoint in the asset mix chart depicted in Figure 2.3.

You will also note two other percentages, a maximum and a minimum, wrapped around the policy statement. These are simply the maximum and minimum commitments you should make to each asset class at any point in time. Each year this book will be updated, and each year we may suggest you over-weight, under-weight or maintain your policy statement for the year ahead. By doing this, we hope to enhance your returns when the economy is strengthening and reduce your risk when the economy is slowing down. In other words, it's another way of trying to smooth your ride through the ups and downs of the business cycle.

Figure 2.3: YOUR PERSONAL INVESTMENT PROFILE

Your Score	Category	Equities Min	Equities Policy	Equities Max	Fixed Income Min	Fixed Income Policy	Fixed Income Max	Cash Min	Cash Policy	Cash Max	Your Category
< 15	Safety	0%	10%	20%	60%	75%	90%	10%	15%	30%	
15-24	Safety / Income	10%	20%	30%	50%	65%	80%	10%	15%	25%	
25-34	Income / Growth	20%	35%	50%	30%	50%	70%	10%	15%	25%	
35-44	Growth / Income	30%	50%	70%	25%	40%	55%	5%	10%	15%	
45-54	Growth	40%	60%	80%	20%	30%	40%	5%	10%	15%	
> 55	Aggressive / Growth	50%	75%	100%	0%	20%	30%	0%	5%	10%	

Remember, your personal policy statement is simply the first step in the selection of an ideal portfolio. By using the FundLine and our Best Bet list, you'll add other dimensions of diversification by breaking down this asset mix into specific geographic regions and investment styles.

PART II

Mutual Fund Basics

CHAPTER THREE

Mutual Fund Categories

There are about 1,800 mutual funds established in Canada, ranging from the traditional equity and bond funds to the more esoteric aggressive growth and specialty funds. The introduction of these new and interesting funds has meant the expansion of investment choices, but it has also made the mutual fund selection process more complex and difficult.

The Basic Features of Mutual Funds

Mutual funds provide four major investment features:

- *Diversification within an asset class*: With one transaction, you can own a portfolio of common stock or government bonds. Well-thought-out fund combinations can provide diversification across geographic boundaries (i.e., U.S. equity funds, international equity funds, global bond funds) and diversification by management style, as in aggressive growth versus a fundamental value style.
- *Convenience*: Mutual funds provide a vehicle that allows investors to buy in dollar amounts rather than 100-share lots. The fact that investors can begin with small initial investments and make periodic contributions—or systematic withdrawals—are advantages not found with other investment vehicles.
- *Mutual funds are cost-effective*: Buy a portfolio of 15 stocks or put together five bonds with staggered maturities, and transaction costs add up. At an average price of $30 a share, and a 100-share board lot of each, this portfolio of 15 stocks would cost $45,000, out of reach for many. Instead, by purchasing shares in a Canadian equity fund you get a portion of a large, already fully diversified investment portfolio. Mutual funds, then, bring size to the equation, and that allows for a cost advantage that individual investors simply cannot compete with.

- And, finally, *mutual funds provide access to the skills of a professional money manager.*

Other mutual fund features include a variety of entry and exit plans, tax-shelter plan eligibility (with some exceptions), liquidity, transferability and record keeping.

But there are costs to these benefits. One of the costs is direct and visible. The fund manager levies an advisory fee, charged monthly against the fund's assets, and there may be a load or commission when you buy the shares.

The Two Types of Investment Funds

An investment fund is the financial term used to define the role of an investment company. An investment fund (mutual fund) is, then, a company that invests in other companies (i.e., equity funds) or other fixed-income investments (i.e., bond funds). There are two types of investment funds: open-end funds and closed-end funds.

Open-End Funds

Open-end funds (usually referred to as mutual funds) sell units or shares to the public on a continuous basis and invest the proceeds in a portfolio of securities according to a published statement of objectives or investment policies. The "open-end" designation means that the mutual fund corporation can keep issuing new shares to purchasers.

Mutual funds are also required to buy back (redeem) shares on demand. You buy and sell the shares of open-end funds at what is called the "net asset value per share" (NAVPS), subject in some cases to a front-end and/or back-end load or commission, if any. Some funds are specifically no-load, and in cases where there is a load, it is negotiable.

The fund managers invest in a portfolio of securities (such as Canadian money market securities, Canadian stocks, foreign stocks and so on) in accordance with the fund's stated objectives and investment policies. Mutual fund units are purchased either through your stockbroker or financial planner, or from the company itself. The minimum initial purchase required is normally $500, with subsequent purchases in the order of $100.

There are more than 1,000 open-end investment funds situated in Canada, classified by various types of objectives. These objectives range from equity funds that invest strictly in common shares to money market funds that invest in money market instruments.

Closed-End Funds

In contrast to an open-end investment fund, closed-end funds are investment company pools for which the number of shares outstanding is fixed (i.e., closed). Since closed-end funds do not sell shares continuously to the public, the shares are traded on the secondary market. You buy and sell in the same manner that you buy and sell publicly traded shares of companies—through a stockbroker—by placing buy-and-sell orders in the auction market. Closed-end investment funds fit in somewhere between holding companies and mutual funds.

Like the open-end fund, the closed-end investment company invests its assets in a portfolio of securities according to an investment plan or strategy. Closed-end funds are typically specialized, holding portfolios in such specific areas as precious metals, foreign countries and foreign currencies. Some, however, hold diversified portfolios of primarily Canadian securities.

Since closed-end fund shares are traded rather than redeemed, the price is determined in the secondary market. Historically, closed-end fund shares have traded at discounts to the net asset value per share. In Canada and the U.S., for example, the discount on foreign country funds has averaged as high as 20% in recent years.

You can buy shares in closed-end funds through your stockbroker. The shares are traded in the same manner as common shares, and commissions will run 1% to 3% of the value of the transaction, depending on the size of your purchase. Net asset values for Canadian closed-end funds are published in The Globe and Mail's Report on Business, Saturday edition.

Why do closed-end fund shares typically trade at a discount? The discount reflects:

- relative optimism or pessimism of investors;
- the cost of liquidating the portfolio and distributing the proceeds to investors;
- the implicit management/advisory fees or other expenses of the fund;
- the preference for brokers to sell open-ended investment funds; and
- the fact that closed-end funds are not awarded the favorable tax treatment of their open-ended counterparts in some countries. As a result, embedded tax liabilities may be inher ited by the purchasers in the form of unrealized stock appreciation.

Mutual Fund Categories

The Canadian reporting services group funds into categories fairly consistently, although there are some minor variations. In general, the funds are categorized as follows.

Money Market Funds

One of the most versatile investment vehicles is the money market fund (MMF). These unique funds invest in money market securities of various maturities. Although there are a large number of money market instruments, the most popular are Treasury bills, issued by the Government of Canada and the provinces; bankers' acceptances; short-term government and high-quality corporate bonds; and the promissory notes of companies with very high credit ratings—a product called commercial paper. These are all considered low-risk investments for which the possibility of a default is relatively remote.

Unlike traditional mutual funds, however, the MMFs (with a few exceptions) attempt to maintain a fixed net asset value per share by using the amortized cost method for valuing some or all of their assets. Traditional mutual funds have floating NAVPS and calculate the value of their portfolio each day (a process called "marking to market").

Money market funds pay only interest, so all distributions are likely to be treated as interest income. Normally, income is distributed through additional shares or units rather than through cash payments.

In addition, MMFs invest virtually all of their assets in money market instruments, including Treasury bills, certificates of deposit, deposit receipts, government short-term bonds and commercial paper.

Bond or Mortgage Funds

Fixed-income funds have virtually all of their assets in fixed-income securities, including bonds, mortgages and money market instruments. The primary objective is stable and regular income.

Dividend Income Funds

Dividend income funds are mutual funds that invest in high-yield preferred and common shares of blue-chip Canadian companies. Some funds also invest a small proportion of their portfolio in fixed-income securities such as money market funds, bonds and debentures. The principal investment objective is to generate investment income for the unit holder. Capital growth may occur, as well, in a favorable interest rate environment.

Although dividend income funds are generally much more stable than equity funds, they will, and do, fluctuate in value. For example, as interest rates rise, the market value of the preferred and common shares and other securities held in the fund will often fall. Furthermore, if unit holders decide to redeem their units at such a time, this could force the fund manager to sell securities at a loss to meet redemptions, further reducing the net asset value per share.

The key investment feature of dividend income funds is the dividend income produced—and the way in which those dividends are taxed. As a unit holder, you are entitled to your proportionate share of the dividends and interest earned on the fund's portfolio, as well as any capital gains (losses) incurred in the fund's trading of securities before their maturity. Normally, dividend income fund distributions are made with additional shares or units rather than cash payments.

Dividend income is given preferential tax treatment at the personal level. That is what makes dividend income and dividend income funds so attractive. The dividend tax credit is discussed later in the chapter.

Balanced Funds

The fund manager maintains a balanced portfolio of stocks and bonds, normally within a specified range. The primary objective is stability of returns. Balanced funds are either formalized, where the portfolio is fixed in some proportion, such as 40% bonds and 60% equities, or semi-discretionary, where proportions can be changed when the advisor deems it wise.

Equity Growth Funds

The funds of an equity growth portfolio are invested in shares that are expected to have above-average earnings and growth potential.

Aggressive Equity Growth Funds

These funds pursue a strategy of investing in very aggressive common shares and look for unusually high growth.

Gold or Precious Metal Funds

These funds hold gold and other precious metals and/or gold mining shares.

Global and International Funds

These are funds that invest a substantial portion of their assets in securities outside the country of domicile. International funds are those that limit their investments to markets and countries outside the domestic country. They might even restrict their investment activities to a specific region, country or continent. In contrast, global funds have no geographic bounds; they invest anywhere that their management believes a bargain can be found—including the host country. Global funds thus offer greater diversification than international funds because of the lack of restriction on investment activities. However, an investor can combine ownership of a diversified domestic portfolio with ownership of international funds to replicate a global portfolio, and can define international allocations among different countries using *single country funds*—funds that invest all of their assets in a specific country.

Specialty Funds

These are funds that invest in a defined industry or asset including gold, high technology, and oil and gas.

Real Estate Funds

These are funds that invest all or most of their assets in real estate.

Index Funds

These are funds whose objective is to replicate the performance of some market index, such as the TSE 300 Composite Index. The fund manager's objectives are to acquire the portfolio at as low a cost as possible, then maintain the portfolio through adjustments to reflect the changes to the index due to substitutions, mergers and takeovers. (We'll provide a more in-depth discussion about index funds in Chapter 4.)

While on the Subject of Taxes . . .

After seeing how tax treatment can skew the investment landscape, we need to spend some time understanding the impact taxes have on more traditional investments. Your return from balanced funds, for example, will be a combination of interest income, capital and dividend distributions and appreciation in the NAVPS—each taxed in its own way. The interest income is taxed as ordinary income. Seventy-five percent of the capital gain distribution is included in income and taxed as ordinary income, while dividend income is subject to the gross-up and dividend tax credit treatment.

Each year you will receive a statement setting out your share of the interest and dividends earned on each fund's portfolio, as well as any capital gains (losses) incurred in the fund's trading of securities before their maturity. All interest, dividend and capital gain income received from the fund, whether it be by cheque or through reinvestment in additional shares, is taxable income. Occasionally a fund makes distributions in excess of its income. These are identified as returns of capital and are not taxable when received. However, they will reduce your cost base of the units, eventually culminating in a larger capital gain.

Your interest income is treated as ordinary income and is taxed in the normal manner. Dividend income is treated as dividend income and is afforded the special treatment that dividend income receives in Canada.

Here is how it works. Dividends received from taxable Canadian corporations are grossed up by 25%, and then a dividend tax credit is applied, computed as 16.67% of the dividend. The net effect of this gross-up and credit is to reduce the effective tax rate to well below that paid for comparable interest income.

The dramatic impact of the dividend tax credit is shown in the accompanying table, which contrasts the tax treatment of $1,000 earned on a term deposit with $1,000 earned in the form of a dividend payment. The amounts are calculated for a Canadian taxpayer who is in the highest marginal tax bracket (taxable income of about $60,000 or more), although the differential is universal (see Table 3.1).

Table 3.1: CALCULATING THE DIVIDEND TAX CREDIT

Income	Interest	Dividend
	$1,000.00	$1,000.00
Gross-Up (25%)		250.00
Taxable Income	1,000.00	1,250.00
Federal Tax (29%)*	290.00	362.50
Federal Dividend Tax Credit (16.67% of $1,000)		166.70
Federal Tax Payable	290.00	195.80
Provincial Tax Payable	159.50	107.69
Total Tax Payable	449.50	303.49
Income after Tax	550.50	696.51
Effective Marginal Tax Rate (%)	44.95	30.35

*These calculations are approximations only for illustrative purposes. They ignore federal and provincial surtaxes.

Capital gains can occur in two ways: the fund may make capital gains distributions based on profitable trading of securities; alternatively, if you sell your units for an amount in excess of your original cost (as adjusted for returns of capital), you will also incur a capital gain. Capital gains are subject to the 25% exclusion rule; that is, only 75% of an eligible gain need be included in income. Capital gains may be offset by allowable capital losses. The amount included is taxed at the marginal tax rate.

What is a dividend?
A dividend is money paid by a company to its shareholders. Common dividends are paid to common shareholders and represent a return on invested capital and are paid out of after-tax profits. Common dividends may fluctuate based on the profitability of the company. Preferred dividends are paid to preferred shareholders and "usually" remain fixed for the life of the preferred shares. Preferred dividends are also paid out of after-tax profits.

Loads and Other Costs

There are two types of potential costs borne by fund holders: loads or sales charges payable at purchase (front end), over the holding period (level load) and/or at sale (back end), and management fees. Sales charges are levied by what are called load funds; firms that charge no sales fees are called no-load. The issue of fees for mutual funds is becoming extremely complex. Part of the problem is the blurring between loads, sales fees and management fees.

Mutual fund loads or commissions are designed as compensation to the broker or agent for advising and arranging the transaction. They come in a variety of packages and options, and since there is no universal truth as to which is best, it is important to understand exactly what you are paying and what you are paying for. The load should also be considered in light of the management fee.

To clarify, loads are sales commissions; management expenses are the charges of the fund manager, including advisory fees, distribution expenses and other operating expenses. These may also include a form of sales commission. Read on.

Both load and no-load groups charge management fees that average, at least for Canadian equity funds, about 2.15% and are deducted from the NAVPS. Load funds, on average, charge slightly higher management fees, as well.

Front-end loads are still widely used in the load category. These are paid at the time of purchase and are calculated on the total investment. If you invest $10,000 in a mutual fund and pay a 5% front-end load, you will pay $500 in commissions.

This represents a load of 5.26% as a percentage of the $9,500 that goes to the purchase of units. Although loads can be as high as 9% (or 9 divided by 91 x 100 = 9.9% effectively), they are negotiable and can normally be reduced depending on the size of your order and your bargaining skills. The most you are likely to pay is 6%, but 3% to 4% is closer to the norm.

Back-end loads or deferred charges have proliferated recently. This option allows you to pay a commission on redemption, typically on a scaled-down basis reflecting the number of years you hold the fund. Therefore, the load is reduced the longer your holding period, falling to zero after a set number of years (normally seven or eight).

For example, the load may be 5.5% if you redeem in the first year, tapering off to nothing if you hold for more than seven years. This deferred method sounds like the way to go, except that there are catches. The management fees are usually higher for the back-end load, so the reduced commission associated with holding the fund is balanced—although not necessarily equally—against the increased management fee paid. Often the fee is based on market value rather than cost, and thus you could, potentially at least, end up substantially increasing the effective fee.

Over 40% of the Canadian mutual funds charge no loads at all (part of the no-load group). The no-load group consists primarily, but not exclusively, of banks and trust companies; they charge no sales commissions but instead sell their products through registered salespersons within their branches or through arrangements with brokers.

A portion of the management fee with many no-load funds may be paid as a commission to selling brokers. These are called trailer fees. So you really are paying some sort of sales fee, whether or not you use a financial advisor, broker or mutual fund agent—it is simply a matter of what you want to call it!

Many funds are now offering choices, as in choose your poison. In some cases, AGF being the classic example, fund companies will offer as many as three different classes of shares or units in the same fund, each providing a different combination of sales commissions and management fees. Options are good, but make sure you understand what you are paying for!

That being said, loads and fees are not critical criteria for selecting funds—your choice should be based on expected return and volatility. However, in choosing among similar funds, it depends on your holding period and strategy. If your investment strategy is to set an asset mix, buy mutual funds to match your needs and hold them for the long term, the more suitable fee package will normally be to pay the front-high load and the lower annual management fee. If your style tends to involve substantial trading and turnover, the no-load fund with the high management fee approach will often yield the best result.

Operating Expenses

The fund's operating expenses can be measured as total operating costs per $100 of assets. Although studies indicate that, in general, high-expense ratio funds tend to slightly underperform low-expense ratio funds, the relationship is not a strong one and is likely to be dominated by other factors. Investors are thus cautioned that a low expense ratio does not necessarily imply above-average performance.

Behind the Numbers:
A *FundLetter** Analysis of Canadian Equity Fund Performance

The Load/No-load Issue

The recent formation of the no-load fund mutual fund group within the Canadian mutual fund industry has focused attention on the load/no-load issue again.

Both load and no-load groups charge management fees that average, at least for Canadian equity funds, about 2.15%. Load funds on average charge slightly higher management fees, as well. How differently do they perform?

A landmark study published by the U.S. Securities and Exchange Commission (SEC) in 1962 concluded that funds with load charges performed no better than no-load funds, and slightly worse after the load. Loads were fixed in those fledgling development days of the mutual fund industry and ran as high as 9.9% on an effective basis. Now commissions are negotiable, and rarely should you pay the top rate.

To check things out, we analyzed performance in the Canadian equity fund category. The results were interesting. Over the past five years, the average no-load fund slightly outperformed the average load fund by about 16 basis points per year (0.16%). Putting it on a practical footing, a $10,000 investment in the typical no-load fund grew to $13,401, while a similar investment in the average load fund grew to only $12,634, assuming a 5% load.

However, over the past 10 years, capturing three market cycles, load funds outperformed the no-loads by a substantial margin—more than sufficient to overcome the load and leave an incremental profit. For example, that same $10,000 investment in the no-load fund grew to $22,443, an annual compounded rate of return of 8.42%, compared with $23,933 for a load fund at 5% commission (an annual rate of return of 9.11%). At a 3% commission, the $10,000 grew to $24,436 (a 9.34% annual rate of return). The typical load fund passed the no-load fund in approximately the seventh year. For both categories, the top-performing funds in terms of return were in the $100 to $500 million category.

So the recent period favored the no-load group, the more extended period the load group.

Table 3.2: CANADIAN EQUITY FUND PAST PERFORMANCE

Category	Total Investment	Amount Allocated to Units	Five-Year Ending Value	Ten-Year Ending Value	Ten-Year Annual Returns
Load at 5%	$10,000	$9,500	$12,634	$22,933	9.11%
Load at 3%	10,000	9,300	12,900	24,436	9.34%
No-load	10,000	10,000	13,401	22,443	8.42%

continued. . .

The bottom line? There are lots of criteria for selecting Canadian equity funds, of which load is only one. Nevertheless, everything else being equal, if you have a short investment horizon (i.e., six years or less), concentrate your research on the no-load group. But if your investment horizon exceeds six years, take a close look first at the load group.

* *The* FundLetter *is a monthly newspaper published by the Hume Group in Toronto (subscription information at 1-800-733-4863). The* FundLetter *focuses on issues and investments within the mutual fund industry, and the contributing editors make specific recommendations on where to invest. Richard Croft and Eric Kirzner are both contributing editors to the* FundLetter.

How many funds in your portfolio?

Another approach is to buy a portfolio of different mutual funds spanning the safety, income and growth objectives. The "family of funds" concept is catching on quickly. The largest mutual fund organizations offer a number of different mutual funds—as many as 30 different ones—that capture the entire objectives spectrum. The notion is that once you have entered the "family" by buying one of the funds, you should be able to revise your portfolio holdings by switching within the family—in some cases at no cost. So, if you wish, you can build your initial portfolio structure with a single fund organization and vary the composition as you see fit.

But some fund organizations offer yet another option—portfolios of their underlying funds that provide diversification on their own. Typical portfolios range from strict income orientation (100% bond and mortgage funds) to heavy growth emphasis (100% equity and real estate funds).

With the advent of the "family of funds" concept, investors can now rebalance their own portfolio with reasonable costs. The purchase of one of the funds within the family enables you to periodically revise your portfolio holdings by allowing you to switch to another fund within the family—in some cases at no cost.

A Special Report on Labor-Sponsored Mutual Funds

Labor-sponsored funds were first developed in 1984 by the Canadian Federation of Labour. The oldest is the Quebec-based Fonds de Solidarité.

Labor-sponsored mutual funds are designed to encourage venture capital investment in small- and medium-size Canadian businesses in part through tax incentives offered to investors. Like other mutual funds, they represent a pool of capital acquired from investors and allocated to a portfolio. However, they can only be sponsored by organized labor organizations.

Labor-sponsored mutual funds, then, invest in small- and medium-size emerging companies, many of which are not publicly traded. As a result, valuation of the portfolio is generally based on security appraisals or market estimates rather than market prices. Unlike most other mutual funds, labor-sponsored mutual funds price their units or shares monthly, rather than daily.

We look at labor-sponsored funds from three perspectives: (1) as a conduit for venture capital, (2) as a questionable investment for a conservative investor, and (3) as an investment vehicle.

And while the government-sponsored tax breaks are attractive, they have a price: a government-imposed penalty if certain investment requirements are not met, a board of directors that must reserve a seat for a labor union and a system that is used to classify investors by type. Prior to the April 1996 federal budget, investors who were retired or who were 65 years of age or older could redeem their labor-sponsored investment fund after only two years and still retain their tax credits. Other investors had to hold the fund for a minimum of five years. In the April 1996 federal budget, Finance Minister Paul Martin eliminated the advantage for senior citizens.

In what looks suspiciously like a pyramid structure, any run on these funds after the minimum five-year holding period without sufficient new money coming in to meet those redemptions would mean that those investors who were the last to enter the game might become the first casualties. Of course, performance of the investments within the fund will go a long way toward determining the retention rate of those early investors.

On the cost side, most labor-sponsored funds come with a back-end load, which means that investors pay a fee to exit the fund. The fee usually starts at 6% of assets after one year and declines by 0.75% each year thereafter. In most cases there is no exit fee if you hold the fund for at least eight years.

The Essentials of the Tax Picture for Labor-Sponsored Funds

Having provided some investment caveats, we have to say that the tax deductions are attractive. On a $3,500 investment, you are immediately entitled to a 20% federal tax credit (up to a maximum of $700), regardless of where you live in Canada. As well, some provinces—notably Ontario, Prince Edward Island, New Brunswick, Nova Scotia and Saskatchewan—offer an additional 20% tax credit, which means that outside of an RRSP, your out-of-pocket cost for a $3,500 investment can be as low as $2,100.

There is one additional issue to bear in mind, and that is the imposition of an alternative minimum tax. Likely not to be a concern for most investors, the tax credits would have no value for individuals faced with paying a minimum tax. Under that scenario, Revenue Canada will add back certain credits and subtract deductions in order to arrive at the alternative minimum tax.

That aside, the sales spin really picks up steam when you look at buying the labor-sponsored fund inside an RRSP. In this case, you are entitled to additional savings. Effectively, your initial investment of $3,500 is deposited into an RRSP and is immediately eligible for the basic RRSP deduction. Depending on the provincial tax rate, investors earning more than $30,000 would receive approximately $1,400 in additional RRSP tax credits, while investors earning more than $68,000 receive as much as $1,855 in additional RRSP tax credits.

A $3,500 labor-sponsored fund investment inside an RRSP can mean as much as $1,400 in federal and provincial tax credits, and an additional $1,855 (the maximum potential benefit) in RRSP tax credits. The net after-tax investment, then, is $245 for those in the highest tax bracket and approximately $700 for individuals earning between $30,000 and $68,000 (depending on the province in which the investor resides).

Another aspect of labor-sponsored funds remains up in the air. At least that's the read we get after talking with a number of accountants. Here's the scenario. You are an Ontario resident (one of the provinces that allow the maximum deductions) and purchase a $3,500 labor-sponsored fund outside an RRSP. Under the new rules, you will receive a 20% federal tax credit ($700) and a 20% provincial tax credit ($700). Your net out-of-pocket cost is $2,100.

Some eight years later, you decide to sell the labor-sponsored fund and the value at the time of sale is $2,600. The question is: do you (1) have a capital loss of $900 (i.e., $3,500 initial unit value less $2,600 receipts at point of sale = $900 loss), or (2) have a capital gain of $500 (i.e., $2,600 receipt at point of sale - $2,100 out-of-pocket expense = $500 profit)? At this time, we have no definitive answer. However, if we were betting advisors, we would tend to err on the side of caution and assume Revenue Canada will take the position that you would in fact have a capital gain.

Understanding the Investment Issues for Labor-Sponsored Funds

Obviously, the tax implications are what make labor-sponsored funds an attractive alternative. And should the labor-sponsored fund actually spin some positive returns over the five years, you would end up with a capital gain and only a portion of the accompanying tax liability. You pay tax only on capital gains above the $3,500 initial investment.

On the other hand, if the fund were to lose 10% compounded annually (not an unreasonable assumption), the value of your investment at the end of five years would be $2,066.72. Assuming your actual out-of-pocket cost after federal and provincial tax credits is $2,100, you would have a total out-of-pocket loss of $33.28. If you redeem your labor-sponsored fund at that point you pay a back-end load of approximately $46.50 (approximately 2.25% of current value of the fund which is $2,020.22). On your initial out-of-pocket cost of $2,100, you would get back $2,020.22. And that does not take into account the lost-opportunity cost attached to your initial investment!

Here's where we have a problem. The labor-sponsored fund could lose 7% compounded annually, leaving you with $2,380.12 (after back-end load charges). On paper you have lost $1,119.88 ($3,500 investment less $2,380.12 at redemption = $1,119.88), but in actual fact, after accounting for the tax credits, you have $280.12 in after-tax profits. That is a net return of 2.5% compounded annually on your initial $2,100 out-of-pocket investment (assuming you received the maximum provincial tax credit at the point of purchase).

A typical investment in a first-year GIC yielding 6% will return about 2.9% to investors in the highest tax bracket. That the after-tax return on a GIC is about the same as the return on a labor-sponsored fund that lost 7% compounded annually illustrates, in our opinion, the problem with tax-driven investments.

In Summary

The Good News

- Diversification: many funds have diversified portfolios; difficult to replicate on your own.
- Asset allocation: you can pursue strategic, dynamic and tactical programs with mutual funds.
- Professional management.
- Record keeping.
- Wide range of choices: you can do most of your financial planning with mutual funds.
- Lots to choose within categories.
- Periodic purchase plans; dollar-cost averaging.
- Numerous withdrawal options: ratio, fixed period, constant dollar.
- Usually small initial purchase ($100 to $1,000); small subsequent purchases, some as low as $25.
- Dividend reinvestment options are extremely valuable.

The Bad News

- Some mutual funds perform poorly.
- Some don't stick to objectives.
- Many are inconsistent.
- Hidden fees are buried in advisory fees.
- Sales reps may be motivated by commission rather than your interest.
- Abuses: cross-selling; twisting; mutual commissions; distributor gifts.
- Improper valuation.
- Internal cross-trading within fund families may be a problem.
- Misleading sales promotions: use of skewed charts, truncated axes.
- Some registered representatives are poorly trained in the skills of effectively mixing and matching funds.
- Hidden switch costs.

CHAPTER FOUR

Equity Funds and Investment Styles

The Risk of Avoiding Stocks

We believe that equity assets, or, if you prefer, *stocks*, should play a role in virtually all investment portfolios. Just how big a role depends on your specific long-range goals and your ability to tolerate the ups and downs of the business cycle.

Notwithstanding those caveats, the fact remains that stocks are a superb investment. Just how good are the performance numbers? Well, over the past 70 years, stocks have been the number-one performing investment asset, outperforming all other investments hands down.

Peter Lynch, one-time portfolio manager of the giant U.S.-based Fidelity Magellan Fund and author of *Beating the Street*, discusses the relative performance of stocks and bonds in the preface of his book. Using the *Ibbotson SBBI Yearbook*, Lynch examines "Average Annual Returns for the Decades 1926–1989"—a summary of returns you would have received using different types of investment vehicles: the 500 stocks in the Standard & Poor's Composite Index, a portfolio of small-company stocks, long-term U.S. government bonds, long-term U.S. corporate bonds and short-term U.S. Treasury bills.

Over the seven decades reviewed in the Ibbotson study, only once (1930-1940) did U.S. bonds outperform U.S. stocks. "By sticking with stocks all the time," writes Lynch, "the odds are six to one in our favor that we'll do better than the people who stick with bonds." And the performance numbers are, well, mind-boggling. "Over the entire 64 years covered in the study, a $100,000 investment in long-term U.S. government bonds would have been worth $1.6 million; the same amount invested in the S&P 500 would be worth $25.5 million."

The key to this discussion is the notion that equity assets must be held for the long term. In the Ibbotson study, we are talking about a 70-year time period, which clearly does not fit within the investing life of an individual. But even over much shorter periods, equity assets have performed admirably. For example, if we look at the five-year track record of Canadian equity funds, only 10 out of 200 funds lost money. The worst of the group[1]—looking at the five-year period ending May 1998—returned -10.8% compounded annually; the best returned 35.1% compounded annually.

Here's where the line between performance and real-world investing begins to blur. We know that over a five-year time period, your equity fund will earn a positive return. We also know, from mutual fund studies, that the average holding period for any mutual fund, including funds that hold equities, is 17 months. And therein lies the problem: individual investors too often sell too quickly and usually at exactly the wrong time.

It appears that individual investors are trying to time the market, or at the very least, their financial advisor is trying to suggest timing when to buy and sell specific funds. Again, according to studies, there appears to be two reasons for this: (1) the need to move in and out quickly, looking for a fast buck from some speculative investment, and (2) the fear of a stock market collapse like the one we witnessed in October 1987 and again in October 1992. A more recent example that should still be fresh in the minds of Canadian investors is the sell-off in both Canadian bonds and stocks leading up to the 1995 Quebec referendum.

Assuming we have been able to convince you of the risks associated with the lottery syndrome, let's for a moment focus on the fears of a stock market collapse.

We trust that the argument to hold stocks in your portfolio is compelling. And we understand that to do so means riding the ups and downs of the business cycle and assuming some risk along the way. We also know that, given a choice, most investors would prefer to avoid risk. If we could play Monday-morning quarterback with our investments, we would all make fortunes in short order—with no risk!

Unfortunately, investments are made with an eye toward the future, which tells us that buy-and-sell decisions are driven by expected changes in the economy or are based on developments that might or might not happen within specific companies. This is another reason why so many investors prefer to avoid stocks in their portfolio. It's simply too hard, despite being overloaded with information, to keep abreast of the ebb and flow of the financial markets.

Let's face it—most investors have neither the time nor the inclination to pore over financial statements and economic trends in search of the diamond in the rough of investment ideas. And while brokerage firms pay top dollar to research analysts whose job it is to forecast the performance of the stock market and/or the earnings of specific companies, many brokers will tell you that even *they* don't have the time to read all the material.

And frankly, we're not sure this type of analysis is the primary issue within the context of your personal investment plan. While we believe that research analysts help maintain efficient financial markets, we question the relevance of short-term earnings forecasts within the context of a long-range investment plan.

---

[1] *According to data from Pal-Trak, the fund with the worst five-year performance record was Cambridge Pacific (-25% compounded annually). The best five-year performance numbers for Canadian equity funds belonged to the AIC Advantage Fund (24.5% compounded annually). Data to the end of September 1997.*

We would argue that there are more important issues to contend with. We believe that individual investors should spend less time searching for the next Microsoft or the newest wave in mutual funds or the next state-of-the-art tax shelter, and instead make a commitment to understanding their own investment personality and develop a cover-all-the-bases investment plan designed from the top down.

Equity Funds Defined

An equity fund is structured to invest primarily in shares of common stock. A Canadian equity fund, for example, invests in the shares of Canadian companies and is considered to be an eligible investment for your Registered Retirement Savings Plan.

There are also equity mutual funds that invest in the common shares of companies outside of Canada, which can be broken into a number of broad categories, including:

1. **U.S. Equity Funds:** Mutual funds that invest primarily in the common shares of U.S.-based companies. Not an eligible RRSP investment, except within the 20% foreign content rules.

2. **International and Global Funds:** Mutual funds that invest primarily in the common shares of companies outside Canada. These funds may invest primarily in U.S. stocks or may focus on other regions around the globe, such as the emerging markets of Latin America and the Far East, as well as mature markets such as Japan and Europe. There is a fine line that distinguishes between international and global funds. International equity funds invest in stocks in countries outside Canada. Global equity funds, on the other hand, invest in stocks in countries outside Canada as well as in stocks domiciled in Canada.

3. **Special Equity Funds:** Sometimes referred to as sector funds, these mutual funds invest in specific industries or sectors of the economy. Examples include the science and technology sector, precious metals and health care, to name a few. We think this is one of the growth areas in the mutual fund industry and would expect to see more of these specialty funds in the future.

We can also distinguish equity funds in terms of their specific objectives, as defined in the fund's prospectus. Some equity fund managers, for example, focus primarily on large-cap stocks; others have a mandate to invest in the shares of small companies with, say, a market capitalization of less than $250 million.

More important, some funds require the manager to maintain a fully invested position, while others allow greater latitude. We don't come down on one side of this debate or the other. There are pros and cons to both positions.

A fully invested fund is useful because it forces the manager to implement an investment strategy that focuses on industries and security selection. That fits well with our asset allocation theme. By establishing the asset mix, we are determining 85% to 90% of our overall return. We are depending on the individual fund managers to provide their expertise on security and industry selection that impacts on the remaining 10% to 15% of our overall return.

To expand on that point, suppose that your portfolio's asset allocation was 50% Canadian equity, 40% Canadian fixed income and 10% Canadian money market. And just to emphasize our point, let's assume you purchased the Ivy Canadian Fund to represent your Canadian equity assets, the Dynamic Income Fund for your Canadian fixed-income requirement and the Elliott & Page Money Market Fund for your cash assets. Your portfolio would break out as follows.

Table 4.1A: SAMPLE ASSET MIX

Fund Particulars	Pct. of Portfolio
Elliott & Page Money Market Fund	10%
Dynamic Income Fund	40%
Ivy Canadian Fund	50%

But on closer inspection, the Ivy Canadian Fund (as of May 31, 1998) was holding about 26% of its assets in cash, the remaining 74% of assets being invested in specific equities. In other words, about one-third of the money you felt comfortable investing in Canadian stocks is not in stocks at all but instead is invested in cash. So your portfolio breaks out as follows (see percentages along the bottom of Table 4.1B).

Table 4.1B: SAMPLE ASSET MIX

Fund Particulars	Equity	Fixed Income	Cash
Elliott & Page Money Market Fund			10%
Dynamic Income Fund		40%	
Ivy Canadian Fund	37%*		13%
Portfolio Breakout	**37%**	**40%**	**23%**

* 74% (fund's position in Canadian equity) x 50% (percentage of asset mix represented by Canadian equity assets) = 37% exposure to Canadian equity

The argument in favor of holding large cash positions is that it helps reduce risk. Equity managers who have the discretion to move in and out of the market—i.e., from stock to cash, etc.—as the business cycle changes, can add value if they are good at timing those changes. This strategy can be particularly useful in a down market, where a high cash position will protect the gains in the mutual fund's portfolio.

Still, all things being equal, we would prefer to hold equity funds that are fully invested in stocks. And while all managers have some latitude as to how much cash they can hold at a point in time, we prefer that equity managers maintain at least 90% of their portfolio in stocks. In short, we prefer that equity managers stick to what they do best—manage their stock picks. We think that you and your financial advisor can establish the correct asset mix, which should provide sufficient cushioning in a market downturn.

Of course, the easiest way to buy Canadian equity assets, and be guaranteed that the fund is always 100% invested in Canadian shares, is to purchase an index fund. That way you determine the asset mix and the portfolio manager takes care of tracking the benchmark index. Such a strategy has gained a large following in the U.S. and we may see that trend expand into Canada over the next few years.

Equity Index Funds—The North and South Debate

When it comes to trends in the Canadian mutual fund industry, much can be learned from our friends south of the border; not because American fund companies are better than their Canadian counterparts, but because trends are often defined by a time line, and in that regard, Americans have been at it longer. And like most things in the business community, trends in the U.S. usually find their way into Canada.

I raise this issue because I am seeing a small but growing movement among Canadian mutual fund investors toward so-called equity index funds. And I find that disturbing, because it's clear to me that the cost savings associated with Canadian equity index funds are not sufficient to justify what amounts to a guarantee of underperformance.

Now, you can argue, as some in the financial press have, that this is simply a case of what goes around comes around. In the 1960s and early 1970s, when the mutual fund industry was in its infancy, investors were sold on the risk-reduction advantages of diversification. Mutual funds simply provided a more efficient cost-effective way to structure an equity portfolio.

As the industry matured and more companies entered the market with new funds, investors began to comparison-shop. Since all broad-based equity funds offered diversification, the allure of one fund over another came down to performance, and that set the stage for the now-famous mountain charts that appear in most mutual fund marketing literature.

Then, in 1976, about the time investors were focusing on money management skills as the primary reason for buying a particular fund, along came the Vanguard Group and the launch of their now-famous Vanguard Index Trust 500 portfolio.

At the time, the concept of indexation was a radical idea! Here was a fund whose objective was to match the performance of the benchmark index, which in this case was the Standard & Poor's 500 Total Return Index. No performance promises, no attempt to highlight the skills of the money manager; just a simple guarantee, low-cost structure and instant diversification.

What Vanguard did was redefine—or shall we say revisit—the way mutual funds were sold, and in doing so set the stage for what today is a widespread debate as to how much value one should attach to management expertise.

The management of Vanguard will tell you that performance by nature is fickle. Too often last year's hot manager becomes this year's outcast. As such, the costs associated with performance in many cases outweigh the benefits. The fact that the Vanguard 500 fund now lays claim to more than U.S.$10 billion in assets illustrates how critical an issue this is to U.S. mutual fund investors.

– R.C.

Index Funds in Canada

Canadian equity index funds have been around since 1983, the first to enter the game being the Great West Life Equity Index Fund. However, to be fair, this is not a pure play on the TSE 300 Composite Index because the fund's objective is to buy the 250 largest companies in the TSE 300 Composite Index. It doesn't say the manager has to buy certain percentages of each stock, percentages that correspond to the percentage weighting within the benchmark index. It simply restricts the manager as to which 250 stocks he can purchase.

The Green Line Canadian Index Fund, on the other hand, is a pure index investment, designed to track the performance of the TSE 300 Composite Index. In this case, the manager attempts to match the weightings of stock in his portfolio to their representative weighting within the TSE 300 Composite Index.

When examining the merits of an index fund, analysts talk in terms of tracking error, which essentially defines how closely the index fund tracks the performance of the benchmark index. How well the manager mirrors the index defines for an investor how well the manager is doing his job. The question of performance, then, becomes a moot point. You won't do any better than the benchmark index, but you shouldn't do any worse, either.

Given the rise in the number of Canadian equity index funds, there is little doubt that Canadian investors share many of the American views on the subject. Like our U.S. cousins, we, too, are asking if the long-term performance numbers are sufficient to justify high management fees. Of course, that assumes that Canadian equity index funds are delivering on their promise of low fees, and that issue is not clear.

When investors buy traditional equity funds, they are buying the manager's performance record, so the fees for traditional equity funds, presumably, compensate a manager for outperforming the benchmark index. But here's where the pay-for-performance debate gets ugly and supports the movement toward equity index funds.

When you look at the five-year track record for Canadian equity funds, you have to ask yourself: "Where's the performance?" Only 37 out of 200 Canadian equity funds with a minimum five-year track record matched or beat the 16.8% compound annual return generated by the TSE Composite Index over the last five years. (All returns are based on a May 31, 1998, year-end.)

Over shorter periods, the pay-for-performance arguments are even harder to justify. Only 64 out of 260 Canadian equity funds had better three-year performance numbers than the TSE 300 Total Return Index. And over the past year, only 24% (84 out of 354) of Canadian equity funds beat the TSE 300 Composite Index. On the surface, those numbers present a powerful case for index funds.

However, if you scratch below the surface, the numbers tell a much different story. Of all three of the pure Canadian equity index funds with five-year records, none was able to equal the performance of the TSE 300 Composite Index (including dividends reinvested). The best of the lot, the Green Line Canadian Index Fund, had a five-year compound annual return of 15.5%, which was 1.3% below the five-year compound annual return on the TSE 300 Index.

Moreover, in terms of performance, the Green Line Canadian Index Fund—which we said was the best-performing Canadian index fund—ranked 63rd out of 200 Canadian equity funds in terms of five-year performance numbers. It is the same story among the other Canadian equity index funds.

Based on these performance stats, two issues seem clear: (1) not all Canadian index funds are created equally, and (2) based on past performance, it appears that Canadian equity index funds guarantee a record of underperformance.

Of course, there is another side to this argument. Fund companies will tell us, quite correctly, that an index has no costs attached to its performance. For the fund company, even though the fund is indexed, there is the cost of buying the securities represented in the index, and there is an annual administrative fee.

In the end, however, the motive for buying an index fund comes down to cost. You might be willing to accept a lower standard if management fees for the index fund are substantially below the average for all Canadian equity funds. But here, too, most Canadian index funds fall down.

Interestingly, the average management-expense ratio (MER) for the five Canadian index funds is 1.66% (ranging from a low of 1.10% for the Green Line Canadian Equity Index Fund to a high of 2.55% for N.N. Canadian 35 Index Fund). Compare that with the 2.13% average MER for the 94 Canadian diversified equity funds that have at least a five-year track record, and the pay-for-performance argument begins to lose clout.

Even assuming the lowest cost structure—i.e., Green Line Canadian Equity Index Fund with an MER of 1.10%—you have to ask just what are you paying for. And, in the best-case scenario, you are paying one percentage point per year for the right to simply track an index. Perhaps rather than asking what costs we should attach to performance, we should ask: "What costs should we save at the expense of guaranteed underperformance?"

Another issue that we cannot understand is the notion that investors should pay a load to buy an index fund. Yet the N.N. Canadian 35 Index Fund has a back-end option that can be as high as 5%.

And consider this: the two Canadian equity index funds that charge a load also hold portfolios that track the Toronto 35 Index. In this case, one has to wonder why investors would not simply buy the Toronto 35 Index Participations (TIPs) that trade on the TSE. Toronto Index Participations comprise a closed-end fund that holds the 35 stocks in the Toronto 35

Index. There is, of course, a brokerage commission attached to buying TIPs, the same cost as would be the case with any stock. However, the annual administrative fees are negligible.

Mind you, TIPs are not as convenient as a mutual fund. For example, you have no mechanism to provide for reinvestment of the dividends. But you have to ask if that inconvenience is worth it as opposed to the management fees and load charges inherent in the mutual fund alternatives.

Coming Full Circle

Having looked at the cost issues attached to Canadian equity index funds, we have come full circle in the pay-for-performance debate. In our opinion, the performance among traditional Canadian equity funds is well worth the cost of admission. In fact, you pay a high price in terms of performance for the benefit of shaving a small amount off your management-expense ratio.

Investment Objectives and Styles

Scanning the Pal-Trak database, we see a number of specific fund objectives related to Canadian equity funds. One such is the very basic "the objective of the fund is to provide investors with superior investment returns over the long term having regard to safety of capital," used by Altamira Equity Fund. In other words, the three-member management team who now manage the Altamira Equity Fund can do just about anything they want as long as they invest in Canadian equity plus 20% foreign. Others prefer to tighten the rules with descriptions like "the fund's principal investment objective is the long-term growth of capital with resultant increase in potential income," used by Imperial Growth Canadian Equity Fund.

Some equity funds prefer to use more complex mission statements to explain their rationale for their fund. For example, the Bullock Optimax USA "A" Fund attempts "to achieve long-term capital appreciation primarily by seeking to provide investment results that exceed the performance of equity securities in the aggregate, as represented by the S&P 500 Index, while reducing overall investment risk. The fund will invest in a dynamic portfolio of large and medium capitalization stocks selected from the S&P 500 through a sophisticated computer optimization program that provides maximum return with S&P Index volatility." There's enough in that sentence to scare the average investor.

Then, of course, we have managers who focus on small-cap stocks, such as the Altamira Special Growth Fund, which "invests primarily in emerging growth companies with small market capitalization," or the Marathon Equity Fund, which attempts to "maximize growth of capital through common shares and other equity securities of Canadian exchange listed issuers. [It] contains some small-cap stocks with potential for significant appreciation. [It] may also invest in U.S. and other foreign securities." Of course, since the Marathon Equity Fund is RRSP-eligible, the managers cannot commit more than 20% of their portfolio to foreign companies. The Sceptre Equity Fund follows a different small-cap investment style by maintaining "a portfolio of high-quality holdings." The manager "invests according to fundamental analysis and value orientation."

As well, many Canadian equity funds focus on specific sectors of the economy. The Royal Canadian Growth Fund, for example, seeks "to achieve rates of return in excess of the TSE 300 Composite Index. The fund invests primarily in the common shares of Canadian companies with a small- to medium-size capitalization. These companies are generally not among the 50 largest market capitalization companies in the TSE 300 Composite Index."

The All-Canadian Consumer Fund looks for "long-term preservation and growth of capital. [It] invests primarily in securities serving consumer interests, but may invest majority of assets in Treasury bills, bonds debentures or other monetary instruments as required by prevailing conditions."

The bottom line is that most fund managers will spend a lot of time explaining the rationale behind their particular approach and why their approach is worth consideration in your portfolio, but few will explain the difference in styles and why that may be significant.

We're not here to defend any particular management style. Quite frankly, we are not really convinced that, over the long haul, one approach is any better than another. However, there is evidence to show that different investment styles can be rewarded at different stages of the business cycle.

Given that, allow us to share some thoughts on just what each management style entails. We break down the numerous management styles into the following six basic categories:

- Top Down
- Bottom Up
- Value Method
- Momentum (formerly referred to as Market Timing)
- Sector Rotation
- Indexation

The Top-Down Approach

A top-down manager generally begins with an overview of the economy. Are we headed for a period of slow growth with no inflation, or rapid growth with high inflation? Perhaps the economy is descending into a recession, which will impair earnings and push up the unemployment numbers. Or maybe we are moving into a period of expansion that will boost sales and lift earnings.

The top-down investment management team will weight each of the potential scenarios and assign a probability rank to each of them. The managers then focus on industries that are expected to profit under a specific macro-economic scenario. And within those industries, management seeks out the companies that look most promising.

The Bottom-Up Approach

A bottom-up manager is also interested in the outlook for the economy. It doesn't do much good to invest in stocks if we are about to enter a major recession that will impact on the profits of all companies. But rather than use the macro-economic scenario to determine investment choices, many bottom-up managers will use it to determine what percentage of the portfolio will be held in cash.

A true bottom-up philosophy seeks out companies that are (1) undervalued, and (2) have exciting long-term potential. The best company is one the manager can buy and never sell. Some bottom-up managers will focus on specific industries and then choose stocks that look particularly interesting at a point in time. Clearly, the technology industry is an example of just such a philosophy in today's market.

The Value Method

Most value managers follow the traditions of Benjamin Graham and Warren Buffett. Graham, the author of *Security Analysis* and *The Intelligent Investor,* is viewed by many as the architect of value investing. Warren Buffett is a strong follower of Graham's philosophy.

Value investing is a defensive approach, as these managers usually seek out long-term investments in out-of-favor companies—stocks that are often overlooked by the general investing public. Ideally, a value investor buys shares in a company that has a strong balance sheet and solid earnings growth at a time when its value on the stock market is less than its break-up value. Most value investors use a bottom-up selection process and often employ a buy-and-hold strategy. This has the added benefit of keeping the costs of managing the fund low.

Momentum

Previously we referred to this style as "market timing." We've changed the label because very few managers want to be pegged as market timers. Given the less than admirable performance numbers of many so-called market timers, the term "market timing" is not in favor on Bay Street these days.

Momentum investing is one of two growth styles—sector rotation being the other. In our work, we have simply divided the growth approaches into the two basic categories.

Many momentum traders follow a technical approach to stock selection. A technician or chartist believes that a picture is worth a thousand words and will often buy a stock or a number of stocks in a specific industry on the basis of a particular technical pattern.

But momentum managers also pay close attention to the direction of a company's fundamentals. For example, a stock may have a high price to earnings (P/E) multiple (i.e., the price of the stock divided by the per share earnings of the company), which would not appeal to a value investor. It may appeal to the momentum investor, however, because the high P/E may be justified because the company has been able to grow its earnings faster than the general market. Microsoft would be an example of a company that has a history of growing earnings faster than the overall market, but the stock price is 50 times the most recent earnings. That's well above the average P/E for the U.S. market, which at the time of writing was about 22 times the previous year's earnings. Does that make Microsoft a bad investment? Not at all! It is simply an investment that will likely appeal to a momentum investor and will not appeal to a value investor.

Generally speaking, momentum investors are more aggressive managers. Their funds are usually higher risk, and the returns reflect that. The momentum manager may use a few or many indicators to make an investment decision. And while the number of indicators is not that important, how often those indicators signal a change in direction is. There is a cost associated with frequent trading in and out of the market, which impacts on the MER of the fund. We prefer momentum managers who stick with positions for long periods, believing that the costs associated with frequent buy-and-sell signals eat away at most of the potential profits.

Sector Rotation

A sector rotator is also applying a growth philosophy to the market, but in this case the manager focuses on specific industries within the overall market. Most generally, a manager following this philosophy uses a top-down approach. The idea is to follow the ups and downs of the economy, moving from one industry to another at different stages of the business cycle.

During the expansion phase of the business cycle, sector rotators usually seek cyclical companies (i.e., referred to as cyclicals), like the auto industry, transportation stocks and consumer durables. These are industries that tend to profit during upturns in the economy and suffer the most during an economic slowdown.

During periods of economic contractions, a sector rotator will move into defensive industries like pharmaceuticals and health care—sectors whose profit margins are not tied as closely to changes in the business cycle.

Elliott & Page is one of the preeminent fund companies in Canada that employs a sector rotation style of management to its equity funds. The company's marketing literature defines "a sector as one of the 14 components that make up the TSE 300 Composite Index. Examples include oil & gas, metals & minerals, and financial services. We target the sectors with the best anticipated returns. We will emphasize [over-weight] those sectors which we can expect to outperform the TSE 300 Composite Index. Our portfolios will typically contain at least 10 sectors, with no sector representing more than 30% of the portfolio."

Indexation

The goal of an index fund manager is to simply track the market. The N.N. Canadian 35 Index Fund attempts to mirror the performance of the Toronto 35 Index. The manager simply buys all 35 stocks, weighting each purchase similarly to the benchmark index. Index managers, then, are more concerned with *tracking error* than they are with performance. Tracking error simply defines how closely the performance of the index fund mirrors the performance of the benchmark index. The strong selling point of the index fund is its low cost, since there is no buy-and-sell decision to make, as well as the tax efficiency of the fund. Because there are few, if any, purchases or sales within the fund, there is not as much capital gain triggered on which tax must be paid at year end. At least capital gains is not as big an issue in a bull market. But what about a bear market?

We have some concern about index funds in a bear market, and it goes back to the comments made earlier in this chapter about equity fund managers who hold excessive amounts of cash.

The cash assets in a traditional equity fund can range from 3% up to 15%, and sometimes higher, depending on how the manager views the stock market at a point in time. Having cash in the portfolio can be helpful during periods when there are net redemptions (i.e., periods when there are more investors redeeming their fund units than there are new investors buying fund units), which usually occurs when the market is falling. The fund can simply draw on the cash reserves to meet those redemptions, and the manager is not forced to liquidate profitable stock positions.

An index fund does not have that luxury. In order for the index fund to mirror the underlying index, the manager has to be fully invested in the index. During a period of net redemptions, the fund is forced to sell stock in order to raise cash. That means unit holders who remain loyal to the fund will get dinged with a T-3 at the end of the year, which raises the question of tax efficiency in a bear market.

Summary

As you might expect, managers may employ a number of investment styles when running a portfolio. Frank Mersch at Altamira is a classic example. Some managers follow a top-down philosophy that focuses on sector rotation for the core of the portfolio. That same manager may take a small percentage of the portfolio and employ some good old bottom-up value methodology to select a stock he may choose to hold for long periods.

One retired manager we spoke with followed a top-down philosophy when he managed a portfolio of Canadian equity funds, yet his largest position in the portfolio was the Loewen Group, a company that manages funeral homes. He bought this stock because (1) he liked the company's style of management, (2) he noticed the company had a very strong balance sheet, and (3) he could see the long-term profit potential in the company's main line of business.

Stock Market Cycles

One of the concerns most investors face when looking at specific equity funds is the degree to which an equity fund will fluctuate in value from one year to the next. When equity funds are hot, the performance numbers sparkle; during not-so-hot years, the numbers can ruffle the feathers of even the most patient investor.

That equity funds traditionally ride a very steep roller coaster is hardly a revelation to the average investor, and for the more experienced investor is a basic investment tenet. History tells us that stocks move in cycles. The question, then, is not that cycles exist, but how to translate each cyclical phase into investment decisions. How well we fare in terms of our long-term performance numbers depends, to a large extent, on how well we interpret each phase of this so-called stock market cycle—a cycle, most analysts agree, that encompasses eight definable stages: three bear market phases and five bull market phases (see Figure 4.1).

The challenge, of course, is to determine where we are on the cycle, which, to be fair, is like trying to find your way through a maze without a map, and quite clearly is more art than science. However, using some historical benchmarks, we can offer a guide that at the very least provides an overview of the investment maze. If nothing else, it should serve to reassure investors that for every ride on the downside there follows another to the top.

Figure 4.1: THE EIGHT PHASES OF THE STOCK MARKET CYCLE

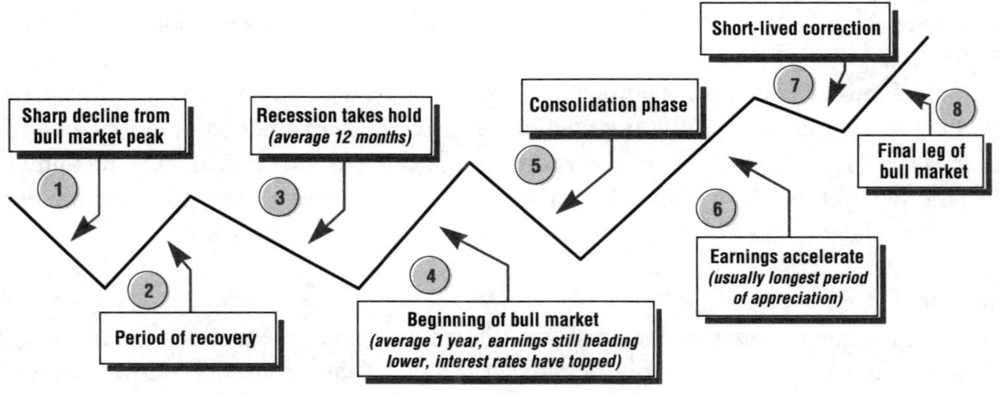

Source: Courtesy of Royal Bank International

The Bear Market Stage

Stock market cycles begin with Phase 1—a bear market. We like to think of this phase as the market's wake-up call—a sharp, relatively short-lived collapse, just when you were starting to feel good about yourself. After a period of strong rallies, where picking the right fund was as easy as throwing darts at the wall, the bubble bursts. In a classic market blow-off, driven in most cases by panic selling, stocks fall sharply.

But don't look for signs of an economic slowdown, because a stock market decline is considered a leading economic indicator. A recession may not begin for another six months to two years. October 1987 was a classic example of just such a market.

While the October 19, 1987, blow-off saw stocks lose 23% of their value in one day, the decline actually began shortly after the August 1987 peak. After "Black Monday," the U.S. Federal Reserve (FED) quickly eased interest rates, effectively delaying the onset of a recession, which didn't come for another 18 months. In retrospect, the FED made the right decision. Delaying the recession no doubt prevented Wall Street's version of economic Armageddon.

The next step in the bear market cycle is Phase 2, which for lack of a better term is the stock market's recovery room. Your stay depends on the severity of the initial decline. Look for stocks to recover 50% to 100% of the initial Phase 1 sell-off. Investors believe that stocks are cheap relative to the recent highs, and prices are supported by rising earnings. Moreover, confidence remains in the system, because the underlying economic fundamentals remain firm and never did support the sell-off.

Phase 3 represents the next wake-up call. At this point, the economy is clearly in a recession and stock prices begin to reflect the fallout. Stock prices usually bottom out about three to six months before the recession ends. The extent of the decline in Phase 3 is also linked to the severity of the recession. For the record, 1990 looks like a classic Phase 3 sell-off.

Finally, we turn the corner. Phase 4 is not what you would call a bull stampede, but stock prices begin to rise, and before you know it they have recovered all of the ground lost in the previous bear market. Surprisingly, stocks are rising while earnings continue to fall and most prognosticators are predicting doom and gloom. What's driving stock prices at this phase is lower interest rates. Which if you think sounds a lot like the period from 1991 through 1993, you're probably right.

Phase 5 is a consolidation period, which can push stock prices down by a third to half of what they gained in Phase 4. The Phase 5 contraction probably took place in 1994, when the U.S. Federal Reserve began to raise interest rates, and stocks and bond funds both lost money.

Fortunately, Phase 5 is soon—some would say not soon enough—followed by another, more sustained, rally: Phase 6. Here we see definite signs that the economy is expanding and earnings are accelerating. It is also a period of high volatility, as earnings become the driving force rather than interest rates. We saw some of that volatility in the technology sector, when high-tech stocks fell as much as 20% in the second quarter of 1997.

Then we come to Phase 7, another short-lived consolidation. How can it be anything but short-lived? At this point in the stock market cycle, investors are really bullish, believing that nothing can stand in the way of continued prosperity. Even bad news is given a positive spin.

Which leads us to the ultimate blow-off, known as Phase 8. That's a point when stock prices rise with no fundamental justification. The outlook for earnings is beyond any rational expectation, and when companies fail to meet those lofty goals, prices fall . . . hard!

Equity Mutual Funds in a Bear Market

A raging bull market is an exciting event, especially if you are in the business of selling mutual funds. Since 1981 (save for the 1987 correction), the equity markets around the world have chalked up record post-war gains. For the most part, equity investors have enjoyed the ride.

While the 1987 stock market crash all but destroyed the retail brokerage business, it only dented the growth in the sales of equity mutual funds. The mutual fund industry continues to be a true growth industry and will probably remain so through to the next millennium.

There's little doubt that this growth has been good for the financial industry. However, there is some question whether the money invested in equity mutual funds is as safe as some people think.

For example, many investors in the 1980s were convinced that they should buy mutual funds with borrowed money. It does, after all, make perfect sense when the stock market is rising. How could you lose? Borrowing money at 10% in order to invest in an equity fund that had grown an average 15% per year seemed as easy as taking cash from a money tree. All that extra growth doesn't even take into consideration the tax benefits. The interest on the borrowed money is deductible, while capital gains have a 25% exclusion.

Unfortunately, those performance numbers have been based in large part on the fact that the market has been in a solid long-term uptrend. While the mutual fund prospectuses, as well as the advertising slogans, are filled with fine print telling you that "past performance is not necessarily indicative of future results," most investors buy with the belief that what was, will continue to be.

The first question is whether equity mutual funds will be able to live up to investors' expectations. Given that equity funds have had such a stellar performance in recent years, investors' expectations may be too high. How much longer can stocks continue to chalk up 15% annual gains?

In a bear market, individual fund holders may want to exit quickly. That means massive redemptions, which in a bear market environment could add fuel to the fire. It was, after all, one of the contributing factors to the October 1987 collapse.

What's more, given the fact that mutual funds have been volatile investments in the past, their explosive growth over the past 10 years may make them even more of a factor in the future. In short, a falling market could be accentuated by the presence of large redemptions, because portfolio managers will be forced to unload shares at any price.

This discussion leads us to an important question. If and when the stock market takes a prolonged slide, will mutual fund investors be hit harder than direct shareholders? The evidence seems to suggest that they will. In 1984, for example, the U.S. stock market, as measured by the Dow Jones Industrial Average, showed a return of 1.3%, including reinvested dividends. However, mutual funds during the same period showed an average loss of 2.9%.

To be fair, the mutual fund numbers included some pretty steep losses—as much as 30% in some cases—that were absorbed by the more speculative funds. The hardest hit group were those mutual funds that dealt in smaller, less established companies, whose shares are not as easy to resell when the market is falling. What's clear is that 1984 was not unique; the same problems surfaced again in 1987.

Still, the popularity of these speculative funds suggests that not everyone believes that the redemption-forced liquidation syndrome is necessarily a greater problem for mutual fund investors than for individual shareholders. After all, traders will argue that when mutual funds are unloading their shares, they depress the price for everyone.

In a bear market, mutual funds, like individual shares, become more volatile. But our asset allocation model that we will discuss later in the book actually thrives on this type of environment. Why? Because it provides more opportunities to rebalance the portfolio during market shake-ups.

Take a look at the chart patterns of the Dow Jones Industrial Average since 1929, and they very closely follow the phases we have just described, proving once again that a picture is worth a thousand words. Examine the accompanying chart for the Standard & Poor's 500 Average since July 1987, and you will see similar results (see Figure 4.2).

Figure 4.2: S&P 500 COMPOSITE INDEX

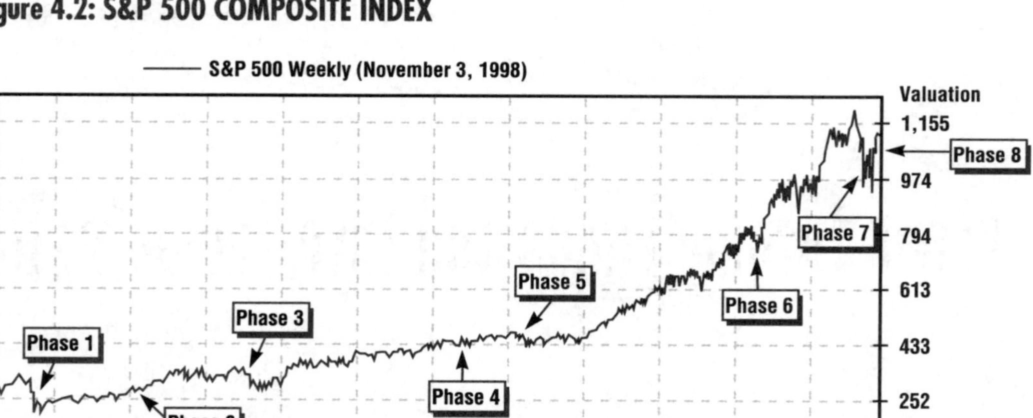

So, where are we now?

If you buy into the eight phases of the stock market cycle, it does appear that October 1987 signaled the end of economic expansion and the high stock market valuations so familiar in the 1980s. If we then assume that 1989 was the beginning of the North American recession, followed by the double dip of 1990, then the rally in late 1991—a rally driven by falling interest rates—was anticipating the end of the recession, an end that officially came in mid-1992.

After a series of rallies, the party abruptly ended in February 1994, when the U.S. Federal Reserve Board raised short-term interest rates by 25 basis points (i.e., 0.25%). What followed were seven additional interest rate hikes that finally ended in February 1995.

In 1998, the markets started with a bang. Up, up and away seemed to be the mood of the market, at least until the problems in Asia, which first surfaced in October 1997 and worsened in August 1998. Fears about a global meltdown were enough to change investor sentiment, which led directly into one of the most gut-wrenching corrections we have seen since 1987.

We said last year that a correction in excess of 10% would be needed to signal the end of Phase Six in this bull market. The 19% correction in the U.S. equity market, and the 29% correction in the Canadian equity market, in our mind, qualifies as the end run for Phase Seven of this bull market cycle. The ensuing rally since the beginning of October 1998 looks to us like the eighth phase of this bull market (read our fearless forecast in Chapter 13). A rally that should take us to a blowoff stage, leading to another sharp correction and eventually to another bull market cycle—probably beginning in the year 2000. That's a best guess, and our timing is clearly more art than science.

CHAPTER FIVE

Fixed-Income Funds and Investment Styles

The "Bond" in Canada Savings Bonds

Here's a question: Why do Canada Savings Bonds (CSBs) that mature in 2006 yield about 5.25%, while Government of Canada bonds maturing in the same year yield about 5.75%? The same government issues both bonds. They have the same term-to-maturity (i.e., they both mature in nine years). The quality of the investments is the same, in that you will receive the face value of the bonds at maturity. So why the disparity in yield?

For a subject that you would think is relatively straightforward—i.e., you buy a bond, you receive interest and, at maturity, your principal investment is returned—there have been volumes written about it. The problem, of course, is not so much for investors who want to buy a bond and hold it to maturity. The problems result when investors buy a bond and want to sell it prior to maturity. Or more commonly, buy a bond fund thinking that it is an alternative to GICs, only to find the value of the bond fund fluctuates with changes in the level of interest rates.

In this chapter we will examine the differences between CSBs and government bonds, explain some terms and help you understand the relationship between long-term bonds, bond funds and interest rates. More specifically, we will focus on what makes a good bond fund and what to look for when buying either Canadian or global bond funds. Think of this chapter, then, as your "fixed-income primer."

Setting the Record Straight

Before entering the fixed-income maze, let's clear up the discrepancy between Canada Savings Bonds and Government of Canada bonds. In point of fact, the investment community is using a loose interpretation of the term "bond" when applying it to CSBs. Having the ability to redeem a CSB any time and receive the full face value plus accrued interest[2] is not how we define bonds. That is how we define cash.

The loose interpretation stems from the fact that while CSBs mature at some point in the future—maturing in 2006 using our hypothetical example—the interest payable is not fixed. The rate payable is adjusted on a needs basis to reflect changes in the rate of interest being paid on savings accounts, one-year Guaranteed Investment Certificates, short-term Treasury bills and money market funds. Again, these are investment comparisons that are normally associated with cash assets.

Bonds are fixed-income instruments. The term "fixed income" refers to the interest or *coupon rate*, which is fixed for the life of the bond. The coupon rate is simply the rate of interest the bond issuer promises to pay as a percentage of the bond's *face value*. For example, if the Government of Canada issues a $1,000 (we refer to the $1,000 as the bond's face or par value) bond with a coupon rate of 10%, the government promises to pay to the bondholder $100 ($1,000 face value multiplied by 10% = $100) in interest each year, and that rate is fixed for the life of the bond. The notion that a bond's coupon rate is fixed is the primary difference between our pure definition of a bond and the rather weak inclusion of the word bond in CSBs.

Making Liberal Use of Examples

Having cleared up the first part of our discussion, let's continue with some hypothetical examples. Consider a hypothetical Government of Canada bond, with a 10% coupon, maturing in September 2007. We'll refer to this bond as a GOC 10% / 2007. What we have, then, is a bond issued by the Government of Canada that promises to pay to the holder 10% per year until September 2007. The coupon rate is paid semi-annually, which simply means half of the 10% interest is paid in March and the other half in September. For the record, almost all bonds pay interest semi-annually.

Here's where it gets interesting. Our GOC 10% / 2007 pays 10% per year while similar government bonds maturing in 2007 are yielding 5.75%. This would appear to be a once-in-a-lifetime investment opportunity. The line forms to the left.

However, before standing too long in this line, realize that as with all aspects of life, there ain't no free lunch. Obviously, for this bond to be available at all, its true yield will have to fall well below the 10% coupon rate.

For some thoughts on this, we return once again to the simplicity of this CSB example. You can cash in your CSB at any time for its full face value. You can do that because when interest rates change the rate payable on the CSB also changes, reflecting the current interest rates available on competing investment vehicles. In short, then, the value of the CSB is unchanged (i.e., you can cash it at any time for its full face value). Only the rate of interest the CSB pays will change.

With our GOC 10% / 2007, we know the rate is fixed for the life of the bond. We also know that our GOC 10% / 2007 should effectively yield the same as other comparable instruments—approximately 7.5%—maturing at the same time.

---

[2] *When you cash your CSB, you are eligible to receive interest for each full month you owned the CSB. As such, you should always wait until the end of the month before cashing a CSB, in order to be eligible to receive interest in that month.*

The question, of course, is how do we get our GOC 10% / 2007 fixed coupon bond to yield only 7.5% compounded annually? Since we can't change the coupon rate, the only alternative is to change what we pay for the bond. And here again is a significant difference between real bonds and CSBs. With CSBs, the rate of interest changes, but the price is fixed. With bonds, the rate of interest is fixed, but the price of the bond fluctuates.

To buy $1,000 face value of the GOC 10% / 2007, we will have to pay a premium, or a price higher than the $1,000 face value. Based on our calculations, which we'll explain in a moment, you should expect to pay approximately $1,310 (rounded) for every $1,000 of face value. Of course, if you talk to a professional bond trader and ask him for the price, you will get a response like $131. This is part of that technical bond market language that serves to confuse most investors. Suffice it to say, bond prices are quoted as a percentage of face value. The $131 price simply means 131% of face value.

Even though you pay a premium, this still looks like an attractive investment. After all, you will earn $100 in annual interest. Divide the annual interest by the price of the bond ($100 / $1,310) and the yield is 7.63%, a calculation that we refer to as the bond's *current yield*. What's interesting about this example is that the current yield is still more attractive than the average yield of 5.75% for other government bonds maturing in 2007. Confused? Still waiting in line to buy? Before you do, consider the next step along this road.

If you hold the GOC 10% / 2007 bond to maturity, you will only receive the $1,000 face value. And there's the rub. Because you paid $1,310, your portfolio will suffer a $310 capital loss over the next nine years. That capital loss has to be factored into your total return, which is what bond traders do when they calculate *yield-to-maturity*.

And while the calculation may be a bit more complicated, the yield-to-maturity is the one measure that allows for an apples-to-apples comparison of all bonds regardless of maturity, coupon rate or price. The yield-to-maturity calculation accounts for all of the facets in the bond's total return, including the semi-annual interest payments as well as the repayment of principal. The yield-to-maturity calculation simply assigns a present-day value to all of the future cash flows including the principal repayment.

For example, if we had purchased our GOC 10% / 2007 bond about the middle of August 1998, we would have received our first interest payment—$50 per $1,000 face value—one month later. Since we also know that similar government bonds maturing in 2007 have a yield-to-maturity of 5.75%, we use this rate to discount our payments to their present value.

Current Date		**Aug-98**
Face Value:		$1,000
Discount Rate:		5.75%
Payment Date	**Payment**	**Present Value of Payment**
Sep-98	$50.00	$49.74

The present value of our first $50.00 semi-annual interest payment then is $49.74. We can then apply the same calculation to the next semi-annual interest payment due in March 1999, the third payment due in September 1999 and so on up to and including the principal repayment due in September 2007. If we add the present values of all future semi-annual interest payments from Table 5.1, the total works out to $725.30. The present value of the principal repayment due September 2007 is $583.60. Add those two figures and we end up with the bond's current price of $1,308.90 (i.e., $131 rounded).

Table 5.1: GOVERNMENT OF CANADA 10% BOND DUE SEPTEMBER 2007—5.75% DISCOUNT

Current Date		**Aug-98**
Face Value:		$1,000.00
Discount Rate:		5.75%
Payment Date	**Interest Payment**	**Present Value of Payment**
Sep-98	$50.00	$49.74
Mar-99	50.00	47.24
Sep-99	50.00	45.92
Mar-00	50.00	44.64
Sep-00	50.00	43.39
Mar-01	50.00	42.18
Sep-01	50.00	41.00
Mar-02	50.00	39.86
Sep-02	50.00	38.74
Mar-03	50.00	37.66
Sep-03	50.00	36.61
Mar-04	50.00	35.58
Sep-04	50.00	34.59
Mar-05	50.00	33.62
Sep-05	50.00	32.68
Mar-06	50.00	31.77
Sep-06	50.00	30.88
Mar-07	50.00	30.02
Sep-07	50.00	29.18
Total		**$725.30**
	Principal	**Present Value of Principal**
Sep-07	$1,000.00	$583.60
Present Value of Principal and Interest		**$1,308.90**

Stating this another way, if we pay $131 to buy our GOC 10% / 2007 bond, our yield-to-maturity will be 5.75%. The yield-to-maturity approximates—after accounting for the decline in the bond's current price—the market rate for similar bonds maturing in 2007. The yield-to-maturity, then, is the principal (pardon the pun) measure used by professional bond traders when comparing fixed-income assets having similar risk factors and maturities. There is one caveat to this discussion. The yield-to-maturity calculation assumes by default (again excuse the pun) that you are able to reinvest those semi-annual interest payments at the 5.75% rate.

When you think about it, with a government bond, there is no real risk of default. Having removed default risk from the discussion means that the only factor impacting the price of the bond will be interest rates. That bond prices are inexorably linked to interest rates lays the foundation for the remainder of our discussion on domestic fixed-income assets. In short, when interest rates rise, bond prices fall, and conversely, when interest rates are falling, bond prices rise. We think of this inverse relationship as the fixed-income teeter-totter (Figure 5.1), with bond prices at one end and interest rates at the other.

Figure 5.1: THE FIXED-INCOME TEETER-TOTTER

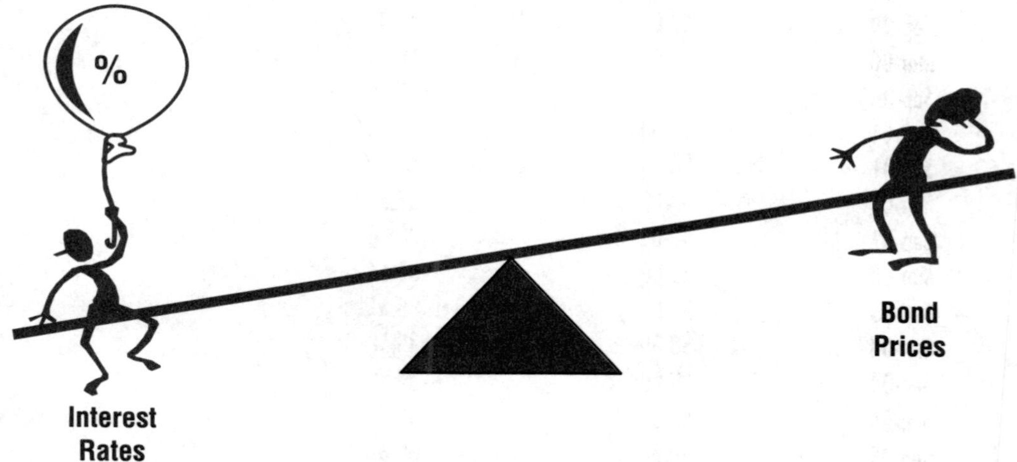

The Term-to-Maturity

When we talk about a bond being long term or short term, we are really talking about the bond's *term-to-maturity*. In August 1998, our GOC 10% / 2007 bond had a term-to-maturity of nine years and one month. A bond maturing in 2023 has a term-to-maturity of 25 years give or take a month or two.

The longer the term-to-maturity, the larger a factor the semi-annual interest payments play in the bond's total return. Indeed, from Table 5.1, you can see that the present value of the interest payments were almost twice as important in the bond's overall price than was the present value of the $1,000 principal repayment due in nine years.

Compare that to a government bond that has, say, a 10% coupon, matures in September 2000 and is discounted at 4.75%, the going rate for similar quality bonds with the same two-year maturity. From the calculations in Table 5.2, we see that the present value of the principal repayment carries a much greater weight in the bond's total price than does the stream of semi-annual interest payments.

Table 5.2: GOVERNMENT OF CANADA 10% BOND DUE SEPTEMBER 2000—4.75% DISCOUNT

Date		**Aug-98**
Face Value:		$1,000.00
Discount Rate:		4.75%
Payment Date	**Interest Payment**	**Present Value of Payment**
Sep-98	$50.00	$49.79
Mar-99	50.00	47.71
Sep-99	50.00	46.60
Mar-00	50.00	45.52
Sep-00	50.00	44.46
Total		**$234.08**
	Principal	**Present Value of Principal**
Sep-00	$1,000.00	$889.26
Present Value of Principal and Interest		**$1,123.34**

Term-to-maturity, then, is significant in terms of portfolio management. The longer the term-to-maturity, the more dramatic will be the shifts in the price of the bond given a change in interest rates.

To understand that, let's return to Tables 5.1 and 5.2, only this time we will assume interest rates have gone up by 1%, which alters our discounting factor. We will discount the GOC 10% / 2007 bond by 6.75% rather than 5.75%, and in Table 5.4 we will discount the bond by 5.75% rather than 4.75%. The price of both bonds will decline. The question is by how much (see Tables 5.3 and 5.4).

Table 5.3: GOVERNMENT OF CANADA 10% BOND DUE SEPTEMBER 2007—6.75% DISCOUNT

Date		**Aug-98**
Face Value:		$1,000.00
Discount Rate:		6.75%
Payment Date	**Interest Payment**	**Present Value of Payment**
Sep-98	$50.00	$49.70
Mar-99	50.00	46.79
Sep-99	50.00	45.26
Mar-00	50.00	43.78
Sep-00	50.00	42.35
Mar-01	50.00	40.97
Sep-01	50.00	39.63
Mar-02	50.00	48.34
Sep-02	50.00	37.09
Mar-03	50.00	35.88
Sep-03	50.00	34.71
Mar-04	50.00	33.57
Sep-04	50.00	32.48
Mar-05	50.00	31.42
Sep-05	50.00	30.39
Mar-06	50.00	29.40
Sep-06	50.00	28.44
Mar-07	50.00	27.51
Sep-07	50.00	26.61
Total		**$704.32**
	Principal	**Present Value of Principal**
Sep-07	$1,000.00	$532.24
Present Value of Principal and Interest		**$1,236.56**

The GOC 10% / 2007 bond went from $131 ($1,308.90 for every $1,000 face value) to approximately $123 ($1,236.56 for every $1,000 face value), a decline of 6.85%.

Table 5.4: GOVERNMENT OF CANADA 10% BOND DUE SEPTEMBER 2000—5.75% DISCOUNT

Date		**Aug-98**
Face Value:		$1,000.00
Discount Rate:		5.75%
Payment Date	**Interest Payment**	**Present Value of Payment**
Sep-98	$50.00	$49.74
Mar-99	50.00	47.24
Sep-99	50.00	45.92
Mar-00	50.00	44.64
Sep-00	50.00	43.39
Total		**$230.93**
	Principal	**Present Value of Principal**
Sep-00	$1,000.00	$867.86
Present Value of Principal and Interest		**$1,098.79**

The 10% Government of Canada bond maturing in 2000 went from $112 ($1,123.34 for every $1,000 face value) to approximately $110 ($1,098.79 for every $1,000 face value), a decline of 2.23%.

The term-to-maturity, then, has a dramatic effect on how a bond's price will change given a change in the level of interest rates. The longer the term-to-maturity, the more volatile the bond's price will be. Using our playground analogy, the longer the term-to-maturity, the greater the movement at each end of the teeter-totter.

The Yield Curve

Bondholders expect a long-term bond to offer higher yields than shorter-term bonds. We saw this in our examples from Tables 5.1 and 5.2. Note that the bond maturing in 2007 was discounted by 5.75% versus a discount rate of 4.75% for the government bond maturing in two years. Generally, we would expect bonds with longer maturities to offer higher yields in order to compensate investors for the increased volatility in the bond's price given a shift in the level of interest rates.

The relationship between interest rates and the term-to-maturity is graphically displayed in the *yield curve* (see Figure 5.2). The yield curve is really just a line on a graph that plots the interest rate paid by bonds with similar risk characteristics but different terms-to-maturity.

There are many yield curves. For example, there is a yield curve for federal government bonds, another for provincial bonds, another for AAA rated corporate bonds, another for AA rated corporate bonds and so on. The most widely followed yield curve is the one that graphs Government of Canada bonds ranging from maturities of one month to 30 years. There are a couple of reasons for this yield curve's popularity: (1) government bonds, as we said, have no default risk to distort the relationship between term-to-maturity and interest rates, and (2) federal government bonds are the most actively traded sector of the fixed-income market, thus providing an up-to-the-minute unbiased measure of the bond market's psychology.

The horizontal axis represents the term-to-maturity, while the vertical axis on the left of the graph represents different levels of interest rates. Note that in July 1998, two-year government bonds are currently yielding 4.75% (see also Table 5.2), while nine-year government bonds are yielding 5.75%. We refer to this as a normal sloping yield curve, in that the rate generally rises from left to right as the term-to-maturity lengthens.

Figure 5.2: YIELD CURVE (JULY 1998)

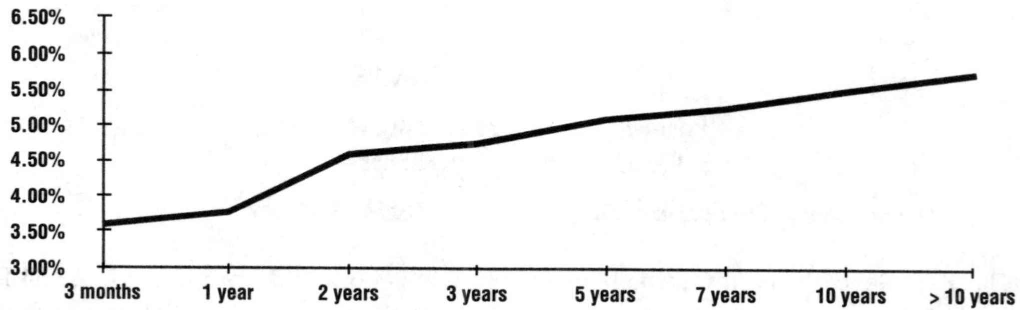

Interestingly, not all yield curves slope up from left to right. And the fact that occasionally the shape of the yield curve changes can tell you a great deal about where the market believes interest rates are headed. And from our perspective, being able to read and understand the yield curve can help us make intelligent choices when investing in fixed-income assets.

In effect, the yield curve paints a picture of the trade-off between risk and reward. It acts as a guide to help investors decide whether it makes more sense to buy bonds offering higher yields but with longer terms-to-maturity. Or perhaps, given some trepidation on the part of the investor, it makes more sense to opt for lower rates on a bond that matures within, say, the next three years. The key is understanding how to read the mood of the market from the yield curve. After all, the yield curve tells us how bond market investors view the future at any given moment. It may not be correct, but it is unbiased, because the participants are painting the picture with their own money.

The Shapes of the Yield Curve

We know in a normal yield curve the line slopes gently upward from left to right. We also know why. The higher interest rates simply compensate the investor for the interest-rate risk associated with longer-term bonds. Long-term bonds are more sensitive to interest rate change than short-term bonds.

When the yield curve slopes downward from left to right, it is said to be inverted. This does not happen often, the most dramatic example in recent memory being the 1981 yield curve (see Figure 5.3), when short-term yields hit 20% while 30-year bonds yielded about 16%. Looking back, earning 16% for 30 years seems almost unbelievable, yet there were few investors willing to risk their capital for that length of time. The 1981 inverted curve reflected the market's belief that the long-term risk of inflation was much less than the short-term threat. The last time this happened, although much less dramatically, was in 1989.

Figure 5.3: INVERTED YIELD CURVE (1981)

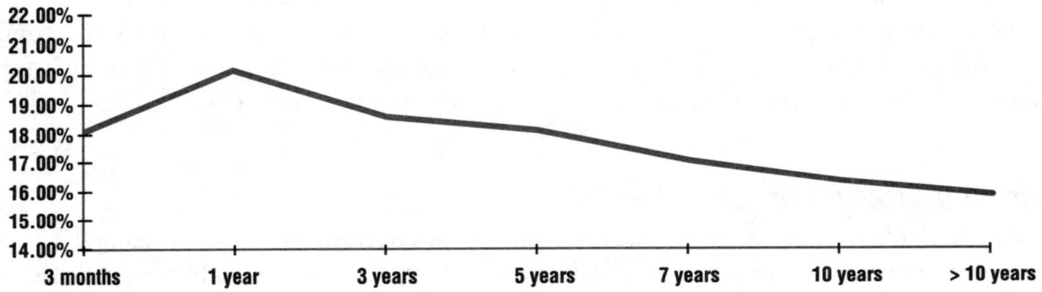

When both short- and long-term interest rates are roughly the same, the curve is said to be flat. An unusual situation to be sure, but one that closely resembles the curve in March 1995, when three-year government bonds yielded 8.24% versus 8.78% for 30-year government bonds. That such a small spread between the three- and 30-year government bonds existed, implied that the market was not anticipating any serious long-term inflationary pressures.

The yield curve in March 1995 was quite different from the one we saw in 1994, when the spread between three- and 30-year government bonds was 1.25 percentage points, and the spread between the three-month Treasury bills and the 30-year bond exceeded 2.64% percentage points (see Figure 5.4).

Figure 5.4: FLAT YIELD CURVE (MARCH 1995)

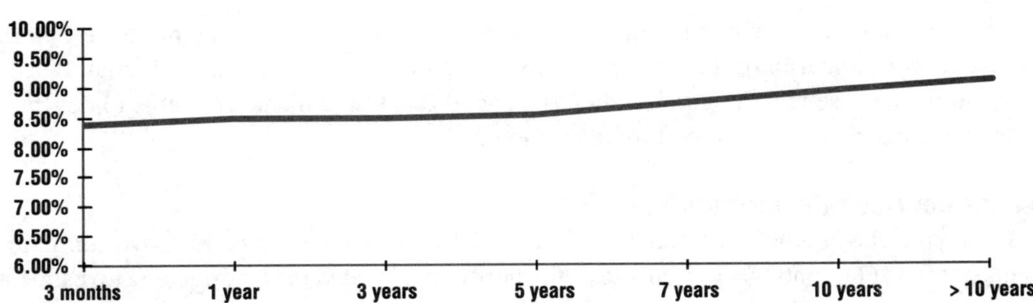

The change in the Canadian yield curve was driven primarily by actions south of the border. This illustrates how closely linked our two economies are, and how dramatic an impact the U.S. Federal Reserve Board can have on Canadian interest rates, especially when Chairman Alan Greenspan gets antsy about the U.S. economy and inflation.

Between February 1994 and February 1995, the Federal Reserve Board raised short-term interest rates seven times, pushing the yield on three-month U.S. Treasury bills from 3.03% to 6%, while the yield on 30-year U.S. government bonds went from 6.23% to around 7.86% in a year. This is what gave us the predominantly flat curve we had in January 1995.

One other telling feature that needs to be examined can also be seen from Figure 5.3. Notice the peak—or, if you prefer the technical term, "hump"—in the one-year maturity spectrum. Typically you find these so-called humps at the point along the yield curve where investors find the ideal combination of the highest yield with the least perceived risk.

And you wanted to trade bonds?

Having read this far, you have now probably come to the conclusion that there is more to fixed-income investing than meets the eye, which is why many investors turn to the professional money management offered by Canadian bond funds.

A bond fund, as the name suggests, simply invests in a portfolio of bonds. A high-grade Canadian bond fund would invest in a portfolio of secure bonds. In fact, some bond fund managers only invest in government bonds and ignore high-grade corporate bonds. Other bond fund managers prefer a mixture of government and high-grade corporate bonds.

Professional bond fund managers practice many different styles to meet the dual objectives of growth and income. (We will discuss management styles later in this chapter.) It is important to understand that the return you get from any high-grade bond fund will be determined, for the most part, by the average term-to-maturity of the fund's portfolio.

If interest rates are high and are expected to fall, bond managers generally lengthen their average term-to-maturity. They want to get the biggest bang for the buck, and from our previous examples, longer-term bonds will rise more dramatically than bonds with a shorter maturity.

If interest rates are low and the manager expects rates to rise, he will tend to shorten the average term-to-maturity of the bond portfolio so that the value of the fund will not fall as far as would be the case with longer-term bonds. A good bond fund manager is able to delicately balance this trade-off between performance and risk.

Caught between Performance and Risk

Those of you who bought Canadian bond funds in 1994 came face to face with two conflicting points of view: (1) wanting a percentage of the portfolio allocated to fixed-income investments to provide income and balance for the overall asset mix, versus (2) a concern that based on 1994's dismal performance numbers, the risks were too high.

To address the first issue, let's understand why domestic fixed-income assets—defined as

Canadian bond funds—should be part of your portfolio. Simply stated, bond funds add stability. And since most bond funds automatically reinvest periodic interest distributions, they compel investors to systematically engage in dollar-cost averaging.

The concept of reinvestment is a key issue, and demands emphasis, particularly if you held bond funds throughout 1994. Thanks to Fed chairman Greenspan, the net asset value of almost every bond fund with at least a three-year track record declined. The average loss among Canadian bond funds was 4.6%.

Among the pieces that make an average, there was the Altamira Bond Fund that fell more than 9% for the full year. Other funds, like the Trimark Government Income Fund, fell only marginally (0.7%). At the end of the day, the result was the same. Massive bond fund redemptions took place during the 1995 RRSP season—just about the time the U.S. Federal Reserve Board was beginning to feel good about itself.

It bears repeating just how important it is to remain calm when riding the ups and downs of the interest rate cycle. February 1995 turned out to be the low watermark for Canadian bond funds. Interest rates had finally stopped climbing, and from that point they began a rather dramatic descent that turned 1994's worst performers into 1995's best performers. Unfortunately, most fixed-income investors had cashed in their chips just as the rally began.

Finding a Silver Lining

If there is a silver lining to the 1994 performance numbers, it is in the exception and not the rule. The exception in this case is the Dynamic Income Fund, the only fund with at least a three-year track record to generate a positive return. Not only did Dynamic Income Fund defy 1994's law of negative gravity, it did so with a vengeance, up 6.4% on the year. A good performance by any measure, and an outstanding performance relative to its peers in 1994.

Pointing out Dynamic Income's rather dynamic performance in 1994 establishes a foundation for understanding what drives bond fund performance in general. And we think that's important (why else would we have spent so much time laying a foundation for pricing bonds earlier in the chapter?) because it helps investors account for performance numbers in any given year. That's more useful than shrugging your shoulders, rolling your eyes and complaining about a manager who didn't live up to expectations.

We think by understanding the cause-and-effect relationship between interest rate cycles and bond fund performance, you will be accorded a measure of comfort through the bad years, which will keep you in the game to profit from the good years. You shouldn't be selling at exactly the wrong time.

We also believe that understanding the past helps us acquire the skills to make sound investment decisions for the future. Depending on your personal tolerance for risk, we can help you construct a portfolio of bond funds that takes advantage of the current interest rate cycle. (More on that in Chapter 13 where we present our forecast for 1999.)

Of course, if you get an uneasy feeling whenever the minister of finance presents a budget laden with rosy economic forecasts, you may be better served with a bond fund portfolio that virtually eliminates all of the risks associated with economic predictions. We have a recipe for that as well. We like to think of this as our way of bringing "insurance" back into the investment management game.

Laying the Groundwork

To start a discussion on what drives bond fund performance, allow us to introduce some hard-nosed bond fund facts.

Fact #1

Solid performance numbers, steady cash flow and reasonable risk make Canadian bond funds an ideal long-term RRSP investment. We mention RRSPs because, as Canadians, we pay a higher tax rate on interest income. Given that, it makes sense to shelter as much of it as possible, hence bond funds inside an RRSP. (See Chapter 9.)

Fact #2

A bond fund's net asset value (NAV) will fluctuate. Canadian bond funds, then, are not an alternative to Guaranteed Investment Certificates (GICs).

Fact #3

Bond funds, and some would say, bond fund managers, do not mature. The fund managers dictate the term-to-maturity of the portfolio, which presumably reflects the manager's view about interest rates within the context of the fund's stated objectives.

Fact #4

There's more to investing in a bond fund than meets the eye, which begs the question: "Will bond fund returns over the next three years match the longer-term historical numbers (five-year performance of the average Canadian bond fund equals 8.7% compounded annually), or will they reflect the dismal performance of 1994?" Like all investments, the answer probably lies between these two extremes.

What drives bond fund performance?

Interest rates drive the performance of a high-grade bond fund. We emphasize the "high-grade" trademark to distinguish between bond funds that invest in government or high-grade corporate bonds from those so-called "high-yield" bond funds that invest in what investment analysts refer to as "junk bonds."

A high-yield bond fund manager will invest in bonds issued by companies that may or may not be able to repay the principal at the end of the term. Therefore, in a high-yield bond fund, there is a risk of default, which adds another dimension to the performance numbers.

However, because we are not supporters of any investment strategy that has the term "junk" associated with it, we will only be recommending high-grade bond funds for your portfolio. As mentioned earlier, these high-grade bond funds invest primarily in government bonds, where the risk of default is not a major concern.

With that in mind, we expect a bond fund's NAV will move inversely to a change in the level of interest rates. If interest rates are rising, the NAV of the bond fund will decline; if interest rates are falling, a bond fund's NAV will rise. Knowing that a teeter-totter relationship exists is one thing; what's more important is knowing how high and low the teeter-totter will go. We need to know this in order to determine just how much of an impact a change in interest rates will have on the NAV of the bond fund.

What we need to know, then, is the bond fund's *average term-to-maturity.* We say average, because unlike the bond examples at the beginning of this chapter, a bond fund does not mature. Moreover, bond fund managers constantly change the bonds within the portfolio, either lengthening or shortening the portfolio's average term-to-maturity. Fund companies keep track of the average term-to-maturity for each of their bond funds, and that information is available to investors and financial advisors for the price of a phone call to the mutual fund's marketing department. In terms of price action, then, the longer the average term-to-maturity, the longer the potential teeter-totter and the more volatile the bond fund will be.

The Tale of Two Bond Funds

Since bond funds invest in bonds and interest rates drive bond prices, we now have some interpretive tools that help explain the difference in the 1994 performance numbers for the Dynamic Income Fund on the one hand, and the Altamira Bond Fund on the other.

Dynamic Income Fund's 6.4% return in 1994 was driven by two important investment decisions. First, Dynamic's managers—Goodman and Company Ltd.—invested about 40% of the portfolio in Canadian foreign pay bonds and foreign-denominated bonds.

Foreign pay bonds, for those not familiar with the product, are bonds issued by provincial or federal governments and other government agencies that are denominated in a foreign currency—usually in U.S. dollars. Since these bonds are issued by Canadian entities, they are not considered a foreign investment, which allows Dynamic Income to remain 100% RRSP eligible. In 1994, the Canadian dollar fell sharply against the U.S. dollar, and thus the value of those foreign pay bonds increased.

Second, and from our perspective the most telling aspect of the 1994 performance numbers, was the decision by Goodman and Company Ltd. to shorten the average term-to-maturity of the bond portfolio early in 1994. That provided a cushion against losses resulting from the rise in interest rates.

At the other end of the spectrum is the Altamira Bond Fund, whose dismal performance in 1994 was the direct result of the fund's long term-to-maturity. The Altamira Bond Fund had a portfolio with an average term-to-maturity in excess of 15 years in 1994. But rather than cashing in their chips, Altamira went into 1995 with a term-to-maturity of 25.9 years.

The rise in interest rates that predominated the financial markets in 1994 had a major impact on the Altamira Bond Fund. When interest rates went up, the value of the Altamira Bond Fund declined. You might say, then, that our tale of two bond funds demonstrates the long and short of it, and supports the rationale behind Fact #3.

A Bond Fund's Duration

When you think about it, assuming a bond fund only invests in high-grade bonds, the term-to-maturity becomes the most important decision the manager has to make. And where the manager places the fund on the yield curve (i.e., invests in short-, medium- or long-term bonds) defines how sensitive the fund will be to changes in interest rates.

We can define that sensitivity, something we do for all bond funds in this book, by calculating a bond fund's duration. Not to complicate the issue with another statistical tool, suffice it to say that duration is a more precise calculation than the average term-to-maturity when measuring a bond fund's sensitivity to interest rates. That's because duration takes into account the portfolio's average coupon (i.e., interest paid by the various bonds in the portfolio), the frequency of interest payments and the current price of the bonds in the portfolio. In mathematical terms, duration tells you how long it will take, in years, to recover your initial investment. Duration is almost always less than the bond fund's average term-to-maturity.

More importantly, from our perspective of wanting the best information at the fingertips of each investor, knowing a bond fund's duration will tell us how much a bond fund should rise or fall given a specific change in the level of interest rates.

Duration is most accurate when used to forecast a bond fund's change in value, given a 100-basis point (i.e., 100 basis points equals 1%) rise or fall in interest rates. For example, if interest rates were to fall by 1%, a bond fund with a duration of 10 years would be expected to rise by approximately 10%. Conversely, a 1% rise in interest rates would approximate a 10% decline in the value of the fund.

While the process of calculating duration can be quite complicated, it is not something you need worry about. For one thing, most bond funds do the calculation for you, and you can usually find out the fund's current duration for the price of a phone call.

Of course, there are exceptions to this. There are still a few fund companies where a phone call to the marketing department gets a puzzled response when asked to supply the bond fund's duration and average term-to-maturity. If you get that response, buy another bond fund.

There are also, of course, international or global bond funds that rarely calculate duration, which in this case makes sense, because the duration number can be rendered meaningless by fluctuations in the foreign exchange rate. (See Chapter 8, where we discuss borderless shopping.)

For our purposes, we need to know how duration helps us quantify a bond fund's potential risk. Looking at risk in terms of volatility, duration will tell you how much the value of your bond fund will change, given a change in interest rates.

Obviously, duration is one of the issues we will look at when recommending specific bond funds. Bond funds with a long average term-to-maturity (i.e., longer than, say, 10 years) would be considered a long-term fund, and we would expect that fund's duration to be anywhere from 5 to 8 years. Bond funds with an average term-to-maturity of, say, 3 to 9 years would be considered medium term (duration would be anywhere from 2 to just less than 5 years), and bond funds with an average term-to-maturity of less than 3 years (duration less than 2 years) would be considered short term.

The idea, of course, is to buy bond funds with long durations in an environment where interest rates are expected to decline (i.e., lower interest rates, higher bond prices), and look for shorter duration bond funds when anticipating a rise in interest rates. But as you might expect, that's easier said than done.

And the last shall be first!

Constructing an econometric model to predict the direction of interest rates is like trying to write a computer program that will predict Wayne Gretzky's next move based on past performance—the answer may be somewhat better than a blind guess, but it is hardly worth the effort.

Fortunately, knowing the next move in interest rates is not as important as making a judgment call on the long-term trend. In January 1994, when U.S. short-term interest rates were at 3.5%, common sense told us that rates would not go too much lower. We simply weren't that far from zero. The point is, you are never going to pick the bottom or top in interest rates—just try to be as close to one end or the other when making an investment decision.

Similarly, when the U.S. Federal Reserve Board raised interest rates seven times between February 1994 and February 1995, that was probably overkill, especially with inflation running at less than 2% annually.

So 1995 would have been the ideal time to buy aggressive bond funds like the Altamira Bond Fund. Obviously, when interest rates begin to decline, bond funds whose main portfolio includes a healthy dose of long-term bonds will produce the biggest bang for your investment dollar. Dramatic changes in interest rates turned some of 1994's worst-performing bond funds into 1995's best performers. During 1995, for example, the Altamira Bond Fund returned 27.5% and was the number-one performing bond fund over that period, reinforcing the notion that "the last shall be first." For the record, the Dynamic Income Fund returned 14.5% in 1995.

Adding *ZIP* to Your Fixed-Income Portfolio

The prospectus of most major bond funds will talk about an active management philosophy. If a manager is not actively trading the bonds in the portfolio to enhance your bottom line, you have to wonder how many investors would be willing to pay the management-expense ratios associated with Canadian bond funds. By the way, the average management-expense ratio for all Canadian bond funds is 1.63%. Interestingly, we notice that among larger bond funds, the management-expense ratio is often below the average. The implication, in the fixed-income fund market at least, is that bigger is usually better.

The goal for most bond fund managers is to outperform some fixed-income benchmark, the most common being the ScotiaMcLeod Bond Universe. The ScotiaMcLeod Bond Universe[3] is simply an index that measures a hypothetical portfolio of high-grade short-, medium- and long-term bonds.

As we have already stated, in a high-grade bond fund, managers normally add value by

[3] *There is also a ScotiaMcLeod Long-Bond Index, a ScotiaMcLeod Medium-Term Index and a ScotiaMcLeod Short-Term Index.*

shifting the average term-to-maturity of their portfolio. And since they are usually measured against the ScotiaMcLeod Bond Universe, more often than not, bond fund managers will maintain an average term-to-maturity that is close to the average term-to-maturity of the benchmark index.

Despite any self-imposed limitations, most domestic bond fund managers have a rather broad mandate in terms of where they can position the portfolio along the yield curve. There are exceptions, of course. And in terms of how we view portfolios, those exceptions can be useful.

As an example, we cite the Green Line Short-Term Bond Fund which "invests in Canadian government and corporate fixed-income securities with maturities of less than three years." Not much room for this manager to maneuver along the yield curve. However, knowing that makes this low-risk bond fund a good choice if you want something to complement a position in a more aggressive actively managed bond fund.

Of course, as was evident with our Dynamic Income example, bond fund managers can also add value holding foreign pay bonds within the portfolio. This provides a currency kicker, so to speak, which can add value in addition to any gains that might be associated by shifts in domestic interest rates.

Fixed-Income Management Styles

We know that domestic bond fund managers attempt to beat the average or benchmark index. They want to do well against their peers, relative to other funds in the same category. While these domestic bond fund managers all have the same goal, they accomplish it using different means. From our perspective, there are basically six management styles associated with both domestic bond fund managers and global bond fund managers.

Top Down: Most bond fund managers use a top-down approach. That's because most bond fund managers attempt to predict the direction of interest rates and set their average term-to-maturity to take advantage of interest rate shifts. Predicting interest rates is a top-down job, which includes an analysis of such macro-economic forces as inflation, jobs and Gross Domestic Product (GDP) growth. Interestingly, a top-down manager would also be sensitive to another macro-economic condition such as currency fluctuations and might buy or sell foreign pay bonds to take advantage of any weakness or strength in the Canadian dollar.

Bottom Up: These managers are not, at least from our perspective, as commonplace as top-down bond fund managers. A bottom-up manager will normally look for opportunities among corporate or provincial bonds. The idea is to find opportunities at different points—the "hump"—along the yield curve.

Value: Bond fund managers who practice a value style generally work from the premise that the portfolio should maintain a consistent duration and credit quality. In other words, the manager might purchase only medium-term high-grade corporate bonds or only long-term high-grade government bonds. The idea is to buy undervalued bonds for yield and capital appreciation within the context of a specific term-to-maturity and credit quality.

Sector Rotation (Spread Trading): We normally associate this style with equity managers. And to be fair, the term sector rotation may be somewhat misleading when applied to bond fund managers. However, we think of sector rotation as a style that engages in "spread trading." The goal is to examine current yield spreads between bonds in different sectors (i.e., what is the spread between Government of Canada five-year bonds and, say, Province of Ontario five-year bonds). The manager compares these spreads with historical spreads in similar interest rate environments, and then seeks out the most attractive sectors, coupons and credit ratings. This is an active management style that generally, although not always, begins with a bottom-up point of view.

Momentum (Interest Rate Anticipation): Most top-down bond fund managers follow a style known as interest rate anticipation. We have simply chosen to define interest rate anticipation in the FundLine as "momentum." Predicting changes in the shape of the yield curve, and then altering the average term-to-maturity to profit from those changes, is the goal of market timers. From our work, we note that most domestic bond fund managers follow a management style defined as top down/market timing.

Indexation: We offer a more liberal interpretation when it comes to defining whether or not a bond fund manager is operating an indexed portfolio. Obviously, for a pure indexed bond fund like the Green Line Canadian Government Bond Fund that "tracks the ScotiaMcLeod Government Bond Index," the distinction is clear. However, there are cases where bond fund managers always maintain the average term-to-maturity of their portfolio within close proximity to their benchmark index. For example, in the case of a long-term bond fund that always maintains its average term-to-maturity within, say, one year of the ScotiaMcLeod Long-Bond Index, we would consider that a long-term bond fund with an indexed management style (note in the FundLine we have a slot to define whether the bond funds average term-to-maturity is short, medium or long term). Similarly, a fund like the Green Line Short-Term Income Fund is, for all intents, indexed to the ScotiaMcLeod Short-Term Bond Index, or some other short-term barometer. It is our opinion, because the manager has so little room to maneuver, that this is an indexed management style.

Global Bond Funds

Looking at the big picture, global bond funds bring to the table another form of diversification. At least that's the way fund companies market this product. Global bond funds generally invest in bonds of other countries where interest rates are perhaps higher than in Canada and, as the thinking goes, this can add some spice to your income needs.

That being said, global bond funds expose the investor to risks not associated with domestic bond funds that do not have any significant foreign pay holdings. The risk that can be present in a global bond fund is foreign currency exposure. We say "can" because some global bond funds actually try to hedge their foreign currency exposure, exposing the investor only to the potential income and capital gains from the bond portfolio.

However, there is a cost to currency hedging and that will have some impact on the performance numbers.

Is currency hedging good or bad? We don't come down on one side or the other in this debate. However, we're not certain that global bond funds offer any real diversification, and we're not certain they are a reasonable alternative to Canadian bond funds. Read on and see what Eric Kirzner and Kelly Rodgers said about global bond funds in October 1996.

Every Person Has His Time and Everything Has Its Place—Except for Global Bond Funds

If you check the mutual fund listings, you'll find there are about 85 global bond mutual funds in Canada. They seem to be popular (there were only a handful a decade ago), but their place in the mutual fund hierarchy is unclear. We know what they are—they invest primarily in foreign government and corporate bonds, and they either fully or partially eliminate the foreign exchange risk (hedged funds) or they don't (unhedged funds). But what exactly do they do? It's hard to get a good fix on what they are supposed to contribute to an investment portfolio.

They are typically promoted by mutual fund companies with statements such as "Investors who purchase only Canadian bonds are excluding themselves from over 95% of the investment opportunities in the international bond market. Since global bond markets have different characteristics and low correlations, global bond funds are ideal for long-term investors seeking portfolio diversification."

Sounds good—particularly the diversification benefits. But what does this mean? Global bond yields, unlike global stock returns, are linked by a common denominator—interst rate parity theory. This "no free lunch" model means that the expected yields on foreign bonds are equal to the expected yields on domestic bonds when measured in the same currency. In light of interest rate parity, correlation factors for bond markets don't have the same effect as they do for stock markets. You may not get portfolio diversification by investing in global bond funds, but you may get additional costs and/or increased risk!

The expected return on an unhedged global bond fund is equal to the expected return on domestic fixed-income securities of comparable average maturity and duration, according to interest rate parity theory. However, the global bond fund has greater expected volatility due to fluctuating underlying exchange rates. Studies indicate that as much as 80% of the return on foreign bond funds is attributable to currency fluctuations. The exchange-rate risk exposure provides some indirect portfolio diversification, but there are better ways to accomplish this.

Fully hedged international bond funds are even less transparent! They have expected returns equal to the expected return on domestic fixed-income securities or domestic bond funds of comparable average maturity and duration. And they offer no diversification benefits. However, the hedging mechanism implies greater operating costs for the international bond fund over the domestic financial products.

It's hard for a bond manager to add value with bonds unless they can forecast interest rate movements, yield curve shifts or exchange-rate movements. There's little evidence that managers can do this consistently across multiple markets.

This doesn't mean we are against currency diversification. Far from it. If you are concerned about Canada's financial future or you want foreign currency exposure for simple diversification purposes, there are a number of useful vehicles. If your required currency is the U.S. dollar, U.S. Treasury Bonds or Notes are ideal. Some mutual fund families have U.S. dollar denominated versions of the Canadian dollar global bond funds. We see a place for these as well. If you are looking for European currency exposure (D-marks, Swiss francs or British pounds) or Far Eastern (Japanese yen, Australian dollar, New Zealand dollar), your best investment vehicle is an AAA issuer (such as the World Bank) Eurobond denominated in your desired currency.

Global bond funds are a puzzle. Investing in unhedged global bond mutual funds is actually a currency play—and it may be a flawed one at that! Furthermore, global bond funds denominated in Canadian dollars are not the right vehicle since the currency exposure is indirect. Although the portfolio is in foreign bonds, the net asset value per share is in Canadian dollars. Investing in hedged global bond mutual funds doesn't seem to make sense. All in all, we suggest taking a pass.

From the standpoint of the fund manager, we'd like to know what they think investors are buying? Where do global bond funds fit into an investor's strategic asset allocation? What client needs do they meet? Is it currency diversification? Why don't you let us know?

—Eric Kirzner and Kelly Rodgers, "Better way to pare currency risk,"
***The Globe and Mail*, October 10, 1996**

Some Thoughts on Mortgage Funds

Mortgage funds are considered low-risk fixed-income assets, and the statistics bear this out. For example, the average three-year standard deviation for mortgage funds is 1.05% versus a three-year average standard deviation for Canadian bond funds of 1.96%.

Because mortgage funds carry less risk, they are often seen as an alternative to GICs. But as we explained in our section on money market funds, perception is quite different from reality. While it is true that mortgage funds are not as risky as bond funds, the price of a mortgage fund can still fluctuate. In 1994, our watershed year for Canadian bond funds, the average mortgage fund lost only 0.04%, well below the 5.8% average loss for Canadian bond funds.

But for a GIC investor that is not appropriate, because a negative return, regardless how small, is not acceptable.

Finally, for the Record—a GIC Substitute

Having talked about why fixed-income funds should not be considered as GIC substitutes, allow us to suggest the mutual fund market's alternative to GICs—the money market fund. Money market funds invest in low-risk Treasury bills, or certificates of deposit issued by major corporations, all of which provide steady, albeit low, monthly returns.

The monthly returns are usually reinvested into additional units of the fund, which effectively suggests that money market funds are all created equal. Given that, the real issue when scouting potential money market funds comes down to the cost of administration and management. Fort the record, the average management-expense ratio for all Canadian money market funds is 0.69%, which includes trading and administrative costs.

In terms of how a GIC investor views the world, the net asset value of a money market is, in most cases, fixed at $10 per unit. Money market funds can be cashed quickly at the $10 per unit price, and that addresses the investor's perception about the variability of returns.

Assuming the GIC investor's primary consideration is variability of return, then the alternative to a GIC is not a fixed-income fund, but the mutual fund industry's equivalent of cash.

CHAPTER SIX

The Outlook for Bond Funds

With interest rates at such low levels—and staying that way—we think it is important to talk about how domestic bond funds are likely to perform in 1998. But more importantly, given the average management-expense ratio (MER) for bond funds, it is useful to look at some alternatives for income-minded investors.

The problem, as we see it, is that whether bonds are issued by the federal or provincial governments, or by municipalities or corporations, bond fund managers are mandated to invest in them. And as we saw in Chapter 5, the price of those bonds is directly affected by changes in the level of interest rates.

Also, we assume that bond fund managers will be invested in bonds at all times. Those bond fund managers who practice a momentum/interest rate anticipation investment style will attempt to produce some capital gains by forecasting the direction of interest rates. But even then, they can only make one fundamental decision, which is whether to shorten or lengthen the average term-to-maturity of the bonds they hold in their portfolio. Momentum/interest rate anticipators will shorten the average term-to-maturity if they expect interest rates to rise and, conversely, lengthen the average term-to-maturity if they expect interest rates to fall.

There are exceptions, of course, as we saw with our tale of two bond funds in the previous chapter. This exception relates to some fund managers who invest part of the portfolio offshore, which brings currency effect into play for the fund. Managers can invest in bonds issued by Canadian governments or Canadian corporations, but these funds are denominated in a foreign currency—usually U.S. dollars. But that approach assumes the Canadian dollar is overpriced, and if anything, we think the Canadian dollar is undervalued.

Another investment option, that quite frankly is not used by many bond fund managers, is to move to convertible bonds. Most bond funds do not allow their manager the latitude to invest in convertible bonds, or as they are referred to in the financial markets, convertible debentures. A convertible debenture combines the high yield of a bond with the capital gains potential of common stock. As the name suggests, convertibles can be exchanged, at the option of the holder, for the common stock of the company.

Generally speaking, convertible debentures are more conservative than common stocks, yet more aggressive than straight bonds. To put this in perspective, the income from a convertible debenture is usually higher than the dividend on the underlying common stock, but less than the available yield on a straight bond.

The value of a convertible debenture—and by extension a fund that invests in convertible debentures—is that it is affected by changes in the price of the underlying common stock, as well as changes in the level of interest rates. Assuming the value of the underlying stock is rising, so too will the value of the convertible debenture, which means that a convertible bond fund has prospects for growth when interest rates are low.

The fixed-income side of the convertible debenture gives it an investment value which helps to support it when the price of the underlying stock is declining. In other words, the convertible debenture would not likely decline as far or as fast as the underlying common stock. At some point, the convertible would begin trading as a straight bond, and then interest rates would be the determining factor in the price of the convertible debenture.

Usually, to find these type of investments in a fund, we have to look at balanced funds, and particularly balanced funds whose primary goal is to provide income and whose secondary concern is growth. We'll say more about this later in the chapter.

As for bond funds, you can expect most bond funds to yield between 4% and 6% per annum. Add to that yield any capital gains potential should interest rates fall, and subtract from that yield any capital losses on the bond fund should interest rates rise.

Bond fund managers who are restricted as to what bonds they can hold—i.e., only government bonds or corporate bonds, etc.—will have a difficult time generating positive sufficient returns to keep income-oriented investors happy, especially after the MER is taken into account.

Are Canadian bond funds missing the mark?

Fees have an impact on the performance of all funds. A fund with a management-expense ratio (i.e., the MER is the total annual cost of operating the fund, including management fees, divided by the total assets in the fund) of, say, 3%, must return at least 3% in any given year just to break even. Another fund with similar objectives that can do the same job for a 2% MER has a 1% advantage before the game even starts. Some funds charge additional administrative fees (i.e., that are not included in the MER), so make sure you read the fund's prospectus carefully.

Within most fund categories, the cost structure of the mutual fund can be offset or mitigated by some adept money management techniques. A good small-cap manager can overcome a high MER with one good stock pick, making the management fees a moot point. If you examine most fund categories, we can't find a discernible relationship between the costs to operate the fund and the fund's actual performance.

We note among Canadian equity funds, as an example, MERs can range from 0.41% to 3.18%; the average for the group is approximately 2.25%. Looking at the five-year performance numbers, among the top 10 Canadian equity funds, five had MERs above the average, and five had MERs below the average. The same holds true for a number of other fund categories, including international/U.S. equity funds, specialty/sector funds and, of course, small-cap equity funds. The bottom line is that the MER is important, but it should not be the most critical issue when examining mutual fund categories.

The exception to this rule is fixed-income funds, including Canadian bond funds, Canadian bond and mortgage funds, Canadian money market funds, and global bond funds. In the fixed-income market, fees play a critical role because they have a direct impact on the performance numbers.

Did you know, for example, that Canadian bond fund managers simply can't beat their respective benchmarks? To see just how poorly Canadian bond funds have performed as a group, compare them with passive indexes for the same pool of securities. In the three-year period ended June 30, 1997, for instance, the average Canadian bond fund returned 11.8%, according to data from Pal-Trak, while over that same period the average Canadian bond and mortgage fund returned 9.8%.

Compare that to the ScotiaMcLeod Bond Universe (an index that tracks the performance of short-, mid- and long-term Canadian government bonds) that returned 13.9% compounded annually. That's quite a difference. Suppose, for example, that you had invested $10,000 in the ScotiaMcLeod Bond Universe Fund three years ago. Today, it would be worth $14,760. That same $10,000 invested in the average Canadian bond fund returned $13,920, and for the average Canadian bond and mortgage fund, the dollar value would have grown to $13,230.

The reason for the differences in return is costs: the benchmark index doesn't have a cost, but the bond fund manager does. Of the 109 Canadian short-, medium- and long-term bond funds with at least a three-year track record, only eight funds outperformed the ScotiaMcLeod Bond Universe, and seven of those eight funds had MERs that were below the average for the group.

How difficult is it to find a Best Bet bond fund? Based on 83 Canadian short-, medium- and long-term bond funds with at least a five-year track record, and representing about $13 billion in assets, only six beat the ScotiaMcLeod Bond Universe in all measuring periods. The measuring periods included one-year, two-year, three-year and five-year returns. Of that group, only the Altamira Bond fund is available nationally with a reasonable minimum initial purchase amount (i.e., $1,000 minimum purchase).

When dealing with fixed-income funds, investors are quite right in asking why they should pay management fees to a bond fund manager for what appears to be a guarantee of underperformance.

These are important issues, because a growing number of investors—most of whom are retired—are looking for income, and based on the statistics, the vast majority of bond funds are simply not adding value. At least not sufficient value to justify the fees.

This fee debate is only relevant if the investor can buy a reasonable alternative to the traditional bond fund. One alternative we like is the so-called "laddered bond portfolio," which is available from most brokerage firms.

For example, suppose you are looking for income, have decided that you need the security of bonds and have a 10-year time horizon. A laddered bond portfolio might be the ideal solution. One of the advantages of a laddered bond portfolio is that you determine the time horizon. You could purchase five bonds, with staggered maturities every two years. By doing so, you control the time horizon. You buy a bond fund, the manager determines the time horizon.

Along the same lines, the laddered portfolio has a defined term-to-maturity. If you hold all of the bonds to maturity, you eliminate the risk of losing your principal investment. A bond fund does not mature, so the principal investment is not guaranteed, although over a three- to five-year time horizon, it is highly unlikely the bond fund will be worth less than you paid for it.

A laddered bond portfolio can also be structured so that it pays income every month, which is another advantage for the investor seeking alternatives to bond funds that distribute income monthly.

The final benefit, of course, is cost. An investor pays an upfront commission that is built into the price of a bond when purchased through a broker. Commissions vary, but figure on about 1%. Once the laddered portfolio is set up, the only additional fees will come when one bond matures, and you pay a commission to buy a replacement bond.

In our 10-year example where we buy five bonds maturing every two years, figure the commission costs to be about 0.25% per annum (assuming you replace each maturing bond over the next 10 years). That's quite a saving when compared to the average costs associated with a Canadian bond fund.

Some brokerage firms will even customize a laddered portfolio, designed to meet the individual investor's income needs and time horizon. All the bonds are purchased at the same time and you pay one commission to buy the entire laddered portfolio. Talk to your broker for more details, and make certain you ask about the costs.

Over the last three years, a passive laddered bond portfolio would have yielded just over 12% compounded annually, based on an average of the ScotiaMcLeod Mid-Term and ScotiaMcLeod Short-Term Bond indices, adjusted for commission costs. Of course, that included periods with double-digit interest rates. Don't expect a laddered portfolio to earn that kind of return today!

It wasn't that long ago that income-oriented investors were restricted to bond funds. But the liquidity, size requirements and commission costs made it difficult for the average investor to buy bonds directly. That has changed in recent years, and with some innovative thinking among the brokerage firms, there are cost-effective alternatives to traditional bond funds. This makes it that much harder to justify the cost of buying a bond fund for income needs.

Other Income Alternatives—Dividend Funds

Having discussed the problems that beset most bond funds, we need to seek out some income alternatives. Fortunately, there are a few possibilities. One of these is dividend funds.

Dividend funds generally have the majority of their assets invested in high-yielding common or preferred shares. A dividend fund, then, has growth potential, especially on the portion of the portfolio that is invested in high-yielding large-cap common stocks.

And you should not underestimate that potential. Last year, for example, dividend funds that held bank stocks—because of their yield—turned in some pretty impressive numbers. Mind you, bank stocks caught more than a few managers off guard, as they were one of the strongest groups on the Toronto Stock Exchange.

What is a dividend?

A corporation's profit is the difference between its revenues or sales and its expenses (including interest payments on its debt and corporation taxes). This profit or net income is either retained by the company for future investment opportunities or is paid out to shareholders in the form of dividends. If a company earns high returns on its operations, it will continuously generate new income for future dividend payments.

Dividends are paid to two types of shareholders. Preferred shareholders are eligible for a set and maximum dividend. For example, an 8% $50.00 par value preferred share would be entitled to a $4.00 dividend per year. These dividends are paid before dividends are paid to the other class of shares, the common shares. However, if the payment of the dividend could impair the ability of the company to function, the dividend could be omitted.

As for the common shares, dividends are paid only after the preferred shareholders' claims are satisfied. The dividend declarations generally reflect the earning power and investment opportunities of the company. For example, if a company retains 60% of its income (paying out 40% as dividends) and earns 12% on its investments, the company's earnings and dividends will expand at a rate of 7.2% per year.

Since dividends are paid out of the company with after-tax dollars, Canadian shareholders are given the dividend tax credit to help equalize the tax incidence.

Understanding the Tax Advantages of Dividends

Aside from the potential growth, the key investment features of dividend income funds are the dividend income produced and the way in which those dividends are taxed. As a unitholder you are entitled to your proportionate share of the dividends and interest earned on the fund's portfolio as well as any capital gains (losses) incurred through the trading of securities in the fund prior to their maturity.

Dividend income, since it is nondeductible at the corporate level, is given preferential tax treatment at the personal level (see Chapter 3 for more details on the tax treatment of dividend funds).

Other Investments Inside a Dividend Fund

In addition to holding blue-chip dividend-paying common and preferred shares, some dividend funds offer additional income-producing strategies such as convertible preferred shares. Like the convertible debentures discussed earlier, convertible preferred shares provide a regular dividend income and are convertible at the option of the holder into the common shares of the company.

The point is, dividend fund managers often have more flexibility than bond fund managers, such as the ability to move from preferred to common shares. Still, dividend fund managers must produce dividend income and so are more restricted in their investment options than balanced funds.

In short, dividend funds are a timely alternative for investors looking for income, and who may be concerned about the erosion of their principal because of the potential loss from holding a bond fund.

The Balanced Fund Alternative

When we think about balanced funds, we usually think about growth. We think of the manager who attempts to maximize return by emphasizing stocks or bonds at a given point in the business cycle. More recently, however, we have seen new funds being categorized as balanced funds, but in reality, these funds are designed to be income alternatives. As a balanced fund that promises to pay regular distributions, the managers have been given wide latitude in terms of what assets they can hold. For example, some balanced funds hold royalty income trust units and, in some cases, managers can utilize covered call option strategies.

Particularly popular are the royalty income trust units (see box on page 97). Currently there is more than $7 billion of royalty trust units on the Toronto Stock Exchange, and many investors have bought into them directly. However, we're not sure that direct ownership of these units is a good strategy for every investor.

In most cases, investors are attracted by the yield, without fully understanding the tax implications or the potential risks. Inside a balanced fund, where the manager is conversant with the product and is able to purchase a diversified portfolio of income trust units, the manager can complement a portfolio of common and preferred shares. Another attraction is the regular cash flow inside a balanced fund, for those funds that pay regular distributions.

An option strategy such as covered call writing is another low-risk alternative used by some balanced fund managers. In this case, the manager buys the underlying stock—usually a blue-chip stock that has a reasonable dividend—and sells a call option that obligates the manager to deliver the stock to the option buyer at a predetermined price and within a specified period of time. (See box on page 98.) Suffice it to say, covered call writing is a low-risk strategy that can yield decent returns on blue-chip stocks.

An example of a fund that can employ covered call writing strategies is the G.T. Global Canada Income Class Fund. This fund pays income on a monthly basis, and that income is in the form of dividends and capital gains. The fund's intent is to protect principal, so that virtually all of the monthly distributions will be in the form of dividends and capital gains. Usually there will be no interest distributions.

The manager is Derek Webb of Chancellor LGT Asset Management. Mr. Webb is a veteran of the investment business, having spent the last five years at LGT. He is a long-time bond trader, making him an ideal manager for a balanced fund that promises a steady flow of income.

Balanced fund managers, especially in those balanced funds that strive to distribute regular income, have more latitude in terms of what strategies they use to produce that income. The more flexibility accorded the manager, the better the chance a fund will meet your income requirements, and thus meet our requirement as an alternative to fixed-income investing.

What is a royalty income trust unit?

With so many investors seeking alternatives to low interest rates, royalty income trust units have become quite popular. There are a number of these units listed on the Toronto Stock Exchange, ranging from iron ore royalty trust units to gold royalty trust units. One of the most recent examples is a royalty trust unit that invests in timberlands.

However, the most common is the royalty income trust unit. For example, with an oil royalty trust unit, the investor is effectively buying a share of a producing oil well. On the surface, it is not that much different from owning shares in Exxon.

When you think about it, Exxon owns a lot of producing oil wells. The money the company earns from the wells is used in one of three ways: (1) the company uses some to pay dividends to its shareholders, (2) the company will plow some of the profits back into retained earnings to fund future growth, and (3) the company will spend some of the profits on new exploration, seeking out new producing wells.

With a royalty trust unit, however, all of the profits from the well are distributed to unitholders in the form of income. The income is simply the profit margin from the well. If oil is selling at U.S. $25 per barrel, and the well can pump it out at a cost of $15 per barrel, than the $10 per barrel profit can be distributed to unitholders.

Seems like a good deal on the surface. But what about the risks? One risk is a change in the price of oil. If oil prices were to fall to, say, $20 per barrel, then your profit margin is cut in half. Remember, it still costs you $15 per barrel to bring the oil out of the ground.

When oil prices are rising, the profit margin increases, and so too does the value of the oil royalty trust unit. In you are a company that markets oil wells, the best time to sell them is when the price of oil is high, which explains why there are so many oil royalty trust units currently on the market.

However, when oil prices are declining, the profit margins shrink and the value of the oil royalty trust unit will fall. These units, then, are not substitutes for GICs whose value will rise and fall with the market.

A second consideration is the oil well itself. It is, after all, a depleting asset. As the oil is brought to the surface, there is less in the well, and so the life of the well is a consideration. Part of your profits, then, is really a return of your principal, and along with that there may be some favorable tax benefits. For example, Revenue Canada allots a depletion allowance to an oil well, and that can be used to shelter some of the income from that well. Ultimately, what you must keep in mind is that the investment may have a limited life. When the oil runs out, so does your investment.

What is covered call writing?

Covered call writing (owning stock and selling a call option against the underlying shares) is the most common option strategy, and this strategy can help increase your yield. The premium received from the sale of the call option increases your cash flow. That cash flow can be paid out or applied to the purchase price of the underlying stock, effectively reducing the cost base of those shares. If you can reduce the price at which you buy the stock, then you presumably reduce the risk of owning the stock. Finally, the exercise (strike) price of the call option establishes a target price at which the manager who is using this strategy is willing to sell the stock.

When fund managers write call options against stock they hold in their fund, they are agreeing to sell the stock at a specific price at some point in the future. For example: assume the manager has 100 shares of Bank of Nova Scotia at $65 per share. Assume further that the manager sells one (each call option contract represents 100 shares of the underlying stock) Bank of Nova Scotia July 70 call option ($70 is the strike or exercise price of the call option) at $2 per share (the $2 per share, or $200 per contract, is the price the option buyer pays and the premium the covered call writer receives).

In this trade, the fund manager has effectively agreed to sell 100 shares of Bank of Nova Scotia at $70 per share until the third Friday in July, which is the date at which the option expires. The advantage, of course, is that no matter where the stock ends up, the $2 per share premium ($200 per option contract) from the sale of the option belongs to the fund.

In this example, the manager has established a set of parameters. If the price of Bank of Nova Scotia is above $70 per share come July, the stock will be called away, and the fund will receive $70 per share. If the stock remains where it is, the fund retains the $2 per share ($200 per option contract) premium, and the manager could theoretically sell another call option expiring in, say, December.

Managers who utilize this strategy must be adept at balancing the trade-off between downside risk (loss) and upside potential (reward). In the Bank of Nova Scotia example, the manager bought the stock at $65 but immediately received $2 per share in premium income. In effect, then, the net cost for the stock was $63 per share ($65 less $2 per share premium = $63).

Five Conservative Funds for Income-Oriented Investors

Having stated our concerns about Canadian bond funds and our views on global bond funds, we wanted to take the time to introduce some hall-of-fame funds (three Canadian dividend funds, one Canadian equity fund and one balanced fund), for income-oriented investors, picked from a list of more than 1,800 mutual funds available to Canadian investors.

To get down to this short list, we applied five exacting *screens*. We used the Pal-Trak mutual fund analysis program to set the screens and then to review the results.

On the first pass, we eliminated all funds that had not been established for at least five years, because we wanted funds that had weathered 1994—one of the worst years for bond and equity funds. The idea was to find managers who can guide funds through bad weather.

In the second pass, we eliminated all funds whose volatility was above average. Again, income-oriented investors are interested first in the safety of their principal and second in the fund's long-term performance. Of course, we were keenly interested in both sides—above-average performance with below-average risk.

In terms of risk, we used the fund's standard deviation when setting up the screen. However, standard deviation doesn't tell the average investor much about the risk associated with a particular fund. Another approach that is visually appealing is to look at the fund's 24-month trailing returns. Why 24 months? Because income-oriented investors should have at least a two-year time horizon before considering the purchase of any mutual fund.

With trailing returns, we looked at every possible two-year performance period since the fund had come into existence. We then asked two questions: What was the worst 24-month period for return, and what was the best 24-month period for return? We were looking for funds that had never experienced a losing 24-month trailing return.

On the third screen we looked at performance. (You knew we would get there eventually.) In this case, we wanted only those funds that had generated double-digit compound annual returns over the last five years. At 10% compounded annually, your money doubles every 7.2 years.

More importantly, we wanted funds that had minimal losses in any of the five previous calendar years (i.e., January to December 1993 year-end to 1997 year-end). If the fund had only small losses in any calendar year, investors would likely continue to hold the fund. And since all of our funds never lost money over any 24-month holding period, the calendar year screen was a useful exercise.

On the fourth screen we looked at the fund's management-expense ratio. In this case, we eliminated any fund whose MER was above the average for the group (2.66% being the average MER for Canadian large-cap value funds). If we are looking at performance and risk, then we think it is also important to seek out funds that are efficiently managed. That can't hurt should we experience a market correction any time soon.

And speaking of the correction that will come at some point, we also screened for funds that had a reasonable amount of cash (i.e., between 5% and 10%) in their portfolio. Just what the conservative income-oriented investor ordered to cushion the blow from a correction and to allow the manager to take advantage of potential buying opportunities after the fact.

And just to make sure that everyone could afford to play the role of a conservative investor, we also screened for funds whose initial investment requirement was no greater than $1,000.

In fact, the last screen eliminated one of our favorite mutual funds for the conservative income-oriented investor, the Phillips, Hager & North Dividend Income Fund. It passed all of our screens with flying colors. Unfortunately, the minimum initial investment requirement is $25,000. If you can afford that much as an initial investment, then this is a good fund to consider. If not, consider one of the other funds from our select list.

The AGF Dividend Fund

AGF is, of course, one of the largest mutual fund companies in Canada. And the AGF Dividend Fund has been one of their stalwart performers, generating above-average returns with below-average risk.

Managed by Gord MacDougall (since the fund's inception December 1985) and Martin Gerber (since January 1991), the fund attempts to provide investors with consistent cash flow, a healthy percentage of which comes from Canadian dividend income, some from capital appreciation and the remainder from interest income. The managers practice a two-way asset allocation strategy, which simply means they focus on only two asset classes—stocks and cash. The fund does not invest in any mid- or long-term bonds.

In terms of risk, the fund passed our trailing return criteria. In its worst 24-month period, the fund returned 5.73% (2.83% compounded annually). That was the return for the period between July 1989 and July 1991. Compare that to its best 24-month period, January 1995 to January 1997, when the fund returned 61.31% (27.01% compounded annually).

The fund has returned a stellar 16.8% compounded annually over the last five years. In dollar terms, a $1,000 investment made in 1992 would have been worth $2,169 by the end of May 1997. More to the point, the AGF Dividend Fund never lost money in any calendar year. In its worst calendar year—1994—the fund still had a positive return of 0.4%.

The fund, at present, has 5.3% of its assets in cash and distributes income monthly.

FUND FACTS

Fund Name: AGF Dividend Fund

Manager: Gord MacDougall (December 1985)
Martin Gerber (January 1991)
Connor, Clark & Lunn Investment Management Ltd.

Address: AGF Funds Inc.
P.O. Box 50, 31st Floor, Toronto Dominion Centre
Toronto, Ontario
M5K 1E9

Telephone: 1-800-520-0620
1-416-367-1900

Net Asset Value: $19.46 (May 31, 1997)

Total Assets: $859.3 million

Performance:

1 Year	2 Year	3 Year	5 Year
33.4%	23.8%	20.0%	16.8%

How Sold: Through financial advisors

Fee Structure: Front- or back-end load, MER 1.91%

Minimum Investment: $500

RRSP Eligible: Yes

BPI Dividend Fund

The BPI Dividend Fund is a must-see for income-oriented investors in that it provides monthly dividend income and has 12% of its assets in cash, one of the lowest management-expense ratios in the industry (MER is 1%), very low risk, and a 15-year track record.

Managed by Eric B. Bushell for BPI Mutual Funds, the fund attempts to provide a high level of current income by investing in a portfolio consisting primarily of preferred shares. That investment style has returned 12.8% compounded annually over the last five years, which means a $1,000 investment made in 1992 would at the end of August 1997 have been worth $1,826.

In terms of volatility, the fund has the lowest standard deviation of the funds on our list, reflecting lower but steadier returns. That shows up in the trailing returns analysis, where the BPI Dividend Fund's worst 24-month period (ending October 1990) yielded a cumulative return of 3.03%, or 1.50% compounded annually. On the best-case scenario, the fund returned 48.84% (22% compounded annually) over the 24-month period ending January 1997.

FUND FACTS

Fund Name: BPI Dividend Income Fund

Manager: Eric B. Bushell
BPI Mutual Funds

Address: BPI Mutual Funds
BCE Place, Suite 3900
161 Bay Street
Toronto, Ontario
M5J 2S1

Telephone: 1-800-263-2427

Net Asset Value: $12.57 (Aug 31, 1997)

Total Assets: $288.4 million

Performance:

1 Year	2 Year	3 Year	5 Year
26%	20.8%	18.3%	12.8%

How Sold: Through financial advisors and direct

Fee Structure: Front- or back-end load, MER 1.00%

Minimum Investment: $500

RRSP Eligible: Yes

Scotia Excelsior Dividend Fund

At first blush, this fund is another in a long line of bank funds designed specifically for conservative income-oriented investors. In the past, we have not recommended many bank funds, and the reason comes down to below-average performance statistics. This is not surprising when you think that bank funds are sold through bank branches to investors looking for alternatives to GICs.

In recent years that trend has begun to change, most likely because investors have been getting more sophisticated. Whatever the reason, it is a positive change, and the Scotia Excelsior family of funds is one group that has been on the cusp of that change.

The principal objective of the Scotia Excelsior Dividend Fund is to provide investors with a high-dividend yield that is paid out on a quarterly basis. The fund accomplishes that goal by investing in various types of preferred shares. Some examples include floating rate preferred shares whose dividend rises or falls so as to be competitive with the current level of interest rates. Also included in the fund's mix are convertible preferreds—shares that can be converted into underlying common stock—and retractable preferred shares. The fund also invests in a selection of good quality, high-dividend-paying common shares.

Managed by the team approach—specifically the M.A. Management team at Montrusco Associates Inc. since 1986—the fund has returned 13.6% compounded annually since 1992 to 1997, turning a $1,000 investment into $1,888 by the end of May 1997.

Filtered through our trailing return analysis, the fund's worst 24-month period was the period ending October 1990, when the fund returned 3.43% or 1.7% compounded annually. The best 24-month span was the period ending February 1997, when the fund returned 52.3% or 23.41% compounded annually.

FUND FACTS

Fund Name:	Scotia Excelsior Dividend Fund
Manager:	M.A. Management Team Montrusco Associates Inc.
Address:	The Bank of Nova Scotia 44 King Street West Toronto, Ontario M5H 1H1
Telephone:	1-800-268-9269
Net Asset Value:	$12.76 (May 31, 1997)
Total Assets:	$319.2 million

Performance:	1 Year	2 Year	3 Year	5 Year
	26.6%	21.1%	15.5%	13.6%

How Sold:	Through financial advisors and direct
Fee Structure:	No-load, MER 1.07%
Minimum Investment:	$500
RRSP Eligible:	Yes

Royal Trust Growth and Income Fund

The second Canadian equity fund that we think belongs in a conservative investor's RRSP is the Royal Trust Growth and Income Fund. The objective of this fund is to provide investors with a balanced portfolio. To accomplish this, the manager—John Kellett of Royal Bank Investment Management Inc.—invests in both common and preferred shares of Canadian corporations. The managers also hold a sprinkling of Canadian convertible debentures.

In addition to the above-mentioned securities, the fund also has a small amount (currently about 7.5% of the fund's assets) allocated to conventional Canadian bonds. And to supplement these diversification techniques, the fund also has about 5% of its assets invested in foreign securities, and more importantly, in terms of risk reduction, the manager has about 10.8% of the assets allocated to cash.

The fund has returned 14.2% compounded annually over the five years to year-end 1997 ($1,000 invested five years ago has, at the end of May 1997, grown to $1,940). In terms of trailing returns, the fund's worst 24-month period ended October 1990. Over that two-year stretch, the fund returned 1.61%, or 0.80% compounded annually. The best 24-month period was between May 1992 and May 1997, when the fund returned 58.24% or 15.79% compounded annually.

FUND FACTS

Fund Name:	Royal Trust Growth and Income Fund
Manager:	John Kellett Royal Bank Investment Management Inc.
Address:	Royal Mutual Funds Inc. Royal Bank Investment Management P.O. Box 7500, Station A Royal Trust Tower, 77 King Street East, 5th Floor Toronto, Ontario M5W 1P9
Telephone:	1-800-463-3863
Net Asset Value:	$14.85 (May 31, 1997)
Total Assets:	$188.3 million
Performance:	1 Year: 38.3%; 2 Year: 25.8%; 3 Year: 18.6%; 5 Year: 14.2%
How Sold:	Through financial advisors and direct
Fee Structure:	No-load, MER 1.77%
Minimum Investment:	$500
RRSP Eligible:	Yes

Global Strategy Income Plus Fund

The Global Strategy Income Plus Fund (the only balanced fund in the group) rounds out our list of five low-risk funds. This is an interesting fund because the manager—Tony Massie (since April 1992) of Global Strategy Financial Inc.—has a mandate to earn high returns from a portfolio of income producing assets, including such things as government bonds (21.7% of the fund's assets), and Canadian common shares (53.8% of assets) as well as a sprinkling of foreign equity and preferred shares. The fund currently has 19% of its assets in cash.

This investment approach is quite different from the way most balanced funds are managed. Indeed, it is a dramatic change in mindset! Unlike traditional balanced funds that are managed for growth, this fund is managed to generate income. And it has done so quite successfully.

The fund has generated a five-year compound annual return of 14.9% to 1997 ($1,000 becomes $2,004 by the end of May 1997). Most impressive is the fund's trailing returns. The worst 24-month period, ended October 1995, returned 9.4% or 4.59% compounded annually. The best 24-month period, ended November 1996, saw the fund return 48.21% or 21.74% compounded annually.

However, one has to be careful when looking at trailing returns in isolation. For example, when compared to other funds on our list, this trailing return report is exceptional. However, this fund has been around for just over five years, unlike the other funds on the list that all have at least a 10-year track record.

The MER for this fund is substantially higher than is the case for the other four funds on our list. We would like to think the MER will come down as the fund ages and the cash flows stabilize. And to some extent, the higher MER may be justified, simply because the manager has a wider mandate than the other funds on our list.

FUND FACTS

Fund Name: Global Strategy Income Plus Fund

Manager: Tony Massie
Global Strategy Financial Inc.

Address: Global Strategy Financial Inc.
33 Bloor Street East, Suite 1600
Toronto, Ontario,
M4W 3T8

Telephone: 1-800-387-1229

Net Asset Value: $22.58 (May 31, 1997)

Total Assets: $724.7 million

Performance:

1 Year	2 Year	3 Year	5 Year
24.5%	20.6%	15.8%	14.9%

How Sold: Through financial advisors and direct

Fee Structure: Front- or back-end load, MER 2.63%

Minimum Investment: $1,000

RRSP Eligible: Yes

CHAPTER SEVEN

The Basics of Cash

Cash Assets

From our perspective, cash assets are represented by any investment in which there is no real risk of losing your principal. It is any security that can be readily sold or turned into cash with very little bother or cost, and generally has a term-to-maturity of less than one year.

A number of assets fit in this category. Bank savings accounts are probably the most common form of cash, but savings accounts may not be an attractive option. For one thing, some savings accounts pay interest on the lowest balance during any particular month. Some pay interest that is compounded daily, while others compound interest weekly, monthly or even semi-annually. Remember, the less frequent the compounding, the lower your return. Second, the interest rates paid on savings accounts are seldom generous. There are other, more attractive, alternatives.

Canada Savings Bonds

Almost every Canadian is familiar with Canada Savings Bonds (CSBs). CSBs have been issued by the federal government every year since 1946. Now, more than 50 years after their introduction, CSBs make up an important component of the federal government's annual financing plans. More important, they make a great deal of sense for the average Canadian investor.

CSBs go on sale every October and the sale usually lasts for about two weeks. They have a number of popular features in that they are:

- backed by the Canadian government and thus are considered risk-free investments;
- easy to buy; you can walk into any bank, trust company or credit union and line up at the CSB wicket, or you can buy the bond in the fall and pay for it over the year through a payroll deduction plan;

- fully registered in the name of the holder. That means that every year you will receive a statement from Revenue Canada that calculates the amount of interest income you must declare on your tax form;
- cashable at any time for their full face value, which, in terms of defining CSBs as cash, is the most important feature. A trip to your local bank and you can receive cash plus any accrued interest within minutes. However, it is always best to wait until the first of the month before cashing your CSB or you will lose some of interest earned on your bond. If you decide on February 16 to cash a CSB, you should wait until March 1 or you will receive only the interest earned until the end of January. You will not be credited with any interest for the 16 days during which you held the bond in February. If you hold on to your bond, interest will be paid every November unless you buy a compound bond. With a compound bond, the interest is not paid out to you but is left to compound at the same interest rate as your principal.

Are CSBs the investment of choice for the cash component of our asset allocation model? (See Chapter 14) A great deal depends on the interest rate of the CSBs. To decide, compare the yield with the rates being offered on T-bills or by financial institutions on GICs. In 1990, for example, CSBs were issued at 10.75%, between 0.25% to 0.75% below the rates available on GICs, and 1.25% below prevailing T-bill rates.

Treasury Bills

Treasury bills are the debt of the federal government. Original issues are delivered every Thursday by auction at the Bank of Canada. T-bills do not pay interest; instead, they are sold at a discount to their face value. The difference in the price you pay and the value of the bill at maturity represents the yield over the term of the T-bill.

For example, a $5,000 90-day T-bill might cost $4,925. At the end of three months you would have $5,000, a return that represents an annual yield of about 6%. T-bills carry terms of 30, 60, 90, 180 or 360 days. You can also purchase nonstandard terms in the secondary market, which is maintained by investment dealers. T-bills can be bought and sold at any time.

T-bills have become very popular in the past few years, particularly since investment dealers relaxed the rules for purchases. At one time, you had to put down between $100,000 and $250,000 to buy a T-bill, but in the past few years investment dealers have been dividing the T-bills issued by the government into smaller offerings, sometimes as little as $5,000. Often there is no commission charge, although you will be paying the dealer's bid/ask spread.

T-bills, unlike CSBs, come in bearer form, meaning they are not registered in your name, and you will not receive any information from Revenue Canada regarding the amount of interest you earned during the year in T-bills. Revenue Canada depends on the honesty of the taxpayer to claim the amount of interest earned on the tax form for the appropriate year.

Money Market Funds

One of the most versatile investment vehicles is the money market fund. These unique funds invest in money market securities of various maturities, including Treasury bills issued by the Government of Canada and the provinces, bankers' acceptances, short-term government and high-quality corporate bonds and the promissory notes of companies with very high credit ratings, a product called commercial paper. These are all considered low-risk investments, for which the possibility of a default is relatively remote.

The investor is entitled to a *pro rata* share of the interest and trading profits earned on the fund's portfolio.

The money market fund is a hybrid between a traditional "mutual fund" and a savings instrument, and is a derived product that was fashioned to meet specific needs. The money market fund has a number of features that are consistent with traditional mutual funds in that it is a pooled, professionally managed, diversified product with normally small dollar-entry requirements, dividend reinvestment plans, periodic purchase plans and no secondary market.

Money market funds debuted in Canada in 1983, although consumer interest appeared to materialize in 1985. In 1987, under amendments to the Bank Act, banks were permitted to manage and sell all categories of mutual funds, including money market funds, without restrictions.

However, unlike traditional mutual funds, Canadian money market funds (with a few exceptions) attempt to maintain a fixed net asset value per share (NAVPS) by using various accounting and trading techniques to accomplish this purpose. For money market funds, instead of a fluctuating NAVPS, it is the interest that fluctuates on a daily basis.

Money market funds only pay interest, so all distributions are likely to be treated as interest income. Normally, income is distributed through additional shares or units rather than through cash payments.

For example, if you bought 100 shares of a money market fund at $10 per share, your total investment would be $1,000. If the yield on the fund was, say, 6%, you would earn approximately 0.5% per month in interest distributions. In most cases you would simply receive a one-half share for each 100 shares held (100 x 0.005 = 1/2 share). At the end of one month, the net asset value of the mutual fund would still be $10 per share, but you would now own 100.5 shares.

Because you could purchase most of the investments that the money market fund will purchase for you, there is normally no fee for buying or selling the shares. The management fees on money market funds are also low relative to other funds. The research and analysis required to buy a basket of money market instruments is not intense or expensive. The management fees cover the administration of the fund and should not be any higher than 0.5% of the funds assets. Some money market mutual funds offer cheque-writing services, which can be an attractive feature.

Money market funds are liquid; you can receive cash for your fund almost immediately, at any time, with no penalty or fees in most cases. You might also consider buying a money market fund that is in the same family as your fixed-income and equity funds. This will make it easier to switch between funds if your changes to your portfolio dictate a change in asset weightings.

Investors use money market funds either as a place to park their money temporarily as they wait for other investment opportunities or as a permanent part of their portfolio.

There are four very good reasons to include money market funds in your portfolio:

1. **Capital Preservation:** Since they invest in very low risk, short term-to-maturity securities, your capital is quite safe with money market funds. You may want to use them as an alternative to a savings account, since you can cash out at any time at the fixed net asset value per share. Only under extremely unusual circumstances would a fund be unable to hold its fixed NAVPS at the $10 per share level.

2. **Competitive Yields:** Money market funds have traditionally provided returns that keep pace with changes in short-term interest rates. You will normally find that the returns are higher than that earned on bank deposits, although often lower than on term deposits. Yields are based on current interest rate movements and will change with the changing interest-rate environment.

3. **Convenience:** The money market fund may be a more convenient product and offers economies of commission and bulk buying over the direct purchase of T-bills or other money market securities. They can be cashed out at any time at the net asset value per share. Your monthly interest payments can be conveniently reinvested in new units. These are ideal as a result for RRSPs or other tax-sheltered plans since you can park small amounts of income temporarily in a money market fund until you decide what to do with it! We recommend that all RRSP investors have a money market fund as part of their plan.

4. **Collateral:** Since they are so stable, money market funds represent excellent collateral for loans.

GICs—Cash or Fixed Income?

This is one of the most hotly debated issues among investors and financial planners. Should we classify Guaranteed Investment Certificates as cash assets or fixed-income assets when constructing an investment portfolio?

The notion that GICs are really fixed-income assets is driven by two major considerations: (1) the so-called accessibility issue, and (2) the maturity spectrum. The fact is, when we think of cash, we think in terms of accessibility: how quickly can you "cash" out your investment? In that sense, CSBs, money market funds and even government Treasury bills can be cashed out within 24 hours, and so defining them as cash assets is relatively easy.

Coupled with the accessibility issue is the investment's term-to-maturity. Again, we think of cash assets as short-term investments, with maturities ranging from 30 days to one year.

Looking at GICs from this perspective makes it difficult to define them as cash assets. When you buy a GIC, you usually lock in your money for periods ranging from one to seven years. In terms of accessibility, you may have the ability to cash out your investments (depending on what interest rates have done in the meantime), but usually in such cases only after absorbing a severe penalty.

Again, following this same theme, we have the term-to-maturity factor. Any investment that ties up your assets for more than a year is hard to define as cash, even more so when you are locking in your assets for five to seven years. So from these perspectives, it is not surprising that investors view GICs as they would fixed-income investments. And there, in our opinion, lies the problem.

Investor perception can be a dangerous thing. In the fall of 1994, after an investment planning presentation, a retired lady approached us and asked what we thought about mortgage funds. For some historical perspective, this was about six months after the U.S. Federal Reserve and the Bank of Canada had begun pushing up interest rates. At this point in the cycle, the value of most mortgage funds had slipped badly.

We found out that this lady, an individual who had always held GICs, had recently rolled her maturing GIC portfolio into a mortgage fund on the advice of her financial advisor.

The advisor had told her—correctly—that she could enhance her yield. The problem was that the advisor also told her that mortgage funds were an alternative to GICs, because both were fixed-income investments. What she did not understand was that the value of a mortgage fund could fluctuate, something that does not occur in a GIC—at least, not on the surface. Having invested a sizable portion of her portfolio (about $100,000) into this mortgage fund, she was now upset to learn that the value of her portfolio had declined sharply.

The same holds true for bond funds. In fact, the variability of return in a bond fund is more dramatic than is the case with mortgage funds. And despite that, we continue to hear of cases where financial advisors recommend a bond fund as an alternative to a GIC, without explaining that a bond fund can fluctuate. And for a long-term investor, perception is everything.

From our perspective, an investor's perception of risk is the primary consideration when classifying investments. We think of cash as a riskless asset. That, too, is the perception of GICs, assuming, of course, they are purchased at a Canadian Deposit Insurance Corporation-insured institution. The GIC principal is guaranteed and will be repaid with interest, on the maturity date.

The second important perception is the variability of return over the holding period. Cash assets, by definition, do not fluctuate in value. On the surface—i.e., there is no active secondary market or price quotes—neither do GICs. The notion that GICs should be viewed as cash, then, comes down to investor perception. And the view that investors and financial advisors should hold, in our opinion, is that short-term GICs are an alternative to cash, but not an alternative to fixed-income investments.

CHAPTER EIGHT

Borderless Shopping

There are major power shifts occurring in the investment world, signaling permanent and elemental changes in how financial planning and investment portfolio building is carried out. The most important implication is that you now need a global orientation to compete successfully in this rapidly changing environment.

There is a relentless march toward globalization of world markets and 24-hour trading. Geographical boundaries have blurred and trading pacts are proliferating. The Internet and electronic trading systems have linked the world in a manner totally unforeseen two decades ago. This globalization process has been marked by securities deregulation, by instant telecommunications and information flows and increased mobility of capital, all of which have served to foster international investing opportunities. Economic growth is shifting toward poorer countries, and knowledgeable investors are becoming increasingly interested in emerging or developing countries. The trend toward free markets, free trade, foreign investment and market deregulation has propelled capital resources to high-growth and low per capita GDP, as well as low-wage countries.

As a result, global investment has become an integral part of the investment asset allocation process. And with good reason. There are tens of thousands of different financial products traded in the world's some 500 bond, stock and derivatives markets. If you limit yourself to only the Canadian market, you are shutting yourself off from rich investment opportunities elsewhere. The Canadian domestic market represents a mere fraction of the world's total investment arena.

Investors who constrain their analysis and selection to domestic instruments severely limit their opportunities. And those investors who do venture forth into the international arena may be discouraged when they discover that their broker or advisor knows less than they do about foreign securities. However, the international investment process, although fraught with pitfalls, is by no means a daunting task.

The Benefits of Global Investment

The smaller the local market, the greater the rewards of global investing. Although Canada is a major investment center, ranking next to the first-tier giants of the United States, Japan and the United Kingdom, it still, as is pointed out so frequently in the financial press, represents only about 2% to 3% of the world, according to how much money is invested here.

There are a number of compelling reasons for investing abroad. Global portfolio investment offers enhanced returns, reduced portfolio risk through the arithmetic of diversification, increased investment opportunities, foreign exchange risk exposure, not to mention the psychic enjoyment of wandering through the global marketplace. But be forewarned. Many foreign markets are volatile and erratic. As of late 1998, Far Eastern markets were still on the defensive in the wake of the 1997 Asian Flu. This underscores the value of concentrating on long-term diversification through a strong, strategic, asset allocation policy.

Enhanced Returns

Canada is one of the world's major industrialized countries and has well-developed capital markets, including the seventh-largest stock exchange in the world, the Toronto Stock Exchange. However, longer-term performance of Canada's equity markets can only be described as fair.

Canadian stocks are subject to a set of domestic economic, political and social factors that cannot be diversified away no matter how large the stock portfolio. These systematic effects, given the relatively tight policies followed by the Bank of Canada in recent years, have conspired to keep Canadian stock returns relatively low. For example, over the recent period from 1986 to 1998, world security markets recorded solid returns, most of them far outstripping Canada. In fact, from a select sample of major markets, Canada ranked near the bottom, ahead of only a handful of markets. While the New York Stock Exchange was registering a return of about 16.1% per year over this period, the Canadian market turned in a more modest 8.5% per annum performance. The leading index of world market performance, the Morgan Stanley Capital International's World Index of 25 major countries, recorded a 15.1% compounded return over that same 10-year period.

In a study published in the *Canadian Investment Review* in 1991, Harry Marmer, a respected researcher and commentator on the global investment scene with the William M. Mercer consulting firm, indicated that over the previous 12 years, using data from 1978 through 1989, non-U.S. foreign stocks as measured by the Morgan Stanley Capital International Europe Asia and Far East (MSCI–EAFE) Total Return Index in U.S. dollars were the top-performing asset class, followed by U.S. stocks, Canadian stocks, Canadian bonds, foreign bonds and Canadian T-bills. Of particular interest was his finding that the correlation between Canadian stocks and non-U.S. foreign stocks was .40. This means that, more often than not, Canadian and non-U.S. stocks are moving independently, reflecting the different forces that drive them.

The bottom line is that global investors realized considerably higher rates of returns than those who confined their investments to strictly Canadian financial products. In a recent study, Keith Ambachtscheer, a well-known chronicler of asset returns and institutional investment strategies and performance, recently pointed out that equity exposure to an investment portfolio increases the potential for greater return without adding to overall risk. Marmer's 1991 study showed that non-U.S. foreign stocks realized 5.4% per annum higher returns than Canadian stocks, with a 2.6% per annum lower volatility.

Diversification

Diversification, as we have pointed out repeatedly, is the cornerstone of successful long-term investing. In simple terms, diversification means that you are selecting securities that do not always move together. Securities with low correlations are valuable diversification products.

Many leading lights in investment finance, including Nobel prizewinners Harry Markowitz and James Tobin, have shown that efficient diversification reduces the risk of a portfolio, assuming that risk is measured by the variance about the returns on the component securities and the portfolio. They have demonstrated that the degree of risk reduction offered by each security added to the portfolio reflects the security's co-variance or co-movement with either the portfolio or an appropriate market index. Therefore, securities that have a low co-variance with the portfolio of securities or a market index are valuable in reducing risk. Thus on any given day, some of your investments may rise and some may fall, and so the chances of major losses are substantially reduced.

This principle of diversification applies quite powerfully to international portfolio diversification. Numerous studies indicate that the correlation between individual stock market indexes and the world stock market index is relatively low. A high degree of the variance in stock indexes is due to the unsystematic (or unique) risk of each country and can therefore be diversified away in an international portfolio of securities.

Bruno Solnik was the first to publish results on the value of global diversification. Using weekly price data for the period from 1966 to 1971, he constructed securities portfolios of various sizes from the U.S., the U.K., France, West Germany, Italy, Belgium, the Netherlands and Switzerland, as well as an international portfolio. He concluded that "The gains from international diversification are substantial. In terms of variability of return an international well-diversified portfolio would be one-tenth as risky as a typical security and half as risky as a well-diversified portfolio of U.S. stocks [with the same number of holdings]." An important caveat is that you have to be prepared to stick it out over the long term because the markets take turns. In general, given differing political and social policies, the longer-run correlations remain low.

Japan and the U.K. are relatively large markets and ideal candidates for internationally diversified portfolios for Canadian investors, based on their low degree of co-movement with Canadian markets.

Concentration on emerging markets is also useful. Since inflation/deflation/recession cycles are normally non-universal, the inclusion of countries with different economic systems and outlooks is valuable. Emerging countries are essentially uncorrelated among themselves and have low correlations with Canadian markets. Emerging countries with particularly low correlations include Argentina, Brazil, China, Greece and India.

The U.S. is the least valuable candidate for Canadians looking for global diversification.

Auger and Parisien, in a study published in the *Canadian Investment Review* in the spring of 1989, showed that although stocks on the Toronto Stock Exchange had relatively low correlation with global asset classes, their correlation with U.S. stocks was relatively high. Their findings were as shown in the table below.

Table 8.1: STOCK CORRELATION

	S&P 500 Unhedged	S&P 500 Hedged	EAFE Unhedged	EAFE Hedged
TSE 300	.70	.70	.40	.50
Canadian Bonds	.50	.50	.30	.30

Are the global effects diminishing?
A strategy of investing globally is to reduce risk. But equity markets are becoming increasingly globalized and homogenous. This has facilitated financial correlation between countries, reduced the effectiveness of domestic monetary policy and made financial markets more rotational. Increased interdependence between markets means that shocks (good and bad) are transmitted much more quickly in domino-type effects. Could common factors cause all markets to act the same way? And, if so, could the value of global diversification be diminishing?

Well, there is bad news and good news. The bad news is that markets tend to move together during economic or political shocks (such as the 1987 global market crash or the 1990 invasion of Kuwait). It seems that when the volatility of global markets rises, the correlation between markets increases. So very short-term diversification effects may be limited. However, the good news is that, in general, given differing political and social policies, the longer-run correlations remain low. Overall, the diversification benefits long extolled for global investing remain intact.

Expanded Investment Opportunities

Global investment also expands your investment opportunities. Many foreign securities have features not available with Canadian domestic investments. Some industries that are at the mature stage in Canada are still at the sunrise level in Europe or Latin America or the Far East. There are numerous securities issued abroad that have different risk/return characteristics from domestic securities or that offer special features not available with Canadian investments. Examples of these include:

- the food and wine industries in Europe
- the efficient textiles and electronics industries of Hong Kong
- the mining industry of Australia
- the robotics, computer and other high-tech industries of Japan
- specialized automobile manufacturing in South Korea

Many investment instruments are readily available—if you know about them! For example, there are a large number of closed-end investment funds traded on the New York and American Stock Exchanges that offer opportunities to trade in single countries such as Chile or Taiwan or in regions such as Europe or Latin America.

Global Leverage

Don Reed, the president of Templeton International in Canada, recently talked about oil consumption in China averaging one barrel per person per year. Doubling that number would increase world oil production by over one billion barrels! Just imagine the leverage associated with this.

Currency Exposure

Global investment means foreign currency exposure. Over the past two decades, the Canadian dollar has fluctuated widely against all major currencies. Investors who hold all of their wealth in Canadian dollars have discovered that as the dollar weakens, the cost of a trip to New York or goods imported from Tokyo has correspondingly risen. If you want to guard against adverse currency fluctuations, you have to hold some of your wealth in something other than Canadian dollars.

For many Canadians, the most important is U.S. dollar investments. If you are looking to hold U.S. dollars, the best bets on the fixed-income side are U.S. dollar-denominated Eurobonds, closed-end bond funds and preferred shares.

U.S. dollar Eurobonds pay periodic interest (normally semi-annually) and mature at their par or face value. Unlike conventional U.S. bonds, they are sold outside the United States. Eurobonds normally offer higher yields than term deposits, bank deposits and similar instruments. The yields on foreign bonds and Eurobonds are sometimes higher than on domestic bond issues as well, although interest-rate parity means that the foreign currency is expected to depreciate at a rate that offsets the differential.

If you are interested in holding other currency-denominated assets such as Swiss francs, you can buy Eurobonds denominated in most major currencies. Eurobonds are relatively easy to buy and provide the highest yields among foreign currency fixed-income investments. You can buy and sell Eurobonds through your brokerage firm. You should also shop around at a few bond dealers at brokerage firms for the best quotes, as they can vary widely.

An important feature about Eurobonds is that the interest income is not subject to withholding tax at source. You simply include the annual receipts as interest income in the equivalent Canadian dollars on your Canadian tax return. If you sell the bonds before maturity, you will trigger a capital gain (or loss), which is subject to the 75% capital gain inclusion rule.

Eurobonds issued by a Canadian government, a corporation and certain international organizations such as the World Bank are RRSP-eligible.

Closed-end bond funds are investment fund units that, like their counterpart, the mutual fund, invest their portfolio assets in a portfolio of bonds and other fixed-income securities according to an investment plan or strategy. A healthy selection of bond funds holding U.S. dollar-denominated bonds are traded on the New York Stock Exchange.

U.S. pay-preferred shares are denominated in U.S. dollars and pay their dividends in U.S. dollars. Because the shares are issued by a Canadian-controlled private corporation, they are eligible for the dividend tax credit. If you sell them for a gain (loss) this will create a capital gain (or loss), which is subject to the 75% capital gain inclusion rule. Foreign exchange gains are taxable, since your purchase price and proceeds of disposition are ultimately translated into Canadian dollars. The first $200 of income attributed to foreign exchange fluctuations are exempt in a taxation year. The shares are eligible for inclusion in an RRSP if they are issued by a Canadian-controlled private corporation, and they are not subject to the foreign property rule.

Does currency matter?
You bet it does!
A reporter who should know better indicated that the TSE, in recording an 11.86% gain in 1995 (not including dividends), "didn't cut it." He pointed out that many markets outperformed Canada, citing, for example, Caracas—up 51%—and Mexico City—up 17%. He went on to say that currency fluctuations would have affected returns for Canadians, but in most cases currency levels don't change the fact that we could have done better elsewhere. Well, here's the truth. Currency fluctuations matter—a lot. When measured in Canadian dollars, Mexico actually recorded a loss of 23.7% in 1995, and Caracas had a loss of 26.2%.

To hedge or not to hedge?

International diversification is important in enhancing the return and reducing the risk associated with your portfolio. One consideration is whether to keep the foreign currency component of your investments exposed or hedged. It depends on what you want. For some, it's the foreign currency exposure; for others, the diversification. It all comes down to demand for foreign currencies—yours. If you travel, buy imported goods or possibly intend to buy a foreign vacation property, then in addition to global diversification, you will also want the currency exposure. If, for example, you have current and future plans to travel in the United States and Europe, then you will want to hold some of your investments denominated in U.S. dollars and, say, Swiss *francs*.

On the other hand, if your spending outlook is domestic, but your investment attitude is global, you will want to manage all or some of the foreign currency exposure, particularly if the foreign currency component is large. Look at the impact on a Canadian investor of a foreign currency change on a U.S.$70,000 (Cdn$100,000) portfolio. If the Canadian dollar were to rise from Cdn$1.40 (i.e., U.S.$.7142) to Cdn$1.30 (U.S.$.7692), the value of U.S.$70,000 in Canadian dollars would drop from $98,000 to $91,000, assuming no other change in the underlying portfolio. This amount is worth hedging. But at what cost?

There are a number of products that can be used in portfolio risk management or, as it is commonly called, "hedging." These products, commonly classified as derivatives, include call options, futures, forwards and swaps.

It's Educational

Let's not ignore a final and important consideration in global investing. There can be great enjoyment associated with learning about things related to global investment. Following political developments in Mexico, reading about the changes in the governments of Asian countries, and assessing the implications of the Indian market reform movement can be highly entertaining and informative in their own right. You can get hooked very quickly on the international economic and market scene.

Global Investment Is Not an Easy Task, However . . .

The idea of international investing in emerging countries is compelling. But it isn't easy to do, at least directly. It's hard enough keeping up with the stocks traded in Canada, let alone the tens of thousands of companies traded on developed and emerging markets.

There are some obvious and severe impediments to foreign investing. These "frictions" include lack of quality information, different accounting and reporting standards, variable transaction costs, withholding and other taxes, liquidity problems, foreign currency risks, political or sovereignty risk, delivery and settlement delays and foreign investor restrictions. The existence of these barriers makes the task of selecting individual foreign securities a difficult one.

There are a number of roadblocks. To invest intelligently in foreign companies, you need access to good-quality information. But current and valuable information on companies in foreign countries can be both expensive and difficult to obtain. Differing accounting and reporting standards make comparisons difficult. On many markets there are no restrictions on insider trading and little protection against manipulative practices. And some markets are completely blocked to small investors.

These and other barriers make it difficult for retail investors to invest directly in foreign securities. For all but the truly dedicated investor, the most efficient route to portfolio diversification is through global, international and specialty country mutual funds.

One of the problems is that large institutional investors are often excluded from trading because they are required to have a custodial bank handle their investing (separation of client funds from management). Many banks refuse to handle investment overseas markets. There are other reasons, including prudent lending standards and industry practices that exclude many institutions. Without institutional participation, the price discovery process is impeded and prices may not reflect value. Coupled with the often rudimentary market structure, weak regulatory environment and lack of local participants, foreign markets are often highly inefficient.

Market inefficiencies include:

1. **Lack of Investor Protection**
   Traders and shareholders are not afforded the same degree of protection as found on developed markets. In many countries there is little protection against trading abuses and market manipulation. Shareholders are often not protected against insider trading and other shady dealings by management. Many countries do not have coattail provisions for minority shareholders on takeovers. In some places there is little or no opportunity for redress if you are treated improperly by a broker.
2. **Lack of Availability and Quality of Information**
   There is very little technical and marketing information on companies published in many emerging countries. The variance in quality, quantity and release of information results in disparate search costs for the investor and the analyst.
3. **Different Accounting and Reporting Standards**
   Accounting standards vary across countries, making the task of comparative analysis on a consistent basis a difficult one. The substantial differences in reporting criteria and timing of releases by corporations add to the complexity of comparative investment analysis. Sometimes notices of rights offerings, special dividends, etc., may not reach the Canadian investor. The most severe challenges are in the area of accounting standards and policies. The quality and quantity of available information vary widely, and differing accounting and reporting standards make comparisons difficult.
4. **Transaction Costs**
   Transaction costs of trading include *visible* costs such as brokerage and institutional fees, stock turnover taxes, exchange taxes, transmittal fees and other miscellaneous agency costs, and *implicit* costs such as bid/ask spreads and impact costs. These levies vary widely by type of investment and country. The issue is complicated by the fact that in some countries, commissions are negotiated and determined by the investor's own bargaining prowess. Most countries levy withholding taxes on interest and dividend income earned by nonresidents on domestic investments. The existence of reciprocal tax conventions between Canada and many countries mitigates the impact, as investors will be eligible for a foreign tax credit for the taxes paid to foreign governments. The withholding tax on dividends in most countries is 15%. To recover it, you have to file a foreign tax return or ask for a special tax credit when filing your tax return.

   Bid/ask spreads are, in general, inversely related to size of market and can be as much as 50% to 100% in some very thin markets! Supply and demand imbalances occur with some regularity on smaller foreign markets.

5. **Liquidity Problems**
   Liquidity, or the ability of an investor to dispose of his or her holdings quickly at market at a reasonable cost, can be a particular problem of investing in emerging countries. Secondary markets in some countries are not particularly active and there can be particular problems involved in selling securities. Wide spreads between the bid/ask prices may exist, sometimes so wide as to render trading impractical. The lack of market makers is often an underlying cause of poor liquidity.
6. **Settlement and Delivery Problems**
   Settlement periods and processes vary widely. Trades made in Canada are normally settled in three business days from the date of the transaction, with theoretical delivery at that time. Trades made in the emerging countries can take weeks or even months to settle. In many countries, a custodian bank or other financial institution is required.
7. **Political and Sovereignty Risk**
   Political risk is the danger of a government taking action that will reduce the value of an investor's assets, either held in that country or invested in that country's resources. The danger extends not only to the existing government, but also to a new one as a result of an election or revolution. The degree of political risk differs greatly across countries, but must be viewed as a major concern when building an international portfolio. With careful portfolio selection, political risk can be sharply reduced through diversification.
8. **Foreign Investor Restrictions**
   Some countries impose restrictions on foreign investing in their domestic markets. These restrictions include position limits that constrain the dollar, unit or percentage amount that a foreigner can invest in a particular security, commodity or investment class; special taxes or levies placed on foreign investors; trading and delivery constraints and outright prohibitions on trading by nonresidents. (India and Pakistan are examples of restricted markets.)

All of these barriers make it difficult for retail investors to invest directly in foreign market securities. The best approach, then, is to invest in investment funds.

Global Investing—Your Various Avenues

Global investing need not be substantially more difficult to the typical investor than is any other means of reaching for profits in securities. There are numerous vehicles available to carry you on to the global stage, many of which require the investment of only a few hundred dollars.

Investors who wish to diversify their portfolios internationally can either trade directly in interlisted securities on domestic markets, securities on foreign markets, or indirectly through American Depositary Receipts and global, international or specific country mutual funds. These methods are briefly described.

Direct Dealings Overseas

There are a number of sources and methods by which you can buy or sell foreign securities directly. These include:

1. **Canadian Brokerage Firms**
   Full-service Canadian brokerage firms will place buy-and-sell orders for clients for foreign securities, typically for a relatively large commission that will reflect the commission schedule on the foreign stock market, plus an increment for the Canadian broker. Investors should expect some time delays, as the broker may have to wire abroad for a quote on the security. One- and two-day lags between the time the order is placed and a confirmation from the broker are not at all uncommon for foreign security transactions. Canadian brokerage firms can buy or sell American Depositary Receipts (ADRs) for clients, as well. ADR holders receive their dividends denominated in U.S. dollars minus the depositary's fee (typically U.S. $.01 per share).

   ADRs are often cheaper to buy than the stocks themselves. For example, the transaction costs associated with the direct purchase of Australian stocks can at times be more expensive than those associated with an Australian company ADR purchased on the New York Stock Exchange. Morgan Guaranty Trust, a major U.S. source for ADRs, also issues International Depositary Receipts, which are similar to ADRs but designed for foreign investors who wish to hold U.S. securities. IDRs, for example, are available in Europe for U.S. equities.
2. **Foreign Banks and Brokerage Firms**
   The more adventurous global investor can open accounts with overseas banks or brokerage firms. Some brokerage firms will allow nonresident clients to trade securities listed on Japanese, Hong Kong, Australian and certain European bourses. Investors who wish to trade directly should contact local branches of foreign banks or trade embassies for the names of reputable banks or brokerage firms. In general, however, this is a cumbersome method of trading in foreign securities, as it will require the search for a reputable firm, making appropriate custody arrangements and foreign currency conversions, and other such annoyances.
3. **Domestic Branches of Foreign Banks**
   The domestic branches of foreign banks will normally handle foreign security transactions for clients, including initial foreign currency conversions, delivery and custody arrangements and currency conversion at time of sale. Typically, however, the banks set minimum transaction amounts at $100,000.

Picking Global and International Funds

Investors who wish to diversify their portfolios internationally can either trade directly in securities on foreign markets, interlisted securities on domestic markets, or indirectly through American Depositary Receipts and indexed products. However, given the barriers and restrictions, we suggest that all but the truly dedicated should capture their global portfolio portion through global and international mutual funds. There are now literally hundreds of such funds domiciled in Canada with varying objectives, track records, load options and portfolios.

Types of Investment Funds

In the global framework, there are a number of global fixed-income funds, including money market and bond funds, with a wide array of objectives and target portfolios.

In the equity category, there are four types of funds. *Global funds* invest their assets in equities of various countries, including their own, while *international funds* invest only in securities of different countries (sometimes limited to a few specific regions) not including their own. *Regional funds* invest in stocks from specific regions of the world. *Specific country funds* invest in securities of a single foreign country.

Single country closed-ended specialized mutual funds have proliferated in recent years. Their introduction and continued popularity mirror three distinct developments in world capital markets: namely, the increased interest of investors in global or foreign equity markets; the strong performance of some of the smaller markets (such as Chile, Korea, Taiwan) relative to the giants (U.S., Japan, U.K.), even after foreign currency adjustments to the investor's currency denomination; and the trend to innovative products and packaging, primarily by major North American and European brokerage firms.

The majority of the closed-ended funds trade at discounts to their net asset values (NAVs), a phenomenon common to closed-ended investment companies.

Some will sell at premiums to their NAV, particularly during strong equity markets. The specialty country funds that invest in smaller countries, and in particular those countries whose markets are blocked or restricted to nonresidents, are valuable investments in that they offer both investment opportunities for globally minded investors and "market completion" devices for fund managers. Closed-ended funds, on the other hand, have a fixed capital structure in that shares are initially sold to the public and the proceeds invested in a portfolio of securities according to a set of objectives. Like the open-ended fund, the management of the closed-ended fund is paid a fee to manage the portfolio, which may be subject to constant revisions. However, unlike the open-ended fund, new shares in the closed-ended fund are only issued in specific cases (such as a new investment opportunity or a takeover), and then only with the approval of the appropriate regulatory bodies. The shares of closed-ended funds are traded on stock exchanges in the same manner as shares of public companies.

Investment Strategies

Canadian-Based Foreign Mutual Funds

There are hundreds of global and international mutual funds domiciled in Canada. Funds can be described by investment objectives categories (safety, income, growth, aggressive growth); geographical orientation (single country, region, global and international); investment philosophy (active vs. passive); investment style (value vs. growth); bottom-up versus top-down; portfolio structure (small vs. medium vs. large capitalization). There are some 105 or so Canadian funds specializing in the United States alone with management-expense ratios ranging from 1.5% to about 3.0%, with the typical fund being about 2.5%.

The 12 Rules of Global Investing

1. Diversify your global portfolio.
2. Invest in countries whose markets have relatively low correlations with those of Canada.
3. Be aware that the U.S. is the least valuable diversification candidate for a Canadian investor.
4. Direct global investing is hazardous to your health. Buy global or international investment funds.
5. Timing probably won't work. Don't be constantly switching from country to country in the search for undervalued securities. The danger is you will miss out on the correlation effects and the advantages of diversification.
6. Select investment funds whose managers build portfolios that really match the stated objectives.
7. Select investment funds whose performance generally remains within a specific risk category.
8. Hold some securities denominated in foreign currency.
9. Always negotiate loads for load funds. Back-end loads are often not the best choice.
10. Review the "hedge or not to hedge" decision.
11. Select management styles (active vs. passive; value vs. growth) that match your tastes.
12. Don't base your selection on the absence of load fees or the size of the management-expense ratio. These are important but by no means critical factors.

1. Investment Objectives Categories

There are foreign funds available in Canada in virtually all of the investment objectives categories. These include money market funds, bond and income funds, balanced funds and equity funds.

Type	Number
Money Market	19
Income	72
Balanced	51
Equity	579
Total	721

2. Geographical Orientation

Funds specialize in countries, regions, the world excluding Canada (international funds) and the world including Canada (international funds).

The general categories are the U.S., international and global, Asia/Pacific Rim, Europe, Latin America and emerging markets.

Geographic Focus	Number
U.S. and Global Money Market	19
U.S. and Global Income	72
U.S. and Global Balanced	51
U.S. Equity	169
North American Equity	25
Global and International	206
Asia/Pacific Rim Equity	79
European Equity	48
Latin American Equity	15
Emerging Markets Equity	37
Total	721

3. Investment Philosophy—Active versus Passive

Active management represents the search for undervalued securities and individual selection. Passive investing focuses on index investing.

In the middle and late 1950s, securities research was dominated by the search for undervalued securities, the predominant investment philosophy of the day. Retail investors—reflecting rising household incomes and general postwar prosperity—started to "play the market" and accounted for nearly 50% of trading volume on the secondary equity market. At the same time, institutional investors expanded their horizons from simple buy-and-hold strategies to a more active trading approach using more sophisticated analytic tools. In 1952, Harry Markowitz, a financial economist, published a paper on diversification techniques and portfolio selection. His theory was called "Portfolio Theory" and forever changed the security analysis process.

The modern era of security markets was launched. The 1960s ushered in the era of growth stocks, the so-called go-go period. The focus among portfolio managers shifted to investment performance from their previous emphasis on safety and security. "Beating the market" became the catchword of the day.

In the 1970s a theory called the "Efficient Markets Hypothesis (or Theory)" came into vogue. This theory held that securities are fairly priced, reflecting at least past and publicly available information. Acceptance of this theory led to a shift to portfolio management and market aggregates from fundamental analysis of individual securities. The theory compared stock prices changes to a giant roulette wheel. Like the wheel, which has no memory, the size and direction of the next market move—so the theory goes—is independent of the previous move. The theory is that stock prices follow a process called a "Random Walk." Do you remember your examination of small particles under a microscope in your chemistry classes? How the particles careered in a seemingly random manner with no predictable direction? That's called the "Law of Brownian Motion" and Efficient Markets Theory says that's how stocks move, as well.

In the early 1980s, as an outgrowth of Portfolio Theory, Efficient Markets and the desire to build diversified portfolios, index funds debuted, with the objective of tracking or replicating the performance of the whole stock market as measured by an index such as the Standard & Poor's 500 Index or the Toronto Stock Exchange 300 Composite Index. Thus we can see the genesis of index investing.

A further impetus came from the deregulation of commissions on May 1, 1975, in the U.S. (1983 in Canada), which shifted the emphasis of portfolio management from return performance to cost minimization, particularly for fund managers pursuing a passive or index-replicating strategy. Suddenly the sloughed-off transaction cost issue became paramount and there was a marked shift from the return component to the cost component of investment management. If a fund manager believes that expected return is primarily passive and uncontrollable, he might shift emphasis to the cost structure of the fund.

What can explain the proclivity of so many investors to choose active over passive management investment—the odds are often against them? Peter Bernstein calls it lottery risk—no one likes to pass up the chance of finding the big return! Could it be . . . better unsafe than sorry? The road to regret is paved with unsure intentions.

There are only a few passive global funds available in Canada.

4. Investment Style—Value vs. Growth

Value and growth have represented the two basic approaches to investing. Two standard demarcations in distinguishing the two are the price/book value and the price/earnings ratios. Benjamin Graham defined value as the lowest third of the DJIA, while managers focusing on growth will pick high P/E stocks. Another approach using two major benchmark indexes of S&P—Barra and Russell 1000 Index—is to designate stocks below the midpoint as value stocks, and those above it as growth stocks. Managers employing a value approach will focus on low price/book and low P/E stocks, often small-cap ones, as well.

Although studies indicate that the value approach seems to outperform growth, value investing may mean unusually high volatility and poorly diversified portfolios. One reason the value approach has yielded a higher return in the long run reflects the principle of "mean reversion," a finding that important factors tend to revert or regress to an average or mean value. For example, low P/E multiple stocks will tend to rise toward the average of all stocks over time, while high P/E multiple stocks will regress to the average. This provides at least one explanation as to why low P/E stocks will outperform high P/E stocks.

5. Investment Style—Bottom-Up versus Top-Down

Portfolio orientation includes bottom up and top down. The bottom-up approach assumes that the entire universe of eligible securities should be monitored and the fund manager will select the securities that he believes offers the best value or prospects. The top-down approach assumes that the best approach is to search for undervalued countries and then select the securities with the best value from that group.

The secret is to diversify by country or region rather than picking individual country stocks. Furthermore, it has been shown that about 85% or so of total global returns are generated by country indexes—currency and individual stock movements have only a small effect on performance. Studies demonstrate that the country factor is the most important in emerging country investments and that it dominates world, currency and industry systematic influences.

Investing in Emerging Markets

Emerging markets offer potentially high returns and diversification benefits over established markets. But they are subject to occasional bubbles: liquidity risk, restricted access and settlement problems. By their very nature they are highly volatile. Accordingly, I believe strongly that they have a place in a diversified portfolio—in a long-term strategic asset allocation strategy. However, I do mean long term; in the short run you will see all kinds of fluctuations.

Why do emerging countries generally perform so well—albeit erratically?

As growth in North America, Europe and Japan decelerates, capital from savings is flowing into emerging countries. Call it the "emerging country" syndrome.

One approach to finding ideal countries is to monitor emerging countries looking for new developments such as political progress, economic liberalization or capital markets developments. For example, political progress in South Africa through the prohibition of apartheid was the appropriate signal for evaluating South Africa investment. Other recent investment signals include the deregulation of markets in Korea, economic and political liberalization in Argentina and Chile and capital market development progress in China and India. Many emerging countries are limiting population growth; are spending a much higher percentage on education; and are seeing the consumer sector rising sharply (the purchase of television sets in many emerging countries is taking place at an extraordinary rate). Over the past 25 years the average rate of economic growth was 5.1% for emerging nations versus 3.5% for developed nations.

What are the emerging countries?

There are some 50 to 60 emerging countries. The largest are Brazil, China and India. The most rapidly developing are Argentina, Chile, South Korea and Taiwan. Others include Ghana, Greece, Jordan, Israel, Pakistan, Turkey and Zimbabwe.

Another way of looking at it is that emerging countries in general have the demographic and economic characteristics of North America in the growth era of the 1950s and 1960s. In fact, the United States was the leading emerging country/market at the turn of the century, as was Japan in the post-war period. Now the pattern should repeat with Argentina, Brazil, China, India, etc. In the 1970s and early 1980s, when we talked about emerging or developing countries it was normally in the context of poor central planning and concomitant debt escalation, inefficient banking systems and debt and currency crises. Now many emerging countries are concentrating on building and improving their equity markets and encouraging the financing of growth with equity issues. Argentina, Brazil, Chile, China, Mexico, and Taiwan are examples of countries focusing on economic growth through equity issues.

The capital markets of an emerging country in general are underdeveloped and inefficient. There are numerous barriers to trading. These barriers have paradoxical implications. On the one hand, they obviously result in increased search, analytic and monitoring "costs" for the investor. On the other hand, they also suggest the existence of market inefficiencies that can provide abnormal returns to the astute trader. The more barriers and problems, the more inefficient the market and the greater the opportunities for the skilled stock (or fund) picker!

Summary

The globalization process of the past two decades has meant a vast array of new and valuable opportunities for investors. The sheer size of the market and the limitless investment opportunities offered have meant that knowledgeable investors can come increasingly closer to the goal of efficient diversification.

Measured against its potential, globalization is still in its infancy. Over the next two decades, we can expect such developments as direct trading access to virtually all of the world's markets from a home video screen (or whatever replaces a screen), and through the next generation of Internet-type networks and a vastly expanded investment opportunity set in the form of new and innovative financial products tied to employment, home ownership and daily life. Investor psychology will continue as a hot research topic, and much more will be learned about why we make the decisions we do. Financial planning will be transformed from a set of poorly connected notions into a science of how to tailor portfolios to closely align them with investment needs.

Global investing should mean higher portfolio returns, enhanced investment opportunities, more efficient diversification, foreign currency exposure or risk reduction and even enriched enjoyment in the investment process. The only limit to product design and new markets is our own imagination. Staying focused and informed as the events unfold will be essential to your investment success.

PART III

Special Reports

CHAPTER NINE

RRSPs and RRIFs

Paradigm Shifts

We recently received a call from a woman in her early eighties. She had built up decent savings over the years and her mutual fund portfolio was providing a steady cash flow to supplement her pension income. She was living quite comfortably. However, her broker had shocked her by suggesting she might outlive her capital when she reaches her middle nineties. (This age is well within her life expectancy.) Although we estimated that the probability of her outliving her income was remote, we suggested some adjustments to her portfolio that would alleviate her concerns.

Her capital sufficiency fears are not unusual today. People are living longer and spending more. They have reduced confidence in government pensions. A recent study (self-interest aside) by a large mutual fund company showed that 76% of respondents do not expect government pensions to provide enough to live on.

The importance of "self-insuring" is evident. Accordingly, it's never too early to start a retirement financial planning program. The best place to start is with a Registered Retirement Savings Plan.

What is an RRSP?

A Registered Retirement Savings Plan (RRSP) allows you to build a fund for your retirement with income and growth which will be tax sheltered until you withdraw the funds from the plan.

A Registered Retirement Savings Plan is defined in the Income Tax Act as "a contract between an individual [called the annuitant] and a person licensed to carry on in Canada an annuity business, or between an individual and a Canadian trust company, bank, or other person who is a member of the Canadian Payments Association, or other approved corporation."

The key to this is what you are allowed to do under the RRSP contract. The rules are quite generous.

The Nine Key RRSP Rules

1. You can open an RRSP at a bank, trust company, credit union, *caisse populaire*, insurance company, brokerage firm or mutual fund company. RRSPs administered by the latter two—brokerage firms and mutual fund companies—are actually issued by a trust company, acting as a trustee.
2. You can deduct your annual RRSP contributions from your taxable income, up to a prescribed limit (which is $13,500 per annum at present).
3. You can invest in a wide range of securities and financial products. Those financial products eligible for inclusion in an RRSP are called "qualified investments."
4. You may open and maintain as many different RRSPs as you wish, although your aggregate annual contributions each year are subject to the prescribed limit as indicated in Rule #2.
5. You can allocate up to 20% of each RRSP to foreign properties.
6. All income (interest, dividends, rents) and profits (realized and unrealized capital appreciation, business gains) recorded within your RRSP are *not* taxable as long as the amounts remain within the plan.
7. You can cash in your RRSP at any time (which is taxable at your personal rate and the proceeds are subject to a withholding tax), but in any case an RRSP must be terminated (matured) by the year in which you turn 69 years old.
8. RRSP funds at the maturity of the plan may be transferred into a number of different retirement options including life and fixed-term annuities, and Registered Retirement Income Funds (RRIFs).
9. RRSPs issued by life insurance companies or that are "locked in" (normally as a consequence of you terminating your employment and taking your vested pension benefits in the form of an RRSP) are protected against creditors during your lifetime. Non-insurance-company RRSPs are not.

Types of RRSPs

There are various types of RRSPs. Many investors, depending on their needs and tastes, maintain two or more of these types.

1. **Guaranteed Principal RRSP**
   In a guaranteed principal RRSP, you invest in savings deposits, term deposits or Guaranteed Investment Certificates (GICs) issued by an underlying financial institution. Typically, the investments in these RRSP accounts will be guaranteed with respect to principal and interest payments by the issuing institution and will furthermore be insured by the Canada Deposit Insurance Corporation (CDIC) up to a limit of $60,000 per account.

2. **Mutual Fund RRSP**
Mutual fund RRSPs are managed and administered by the selling institution. These plans are available in every mutual fund category (money market, bond, mortgage, income, balanced, equity, specialty and asset allocation). These RRSPs do not have financial institution guarantees and are not subject to CDIC coverage. Normally, no administration fees are paid on these plans.

3. **Self-Directed RRSPs**
Self-directed RRSPs are plans in which you determine the asset allocation and security selection of your portfolio. Self-directed plans provide the greatest flexibility since you control the investments.
The plan must be administered by a trustee. An annual administration fee is paid. If you pay the fee outside your RRSP, the fee is deductible from taxable income.

4. **Group RRSPs**
Group RRSPs are plans sponsored by an employer, usually structured as an alternative or supplement to a pension plan and customized to company requirements.

Eligible RRSP Investments

Only certain investments, called *qualified investments*, are eligible for RRSPs. These include:

- savings and term deposits
- Guaranteed Investment Certificates
- Banker's Acceptances
- limited partnership units traded on exchanges
- domestic bonds and debentures
- shares of companies listed on prescribed stock exchanges in Canada
- some annuities
- some life insurance policies
- a share or similar interest in a credit union
- some over-the-counter stocks
- all classes of Canadian mutual funds
- Canadian basket investments such as Toronto Index Participation Units (TIPs)
- Canadian convertible bonds
- warrants
- real estate investment trusts (REITs)
- personal mortgage loans (from the RRSP to the annuitant, as long as the mortgage is insured and there are reasonable market terms as well as market rates of interest)
- debt obligations and shares of companies listed on prescribed foreign stock exchanges

- investment-grade quality (as established by a qualified rating agency at the time of purchase) foreign government bonds
- royalty trusts.

Items that are *not* qualified investments for RRSPs include futures contracts, collectibles, gold and silver bullion, real estate, shares of most private corporations and foreign basket product trusts (such as the Standard & Poor's Depositary Receipts or SPDRs).

Foreign Property Restrictions

You are entitled to invest up to a maximum of 20% of the book value of each RRSP in foreign properties. RRSPs that hold foreign property investments in excess of that limit at the end of any month incur a 1% per month penalty tax. Canadian mutual funds are permitted to invest up to 20% of their portfolio assets in foreign securities without being designated as a foreign property. So if you invest in Canadian mutual funds that hold 20% of their portfolio in foreign securities, you can end up with 36% in foreign securities as follows:

Portfolio Allocation	Percent of Portfolio	Percent Foreign	Percent Total
Foreign Property Funds	20%	100%	20%
Canadian Funds	80%	20%	16%
Total	100%		36%

Spousal Contributions

You are allowed to contribute to an RRSP in the name of your spouse as long as she has not reached the age of 70. The amount contributed to your spousal plan reduces the amount you can contribute to your plan since the annual contribution limit reflects the aggregate of the two. Spousal plans represent one of the few opportunities for family income splitting (albeit on a deferred basis) in Canada.

Annual Contribution Limits

If you are not a member of a pension plan or a deferred profit-sharing plan (DPSP), the maximum amount that you can contribute to an RRSP each year is calculated as 18% on your previous year's earned income. For example, your annual contribution limit for 1998 is based on your 1997 earned income.

If you are a member of a pension plan or a deferred profit-sharing plan, your contribution limit is 18% of your earned income from last year up to a maximum of $13,500 less your PA or pension adjustment (the total of your pension and DPSP credits for the year). You usually will receive a notice from Revenue Canada early in the year specifying what your PA and your maximum RRSP contributions are.

Earned income includes most forms of remuneration, including employment income, income from owning a business, net rental income, taxable alimony and maintenance payments *minus* all allowable traveling expenses, annual union and professional dues, allowable legal expenses, net business and net rental losses, and deductible alimony and maintenance payments made.

You have the first 60 days of the calendar year to make RRSP contributions that would be deductible (if you wish) in the previous year. For example, contributions made in the first 60 days of 1998 may count toward either the 1997 or 1998 taxation year, or may be allocated between the two.

Although contributions are normally made in cash, you can contribute investments (as long as they are qualified) to your self-directed plan. The amount is assumed to be allocated to your RRSP at the fair market value at the time of transfer and is part of the contribution for the year. The transfer may trigger capital gains or losses in your personal account.

The maximum amount you may contribute to your own RRSP, a spousal RRSP or any combination of the two is subject to the following dollar limits:

Years	Amount
1997-2003	$13,500
2004	$14,500
2005	$15,500
2006	Indexed

Recent studies indicate that only a small percentage of Canadians contribute the maximum allowable amount.

The Benefits of RRSPs

The overall benefits of RRSPs are these:

1. You can deduct your RRSP contributions from your taxable income.

2. The funds accumulate on a tax-sheltered basis within your RRSP (i.e., all earnings and growth are not taxed as long as they remain within the plan). This effect can be dramatic. Let's compare what happens when you invest in a tax-sheltered plan versus investing in a non-tax-sheltered portfolio.

   Suppose you invest $10,000 in a 25-year government bond that pays 8% ($800) per year in interest and hold it for 25 years until it matures. Let's assume that you pay tax at a rate of 45% (a typical average combined federal and provincial marginal tax rate for Canadian investors). After paying tax every year, you will end up with $29,344 as shown in the table below. If, however, the $10,000 is invested in an RRSP, the interest income will be tax sheltered and the portfolio will grow to $68,485 over that same period!

Table 9.1: VALUE OF $10,000 INVESTED TO EARN 8% PER ANNUM FOR 25 YEARS; NON-TAX SHELTERED; TAX RATE 45%

Year	Cumulative Value
1	$10,440
2	10,899
3	11,379
4	11,880
5	12,402
6	12,948
7	13,518
8	14,113
9	14,733
10	15,382
11	16,059
12	16,765
13	17,503
14	18,273
15	19,077
16	19,916
17	20,793
18	21,707
19	22,663
20	23,660
21	24,701
22	25,788
23	26,922
24	28,107
25	29,344

Table 9.2: VALUE OF $10,000 INVESTED TO EARN 8% PER ANNUM FOR 25 YEARS; TAX SHELTERED

Year	Cumulative Value
1	$10,800
2	11,664
3	12,597
4	13,605
5	14,693
6	15,869
7	17,138
8	18,509
9	19,990
10	21,589
11	23,316
12	25,182
13	27,196
14	29,372
15	31,722
16	34,259
17	37,000
18	39,960
19	43,197
20	46,610
21	50,338
22	54,365
23	58,715
24	63,412
25	68,485

The results are even more dramatic if you compare tax-sheltered and non-tax-sheltered investments, assuming a periodic purchase plan. For example, if you invest $10,000 in an RRSP and $5,000 per annum at the end of every year thereafter, you will end up with $434,105 after 25 years at 8%! If, instead, you invested personally and paid interest on the income, the amount will only have grown to $249,156.

Table 9.3: VALUE OF $10,000 PLUS $5,000 PER ANNUM INVESTED TO EARN 8% PER ANNUM FOR 25 YEARS; NON-TAX SHELTERED; TAX RATE 45%

Year	Cumulative Value
1	$15,440
2	21,119
3	27,049
4	33,239
5	39,701
6	46,448
7	53,492
8	60,845
9	68,523
10	76,538
11	84,905
12	93,641
13	102,761
14	112,283
15	122,223
16	132,601
17	143,436
18	154,747
19	166,556
20	178,884
21	191,755
22	205,192
23	219,221
24	233,866
25	249,156

Table 9.4: VALUE OF $10,000 PLUS $5,000 PER ANNUM INVESTED TO EARN 8% PER ANNUM FOR 25 YEARS; TAX SHELTERED

Year	Cumulative Value
1	$15,800
2	22,064
3	28,829
4	36,135
5	44,026
6	52,548
7	61,752
8	71,692
9	82,428
10	94,022
11	106,544
12	120,067
13	134,673
14	150,447
15	167,482
16	185,881
17	205,751
18	227,211
19	250,388
20	275,419
21	305,453
22	331,649
23	363,181
24	397,236
25	434,014

Now, as illustrated in Figure 9.1, the longer the period you invest, the more dramatic the difference between the tax-sheltered and non-tax-sheltered return.

Figure 9.1: INVESTMENT GROWTH—TAX SHELTERED VS. NON-TAX SHELTERED

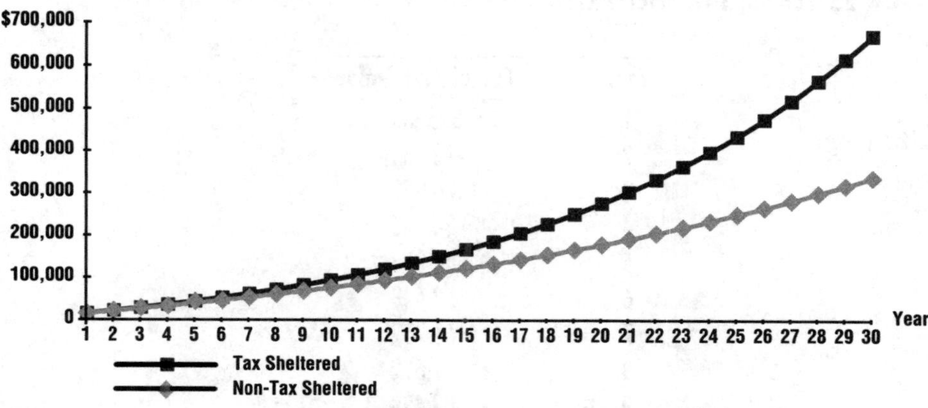

Year	Tax Sheltered Cumulative Value	Non-Tax Sheltered Cumulative Value
1	$15,800	$15,440
2	22,064	21,119
3	28,829	27,049
4	36,135	33,239
5	44,026	39,701
6	52,548	46,448
7	61,752	53,492
8	71,692	60,845
9	82,428	68,523
10	94,022	76,538
11	106,544	84,905
12	120,067	93,641
13	134,673	102,761
14	150,447	112,283
15	167,482	122,223
16	185,881	132,601
17	205,751	143,436
18	227,211	154,747
19	250,388	166,556
20	275,419	178,884
21	302,453	191,755
22	331,649	205,192
23	363,181	219,221
24	397,236	233,866
25	434,014	249,156
26	473,736	265,119
27	516,634	281,785
28	562,965	299,183
29	613,002	317,347
30	667,043	336,310

3. At retirement, or when you mature your RRSP (sometimes called "collapse" or "re-register"), taxes on the accumulated funds within the plan are normally taxed at a lower rate.

4. A wide range of maturity options are available, including lump-sum receipts, life annuities, fixed-term annuities, Registered Retirement Income Funds and Life Income Funds.

5. You can use spousal RRSPs to effectively split income. You and your spouse will receive benefits from the RRSP with the proceeds to the lower income-earning partner taxed at the lower rate.

RRSP Withdrawals

If you wish, you may take out all or part of the funds accumulated within your RRSP. You can withdraw funds from your RRSP at any time; however, when the funds are withdrawn, they must be included as income for that taxation year. The institution holding your RRSP is required to deduct tax (called withholding tax) at the time the funds are withdrawn.

However, in any circumstances, you must mature or collapse your RRSP by December 31 of the year in which you turn 69. For example, if you were born on January 17, 1945, you must collapse your plan by December 31, 2014. The following are your withdrawal options.

Lump-Sum Withdrawal

This normally is not the most appropriate approach to take since the full amount of your RRSP proceeds will be added to your taxable income. This could mean, for example, a tax bite in the order of about $230,000 on a $500,000 RRSP.

Life Annuity

Instead of taking a lump-sum payment, you can buy a life annuity contract with all or some of your RRSP proceeds.

The life annuity is the product you cannot possibly outlive. Life annuities pay you periodic (normally monthly) payments for as long as you live.

Life annuity contracts are for the life of one or more persons (for example a buyer and his spouse) and are sold only by life insurance companies. If you are single, a widow or widower, and your children are already well provided for and you have no plans to leave an estate, then the single life annuity is an important addition to your retirement portfolio. The single life annuity will go a long way to ensuring that your money doesn't disappear before you do! *But remember that there will be no residual from this annuity after your death.* In other words, when you die, the life annuity ends.

Life annuity contracts are covered by the industry-wide CompCorp protection plan that provides for $2,000 a month in coverage for non-commutable contracts (i.e., contracts that cannot be converted or cashed).

If you purchased the annuity with the proceeds from an RRSP or other tax-deferred plan, you will be taxed on the entire annuity receipts (which includes both principal and interest) you receive each year.

A typical annuity contract calls for monthly payments, although quarterly and semi-annual payments are available. The various types of life annuities include the following:

- A *single straight life annuity* provides you with payments for as long as you live.
- A *life with guaranteed term* contract provides you or your beneficiary with payments for your life or for a fixed number of years (the guaranteed term), whichever is greater. If you buy a life annuity with a 15-year guaranteed term with your spouse as the beneficiary and you die six years later, your spouse receives the equivalent of nine additional years of payments. Typical guarantee periods are five, 10 and 15 years.
- *Straight life with joint and survivor* are life annuities in which you and a specified person (typically your spouse) receive the annuity payments until the second person's death. These contracts can also have a guaranteed term.

There are a number of factors that will determine the monthly payment stream for a given annuity purchase. These factors are:

1. *Your age*. The older you are, the lower the price (premium) that you will pay to buy a specific monthly stream of annuity payments.

2. *Your sex*. Women have higher life expectancies than men and receive lower annuity returns than males of comparable age. For example, females in their sixties can expect about $20 to $30 a month less than comparable age males for typical 10-year guaranteed term annuities.

3. *Type of annuity*. There are numerous types of annuities and this leads to different pricing. You'll earn the highest return with single life annuities while your receipts will be reduced if you take a guarantee option. Your return will be lower still with a joint and survivor option with a guaranteed term.

4. *The issuer*. Quotes vary considerably by issuer, reflecting supply and demand for funds particular to the issuer at that time.

5. *The current level of interest rates*. The higher the level of prevailing interest rates, the larger the payments on your annuity at the time of purchase.

Fixed-Term Annuities

Another choice is to buy a fixed-term annuity with your RRSP proceeds.

Fixed-term annuities are sold by life insurance companies, banks, trust companies and credit unions.

The fixed-term annuity cannot have a maturity date past the year in which you turn ninety. In the event of the death of the annuitant prior to the end of the term, payments will be either continued to the surviving spouse or commuted as a lump-sum payment to the estate.

Term annuity contracts include:

- A *single fixed-term contract* that has characteristics closer to fixed-term investments such as mortgages. Term annuities simply offer payments for a specified number of years.
- *Joint fixed-term contracts* provide you and another person or persons with payments until the last survivor reaches the term or specified age. If both die before the term is up, the payments are commuted (their present value calculated) and the lump sum is paid to your stated beneficiaries.

The Bottom Line on Annuities: Six Annuity Planning Ideas

Selecting the right annuity for you (and your family) is not an easy task because the choice is not strictly a financial one. Emotions and special needs will play a large part in your ultimate decision. Remember an annuity eats up capital and there is nothing left when the final annuity payment is made. Here are some tactical suggestions.

Idea #1

If you are single, a widow or widower, your children are already well provided for and you have no plans to leave an estate, then the single life annuity is the best bet for you. This will give you the highest possible monthly income. But remember that there will be no residual from this annuity after your death.

Idea #2

If you are married and have no estate concerns, then the right vehicle will be the life annuity with joint and survivor clause. Your monthly receipts will be relatively high and payments will continue to be made to your spouse if you die first.

Idea #3

If you are married and have children that you wish to provide for, your choice is not as straightforward. The type of annuity that you will select will reflect an important trade-off between your needs for the future and those of your selected beneficiaries. If you wish to provide some residual to your children if you were to die early, consider the life annuity with a guaranteed term, or a term annuity.

Idea #4
Because you are locked in for life it is dangerous to commit substantial funds to one annuity with a fixed embedded interest rate. If the rate of inflation increases and interest rates rise, you will watch the purchasing power of your annuity receipts steadily erode. So allocate your annuity purchases over a reasonable time frame such as two to three years.

Consider buying indexed or variable-rate annuities. If interest rates are moving with changes in the inflation rate, then you will be reducing the variance about your purchasing power of your receipts. The drawback is that you won't know precisely what your monthly receipts will be. We recommend a mixed approach. Put most of your annuity money (75%-80%) in appropriate fixed-rate annuity contracts and the remainder (20%-25%) in the variable-rate ones. You will know within about 90% what your monthly (or periodic) receipts will be. A small component of your receipt will fluctuate, reflecting changes in interest rates.

Idea #5
It pays to shop for an annuity. If you compare annuity quotes among a number of institutions you will discover that there will be a wide variance. You will find that the high to low spread can be anywhere from $15 to $30 a month for, say, a joint and last survivor annuity with a 15-year guarantee, for a male and female age 65 at present, and higher when rates are higher.

There are two approaches to shopping for an annuity. If you know what you want and you like to do your own research, call a number of institutions and get firm quotes. Make sure that you are getting quotes on an annuity with identical terms with no hidden costs or fees. Alternatively, go to an annuity broker or service and let them do the work for you. They deal with annuities and issuers constantly and will know how to get you the best quotes. There are a number of annuity brokers and advisory services listed in your yellow pages under "Annuities."

Idea #6
In general, persons who buy life annuities are "healthier" than the average for the population, or in the lingo of the actuaries, these people have higher mortality rates (they live longer). But there is an important implication of this so-called "reverse adverse selection." If you are unhealthy, you should shop around to find a company willing to quote you higher rates than the norm because your life expectancy is lower than average.

Registered Retirement Income Funds (RRIFs)

The most popular choice of the RRSP maturity options is the RRIF. RRIFs are offered by most institutions eligible to issue RRSPs. They allow the annuitant some control over the investment made within the plan. Just like a self-directed RRSP, you decide what investments you want to have in your plan. Investments that qualify are similar to those of an RRSP.

To set up an RRIF, you transfer your RRSP proceeds to a RRIF and withdraw funds each year (subject to a required minimum) for your personal use. Only the actual RRIF payments you receive each year are taxable.

RRIFs are the most flexible of the options since you control the cash flow of the pool, although you are required to maintain a minimum level of payment each year according to a minimum withdrawal formula.

As with RRSPs there are different RRIF structures. These include the following:

1. **Guaranteed Principal RRIFs**
   RRIFs based on term deposits, Canada Savings Bonds and GICs are the lowest cost but returns may be very modest in low interest rate environments. The investments in these RRIF accounts will be guaranteed with respect to principal and interest payments by the issuing institution and will furthermore be insured by the Canada Deposit Insurance Corporation (up to a limit of $60,000 per account).

2. **Pooled or Mutual Fund RRIFs**
   These are mutual fund RRIFs that are managed and administered by the selling institution. These plans do not have financial institution guarantees and are not subject to CDIC coverage.

3. **Self-Directed RRIFs**
   Your RRIF can be self-directed in which you make all the decisions and you control the investments.

4. **Professionally Managed RRIFs**
   Professionally managed RRIFs are those for which advisors at your financial institution or brokerage firm make the decisions.

Life Income Fund (LIF)

This alternative is applicable only to locked-in RRSPs and is essentially an RRIF that has been modified to comply with locking-in requirements of pension legislation. An LIF must be converted, no later than the end of the year when the LIF holder turns 80, into a life annuity.

Some RRIF Planning Ideas

1. You can base your minimum annual withdrawals on the age of your spouse rather than your own age.
2. Make sure you structure your RRIF so that it provides the cash flow you require.
3. Shop carefully before committing. There is substantial competition for your retirement dollars and rates and costs vary considerably.

Your *FundLine Advisor* Team's Tips for Effective RRSP and RRIF Investing

Strategy #1: Hold High-Yield Investments in RRSPs
High-yield investments with little growth prospects are ideal for RRSPs, where the income is sheltered and the 25% capital gain exclusion is unimportant. High coupon, high-yield bonds are ideal.

Strategy #2: Always Have Some Equities—Even in an RRIF
There is a strong argument for including equities in your retirement portfolio. Equities are important in leveraging the return on your overall portfolio and in dealing with inflation concerns. An appropriate allocation is anywhere from 15% to 30%, with the latter targeted to a healthy single female at age 65 (she has a long life expectancy), and the former to a healthy male at age 65.

Strategy #3: Maintain Inflation Rate Protection
The last thing you want to see at retirement are rising interest rates. In addition to sending security prices lower, they may also represent rising consumer prices. The twin specters of rising interest rates and rising inflation would be the primary reason for the erosion of your purchasing power. Analysts have been consistently wrong for years in predicting inflation movements. You can immunize or guard your portfolio against rising interest and inflation rates with floating rate securities—securities whose yield fluctuates with changing rates.

For example, Treasury bills have low yields at present, but given the short average term-to-maturity, they will generally provide returns that closely approximate current short-term interest rates.

Strategy #4: Avoid High-Dividend-Paying Investments
The dividend tax credit allowed for investing in dividend income from Canadian preferred and common shares only applies to personal holdings. Within an RRSP or RRIF the advantage is lost. The 25% exclusion rule for capital gains is also lost within an RRSP.

Strategy #5: Include a Money Market Fund
Although money market funds are suitable anywhere, they are powerful savings vehicles within RRSPs. With the interest income reinvested in new shares, you avoid the inconvenience of small dollar reinvestments.

Many Canadian money market funds are designed to maintain a fixed net asset value per share at $10. The yield fluctuates each day to reflect the average yield on the fund's portfolio and changing short-term interest rates.

Strategy #6: Go for Strip Bonds in Your RRSP

One exception to the high-yield case is strip bonds, which pay no interest and mature at par value. These bonds are packaged by brokerage firms, banks and trust companies, who take full conventional bonds and split them into the coupon bonds or strips or the residual maturity value or stripped bond. They sell at discounts to reflect the no-interest feature and provide a specific and definite yield-to-maturity since there is no reinvestment risk.

If you hold stripped bonds outside a tax shelter, you will be required to report the capital appreciation (deemed to be implicit interest income) as taxable income every year. Therefore, strips should be confined to RRSPs and other tax shelters.

Strategy #7: Foreign Property Limits

Don't allow your foreign property percent to rise much above 18%. Even though the limit is 20%, you want to leave room for additions to the cost base. Such additions may result from rights offerings or from special distributions.

CHAPTER TEN

The Rebirth of Segregated Funds

Until recently, there wasn't a whole lot of talk around investment funds sponsored by insurance companies, or as they are called in the industry, segregated funds (mostly because the performance of segregated funds tended to be, well, average). That being said, the fact that segregated funds tend to, on average, be average, has a lot to do with how they are managed and the costs associated with insurance-type guarantees.

Segregated funds are really insurance contracts that provide death benefits and principal guarantees. Because of those guarantees, which we will speak to in a moment, the funds were conservatively managed, to the point where managers were mandated first to avoid loss of principal and second to produce positive returns.

Good segregated fund managers tended to weather downturns in the market reasonably well but often fell short during periods when the financial markets were rising. Because of that, you rarely read much about segregated funds in the financial press, since they were at the bottom of the performance parade during any particular measuring period.

That's changed in recent years, and especially in the last year, when a whole new series of segregated funds have come to the market. Some, such as the new Guaranteed Investment Funds (GIFs) from Manulife Financial, are really just well-known mutual funds from a number of different families with an insurance wrapper.

Since the introduction of GIFs, some mutual fund companies have enlisted the assistance of an insurance company and have begun to market their own in-house family of segregated funds. Performance, then, is not the issue it once was. The issue today is the guarantee on your investment principal. A guarantee with a cost!

We think it is a mistake to dismiss segregated funds out of hand, simply because of performance issues. We also think it is a mistake to buy segregated funds because of the guarantee. At the end of the day, segregated funds may deserve a place in your portfolio for reasons you never thought of. As a result, investors should take some time to understand what these products offer and at what cost.

From an estate planning perspective, segregated funds offer a couple of interesting twists. As long as you name a beneficiary, there will be no probate fees on your death. The value of the fund, or the minimum guarantee, will go directly to the beneficiary on your death.

The minimum guarantee relates to your principal investment. Most segregated funds will guarantee that your estate receives the greater of 100% of the entire amount, although some segregated funds only guarantee 75% of your principal investment (see accompanying tables for more complete descriptions of the various segregated fund families), deposited by the investor, or the current market value of the segregated fund.

For example, suppose you invested $10,000 in the XYZ segregated Canadian equity fund, and two years later, upon your death, the value of the fund had declined to $9,000. Assuming your fund family has a 100% deposit guarantee, your beneficiary would receive $10,000, because the initial deposit was greater than the current market value of the fund.

Many segregated funds also offer deposit guarantees for specific time periods, 10 years being the most common time frame. In effect, the insurance company guarantees, at a minimum, the greater of 100% of the deposit or the market value of the funds, for money that has remained on deposit for 10 years.

The deposit guarantee clearly has value in terms of estate planning, but let's be realistic. In terms of investment planning, how much value is there with a guarantee that basically says: "If you hold our fund for at least 10 years, we guarantee, that at a minimum, your principal investment is returned to you."

For the record, there are over five hundred mutual funds in Canada with a 10-year track record. Only 14 funds out of that total had negative returns over the past 10 years (see table 10.1). Of the 14 funds that failed to earn a positive return, five were either resource or precious metals funds, and three were based in either the Pacific Rim or Japan. If fact, if you were able to steer clear of the Cambridge family of funds, you probably could have escaped any of the problems that go with earning money long term in the equity markets. Given that background, chalk up one positive characteristic for segregated funds (the guaranteed death benefit) and one not-so-positive characteristic (the 10-year deposit guarantee).

Table 10.1: FUNDS WITH LOSING 10-YEAR RECORDS

Fund Name	MER	10-Year Return	% Return 1998*	% Return 1997	% Return 1996	Total Assets ($millions)
Cambridge Pacific	3.7%	-15.2%	-50.8%	-44.7%	3.9%	0.40
Cambridge Resource	3.4%	-6.2%	-59.1%	-42.3%	36.3%	4.30
Cambridge Special Equity	3.5%	-5.7%	-33.4%	-43.9%	5.0%	2.60
Cambridge Growth	3.5%	-3.3%	-44.9%	-31.5%	6.7%	7.60
Royal Japanese Stock	2.8%	-2.8%	-1.2%	-7.8%	-15.8%	33.80
Goldfund Limited	2.2%	-2.6%	-20.2%	-36.8%	14.0%	2.30
Cambridge Global	3.5%	-2.4%	39.4%	-52.0%	-7.6%	0.60
First Heritage	4.0%	-2.3%	-39.7%	-19.4%	19.2%	2.40
Cambridge Balanced	3.5%	-2.3%	-46.1%	-27.5%	12.8%	3.60
All-Canadian Resources Corp	2.0%	-2.1%	-22.6%	-18.3%	-1.0%	2.50
Industrial Equity	2.4%	-2.0%	-32.3%	-26.6%	19.7%	44.60
Goldtrust	1.8%	-2.0%	-17.8%	-33.8%	21.6%	5.60
Investors Japanese Growth	2.5%	-1.7%	-3.0%	-20.6%	-15.6%	404.10
Dynamic Precious Metals	2.5%	-1.2%	-28.6%	-45.9%	24.8%	146.00

* to August 31, 1998

Keeping with the same theme, one of the more talked-about benefits of segregated funds is the fact they are, to a point, creditor proof. This, of course, relates to the fact that segregated funds are insurance contracts and they belong to the beneficiary on the death of the fund holder.

That's an interesting advantage for some investors, particularly business owners or professionals such as doctors or accountants, who may from time to time be subjected to bankruptcy or litigation. In these cases, the courts have generally ruled—with some caveats—that liens cannot be attached against insurance contracts like segregated funds. It is best to ask your financial advisor about any caveats.

Now, of course, these benefits have a cost that is factored into the management-expense ratio (MER). The average MER on segregated funds is generally higher than it would be for traditional mutual funds in the same category. The extra costs cover the segregated fund guarantees.

What we have, then, are a group of funds that in some cases are more conservatively managed—to protect the financial integrity of the insurance company that stands behind the guarantees—and that have, on average, higher management-expense ratios (which explains why the performance numbers may be less than stellar over long periods). The question is whether the guarantees are worth the cost.

Manulife Guaranteed Investment Funds

Having laid the foundation as to why segregated funds may belong in your portfolio, we want to introduce you to the family of segregated funds that changed the segregated fund industry: Manulife Guaranteed Investment Funds.

For the record, we should note that Richard Croft has a long-term consulting relationship with Manulife Financial. In this chapter, we are not making recommendations for any specific fund product. As well, Richard Croft was not involved in the development of Manulife Guaranteed Investment Funds. What is clear, and why we need to examine this particular family of funds, is that Manulife GIF revolutionized the segregated fund industry.

Guaranteed Investment Funds (GIFs) are a new investment fund family. Well almost! With GIFs, Manulife has offered some of the better-known mutual fund companies—like Trimark, Talvest Fidelity, GT Global, AGF, Elliott & Page—as another way to distribute their product.

The investor buys either a front-end or back-end loaded GIF from Manulife. The money flows through Manulife directly to the mutual fund company and is invested directly in the fund of choice. For example, if you bought the Trimark Select Growth Fund GIF, you end up with units in the Trimark Select Growth Fund; not a fund that mirrors the Trimark Select Growth Fund, nor a similar fund managed by the same portfolio manager, but the actual fund. As such, your performance will effectively mirror the performance of the Trimark Select Growth Fund (that is, after accounting for the charges levied by Manulife to affect the guarantees and any costs associated with the timing of the flow of funds through Manulife to the underlying fund).

Keeping with our Trimark Select Growth Fund GIF, Manulife guarantees a minimum of 100% of the principal investment to your beneficiary upon your death, or at maturity, which for the GIF is ten years. In other words, 10 years hence, you are guaranteed that at least your principal will be returned.

One of the unique twists pioneered by the Manulife GIF is the so-called reset feature. You can choose a new "principal" amount to be guaranteed—with some age restrictions that are detailed in the prospectus—at any point during the initial 10-year guarantee. For example, if your Trimark Select Growth Fund GIF had a couple of good years and your initial $10,000 investment was now worth, say, $12,000, you can reset your principal guarantee to the new $12,000 amount, guaranteed 10 years from the date of the reset. The reset guarantee also applies to the GIF death benefit payable to your beneficiary.

This is one of the features that has become quite popular among investors. Indeed, it is one of the strong selling points from other mutual fund companies that offer their own specific segregated funds.

Another advantage GIF brought to the table was a switching privilege. If you chose to sell your Trimark Select Fund GIF and buy, say, the Fidelity True North GIF, there is no cost to switch. The reason is that you are effectively remaining within the GIF family of funds. Again, this was revolutionary and quite unique to Manulife. Mutual fund companies offer switching privileges but only within their funds, not with other fund families.

The ability to switch at no cost is an advantage. The cost to switch from a fund in the Trimark family to another in the Fidelity family can be quite high, especially if there are deferred sales charges that have to be paid out upon redemption. Inside the GIF family this can all take place with no redemption charges, and you can still retain the 10-year minimum guarantee.

Of course, the creditor proofing—again within reasonable limits—remains intact, and when you die, the money will be passed on to the beneficiary outside the estate and free of any probate fees.

The additional costs are reflected in the higher management-expense ratios of the GIF products. Look for the average MER within the GIF family to be between 0.75% to 1% higher than if you bought the fund directly. With the Trimark Select Growth Fund example, the MER inside the GIF family is 3.25% compared with an MER of 2.25% for direct purchase.

Over time, those additional costs will impact your performance. Remember 1% per year in additional costs, when compounded over long periods, can be a substantial hit against performance. On the other hand, the GIF product is managed aggressively just like the underlying fund, which removes any conservative biases that impact the performance of the more traditional segregated fund.

Look for more funds to be included under the GIF umbrella in the coming years. Already there are more than 50 funds available from a wide range of fund families. (See Manulife table at the end of this chapter). Do they fit in your portfolio? Let's see!

In summary, Guaranteed Investment Funds:

- offer 100% deposit guarantee—Manulife guarantees the greater of 100% of the deposit or the market value on funds remaining on deposit for 10 years;
- allow the investor to lock in investment growth twice a year by renewing the 10-year deposit guarantee;
- guarantee a minimum death benefit based on the greater of the market value of the fund or the principal amount deposited;
- provide estate planning advantages—no probate fees when a beneficiary is named;
- provide protection from creditors—within limits—in the event of personal bankruptcy;
- provide the ability to move between fund families without a deferred sales charge or a switching fee.

The question is simple: Are the guarantees, the creditor proofing, the estate planning issues and the switching privileges worth the cost of admission (i.e., the higher MER)?

A Segregated Fund Portfolio
Aggressively Buying the Guarantee

Now that there are a number of mutual fund companies distributing segregated funds by selling the maturity guarantees, we need to examine the guarantee more closely. Remember, mutual fund companies market segregated funds; they don't insure them. In the end, the guarantee is issued by an insurance company, and the value of the guarantee is directly related to the financial strength of the insurance company.

The problem, as we see it, is not in the concept of the guarantee, but rather in how investors use the guarantee in their portfolio. The fact a guarantee exists differentiates a segregated fund portfolio from a traditional mutual fund portfolio (if not in terms of the real-world usefulness of the maturity guarantee, at least in terms of the role the guarantee plays on your psyche).

When we build traditional mutual fund portfolios we are interested in building diversification. The idea is to try and smooth out the fluctuations in your portfolio, in an attempt to keep you invested over the long haul. A comfortable investor is a long-term investor.

With a segregated fund, you can argue that the guarantee serves the same purpose as portfolio diversification for the traditional mutual fund portfolio. This suggests that a portfolio of segregated funds can carry higher risks than a portfolio of traditional funds, because there is, presumably, no downside in the long term.

What we find most interesting is how so many investors are drawn to balanced segregated funds. Mutual fund analyst Duff Young wrote in a *Globe and Mail* column (*Report on Business* August 1, 1998), "balanced funds in Canada generally have only about half their money invested in stocks, with the rest in government guaranteed bonds and Treasury bills."

The point is that the balanced fund already has a built-in guarantee. The bond component will eventually return the investor's principal. So, in reality, only half a balanced fund is actually at risk, at least in terms of how the segregated fund investor defines risk. Only the equity component of the balanced fund has any real chance of losing money.

Young walks his readers through some of the math in that *Globe and Mail* column. Normally, a balanced fund has half the portfolio in equities and the other half in fixed-income investments like government bonds. "The value of the bonds are guaranteed to grow in value over a 10-year period (the length of time to the maturity guarantee on most segregated funds), in the ballpark of 70% on a cumulative basis. That means that the bond holdings alone will be worth about 85% of the original capital anyway." If the stocks representing the other half of the portfolio were to lose all their value, the most the investor would lose is 15%. And for that you pay up to 1% annually to effect the maturity guarantee.

Again, as we have said, any real advantage is the guaranteed death benefit. But there, too, why pay for a guarantee on such a conservative type of fund? Why not use the guarantee to buy more aggressive funds? Ratchet up the potential performance, because you are paying for the downside guarantee.

Now to be fair, insurance companies charge more to guarantee a more aggressive fund. But we think, over the long term, the more aggressive fund will overcome the extra costs with better performance numbers.

Our Segregated Fund Listings

Segregated funds have been around for three decades, and in some cases even longer. Yet it took the mutual fund industry to redefine the way segregated funds are structured and ultimately sold. The marketing of the maturity guarantee as a no-risk way to invest in stocks is a case in point. It's always been there, but insurance companies used to sell the product from an insurance angle, and thus the focus was on the death benefit and the avoidance of probate.

The idea that one can reset their guarantee is another marketing ploy used with great success in the selling of the newer segregated funds. The reset option is now available on almost all segregated funds, with only minor differences such as the maximum number of resets an investor can initiate during any year.

With the recent volatility in the stock markets, mutual fund companies have been quick to capitalize on the maturity guarantee. Advertisements talk about safety nets, the idea of risk-free investing and having the best of both worlds. And the message has been paying off as segregated fund sales have been one of the fastest-growing segments of the mutual fund industry.

With that in mind, we've included a list of segregated funds to help you do some comparison shopping. This is by no means an exhaustive list. In fact, one of the more interesting programs we have come across is the Talvest model, which at the time of writing was not approved for sale.

Talvest intends to offer a series of five segregated fund portfolios, three non-RRSP portfolios and two RRSP model portfolios. Each portfolio combines the best Talvest funds in a specific class plus the best Maritime Life segregated funds. Maritime Life Assurance Company then provides the insurance guarantee for the product.

Table 10.2: SEGREGATED FUND PORTFOLIOS

Conservative Nonregistered Portfolio

Min.	Benchmark	Max.	Benchmark Composition
0%	0% Cash	30%	Maritime Money Fund
10%	25% Cdn. Bonds	40%	25% Maritime Bond Fund
0%	10% Int'l Bonds	30%	10% Talvest Foreign Pay Bond Fund
10%	25% Cdn. Equity	40%	10% Maritime Diversified Equity Fund 15% Talvest Cdn. Equity Growth Fund
5%	15% U.S. Equity	30%	15% Maritime Mer. Growth & Income Fund
10%	25% Int'l Equity	40%	25% Talvest Global Equity Fund

Conservative Registered Portfolio

Min.	Benchmark	Max.	Benchmark Composition
0%	0% Cash	30%	Maritime Money Fund
20%	35% Cdn. Bonds	50%	35% Maritime Bond Fund
0%	0% Int'l Bonds	15%	Talvest Foreign Pay Bond Fund
30%	45% Cdn. Equity	60%	10% Maritime Diversified Equity Fund 35% Talvest Cdn. Equity Growth Fund

0%	10% U.S. Equity	20%	10% Maritime Mer. Growth & Income Fund
0%	10% Int'l Equity	20%	10% Talvest Global Equity Fund

Growth and Income Portfolio

Min.	Benchmark	Max.	Benchmark Composition
0%	0% Cash	30%	Maritime Money Fund
20%	35% Cdn. Bonds	50%	10% Talvest High-Yield Bond Fund
			25% Maritime Bond Fund
0%	0% Int'l Bonds	15%	Talvest Foreign Pay Bond Fund
30%	45% Cdn. Equity	60%	15% Maritime Diversified Equity Fund
			30% Talvest Cdn. Equity Growth Fund
0%	10% U.S. Equity	20%	10% Maritime Mer. Growth & Income Fund
0%	10% Int'l Equity	20%	10% Talvest Global Equity Fund

Aggressive Nonregistered Portfolio

Min.	Benchmark	Max.	Benchmark Composition
0%	0% Cash	30%	Maritime Money Fund
0%	10% Cdn. Bonds	30%	10% Maritime Bond Fund
0%	10% Int'l Bonds	30%	10% Talvest Foreign Pay Bond Fund
20%	40% Cdn. Equity	60%	15% Maritime Diversified Equity Fund
			15% Talvest Cdn. Equity Growth Fund
			10% Talvest Canadian Small Cap Fund
5%	15% U.S. Equity	30%	10% Maritime Mer. Growth & Income Fund
			5% Maritime Discovery Fund
10%	25% Int'l Equity	40%	20% Talvest Global Equity Fund
			5% Talvest Global Small Cap Fund

Aggressive Registered Portfolio

Min.	Benchmark	Max.	Benchmark Composition
0%	0% Cash	30%	Maritime Money Fund
10%	20% Cdn. Bonds	40%	10% MLAC Bond Fund
			10% Talvest High-Yield Bond Fund
0%	0% Int'l Bonds	15%	Talvest Foreign Pay Bond Fund
45%	60% Cdn. Equity	70%	20% Maritime Diversified Equity Fund
			30% Talvest Cdn. Equity Growth Fund
			10% Talvest Small Cap Fund
0%	10% U.S. Equity	20%	5% Maritime Discovery Fund
			5% MLAC Amer. Growth & Income Fund
0%	10% Int'l Equity	20%	5% Talvest Global Equity Fund
			5% Talvest Global Small Cap Fund

Instead of the guarantee applying to a specific fund, the maturity and death benefit guarantee is applied to the overall portfolio. And rather than allowing the investor to initiate a reset option, the maturity guarantee for each portfolio is automatically reset when the value is at its highest level (specific age restrictions apply). In effect, Talvest and Maritime Life guarantee you the highest market value of each portfolio based on the previous 10 years' performance. For example, suppose you buy the Growth and Income portfolio on January 1, 1999. You want to sell the portfolio on January 1, 2014. You would receive the portfolio's ending value on the highest level between January 1999 and January 2004. That 5-year period represents the resell guarantee, being the highest level in the period preceding the previous 10 years. We're not sure we can explain this guarantee that effectively, so we're clearly of the opinion it has little value to the investor. Of course, each time you initiate, the maturity guarantee is reset; so, too, is the 10-year time period on which the maturity guarantee is based.

In the following pages, we have included a listing of segregated funds. We have included some of the larger families and some of the up and comers. We were not always able to get information on the old-line insurance company funds.

In each case we name the fund, its categor, and management-expense ratio. When looking at many of the funds, you will notice that they are guaranteed versions of funds that already exist. Compare the MER on the segregated fund with the MER on the traditional fund, and you will get an idea as to how much you are paying for the guarantees. We like the transparency.

We then look at the guarantees for both the death benefit and the maturity benefit. The question here is what percentage of the initial investment is guaranteed? Usually the maturity guarantee is for 100% of the initial investment less any withdrawals plus any contributions. The death benefit is almost always 100% guaranteed, except from some companies with certain age restrictions .

Finally, we look at the term to maturity and investment options. How many times in a year can you reset your principal guarantee? How many times can you switch from one fund to another in the same family, and is there a cost to switch? Usually there is no cost to switch, although most companies allow your advisor to charge a switch fee at their discretion. For example, Templeton and Trimark do not charge to switch, but they allow the advisor to charge up to 2% per annum for each switch. Be aware of that when dealing with your advisor.

Table 10.2: SEGREGATED FUND LISTINGS

BPI SEGREGATED FUNDS

Fund Name	Fund Type	MER	Death Benefit Guarantee	Maturity Benefit Guarantee	Term to Maturity	Reset Options	Cost to Switch	Number of Allowable Switches
BPI Canadian Equity Value Segregated	Cdn Equity	2.25%	100%	100%	10 years	4	Nil	Unlimited
BPI Canadian Mid-Cap Segregated	Cdn Equity	2.40%	100%	100%	10 years	4	Nil	Unlimited
BPI American Equity Value Segregated	US Equity	2.40%	100%	100%	10 years	4	Nil	Unlimited
BPI Global Equity Value Segregated	Intl Global	2.35%	100%	100%	10 years	4	Nil	Unlimited
BPI International Equity Value Segregated	Intl Equity	2.35%	100%	100%	10 years	4	Nil	Unlimited
BPI Global Balanced RSP Segregated	Global Bal	2.10%	100%	100%	10 years	4	Nil	Unlimited
BPI Income and Growth Segregated	Cdn Bal	2.15%	100%	100%	10 years	4	Nil	Unlimited
BPI High Income Segregated	Domestic F.I.	1.45%	100%	100%	10 years	4	Nil	Unlimited
BPI Dividend Income Segregated	Dividend	1.15%	100%	100%	10 years	4	Nil	Unlimited
BPI Canadian Bond Segregated	Domestic F.I.	1.40%	100%	100%	10 years	4	Nil	Unlimited
BPI T-Bill Segregated	Money Market	0.70%	100%	100%	10 years	4	Nil	Unlimited

Insurance Underwriter: TransAmerica Life Insurance

C.I. SEGREGATED FUNDS

Fund Name	Fund Type	MER	Death Benefit Guarantee	Maturity Benefit Guarantee	Term to Maturity	Reset Options	Cost to Switch	Number of Allowable Switches
C.I. American Segregated	US Equity	3.16%	100%	100%	10 years	6	Nil	Unlimited
C.I. Global Segregated	Intl Global	3.30%	100%	100%	10 years	6	Nil	Unlimited
C.I. Hansberger Value Segregated	Intl Global	3.30%	100%	100%	10 years	6	Nil	Unlimited
C.I. Harbour Growth & Income Segregated	Cdn Balanced	2.97%	100%	100%	10 years	6	Nil	Unlimited
C.I. Harbour Segregated	Cdn Equity	3.05%	100%	100%	10 years	6	Nil	Unlimited
C.I. Money Market Segregated	Money Market	1.50%	100%	100%	10 years	6	Nil	Unlimited

Insurance Underwriter: Toronto Mutual Insurance Company

LONDON LIFE SEGREGATED FUNDS

Fund Name	Fund Type	MER	Death Benefit Guarantee	Maturity Benefit Guarantee	Term to Maturity	Reset Options	Cost to Switch	Number of Allowable Switches
London Life American Equity (Maxxum)	USEq	2.60%	75%	75%	10 years	None	Nil	Unlimited
London Life American Growth (AGF)	USEq	2.70%	75%	75%	10 years	None	Nil	Unlimited
London Life Asian Growth (AGF)	FgnEq	2.60%	75%	75%	10 years	None	Nil	Unlimited
London Life Balanced (BG)	Balan	2.45%	75%	75%	10 years	None	Nil	Unlimited
London Life Balanced (Sceptre)	Balan	2.45%	75%	75%	10 years	None	Nil	Unlimited
London Life Balanced Growth (LLIM)	Balan	2.35%	75%	75%	10 years	None	Nil	Unlimited
London Life Bond	FixInc	1.75%	75%	75%	10 years	None	Nil	Unlimited
London Life Canadian Balanced (Maxxum)	Balan	2.40%	75%	75%	10 years	None	Nil	Unlimited
London Life Canadian Equity	CdnEq	2.35%	75%	75%	10 years	None	Nil	Unlimited
London Life Canadian Equity (GWLIM)	CdnEq	2.35%	75%	75%	10 years	None	Nil	Unlimited
London Life Canadian Equity Growth (Maxxum)	CdnEq	2.40%	75%	75%	10 years	None	Nil	Unlimited
London Life Canadian Opportunity (MF)	FgnEq	2.50%	75%	75%	10 years	None	Nil	Unlimited
London Life Diversified	Balan	2.35%	75%	75%	10 years	None	Nil	Unlimited
London Life Dividend (LLIM)	CdnEq	2.25%	75%	75%	10 years	None	Nil	Unlimited
London Life Dividend (Maxxum)	CdnEq	2.30%	75%	75%	10 years	None	Nil	Unlimited
London Life Equity (MF)	CdnEq	2.50%	75%	75%	10 years	None	Nil	Unlimited
London Life Equity (Sceptre)	CdnEq	2.45%	75%	75%	10 years	None	Nil	Unlimited
London Life Equity/Bond (GWLIM)	Balan	2.35%	75%	75%	10 years	None	Nil	Unlimited
London Life European Equity (Sceptre)	FgnEq	2.65%	75%	75%	10 years	None	Nil	Unlimited
London Life Global Equity (LLIM)	FgnEq	2.50%	75%	75%	10 years	None	Nil	Unlimited
London Life Global Equity (Maxxum)	FgnEq	2.60%	75%	75%	10 years	None	Nil	Unlimited
London Life Government Bond (GWLIM)	FixInc	1.75%	75%	75%	10 years	None	Nil	Unlimited
London Life Growth & Income (AGF)	Balan	2.50%	75%	75%	10 years	None	Nil	Unlimited
London Life Growth & Income (MF)	Balan	2.30%	75%	75%	10 years	None	Nil	Unlimited
London Life Growth Equity (AGF)	CdnEq	2.90%	75%	75%	10 years	None	Nil	Unlimited
London Life Growth Equity (LLIM)	FgnEq	2.35%	75%	75%	10 years	None	Nil	Unlimited
London Life Income (LLIM)	Balan	1.90%	75%	75%	10 years	None	Nil	Unlimited
London Life Income (MF)	Balan	2.05%	75%	75%	10 years	None	Nil	Unlimited
London Life Income (Maxxum)	FixInc	1.80%	75%	75%	10 years	None	Nil	Unlimited
London Life International Equity	FgnEq	2.50%	75%	75%	10 years	None	Nil	Unlimited
London Life Larger Company (MF)	CdnEq	2.50%	75%	75%	10 years	None	Nil	Unlimited
London Life Mid Cap Canada (GWLIM)	CdnEq	2.35%	75%	75%	10 years	None	Nil	Unlimited
London Life Money Market	FixInc	1.20%	75%	75%	10 years	None	Nil	Unlimited
London Life Mortgage	FixInc	2.00%	75%	75%	10 years	None	Nil	Unlimited
London Life Natural Resource (Maxxum)	CdnEq	2.65%	75%	75%	10 years	None	Nil	Unlimited
London Life Ninth American Balanced (LLIM)	Balan	2.35%	75%	75%	10 years	None	Nil	Unlimited
London Life Ninth American Equity (BG)	FgnEq	2.45%	75%	75%	10 years	None	Nil	Unlimited
London Life Precious Metals (Maxxum)	CdnEq	2.65%	75%	75%	10 years	None	Nil	Unlimited
London Life Real Estate (GWLIM)	Spclty	2.70%	75%	75%	10 years	None	Nil	Unlimited
London Life U.S. Equity	USEq	2.55%	75%	75%	10 years	None	Nil	Unlimited

Insurance Underwriter: London Life Insurance Co.

MANULIFE SEGREGATED FUNDS

Fund Name	Fund Type	MER	Death Benefit Guarantee	Maturity Benefit Guarantee	Term to Maturity	Reset Options	Cost to Switch	Number of Allowable Switches
MLI AGF American Growth GIF	USEq	3.25%	100%	100%	10 years	2	Nil	2
MLI AGF Canadian Bond GIF	FixInc	2.35%	100%	100%	10 years	2	Nil	2
MLI AGF Canadian Equity GIF	CdnEq	3.20%	100%	100%	10 years	2	Nil	2
MLI AGF Dividend GIF	CdnEq	2.80%	100%	100%	10 years	2	Nil	2
MLI AGF Global Government Bond GIF	FixInc	2.35%	100%	100%	10 years	2	Nil	2
MLI AGF Growth & Income GIF	Balan	2.95%	100%	100%	10 years	2	Nil	2
MLI AGF High Income GIF	CdnEq	2.35%	100%	100%	10 years	2	Nil	2
MLI AIM GT America Growth Class GIF	USEq	3.15%	100%	100%	10 years	2	Nil	2
MLI AIM GT Canada Growth Class GIF	CdnEq	3.00%	100%	100%	10 years	2	Nil	2
MLI C.I. Harbour GIF	CdnEq	3.00%	100%	100%	10 years	2	Nil	2
MLI C.I. Harbour Growth & Income GIF	Balan	2.95%	100%	100%	10 years	2	Nil	2
MLI Canadian Equity Index GIF	CdnEq	1.75%	100%	100%	10 years	2	Nil	2
MLI Dynamic Dividend Growth GIF	CdnEq	2.94%	100%	100%	10 years	2	Nil	2
MLI Dynamic Global Bond GIF	FixInc	2.45%	100%	100%	10 years	2	Nil	2
MLI Dynamic Partners GIF	Balan	3.37%	100%	100%	10 years	2	Nil	2
MLI Elliott & Page American Growth GIF	USEq	3.05%	100%	100%	10 years	2	Nil	2
MLI Elliott & Page Balanced GIF	Balan	2.75%	100%	100%	10 years	2	Nil	2
MLI Elliott & Page Equity GIF	CdnEq	2.75%	100%	100%	10 years	2	Nil	2
MLI Elliott & Page Money Market A GIF	FixInc	1.35%	100%	100%	10 years	2	Nil	2
MLI Elliott & Page Money Market B GIF	FixInc	1.25%	100%	100%	10 years	2	Nil	2
MLI Elliott & Page Value Equity GIF	CdnEq	2.80%	100%	100%	10 years	2	Nil	2
MLI Fidelity Canadian Asset Allocation GIF	Balan	2.95%	100%	100%	10 years	2	Nil	2
MLI Fidelity Canadian Bond GIF	FixInc	2.15%	100%	100%	10 years	2	Nil	2
MLI Fidelity Cap Builder GIF	CdnEq	3.00%	100%	100%	10 years	2	Nil	2
MLI Fidelity Growth America GIF	USEq	3.15%	100%	100%	10 years	2	Nil	2
MLI Fidelity International Portfolio GI	FgnEq	3.38%	100%	100%	10 years	2	Nil	2
MLI Fidelity True North GIF	CdnEq	3.00%	100%	100%	10 years	2	Nil	2
MLI Hyperion Value Line U.S. Equity GIF	USEq	3.15%	100%	100%	10 years	2	Nil	2
MLI O'Donnell Canadian GIF	CdnEq	3.00%	100%	100%	10 years	2	Nil	2
MLI O'Donnell Select GIF	CdnEq	3.00%	100%	100%	10 years	2	Nil	2
MLI Talvest Canadian Asset Allocation GIF	Balan	2.95%	100%	100%	10 years	2	Nil	2
MLI Talvest Income GIF	FixInc	2.25%	100%	100%	10 years	2	Nil	2
MLI Trimark Select Balanced GIF	Balan	2.98%	100%	100%	10 years	2	Nil	2
MLI Trimark Select Canadian Growth GIF	CdnEq	2.98%	100%	100%	10 years	2	Nil	2
MLI Trimark Select Growth GIF	FgnEq	3.33%	100%	100%	10 years	2	Nil	2
MLI U.S. Equity Index GIF	USEq	1.80%	100%	100%	10 years	2	Nil	2

Insurance Underwriter : Manulife Financial

MARITIME LIFE SEGREGATED FUNDS

Fund Name	Fund Type	MER	Death Benefit Guarantee	Maturity Benefit Guarantee	Term to Maturity	Reset Options	Cost to Switch	Number of Allowable Switches
Maritime Life Aggressive Equity A&C	CdnEq	2.55%	100%	100%	15 years	Automatic	0	5
Maritime Life Aggrresive Equity B	CdnEq	2.55%	100%	100%	15 years	Automatic	0	5
Maritime Life American Growth & Income A&C	USEq	2.55%	100%	100%	15 years	Automatic	0	5
Maritime Life American Growth & Income	USEq	2.55%	100%	100%	15 years	Automatic	0	5
Maritime Life Balanced A&C	Balan	2.45%	100%	100%	15 years	Automatic	0	5
Maritime Life Balanced B	Balan	2.45%	100%	100%	15 years	Automatic	0	5
Maritime Life Bond Series A	FixInc	1.80%	100%	100%	15 years	Automatic	0	5
Maritime Life Bond Series B	FixInc	1.80%	100%	100%	15 years	Automatic	0	5
Maritime Life Bond Series C	FixInc	2.15%	100%	100%	15 years	Automatic	0	5
Maritime Life Canadian Equity Series A&C	CdnEq	2.55%	100%	100%	15 years	Automatic	0	5
Maritime Life Canadian Equity Series B	CdnEq	2.55%	100%	100%	15 years	Automatic	0	5
Maritime Life Discovery A&C	USEq	2.55%	100%	100%	15 years	Automatic	0	5
Maritime Life Discovery B	USEq	2.55%	100%	100%	15 years	Automatic	0	5
Maritime Life Diversified Equity A&C	CdnEq	2.55%	100%	100%	15 years	Automatic	0	5
Maritime Life Diversified Equity B	CdnEq	2.55%	100%	100%	15 years	Automatic	0	5
Maritime Life Dividend Income Series A	CdnEq	2.10%	100%	100%	15 years	Automatic	0	5
Maritime Life Dividend Income Series B	CdnEq	2.10%	100%	100%	15 years	Automatic	0	5
Maritime Life Dividend Income Series C	CdnEq	2.25%	100%	100%	15 years	Automatic	0	5
Maritime Life EurAsia A&C	FgnEq	2.40%	100%	100%	15 years	Automatic	0	5
Maritime Life EurAsia B	FgnEq	2.40%	100%	100%	15 years	Automatic	0	5
Maritime Life Europe Series A&C	FgnEq	2.40%	100%	100%	15 years	Automatic	0	5
Maritime Life Europe Series B	FgnEq	2.40%	100%	100%	15 years	Automatic	0	5
Maritime Life Global Equities Series A&C	FgnEq	2.75%	100%	100%	15 years	Automatic	0	5
Maritime Life Global Equities Series B	FgnEq	2.75%	100%	100%	15 years	Automatic	0	5
Maritime Life Growth Series A&C	CdnEq	2.55%	100%	100%	15 years	Automatic	0	5
Maritime Life Growth Series B	CdnEq	2.55%	100%	100%	15 years	Automatic	0	5
Maritime Life Money Market Series A	FixInc	1.00%	100%	100%	15 years	Automatic	0	5
Maritime Life Money Market Series B	FixInc	1.00%	100%	100%	15 years	Automatic	0	5
Maritime Life Money Market Series C	FixInc	2.00%	100%	100%	15 years	Automatic	0	5
Maritime Life Pacific Basin Equities A	FgnEq	2.75%	100%	100%	15 years	Automatic	0	5
Maritime Life Pacific Basin Equities B	FgnEq	2.75%	100%	100%	15 years	Automatic	0	5
Maritime Life S&P 500 Series A&C	USEq	2.20%	100%	100%	15 years	Automatic	0	5
Maritime Life S&P 500 Series B	USEq	2.20%	100%	100%	15 years	Automatic	0	5

Insurance Underwriter: Maritime Life Assurance Company

TRIMARK SEGREGATED FUNDS

Fund Name	Fund Type	MER	Death Benefit Guarantee	Maturity Benefit Guarantee	Term to Maturity	Reset Options	Cost to Switch	Number of Allowable Switches
Trimark Advantage Bond Segregated	FixInc	1.64%	100%	100%	10 years	4	Nil	Unlimited
Trimark Americas Segregated	FgnEq	3.34%	100%	100%	10 years	4	Nil	Unlimited
Trimark Canadian Bond Segregated	FixInc	1.44%	100%	100%	10 years	4	Nil	Unlimited
Trimark Canadian Resource Segregated	CdnEq	3.20%	100%	100%	10 years	4	Nil	Unlimited
Trimark Canadian Small Cos. Segregated	CdnEq	3.20%	100%	100%	10 years	4	Nil	Unlimited
Trimark Discovery Segregated	Spclty	3.30%	100%	100%	10 years	4	Nil	Unlimited
Trimark Europlus Segregated	FgnEq	3.55%	100%	100%	10 years	4	Nil	Unlimited
Trimark Government Income Segregated	FixInc	1.44%	100%	100%	10 years	4	Nil	Unlimited
Trimark Indo-Pacific Segregated	FgnEq	3.75%	100%	100%	10 years	4	Nil	Unlimited
Trimark Interest Segregated	FixInc	0.75%	100%	100%	10 years	4	Nil	Unlimited
Trimark Select Balanced Segregated	Balan	2.69%	100%	100%	10 years	4	Nil	Unlimited
Trimark Select Canadian Growth Segregated	CdnEq	2.75%	100%	100%	10 years	4	Nil	Unlimited
Trimark Select Growth Segregated	FgnEq	2.77%	100%	100%	10 years	4	Nil	Unlimited

Insurance Underwriter : American International Group

TEMPLETON SEGREGATED FUNDS

Fund Name	Fund Type	MER	Death Benefit Guarantee	Maturity Benefit Guarantee	Term to Maturity	Reset Options	Cost to Switch	Number of Allowable Switches
Templeton Growth Fund	Intl Equity	2.37%	100%	100%	10 years	4	0	Unlimited
Templeton International Stock Fund	Intl Equity	2.86%	100%	100%	10 years	4	0	Unlimited
Templeton Mutual Beacon Fund	US Equity	2.90%	100%	100%	10 years	4	0	Unlimited
Templeton Canadian Stock Fund	Cdn Equity	2.84%	100%	100%	10 years	4	0	Unlimited
Templeton Canadian Balanced Fund	Cdn Balanced	2.65%	100%	100%	10 years	4	0	Unlimited
Tempeton T-Bill Fund	Money Market	1.15%	100%	100%	10 years	4	0	Unlimited

Insurance Underwriter: Alliance Insurance Company

CHAPTER ELEVEN

Bank Packages

Trends within the Banks and Trust Companies

Size does matter! Just ask Canada's big five, soon to be big three banks. As a group, they are quickly becoming Canada's largest mutual fund distributors, despite starting well after many of the other long-term players in the mutual fund industry.

The Royal Bank of Canada currently ranks number 3 in terms of mutual fund assets under administration, and this does not take into account the assets that would fall under the Royal umbrella should the merger with the Bank of Montreal pass mustard. And even if that merger fails, Royal Bank has Trimark—the number 2 provider of mutual funds—squarely in its sites.

Table 11.1 looks at the current state of affairs in the mutual fund industry.

TABLE 11.1: TOP TEN MUTUAL FUND DISTRIBUTORS AS OF MARCH 31, 1998

Company	Assets under Administration* ($billions)	Industry Rank
Investors Group	35,618	1
Trimark	29,155	2
Royal Bank **	28,374	3
Mackenzie	24,290	4
Templeton	19,128	5
Fidelity	14,852	6
AGF	14,719	7
Toronto Dominion Bank	14,494	8
Canadian Imperial Bank of Commerce	12,932	9
CT Funds (Canada Trust)	11,930	10

* Source IFIC
** Includes Royal Trust Funds

So the banks are becoming bigger players in the mutual fund arena. What else is new? It seems clear that they want to dominate mutual funds as they do other areas in the financial services industry. And sooner rather than later, they will likely dominate, both in terms of manufacturing new funds and distributing third-party funds.

Not that this is necessarily a bad thing. The branch system is convenient, as is the notion of having a range of financial services under one roof. On the other hand, being all things to all people usually means you are never the best at any one thing.

But let's be clear, we are not here to bash banks. If you are looking for that, buy any number of financial magazines, and we're sure you will find some article that trashes banks in one form or another.

What we would like to do is examine how mutual funds are sold in the big five Canadian banks, look at some of the programs they have to offer, talk about the positives, provide some insight into costs, and then let you be the judge. At the end of the day you pay the financial freight. We simply want to give you the tools to judge how much value you are getting for your money.

To begin, we need to make it clear that we're not convinced you will always get the best financial advice from a jack-of-all-trades system. Having someone at the branch level trained in mutual fund basics might help you understand the basics, but how much more? Is that person best qualified to help you build an optimum mutual fund portfolio? In most cases, probably not!

We think that's an important point, because we would expect you to get solid advice on portfolio building from a full-service financial advisor. Mind you, what we expect is not what consumers always get, even from so-called full-service advisors.

We tend to think of good financial advisors like we think of good doctors. You probably like your family doctor, but normally you only visit when you have a specific problem, or when you go for your annual check-up.

Good financial service will provide your annual financial check-up. This is an important component within any long-term financial plan. And to be fair, an annual financial check-up is probably available from some bank branches.

However, in all too many cases, you enter a branch system and speak with someone on the other side of the counter. You discuss on some basic level your financial circumstances, and on some basic level, a portfolio of mutual funds is recommended. We're not convinced that's the person you will want to sit down with a year from now to evaluate how your portfolio has performed, and to assess what you should do in the future. In fact, it's quite likely that person will have moved to another branch by the time a year rolls around.

The other major role a good financial advisor plays is that of a mentor; someone to guide you through periods when the financial markets are particularly volatile. What are you to do when the stock market falls 10%, for example? It's easy to say you should hold for the long term. It is much more difficult to actually do that, when you are spooked by a major sell-off.

Just as you attempt to catch your breath, you pick up your favorite financial newspaper and there, on the front page, stoking your worst fear is a headline proclaiming that the worst is yet to come.

Wouldn't it be nice to have someone to talk with? To give you another perspective? Some solace when everyone around you is heading for the exit? But that only works if the advisor can provide you with concrete reasons as to why the market is correcting. And to tell you that contrary to popular belief, the world is not coming to an end.

Your financial advisor is there to provide that measure of comfort during turbulent times, which supports the notion of holding for the long term. This is an important role that good financial advisors play. And that's why financial advisors are compensated for their assistance by the ongoing trailer fees paid by the mutual fund companies. We believe that kind of assistance is worth the price of admission.

Speaking of costs, remember that loads are only one side of the issue. Just because a bank is selling no-load funds doesn't mean you are buying without a cost. The real cost is the management-expense ratios (MER) which include the annual trailer fees paid to financial advisors. You are paying these fees with all funds.

Banks don't normally distribute trailer fees. So that fee goes directly into the bank's bottom line. So think of it this way: the MER you pay to buy a no-load fund from the bank's family of funds is compensation to the bank for the convenience of being able to buy at a branch level. It also pays for the on-site service of mutual fund specialists who may or may not be available in certain branches. So know what you are paying for and what services you are receiving in return.

We believe that, over the next few years, banks will bring more specialists into the branch system. They are after all, getting better at marketing all their services.

Both Manufacturers and Distributors

Banks manufacture and distribute mutual funds. By that we simply mean that the bank creates the fund—i.e. the Royal Canadian Equity Fund—and then distributes the units through the branch network.

It is a powerful one-two punch, especially when you consider that the branch system provides so many other services to clients. Clients can make deposits and withdrawals, open savings and chequing accounts, arrange personal loans and mortgages, open an RRSP, and even buy guaranteed GICs where performance is linked to a stock market index. Thus banks can advertise "marketing the growth without risk" scenario. These are all profit centers for the bank.

With such a streamlined delivery system, banks have been quite efficient in how they price their mutual fund products. Remember that banks are interested in cross-selling services. If you are holding bank mutual funds, you can often get favorable rates on personal loans, mortgages, and general banking services. Like we said, Canadian banks want to be your one-stop financial center.

So we'll concede that banks have, in general, done a good job manufacturing and pricing their mutual fund products. They are not always the best-performing funds as a group. There are some top performers, others at the bottom, and others that are just average. Across the board, the performance of all bank funds has been average.

In the last couple of years, a couple of banks—notably CIBC and ScotiaBank—have offered third-party funds to their clients. When we talk about third-party funds, we mean funds manufactured at other dealers like Trimark, Altamira, Dynamic, etc.

The problem banks have with third-party funds is in how the revenue is distributed. As a comparison, think of General Motors. GM can make more money selling cars they manufacture, rather than cars manufactured by another company. So it is with banks, who can make more selling their in-house funds than they can selling third-party funds.

But keeping with our innovative theme, banks have come up with a way to leverage their position while marketing third-party funds. Something to compensate them for selling a competitor's product on a no-load basis.

How can this be done? Create a portfolio management service, using a high-profile mutual fund expert, and charge an additional administration fee on top of the normal MERs charged by the third-party funds.

That's a lot of fees to the end user, and we're not sure the fees justify the added value. But you be the judge, as we review two prominent portfolio products, the Scotia Leaders program, and the CIBC Choice Funds program.

The Scotia Leaders Program

The ScotiaBank Leaders program offers two pre-packaged mutual fund portfolios: (1) a Canadian equity portfolio and (2) a global equity portfolio. Both portfolios are structured using Ranga Chand's heavy hitter funds.

According to literature from ScotiaBank, inside the Scotia Leaders Program you pay no purchase fees, no redemption fees, no monitoring fees, no switch fees, no RRSP fees and no transaction charges—just one annual administration fee charged quarterly. And all or partial redemptions are allowed with no penalty.

Seems like they are eliminating a lot of fees. And they are. But they are also adding back an administration fee. The administration fee is 1% for the first $50,000, 0.75% on the next $50,000 and 0.50% on amounts in excess of $100,000. The administration fee is in addition to the MERs charged by the individual funds in the program.

The program started in October 1996. From the end of October 1996 to April 1998, the total return on the Scotia Leaders Canadian equity portfolio was 18.45%. The Scotia Leaders global equity portfolio did better, for a total return of 35.24%. These returns are net of the MERs charged by the funds but before the administration fee charged by the Scotia Leaders program.

If we subtract the administration fee, the net return on the Scotia Leaders Canadian Equity portfolio over that 18-month period (October 1996 to April 1998) period was 16.95%. For the Scotia Leaders global equity portfolio, the net return after administration fees was 33.74%. We are assuming a 1% annual fee—1% annually equals 1.5% for the 18-month period we are looking at—for each Scotia Leaders portfolio. The 1% per annum fee represents the amount payable by the smallest portfolio, which is $50,000 in assets or less.

But those numbers still don't tell us anything about value. As we have discussed in other parts of this book, investors can only make informed judgments about value when they have some benchmark against which to measure performance.

What we need to do is compare the Scotia Leaders Canadian equity portfolio to the performance of the average Canadian equity fund over the same period, and compare the Scotia Leaders global equity portfolio to the average global equity fund.

Looking at comparables, the average Canadian diversified equity fund returned 31.4% for the period from October 31, 1996 to April 30, 1997. Those returns are net of MERs, and of course, there is no administration fee.

These returns assume you purchased the average Canadian diversified equity fund during that 18-month period. Not an overachiever, not an underachiever, just the average fund in the Canadian equity category.

Interestingly, since the program began, the average Canadian equity fund has beaten the Scotia Leaders Canadian equity portfolio hands down. In fact, the average Canadian equity fund has almost doubled the performance of the Scotia Leaders Canadian equity portfolio after accounting for the administration fees.

The average global equity fund returned 35.0% over that 18-month period. Again, the returns are net of MERs. And again, the average performing global equity fund has beaten the Scotia Leaders global equity portfolio after accounting for the administration fees. Not by much mind you, but the average for the category did beat the so-called heavy hitters.

And just so that we play fair in this analysis, we also looked at the performance of the average international equity fund. We did this because when ScotiaBank quotes from Mr. Chand's book about overachievers and underachievers, they look at the five-year performance numbers for international equity funds.

So how did the Scotia Leaders global equity portfolio do against the average international equity fund? Well, over the 18 months from October 31, 1996, to April 30, 1998, the average international equity fund returned 31%, net of MERs. Based on those numbers, it would appear that the Scotia Leaders global equity portfolio did in fact add value over the first 18 months of the program. Not much value, but the program did outperform the averages.

Presumably, the reason you pay the administration fee is because the bank will add value. The bank will help you put together a model portfolio of heavy hitters that will allow you to do better than you could on your own. Based on what we have seen so far (and that is only for the first 18 months), we think that the Scotia Leaders program has been, at best, a program of average achievers.

But let's be fair. Past performance is not necessarily indicative of future performance. And we're not about to chastise Mr. Chand for the performance numbers so far. People in glass houses and all that sort of thing. So this is not about the performance numbers since inception, but rather on how the program is structured. Indeed, how any celebrity managed program is structured.

Go into ScotiaBank's web site and you will see how overachievers, underachievers and average funds in a specific category performed over the past one-, three- and five-year periods (see Figure 11.1). The implication is that the Scotia Leaders program will help you attain results befitting an overachiever.

FIGURE 11.1: OVERACHIEVERS VS. UNDERACHIEVERS

Overachievers vs Underachievers Canadian Equity Funds (returns %)*			
	1 Year	3 Years	5 Years
Overachievers	28.5%	18.1%	18.1%
Underachievers	11.8%	10.0%	11.9%
Average for Canadian equity funds	20.9%	14.2%	14.7%

Overachievers vs Underachievers International Equity Funds (returns %)*			
	1 Year	3 Years	5 Years
Overachievers	19.6%	14.5%	16.2%
Underachievers	1.4%	4.2%	9.0%
Average for international equity funds	12.9%	9.7%	12.8%

* to July 31, 1998

That causes us some concern. Anyone can pick a fund with the best five-year rate of return, and then say, "Had you held this fund for the last five years, this is what you would have earned." But how does that tell us anything about the future?

Another concern we have is the notion that the program will eliminate underachieving funds. That, presumably, is a selling feature. If a heavy-hitter fund doesn't continue its heavy-hitting performance, then it will eventually be classed as an underachiever. If the fund underachieves for one full year, then it is cast aside, and sent quietly off to the recycling bin.

As you might imagine, given the rather poor performance of the Scotia Leaders Canadian equity portfolio since inception, there was at least one underachiever in that mix. Pity the poor BPI Canadian Small-Cap Fund. The fund is now history. And we assume it will be replaced by another heavy-hitter fund with a top-notch five-year track record. At the time of writing, we were not sure what that fund was.

Two things come to mind. First, with this program, are you not paying an administration fee to the bank to systematically manage your mutual fund portfolio, using a buy high, sell low philosophy? This is something we think goes against all conventional investment wisdom.

Second, this is what happens when the Scotia Leaders program has five years behind it. Will the marketing literature still rely on a table that defines overachievers, underachievers and average funds?

In fairness, we noted that on the ScotiaBank web site, investors can actually calculate the performance of the program using any start date and any finishing date. That's a good thing, because the best program is one in which investors fully understand the potential and the pitfalls.

Finally, in defense of the BPI Canadian Small-Cap Fund, don't be too quick to dismiss it. We have often found that underachievers of today become the heavy hitters of tomorrow. Kind of like buying low and selling high.

The CIBC Choice Funds Program[4]

The CIBC program is more expensive than the Scotia Leaders program, and it is too early to tell whether this program offers any additional pizzazz.

CIBC will charge investors with less than $50,000 in the program an annual administrative fee of 1.5%. On a $50,000 portfolio, you will pay CIBC an annual $750 "administration fee." Again, this is in addition to the MERs charged by the mutual funds.

The administration fee is set on a sliding scale, falling to 1.25% for amounts from $50,000 up to $100,000, to 1.0% for amounts from $100,000 to $150,000, and for amounts over $150,000, the administration fee is 0.75%. Again like the Scotia Leaders program, there is no commissions to buy or redeem units, no charges for partial redemptions, no RRSP fees and no switching fees.

Just so we are clear, the load/no-load debate is a moot point. We ask you: Who is better off over the long term? The investor who pays a 3% front-end load, and pays an annual 2% MER? The investor who buys the fund using a 3% back-end load (remember there is no out-of-pocket cost to the investor when purchasing the fund on a deferred sales charge basis) and then pays an annual 2.5% MER for the next six years? Or finally, the investor who buys no-load, but has a 2.5% MER indefinitely?

There are formulas one can use to determine which is most cost-effective at a point in time. But in reality, any formula must make certain assumptions about the performance of the fund over the long haul. Generally speaking, assuming the fund is an average long-term performer, and you are an average long-term investor, one approach is about the same as another.

If we assume no net affect from the load/no-load issue, the next question comes down to the total ongoing costs associated with the Choice Funds program. Investors need to ask how much are they really paying to have a pre-canned portfolio selected by a mutual fund expert. Or put another way, how much of they ongoing return must be sacrificed in order to cover the annual expenses?

When you add an administration fee on top of the MER, the costs can run about 3%-plus per year. Surprisingly, investors seem only too eager to jump on these portfolio bandwagons, probably because equity mutual funds have been returning double-digit numbers for the past several years. However, we're not so sure that investors will be so forgiving when their portfolio returns come back down to more normal levels.

---

[4]*Both Richard Croft and Eric Kirzner as independent members on the CIBC Investment Committee. Neither has been involved previously or now with the CIBC Choice Funds Program.*

So, what do you get for your money? At present, one of five pre-selected mutual fund portfolios, each including up to six mutual funds. The model portfolios are really just versions of the same theme; that is, to build a balanced mutual fund portfolio "that is specifically designed for your needs."

Gordon Pape is the expert attached to this program. Along with Mr. Pape, CIBC personnel and William Mercer Co. will act as advisors to the program. The advisors can pre-select from any of 1,800 available mutual funds. Most of these are third-party funds. The program is available through the branch system.

What we find odd, is why investors need to pay that kind of annual fee for Gordon Pape's expertise? Why not simply buy his *1999 Mutual Fund Buyers Guide*? Presumably, the funds listed in his book are his best choices for the year ahead. Even if you want more up-to-date advice, Gordon has his own mutual fund newsletter and a web site (www.gordonpape.com). No matter how you slice it, the costs are much less than the CIBC annual administration fee.

The bottom line for most investors is this: The best approach is not to get caught up in the hype that you are somehow saving something because you can buy the funds on a no-load basis. Look to the long term and understand the ongoing costs. Take the time to develop a long-term financial plan that includes, among other things, estate planning, tax advice, and a long-term investment portfolio. And the banks offer programs to help you do that. We also have such a program in our personality profile at the beginning of this book. Get prepared, and then buy.

Canada Trust: One-Stop Fund Solutions

Can it be true? A major financial institution offering mutual funds on a no-load basis, with no additional charges, access to your account from the Internet or by touch-tone phone, and if you want to talk to a real person, a mutual fund specialist?

Sounds like a commercial. Well, it is! A C.T. Securities media event, in fact. The program entitled "One-Stop Fund Solutions" is being marketed by C.T. Securities, a subsidiary of Canada Trust. The idea is to make it easier for the average investor to access mutual funds at a reasonable cost. An investor may access 26 fund families at last count, including names like AGF, AIC, Dynamic, Fidelity and Trimark.

The marketing campaign describes One-Stop Fund Solutions as a place to buy the same funds that financial advisors normally charge a load to buy, but now through C.T. Securities, can be purchased on a no-load basis. It's a good pitch and probably a decent product, but again, you know our views on the load/no-load debate.

And just to add some further grist for the no-load mill, investors have always had the ability to buy a fund on a no-load basis, even from a so-called load fund company. Financial advisors, if they choose, can sell a fund using a level load option. This means they receive a higher trailer fee forever, but no upfront commission.

Another approach that is used by financial planners is to charge a fee for the financial plan, and then waive the load costs if the plan is implemented. The point is you will pay for financial advice. It is just a question of when and how.

The C.T. Securities program does not provide a celebrity mutual fund expert to put together a portfolio of funds on your behalf. So there is no advice as to how to structure a portfolio. You are on your own in terms of setting up the program. Well, not really on your own. You can use the information from *The FundLine Advisor* to build your portfolio.

However, there is no advice or ongoing monitoring of your mutual fund portfolio. No hand holding during market corrections. Yet C.T. Securities still expects to receive the trailer fees, which led at least one mutual fund company to take out a series of one-page ads. Goodman and Company—Manager of the Dynamic Mutual Funds—said in the ad that "C.T. Securities still expects to receive full-service commissions from Goodman and Company Ltd., who like all managers of load mutual fund companies, pay dealers a deferred commission for providing ongoing service."

The implication is this: Why should C.T. Securities earn a trailer fee if they provide no advice? Why indeed? Whether you want to admit it or not, there is value to having a good financial planner working with you. You need to judge how much value.

There are some restrictions with the One-Stop Fund Solutions program. You must have an account at C.T. Securities, and the net equity in the account must be at least $15,000. Not unduly restrictive for most investors.

The minimum purchase for each mutual fund is $2,500, and there is a 1% redemption charge if you redeem or switch your fund within the first 90 days. After 90 days, there is no cost to switch or to redeem units.

You can talk with a C.T. Securities mutual fund specialist, who will walk you through the pros and cons of various funds. And those specialists presumably have access to Steve Kangas, employed by C.T. Securities' parent company, Canada Trust. Kangas is certainly a respected mutual fund expert in Canada.

What the One-Stop Solutions Program does is provide a cost-effective vehicle on which to buy a mutual fund portfolio. Apparently, the funds are bought on behalf of the client on a front-end load basis, with zero commission.

Summary

You can't argue with the merits of any program that helps investors lower their costs. That's called competition. And the financial-services industry is just beginning to feel the full brunt of such competitive pressures.

Is the service no-fee? Well, to a point. No loads, but you are still funding the ongoing commissions which are paid by the fund companies to the dealer. You might ask yourself, "If I'm going to be paying these fees anyway, shouldn't I get some advice in return?"

Royal Bank: Strategy Index Funds

Apparently strategy indexing is what works on Wall Street. At least on paper! If nothing else it has David Chilton—*The Wealthy Barber*—excited about it. For the record, Mr. Chilton is paid by O'Shaughnessy Capital Management (OCM) to promote its funds on behalf of the Royal Bank of Canada.

Now that we have dispensed with the legalese, let's take a look at this program. Strategy indexing is a relatively new concept developed by James P. O'Shaughnessy, and is described in detail in his best-selling book *What Works on Wall Street*.

Essentially, based on information from Royal Bank's web site, OCM believes that a disciplined investment strategy is the only way to outperform the Standard & Poor's 500 benchmark in the U.S. or the TSE 300 Composite Index benchmark in Canada.

The S&P 500 Index consists of 500 U.S. stocks chosen for market size, liquidity, and industry group representation. It is a market-capitalization weighted index (stock price times number of shares outstanding), with each stock's weight in the index proportionate to its market value. The S&P 500 is one of the most widely used benchmarks of U.S. equity performance.

The TSE 300 is a capitalization-weighted index of 300 stocks that trade on the Toronto Stock Exchange. Capitalization weighted means that a company with a large market capitalization (company's market value) will make up more of the total market value of the index and will therefore have a greater impact on the movement of the overall index.

According to OCM, the reason so many traditional money managers and the funds they manage fail to beat the S&P 500 Index is because fund managers lack the necessary discipline and consistency.

"Money managers still have no coherent, understandable strategy that guides their stock selections. They have no mechanism to help them rein in their emotions or to guarantee that their good ideas work. Too often their picks are based on hope rather than experience. As an investor, you don't really know how your money is managed or if a manager's past performance is just a fluke," writes OCM.

OCM employs stock-selection strategies based on long term, empirical evidence. What's more, these strategies are explicitly stated, historically tested and rigorously implemented. These disciplines will never deviate. With these strategies, you essentially align your portfolio to a superior strategy, making style drift impossible. Knowing how a stock-selection strategy performs historically helps you understand, estimate and control risk and return when planning your portfolio. So much for the marketing pizzazz.

Lest we forget, all that we have talked about so far is based on a paper-driven trading system. This program has not as yet been proven to work in the real world with real transaction costs. Nor has it accounted for the normal purchase and redemption routines that impact all mutual funds.

Strategy indexing comes in two flavors: value and growth. This presumably helps you deal with the issue of diversification among management styles.

With the value approach, the manager buys the 50 highest dividend-yielding companies from a database of 568 stocks known as the O'Shaughnessy Market Leaders Universe. Value stocks in the database are selected on the basis of (1) market capitalization; (2) number of shares outstanding; (3) cash flow; and (4) 12-month sales being 50% greater than the average for S&P 500 Composite Index. Utility and power companies are not included in the database.

These 50 companies presumably represent the best of the best over any one-year period. At the end of each year the portfolio is rebalanced with a revised top 50 list. Rebalancing takes place on the 20th business day of each new calendar year.

Historically this strategy—again all on paper—has outperformed the S&P 500 Composite Index over three-, five- and 10-year periods to the end of December 1996. You can buy this approach through the Royal U.S. Value Strategic Index Fund.

The other side of this investment strategy is the so-called growth component. In this case, OCM buys the 50 stocks with the highest one-year price increase as of the date of purchase. These 50 high-growth picks are selected from the "O'Shaughnessy All Stocks Universe," which includes some 4,243 stocks. To be included in the index, the companies must have (1) annual earnings higher than the previous year, and (2) a price-to-sales ratio below 1.5. This portfolio is also rebalanced on the 20th business day of each calendar year.

Again, according to marketing literature from Royal Bank, the U.S. Growth Strategy Index has outperformed the S&P 500 Composite Index on a one-, five- and 10-year basis, to the end of December 1996. You can buy this approach in the Royal U.S. Strategic Growth Index fund.

The final frontier in this strategic indexing universe is the Royal Canadian Strategic Index Fund. This is a potpourri of strategy indexing. In this fund, the manager will invest 10% of the assets in each of the U.S. Strategic Value and U.S. Strategic Growth indexes. That will take care of the 20% maximum foreign content allowed in Canadian equity funds.

The rest of the assets in the Royal Canadian Strategic Index Fund will be used to buy 25 Canadian growth stocks (selected from the 404 issues in the Canadian growth universe) and 25 Canadian value stocks (selected from the 78 issues in the Canadian value universe). As one would expect, Canadian strategy indexing outperforms the TSE 300 Composite Index over all relevant rating periods (1, 3, 5 and 10 years). With such powerful numbers supporting this program, no wonder the wealthy barber is excited.

For us, we look at this program as a two-sided coin. On the one side, we like the concept of a disciplined strategy. It takes any biases that the manager may have and removes them from the equation. And we believe that investors are best served when they build a well thought out diversified portfolio. Hence the logic behind the FundLine. Having a manager who is dedicated to a specific system helps that process. Why? Because we have a clear understanding as to those elements of diversification that manager brings to the table.

We like the fact that OCM promises to cap the annual MER at 1.5%. This is well below the 2.17% average for U.S. equity funds and 2.20% for Canadian equity funds.

We also like the idea of having the fund fully invested all the time. If you are buying an equity fund, it should be invested in stocks. It should not be holding a substantial portion of the portfolio in cash.

On the performance side, the jury is still out. We continue to emphasize that these performance numbers are hypothetical. This is a paper-based trading system, and to this point, does not have a long track record in the real world.

Applying a well-thought-out analytical tool to a successful real-world mutual fund is not easy. Just ask Value Line, the giant U.S. based Investment Advisory Service that utilizes a complex algorithm to rank the year ahead performance of each of 1,700 stocks it follows. The stocks are divided into five quintiles with a 1 rank being the best and a 5 rank the worst.

For more than 30 years, performance numbers have defied efficient market theory; the stocks ranked 1 outperformed stocks ranked 2, which outperformed the 3-ranked stocks, and so on. Indeed, the Value Line system stands as an exception to the rule that no forecasting tool can beat a passive index over long periods.

The market was so impressed with the Value Line system, that when the company decided to launch its first mutual fund, investors were lining up for a piece of the action. But it is here where the real world of investing conflicts with the theoretical world of forecasting. The fund never lived up to its lofty expectations, and for the first 15 years, underperformed the S&P 500 Composite Index by about 1.5% compounded annually.

In terms of performance, the marketing literature speaks loudly about the potential returns from strategy indexing. The marketing literature supplied by Royal Bank compares the performance of the U.S. Strategic Growth and the U.S. Strategic Value indexes with that of the S&P 500 Composite Index. The numbers are compelling: U.S. $10,000 invested in the growth strategy over 44 years yields $20 million pre-tax. The value strategy returns U.S. $6.4 million. The U.S. $1.4 million one would have gotten by simply investing in the S&P 500 Composite Index pales by comparison. As you might have guessed, we have some concerns about this type of analysis. Despite warnings to the contrary, such comparisons are not designed to educate investors, but rather to raise expectations.

Whether strategy indexing turns out to be a real-world superior system, time will tell. And speaking of time, we note that OCM makes a strong case that investors who buy into this philosophy should be willing to commit to it for the long term — as in five years or longer. We suggest you heed that advice!

We would also raise a flag about the risk factors. Amidst all of the talk about performance, investors need to understand that all three of the Royal strategy index funds are riskier than the underlying benchmark index.

The U.S. Growth Strategy Index is fully one-third riskier than the S&P 500 Composite Index. And one could argue that the paper-based performance numbers generated by the Growth Strategy Index are directly linked to the excess risk characteristics, as opposed to any new enlightened investment approach.

The Value Strategy Index is another matter. While riskier than the underlying S&P 500 Composite Index, the Value Strategy Index did show positive risk-adjusted performance numbers relative to the S&P 500 Composite Index.

But here, too, much of that can be explained by the high interest rate environment from the mid-1970s to the late-1980s. High interest rates favor high dividend-yielding stocks. If you look closely at the long-range performance graphs (see the Royal Bank's marketing literature), that's the period when the value returns started to really pull away from the returns generated by the S&P 500 Composite Index. Again we emphasize that investors need to have a long time horizon.

Finally, we have some concerns about the terminology. The idea of calling these funds "index funds" can be misleading. An index fund is traditionally thought of as a low-cost fund that mirrors the performance of some underlying index. Because an index fund manager rarely trades the portfolio, unit holders are not subjected to significant capital gains (or losses) distributions in any one year.

However, the Strategy Index funds could theoretically turn over the entire portfolio on the 20th business day of the new calendar year. This is a situation that could generate substantial capital gains to the unit holders.

We're not ready to recommend these funds — yet. Our qualifying period is three years, which should be enough time to tell whether or not this system lives up to its billing. But, we are intrigued with the concept, and applaud Royal Bank for trying something new and innovative. We intend to revisit these funds at a future date.

Summary

Yes, size is important. But with book writing, quantity takes a back seat to quality. Think of this chapter as a small, quick-fisted review of some mutual fund products and programs offered by banks and trust companies. A small guide through the bank maze.

While only a short chapter this year, we expect this chapter to grow in the future as more products and new ideas come to market. And you can be sure that we will continue to review new concepts or programs from all sides.

CHAPTER TWELVE

Ethical Investing and Ethical Funds

In the wake of the "greed" era of the 1980s, the cold realities of the 1991 recession and the 1997/98 Asian Flu, some investors have begun to reassess their priorities. It's a new world where wealth maximization may not be the only decision-making principle.

One of the most interesting phenomena of these changing times is the growing interest in socially responsible investing and investments. The annual report of one of the largest ethical mutual funds in Canada provides a good definition on the subject: "Can Canadian investors reap financial rewards while remaining true to their moral beliefs?"

There are different definitions of socially responsible investing. Ultimately it means investing in accordance with your conscience and your morals.

Some investors attempt to do it on their own by building their own screening process to weed out undesirable and unacceptable companies. Others rely on mutual funds to do the screening for them. The first such socially responsible fund, the Vancouver-based Ethical Funds Inc.'s Ethical Growth Fund, was introduced in Canada in 1986. A handful of similar funds have followed, including two new ones in 1992. There are now five families that offer such funds, although only two, Ethical Funds and the Clean Environment Group, specialize in this area.

Types of Socially Responsible Funds

What are socially responsible funds, what do they do, and how have they done?

Socially responsible funds state their investment philosophy variously as active or exclusionary.

The first are the so-called ethical funds that employ social screening to exclude certain types of companies from the fund's list of eligible investments. Typically, the screened or banned companies include those involved in the manufacture and distribution of alcohol and tobacco products; in the manufacture of weapons systems; in the production, importation and distribution of pornography; companies who do not practice effective pollution control and environmental protection; companies who support repressive regimes; and companies who have unsound or ungenerous labor practices. Companies involved in nuclear power are often on the prohibited list as well. The Ethical Funds Group is the leader of the exclusionary type.

The inclusionary type are sometimes affectionately, or derisively, depending on your want, called "do-gooder" funds. "Do-gooders" look for specific types of companies, typically including investments in companies that have environmentally progressive policies; that have fair labor practices; that have enlightened industrial and stakeholder relations programs; and that are involved in recycling and waste management research in environmental clean-up. The Clean Environment Group is an active participant in this area.

The exclusionary screens and inclusionary targets often result in companies appearing on both ethical and do-gooder lists. For example, some of the Canadian banks and a number of oil-producing companies are fixtures in socially conscious portfolios.

There are definitional issues involved in the ethical investment process. The issue of ethical practice and companies can be a very personal thing. A Christian Scientist might consider a firm involved in medical research as unethical, while others would consider firms that experiment with live animals to search for new drug cures as unacceptable. On what side would the manufacturer of military defense equipment such as Patriot Missiles fit on the ethical scale? Which, for example, are the repressive regimes and what constitutes "supporting" a repressive regime?

The Socially Conscious Record

The four socially conscious Canadian equity mutual funds with a sufficient track record for evaluation have relatively impressive performance numbers. Over the period July 1995 through July 1998, the four funds achieved an average return of 22.5% as compared to 16.3% for the average Canadian equity mutual fund (16.9% for the median) and 19.9% for the TSE 300 Composite Index.

Furthermore, on a risk-adjusted basis (3-year return divided by standard deviation), the four ethical funds yielded up a 6.5 times return per unit of risk ratio, well above the 4.4 times average for the Canadian equity fund category and the 5.5 times ratio for the TSE 300 Composite Index. The MVA (Manager-Value Added) indexes for the funds are also impressive: Clean Environment Equity, 113.8; Desjardins Environment, 100.8; Ethical Growth Fund, 100.9; and Investors Summa, 110.5.

In addition, over the period July 1993 through July 1998, the socially conscious group recorded a 16.3% average as compared to 11.9% for the equity funds and 11.0% for the TSE 300 Composite Index. The two funds with 10-year records, Ethical Growth and Investors Summa, have outperformed the equity mutual fund average by about 2% per year on average and about equaled the TSE 300.

The handful of socially conscious funds in the money market, balanced and global categories have also realized above-average returns as well.

Virtue has indeed paid off over the past decade. Ethical investing is neither a fad nor a curiosity—it's for real. Socially conscious investing is an interesting phenomenon and is certainly a mirror on these changing times.

The Social Index

The Domini 400 Social Index is an index of 400 "socially screened" corporations. The index, available in total return and price-only forms, is maintained by Kinder, Lydenbereg, Domini & Co., is compiled by Wilshire Associates, and has been published since May 1990. Since its first publication, the index has outperformed the S&P 500 and the Russell 1000 by a small margin.

The Track Record

Why have the socially conscious funds done so well? Common sense would suggest that ethical funds will earn lower rates of returns for their investors in the long-run since their investment choices are restricted. The superior performance of the funds thus far could be a fluke. Or it may mean that ethical funds are employing more skillful and thoughtful management. Or possibly, ethical funds are good bull market performers and weak bear market ones.

In theory, a nonrestricted fund can replicate the portfolio of an ethical fund while still investing in profitable and promising other companies. Thus, its performance should dominate the ethical fund. Furthermore, some of the fund's managers research efforts presumably go towards checking whether companies are depleting the rain forest, or testing products on animals, or are affiliated with other "offenders." These moral audits involve time and money. But it seems that fund managers of socially conscious funds are doing a particularly good selection job. By selecting companies that are not only environmentally friendly but also cost effective, they have better relations with employees, neighbors and clients, and reduce the probabilities of facing fines and lawsuits. Lean, mean, ethical and responsible isn't just a 1990s fad—this may well be the low cost, high-profit paradigm of the future.

Socially conscious investment fund managers may well be investing in the frontier. Typically, these companies are ahead of the times as well. Companies that have already installed pollution control equipment will be prepared when environmental rules are tightened in the future. One of my University of Toronto MBA portfolio groups had a strong background in ethical investing and in a recent report added some valuable ammunition to the argument from a land development and First Nations' perspective. They pointed out that some ethical companies are "initiating negotiations with native groups prior to the development of a project on lands, subject to land claims. Thus they will have pre-empted future costs arising from legal challenges as well as potential future consumer ill-will."

Maybe there is a "first in" effect taking place. Possibly the fund managers of ethical mutual funds are particularly adroit at being first in place in finding and selecting these innovative firms—at least for now. The results over the past few years suggest that this "first in" approach may reflect superior effort or ability of the ethical fund managers at security selection. It's almost as if increased effort or skill are present to combat the obvious operating constraints.

The Clean Environment Group

The Clean Environment Equity Fund and Clean Environment Balanced Fund, managed by Acuity Investment Management, are interesting funds. Launched in January 1992, the funds' managers employ both financial and environmental criteria in their investment mission. They search for growth-oriented firms that are cash rich and generally debt free and where management are significant stakeholders. They avoid leveraged firms. This might suggest why the "Clean" appellation is applied, but that term actually refers to the managers' investment philosophy of concentrating on companies in the environment services and products area (recycling, waste management, alternative energy) and companies that are adopting innovative approaches to dealing with environmental issues through the use of environmentally clean raw materials and the like.

Ethical investing is an admirable strategy. But I caution that your returns might be more moral than monetary. If you are prepared for this, I say go for it. Evidence so far is that you will at least have energetic and adroit fund managers. I wonder if they smoke or drink or fail to recycle their garbage?

The Socially Conscious Universe

Canadian Equity Funds
Clean Environment Equity
Desjardins Environment
Ethical Growth
Investors Summa

Canadian Equity Funds (Small Cap)
Ethical Special Equity

Canadian Balanced Funds
Clean Environment Balanced
Ethical Balanced

U.S. Equity Funds
Ethical North America

Foreign Equity Funds
Ethical Pacific Rim

Fixed Income
Clean Environment Income
Ethical Money Market
Ethical Income
Ethical Global Bond

CHAPTER THIRTEEN

The 1999 FundLine Forecast

To the abyss and back?

As we write this forecast the world stock markets have just gone through a gut-wrenching correction. On August 31, the U.S. stock market, as measured by the Dow Jones Industrial Average, fell 512 points in one day. And to make matters worse, 300 of those points were shaved from the market during the last hour of trading. It was a classic capitulation. And it was the second time in less than a year that the market had fallen 500 points (as measured by the Dow Industrial Average) in one day. We'll talk about this major correction, what caused it, what to look for in the future, and how to invest your mutual fund portfolio in 1999.

But before we do, we want to review some of the things we said last year to provide some perspective as to how well we did or didn't do, and to lay the foundation for some of our long-term positions.

The year that was ...

In last year's forecast, we talked about a singular fundamental point of view—that it is possible to have long-term growth without inflation. A growth-without-inflation scenario means lower interest rates, higher wages, and earnings growth—the best of all possible scenarios. And we continue to believe that position on a long-term basis, but with some caveats for 1999, which we will talk about a little later.

We also said last year that we didn't think inflation would be a problem for the stock market, believing instead that the ultimate slayer of the bull market would most likely be deflation. We also said that interest rates would likely be lower at the end of 1998 than they were at the beginning of 1998, which has come to pass, as long-term 30-year U.S. government bonds were yielding 5.3% at the end of August 1998 (see Figure 13.1). Indeed, the U.S. Federal Reserve cut short-term rates.

Figure 13.1: U.S. YIELD CURVE (SEPTEMBER 1998)

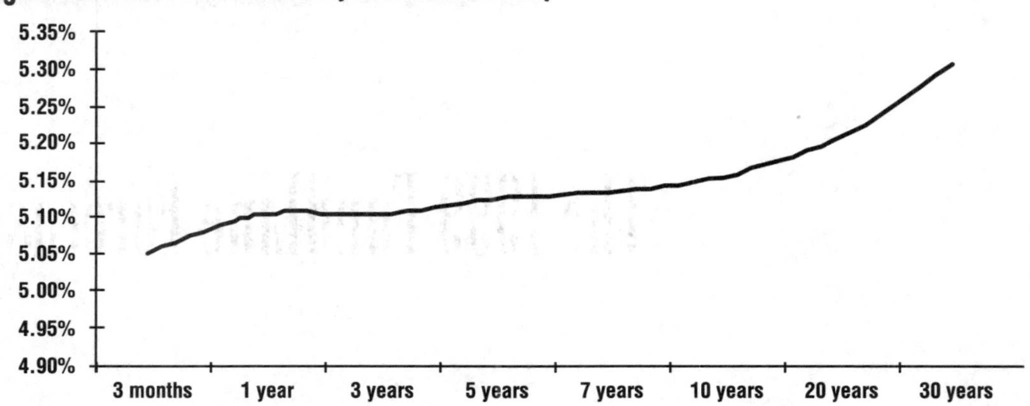

It is interesting how the position of so many analysts has changed over the last year. When we wrote the 1998 forecast, we were quick to point out that we were in the minority. After the stock market sell-off at the end of August, it seems that our position is now the most commonly held view of the future.

We pointed to labor costs as the main cause for concern on the inflation front. But we said, and still believe, that North American labor costs will remain relatively benign. Wages will rise, but not faster than productivity.

We see a growing number of companies tying productivity to compensation packages for both union and non-union workers. As we noted in last year's edition, more than half of the Fortune 500 companies partially compensate their workers with bonuses. As long as this trend continues, wage pressure should not lead to higher prices. If profit margins increase because workers are more productive, then companies do not have to raise prices in order for their earnings to increase. If companies aren't raising prices, inflation will not occur, and over the longer term, interest rates will remain low.

We also made an observation last year that the Canadian government would have a budget surplus by the end of the 1998-99 fiscal year (fiscal year ends March 1999) because of a powerful combination of higher than expected revenue, reduced government spending and lower interest costs on the debt. Indeed, the government actually reached its surplus before our target date.

We were quite close on our views for Canadian interest rates as well. We thought that Canadian Treasury bills would fall to 3.5%, which is where they were before rates were jacked up in August to defend the Canadian dollar. We also thought that Canadian bond rates (as measured by 10-year Government of Canada bonds) would fall to about 5.25%. At the time of writing, 30-year Government of Canada bonds are yielding about 5.75%, and 10-year bonds about 5.35%. Scary, isn't it?

What we didn't see coming ...

The blip that we didn't see coming was the collapse of the Canadian dollar. But then, apparently, neither did many other analysts. At the time of writing, the Canadian dollar has recovered from its low to close above 65 cents U.S. (see Figure 13.2). Even 65 cents U.S. is just above the lowest point in history. Gives you a sinking feeling at a time when the Canadian dollar was actually doing quite well relative to other curencies

Figure 13.2: CANADIAN DOLLAR VS. U.S. DOLLAR (1 YEAR)

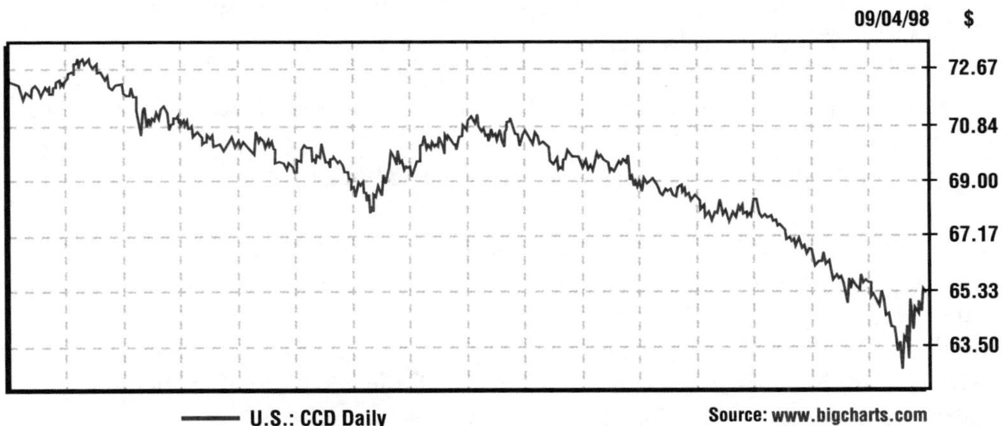

The problem, of course, is that we are faced with being compared to the most powerful economy in the world. Kind of like we imagine it would be for a son of Bill Gates (Gates being the chairman of Microsoft Corp., whose personal fortune is closing in on U.S. $60 billion) trying to live up to his father's accomplishments. What do you do for an encore?

So the Canadian dollar is rising against almost all the Asian currencies, and against some European currencies. Yet we compare our results against the U.S. dollar that has risen even more dramatically. Based on these assumptions you might argue, as the Canadian government has been so adept at doing, that the dollar's fall looks worse than it actually is.

But try telling that to Canadians who spend their winters in Florida. Tell that to Canadian businessmen who rely on U.S.-made products and have to pay their bills in U.S. dollars. Tell that to Canadian investors who hold Canadian equity funds, that have fallen harder and faster than equivalent U.S. equity funds. The impact from a weak Canadian dollar is spilling over into the financial markets.

We find it disconcerting that neither the Bank of Canada nor the Canadian minister of finance has taken a tougher stance against the loonie's free fall. At the time of writing, we had seen some intervention by the Bank of Canada, but most of that was intended to slow the slide — not stop it. We particularly like the characterization made by Dr. Sherry Cooper, chief economist at Nesbitt Burns in Toronto, when she suggested that there was a "malaise" surrounding the Canadian dollar.

Call it Canadian complacency, call it a negative self image. Call it what you will, but we agree with Dr. Cooper: It is time for the Canadian government to take the necessary steps to rigorously defend the Canadian dollar.

The weakness of the Canadian dollar is the result of a number of factors, some of which are domestic in nature and over which we have some control. Others are global events over which we have little control. Talk with 10 economists, and you will likely get 10 different reasons as to why the Canadian dollar is weak. The factors we have seen most often include the following (in no particular order):

- Weak commodity prices — as in gold, coal, nickel, copper, oil, lumber — all products which Canada exports.
- Low Canadian interest rates when viewed in the context of U.S. interest rates.
- Hesitation on the part of the Bank of Canada to intervene to protect the value of the loonie.
- A slowing domestic economy, desperately in need of tax relief.

The Asian Flu, which has already caused weakness in Asia, Japan, Russia and now Latin America, has caused a flight to quality on the part of investors. And the flight to quality road leads directly into the U.S.

Probably all of the above have had some impact on the loonie. But we believe the chief cause for concern is the flight to quality issue. To put this in perspective, consider the plight of, say, an average working-class Japanese investor, who we will call Mr. Samori. Now Mr. Samori has *yen* to spend and a yen to invest. Pardon the pun.

Mr. Samori has a number of investment alternatives to look at. For example, he could buy Japanese stocks. But the Japanese stock market, as measured by the Nikkei 100 Index, has been trading between 13,000 *yen* and 20,000 *yen* for the past eight years. This is a typical stock market reaction to an economy that is in a severe recession. The point is, if Mr. Samori buys Japanese stocks, he is essentially boarding a train that is going in circles. Not very appealing for a long-term investor saving for retirement.

Mr. Samori could also buy Japanese short-term Treasury bills. Guaranteed safety of principal and steady cash flow, with only a small blip should Japanese interest rates rise. On the surface it seems like a reasonable alternative to a Japanese stock market going nowhere. The problem is the rate of return. Japanese short-term Treasury bills are also going nowhere, yielding about 0.50% per annum. Using our rule of 72, that means Mr. Samori will double his initial investment about every 140 years, give or take a decade. Again, not a very appealing alternative for someone who is investing for retirement.

Mr. Samori is caught in an investment trap. For Mr. Samori to retire comfortably, he needs to save more because he is simply not earning enough of a return on the money he has already set aside. Mr. Samori is typical of the average Japanese investor, which explains why the savings rate in Japan has been rising. Today, average Japanese workers who historically have put aside 10% to 15% of their income are now socking away upwards of 23% of their income.

A savings rate that high will have a long-term impact on the Japanese economy. If Japanese are saving, they are not spending. If Japanese consumers are not spending, then you are missing one of the key ingredients in any economic turnaround. The domino effect continues, with a stock market going nowhere, interest rates hovering just above zero, and an economy continuing to reel from the effects of dis-inflation.

Well so much for the economics lesson. What is Mr. Samori to do? The answer is to invest abroad, outside the Japanese economy, where he can achieve some global diversification.

But where to invest? Mr. Samori will look for markets where there is a higher rate of return and a strong domestic currency. Any place come to mind?

Mr. Samori can purchase U.S. government Treasury bills which, at the time of writing, yielded more than 5% per annum; at least 10 times the return he can get from investing in Japanese government bonds. His retirement portfolio will double about every 14 years instead of every 140 years. This is a powerful inducement to invest in the United States, especially when you add to that the performance of the U.S. dollar relative to the Japanese *yen*.

If you were in the Canadian investment business, what would you offer Mr. Samori as a low-risk alternative to U.S. Treasury bills? The answer is Government of Canada Treasury bills. But Government of Canada Treasury bills are only yielding 4%, at least a full percentage point less than similar U.S. government Treasury bills. If you were in Mr. Samori's shoes and were looking for a low-risk investment alternative, where would you invest? Like Mr. Samori, probably in the highest quality security in the world, U.S. Treasury bills. Hence our definition of flight to quality.

There are literally hundreds of thousands of investors like Mr. Samori, from all parts of world. All have the same concerns, some more pressing than others, especially in lesser developed countries that have devalued their currencies, namely South Korea, Indonesia, the Philippines, Thailand, and most recently, Russia.

This flight to quality into the U.S. means that investors are buying U.S. dollars and selling their domestic currencies. The impact of this buying and selling raises the value of the U.S. dollar against almost all the world's currencies. And since more investors are buying into the U.S. than are buying into Canada, our loonie weakens against the U.S. dollar, and at a time when the loonie has actually done reasonably well against most Asian currencies. If we can attract more of these investors to Canada, that will help strengthen the loonie vis-à-vis the U.S. dollar. U.S. rates will have to fall!

The problem, of course, is that higher interest rates can slow down the domestic economy, at a time when the Canadian economy is already slowing because of low commodity prices. If you simply raise interest rates and take no further action, it may do very little to help the loonie longer term. If higher interest rates help the loonie short term but slow down the Canadian economy in the process, then over time investors will flee Canada — thus lowering the value of the loonie — because the investment climate is not appealing. It is a difficult situation to be sure. Damned if you do raises rates, damned if you don't raise rates.

To stand toe to toe with the rest of the world, the Canadian government would have to take some unprecedented steps. Along with higher interest rates, there would also need to be significant tax cuts. The government has moved on the interest rate front, so let's see if they give us some tax relief in the next federal budget.

Depending on how well the loonie performs — which is a wild card — we think Canadian interest rates will most likely remain in a narrow range, say no more than 1% higher than current rates, and no more than 50 basis points (0.50%) lower than current rates.

Figure 13.3: CANADIAN YIELD CURVE (SEPTEMBER 1998)

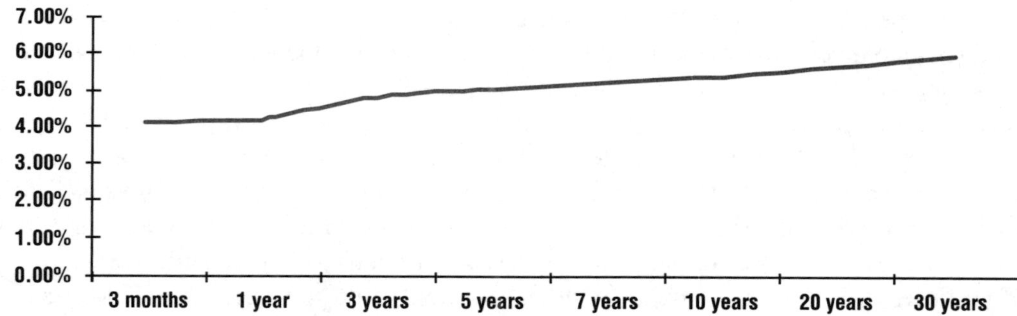

Table 13.1 looks at the current interest rate environment, as well as our range in which we would expect rates to remain until the end of 1999.

Table 13.1: FORECAST OF INTEREST RATE YIELDS

Term	Current Yield	Low	High
3 months	4.00%	3.20%	4.50%
1 year	4.10%	3.60%	5.10%
3 years	4.70%	4.20%	5.70%
5 years	4.90%	4.40%	5.90%
7 years	5.10%	4.60%	6.10%
10 years	5.25%	4.75%	6.25%
20 years	5.50%	5.00%	6.30%
30 years	5.80%	5.20%	6.60%

Based on these assumptions, we would steer clear of bond and mortgage funds for performance-oriented accounts. Of course, for the more conservative investor, we see the bond and mortgage fund as a defensive component within the portfolio, and, therefore, something the conservative investor should have.

The other alternative for the lower risk component of your portfolio is dividend funds. These are funds that invest in blue-chip dividend-paying Canadian common and preferred shares. We'll talk about how you might use dividend funds a little later in this chapter.

The year that is ...

At the time of writing, the most befitting symbol for the average investor was the Russian BEAR. Investors were bitten by that bear on August 31, 1998. This date saw the end of one of the longest running bull markets in history.

There is no doubt that the bull will return again, and perhaps sooner than we think. But for now, the footprints of the bear are all over the world financial markets, and we believe investors should maintain a defensive stance over the coming year.

We'd like to blame Russia for our current state of affairs. It is an easy target, and quite symbolic, what with the bear and all. But in reality, there has been a marked change in investor sentiment, and not simply because of Russia.

In the past we have likened the stock market to a four-legged chair. When all four legs are firmly planted, the market will rise. Indeed, a bull market can sustain itself on three firmly planted legs. But, on two legs, the chair falls. A bear trend takes precedence.

The four legs that we speak of are (1), the inherent bullish bias of the economy, (2) interest rates, (3) the outlook for corporate earnings, and (4) sentiment.

Over the long term, because the stock market represents investors' stake in the economy, values will rise. History supports that position, and to believe otherwise assumes, by definition, that the economy itself will not grow. To be sure, there are periods when stock values increase more rapidly and with greater intensity than others, just as there are shorter term periods when stock values will fall. Over long periods, however, history proves that markets rise. Hence the inherent bullish bias is a given.

Interest rates in our mind are also a given. For some time we have suggested that interest rates are too high, particularly in the U.S. And whether we like it or not, interest rates in the U.S. set the tone for interest rates around the world.

Figure 13.1 shows the U.S. yield curve. The graph tells us that the market believes that U.S. short-term interest rates are too high and must come down. Today, the rate paid on 30-year U.S. government bonds is just slightly below the rate paid on U.S. Treasury bills. The yield on U.S. government bonds is determined by market forces. The yield on short-term U.S. government Treasury bills is determined, for the most part, by the U.S. Federal Reserve. We believe the U.S. Federal Reserve will eventually lower rates at the short end of the U.S. yield curve, probably to the point where U.S. Treasury bills yield 4.0% to 4.5%. Based on that cursory analysis, we believe that the interest rate leg remains firmly planted.

Earnings, or more importantly, the expectation for future earnings, determine the speed and intensity of the stock market. This leg has been severely sawn off in recent months. This is partly due to the slowdown in Asia, which weakens demand for U.S. exports. It is also partly due to the strong U.S. dollar, which makes it more difficult for U.S. companies to compete at home. The strong U.S. dollar also directly impacts the performance of U.S. companies who derive their earnings offshore and must translate those offshore earnings back into U.S. dollars. Given these impediments, it is hard to imagine how U.S. corporate earnings can meet the lofty expectations that are still priced into the U.S. equity markets.

Our Canadian stock market has suffered a more severe correction than has the U.S. equity market. And much of that stems from perception. The world, rightly or wrongly, views Canada as a commodity-based economy. Commodity prices like oil, gold and base metals are at or near historic lows. There is very little room to raise prices in the foreseeable future.

The fourth leg is market sentiment, which some analysts refer to as momentum. Whatever the name, it comes down to whether investors see earnings and interest rates as a glass half full, or one half empty. At this point, the half empty analogy has taken center stage.

To be sure, sentiment can change quickly. We note with interest, that at the end of July 1998, the financial markets were awash in bullish overtones. At the end of July, investors were almost giddy, looking at every new hot spot in the world, as an ember to add spark to the bullish engine. They no longer see hot spots with such tainted eyes. Sentiment can again change quickly, but without earnings supporting the market, we are hard pressed to see how North American equity markets can rise dramatically over the foreseeable future.

More likely we will see prices trade in a wide range say between a low of 7,000 and a high of 10,000 on the Dow. On the TSE 300, this is between a low of 5,000 and a high of 7,500.

We are giving this market a much wider girth than normal, because there remains some very positive demographics underpinning the North American and European economies — specifically the baby boomers and their retirement savings plans. Baby boomers must save for their retirement, and there are really no viable long-term alternatives to the stock market. So money continues to flow into savings and investments, and much of that flows into equity markets via mutual funds, which could help bolster the markets through a very turbulent winter.

What Now?

Knowing where we are is one piece of the puzzle. The real question is what to do now. Or more specifically, how do we make money in a bear market?

We begin with what we know. In the current market environment, we know that the Canadian stock market has corrected more than 29% from its high. Anything over 20% defines a bear market (see Figure 13.4).

The U.S. market as measured by the Dow Industrial Average or the S&P 500 Composite Index had corrected—at the time of writing—more than 19% from its 52-week high. This is not quite enough to qualify as an official bear market. For this to be officially designated a bear market, we will have to see the Dow Industrial Average close below 7,450 and the S&P 500 Composite Index to close below 952. At the time of writing, both indexes were just slightly above those levels. But really, we're talking semantics. The S&P 500 Composite Index has broken through its 200-day moving average (see Figure 13.5).

Note that the index did not break its moving average during last October's mini-crash, or during the slide in mid-January of 1998. In both cases, the market bounced off the 200-day moving average and then resumed its upward trend. The 200-day moving average is considered by many technicians to be the definitive line to measure the trend. Based on the fact the S&P 500 breached the 200-day moving average before the sell-off at the end of August, we believe it is fair to say that the bear has come out from hibernation and is currently dominating the U.S. equity markets.

Figure 13.4: TSE 300 COMPOSITE INDEX + 200-DAY MOVING AVERAGE (1 YEAR)

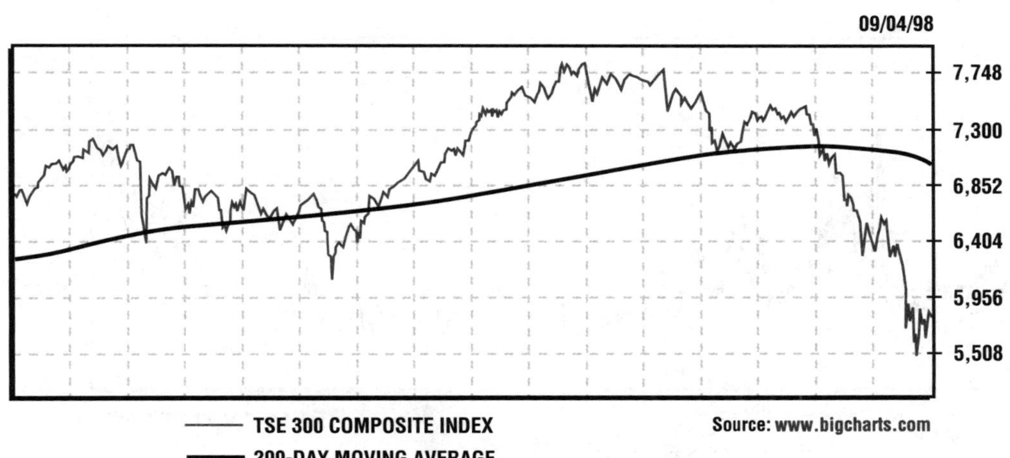

Figure 13.5: S&P 500 COMPOSITE INDEX + 200 DAY MOVING AVERAGE (1 YEAR)

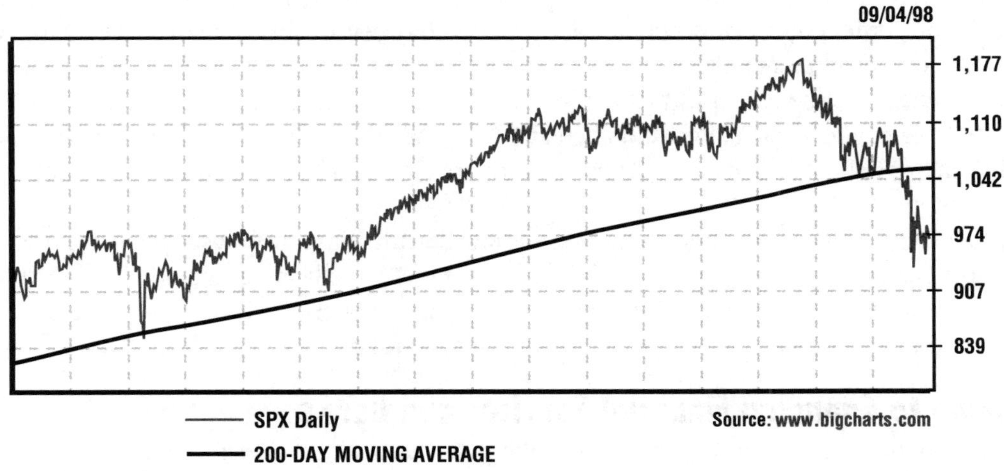

We know that there is a great deal of uncertainty in the markets, which means much higher risk than is normal. We note for example, that option premiums were very high in August and during September. The Volatility Index (symbol VIX) was trading at 44.6%. The 50-day moving average for the VIX (the smooth line on the chart) is at 26%. That tells us that option premiums are 1.7 times normal levels (see Figure 13.6).

One of the main factors that goes into pricing an option is volatility. Volatility is how the financial markets quantify risk. Simply stated, when option premiums are high, traders believe that the risks in the market are also high.

Figure 13.6: CBOE VOLATILITY INDEX + 50-DAY MOVING AVERAGE (1 YEAR)

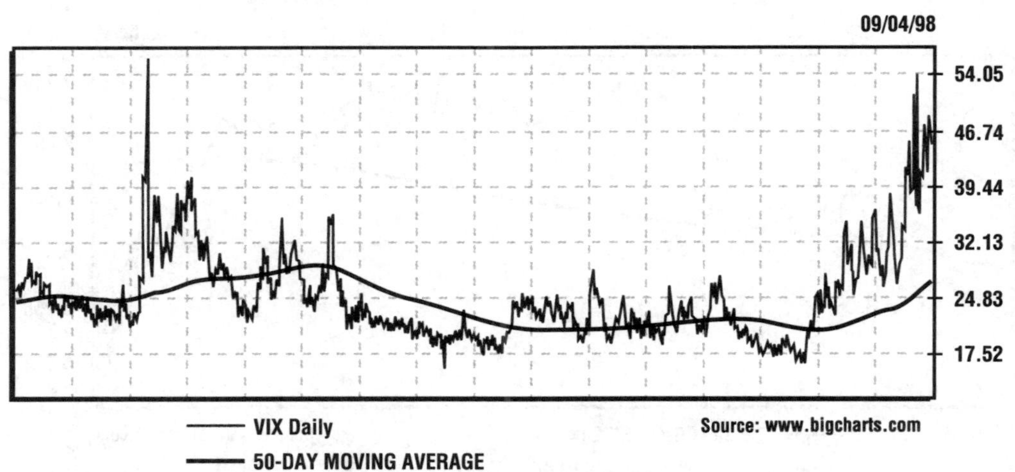

We know that inflation is dormant. In fact, deflation may have more of an impact on financial markets going forward. In this environment, interest rates will remain low, which makes it difficult to find reasonable long-term alternatives to the equity markets.

Here's what we don't know: When will this bear market end? How much further will the North American equity markets fall? Unless you are particularly adept at market timing and have a short-term point of view with lots of capital to risk, we're not going to be trying to pick tops and bottoms in this market.

Experience has also taught us that decisions made in a bear market almost always look bad two weeks later, and almost always look great 18 months to two years down the road. This tells us that any decision we make will focus on some specific point in the future—preferably the distant future.

One thing we can do to fine-tune our mutual fund portfolio is to look at sectors in the market that have been particularly hard hit, meaning sectors that have been driven down by extreme investor sentiment. We can put a small amount of money to work in those sectors, in order to provide some real oomph to the bottom line of your portfolio.

Looking to Canadian Financial Services and Banks

As a case in point, consider the Canadian banking sector. Banks stocks have been taken down *hard* (see Figure 13.7), because traders are concerned about the potential for losses due to excess credit being extended to Russia. And if that weren't enough, there was also concern about potential trading losses from the banks' brokerage subsidiaries — losses from playing Russian roulette on the Russian stock market. We think the market has overestimated those potential losses.

Figure 13.7: TORONTO FINANCIAL SERVICES + 200-DAY MOVING AVERAGE (1 YEAR)

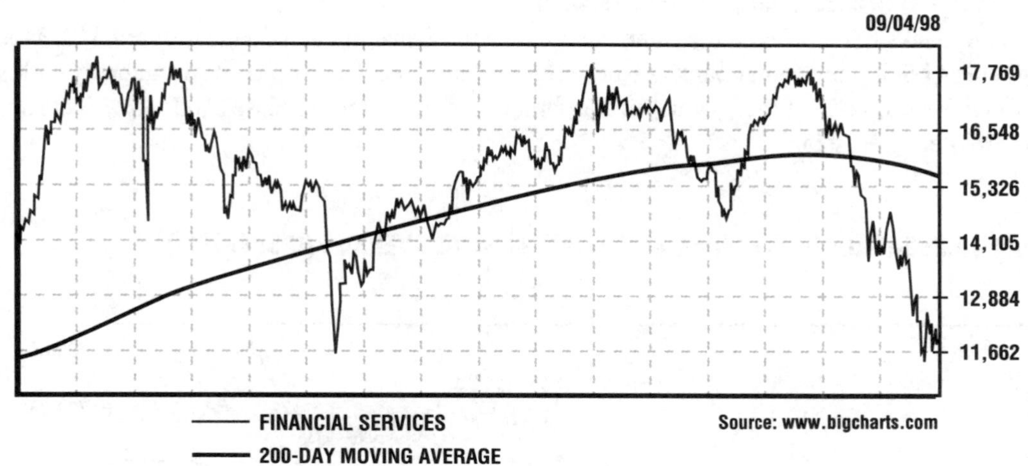

For example, the Bank of Nova Scotia (symbol BNS) had a market cap of $21.9 billion in April 1998. By September 1998, the market cap of BNS was $12.9 billion. Are we to believe that BNS had 40% of its assets at risk in Russia? Obviously, I'm using BNS as an example, but what I am suggesting here applies equally to any of the big five Canadian banks (see Table 13.2).

Table 13.2: BANK STOCK YIELDS

Bank Stock	Symbol	Friday's Close	Dividend	Yield
Bank of Nova Scotia	BNS	$25.90	$0.80	3.09%
Bank of Montreal	BMO	55.10	1.75	3.19%
Canadian Imperial Bank of Commerce	CM	30.75	1.20	3.90%
Royal Bank of Canada	RY	60.45	1.84	3.04%
Toronto Dominion Bank	TD	40.45	1.36	3.36%

At the end of August, BNS had earned $3.02 per share or $1.484 billion over the previous four quarters. Note we said earned, not expected to earn. That means that at the beginning of September, BNS was trading at 8.73 times last year's earnings. BNS pays out a dividend of 80 cents per share, or about 25% of what it makes. Can we all agree for the moment that BNS — as with all the other big five Canadian banks — will be able to maintain its dividend at current levels? If we can agree to that, BNS has a current dividend yield of 3.13% per annum. Do you know of any money market funds earning that much year over year?

Learning from the U.S. Bank Model

The U.S. banks have suffered the same fate as have the Canadian banks (see Figure 13.8). Most of the big U.S. money center banks — i.e., Chase Manhattan, Citicorp, J. P. Morgan etc. — lost between 30% to 40% of their value for the same reasons — trading losses and loan loss provisions related to Russia.

Figure 13.8: S&P BANKING INDEX + 200-DAY MOVING AVERAGE (U.S. BANKS)

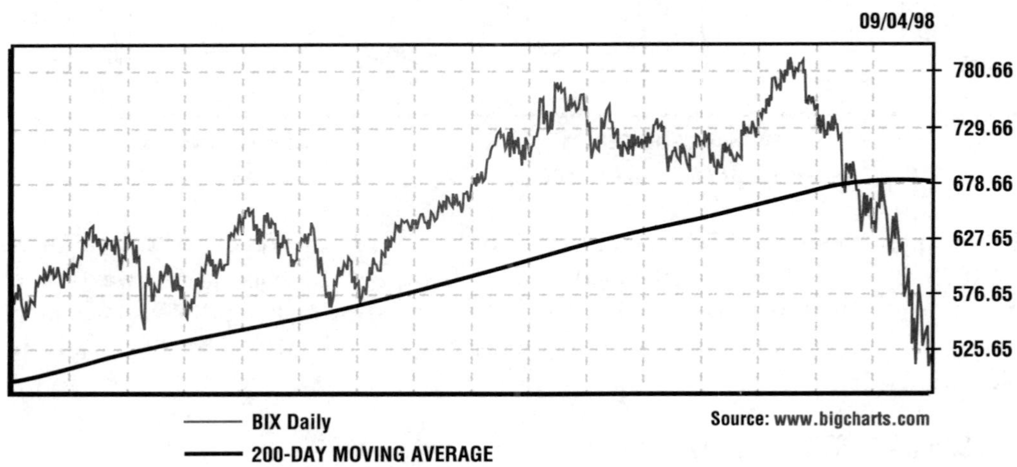

The difference is that U.S. banks have already come clean. In the case of Citicorp, for example, losses from Russia will reduce the next quarter's earnings by approximately U.S. $350 million. That's on a company that earns about U.S. $1 billion per quarter. In other words, instead of earning U.S. $1 billion next quarter, Citicorp will earn U.S. $650 million.

Now think about those numbers for the year. We are saying that Russia will have less than a 10% impact on the year-over-year earnings of Citicorp. Yet the market reduced the value of the stock by four times that amount. Based on the percentage of total earnings, the net impact will be similar for both Chase Manhattan and J.P. Morgan.

We don't believe that the Canadian banks have any more exposure to Russia than do the U.S. money center banks. So let's assume a worst-case scenario, that Canadian banks will have to set aside 10% of next year's earnings as a loan loss provision. And further, let's assume that BNS earnings don't grow next year. So instead of earning $1.484 billion, BNS earns $1.335 billion or $2.71 per share. At current prices, the stock is trading at less than 10 times next year's reduced earnings estimate. Think maybe the market has taken more than a pound of flesh from the financial services sector? We do!

This analysis has a couple of implications for mutual fund investors. Dividend funds that invest heavily in bank stocks will likely do quite well next year (see The Dividend Fund

Alternative). So, too, should Canadian equity funds that are overweighted in the financial services and banking sector.

The Dividend Fund Alternative

Looking for a secure place for your investment dollars? Something that promises a better return than, say, Canadian bond or mortgage funds? Throw in some tax advantages, and what more could the average investor ask for.

Indeed that was the promise from Canadian dividend funds that invested in blue-chip preferred shares. The index funds promised a slightly higher yield than government bonds before tax. Ramp up the return with the dividend tax credit, and dividend funds took off as the conservative investment of choice through most of the 1990s.

Dividend funds became so popular that some fund companies had to begin capping their funds, which is something no fund company likes to do. The problem was really quite simple. The portfolio managers were getting all kinds of new money to invest, but they couldn't find good quality Canadian preferred shares to buy.

With low interest rates, Canadian companies began to issue new bonds rather than preferred shares. It was simply a more cost effective way to raise capital. So dividend funds went about chasing a few good preferred stocks, and in the process pushed the price of preferred stocks above what they were worth on any rational basis.

When there is a shortage of a particular commodity, mutual fund companies often change the investment philosophy of their funds to meet the current needs of the market. Many of the so-called dividend funds changed their name to dividend growth funds, which allowed the portfolio managers to seek out dividend-paying common stocks to help augment the performance of the portfolio.

Now common stocks are riskier than preferred stocks, meaning that the dividend fund — or the renamed dividend growth fund — would likely move up and down more dramatically over the course of a business cycle. But, since there was an abundance of good quality blue-chip common stocks that paid decent dividends, that was an acceptable risk for investors looking for alternatives to bond and mortgage fund.

The most popular sector in which dividend funds began to invest was financial services and banking. In the early to mid 1990s, dividend funds began to roll. Not only were they able to distribute regular dividends, but because of the growth in the financial services sector, dividend funds became some of the hottest performing funds. Double-digit returns became the norm. This was quite an about-face for a group of funds that sold themselves as conservatively managed alternatives to bond and mortgage funds.

Then came the inevitable market correction. As the Canadian stock market tumbled, bank stocks were particularly hard hit (see section "Looking to Canadian Financial Services and Banks"). And by extension, so too were those conservatively managed dividend/dividend growth funds. Conservative investors learned first-hand the cost of growth.

But now that the banks and financial companies have taken their lumps, and so dividend funds are no longer the darlings of Bay Street. Perhaps it's time to take a second look at this sector as a conservatively managed fund going forward.

Here's the way we see it. If you believe as we do that the worst may be over for the Canadian banking sector, then you have to like the longer term prospects for dividend funds.

Based on the information presented here, we have included a list of dividend funds along with the current percentage of their portfolio in the Canadian financial services sector. In Table 13.3 we show nine dividend funds with the highest concentration of financial services. The MER column is the management-expense ratio, which tells us how expensive the fund is to operate.

The table is broken down into percentages of the overall portfolio for cash, Canadian equity, preferred equity and financial services. We felt it was important to break down the percentage of the fund in Canadian equity versus preferred shares, so that we can get an idea of what percentage of the portfolio is actually invested in the common stock of Canadian financial service companies. For example, the Standard Life Canadian Dividend Fund has no preferred shares, which means that the 44.9% of the fund is invested in the common shares of financial-service companies. We would expect this fund to provide unit holders with the biggest bang for this investment dollar, if you accept our view that Canadian financial-service stocks, and Canadian bank stocks, are really oversold.

Table 13.3: CANADIAN DIVIDEND FUNDS WITH EXPOSURE TO FINANCIAL SERVICES

Fund Name	MER	MVA Index	% Cash	% Canadian Equity	% Preferred Equity	% Financial Services
Standard Life Canadian Dividend	1.50%	122.00	8.8%	91.4%	0.0%	44.9%
Royal Dividend	1.77%	117.70	4.7%	78.1%	6.2%	35.7%
Green Line Dividend	2.00%	110.40	1.6%	91.7%	5.0%	31.6%
PH&N Dividend Income	1.21%	126.70	8.4%	90.6%	0.3%	30.8%
Altamira Dividend	1.56%	116.60	1.2%	58.8%	37.7%	28.7%
Northwest Dividend	1.75%	121.10	2.1%	64.8%	8.7%	27.4%
Investors Dividend	2.37%	116.80	16.7%	51.2%	15.7%	25.2%
MAXXUM Dividend	1.73%	114.90	1.6%	85.5%	6.0%	25.2%
First Canadian Dividend Income	1.66%	121.00	8.5%	88.3%	0.7%	24.3%

Source: Pal-Trak

The U.S. Markets

Year 2000, Y2K, the millennium bug. Whatever you choose to call it, the date stamp problem with the world's computer systems will be on the minds of investors throughout 1999. We believe the Year 2000 problem will create uncertainty, which will impact the world's financial markets—including, we think, the U.S. stock market.

We're not here to suggest that the problem will be catastrophic. In fact, when the millennium clock strikes 12 midnight, the bug may turn out to be a non-event. That's a best-case scenario, mind you. And not the most likely scenario. The worst-case scenario would see the world come to a stop. That, too, is not likely. Look for something in the middle.

Unfortunately, we will not know the true extent of the problem until we reach the Year 2000. And the real concern we have is the uncertainty around the event. Financial markets do not like uncertainty, and that will play on the minds of investors throughout most of 1999, but certainly by the third quarter of 1999.

We see the Year 2000 question mark as another problem on top of the Asian situation, on top of the infrastructure problems within Russia, and what will likely be weakness in Latin America. All of which supports our conservative stance on the markets in 1999. It may be the first real opportunity for investors to experience what it is like to be in a bear market.

Now a bear market need not strike fear in your heart, especially if you are what you say you are—a long-term investor. In fact, for the long-term investor, bear markets are actually healthy. They help to shake out the weaker investors who cannot handle the risks associated with equity investments, and in the process build a base on which stocks can make their next major move to the upside, when the bull re-emerges.

We define a bear market as one in which stock prices fall at least 20% from their highs. Consider, for example, the Standard & Poor's 500 Composite Index. As we have already pointed out, the U.S. equity market had, at the time of writing, fallen more than 19% from its high. Not quite enough to be characterized as a bear market.

Mind you, the 20% demarcation line is the traditional definition of a bear market. We think a bear market has already taken hold. We say this given the way the performance of the major indexes has been distorted in recent years, particularly in terms of the performance of large-cap stocks versus small- to mid-cap stocks. The fact is, the performance of the S&P 500 Composite Index has been driven almost entirely by the big-name companies.

When the S&P was at its peak, more than half the gains could be traced to the 50 largest companies in the index, which means that 450 companies in the S&P 500 Composite Index have averaged about half the returns of the big names.

A similar and even more glaring distortion could be seen in the U.S. over-the-counter market. Do you remember when the NASDAQ composite index crossed the 2,000 plateau for the first time in history? Almost 70% of the NASDAQ composite's performance numbers could be traced to the 100 largest companies represented in that index (there are about 2,000 companies in the index)—companies like Dell Computer, Microsoft and Cisco Systems.

Need more convincing? Look at the Russell 2000 Index, one of the best proxies for small to mid-size U.S. companies. It has lagged badly in the performance parade. At the height of the market, when the S&P was up more than 22.2% on the year, when the NASDAQ 100 index was up more than 46% on the year, the Russell 2000 Index was able to only muster a 6.1% year-to-date return. The bear market was here; we just weren't able to see it. The market doesn't like to see divergences. And the market marked its disapproval on August 31, 1998.

If you buy into our position that we are in a bear market, then we need to define what to look for as we move forward. Bear markets don't automatically mean sharply lower stock prices. In effect, what happens is that the value of a stock relative to its earnings begins to shrink.

For example, if XYZ is trading at $100 per share and XYZ earns $4.00 per share annually, then XYZ is said to be trading at 25 times earnings ($100 per share divided by $4.00 per share in earnings equals 25 times earnings). We refer to this calculation as the stock price to earnings multiple (P/E).

A stock's P/E will normally expand in a bull market and contract in a bear market. That P/E contraction can take place in one of two ways. The stock price can decline while the earnings remain the same. For example, if XYZ is trading at $80 per share but still earns $4.00 per share, the P/E multiple for XYZ has contracted from 25 to 20.

The P/E multiple can also contract if the earnings continue to rise but the stock price remains flat. For example, if XYZ remains at $100 per share, but the earnings come in at $5.00 per share, than the P/E multiple has also contracted from 25 to 20.

These are important distinctions for investors to contemplate. What we are saying is that the stock market could actually move sideways as long as earnings are rising. And that would still meet Croft and Kirzner's definition of a bear market. The point is, stock prices don't automatically collapse simply because we are in a bear market. And since the real fear investors face is that stock prices will collapse and the value of their portfolio will decline significantly, we need to reinforce the view that one needs to always maintain a long-term perspective and never get caught up in the news of the moment.

We see the U.S. market from two perspectives. On the one hand, there is genuine concern that U.S. corporate profits will not meet expectations because of the slowdown in Asia and the effect the slowdown is having on the rest of the world. That has the potential to cause U.S. stock prices to decline.

On the other hand, we think there will continue to be a flight to quality into U.S.-denominated assets by investors making the best of a bad situation. And the U.S. market is still the best and biggest game in town. That capital inflow should help support U.S. stock prices.

Keeping with the capital inflow position, we need to also focus on the long-term demographics. There is still a vast pool of capital that is sitting on the sidelines waiting to be invested. That pool should grow substantially over the next decade as more baby boomers near retirement. The point is, these investors need to invest somewhere. And for most of those investors, a 5.3% yield, which is the current yield on long-term U.S. government bonds, or 5.8% on long-term Government of Canada bonds, just doesn't provide sufficient returns to meet those long-term retirement goals.

So from the North American perspective, we are taking a more conservative stance in 1999 by reducing our equity exposure and buying into assets that we believe will help investors cope with volatile markets.

The Global View

Economic and Market Contagion

Markets opened generally strong in 1998. However, a series of aftershocks from the 1997 "Asian Flu" and new quakes stemming from problems in Russia and Latin America sent markets reeling. By late August, world stock markets were under severe pressure and most markets had lost considerable ground on the year to date.

The economic and political events leading up the current problems started in Thailand in June 1997 when the Thai currency collapsed. The smaller Southeast Asia countries were each hit one by one as each of their currencies in turn came under pressure due to their own escalating deficits and weakening economies.

The problems then spread to the stronger countries in the region, engulfing two of the economic powers—South Korea and Taiwan. Then the currency problems struck Hong Kong in late October, and the Hong Kong stock market lost over 10% in one single-day plunge on October 23. Events spilled over into Europe and North America in a domino effect—and the term "Asian Flu" was coined.

The "Asian Flu" is another one of the market cascades that occur from time to time after strong market run-ups or bubbles. There have been a number of examples in recent years. These include:

- On October 19, 1987, we witnessed the largest single-day market crash in history (in points but not percent) when major markets were led down by the resounding 22% break in New York on Black Monday. Most of the 500-point-plus slide in 1987 was attributed to market rather than economic forces as "program trading," the antiquated floor-based manual trading system and even the New York Stock Exchange "Specialists" system, were variously fingered as the culprits.
- In early December, 1994, the Mexican *peso* was under pressure from a number of forces including a sharply escalating current account deficit. By early January 1995, the currency had depreciated by over 45% and a financial crisis was in full bloom. The problems spread to other Latin America countries, and then to emerging countries, all of which experienced significant market breaks.
- The latest market crisis struck the week of August 23, 1998. The Russian *ruble* virtually collapsed, plunging world stock and currency markets into disarray. None of the world's major markets were immune from the selling onslaught as investors bailed out of stocks and bonds (except U.S. bonds.) Investors searching for a haven for their money have shunned the Canadian dollar and the currencies of other resource-based economies.

Contagion

Why would the collapse of the Russian economy affect countries that do not trade with Russia and aren't in any way dependent on the Russian economy? Infection can occur in two ways — through direct real events in real markets and through events in financial markets.

Russia is a major importer of basic commodities, and its financial woes probably mean a reduction in commodity purchases with its resulting effect on already depressed commodity prices. Furthermore, concerns of defaults on Russia on U.S. and European debt cause risk premiums for risky debt to rise in a domino-like financial effect. A previous example was the events surrounding the 1982 recession which was brought on by an emerging country, world-debt crisis.

The 1999 Global Outlook

Overall world growth is likely to shrink to about 2.2% in 1999 from the healthy 4.0% level reached in 1997. We believe the global bull market, which started in October 1990 (in the midst of the Persian Gulf Crisis), has finally come to an end. Global asset class returns are likely to be modest in 1999.

Despite the less than stellar outlook for markets, we strongly urge that you build and keep a diversified portfolio. Pick a good asset allocation (such as a 20%/30%/50% cash /bonds/equity) and then select suitable investments or funds to satisfy your program. Diversification works as countervailing forces reduce the overall volatility of your portfolio, letting you sleep better at night. While stocks were plunging during the August "Volga Virus," long-term U.S. government bond prices were rising as were money market fund yields.

Change your asset allocation mix when your life style or cycle is changing (retirement is drawing closer; your employment situation has changed) or when your risk tolerance changes.

Similarly, the rewards of global investing consist of striking a good portfolio balance. A large portion of the variance in overall stock prices is due to the unique risk of each country and can therefore be diversified away in a security portfolio. Nevertheless, on the global front, changing world patterns cannot be ignored and some rotation is essential.

Our advice is to focus on the long term and stay globally diversified. Our general principles are twofold: global investing should represent about 10% to 30% of your portfolio holdings; and your strategy must be long term. The biggest danger for investors is what is called "Gambler's Ruin," or being right in the long term but losing out because you sold in the short term due to undercapitalization or fear.

Overall, we expect equity markets to show increased volatility and nervousness and that 1999 will not be a great year. Nevertheless, long-term investors should maintain an appropriate global mix in their portfolio. Our recommended global—that is, non-North American—mix for 1999 is shown at the end of this chapter as part of our model portfolios.

The Asia Pacific/Far East Outlook

The Asia Pacific/Far East region remained weak in 1998 in the wake of the devastating 1997 Asian Flu. The area was, and is, marked by recessions, most notably in Japan, Malaysia, Thailand and South Korea. The most likely scenario is that the "Asian Flu" recession could last well into the year 2001.

Furthermore, many Asian governments are intervening in their own domestic stock markets—a very dangerous sign!

The history of this region is one of volatility, spectacular returns some years and dramatic losses in others. But given its low correlation with North American markets, we nevertheless suggest a permanent, albeit modest, Asia Pacific/Far East allocation for your portfolio.

Japan

Japan's economy has been in a recession throughout the 1990s and the Tokyo market has stagnated as the country has suffered through its worst downturn since World War Two. Unemployment, at about 4.3%, is running at a record rate and most economic indicators continue to show that the recession remains in force — possibly even deepening. Real GDP growth turned negative in the fourth quarter of 1997 and overall the economy should retract in 1998. Japanese authorities were predicting zero growth for the fiscal year ended March 1999; however, in the wake of the Russian *ruble* crisis, the result is likely to be worse.

Japan's Ministry of Finance, in conjunction with the Bank of Japan, has launched a series of economic initiatives over the past four years designed to stimulate the economy and help keep interest rates down. The problem is that the low interest rate policy designed to bolster the U.S. dollar, keep the *yen* weak and stimulate exports, has sent domestic capital abroad. The Japanese banks lost business on both sides of the balance sheet when their loans to Asian countries started to sour. Corporate bankruptcies were at a record level in 1998.

In late August, the cabinet approved another broad financial plan aimed at the weak financial sector and in restructuring the crippled banking system. Personal spending has been declining as well, and spending initiatives and tax cuts are planned to stimulate the weak household sector.

Japan's economy is still the key to world health. It is the world's largest creditor in terms of foreign currency reserves and personal savings. Despite this, Japan was placed on credit watch review by Moody's Investor service in late July 1998.

The Outlook for Europe

The outlook for Europe is mixed as countries react to differently forces, ranging from currency unification in the European Community to restructuring in central Europe and the fallout from the Volga Virus. European growth is likely to level out at about 2.5% to 2.7% in 1999. Overall, we have a relatively high weighting to Europe.

The members of the European Community have now agreed on the long-awaited economic and monetary union, which will include 11 of the 15 EC countries. These countries are Austria, Belgium, Finland, France, Germany, Ireland, Italy, Luxembourg, Netherlands, Portugal and Spain. Greece does not meet the entry conditions at present, and Britain, Denmark and Sweden have temporarily opted out. Countries such as Italy and Portugal, that as recently as two years ago appeared to have no chance of meeting the stringent fiscal and monetary entry conditions set out in the Maastricht agreement in 1992, tightened their economic policies and have made the cut.

The focal point to European economic confederation is the unified currency. The *Euro* officially came into existence in May 1998 as a notional currency fixing the exchange rates of the 11 participating EU members. By January 1, 1999, the *Euro* will be used in actual transactions. The transition to the *Euro* replacing all existing European currencies is forecast to take three years. By 2002, all EC national currencies should disappear.

The benefits associated with a single currency and fixed exchange rates are enormous. Prices for identical goods sold in different European countries will be comparable since all products will be priced in *Euro* dollars. European and multinational firms transacting in different European currencies will no longer have to engage in hedging transactions to manage foreign-exchange risk. It is likely that the *Euro* will rival the U.S. dollar in importance in global markets.

Currency unification will pose challenges for some of the weaker countries since they will lose the flexibility of depreciating their currencies to deal with economic crises. Furthermore, there are no provisions for what happens to countries that cannot maintain economic integrity in the Union. But, despite these uncertainties and the wrangling over issues such as how the current central banks will integrate with the unified European central bank, the new European community will be a mighty force and could emerge as the most powerful economic unified entity in the world, with approximately 30% of world output based on current conditions. Most European countries are in the midst of a North American-style restructuring and reengineering program that has led to tighter and more profitable corporations. The takeover parade has bolstered returns as well.

Not everyone is buoyant about Europe's prospects. John Kenneth Galbraith, one of the world's best-known economists, believes the European bubble will soon burst and that we can anticipate higher interest rates in Europe when a unified central bank gets the house in order. Furthermore, Europe's, particularly Germany's, exposure to Russian loans is a cause for concern.

However, European economic growth, currently running at about 3% per annum, should remain healthy and steady. Interest rates should remain low, given the relatively high level of unemployment. We expect Europe to retain its healthy investment climate and recommend you maintain a permanent investment allocation in the region.

Germany remains the leader of the European community and should continue as such in the unified Europe. Growth is steady, inflation is well controlled and all economic indicators are healthy. Germany has benefited from lower energy and commodity prices. However, high unemployment remains the thorn in the side.

France, in particular, has regained its role as a world leading economy. The economy is growing at a rate of about 2.75% per annum and the rate inflation is among the lowest of the world's major industrialized countries. France's chronically high unemployment rate is showing some signs of abating. The weak *franc* has meant strong exports and a healthy current account surplus.

The Outlook for Latin America

Latin America usually reflects its own unique developments rather than the systematic pull of North America. The outlook at present is pessimistic. Commodity-based countries such as Mexico and Venezuela were hard hit by the commodity price declines and the Russian *ruble* crisis. For example, Latin America bonds plunged in the midst of the Russian crisis as risk premiums soared!

Latin America's problems started in 1997 when oil and copper prices, two major export staples of the region, started to plunge. Countries such as Mexico, Brazil, Chile and Venezuela all face similar currency problems. As borrowing costs start to escalate, reflecting both domestic inflation and escalating risk premiums, the pressure on the currency rises leading to devaluation pressures.

Mexico is the most representative country in the region. In Mexico, the economic reform program implemented in 1995 in the wake of the December 1994 currency crisis has been relatively successful. Confidence has been restored as investors have bought in to the plan and the Bolsa Mexicana de Volores. However, the Volga Virus has triggered yet another crisis in Mexico. Financial crises are not new to Mexico — in recent years they have come in six-year waves. (The *peso* had been devalued in 1976, 1982, 1988 and 1994!)

The good news is that employment is on the rise, real GDP is running at a relatively high rate and household spending is strong. However, inflation rates remain in the double-digits and the downward pressure on the *peso* in the wake of the Asian flu and Volga are likely to result in upward pressure on prices. Furthermore, interest rates are high and likely to stay there, reflecting both high domestic inflation rates and concerns about the *peso*. The floating-rate system introduced in 1995 after the 1994 devaluation has helped, but inflation is being imported. Devaluation of the currency, either voluntary or forced through depreciation, is possible.

Maintain only a small weighting to the Latin America region.

The FundLine Forecast Summary

Over the years we have stressed the role diversification plays in your mutual fund portfolio. And it bears—pardon the pun—repeating here. If you can build a mutual fund portfolio that is diversified by asset class, geographic region, fund objectives and management styles, you have done all you can do to protect a portfolio during turbulent times.

When we talk about asset classes, we are referring to equity funds, bond funds and money market funds (representing stock, bond and cash assets). Geographic region is defined as Canada, the U.S. and international investing.

When we talk about fund objectives, we are talking about where managers invest. In your bond fund, what is the maturity spectrum—short, medium or long term? In an equity fund, does the manager focus on small-, mid- or large-cap stocks? Is there a currency impact on your portfolio? A U.S. equity fund is invested in U.S. dollars, and when it is converted into Canadian dollars, this affects your portfolio, probably adding 5% to the performance numbers of the U.S. fund.

Finally, there is the style of the manager. Does the portfolio manager follow a value or momentum style? Does the manager buy stocks following a top-down philosophy? Or does the manager favor a bottom-up approach?

We are not coming down on one side or the other of the management debate. We are simply saying that the market rewards different styles of fund management at different points in the cycle. In the current downturn, value managers who were holding a substantial percentage of their portfolio in cash were big winners. During the first six months of this year, and most of last year, momentum managers were producing some of the biggest gains.

The problem for investors, is what to do when confronted with a correction, when torn between the bulls and the bears. And the answer, assuming you were properly diversified to begin with, is nothing. Stay the course, because the investmemnts that may look weak today may well be the big winners of tomorrow.

A Time for Reflection

A bear market provides an opportunity for you to reassess your goals and risk tolerances, a chance to review your fund's philosophy. For example, many of those equity managers who follow a value approach have been holding 20% to 25% of their portfolios in cash. And those managers did better during the August sell-off than the managers who had 90% to 95% of the fund's money invested in equities.

But remember why the equity manager was holding such massive amounts of cash in the first place—managers such as Johnathan Goodman of the Dynamic Fund (17.3% cash), and Jerry Javasky of the Ivy Canadian (33.9% cash), Ivy Enterprise (24.5% cash) and Ivy Growth and Income (27% cash) funds (all numbers were from Pal-Trak at the end of June 1998). These managers, and others like them, were holding cash in the hopes of buying good-quality stocks at lower prices.

Well, we now have lower prices, especially among Canadian stocks. Let's see how much of that cash gets invested over the next few weeks. If those same managers come out of this correction with the same cash levels they had going in, then where's the value added? Let's face it: Over the longer term, cash is the worst-performing asset. And if you are buying a Canadian equity fund and paying a 2.25% management-expense ratio, we think that fund ought to be invested longer term, in Canadian equities—not cash!

As for reassesing your goals and risk tolerances, a correction provides an opportunity for a gut check. Did the ups and downs of the market have you laying awake at night? Or was it simply a blip on a long-term radar screen? How you answer this question will go a long way towards helping you ascertain the right asset mix going forward. If this correction is a non-event, then you are where you should be. If it is a problem, then maybe you should add more bond and dividend funds, and reduce your equity holdings.

Safety — Score: <15

Equities			Fixed Income			Cash		
Min	Policy	Max	Min	Policy	Max	Min	Policy	Max
0%	10%	20%	60%	75%	90%	10%	15%	30%

	Non-RRSP	RRSP
Canadian Equity	2.5%	2.5%
U.S. Equity	4.0%	4.0%
International Equity	3.5%	3.5%
Special Equity	0.0%	0.0%
Total Equity Assets	**10.0%**	**10.0%**
Dividend Funds	10.0%	22.5%
Domestic Bond	20.0%	25.0%
Global Bond	30.0%	12.5%
Total Fixed Income Assets	**60.0%**	**60.0%**
Money Market	30.0%	30.0%
Total Cash Assets	**30.0%**	**30.0%**

Safety / Income — Score: 15–24

Equities			Fixed Income			Cash		
Min	Policy	Max	Min	Policy	Max	Min	Policy	Max
10%	20%	30%	50%	65%	80%	10%	15%	25%

	Non-RRSP	RRSP
Canadian Equity	2.5%	2.5%
U.S. Equity	5.0%	5.0%
International Equity	2.5%	2.5%
Special Equity	0.0%	0.0%
Total Equity Assets	**10.0%**	**10.0%**

Income / Growth — Score: 25–34

Equities			Fixed Income			Cash		
Min	**Policy**	**Max**	**Min**	**Policy**	**Max**	**Min**	**Policy**	**Max**
20%	**35%**	**50%**	**30%**	**50%**	**70%**	**10%**	**15%**	**25%**

	Non-RRSP	RRSP
Canadian Equity	5.0%	5.0%
U.S. Equity	10.0%	5.0%
International Equity	5.0%	5.0%
Special Equity	0.0%	0.0%
Total Equity Assets	**20.0%**	**20.0%**
Dividend Funds	15.0%	15.0%
Domestic Bond	15.0%	30.0%
Global Bond	25.0%	10.0%
Total Fixed Income Assets	**55.0%**	**55.0%**
Money Market	25.0%	25.0%
Total Cash Assets	**25.0%**	**25.0%**

Growth / Income — Score: 35–44

Equities			Fixed Income			Cash		
Min	**Policy**	**Max**	**Min**	**Policy**	**Max**	**Min**	**Policy**	**Max**
30%	**50%**	**70%**	**25%**	**40%**	**55%**	**5%**	**10%**	**15%**

	Non-RRSP	RRSP
Canadian Equity	5.0%	10.0%
U.S. Equity	10.0%	10.0%
International Equity	10.0%	5.0%
Special Equity	5.0%	5.0%
Total Equity Assets	**30.0%**	**30.0%**

Growth — Score: 45–54

Equities			Fixed Income			Cash		
Min	Policy	Max	Min	Policy	Max	Min	Policy	Max
40%	60%	80%	20%	30%	40%	5%	10%	15%

	Non-RRSP	RRSP
Canadian Equity	10.0%	15.0%
U.S. Equity	20.0%	10.0%
International Equity	15.0%	10.0%
Special Equity	0.0%	10.0%
Total Equity Assets	**45.0%**	**45.0%**
Dividend Funds	5.0%	15.0%
Domestic Bond	15.0%	25.0%
Global Bond	20.0%	0.0%
Total Fixed Income Assets	**40.0%**	**40.0%**
Money Market	15.0%	15.0%
Total Cash Assets	**15.0%**	**15.0%**

Aggressive / Growth — Score: >55

Equities			Fixed Income			Cash		
Min	Policy	Max	Min	Policy	Max	Min	Policy	Max
50%	75%	100%	0%	20%	30%	0%	5%	10%

	Non-RRSP	RRSP
Canadian Equity	10.0%	25.0%
U.S. Equity	25.0%	10.0%
International Equity	15.0%	10.0%
Special Equity	10.0%	15.0%
Total Equity Assets	**60.0%**	**60.0%**

PART IV

Building Your Own Mutual Fund Portfolio

CHAPTER FOURTEEN

Balancing Risk and Return

The Simple Case for Asset Allocation

Imagine a pie baked with 4 cups of flour and 10 pounds of sugar. Even those of us with a sweet tooth—something we have often been accused of—would find that a little rich! Unfortunately, we all too often find that investors are willing to mix their assets with the same regard for taste as was shown in our imaginary pie.

When portfolio managers talk about investments, they talk in terms of assets like equities, fixed income, cash, hedges, real estate, etc. If you own shares of the Altamira Equity Fund,[5] that would be considered an equity asset. Similarly, if you own shares in Northern Telecom, General Motors or IBM, these too would be considered equity assets. In short, then, equity assets are long on growth, can be quite volatile—more on that later— and, generally speaking, are not considered income-producing investments.

On the other hand, let's say you owned shares of the Dynamic Income Fund.[6] Since this fund invests in bonds and other fixed-income investments, it would be considered a fixed-income asset within our portfolio. Fixed-income assets produce income, generally have less risk and, at times, produce better-than-average capital gains.

In short, these so-called assets are the "ingredients" of your portfolio. Just as with our imaginary pie, and so with your portfolio: choosing the right recipe—or asset mix—is the most important decision you and your manager will make.

When we talk about asset mix, we are really focusing on the percentage of a portfolio represented by each class of investment. For example, a portfolio mix might look something like "40% equities, 50% fixed income and 10% cash."

---

[5] *Altamira Equity Fund is an open-ended mutual fund that, for the most part, invests in good quality Canadian stocks.*

[6] *The Dynamic Income Fund invests in short-, medium- and long-term bonds of Canadian governments (federal and provincial) as well as investment-grade Canadian corporate bonds and debentures.*

There is a reason for choosing that kind of description—and it's not because it's easier to say than "I'm holding $40,000 of the Altamira Equity Fund, 500 shares of General Motors, $50,000 in government bonds and $50,000 in GICs . . ." Managers describe portfolios in terms of asset mix because they understand the importance that asset mix decisions play on the portfolio's overall return.

Just how important? Studies have shown that 85% (some studies have suggested as much as 90%) of your overall return can be pegged to your asset mix decision, another 5% to 10% comes from market timing (i.e., shifting in and out of investments in response to economic changes), and the remaining 5% to 10% from selecting one specific security over another (i.e., buying IBM rather than General Motors, or Microsoft rather than Northern Telecom).

In other words, by determining what percentage of your portfolio is committed to fixed-income assets, what percentage to equity assets and what percentage to any other asset class, you have laid the basis for 85% of your total return.

To make the point, consider a hypothetical two-asset portfolio that includes equities (stocks) and fixed-income assets (bonds). We'll use the Toronto Stock Exchange (TSE) 300 Composite Total Return Index[7] to represent our equity assets, and the ScotiaMcLeod Bond Universe Total Return Index[8] to represent our fixed-income assets.

For the 10-year period between May 1986 and May 1996, the ScotiaMcLeod Bond Universe returned 10.7% compounded annually. A $10,000 investment, for example, in fixed-income assets went up 2.7 times over that 10-year period.

Now, over that same time frame, the TSE 300 Composite Total Return Index grew by 8.6% compounded annually. In other words, a $10,000 investment in an index representing Canadian stocks would have grown to just under $23,000 during that period.

Now, what we are going to do is to mix and match these two assets in a homegrown portfolio. Think of it as our version of investment taste testing. Based on Table 14.1, we'll examine a number of variations on this theme, hoping in the end to make the point about the importance of asset mix decisions.

---

[7] *The Toronto Stock Exchange 300 Composite Index measures the performance of 300 of Canada's largest companies. When we speak of total return, we are assuming that all the dividends received from those 300 companies are reinvested into the index, much like a dividend reinvestment program offered by many mutual funds.*

[8] *The ScotiaMcLeod Bond Universe Total Return Index assumes the investor purchased an equally weighted basket of Canadian government bonds (i.e., Government of Canada bonds that mature in 3 years or less, an equal percentage that mature in 5 to 10 years and another group of long-term bonds that mature in 20 years), and that all interest payments were reinvested into the index.*

Table 14.1: IMPACT OF THE ASSET MIX DECISION

	Canadian Bond Funds	Canadian Equity Funds	Compound Annual Return	Value of $10,000
Portfolio A	100%	0%	10.70%	$27,636.07
Portfolio B	80%	20%	10.28%	$26,605.26
Portfolio C	60%	40%	9.86%	$25,609.20
Portfolio D	50%	50%	9.65%	$25,123.86
Portfolio E	40%	60%	9.44%	$24,646.82
Portfolio F	20%	80%	9.02%	$23,717.11
Portfolio G	0%	100%	8.60%	$22,819.09

Forgetting for the moment that fixed-income assets would have provided a decent retirement nest egg over our test period, we want you to look closely at Table 14.1 and note the impact of the asset mix decision.

If, for example, you modeled your asset mix based on Portfolio D—50% equities and 50% bonds—you would have locked in a base return of 9.65% without ever having selected a single security. Your $10,000 investment in May 1986 would have been worth $25,123.86 by May 1996.

Perhaps, rather than holding a Canadian equity fund whose returns matched the TSE 300 Composite Index, you practiced some nimble trading. If you were buying and selling individual securities at each phase of the business cycle, perhaps you could enhance those returns. For example, you might purchase financial stocks at the beginning of a cycle, then switch to cyclical stocks as the economic recovery picks up steam and finally go into defensive stocks when the economy begins to peak.

Of course, that assumes you can consistently pick winning stocks and have the ability to recognize where we are on the business cycle. For most of us, that is simply too much to expect, especially since many professionals who are paid to forecast the current direction of the economy have difficulty being in the right place at the right time.

More importantly, we would argue, as do so many academic studies, that over the long haul the impact from that trading strategy would be marginal at best, especially when compared with the asset mix decision.

Looking at Table 14.1, note what happens when you simply shift your asset mix from Portfolio F to Portfolio D. That one decision adds 0.63% compounded annually to your bottom line. And while that may not seem like much, on our $10,000 initial investment, it adds $1,406.75 to your pocket over a 10-year period.

But the incremental return that comes from the right asset mix goes beyond year-over-year excess returns. The reason? As was explained in Chapter 2, changes in compound return compound over time. The value of the $10,000 invested in Portfolio B is worth 5.9% more than Portfolio D at the end of the 10-year period.

If those returns remained consistent over the next 10 years, Portfolio D would be worth

$70,784.01 compared with $63,120.83 for Portfolio F. That's a difference of $7,663.17, which means that Portfolio D would then be worth 12.14% more than Portfolio F. That's what we mean when we say returns compound over time, and explains a professional money manager's obsession with small improvements in annual rate of return.

It also speaks volumes about the importance asset mix plays in your long-range investment plan. Even modest changes in asset mix can lead to significant changes in return over the life of your portfolio. In our opinion, then, the asset mix decision is key to your financial well-being.

Normally, you should expect an asset mix that puts more emphasis on equities to outperform other investments over the long term—something, we might add, that didn't happen over our test period but, as we learned from the experience of Peter Lynch in Chapter 4, will occur over the long haul. On the other hand, if you cannot tolerate high levels of risk, then you should opt for an asset mix like portfolios A, B or C.

And don't forget, Canadian bonds and stocks are only two potential classes of investments. Your selection of portfolio ingredients might also include short-term, interest-bearing securities (referred to as "cash" or money market funds), U.S. and international equities, real estate, gold, etc.

Thus, conservative investors will probably add a generous dab of T-bills to provide additional safety. One low-risk asset mix might include 20% equities, 50% bonds and 30% cash. More speculative investors might choose a spicier mix, say, 5% cash, 25% bonds and 70% equities.

Having determined your asset mix, you should then look at particular securities, or better yet, specific funds, to represent each asset class. Unfortunately, if you're like most investors, you will probably reverse the process, focusing on security and/or fund selection to the exclusion of all other considerations. The result? When you add up the percentage committed to each asset class, you find that your asset mix has been determined by default. And that means that greater than 85% of your return has been determined without your conscious control, which is probably a recipe for disappointment.

Homemade versus Store-Bought Diversification

Diversification is, in our opinion, the cornerstone of successful long-term investing. It is the process of getting a suitable mix of safe, liquid assets such as savings accounts and money market funds, income-producing securities such as term deposits or bond mutual funds, and growth assets such as equity mutual funds and common shares into your combined personal and RRSP portfolio. The question is, how do you actually get your desired mix? Do you do it yourself, from the asset mix decision, right through to the security selection process, or do you simply buy it? We'll examine both approaches in this section.

If you have the knowledge and the time, you could even structure your own portfolio by hand-selecting the proper securities. You could, for example, attempt to structure a balanced portfolio by purchasing shares of, say, General Motors, Bank of Montreal and IBM. But understand this approach is very expensive and is not a simple procedure.

Remember, when buying stocks, you should purchase, at a minimum, a round lot. For most investors, a round lot is considered to be 100 shares. And to do it right, you will need to buy shares in more than the three companies we cite in our preamble. The Value Line Investment Survey, a well-respected U.S. advisory service, recommends that a well-diversified portfolio include at least 15 separate stocks in different industries. Other studies suggest you need at least 30 different stocks in your portfolio, which means that a properly diversified common stock portfolio could require upward of $40,000 to $50,000 in capital. And that is before you make any commitment to fixed-income assets or cash reserves.

On the other hand, you can buy diversification. One method is to simply buy a balanced mutual fund. These are funds that practice asset allocation by holding a portfolio of stocks and bonds. The balanced fund manager can then alter the weightings within the asset mix within the guidelines of the fund's prospectus. For example, the Sceptre Balanced Fund,[9] according to *BellCharts*, "maintains a steady asset mix with equities at a maximum of 65% and a minimum of 35% of the portfolio."

Balanced fund managers, then, not only decide on which securities are held in the portfolio—i.e., how much General Motors, how much IBM and so on—they also allocate the percentage of the portfolio to be committed to any one asset class (i.e., equities, fixed income or cash).

When you think about it, balanced funds would seem to be the ideal approach. Let the portfolio manager decide not only the asset mix, but also the securities to buy within each asset class.

However, it isn't quite that straightforward. At the outset, you are leaving an asset mix decision to the portfolio manager, and that asset mix may not be suitable for your current situation and long-term goals. For example, if you are a conservative investor, your personal policy statement might be 20% equity, 65% fixed income and 15% cash. The balanced fund manager may be holding a portfolio that is 65% equity, 25% fixed income and 10% cash. The point is, the balanced fund manager is not reflecting your specific circumstances and we believe that may not be in your best long-term interest.

There are also some issues on the performance side. For some thoughts on that, we take you to Table 14.2, which looks at the average compounded return over the last 10 years (to August 31, 1997) for Canadian balanced funds, Canadian bond funds, Canadian equity funds, Canadian money market funds and U.S. equity funds. We have weighted the returns on the basis of assets under management. In other words, a fund with $50 million under management will not carry as much weight in the calculation as a fund with, say, $200 million under management. The idea behind weighting the performance is to examine the numbers on the basis of the funds most often purchased by investors.

[9] *Sceptre Balanced Fund is managed by Sceptre Investment Counsel Limited in Toronto.*

Table 14.2: AVERAGE RETURNS AMONG VARIOUS FUND CATEGORIES*

Canadian Balanced	Canadian Bond Funds	Canadian Equity Funds	Canadian Money Market	U.S. Equity Funds
8.5%	10.1%	9.0%	7.1%	10.5%

* to August 31, 1997

From Table 14.2, we know that the average Canadian balanced fund returned 8.5% compounded annually over the past 10 years (to August 31, 1997). What that means is a $10,000 investment made in the average Canadian balanced fund 10 years ago would be worth $22,609.83 by August 31, 1997.

Now let's examine what would have happened with a typical asset mix based on the personal investment profile from Chapter 2. Let's assume your score was close to the average of most investors: say, 50% equity, 40% bonds and 10% cash. And since balanced funds can invest in markets other than Canada, we'll establish the following model portfolio:

Model Portfolio	
Average Canadian Equity Fund	30%
Average U.S. Equity Fund	20%
Average Canadian Bond Fund	40%
Average Canadian Money Market Fund	10%
Total	**100%**

The question is, how did the performance of a model portfolio of average funds in each category compare with the performance of the average balanced fund over the past five years? If we assume you earned 30% (the weighting within the model portfolio) of the return from the average Canadian equity fund over the past five years (i.e., 9.0% x .30 = 2.70%), 40% of the return from the average bond fund (10.0% x .40 = 4.04%), 10% from the Canadian money market (7.1% x .10 = 0.71%), and 20% from the average U.S. equity fund (10.5% x .20 = 3.00%), your overall portfolio would return 10.45% (2.70% + 4.04% + 0.71% + 3.00%) compounded annually. A $10,000 investment that was made 10 years ago in this model portfolio would, today, be worth $27,018.25. When you compare this performance with the average balanced fund (i.e., 8.9% compounded annually) over the same 10-year period, you can see why we encourage you to design your own personal portfolio, and why we will give you the tools to do just that.

Moreover, by determining your personal asset mix, you tailor your investments to your personal policy statement. And coincidentally, the numbers tell us that by selecting funds to represent your own personal asset mix, you enhance your overall return. And that assumes you purchase only the average funds in each class and make no changes to the asset mix for the 10-year holding period.

From our perspective, then, we think most investors are better off using mutual funds for their security selection. We believe that over the long haul, buying a Canadian equity fund makes more sense than trying to buy a portfolio of 30 Canadian stocks in different industries. Furthermore, the availability of dividend reinvestment programs makes mutual fund investing more convenient, and the diversification that comes from an investment in a mutual fund is generally more cost-effective than you could achieve by purchasing your own handpicked portfolio.

We also believe that mutual fund managers add more value by bringing their stock picking or bond selection ability to the table than they do by arbitrarily deciding what asset mix makes the most sense at a point in the business cycle.

Basic Investment Planning

If you accept our notion that mutual funds should be used in place of security selection, then our most important decision once again comes down to the asset mix—the percentage of stocks, bonds and T-bills in the portfolio.

An investment strategy that allocates your financial resources among asset classes is referred to as asset allocation. And there are three basic formats your investment strategy can take:

1. Strategic Asset Allocation
2. Tactical Asset Allocation
3. Dynamic Asset Allocation

Strategic asset allocation means the process of apportioning the fund's investment portfolio among the broad investment classes—T-bills and other money market securities, fixed income, equities, real estate and international securities. The introduction of different types of securities, particularly those that are less than perfectly correlated with each other, will reduce the variability of the portfolio and increase the likelihood that the portfolio will earn the required rate of return.

When we talk about strategic asset allocation, we are talking about an investment philosophy where you structure a portfolio based on your personal investment objectives and risk tolerances. (Refer to the personal investment profile from Chapter 2.)

For most strategic investors, the range of appropriate asset allocation mixes is somewhere between 35%/65% to 65%/35% fixed-income assets relative to equity assets, spanning the very conservative to the highly aggressive.

Tactical or timing allocation is the sometimes controversial policy of changing the asset mix to capture perceived market cycle shifts or opportunities. Tactical asset allocation is practiced by a number of balanced funds, and in most cases these managers utilize sophisticated computer models to evaluate the relative value of equities to fixed-income investments to cash at a point in time. When, according to the computer model, equities are undervalued relative to bonds, for example, the manager will add stocks to the portfolio and reduce the commitment to bonds.

AGF Management practices tactical asset allocation and utilizes a computer model developed by the giant U.S. brokerage firm Paine Weber. This computer model draws on 70 years of historical performance statistics for stocks, bonds and cash, and evaluates the merits of one asset class relative to another at a point in time. Quite often, AGF will announce a major shift in its emphasis from stocks to bonds to cash, and when it does, it is newsworthy.

Obviously these managers believe they can identify market cycles, and thus can add value by adjusting the asset allocation mix by buying or selling equities, cash and bonds with the changing times. Tactical asset allocation is obviously an active strategy.

There are also passive approaches to asset allocation. For example, managers who believe in efficient markets where security prices reflect all information and are properly priced and that economic cycles cannot be accurately forecast don't spend time searching for undervalued securities or looking for changing economic cycles. Instead, they attempt to add value by constructing and maintaining the portfolio in the most cost-efficient manner.

Passive asset allocation strategies attempt to rebalance the portfolio at set intervals, say once a year or every six months, etc. The idea behind rebalancing is to bring the portfolio back to its original weighting. In other words, if equity funds outperformed the other assets over the preceding period, then equities would have a greater weight in the portfolio. In order to rebalance, you would sell some of the equity funds and buy more of the assets that underperformed. Think of it as a disciplined approach that forces you to buy low (i.e., assets that have underperformed) and sell high (i.e., assets that have outperformed).

On the question of which style we favor, we lean toward a combination approach. We believe in the "strategic" decision to structure an asset mix in line with your investment personality. But you will also note, from Chapter 2, that we provided a range for each asset class. That's to allow us the latitude to dynamically rebalance the asset mix while maintaining the long-term strategic intent of the portfolio.

We will make recommendations each time we update this book as to whether you should over-weight, under-weight or maintain your policy statement during a particular year. These periodic changes in weighting attached to each asset class, based on our year-ahead view about the economy, is how we define the "dynamic" aspect of our asset allocation philosophy.

But we should point out that studies thus far have indicated that market timing is extremely difficult. The rewards of timing are high—but as Nobel prizewinner Paul Samuelson has pointed out, timing can be hazardous to your health.

The key is to choose the style you are most comfortable with and to stick with it. If you do not want to follow our dynamic model, then simply rebalance the asset mix once a year bringing it back in line with your policy statement. So, assess yourself honestly, stay within your comfort zone and stick by your convictions.

Defining Your Asset Mix

Having laid some of the foundation for asset allocation, we want to move into defining asset allocation as it pertains to the individual investor. Basically, there are four broad asset categories (see Figure 14.1):

1. Equity Assets
2. Fixed-Income Assets
3. Cash Assets
4. Real Estate Assets

Figure 14.1: YOUR ASSET MIX

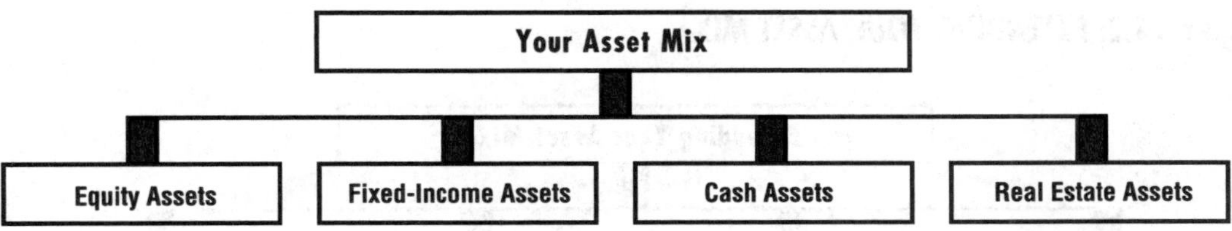

Most investors, at least from the ones we've talked with over the years, prefer to separate the family home from their investment portfolio. Indeed, we talked about that when formulating your personal investment profile. The fact is, most investors would prefer not to depend on the sale of their family home to provide for their retirement income. That's not to say they won't sell the home at retirement; we're simply saying that it's nice not to have to sell it. As such, when we talk about real estate assets, we're really talking about investments in real estate mutual funds, or Real Estate Investment Trusts (REITs) or perhaps an investment property, we're not talking about the family home.

Another factor which bears consideration is the so-called liquidity crisis that can prevent you from cashing out at a given point in time. We note, for example, the so-called "stabilization measures" imposed in August 1995 by two real estate funds managed by Roycom Advisors Inc.—Roycom-Summit TDF Fund and the Roycom-Summit Realty Fund. The goal, according to management, was to stem the tide of redemptions: "The stabilization process allows the funds to pay redemptions only out of money coming into the fund, which can result from new units being sold, or from rental income received on the properties in the fund's portfolio." (*The Globe and Mail*)

Without a provision of this sort, real estate funds would have to sell off properties at distressed prices, which could result in advantaging one group of unitholders to the detriment of others. Because real estate funds do not have the liquidity of a stock or bond fund, managers cannot move adeptly in and out of the market, and for investors who want the right to redeem, that's a risk factor. Accordingly, a Real Estate Investment Trust is generally a preferred investment vehicle.

Extending the Asset Mix

Having ascertained a reasonable asset mix from your personal investment profile, we find it helpful to broaden our definitions by extending the asset mix, effectively subdividing the assets by geographic region. Similarly, we want to segment our fixed-income assets into domestic fixed income and foreign fixed income: how much in Canada, how much in the U.S. and how much overseas. In both cases, of course, we face some restrictions in terms of the foreign content rules within RRSPs.

The idea is to fine-tune the portfolio, so that we can take advantage of our view about the world financial markets. Obviously, this is a judgment call, and for lack of a better term, represents the tactical aspect of our asset allocation model (see Figure 14.2 and Table 14.3).

Figure 14.2: EXTENDING YOUR ASSET MIX

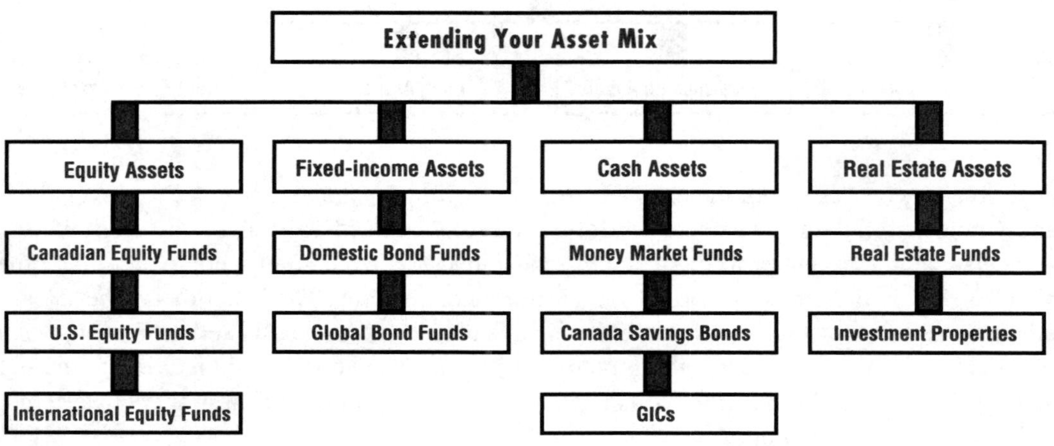

A couple of points come to mind. Holding U.S. equities is an important part of almost any investment package, simply because of the impact the U.S. economy has on the world stage and, more specifically, on Canadian equities. Global equities provide us with further diversification and some negative correlation within the portfolio. In simple terms, global markets rarely move in sync. Often, one market will rise when another falls (i.e., negative correlation), which tends to stabilize the overall portfolio.

There are also advantages from the performance side. International diversification allows us more flexibility and provides an opportunity to enhance long-term returns without significantly altering our risk pattern. This is particularly useful when a sizable portion of the assets are held outside tax-sheltered plans.

Table 14.3: A TYPICAL EXTENDED ASSET MIX

Asset Groups	Pct of Portfolio
Canadian Equity Funds	25%
U.S. Equity Funds	20%
International Equity Funds	10%
Total Equity Component	***55%***
Global Bond Funds	10%
Domestic Bond Funds	25%
Total Fixed-Income Component	***35%***
Money Market Funds	10%
Total Cash Component	***10%***
Total Portfolio	***100%***

Security Selection

Equities

The final stage is the selection of securities to represent each of the asset classes, and ultimately each segment within that asset mix. Here you will decide which funds will provide the best fit in your portfolio. We will offer a number of potential funds, plus the necessary tools to mix and match these funds to give you the most *oomph* for your investment dollar, while always maintaining a tight rein on the risk side of the equation.

Fixed Income

In Canada, most bond funds invest in government securities. Since there is no default risk, the fixed-income manager focuses on the portfolio's duration or, put another way, the term-to-maturity. Portfolio managers lengthen the term-to-maturity if they feel interest rates will fall, and will generally shorten the maturity if they fear a rise in interest rates. Later on in this book, we'll be providing the tools to help you mix and match domestic and global bond funds in your portfolio.

Global bonds fall into a different category. Because size is a more important issue and exchange-rate risk is a consideration, we believe that global bond fund managers bring an expertise that can add value to your investment decisions.

Cash

Cash is considered a hedge. It helps us smooth out the fluctuations in the overall portfolio and provides a buffer should we wish to add to any of our asset classes. There are three approaches to the cash component: money market funds, GICs, Canada Savings Bonds/Government of Canada Treasury bills.

More Risk—More Return

Having defined the typical makeup of an asset mix, and then extending that mix into various securities, we would like to once again return to Table 14.1. We simply believe that it is necessary to explain the rationale behind equity assets in a long-term growth portfolio, especially since our test period defies some long-standing investment truisms, specifically the relationship between risk and return. Equities, considered a higher-risk investment, underperformed lower-risk bonds, and more importantly, underperformed risk-free Treasury bills during the period from 1986 to 1996.

If we told you in May 1986 that you had two investment choices—Government of Canada Treasury bills that would generate a compound annual yield of 8.43% with no risk, or Canadian equity funds that could generate an 8.60% return, with no guarantees—which would you choose?

And just for good measure, let us add another factor to this dilemma. With equity funds, there might be periods where you would earn nothing, and there is a good chance that you might even lose money in any given year! Using that as a sales pitch, equities would not look very attractive. Let's face it; who would be willing to risk their capital when investments with no risk offer better returns?

And therein lies the rationale behind equity funds. Over the long haul, higher-risk equity investments must substantially outperform lower-risk investments. To suggest otherwise would mean that all investors, because we all fear financial risk, would simply buy risk-free assets. In the long run, risk capital would dry up. Based on our experience, 10 years is, in terms of risk, about as long a time horizon as most investors are comfortable with.

We believe that all portfolios should contain some equity securities. The appropriate amount or allocation varies, although the suggested range is normally 30% to 70% depending on your goals, tastes and financial plans.

What is the best way to achieve this? This depends to a large extent on your beliefs. Our view is that your investment philosophy should reflect your beliefs. If you think you can find undervalued securities, or that there are mutual funds managers who can, then you should pursue what is called an "active" strategy, searching for value by either hand-selecting your stocks or by selecting equity mutual funds that pursue an active policy of searching for undervalued securities.

On the other hand, if you believe that markets are efficient and that stocks prices reflect all information, save the money and effort associated with stock and/or fund valuation, then take a "strategic" approach where you mix and match mutual funds within a portfolio where the asset mix is defined by your personal policy statement.

We believe that the financial markets will come full circle over the next decade. Indeed, over the next decade we will probably find ourselves in a very different environment, and with interest rates at 30-year lows, we can make a strong case that Canadian equities will once again resume their role as the dominant Canadian asset within your portfolio.

Which brings us one step further down this road. There is a view expressed by some financial commentators that "because equities are the best long-term investment, why buy anything else?" And to be fair, given our views about equities for the next decade, for individual investors who want to maximize their total long-term return, have no need for investment income and can accept a degree of risk, an all-equity portfolio may indeed be the answer.

However, for some thoughts on that, take a close look at Table 14.4 which looks at the annual returns of selected assets from the beginning of 1984 to the end of 1995. For six of the 12 years in question, Canadian equities produced double-digit returns. That is the attraction of equities. But again, while most of us like the potential of double-digit returns, not many can accept the risk associated with a major stock market correction. We point to the performance of 1987, and draw your specific attention to the performance of equities late in the year (see Figure 14.3). Could your pocketbook withstand that type of correction?

Interestingly, for the entire year, because of the strong performance of equities up to and including August 1987, Canadian and U.S. equities actually turned in a positive year-over-year return. More disturbing in terms of year-over-year performance was the 1990 bear market for equities, when U.S. stocks fell 4.09% (as measured by the S&P 500 Composite Total Return Index) and Canadian stocks fell 14.80% (as measured by the TSE 300 Total Return Index).

Table 14.4: PERFORMANCE OF SELECTED FINANCIAL ASSETS

	Canadian Equities		U.S. Equities		Canadian Bonds		Cash	
Year	$ Return	% Return	$ Return	% Return	$ Return	% Return	$ Return	% Return
1/1/84	10,000		10,000		10,000		10,000	
1984	9,761	-2.39	10,458	4.58	11,466	14.66	11,162	11.62
1985	12,208	25.07	13,614	30.18	13,900	21.23	12,267	9.90
1986	13,301	8.95	16,066	18.01	15,944	14.70	13,425	9.44
1987	14,083	5.88	16,861	4.95	16,588	4.04	14,558	8.44
1988	15,643	11.08	19,482	15.54	18,212	9.79	15,967	9.68
1989	18,986	21.37	25,463	30.70	20,545	12.81	17,982	12.62
1990	16,176	-14.80	24,421	-4.09	22,094	7.54	20,439	13.66
1991	18,121	12.02	31,640	29.56	26,985	22.14	22,370	9.45
1992	17,861	-1.43	33,852	6.99	29,640	9.84	23,896	6.82
1993	23,675	32.55	37,061	9.48	35,017	18.14	25,139	5.20
1994	23,628	-0.20	37,543	1.30	33,511	-4.30	26,496	5.40
1995	27,054	14.50	51,659	37.60	40,448	20.70	28,510	7.60
Standard Deviation*		13.17%		13.70%		7.81%		2.65%

* Standard deviation of annual returns

Of course, when we talk about the volatility of annual returns, we are talking about risk, which we defined in Chapter 2 as the standard deviation of those returns. By looking at Table 14.4, we can see that stocks were substantially more volatile than bonds over the period in question.

Indeed, the annual standard deviation of U.S. equities was 13.17% vs. 7.81% for Canadian bonds and 2.65% for Government of Canada Treasury bills. What that means, from our lesson in Chapter 2, is that we could expect the value of our U.S. equity funds to rise or fall within 13.17% (one standard deviation) of their mean 66% of the time.

Similarly, we would expect the value of a Canadian bond fund with a standard deviation similar to the ScotiaMcLeod Bond Universe to rise or fall within 7.81% of their mean 66% of the time. Interestingly, in support of the view that you should always expect the unexpected, we draw your attention to the performance of Canadian bond funds during the month of February 1994. For the record, in that one month, the average Canadian bond fund fell about 8%.

This just goes to show how performance numbers can get skewed when the unexpected happens. In this case, it was an unexpected hike in short-term interest rates by the U.S. Federal Reserve Board. And if you own a bond fund (see Chapter 6), rising interest rates mean lower bond prices.

Of course, Government of Canada Treasury bills have the lowest standard deviation of any asset. In the vernacular of the average investor, Treasury bills are low risk. That's not to suggest that the value of your money might not be eroded by the onset of inflation, which we contend is a significant risk factor. But in terms of repayment principal and interest, the annual standard deviation on Treasury bills suggests a risk-free asset.

Figure 14.3: ANNUAL RETURNS ON SELECTED FINANCIAL ASSETS (1984–1995)

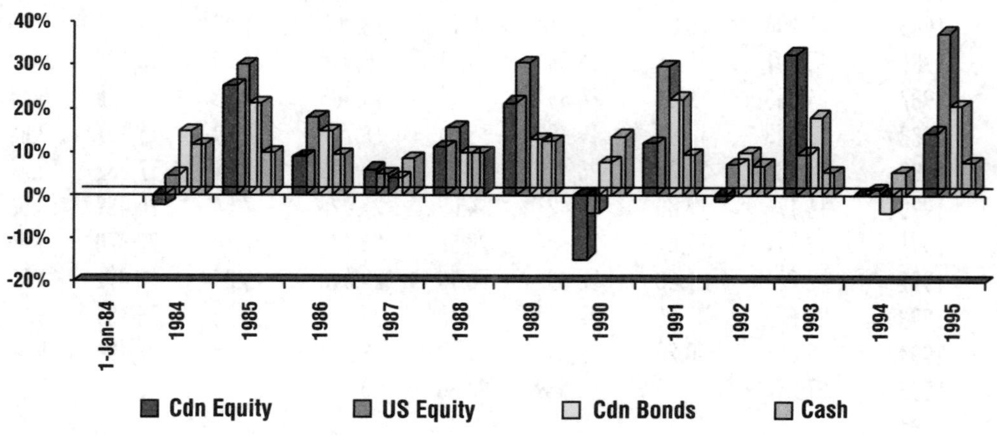

Figure 14.3 takes us another step along the road to asset allocation by graphically displaying the annual performance of all four of our selected assets. Note that all four assets had their "day in the sun" over the past decade. It was, for each of these assets, "the best of times and the worst of times."

By spreading your investment dollars across all four financial assets, we are able to reduce the overall volatility in the portfolio. Taking that one step farther, because asset allocation reduces your overall risk, you need not be as concerned about the volatility of the funds you hold in the portfolio. You could, for example, buy an aggressive Canadian equity fund to represent your equity assets, and an aggressive bond fund to represent your fixed-income assets.

In portfolio management terms, by purchasing aggressive equity or bond funds, we are raising the beta of our portfolio. Now before we get caught up in another statistical concept, beta is not that complex. To review, beta simply measures the systematic risk of a fund, or more specifically, measures the performance of a particular fund relative to some benchmark index.

Most Canadian equity funds, for example, are measured against the TSE 300 Composite Index. And benchmark indexes, like the TSE 300 Composite Index, have a beta of 1.00. A Canadian equity fund with a beta of, say, 1.20 would be considered an aggressive equity fund.

We would expect, then, if the TSE 300 Composite Index went up 10%, our aggressive Canadian equity fund would rise by 12% (10% x 1.20 beta = 12%). So, in a rising market, the aggressive growth equity fund should outperform the benchmark index (i.e., the TSE 300 Composite Index) and, conversely, in a down market, should underperform the benchmark.

This is a reasonable approach if we accept the basic tenet that diversification within the asset allocation model addresses our concern about volatility, allowing us to select individual funds on the basis of above-average performance. We can, then, buy so-called "aggressive growth funds" for the equity component of our asset allocation model because we have reduced our risk through diversification across a number of asset classes.

With that in mind, let's look at what happens to an asset allocation model from January 1, 1984, to December 31, 1995. In this case, we divided our model portfolio between equities (25% in Canadian equities, 25% U.S. equities), Canadian fixed income (25% domestic bonds) and cash (25% Government of Canada Treasury bills). We raised the beta on our equity assets from 1.00 to 1.20 by purchasing an aggressive Canadian equity fund and an aggressive U.S. equity fund. The returns and standard deviation are found in Table 14.5.

Table 14.5: ASSET ALLOCATION

Year	Cdn Equity	US Equity	Cdn Bonds	Cash	Portfolio
1/1/84	$10,000	$10,000	$10,000	$10,000	$10,000
1984	9,713	10,550	11,466	11,162	10,723
1985	12,635	14,370	13,900	12,267	13,293
1986	13,992	17,476	15,944	13,425	15,209
1987	14,980	18,514	16,588	14,558	16,160
1988	16,971	21,967	18,212	15,967	18,279
1989	21,323	30,059	20,545	17,982	22,477
1990	17,536	28,584	22,094	20,439	22,163
1991	20,066	38,723	26,985	22,370	27,036
1992	19,722	41,971	29,640	23,896	28,807
1993	27,425	46,746	35,017	25,139	33,582
1994	27,359	47,475	33,511	26,496	33,710
1995	32,119	68,895	40,448	28,510	42,493
Standard Deviation*	15.80%	16.44%	7.81%	2.65%	9.40%

*Standard deviation of annual returns

Compare the performance of the asset allocation model portfolio (far right column in Table 12.5) with the performance of each of the assets in Table 14.4. In this case, the asset allocation portfolio outperformed Canadian equities, T-bills and Canadian bonds, and underperformed an all-U.S. equity portfolio.

However, and this is the point of the exercise, the risk associated with the asset allocation model portfolio in Table 14.5 was similar to the risk of the bond portfolio from Table 14.4, and substantially below the risk of either an all-Canadian or all-U.S. equity portfolio. That's because 25% of the asset allocated portfolio includes cash, which dramatically reduces the portfolio's overall risk.

An Intuitive View of Investing

Suppose you are holding three funds, each of which has a net asset value of $10. Let's call them fund A, B and C. Suppose that you paid $4, $10 and $12 respectively for each of the three.

What decisions should you make? Should you sell "A" to lock in a 150% gain? Should you sell "B" because it has done nothing for you? Should you sell "C" because you have lost 16.7% of your investment?

The answer is none of the above. With the exception of a possible tax issue, none of the three choices makes sense as an independent decision. The point is, the portfolio of three funds is currently worth $30 against an initial cost of $26. The portfolio has risen by 15.4%. The relevant question is whether this portfolio is performing the way you had hoped and whether it is still suitable, given your objectives. This is the principle of mutual fund diversification, and the reason decisions should normally be made on a portfolio basis.

If we can get you to think of your portfolio as an all-weather vehicle, then you will become a longer-term investor who pays little attention to one-day, one-week, one-month or one-year fluctuations. You will hold a portfolio that gets you where you want to go, and does so while letting you sleep nights.

CHAPTER FIFTEEN

Higher Performance—The Concept of Manager Value Added (MVA)

The Search for Performance

When investors talk about mutual funds, the conversation never fails to turn to performance numbers. This is not really surprising, since returns over a given period are the most visible factor relating to a mutual fund's performance. Past returns are easy to quantify.

For example, let us say that XYZ Fund returned 10% year-to-date in 1998, 25% in 1997 and 15% in 1996. This is straightforward. With the raw numbers in hand, financial advisors or agents who sell mutual funds can quantify and personalize the returns by translating the percentages into dollar values. Had you invested $1,000 in XYZ Fund at the beginning of 1996, your portfolio would, today, be worth $1,581. Impressive performance numbers appeal to the most basic investor instinct—greed.

What seems to get lost in this hype is the disclaimer attached to these performance numbers that states, "Past performance is not necessarily indicative of future performance." We think there needs to be some balance between the raw performance numbers and the associated risks.

Obviously, over the long term, a portfolio of top performing funds will add value. For example, let's assume $1,000 invested in a hypothetical portfolio that is 50% invested in Canadian equity funds, 40% in Canadian bond funds and 10% in Canadian money market funds has returned 9.18% compounded annually over the last 10 years. That $1,000 investment, made 10 years ago, would today be worth $2,406 (see Figure 15.1).

Figure 15:1: A HYPOTHETICAL PORTFOLIO'S PERFORMANCE

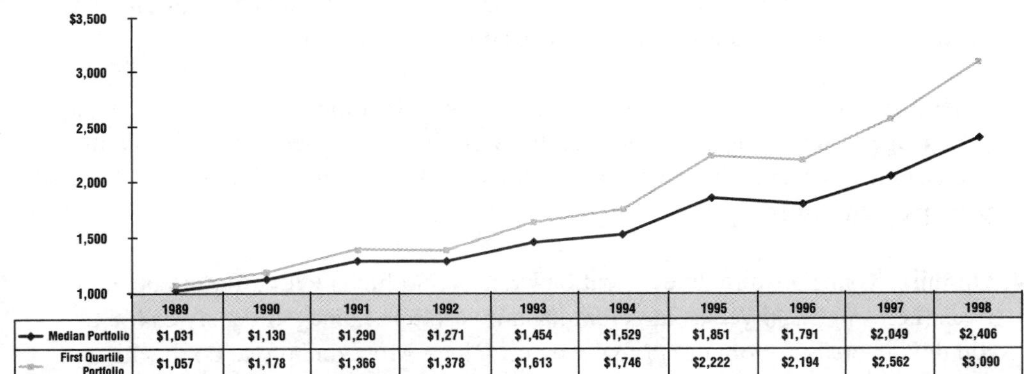

	1989	1990	1991	1992	1993	1994	1995	1996	1997	1998
Median Portfolio	$1,031	$1,130	$1,290	$1,271	$1,454	$1,529	$1,851	$1,791	$2,049	$2,406
First Quartile Portfolio	$1,057	$1,178	$1,366	$1,378	$1,613	$1,746	$2,222	$2,194	$2,562	$3,090

This is not a bad performance for a passive portfolio. But look what happens if you are able to buy funds that, over the long term, were better-than-average performers. If you were able to find and hold funds that were first-quartile performers over that 10-year period, your portfolio would have returned at least 11.94% compounded annually, taking your $1,000 investment to $3,090. The trick is to find those better-than-average performers—and that can be a daunting task.

Looking at our hypothetical portfolio at the time of writing, you would be choosing your fund portfolio from any one of 501 Canadian equity funds, 186 Canadian bond funds and 143 Canadian money market funds. Separating the wheat from the chaff is easy if you are looking at past performance; it is much harder when trying to find funds that will outperform the benchmarks in the future.

For the record, then, we think that performance is important, but only to a point. We believe that performance is one consideration in the selection process—it is not the only consideration.

Understanding How We Select Funds

During the first eight months of 1998, AIM Global Health Services Fund returned 24.7%, making it a top performing funds for Canadian investors. The three-year return is equally impressive at 25.1%.[10]

Should you buy this fund? Well, it depends! If your decision to buy hangs on the performance numbers, without understanding how that fund fits into your portfolio, then the answer is no. To buy on that basis, we think, is rainbow chasing of the worst kind. And we might add, this is a specialty resource equity fund, which means in terms of diversification, it adds very little to the portfolio.

Our investment philosophy is simple:

1. Set your financial objectives and understand your risk tolerances. In short, define your investment personality.

---

[10] *Returns are to the end of August 1998.*

2. Establish an appropriate asset mix (i.e., what percentage of your assets should be invested in money market funds, what percentage in fixed-income funds and what percentage in equity funds), based on your investment personality.

3. Extend your asset mix to include geographic diversification. In other words, what percentage of funds earmarked for equity assets should be used to buy Canadian equity funds, what percentage for U.S. equity funds, international equity funds and perhaps Latin American funds.

4. Optimize your portfolio diversification by selecting funds with different objectives (i.e., small-cap versus large-cap) and investment management styles (i.e., top down versus bottom up, growth versus value). More on how to do this in Chapter 16.

5. Finally, seek out the best managers in each category. At this point, performance becomes an issue because you have clearly defined the role the fund will play in your portfolio.

If we could summarize our philosophy, it comes down to a selection process. We think that an understanding of the role a particular fund plays in your portfolio is more important than the specific performance numbers of that fund.

To emphasize the point, consider the following analogy. Suppose you liked the prospects for General Motors, because the company was gaining market share and improving profit margins. The basis of your rosy forecast for General Motors is your analysis of historical trends—specifically market share and profit margins. Now think about this: is that any different from analyzing the historical returns of a mutual fund, and then based on that analysis, concluding that that fund will be a strong performer in the future?

Now here's where the selection process comes into play. Would you buy shares of General Motors if you already owned shares of Ford and Chrysler? It depends! On the one hand, you already own shares in two of the "Big Three" North American carmakers. If General Motors is gaining market share, it is likely at the expense of Ford and Chrysler. Therefore, General Motors brings nothing to the table in terms of diversification.

On the other hand, if you think the outlook for General Motors is better than the outlook for Ford and Chrysler, there is a compelling argument for buying the stock. But in terms of your overall portfolio, would it not make more sense to first sell the shares of Ford and Chrysler, and then use the proceeds to buy General Motors?

Mutual fund portfolios are no different. We need to first understand what role a specific mutual fund plays within the context of the overall portfolio. In other words, what elements of diversification does it bring to the table? We would then analyze the historical returns of the mutual fund, just as we would analyze profit margins, earnings and market share for a stock. And in all instances, we need to recognize the shortfalls of the analysis—which in no small way explains the rationale for the "past performance caveat" expressed at the beginning of this chapter.

Our bottom line is that returns expressed over a given period are the most visible and least predictable aspect of a mutual fund's performance, just as earnings and profit margins are for a company. We are not here to diminish their importance but only to suggest that performance numbers, and by extension, the manager who generated those performance numbers, are not as important as proper diversification on your long-term investment objectives.

Having summarized our views about portfolio building, the rest of this chapter will be devoted to laying out a process that will help you find the right manager for the right job.

To Measure Is to Know

There is a story about the great economist Frank Knight. He was walking around the grounds of the University of Chicago and saw a plaque dedicated to Lord Kelvin that read: "Which cannot be measured, cannot be known." On seeing the plaque, Knight said, "Oh, well, if you can't measure it, go ahead and measure it anyway."

Even Knight, who was so accustomed to precision, was willing to accept the fact that something is better than nothing, which suggests that the search for the perfect performance measure is more like the search for the Holy Grail rather than the needle in the haystack. Both are about as hard to find, but at least the performance measure is worth the effort. And even if you can't find the perfect performance measure, the search is still worth the effort because, in the end, some measures are clearly better than others.

With that in mind, allow us to return to the General Motors analogy, and imagine for a moment, that you are the chairman of the board. Your job is to (1) manufacture quality cars in a cost-effective manner, and (2) market those cars through the GM distribution network.

To fairly evaluate your performance, we need to determine whether or not you are meeting those dual objectives. For example, the company's profit margin (i.e., the difference between the cost of manufacturing the vehicle and its selling price) will tell us how cost-effective your manufacturing plants are. The key is the trend in profit margins: are they increasing or decreasing? At the same time, by analyzing whether the company is gaining or losing market share will tell us how well you are maintaining the distribution network. Both of these factors can be quantified mathematically.

Of course, simply knowing what your profit margins are tells us nothing about value. Only if we can compare those margins against a relative benchmark can we assess whether the margins are good or bad. The question is, what's the benchmark?

Obviously, we cannot evaluate performance by comparing the profit margins of your automobile manufacturing company to, say, the profit margins of software maker Microsoft Corp. We would be comparing apples to oranges. For performance evaluations to be relevant, we need to compare the efficiency—i.e., profit margins—of your manufacturing plants, with the margins of the automobile manufacturing industry.

The same is true of the distribution network. We need to establish a basis of comparison. We cannot compare the volume of traffic and the one-on-one contact in a car dealership with the traffic flow and self-service of a Wal-Mart. One has nothing to do with the other. Again, the basis of comparison must be relevant, and again we would compare your numbers with the average of the industry.

As with any evaluation, there are limitations. Being able to measure those contributions that are mathematically quantifiable does not, by itself, tell us how well you are doing your job. Some aspects of your job are simply not quantifiable.

For example, in your position as chairman of the board, you are also responsible—at least on a macro scale—for making sure your customers are satisfied and that your employees are happy and remain loyal to the company's objectives. Both of these issues can have a dramatic impact at some point in the future, yet neither can be quantified today. Such are the limitations of any model that measures value.

Now let's consider how we might apply what we have learned so far as we search for value among mutual fund managers. We begin by looking at a mutual fund as a company. The fund's prospectus defines the company's objectives, and the portfolio manager is the person responsible for guiding the company within the context of those objectives. The prospectus is a unique document, in that it acts as a sort of job description for the portfolio manager.

Finding the Right Benchmark

Suppose you are holding a Canadian equity fund in your portfolio. The objective, as defined by the fund's prospectus, is to invest in Canadian stocks. The manager invested within those guidelines and the fund returned 18% last year. Is that good or bad?

We don't know, because at this point, we have no frame of reference. As with the profit margins for General Motors, we can only determine value by comparing that return to a relative benchmark. Against Guaranteed Investment Certificates (GICs) that returned 4% over the same period, the fund's return was sensational. But that is not a fair comparison. Measuring a Canadian equity fund against GICs would be akin to comparing a carmaker with a manufacturer of computers. The businesses are not related.

Similarly, you cannot compare a portfolio that is divided equally between stocks, bonds and cash with the TSE 300 Composite Total Return Index, or with the yield on risk-free Treasury bills, or any other single barometer. Again, apples and oranges!

What we need to do is look at the returns of a comparable benchmark. In the case of our Canadian equity fund, we need to look at the returns on the Canadian stock market over a similar period. If Canadian stocks, on average, returned 25%, then the 18% return recorded by our Canadian equity fund pales by comparison. Had Canadian stocks returned 15%, then it would appear on the surface, at least, that the fund manager added value. The point is that we need reasonable benchmarks in order to make reasonable comparisons.

So, what makes a reasonable benchmark? Most importantly, categories and benchmarks should reflect what managers do, rather than what they *say* they do! A benchmark, then, should be:

1. Unambiguous: The TSE 300 Composite Index is an unambiguous benchmark. Its composition is published, and investors know how it is comprised and how its value is determined.

2. Investable: The benchmark should represent a passive alternative to a fund manager. Ideally, you should be able to actually buy the benchmark or a proxy for it.

3. Measurable: The benchmark should be calculated, published periodically and subject to precise calculations.

4. Appropriate: The benchmark selected should match the objectives of the mutual fund. A Canadian equity fund that specializes in small-cap stocks should be compared to a Canadian small-cap index. Similarly, a U.S. equity fund that invests in a diversified portfolio of U.S. stocks should be compared to a broad-based U.S. stock index.

A model that rates mutual fund managers has to evaluate and contrast the returns realized by a fund manager with the returns that could have been obtained if a reasonable alternative passive portfolio had been selected. To justify paying a manager of a Canadian equity fund, you would like to have that manager outperform a passive alternative, which in most cases would be the TSE 300 Composite Index. Now, what are your alternatives if the manager of a Canadian equity fund doesn't do as well as the TSE 300 Composite Index?

Well, the alternatives are these. There are two exchange-traded index funds listed on the Toronto Stock Exchange. The first, Toronto Index Participation Units (TIPs), invests in the 35 largest companies in the TSE 300 Composite Index. The second index fund is the One Hundred Index Participation Units (HIPs) which, like TIPs, is an index fund that invests in the 100 largest companies in the TSE 300 Composite Index. Neither TIPs nor HIPs charges much in the way of management fees, although there is a regular brokerage commission to buy and sell these products, just as there would be with any exchange-traded stock.

The Quest for Value

Having laid the foundation for choosing an appropriate benchmark, and defining some of the issues related to evaluating managers, let's look at three different funds with very different performance records during a defined time period of five years, from 1992 to 1996.

The first on our list is the AGF International Group American Growth Fund, which has been managed by Stephen Rogers since March 1993. In looking at the data in Figure 15.2, the AGF fund returned 16.8% compounded annually to 1996, enough to turn a $1,000 investment made at the beginning of 1992 into $2,172.96 by the end of 1996. Looking at these performance numbers, few investors would have been disappointed. Indeed, we suspect that most investors would vote Mr. Rogers into the managers' hall of fame.

Figure 15.2: AGF INTERNATIONAL GROUP AMERICAN GROWTH FUND

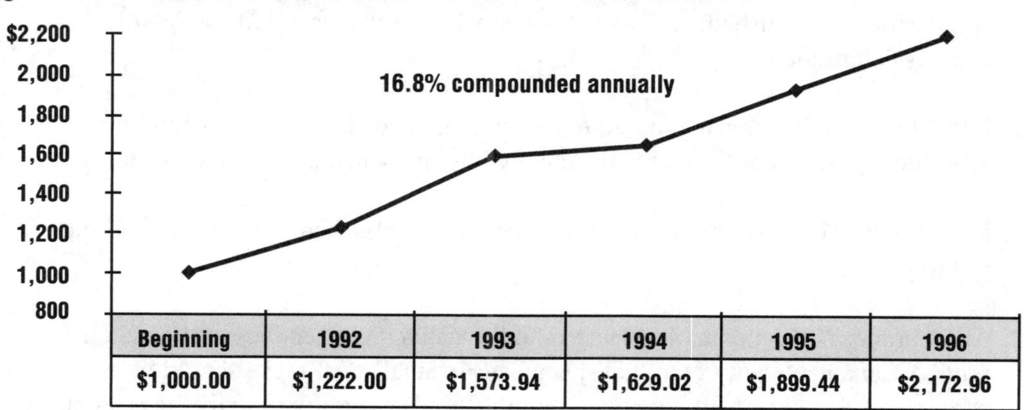

Beginning	1992	1993	1994	1995	1996
$1,000.00	$1,222.00	$1,573.94	$1,629.02	$1,899.44	$2,172.96

Mind you, not all mutual funds experience such spectacular returns. We note, for example, the Royal LePage Commercial Real Estate Fund from 1992–1996 had been lucky to break even. In fact, the Royal LePage Commercial Real Estate Fund (managed by Morris Mostowyk of Royal LePage Capital Property Services) produced a compounded annual return of just 0.5%, enough to grow a $1,000 investment made at the beginning of 1992 into $1,024.84 by the end of 1996 (see Figure 15.3).

Figure 15.3: ROYAL LEPAGE COMMERCIAL REAL ESTATE FUND

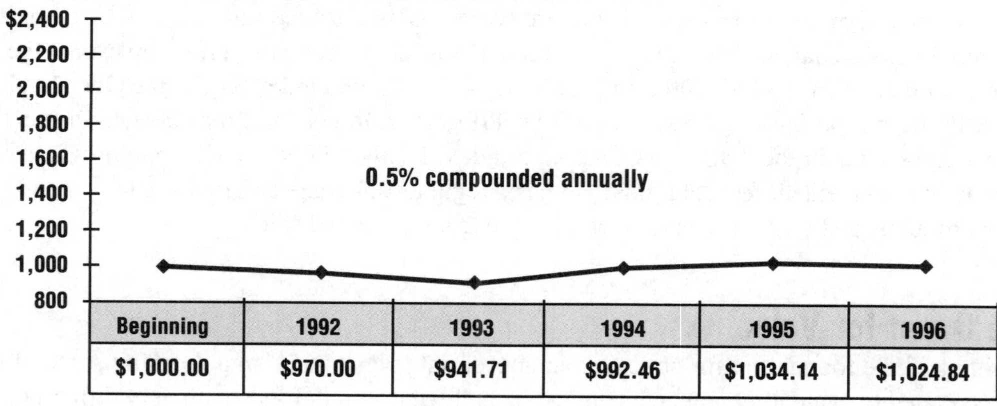

Beginning	1992	1993	1994	1995	1996
$1,000.00	$970.00	$941.71	$992.46	$1,034.14	$1,024.84

Finally, let's examine the Investors Group Japanese Growth Fund, which has been anything but a growth fund. This fund, managed by Colin Abraham of Carlson Asset Management Far East, returned 4.0% compounded annually in the period 1992–1996, growing a $1,000 investment at the beginning of 1992 into $1,215.11 at the end of 1996.

Figure 15.4: INVESTORS GROUP JAPANESE GROWTH FUND

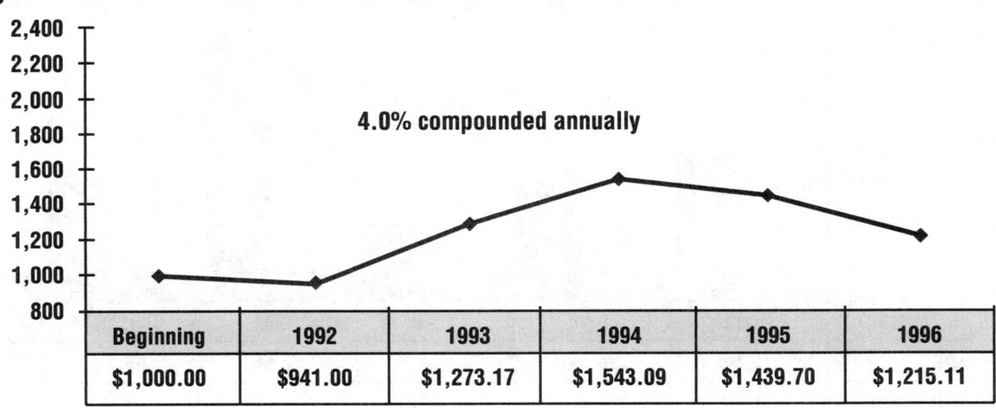

Beginning	1992	1993	1994	1995	1996
$1,000.00	$941.00	$1,273.17	$1,543.09	$1,439.70	$1,215.11

So three very different funds, with three very different performance records. If we were to only look at past returns of one fund relative to all other mutual funds, then it would appear that Stephen Rogers has added value, while both Mr. Mostowyk and Mr. Abraham have fallen down on the job.

Of course, we are painting this picture with far too broad a brush. The fact is, at this point, we have no way of evaluating any of the managers, because at this point we have no benchmark against which to measure their performance. Comparing Mr. Rogers' U.S. equity fund against Mr. Mostowyk's real estate fund or Mr. Abraham's Japanese equity fund is simply another of our apples-to-oranges comparisons. These are three very different funds investing in very different markets. Or stated another way, the job descriptions of each manager—as defined by the fund's prospectus—cannot be compared.

What we really want to know is how much of Mr. Rogers' stellar performance was the result of his shrewd stockpicking ability, and how much was the result of simply investing based on the objectives as defined by the prospectus. Remember, this is a U.S. stock fund, and Mr. Rogers is expected to invest in the U.S. market.

To make a fair apples-to-apples comparison, then, we need to evaluate Mr. Rogers against a reasonable benchmark, which in this case would be the Standard and Poor's (S&P) 500 Composite Total Return Index[11] (adjusted for $Cdn). From 1992 to 1996, the S&P 500 returned 19.1% compounded annually, or 2.3% more than the AGF International Group American Growth Fund over the same period. Over that five-year period, a $1,000 investment in the S&P 500 would have returned $2,399.35 by the end of 1996. Figure 15.5 shows the annual returns for both the AGF International Group American Growth Fund and the S&P 500 Composite Total Return Index over that five-year period.

---

[11]The Standard & Poor's 500 Composite Total Return Index tracks the performance of 500 of the largest companies that trade in the U.S. The total return component assumes all dividends paid by the companies are reinvested back into additional shares.

Figure 15.5: AGF AND THE S&P 500: ANNUAL RETURNS

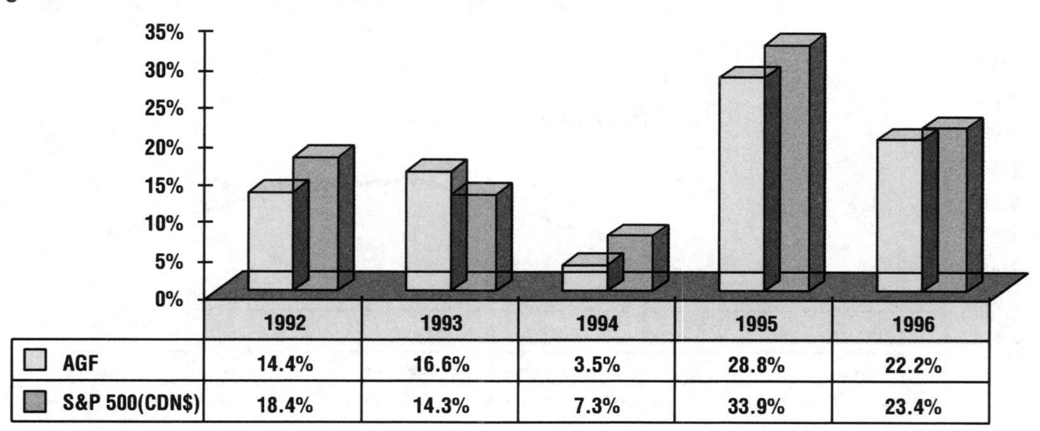

	1992	1993	1994	1995	1996
AGF	14.4%	16.6%	3.5%	28.8%	22.2%
S&P 500(CDN$)	18.4%	14.3%	7.3%	33.9%	23.4%

By comparing the annual returns for the AGF International Group American Growth Fund to an appropriate benchmark, some interesting trends develop. Note, for example, that Mr. Rogers underperformed the S&P 500 Composite Total Return Index in four of the five years up to the end of 1996. Based on the first pass of our evaluation, the investor would have been better off buying the passive alternative, which in this case would be the S&P 500.

For the record, investors can buy an exchange-traded proxy for the S&P 500. A product called the Standard & Poor's Depositary Receipts (symbol SPY) is traded on U.S. stock exchanges. It's an index fund that mirrors the performance of the S&P 500, with annual management fees of approximately 40 basis points (0.40%), compared with an average management-expense ratio for the AGF International Group American Growth Fund of 2.79%.

Figure 15.6 compares the performance of the Royal LePage Commercial Real Estate Fund with an appropriate benchmark, which in this case is the TSE Real Estate Index. What becomes clear when making this comparison is that Mr. Mostowyk's performance is not as disappointing as you might have first thought. While the performance numbers leave a lot to be desired, they are the result of declines in real estate values, and not the consequence of poor investment decisions.

To knock Mr. Mostowyk's numbers, without recognizing that the prospectus of the fund obligated him to invest in an underperforming asset over the last five years, would not be fair. If we could return once again to the General Motors example, it would be the same as penalizing you as chairman of the board because the company's profits were down, without giving any consideration as to why they were down. If profits were down because car sales across the industry were down, then we would be blaming you as chairman for a weak economy, which is something you have no control over.

If we are to devise a model to evaluate a manager, the model must be based on only those factors over which the manager can exercise some control. In Mr. Mostowyk's case, his element of control is his ability to make better-than-average investments in the real estate sector. And looking at the numbers, we believe he did.

From 1992 to 1996, the Royal LePage Commercial Real Estate Fund outperformed the TSE Real Estate Index in four of the five calendar years. The exception is 1996, when the TSE Real Estate Index rallied 41.7%. Interestingly, had you invested in the TSE Real Estate Index (i.e., bought each of the stocks that make up the index), your portfolio would have declined at a 14.5.% compounded annual rate in that five-year period. A $1,000 investment in the TSE Real Estate Index would have dropped to $455.82 some five years later. At least Mr. Mostowyk was able to keep your principal investment intact.

Figure 15.6: ROYAL LEPAGE AND TSE REAL ESTATE: ANNUAL RETURNS

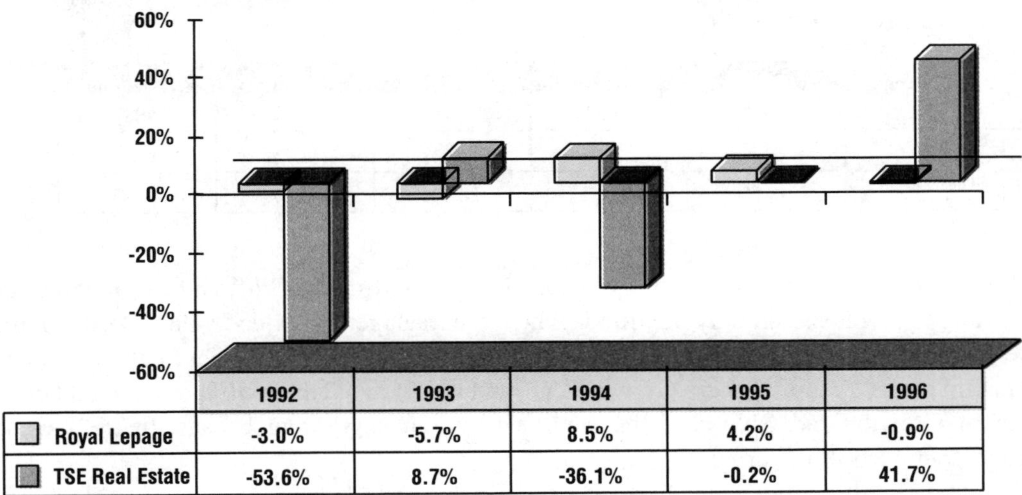

	1992	1993	1994	1995	1996
Royal Lepage	-3.0%	-5.7%	8.5%	4.2%	-0.9%
TSE Real Estate	-53.6%	8.7%	-36.1%	-0.2%	41.7%

Finally, let's review the performance numbers of the Investors Group Japanese Growth Fund relative to a Japanese equity index. In this case, we will use Salomon Brothers Japanese Equity Index as our benchmark. Note from Figure 15.7 that Mr. Abraham outperformed the Japanese index in three of the five years.

In 1992, for example, the Investors Japanese Growth Fund lost 5.9% of its value. Over the same period (1992) the Saloman Brothers Japanese Equity Index lost 15.5%. The Investors Group fund lost money, but it did better than the benchmark. So it would appear that, based on these five years, Mr. Abraham was able to add value to the portfolio, relative to the benchmark.

Figure 15.7: INVESTORS JAPANESE GROWTH AND SALOMON JAPAN EQUITY: ANNUAL RETURNS

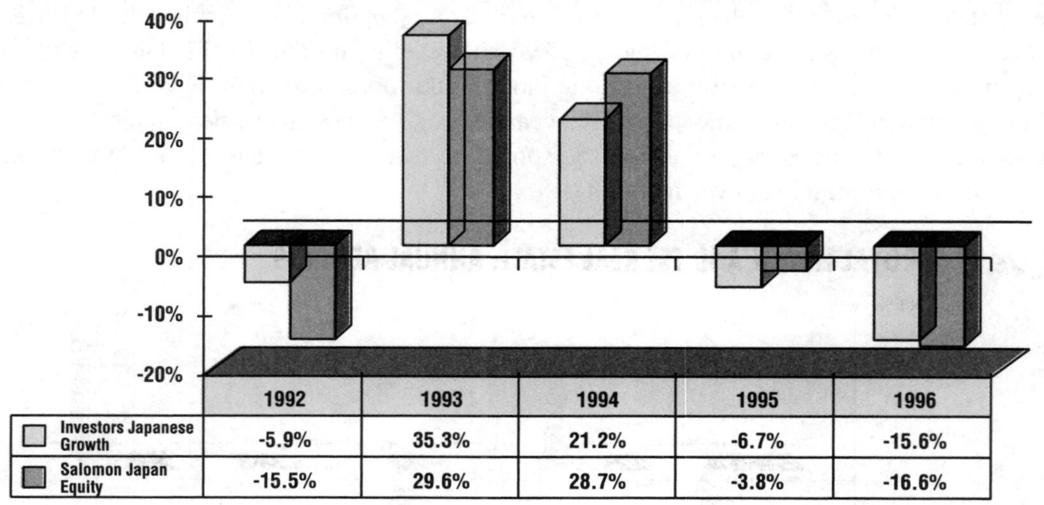

	1992	1993	1994	1995	1996
Investors Japanese Growth	-5.9%	35.3%	21.2%	-6.7%	-15.6%
Salomon Japan Equity	-15.5%	29.6%	28.7%	-3.8%	-16.6%

At this point in the discussion, you may be asking yourself if Mr. Croft and Mr. Kirzner are suggesting that you should only buy funds where the manager has added value. Based on the three examples just cited, you would purchase the Royal LePage Commercial Real Estate Fund and the Investors Group Japanese Growth Fund, and would avoid the AGF International Group American Growth Fund. Obviously, that is not what we are suggesting, because to do so would damage your portfolio returns.

If you buy funds simply on the basis of a superior rating for a manager's performance, then you are committing a sin equal to buying funds solely on the basis of past performance. Screening funds on the basis of MVA ratings alone is still rainbow chasing.

Before moving on, we would suggest that you reread our five-step investment philosophy described earlier in this chapter. Note steps 2 and 3 where we talk about establishing the appropriate asset mix, and then selecting funds that fit within that mix. If your asset mix does not include real estate, then don't buy a real estate fund, regardless of the MVA rating for that manager. On the other hand, if your asset mix suggests that you should own a real estate fund, then, and only then, look for a real estate fund where the manager has added value.

The same holds true for U.S. equity funds and Japanese growth funds. If you want to have some U.S. exposure in your portfolio, then look for U.S. fund managers who have added value. If you want to have exposure to the Japanese market, then look for a Japanese fund manager who has added value. What's important is that you follow the process from start to finish.

Bringing "Risk" into the Discussion

While most investors understand that a trade-off between risk and return exists, few know how to describe that relationship in concrete terms. We know, for example, that an investment in pork belly futures could double or triple in a short period of time. We also know that speculating in commodity futures carries great risk, and we could lose our entire portfolio, and then some, in an equally short period of time.

On the other hand, we know that an investment in Canada Savings Bonds is, in terms of the principal investment, a risk-free exercise. We will receive a fixed rate of interest on our investment and recoup our principal investment when we sell them.

The decision to buy or not to buy either or both of these investments is driven by a conscious assessment of the trade-off between risk and return, a trade-off that can only be made with certainty when looking at extreme situations. Unfortunately, most investors and most investments fall somewhere between speculation in commodity futures and risk-free CSBs. As such, the trade-off between risk and return becomes blurred and difficult to describe.

However, risk is an important consideration as we attempt to evaluate a mutual fund manager. It is one thing to assess whether a manager performed well relative to a benchmark, but it is quite another to look at risk-adjusted returns relative to a benchmark.

To make the point, consider the performance numbers for the Phillips, Hager & North (PH&N) Canadian Equity Plus Fund when compared to the TSE 300 Composite Total Return Index. The PH&N Canadian Equity Plus Fund returned 14.4% compounded annually from the beginning of 1992 to the end of 1996. A $1,000 investment would have grown to $1,957.91.

Over that same period, the TSE 300 (the comparable benchmark) returned 13.9% compounded annually, a $1,000 investment at the beginning of 1992 growing to $1,915.38 by the end of 1996.

Looking at the performance numbers, the return from the fund was almost identical to that of the benchmark. Based on what we have learned so far, it would seem that Peter Guernsey, PH&N's fund manager since 1971, really did nothing more than keep pace with the benchmark index. And the cost of doing so was an average management-expense ratio of 1.18% annually.

However, before we draw any conclusions, consider a comparison of the annual performance numbers in Figure 15.8. At first glance, we see that the PH&N Canadian Equity Plus Fund outperformed the benchmark in three of the five years from 1992 to 1996. But on closer examination, take a look at the returns for 1992 and 1994. In both years, the TSE 300 Composite Total Return Index recorded small losses in 1992 (-1.4%) and 1994 (-0.2%), while the PH&N Canadian Equity Plus Fund generated positive returns. In fact, over that five-year period, the PH&N Canadian Equity Plus Fund never had a losing year.

Figure 15.8: PH&N CANADIAN EQUITY PLUS FUND AND THE TSE 300: ANNUAL RETURNS

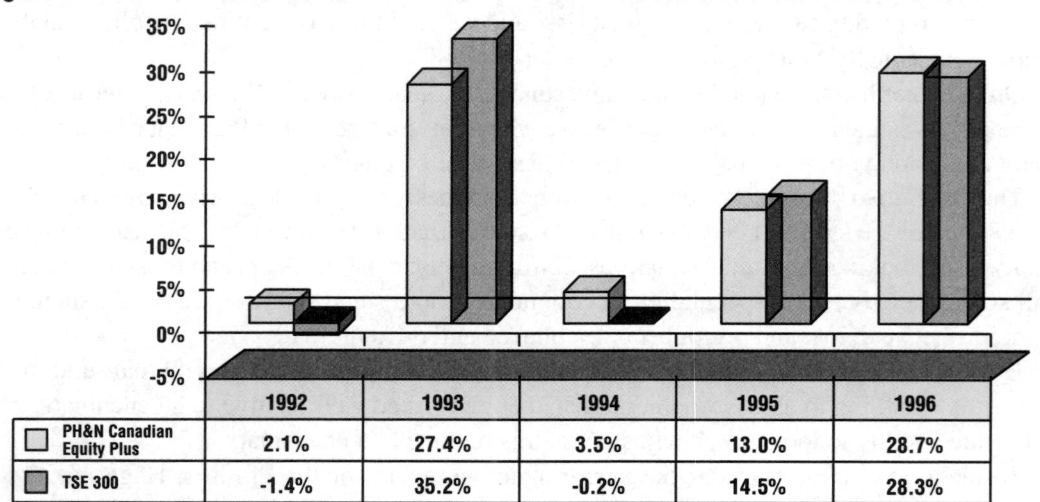

	1992	1993	1994	1995	1996
PH&N Canadian Equity Plus	2.1%	27.4%	3.5%	13.0%	28.7%
TSE 300	-1.4%	35.2%	-0.2%	14.5%	28.3%

Did this manager add value? Well, consider the facts. We have a Canadian equity fund manager whose returns were slightly better than the benchmark index. Equally important, though, we see that in the process of attaining those returns, the fund never had a losing year. A period without loss is worth something to the average investor; in our view worth enough so that to characterize the fund manager as average when he was able to equal the performance of the benchmark index, with less risk, would be unfair.

Risk, then, is the other issue we need to understand in order to assess whether or not a manager added value. We define risk as the volatility of returns of the underlying fund, and we quantify risk mathematically using standard deviation. Standard deviation statistically quantifies the percentage return that the fund can vary from one month to the next. The higher the standard deviation, the more volatile and, by definition, the more risky the fund is.

Of course, for the average investor, risk is defined as the potential for loss over any given period of time. Figure 15.9 looks at the trailing 24-month cumulative returns of our PH&N Canadian Equity Plus Fund. What this shows is all of the possible 24-month holding periods since the fund's inception. We then pose these questions: what was the best 24-month return (81.23%), what was the worst 24-month return (-4.76%) and what was the average 24-month return (26.75%)?

Figure 15.9: TRAILING 24-MONTH CUMULATIVE RETURNS FOR PH&N CANADIAN EQUITY PLUS FUND

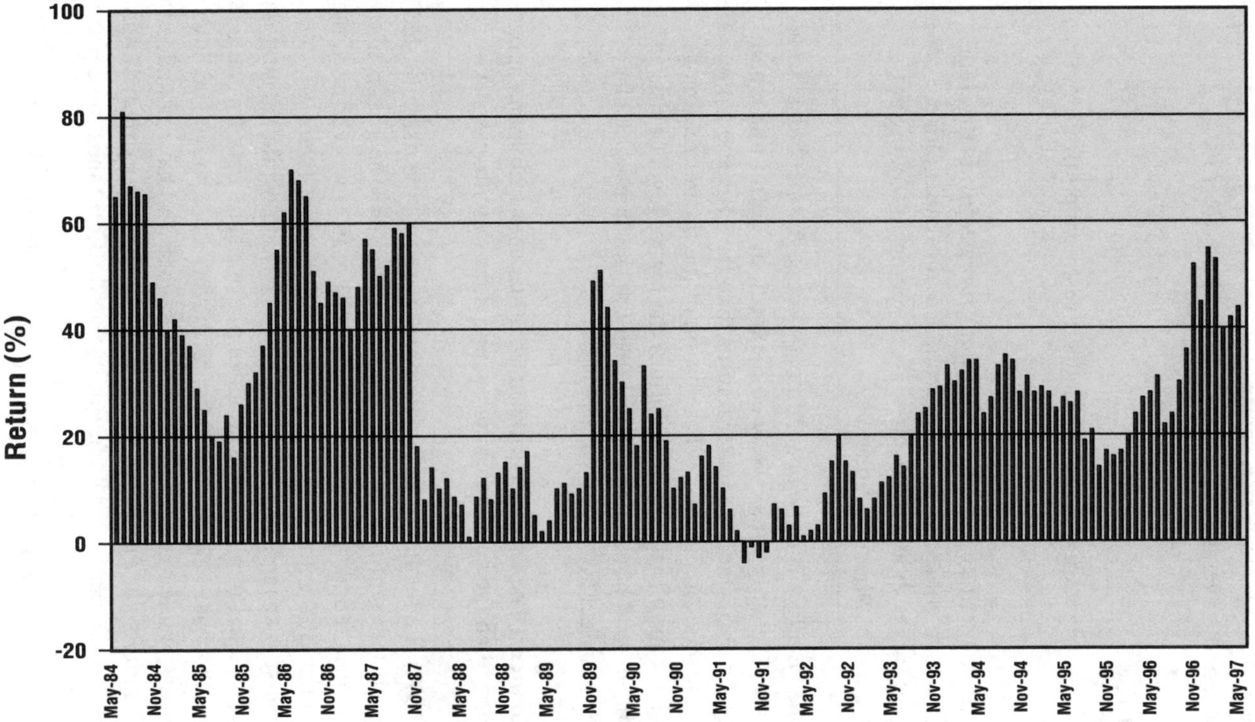

	Total Change	Annual Cmpd Rate	$10,000 Invested	24 Months Ending
Best	81.23%	34.62%	$18,123.27	June 1984
Worst	-4.76%	-2.41%	$9,524.19	September 1991
Average	26.75%	12.58%	$12,674.57	n/a

Trailing returns provide a foundation for investors to make a rationale decision about risk. You simply pick your time horizon (i.e., 24 months in this case) and ask yourself if you could withstand a loss of -4.76% (worst case) over a two-year period, if there was the potential to earn 81.23% (best case) and where the average return was—in this case, 26.75%.

Manager Value Added

When you think about it, the total return of a mutual fund's investment portfolio can be affected by three factors:

1. *Where the portfolio is invested as defined by the fund's prospectus.* Is this fund mandated to hold Canadian equity, U.S. equity, bonds, real estate, gold, etc.? We can evaluate what returns we should expect in a given sector by looking at the returns earned on the comparable benchmark.

2. *The degree of risk the manager is assuming.* A most basic investment tenet states that "higher risk begets higher returns." We would expect, by definition, a high-risk Canadian equity fund to generate greater returns than the TSE 300 Composite Total Return Index. The question is this: What portion of the greater returns generated by the Canadian equity fund was the result of the higher level of risk assumed by the manager, and how much was the result of the shrewd stock-picking ability of the manager?

3. *The ability of the manager.* The best scenario is a fund manager who manages to generate higher returns than the benchmark index, and does so with less risk.

Manager Value Added (MVA) is a mathematical model that quantifies the risk-adjusted return of the fund with the risk-adjusted return of the comparable benchmark. The goal is to evaluate how much the manager contributed to the returns in the portfolio. In other words, of the three factors cited above, how much of the portfolio's return was the result of factor #3.

MVA is an index that ranks managers on their ability to add value, while keeping risk to a minimum. The index is calculated monthly and includes performance data for the last three years. All managers start with a base value of 100. Managers who score above 100 have added value over the last three years, while managers who score less than 100 have not added value.

To understand the calculations, let's examine two giant Canadian equity mutual funds; the Altamira Equity Fund and the Trimark Canadian Equity Fund. Both funds have about $2.5 billion Cdn. in assets, and have diversified portfolios of Canadian stocks. A reasonable benchmark for both funds would be the TSE 300 Composite Total Return Index.

The three-year standard deviation for the Altamira Equity Fund is 3.33%, compared with 2.94% for the Trimark Canadian Equity Fund and 3.38% for the TSE 300. Both the Altamira Equity Fund and the Trimark Canadian Fund exhibited less variability than the TSE 300.

Looking at traditional return measurements, each fund, based on its five-year performance, outperformed the TSE 300 (see Table 15.1). Over shorter periods, however, the results are less impressive; specifically, the 3-year, 1-year, 6-month and 1-month returns for both funds were less than the returns on the TSE 300.

Table 15.1: ALTAMIRA EQUITY, TRIMARK CANADIAN, TSE 300: COMPARISON OF RETURNS*

	5 Years	3 Years	1 Year	6 Months	1 Month
Altamira Equity Fund	17.7%	11.8%	7.7%	4.4%	5.3%
Trimark Canadian Equity Fund	16.4%	14.0%	21.8%	6.5%	4.3%
TSE 300 Composite Index	16.3%	16.4%	24.1%	7.1%	7.0%

* Returns to May 31, 1997

Why does this anomaly exist? The larger a mutual fund gets, the harder it is for that fund to outperform the comparable benchmark. It is simply more difficult for the fund manager to buy a large position in any given stock, particularly small stocks that tend to have more dramatic moves than larger stocks. Even if you are able to buy a significant position in a small company, how do you sell the shares without affecting the price of the stock in the market? And quite often that's just the kind of shrewd move a manager will make in the early days of the fund, and those early performance numbers still form part of the long term (i.e., five-year track record).

As the fund gets bigger, the manager will tend to buy more large-cap stocks because of those liquidity concerns. And because the manager will endeavor to be diversified, a portfolio of large-cap stocks will begin to look a lot like the benchmark index the manager is trying to beat, compounding the problems with shorter-term performance numbers. But we digress!

The MVA index is a four-step process. In step #1, we begin by listing the last 36 monthly returns for each fund, as well as the most recent 36 monthly returns for the benchmark index (example shown in Table 15.2).

Table 15.2: MVA EXAMPLE*

	Jan-97	Feb-97	Mar-97	Apr-97	May-97
Altamira Equity Fund	2.8%	3.0%	-4.8%	0.2%	5.3%
Trimark Canadian Equity Fund	1.7%	1.9%	-3.1%	1.8%	4.3%
TSE 300 Composite Index	3.1%	1.0%	-4.6%	2.1%	7.0%

* Actual calculations include data for 36 months ending May 1997

* * *

At this point we have only examined the actual returns of our two funds relative to the comparable benchmark. We have not taken risk into account. We know that both our funds have experienced less variability than the benchmark index, but we have yet to factor those differences into our model.

To bring risk to the table, we ask a very basic question: how much return should I expect to earn given the risk assumed by each fund? We would then apply that same analysis to the benchmark index. In other words, we know that the Trimark Canadian Equity Fund has a monthly standard deviation of 2.94%, but we don't know what rate of return is reasonable for that level of risk.

That's what we attempt to tackle in step #2 of our model. The objective here is to establish an expected monthly return based on the risk assumed. A number of assumptions go into the algorithm used to establish this expected monthly return, that includes among other things:

1. Establishing a specific time period (i.e., monthly returns).
2. Incorporating the risk-free rate of return available on 91-day Treasury bills.
3. Adjusting the standard deviation for the time period in question (i.e., monthly).

Using this algorithm, we calculate a monthly return based on the risk assumed by the fund manager and the risk inherent in the benchmark index. In Table 15.3, we define a monthly return that reflects the variability of the fund and the index.

Table 15.3: MONTHLY RETURNS WITH VARIABILITY FACTOR*

	Jan-97	Feb-97	Mar-97	Apr-97	May-97
Altamira Equity Fund	0.95%	0.93%	0.97%	0.94%	0.97%
Trimark Canadian Equity Fund	0.86%	0.85%	0.87%	0.86%	0.88%
TSE 300 Composite Index	0.96%	0.95%	0.98%	0.95%	0.99%

* Actual calculations include data for 36 months ending May 1997

There are a couple of things to note. First, the 0.95% average expected monthly return for the Altamira Equity Fund translates into a compound annual return of about 12.01%, which, interestingly, is close to what the fund actually achieved over the three years to May 1997.

Second, we can expect a lower monthly return for the Trimark Canadian Equity Fund than either the Altamira Equity Fund or the TSE 300 Composite Total Return Index. The reason is this: the Trimark Canadian Equity Fund has exhibited lower variability over the years 1995 to 1997, and therefore the return requirement to compensate for the risk assumed is not as great. As a like comparison, we would not expect a low-risk money market fund to produce returns equal to a higher-risk equity fund.

Obviously, with the exception of a money market fund, we would not expect any mutual fund to consistently produce a positive monthly return. In some months the fund will do much better than the expected return, as happened in January, February and May for the Altamira Equity Fund (see Table 15.2).

In other months, the funds will do much worse than the expected rate of return, something that happened to both funds and the benchmark index in March 1997. However, over the course of one, two or three years, we would expect to see the fund's actual numbers average out to—or preferably beat—the expected monthly return data.

In step #3, we compare the actual return data for each fund and the benchmark index with the expected return data calculated using our algorithm. We divide the fund's actual monthly return by its expected monthly return. For example, using the Altamira Equity Fund data for February 1997, we divide the actual return during that month (3.0%) by the expected return (0.93%). The resulting value is 3.15. Table 15.4 shows a sample of the remaining calculations for step #3.

Table 15.4: ACTUAL MONTHLY RETURNS DIVIDED BY EXPECTED MONTHLY RETURNS*

	Jan-97	Feb-97	Mar-97	Apr-97	May-97
Altamira Equity Fund	2.95	3.23	-4.95	0.21	5.46
Trimark Canadian Equity Fund	1.98	2.24	-3.56	2.09	4.89
TSE 300 Composite Index	3.23	1.05	-4.69	2.21	7.07

* Actual calculations include data for the 36 months ending May 1997

In step #3, we are bringing risk into the model by adjusting the actual monthly returns for the risk assumed. We are attempting to break down the monthly returns to ascertain how much of the actual return was affected by risk. Remember, at the beginning of this section, where we listed three factors that affect a fund's total return, the second of those three factors was risk. We apply the same criteria to the benchmark index, because we will eventually compare a manager's risk-adjusted returns to the risk-adjusted returns of the index—which leads us to the next step.

In step #4, we begin to make the comparisons on which the MVA index is based. We compare the risk-adjusted scores for each fund (taken from Table 15.4) with the risk-adjusted score of the benchmark index (also from Table 15.4). In each case we take the risk-adjusted score for the fund and subtract the risk-adjusted score for the benchmark index.

For example, using the data from January 1997, we would take the Trimark Canadian Equity Fund's risk-adjusted score (i.e., 1.98), and subtract the risk-adjusted score for the TSE 300 (i.e., 3.23). The resulting value is -1.25. Table 15.5 shows a sample of the remaining calculations for step #4.

Table 15.5: RISK-ADJUSTED SCORES FOR ALTAMIRA EQUITY FUND AND TRIMARK CANADIAN EQUITY FUND*

	Jan-97	Feb-97	Mar-97	Apr-97	May-97
Altamira Equity Fund	-0.28	2.17	-0.25	-2.00	-1.61
Trimark Canadian Equity Fund	-1.25	1.18	1.13	-0.12	-2.18

* Actual calculations include data for the 36 months ending May 1997

The logic behind step #4 is relatively straightforward. We are simply comparing the fund manager's performance to the benchmark, after adjusting both the fund and the benchmark for risk. It is important to bring the index into the evaluation, because we are trying to find out if the manager added value—not whether the fund was necessarily a good investment over the last three years.

The MVA index has a base value of 100. We then add the 36 data points from Table 15.5 (going back over the last three years) and add (or subtract) that total from 100. The result is the MVA index for that particular fund manager. The MVA index tells us whether or not a fund manager added value when measured on a risk-adjusted basis against a reasonable benchmark. If the fund's MVA index is above 100, the manager has added value. If the fund's MVA index is less than 100, the manager has not added value.

For the record, in the period 1995–1997 the MVA index for the Altamira Equity Fund was 89.42, and for the Trimark Canadian Equity Fund, 98.63. In both cases, the managers failed to add value over those three years when compared to a reasonable benchmark. The complete MVA index of all funds with at least a three-year track record is provided in Appendix III.

Performance Measures—Uses and Abuses

Performance measures can be used to evaluate performance during both bull and bear markets. However, determining the appropriate benchmark and selecting an appropriate time frame is not a simple matter. Studies have shown that high-performing funds in one year are sometimes the big losers the next year. We cite our tale of two bond funds from Chapter 5.

Taking that analysis one step further, some funds outperform the averages in strong markets but underperform when markets are weak. And more often than not, mutual funds on average do not outperform a randomly selected portfolio of securities. A key criterion in selecting a good fund is consistency of performance. How well does the fund perform in bad markets? In good markets? As a result, the fund's beta, variance and reward-to-risk measures are all important tools.

You should also examine the tenure of the fund's manager and whether the person who managed the fund's portfolio when it produced big gains is still at the helm. Often, good managers are lured into a better-paying competitor's camp, while poor managers often find themselves out of a job. In other instances, the portfolio is managed by a management team, as is the case with the Trimark Canadian Equity Fund. This can be a plus because it provides a degree of consistency.

We believe, because we only track the most recent 36 monthly performance numbers, that the MVA index will incorporate a new manager's track record quickly into the model, particularly if the manager excels over a short period of time.

At all costs, avoid the mistake of selecting funds strictly on the basis of recent quarterly or annual performance numbers cited in the financial press. The star performers this quarter or this year may well be the laggards next period.

Some Final Thoughts

We believe that the MVA index is an excellent model for rating fund managers. But, as with any rating model, it is not intended to be a guide for future performance. As we have stated, investments ought to be approached from the top down. Rather than selecting funds on the basis of any measurement standard, investors should first look at how those funds fit within the context of their long-range objectives and risk tolerances.

The MVA index is but one piece of the fund selection puzzle. We believe investors should follow our 5-step investment guide, and then purchase quality funds in the selected categories based on the MVA index.

The MVA index ranks funds on the basis of return per unit of risk over the past three-year period. Obviously, we have to be careful not to infringe on our real-world view that no ideal time period on which to measure funds exists. However, since our model required reasonable risk measurements, we were drawn to the three-year standard deviation numbers widely available in Pal-Trak.

Quantity was also a factor. In the current Pal-Trak database, there are 1,100 funds with three-year track records versus 748 funds with at least five-year records. By using the three-year numbers, we were able to rank more funds without, in our opinion, sacrificing the validity of the index. Because one of the risk measures used in Pal-Trak is calculated using price and return data from the most recent 36 months, the three-year time period appears to be a reasonable compromise.

If the calculations seem complicated, they are. But, fortunately, they are not something you have to do yourself. The MVA indexes are calculated monthly by Portfolio Analytics (1-800-531-4725 or 416-489-7074 and via e-mail: paltrak@pal.com), the Toronto-based company that distributes Pal-Trak mutual fund data disks. And, of course, we will provide annual updates to the MVA indexes in future editions of this book and through Richard Croft's newsletter, *Money Matters*.

CHAPTER SIXTEEN

The FundLine

The Many Forms of Diversification

To maintain investments for the long term, we need a portfolio that will smooth the ride over the hills and valleys of the business cycle. Investors who hold portfolios that rise substantially one year, only to fall sharply the next, don't sleep well at night—and don't stay invested for the long term. The only way to counter this volatility is to diversify your portfolio. In short, diversification reduces risk.

To put another spin on the advantages of diversification, we can't dismiss the fact that different asset classes perform differently over time. We can say with reasonable certainty that, over the long term, equity funds will outperform bond funds, and bond funds will do better than money market funds. What we cannot forecast is which asset class will dominate in any given year.

Table 16.1: FUND GROUPS PERFORM DIFFERENTLY OVER TIME

Year	Small-Cap Funds	Large-Cap Funds	Canadian Bond	Money Market
1997	13.6%	**13.7%**	8.1%	2.4%
1996	**33.5**	25.1	10.0	4.0
1995	**19.4**	13.0	18.5	6.3
1994	-10.4	-2.7	-5.5	**4.2**
1993	**64.1**	25.2	15.7	4.6
1992	12.0	**50.0**	8.7	6.0
1991	15.6	12.9	**19.0**	9.1
1990	-15.8	-12.1	6.9	**12.2**
1989	15.0	**17.5**	11.4	11.1
1988	-1.3	**12.7**	8.5	8.4
1987	5.7	1.5	3.0	**7.6**

That being said, the risk-reduction benefits of diversification are meaningless if performance suffers. And therein lies the most basic investment paradox. We know from our discussion about Manager Value Added that we can mathematically quantify an expected rate of return for a given level of risk. Lower-risk investments produce lower returns, and higher-risk investments produce higher returns.

For diversification to add value, it has to be done in such a way as to balance the relationship between risk and return. What we want, ideally, is a lower-risk portfolio that generates above-average returns. To accomplish this goal, we suggest is a four-dimensional approach to diversification that includes:

- Diversification by asset class or mix
- Diversification by geographic region
- Diversification by fund objectives
- Diversification by investment style

Figure 16.1: THE FOUR DIMENSIONS OF DIVERSIFICATION

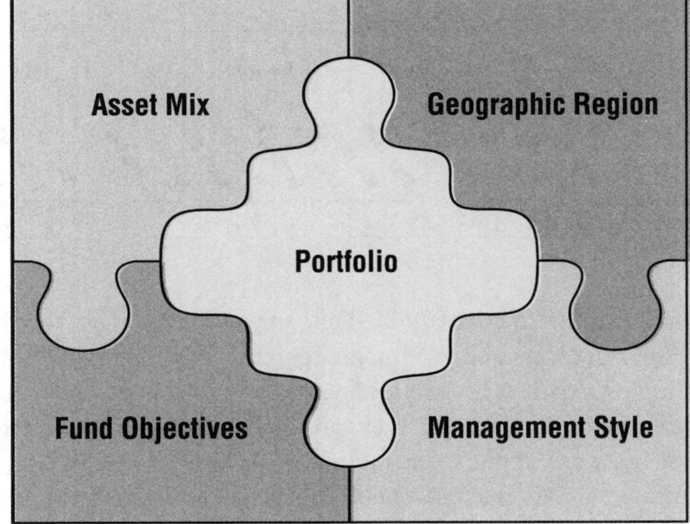

Diversification by asset class (discussed in Chapter 14) is the most important consideration when constructing a well-balanced portfolio. We can further reduce risk by extending the asset mix to include geographic regions—as in borderless shopping (see Chapter 8).

We believe that diversification by fund objectives and investment management style is another important consideration. The purpose of this exercise is not to judge the merits of any particular investment style but rather to mix and match styles that bring a measure of balance to the portfolio. We discussed these elements in Chapter 4, which focused on equity funds, and in Chapter 5, which focused on fixed-income funds.

Now we will attempt to bring all of these elements together. We will break down and graphically display this four-dimensional approach to diversification in an easy-to-read format entitled the *FundLine*.

The FundLine provides an interpretive view of the risk-reduction elements a particular fund brings to your portfolio. We believe that investors who mix and match above-average funds, as measured by the MVA index, and utilize the diversification techniques spelled out by the FundLine will be able to construct a well-balanced portfolio that should, over the long haul, provide above-average, risk-adjusted returns.

The FundLine

The goal of the FundLine is to graphically illustrate the elements of diversification brought to the portfolio by each mutual fund reviewed in this book. It is our way of streamlining the selection process so that all factors that come into play for the construction of a portfolio can be found in the FundLine. If you want to build an optimum portfolio, simply fill in the boxes.

Figure 16.2: THE FUNDLINE

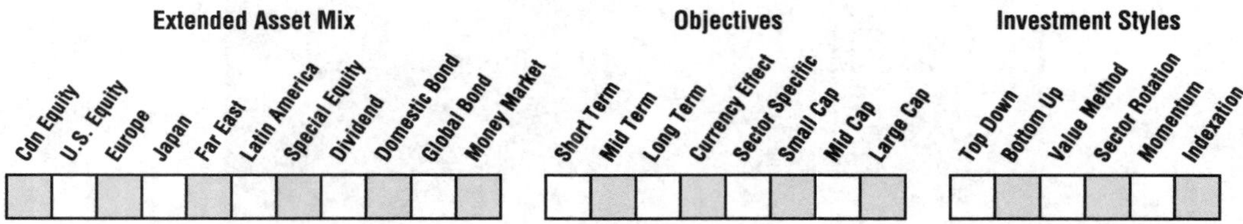

The FundLine is comprised of 25 boxes divided into three sections. The first section, *Extended Asset Mix*, defines the asset class and geographic region in which the fund invests.

The second section, *Objectives*, broadly defines those investments the fund is emphasizing in the portfolio. For some funds, the objectives can change. For example, a bond fund manager who thinks interest rates are about to fall might have a large percentage of the portfolio invested in long-term bonds. As interest rates fall, that same manager may sell the long-term bonds at a profit and move the portfolio into short-term bonds. The attributes of a particular fund are categorized based on the portfolio at the time of writing.

The third section categorizes a number of different *Investment Styles*. Generally speaking, the investment style of a successful fund will remain constant. We are hedging our position on this subject somewhat. While we would not expect successful portfolio managers to willingly change their approach to investing, there are times when managers are forced to rethink their approach.

We note, for example, that in May 1997, Gerald Coleman tendered his resignation to Mackenzie Financial Corporation in order to take up a new position as president of C.I. Capital

Management's money management unit. Mr. Coleman was the lead manager on the very successful Ivy Canadian Fund.

The funds in the Ivy family are considered "value" funds. Value is an investment style, where managers seek out so-called undervalued companies. Potential investments are analyzed according to a strict set of fundamental principles. Value managers look at such things as a company's stock price as a percentage of its book value, corporate debt relative to equity, etc.

It's hard to argue with the concept of value investing, because in theory the manager is buying a company for less than its actual worth. Value funds are also more conservative than growth funds, which means they will not likely experience dramatic declines in a down market and will underperform growth funds in a rising market.

In recent years, however, value managers have been hitting on all cylinders. Value funds by nature are less volatile and thus are preferred by conservative investors, but they have also been top quartile performers. This is beneficial for the investor's bottom line, and as Mr. Coleman learned, such numbers can do wonders for your market value if you're considering a job change.

Over the past few years, Mr. Coleman has been practicing the right management style at the right time. But now, with North American stock markets at record levels, it is harder for value managers to find undervalued stocks. When value managers can't find good investments after filtering stocks through a strict set of fundamental criteria, those managers will simply hold cash. We note, for example, that at the end of June, 1998, the Ivy Canadian Fund had 33.9% of its assets in cash.

Now, here's the problem. If your equity fund is holding substantial amounts of cash when the stock market is rising, your future performance numbers will suffer. And that raises the question that takes us full circle: can value managers continue to deliver top quartile performance numbers in the future without changing their investment style?

A Closer Look at the Extended Asset Mix

As you can see from the FundLine in Figure 16.2, we have subdivided or extended the asset classes into 11 categories. Recall that in Chapter 14 we extended the traditional asset mix from equity/fixed income/cash to include geographic diversification. The FundLine simply builds on that foundation by broadening our international equity categories to include Canada, the United States, Europe, Japan, the Far East and Latin America. We have also included a special equity class that represents sector-specific funds, including real estate, precious metals, resources and any other special equity type of fund.

Fixed-income assets are also represented in the asset class section of the FundLine. In this case, we have subdivided the fixed-income component into three categories: dividend funds, domestic bond funds and global bond funds. And the final category is money market, which represents any cash assets in your portfolio.

The Fund's Asset Mix

The notion that funds are required to invest by asset class seems straightforward enough. A Canadian equity fund invests, for the most part, in Canadian stocks. A domestic bond fund invests in Canadian bonds, and so on. And rarely would that asset mix change.

But there are exceptions to the rather narrow definition associated with Canadian equity funds and Canadian bond funds. An example would be global balanced funds. The asset mix for global bond funds is not always neatly defined, and it does not necessarily remain static.

For example, the Elliott & Page Global Balanced Fund invests in a diversified portfolio of equity and fixed-income investments from around the world. While David Boardman and Ian Henderson, the fund managers, have a mandate to invest anywhere in the world, they have focused their attention on equity and fixed-income investments in the U.S., Europe and Japan (see Figure 16.3).

Figure 16.3: ELLIOTT & PAGE GLOBAL BALANCED FUND: APPROXIMATE WEIGHTINGS

Cash	2%
Canadian Equity	1.3%
U.S. Equity	17%
Europe Equity	25%
Japan Equity	10%
Canadian Bonds	16%
Foreign Bonds	28.7%

The Elliott & Page Global Balanced Fund, then, represents equity and fixed-income assets, as well as providing a measure of geographic diversification (see Figure 16.4).

Figure 16.4: ELLIOTT & PAGE GLOBAL BALANCED FUNDLINE

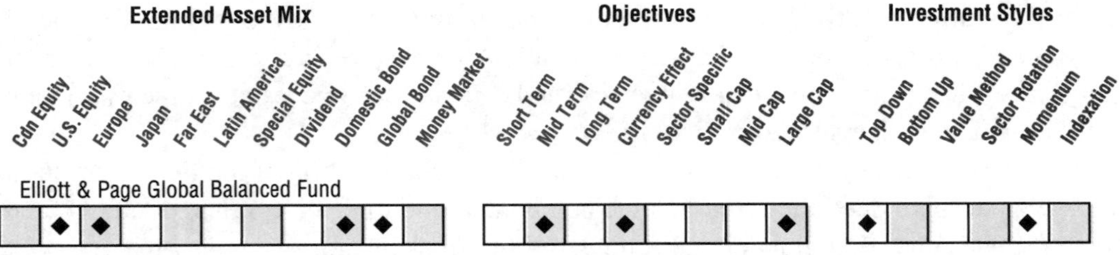

The G.T. Global Growth and Income Fund also represents both equity and fixed-income investments, and has a mandate to invest worldwide. Fund managers Soraya M. Betterton, Nicholas S. Train and Gary Kreps have been focusing their attention on equity and fixed-income investments only in the U.S. and Europe. The managers also had approximately 13% of the fund's assets invested in the Asia Pacific region (including 8% in Australia). We categorize the Asia Pacific region under the Far East category in the FundLine.

Note, however, in Figure 16.5, that we have not marked off the Far East category. We believe that a fund must have at least 15% of its assets invested in a specific region or asset before we recognize its diversification potential in the FundLine.

Figure 16.5: G.T. GLOBAL GROWTH & INCOME FUNDLINE

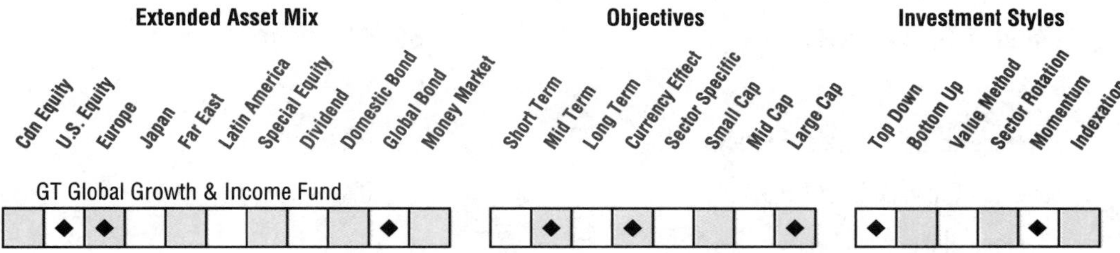

Some Thoughts on One-Stop Shopping

In looking at the FundLine categories that pertain to global balanced funds (the terms "balanced," "growth & income" and "diversified" are interchangeable), an interesting question is raised. Why not simply buy a global balanced fund and nothing else? The point is this: is there an advantage to buying funds that offer many forms of diversification?

In Figure 16.4, for example, we see that the Elliott & Page Global Balanced Fund falls into nine of the 25 categories in the FundLine, while the G.T. Global Growth and Income Fund provides exposure to eight FundLine categories. The mutual fund industry sees this as one-stop shopping. We see it as a "handyman special" that best serves small investors who are just starting out. It is not clear that global balanced funds add value for investors who have the wherewithal to buy a diversified portfolio of six to eight quality mutual funds.

In terms of performance, we see advantages to buying good-quality funds that specialize in specific markets (i.e., equity funds, bond funds, international equity funds, small-cap funds, etc.). Funds that strive to be all things to all investors suffer from what we call the "jack-of-all-trades, master-of-none syndrome." The more diversification a fund manager brings to the table, the less likely it is that the manager will excel at any investment strategy that focuses on specific areas.

To illustrate, consider a hypothetical portfolio of eight mutual funds using only the FundLine as our portfolio building tool. (By that we mean that no effort has been made to find above-average performing funds using, among other things, the MVA index.) We have simply chosen a portfolio of *average performing funds* that represent elements of diversification as defined by the FundLine. The allocation of our FundLine portfolio is laid out in Table 16.2, and the diversification breakdown is given in Figure 16.6.

Table 16.2: FUNDLINE PORTFOLIO ALLOCATION

Funds	Percentage
Average Canadian Large-Cap Equity	15.0%
Average Canadian Small-Cap Equity	15.0%
Average U.S. Equity Funds	15.0%
Average International Equity Funds	15.0%
Total of Equity Assets	**60.0%**
Average Canadian Dividend Funds	15.0%
Average Canadian Bond Funds	15.0%
Average Global Bond Funds	5.0%
Total of Fixed-Income Assets	**35.0%**
Average Canadian Money Market Funds	5.0%
Total of Cash Assets	**5.0%**

Figure 16.6: SAMPLE FUNDLINE PORTFOLIO ALLOCATION

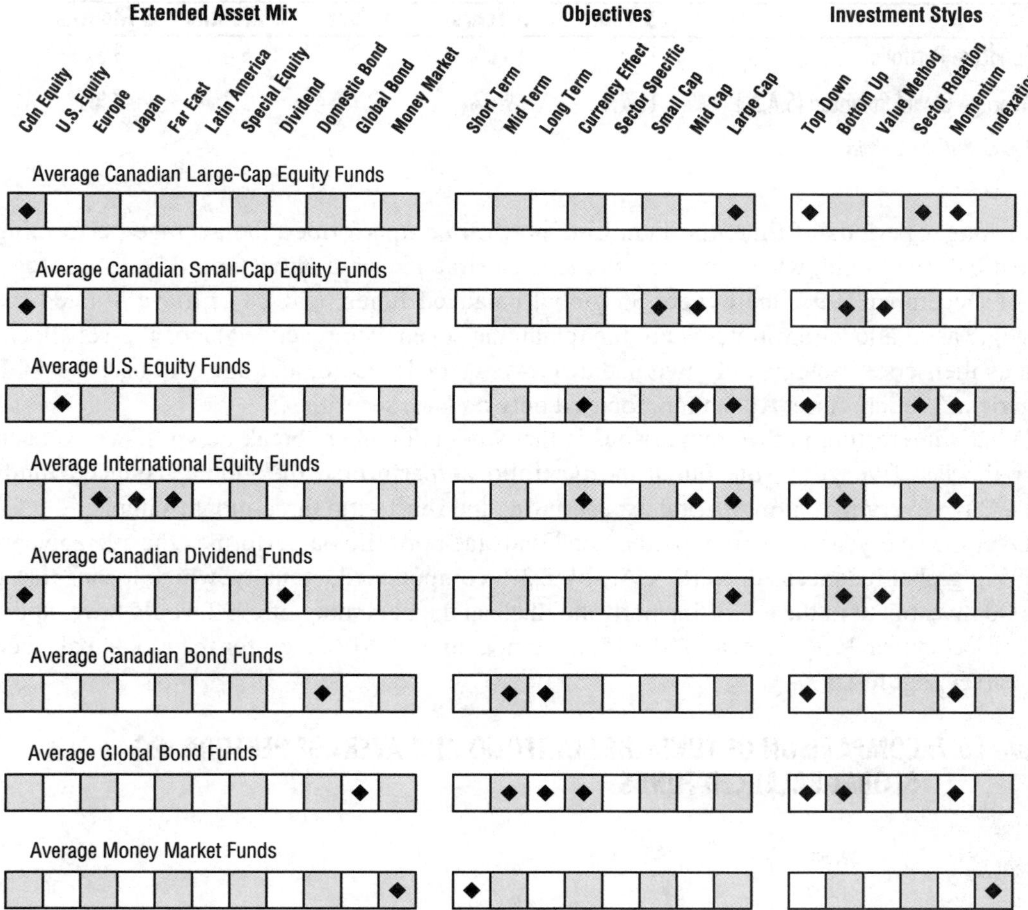

Our hypothetical FundLine portfolio includes only average performing funds in a specific category. Now, let's do a comparison of this passive portfolio against the performance of average performing global balanced funds over a similar time frame. The results are interesting (see Table 16.3).

Table 16.3: PERFORMANCE COMPARISONS

	5 Years	3 Years	1 Year	6 Months	3 Months
FundLine Portfolio	13.5%	13.0%	6.0%	6.4%	3.3%
Average Global Balanced (S.A.A.)	11.2%	9.4%	12.1%	5.9%	3.8%

Source: Portfolio Analytics

Over longer periods of time, the FundLine portfolio outperformed the average performing global balanced fund, whose managers practice a strategic asset allocation (S.A.A.) strategy. As of December 1997, there were 35 global balanced funds, and 28 of those utilized the strategic asset allocation strategy. For the remaining seven who practiced tactical asset allocation as their core strategy, only two had a five-year track record, and one of those, the AGF American Tactical Asset Allocation, focused only on U.S. securities.

What's interesting in the comparisons is the way the numbers break down. If we go back over the last five years, the FundLine portfolio outperformed the global balanced funds (S.A.A.) in every measuring period except during the short-term three-month sample.

Over the five-year measuring period, the FundLine portfolio outperformed the average performing global balanced funds (S.A.A.) by 2.3% compounded annually, which means that a $1,000 investment in the FundLine portfolio made at the beginning of 1992 would have, at the end of December 1996, grown to $1,815.52 compared with $1,632.69 for the global balanced funds (see Figure 16.7).

Figure 16.7: COMPARISON OF FUNDLINE PORTFOLIO AND AVERAGE PERFORMING GLOBAL BALANCED FUNDS

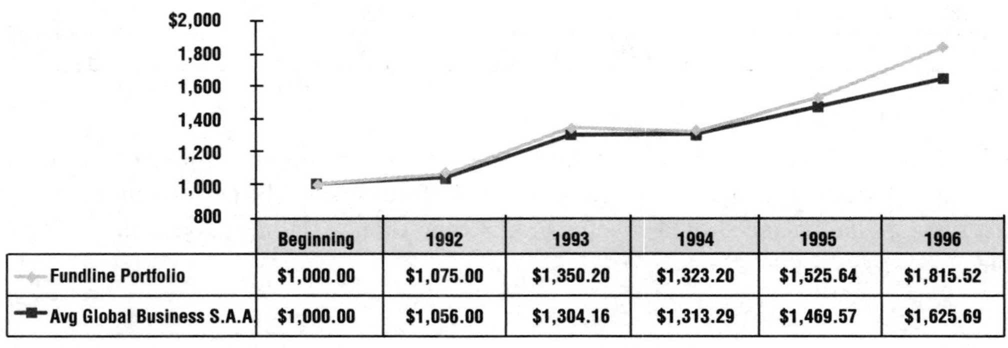

	Beginning	1992	1993	1994	1995	1996
Fundline Portfolio	$1,000.00	$1,075.00	$1,350.20	$1,323.20	$1,525.64	$1,815.52
Avg Global Business S.A.A.	$1,000.00	$1,056.00	$1,304.16	$1,313.29	$1,469.57	$1,625.69

Let's take this discussion one step further. Table 16.4 looks at the performance numbers for global balanced funds by quartile for the same measuring periods used in Table 16.3. We have also included the FundLine portfolio for comparison purposes and calculated what performance quartile the FundLine portfolio would have fit into over those measuring periods.

Note that over longer time periods (three and five years), the FundLine portfolio is solidly positioned in the first quartile. It is also solidly entrenched in the first quartile performance numbers for the one-year time period. Only over shorter periods—i.e., six months and three months—do we see some volatility in the quartile ranking of the FundLine portfolio. Again, that is something we would expect, because performance anomalies often occur over shorter time periods. And remember, we have only included average performing funds in the FundLine portfolio.

Table 16.4: QUARTILE BREAKDOWN

	Average Global Balanced S.A.A.				
	5 Years	**3 Years**	**1 Year**	**6 Months**	**3 Months**
1st Quartile	12.7%	12.0%	14.5%	7.3%	4.6%
2nd Quartile	12.4	9.0	11.1	5.6	3.6
3rd Quartile	10.4	7.4	8.3	4.5	3.2
4th Quartile	9.0	5.7	5.8	3.4	1.7
FundLine Portfolio	**13.5%**	**13.0%**	**16.0%**	**6.4%**	**3.3%**
FundLine Portfolio by Quartile	**1**	**1**	**1**	**2**	**3**

These numbers make more sense when you think of the complexities of managing a global balanced fund. Global balanced (diversified) managers must determine the weights of each asset class within the portfolio (i.e., stocks, bonds and cash), decide which country offers the best opportunity for growth and then select the right stocks and bonds within that geographic region. And in many cases, these funds attempt to hedge currency risk.

We think it is a stretch to expect a manager, who is required to invest by asset mix and geographic region, to manage the exchange-rate risk and also be adept at picking individual stocks and bonds that offer above-average performance.

In short, we concede that 85% to 90% of your overall return is dependent on your asset mix decision and emphasize that the asset mix decision is the core strategy of the balanced or global balanced (diversified) fund. But, in our opinion, purchasing a balanced fund or a global balanced (diversified) fund eliminates any possibility of finding a good manager who can add value for the other 10% to 15% of your overall performance numbers. We think the FundLine provides a solid, straightforward foundation on which to optimize your asset mix within your own personal guidelines, allowing you to then focus on the funds that specialize in certain investment areas.

The Fund's Objectives: Small, Medium and Large Cap

The next section of the FundLine defines for us the makeup of the investments held by the individual funds. We're not talking about the specific stocks an equity fund might hold or the specific bonds in a bond fund, but rather the general structure of the portfolio.

For example, a fund manager may focus specifically on large-cap or small-cap stocks. The Manulife Cabot Canadian Equity Fund, for example, has a clear large-cap mandate; the manager is restricted to the top 100 funds listed on the Toronto Stock Exchange. The Global Strategy Canadian Small-Cap Fund, on the other hand, focuses entirely on shares of small-cap companies.

We find that equity managers usually have a blended portfolio that includes, say, small- and medium-cap stocks, or medium- and large-cap stocks. Some managers will tell you they hold a blended portfolio that includes small-, medium- *and* large-cap stocks.

However, we have found on closer examination that all fund managers express some bias in their selection process. As such, the bulk of any blended equity portfolio is usually weighted between two groups—say, small- and medium-size firms, or medium- and large-cap companies.

We expect equity funds that focus on small-cap stocks, on average, to be more volatile than equity funds with a large-cap focus. In fact, the average monthly standard deviation (calculated over the period 1995–1997) for small-cap Canadian equity funds is 4.19%, versus an average monthly standard deviation of 3.26% for Canadian equity large-cap funds.

While we do not endorse one type of fund portfolio over another, we would expect, over long periods of time, that small-cap funds will outperform large-cap funds. Higher returns compensate you for the increased risks.

The calendar year numbers have been decidedly in favor of small-cap stocks over the period 1992–1996. For example, a $1,000 investment in Canadian small-cap funds would have grown to $2,446.64. A $1,000 investment in the average Canadian large-cap fund, over the same five-year period would have been worth $1,734.41.

Figure 16.8: AVERAGE CANADIAN SMALL- AND LARGE-CAP FUNDS: A COMPARISON

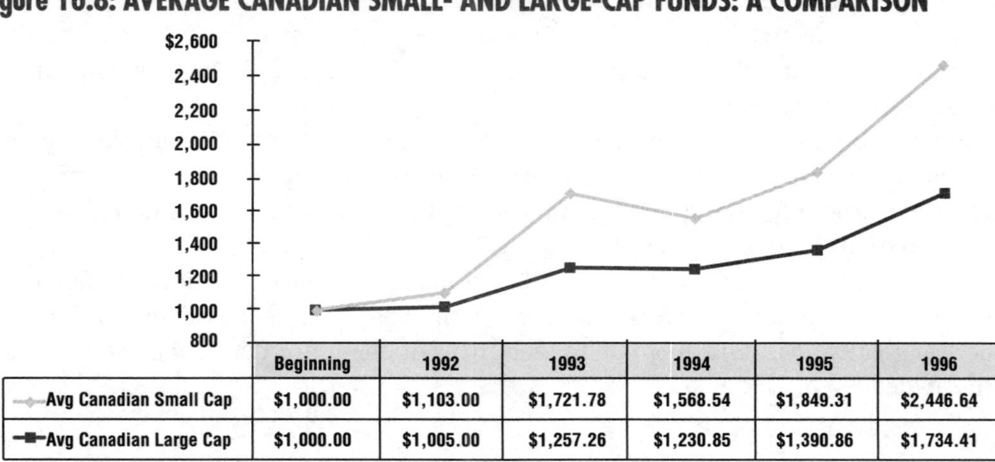

	Beginning	1992	1993	1994	1995	1996
Avg Canadian Small Cap	$1,000.00	$1,103.00	$1,721.78	$1,568.54	$1,849.31	$2,446.64
Avg Canadian Large Cap	$1,000.00	$1,005.00	$1,257.26	$1,230.85	$1,390.86	$1,734.41

That being said, history also tells us that there are periods when small-cap funds will underperform large-cap funds, and sometimes those periods of underperformance can be quite lengthy. The three-year performance numbers (to May 31, 1997) support that position and explain why we have been reading in the financial press for some time that investors have been having a love affair with large-cap stocks.

Table 16.5: SMALL CAP VS. LARGE CAP: PERIOD RETURNS*

Small Cap vs. Large Cap	5 Years	3 Years	1 Year	6 Months	3 Months
Average Canadian Small Cap	18.4%	13.9%	12.8%	6.6%	1.0%
Average Canadian Large Cap	13.9%	15.3%	23.8%	7.7%	4.9%

*Period returns ending May 31, 1997

When constructing an optimum portfolio, we suggest you balance your portfolio by including a small-cap fund as well as a large-cap fund.

Fixed-Income Portfolios: Short, Medium and Long Term

As is the case with equity funds, the FundLine provides three boxes that represent the portfolios of fixed-income managers. Fixed-income managers, whether mandated to invest globally or domestically, tend to pick their spots along the yield curve. These three categorizations are representative of virtually all fixed-income portfolios and, in short, pigeonhole the average term-to-maturity of the bond fund being analyzed.

You will recall from Chapter 5 that term-to-maturity and, more specifically, duration have a dramatic impact on the profitability of a bond fund, given a change in the level of interest rates. Simply stated, a domestic bond fund with a portfolio of long-term bonds will be more volatile, and offer greater capital gains potential than a domestic bond fund with a short term-to-maturity.

For purposes of the FundLine, we define "short term" as those bond funds where the average term-to-maturity is three years or less. "Mid term" is defined as a bond fund with an average term-to-maturity of three to 10 years, and "long term" represents fixed-income funds where the average term-to-maturity is greater than 10 years.

We have also included a box entitled "Currency Effect" in the middle of the *Objectives* section. This tells us whether the fund's performance will be affected by fluctuations in a foreign currency. Whether you view that box as currency risk or currency hedge depends on your point of view. If you go south every winter, you may look for funds that are diamond-marked under Currency Effect, viewing that as a tool to hedge yourself against changes in the value of the Canadian dollar.

Of course, the significance of currency effect in the fund's performance hinges on the type of investments held in the fund. For example, we would expect over most long periods that the bulk of the performance numbers generated by international equity funds are the result of the overall performance within a specific equity market, rather than from currency fluctuations. If the equity market in a particular country is doing well, it usually means that the country's currency is also strong.

This approach would seem to fly in the face of comments we made in Chapter 14. Remember how currency fluctuations had such a dramatic impact on funds invested in Mexico? Still, in general terms, an international fund (remember Latin American Funds have their own category) generally invests in mature markets (i.e., Europe, Japan and parts of the Far East) and, as such, the manager has the ability to hedge against currency fluctuations. As a result of that, we believe that the performance numbers from an international equity fund are driven largely by the performance of the stock market in the countries where the fund invests, and not as much by currency fluctuations.

In 1996, for example, the performance of the U.S. dollar vis-à-vis the Canadian dollar had some impact on the Canadian dollar-adjusted performance numbers generated by U.S. equity funds. However, the impact from changes in the U.S. dollar/Canadian dollar exchange rate paled in comparison with the returns produced by a hot U.S. equity market. On the other hand, exchange-rate risk has, in the past, played a major role in the performance of equity funds that invest in smaller markets, such as Latin America.

Currency fluctuations also play a major role in the performance of global bond funds. There are periods where currency exchange has a greater impact on the global bond fund's performance than does the term-to-maturity of the fixed-income portfolio. In some cases, global bond fund managers actively manage currency exposure in an attempt to enhance returns from profitable currency trading.

Other global bond funds go to great lengths to hedge against exchange-rate risk, which implies that most of the performance numbers from such funds will be the result of changes in the level of interest rates within a specific geographic region. An example is the Universal World Tactical Bond Fund, where the manager "uses active currency management to protect gains." Presumably, Mr. Williams is protecting the gains earned by actively managing the fixed-income part of the portfolio and is not attempting to enhance total returns by trading currencies.

The point is whether the manager is actively managing the portfolio to profit from currency fluctuations or to protect against currency fluctuations, we believe that all global bond funds will be affected one way or another by currency fluctuations, and as such all global bond funds will have a diamond mark in the Currency Effect box.

Finally, most U.S. and international equity funds, global bond funds and global balanced (diversified) funds are valued in Canadian dollars. There are exceptions, however, with AGF being the classic example. AGF offers investors a choice. Many AGF funds can be purchased in U.S. or Canadian dollars.

The Dividend Box: A Fixed-Income Alternative

Last year we added a *Dividend* box to the FundLine. Dividend funds, like bond funds, promise to deliver income. However, with dividend funds the income is in the form of preferred and/or common dividends paid by stocks held in the fund.

We believe a dividend box is an important addition, because we were striving to find alternatives to fixed-income investments. With interest rates at historically low levels, we are not expecting the performance of generic bond funds to be as strong in the future as they have been in the last 10 years.

We also feel that dividend managers fill a niche, because they have more latitude in terms of where they can place new money in order to produce income. Think about it! Bond fund managers, in general, have very restrictive policies in terms of what they can and cannot invest in. They can change the term-to-maturity of their portfolio—i.e., hold shorter-term bonds when rates are expected to rise and longer-term bonds when rates are expected to decline—but at the end of the day, they must hold bonds. When rates rise, the value of a bond portfolio will decline. It is simply a matter of degree.

Contrast that position with that of dividend fund managers, who must invest in dividend-paying stocks. If dividend fund managers were required to only hold preferred shares—which tend to rise and fall based on the prevailing rate of interest—they would have the same problem our bond fund managers have: higher interest rates would mean the value of their preferred share portfolio would decline.

Dividend fund managers have more flexibility than simply investing in preferred shares. They are only required to hold dividend-paying stocks, and those stocks can be preferred or common shares.

If you are going to hold common shares that pay reasonable dividends, you will hold companies like BCE Inc. and the shares of Canadian chartered banks. Since Canadian bank stocks have been on fire for the last two years, and with BCE Inc. beginning to act like a growth company, is it any wonder dividend funds have done so well recently? In 1996, for example, Canadian dividend funds, on average, returned 25.1% compared with 10.0% for the average Canadian bond fund.

Because some dividend funds pay regular monthly dividend distributions and because dividends have certain tax advantages for high-income earners, these are attractive alternatives for investors seeking income.

We think that investors who are seeking income-producing funds ought to look for those funds whose manager has the greatest degree of flexibility. That is, funds that acknowledge the significance of the manager's role in determining the right mix of income-producing investments. Dividend fund managers simply have more flexibility than bond fund managers.

Keeping with that same theme, there are a few funds that are classified as Canadian balanced funds, but we believe they should be classified as income-producing funds. Three that come to mind include the G.T. Global Canada Income Class Fund, the Global Strategy Income Plus Fund, the Guardian Monthly High Income Fund.

All three funds have been given a mandate to invest in a "full range of income-producing investments, including preferred and common shares, short-term debt obligations, royalty income trust units and certain 'derivative strategies.'" Investments include, in some cases, convertible debentures, common and preferred stock, and, in the case of the G.T. Global Canada Income Class Fund, covered call writing strategies to enhance income and reduce risk. Think of covered call writing as a low-risk strategy that can yield decent returns on blue-chip common stocks—returns that, for the record, are taxed as capital gains.

We like to think of these as non-traditional balanced funds whose goal is to produce a regular stream of income, as opposed to traditional balanced funds that focus on growth first and income second.

Figure 16.9: FUNDLINES FOR G.T. GLOBAL CANADA INCOME CLASS, GLOBAL STRATEGY INCOME PLUS, GUARDIAN MONTHLY HIGH INCOME FUND

Extended Asset Mix

Fund	Cdn Equity	U.S. Equity	Europe	Japan	Far East	Latin America	Special Equity	Dividend	Domestic Bond	Global Bond	Money Market
G.T. Canada Income Class Fund	◆							◆			
Global Strategy Income Plus Fund	◆							◆	◆		
Guardian Monthly High Income Fund	◆							◆			

Objectives

Fund	Short Term	Mid Term	Long Term	Currency Effect	Sector Specific	Small Cap	Mid Cap	Large Cap
G.T. Canada Income Class Fund								◆
Global Strategy Income Plus Fund		◆						◆
Guardian Monthly High Income Fund						◆	◆	

Investment Styles

Fund	Top Down	Bottom Up	Value Method	Sector Rotation	Momentum	Indexation
G.T. Canada Income Class Fund		◆	◆			
Global Strategy Income Plus Fund	◆	◆			◆	
Guardian Monthly High Income Fund		◆	◆			

Sector-Specific Funds

Finally, under the *Objectives* section, we have a box entitled "Sector Specific," which represents funds that do not provide much in the way of diversification but can add some real oomph to your bottom line. Funds that receive a diamond mark in the Sector-Specific box will likely also have a diamond mark in the Special Equity box under the *Extended Asset Mix* section.

Investors should give careful consideration to using this box in constructing a portfolio. For example, the Green Line Science and Technology Fund, because of its narrow focus, would receive a diamond mark in the Special Equity and Sector-Specific boxes. However, while we would expect a U.S. science and technology fund to be more volatile than the overall market, it will tend to move in the same direction as, say, the S&P 500 Composite Index, because the boom or bust in the technology sector is driven by the strength or weakness of the overall economy.

On the other hand, funds that specialize in precious metals or natural resources tend to move opposite to the general trend and can provide reasonable diversification to the broader market.

We would generally expect these types of special equity funds to perform quite differently from the broader equity market, perhaps rising when stocks are generally falling, and performing poorly as has been the case in recent years when the market, in general, is rising.

In 1996, for example, resource funds returned on average 30.0% for the year, while the average for precious metals funds was 38.1%. However, in 1997, as the price of gold began to decline, and with the Bre-X fiasco having such an impact on the market, the shine that was on Canadian precious metals funds began to tarnish. Still, we cannot escape the fact that the Canadian economy is very dependent on natural resources, and therefore, any Canadian equity fund will have some exposure to this sector. We suggest that it might not be necessary to have funds that specialize in precious metals or resources.

Using Special Equity Funds in Your Portfolio

They are the best of funds; they are the worst of funds. Check the three-month, six-month and one-year performance numbers, and at the top of the list you will usually find a special equity fund. In fact, looking at the 1997 year-to-date (to May 31, 1997) performance numbers, the top performing fund at +38.6% was indeed a special equity fund—the Green Line Resource Fund.

Check the same performance periods and at the *bottom* of the list you will usually find a special equity fund. In this case, the worst 1997 year-to-date (to May 31, 1997) performer was a special equity labor-sponsored fund, the Tourism and Entertainment Fund at -74.6%. There were also a number of precious metals funds that fared poorly, including The Cambridge Precious Metals Fund at -28.3% and the CIBC Precious Metals Fund at -21.2%.

It's not surprising we find this much diversity among special equity funds. They do, after all, focus on a specific industry or economic sector. And in any given period, some sectors will be doing quite well—resources, metals and technology being cases in point—while other sectors are simply out of favor (real estate, for example). Critics of special equity funds see them as a collection of shooting stars, rocketing to the top of the charts one quarter, plummeting the next, seemingly going nowhere. The implication, then, is why take the risk?

And the risks are significant. The three-year standard deviation of the average Canadian sector fund is 6.03%; for the average Canadian precious metals fund, 7.3%; and for Canadian resource funds, 5.69%. Compare that with the 4.19% for the average small-cap fund, which is the next most volatile category. In addition, special equity funds simply do not provide the risk-reduction advantages normally associated with an investment in mutual funds.

In most cases, special equity funds have more than 5% of their portfolio invested in a single stock. The Cambridge Precious Metals Fund, for example, had 11.1% of the portfolio (as of the end of December 1996) invested in the common shares of Corsair Petroleum and another 7.9% invested in Carmanah Resources. If either of these companies falls sharply, so, too, does your special equity fund. Kind of like putting your eggs in one basket.

We acknowledge that special equity funds are not a balanced mutual fund. What motivates an investment in special equity funds is performance. And with some careful selections, special equity funds can add value, but not as a stand-alone investment. But assuming you already have a well-balanced portfolio of funds, a carefully selected special equity fund can add nicely to your bottom line. To get the extra kick from special equity funds, however, you need to focus on sectors that are likely to outperform the general market.

Another consideration is the management expertise of the fund. Don't assume, when focusing on a specific sector, that all funds in that sector will perform the same way. In the case of precious metals funds, for example, it depends on what percentage of the portfolio is invested in gold mining stocks and what percentage is in gold bullion.

In addition, how long do you want to hold the fund? In many cases, a good high-quality resource, technology or health-care fund could be a long-term hold. That being said, many special equity investments are viewed as cyclical in nature, because the stocks of many industry sectors tend to rise and fall as investors anticipate the expansion and contraction of the economy.

And finally, you need to understand how an investment in a special equity fund fits within your broader portfolio. Some funds, like precious metals or resource funds, might not be acceptable as stand-alone investments but can be great additions to an already diversified portfolio. Adding funds that do not tend to move in sync with the broader market can reduce overall portfolio risk.

Of course, the amount of risk reduction depends on what other funds are already in your portfolio. For example, the Marathon Equity Fund is categorized as a small-cap fund, but many of the assets in this portfolio are invested in mining and resource companies.

The point is, does a precious metals fund really make sense as an addition to a portfolio that already includes the Marathon Equity Fund? Special equity funds really make sense when they provide your portfolio with a better mix. If you understand that balancing act, special equity funds can add value to your portfolio.

The Importance of Investment Styles

A number of studies have looked at the importance of investment styles. The bottom line for virtually all of these studies is that no single investment strategy or style will consistently outperform others (see Figure 16.10). More to the point, it would be virtually impossible to predict the leading investment style in any given year.

Figure 16.10: TOP PERFORMING STYLE VARIES FROM YEAR TO YEAR

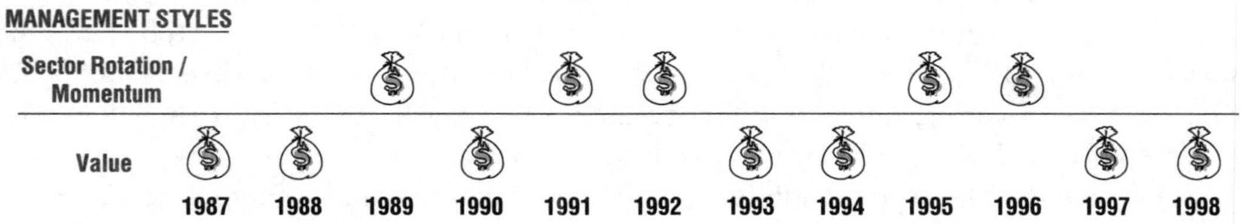

MANAGEMENT STYLES

Sector Rotation / Momentum

Value

1987 1988 1989 1990 1991 1992 1993 1994 1995 1996 1997 1998

Diversification by investment style plays a major role in pension fund management, institutional portfolio management and in the management of high-net-worth individual portfolios. This is why we think diversification by investment style is so important.

In Chapter 4, we discussed the six investment styles on a general basis. In this section, we want to expand the discussion to include some intricacies that may change the way you look at investment styles. We will make liberal use of examples of investment styles as they relate to balanced funds, global balanced funds, global fixed-income funds, international equity funds and money market funds. For the record, the six investment styles are presented at the far right of the FundLine.

When categorizing portfolio managers by their investment style, we came across some interesting concepts that need to be explained. For example, we generally assume that bottom-up equity fund managers focus most of their time ferreting out business opportunities and much less time predicting the short-term direction of the business cycle.

They buy a business because it is undervalued, based primarily on the long-term fundamentals, and also because the economy is about to rebound. Given that position, we generally find that bottom-up managers also practice a value style of investing.

Examples of this investment philosophy include the Trimark family of funds, where all of the equity funds are managed using a bottom-up/value style. In fact, this is the investment philosophy in which Trimark prides itself and spends a great deal of money to market (see Figure 16.11).

When looking at the Trimark balanced (income/growth) funds, you can see that the firm practices a top-down/momentum philosophy to determine what percentage of the portfolio will be dedicated to stocks and what percentage to bonds over the course of the business cycle. At that point, the managers employ the traditional Trimark bottom-up/value style to select individual stocks in the portfolio.

In a similar vein, global funds are difficult to pigeonhole in terms of investment style. A number of global equity fund managers, for example, will use a top-down investment approach to determine which country offers the best investment opportunities. Having settled on a specific country, some of those same managers will employ a bottom-up/value style to select the individual stocks within that country. An example of this type of investment philosophy can be found in Mackenzie's Universal World Emerging Growth Fund that specializes in medium-size companies. Medium-size companies, as is the case with small-cap stocks, require the managers to make some value judgments about the merits of a particular business, and that lends itself nicely to a bottom-up/value style of investing to complement the top-down philosophy used to select the appropriate geographic regions.

Figure 16.11: THE TRIMARK FAMILY OF FUNDS

TRIMARK FAMILY OF FUNDS		Extended Asset Mix											Objectives								Management Style					
Fund Name	MVA Index	Canadian Equity	U.S. Equity	Europe	Japan	Far East	Latin America	Special Equity	Dividend	Domestic Bond	Global Bond	Money Market	Short Term	Mid Term	Long Term	Currency Effect	Sector Specific	Small Cap	Mid Cap	Large Cap	Top Down	Bottom Up	Value	Sector Rotation	Momentum	Indexation
Trimark Advantage Bond	103.5									◆				◆								◆		◆		
Trimark Americas	79.5		◆				◆									◆		◆				◆			◆	
Trimark Canadian		◆																		◆		◆	◆			
Trimark Canadian Bond	96.5									◆				◆							◆			◆	◆	
Trimark Discovery		◆	◆															◆	◆			◆			◆	
Trimark Europlus	95.6			◆												◆				◆		◆	◆			
Trimark Fund	92.4	◆	◆													◆				◆		◆	◆			
Trimark Government Income										◆			◆								◆		◆	◆		
Trimark Income/Growth		◆								◆				◆					◆	◆	◆		◆		◆	
Trimark Indo-Pacific	94.7					◆										◆			◆	◆		◆	◆			
Trimark Interest	92.4											◆	◆													◆
Trimark RRSP Equity	95.4	◆																		◆		◆	◆			
Trimark Select Balanced	97.2	◆								◆				◆						◆	◆				◆	
Trimark Select Canadian Growth		◆																		◆		◆	◆			
Trimark Select Growth		◆	◆		◆											◆				◆		◆	◆			

Figure 16.12: MACKENZIE'S UNIVERSAL WORLD EMERGING GROWTH FUNDLINE

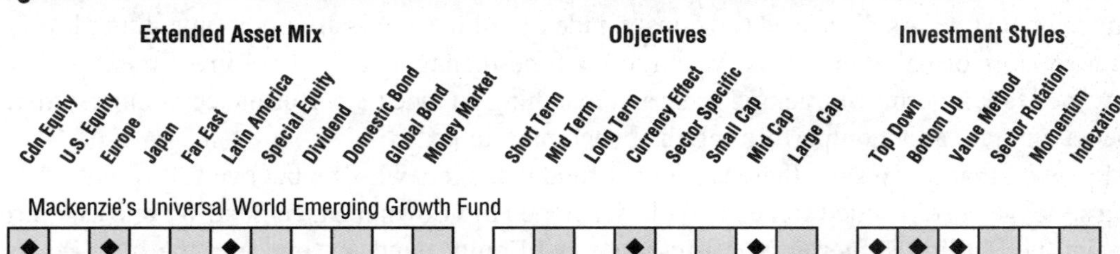

Another style that global fund managers use is "sector rotation." This is particularly well suited to global equity funds such as the Global Strategy World Equity Fund, which uses a multi-manager approach focusing primarily on country selection and followed by specific sectors within those countries.

Figure 16.13: GLOBAL STRATEGY WORLD EQUITY FUNDLINE

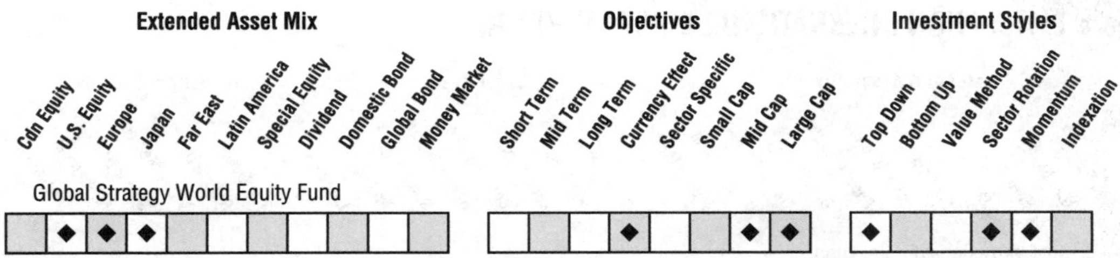

Indexation is a style that usually stands alone. We assume, for example, that money market funds employ an index style in that they attempt to track short-term interest rates. For our purposes, nearly all money market funds follow a FundLine similar to the one found in Figure 16.14.

Figure 16.14: FUNDLINES FOR G.T. SHORT-TERM INCOME CLASS FUND AND PH&N CANADIAN MONEY MARKET FUND

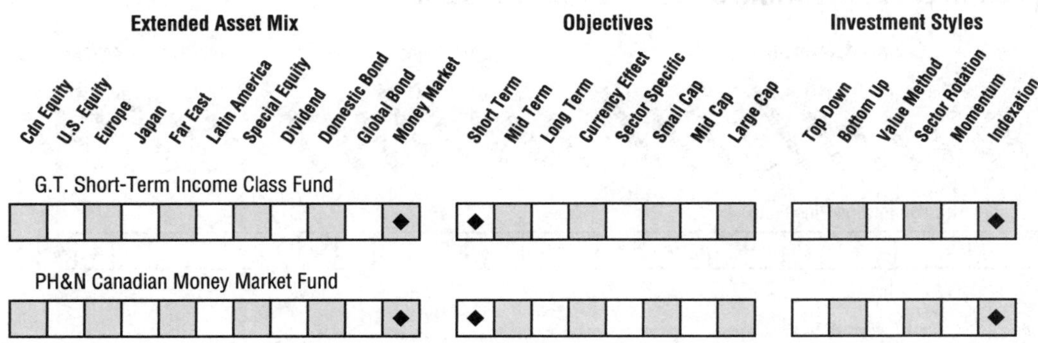

Keeping with the same theme, index fund managers are not normally associated with any other management style. As discussed previously, index fund managers are not momentum players, sector rotators or value investors. When index fund managers talk about investment philosophy, they talk in terms of tracking error and matching an index's performance numbers; there is never any talk about outperforming the benchmark index.

However, that being said, there are global fund managers who we believe follow an indexation style, yet also practice some good old-fashioned top-down management. We cite as a case in point the Phillips, Hager & North International Equity Fund. In this case, the fund's managers employs a top-down philosophy to select the one country whose equity market offers the most potential. Having selected a specific country, the managers will use derivatives (i.e., index futures contracts or index-linked products from companies like State Street Bank) to implement a position in that country. The managers seek to match the performance of the index in that particular country. At the same time, the managers attempt to outperform other managers by profiting from currency fluctuations and by selecting the optimum investment mix in that country.

Figure 16.15: PH&N INTERNATIONAL EQUITY FUNDLINE

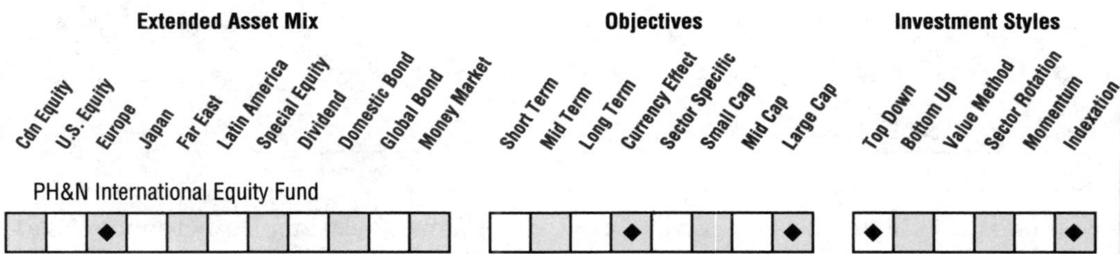

Another variation on that theme can be seen in the Global Strategy Europe Plus Fund, where the managers actually purchase a number of good quality, large-cap stocks employing a top-down/sector rotation management style, and then augment those selections with the purchase of index futures contracts on the various European bourses.

Figure 16.16: GLOBAL STRATEGY EUROPE PLUS FUNDLINE

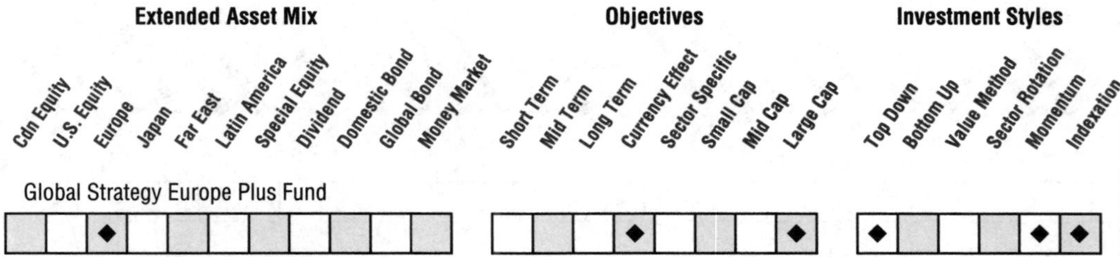

Momentum is a strategy well-suited to bond funds. Bond fund managers refer to their style as interest rate anticipation (see Chapter 5). The fact is, most domestic fixed-income funds invest in high-grade government bonds, effectively eliminating default risk, and tying capital gains or losses to changes in the level of interest rates. The reason? A change in the level of interest rates is considered a macro-economic event that would, by definition, require the manager to follow a top-down philosophy. Simply stated, then, interest rate anticipators attempt to time the movement in interest rates, then take a position along the yield curve that will earn the maximum return should that scenario unfold. Examples of this type of fund managers can be found in Figure 16.17.

Figure 16.17: FUNDLINES FOR ELLIOTT & PAGE BOND FUND AND TALVEST FOREIGN PAY CANADIAN BOND FUND

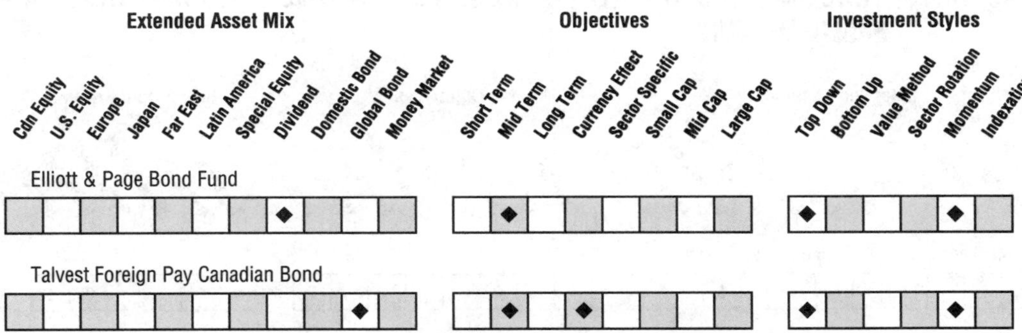

We also find some fixed-income fund managers who practice a bottom-up/value style. Examples include a high-yield bond fund, where the manager looks for corporate bonds that offer high rates of interest. However, when investing in a high-yielding corporate bond, you must accept the possibility of default.

High-yield bond fund managers diversify across a number of companies in different industries in order to reduce the risks associated with defaults. Therefore, high-yield bond fund managers are keenly interested in the fundamentals underlying the company issuing the bond, because those fundamentals will dictate whether or not the company will be able to meet its obligations.

We have slotted most mortgage fund managers into a top-down/value investment philosophy, even though they tend to invest in higher-grade mortgages. Contrary to that position, we view mortgage funds as an income vehicle. If you accept that premise, then mortgage fund managers should focus on maintaining a steady and reasonable monthly income for unitholders. Any potential capital gains resulting from the manager's inability to time changes in the direction of interest rates will normally pale in comparison with the long-term goals of steady monthly income for the unitholder.

We also note that some balanced funds, like the Mackenzie Industrial Income Fund, practice a top-down/sector rotation (spread trading)/momentum philosophy. In this case, the Mackenzie Fund management team attempts to provide unitholders with a "steady flow of income consistent with reasonable safety of capital. The portfolio consists mainly of corporate and government bonds and short-term notes, as well as common and preferred shares of established Canadian companies."

It is the last part of the statement where investment in large and established Canadian companies is given as an objective that brings sector rotation into the picture. We believe the sector rotation philosophy is a minor consideration in this fund's overall investment philosophy, with more emphasis being placed on the top-down/market timing components of the investment plan.

Of course, many balanced fund and global fund managers use market timing when making investment decisions, particularly (1) when it comes to weighting the stock and bond components of the balanced portfolio, and (2) when it comes to country allocation and interest rate anticipation within specific countries for the global funds.

Figure 16.18: FUNDLINES FOR MACKENZIE INDUSTRIAL INCOME FUND AND INDUSTRIAL MORTGAGE FUND

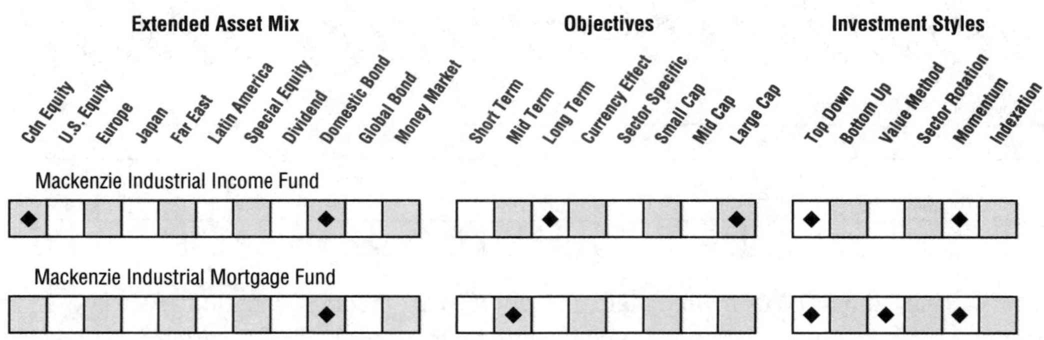

Building a Portfolio with the FundLine

Knowing how the FundLine works, you now have at your fingertips all the information you need to construct an optimal portfolio. You simply fill in the boxes using the highest-ranking funds from those we have included at the back of the book.

To see how easy the process is, follow the *hypothetical* example of Mr. Jones. He has filled in his personal investment profile and, according to his answers, has a score of 53. Based on his score, his personal investment profile and extended asset mix are as follows:

Figure 16.19: MR. JONES' PERSONAL INVESTMENT PROFILE

Growth / Income								
Equities			Fixed Income			Cash		
Min	**Policy**	Max	Min	**Policy**	Max	Min	**Policy**	Max
30%	**50%**	70%	25%	**40%**	55%	5%	**10%**	15%

Figure 16.20: MR. JONES' EXTENDED ASSET MIX

	Non-RRSP	RRSP
Canadian Equity	20%	30%
U.S. Equity	20%	10%
International Equity	20%	10%
Total Equity Assets	**60%**	**50%**
Domestic Bond	15%	25%
Domestic Bond Funds	10%	20%
Global Bond	10%	0%
Total Fixed-Income Assets	**35%**	**45%**
Money Market	5%	5%
Total Cash Assets	**5%**	**5%**

Non-RRSP Extended Asset Mix

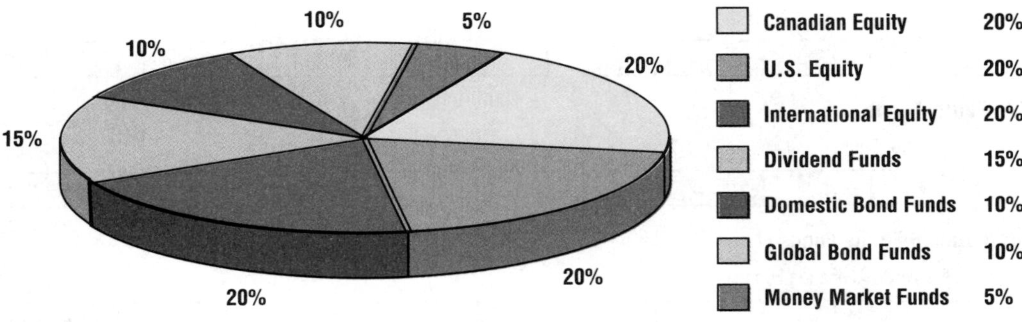

RRSP Extended Asset Mix

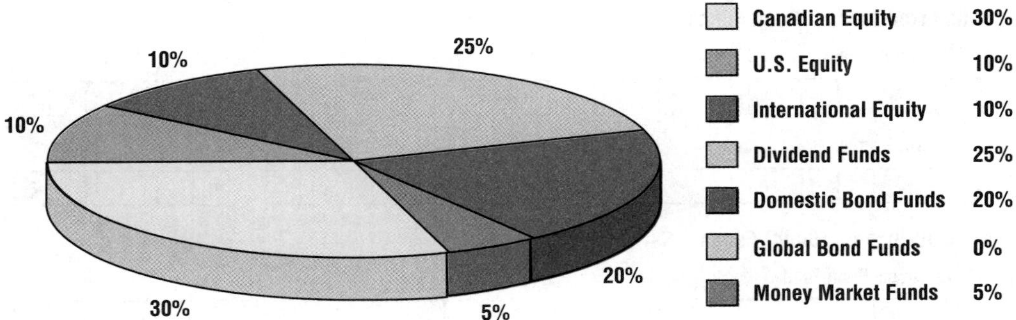

Having determined the extended asset mix, Mr. Jones' next step is to select securities—specifically, which funds, representing each asset class, he wants his portfolio to hold.

Mr. Jones would begin with the best-ranked funds in each category as described in Appendix I. To illustrate how the FundLine portfolio is built, follow Mr. Jones through the process. (Note that the portfolio lines are fictional examples.)

Figure 16.21: MR. JONES' BEST BET FUNDS SELECTION

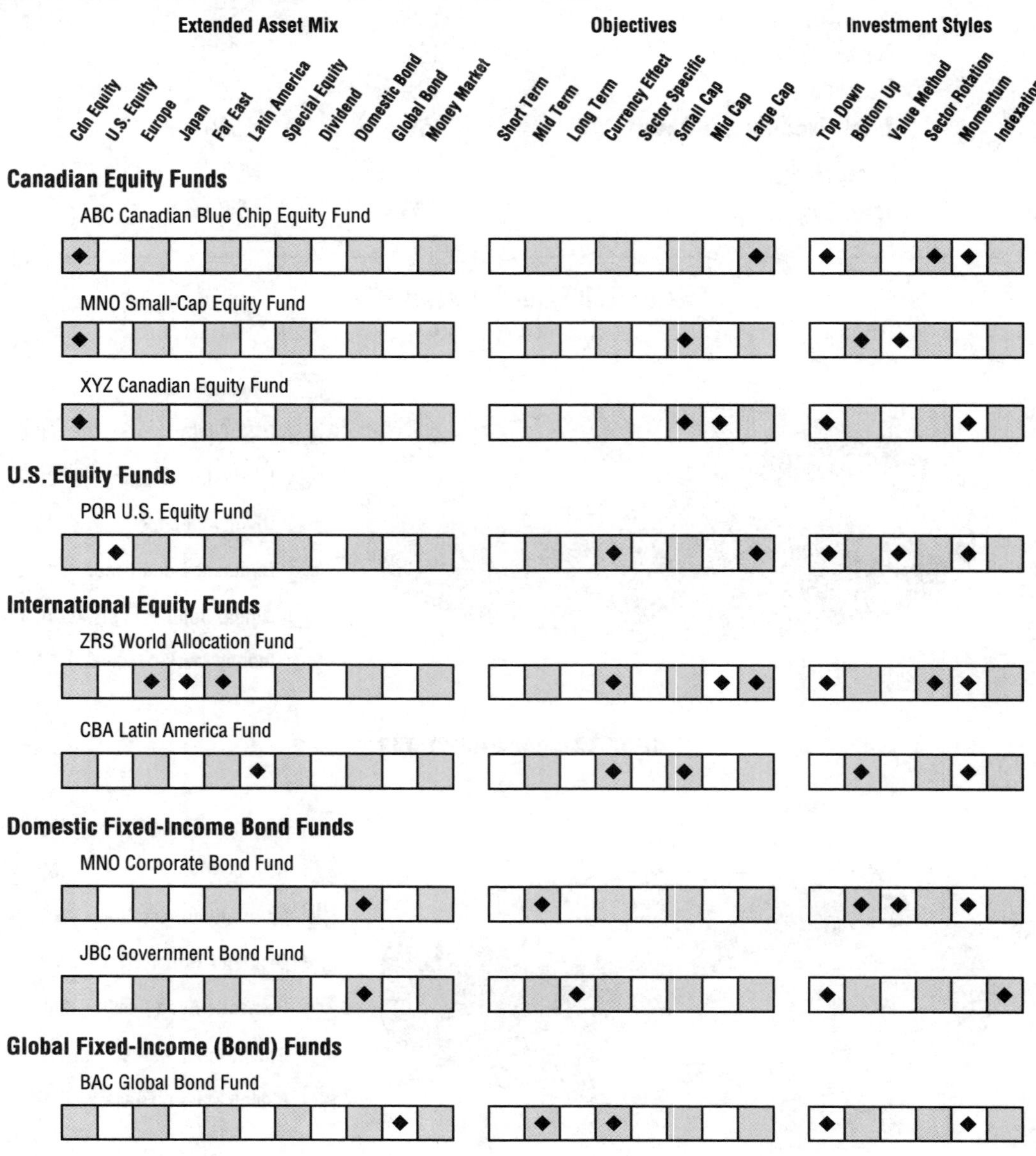

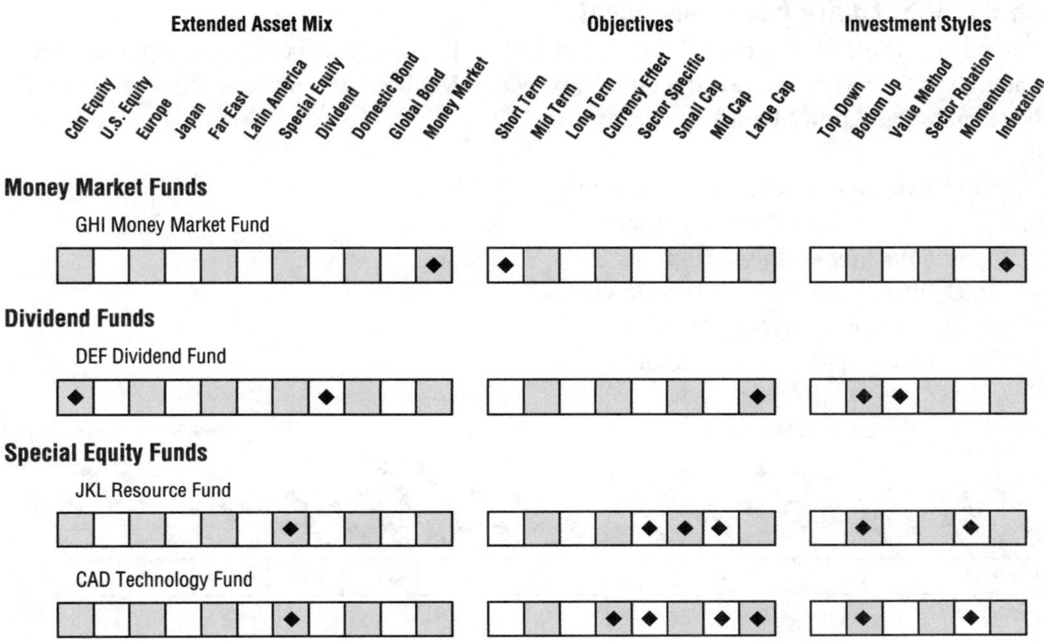

Now Mr. Jones will begin to fill in as many boxes as possible along his Portfolio Line. (Note that boxes do not get checked off more than once.) To do this, he will determine those funds—usually no more than eight or nine—that (1) meet his ideal asset mix, and (2) provide diversification.

Step #1: Canadian Equity Fund component

Mr. Jones chooses the MNO Small-Cap Equity Fund for his Canadian component. He fills in four boxes along his Portfolio Line:

1. under *Extended Asset Mix*—Canadian Equity
2. under *Objectives*—Small Cap
3. under *Investment Styles*—Bottom Up
4. under *Investment Styles*—Value Method

Figure 16.22: MR. JONES' PERSONAL FUNDLINE

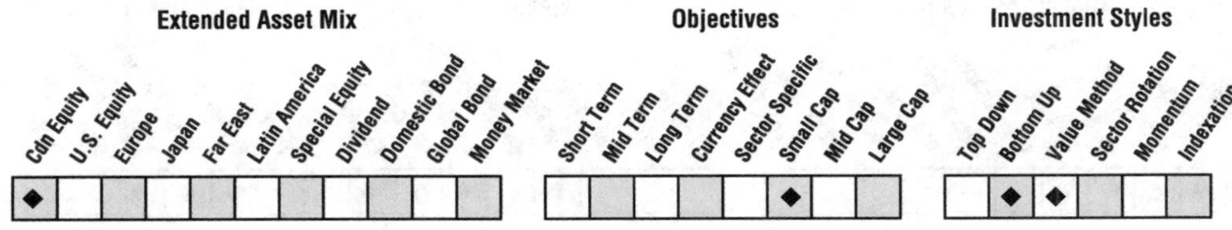

Step #2: U.S. Equity Fund component

Mr. Jones' next selection is the PQR U.S. Equity Fund, which has six boxes along its fundline. He actually fills in five boxes (the other box, Value Method, was already filled in under the MNO Small-Cap Equity Fund):

1. under *Extended Asset Mix*—U.S. Equity
2. under *Objectives*—Currency Effect
3. under *Objectives*—Large Cap
4. under *Investment Styles*—Top Down
5. under *Investment Styles*—Value Method
6. under *Investment Styles*—Sector Rotation

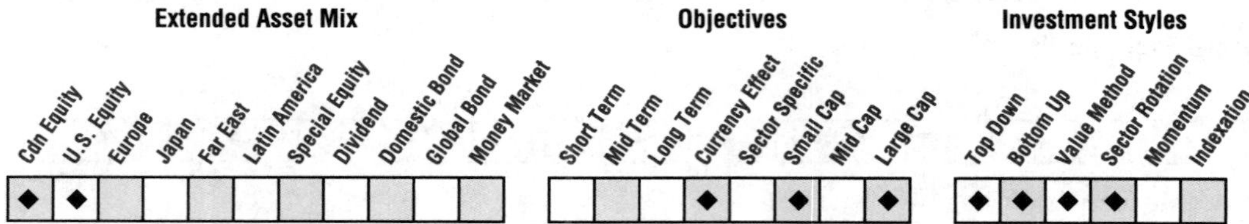

Step #3: International Equity Fund component

With his first two selections, Mr. Jones has filled in nine of the 25 boxes. He then chooses the ZRS World Allocation Fund as his third selection, which has nine boxes in its fundline. Mr. Jones will fill in five of the nine boxes:

1. under *Extended Asset Mix*—Europe
2. under *Extended Asset Mix*—Japan
3. under *Extended Asset Mix*—Far East
4. under *Objectives*—Currency Effect
5. under *Objectives*—Mid Cap
6. under *Objectives*—Large Cap
7. under *Investment Styles*—Top Down
8. under *Investment Styles*—Sector Rotation
9. under *Investment Styles*—Momentum

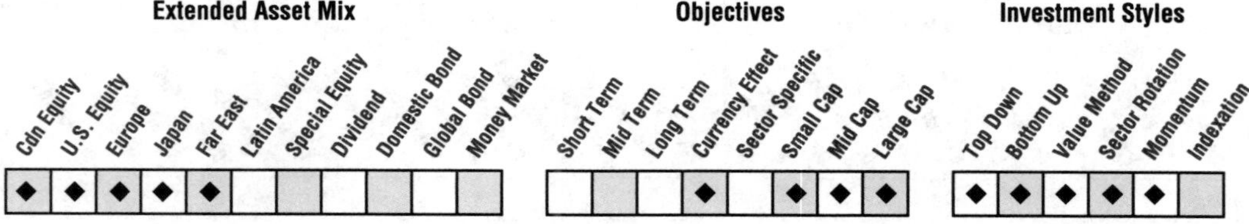

Step #4: Domestic Fixed-Income (Bond) Fund component

Having made these selections, Mr. Jones has now filled in 14 of the 25 potential boxes. If he then chooses the JBC Government Bond Fund for his domestic fixed-income asset, he will fill in three new boxes:

1. under *Extended Asset Mix*—Domestic Bond
2. under *Objectives*—Long Term
3. under *Investment Styles*—Top Down
4. under *Investment Styles*—Indexation

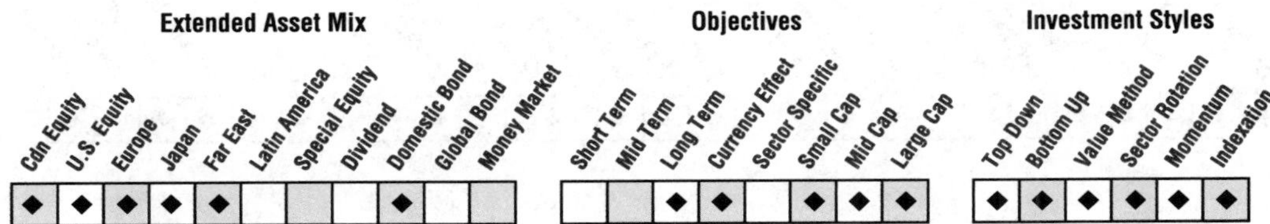

Step #5: Global Fixed-Income Fund component

Mr. Jones next selects the BAC Global Bond Fund for his global fixed-income component, which has five boxes in its fundline (three of which Mr. Jones has already filled in along his Portfolio Line):

1. under *Extended Asset Mix*—Global Bond
2. under *Objectives*—Mid Term
3. under *Objectives*—Currency Effect
4. under *Investment Styles*—Top Down
5. under *Investment Styles*—Momentum

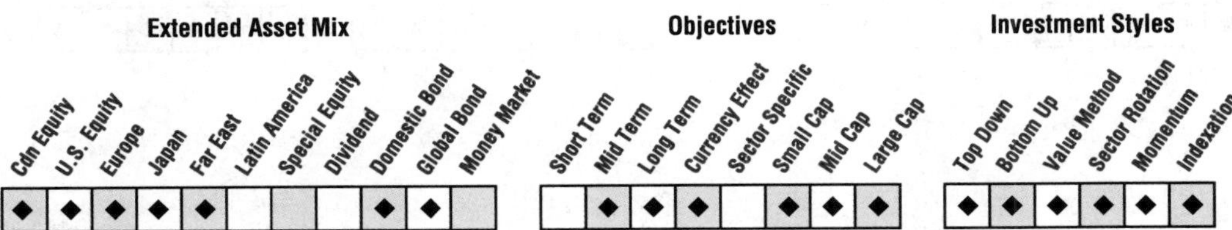

Step #6: Money Market Fund component

Mr. Jones adds the GHI Money Market Fund to his portfolio and fills in two more boxes along his Portfolio Line:

1. under *Extended Asset Mix*—Money Market
2. under *Objectives*— Short Term
3. under *Investment Styles*—Indexation

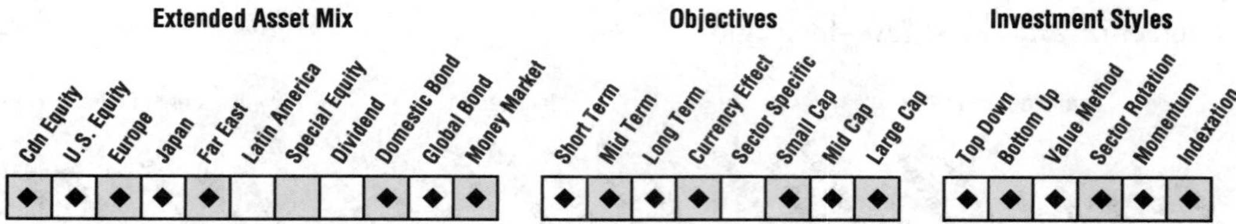

Step #7: Dividend Fund component

Mr. Jones selects the DEF Dividend Fund, which has five boxes along its fundline. One new box—Dividend— is filled in:

1. under *Extended Asset Mix*—Canadian Equity
2. under *Extended Asset Mix*—Dividend
3. under *Objectives*—Large Cap
4. under *Investment Styles*— Bottom Up
5. under *Investment Styles*—Value Method

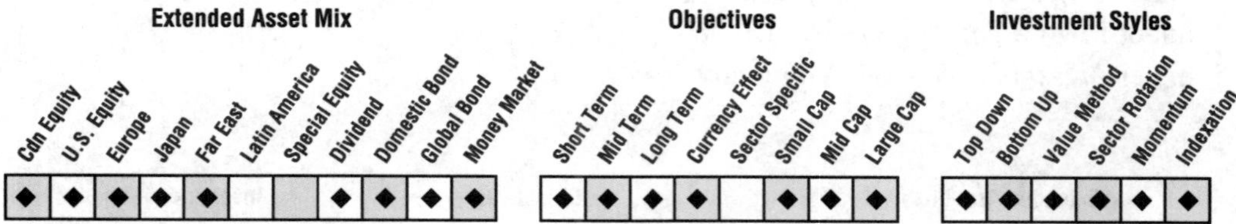

Step #8: Special Equity Fund component

Mr. Jones has selected seven funds for his portfolio and has completed 22 of 25 boxes for his Portfolio Line. The three boxes yet to be filled in are: under *Extended Asset Mix*—Latin America and Special Equity; and under *Objectives*—Sector Specific. Since 22 of the 25 boxes have been completed, Mr. Jones has a well-diversified portfolio. His next selection can probably be made simply on the basis of performance, and he selects the CAD Technology Fund. The CAD Technology Fund represents another seven boxes, two of which Mr. Jones has not filled in along his Portfolio Line:

1. under *Extended Asset Mix*—Special Equity
2. under *Objectives*—Currency Effect
3. under *Objectives*—Sector Specific
4. under *Objectives*—Mid Cap
5. under *Objectives*—Large Cap
6. under *Investment Styles*—Bottom Up
7. under *Investment Styles*—Momentum

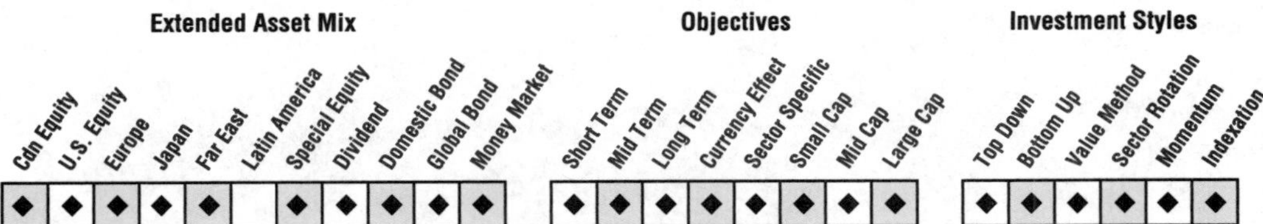

Mr. Jones now has completed 24 of the 25 potential boxes and has built a well-diversified portfolio of solid funds.

So you see, the concept of the FundLine is straightforward: complete as many boxes as possible with the number of funds you would like to purchase. If Mr. Jones chooses, he could add a final selection to his portfolio—the CBA Latin America Fund—and that would fill in the one remaining box (*Extended Asset Mix*—Latin America). With nine funds in his portfolio, Mr. Jones has completed all 25 boxes in his Portfolio Line.

The FundLine method combined with the Portfolio Line make fund selection simple. We have provided a worksheet in the Appendix, so that you can begin to build your own personalized mutual fund portfolio that is optimally diversified.

Before you begin, please review our economic forecast for 1999, as well as our suggested weightings for each portfolio for the year ahead.

A Guide to the Appendices

The Worksheet

To use the appendices, fill out the worksheet on page 280, based on your own investor category. Then set your asset mix using the recommended weightings discussed in Chapter 12 or your own preselected weightings. But remember, use weightings that fit within the minimum and maximum parameters of your personal investment profile.

There are three appendices in this year's edition of *The FundLine Advisor*. Appendix I is our Best Bet list of funds. There are 100 Best Bet funds in this year's list, and we provide essential information about each of them.

All of the funds in our Best Bet list have reasonable minimum initial investments. In this edition of *The FundLine Advisor*, we wanted to make certain that all of the funds on our list were within reach of every investor. The average minimum investment for the Best Bet list is between $500 and $1,000, the highest being $5,000. In addition, we focused on funds that were available for sale in every province. No matter where you live in Canada, you should be able to buy any of the Best Bet funds.

Naturally, the MVA score was relevant in the decision process. However, it was not as important as making certain that we provided you with a list of funds that could cover all of the categories in the FundLine. In this year's edition, the Best Bet list provides representation in all of the categories, except money market. However, we feel that there is not a significant difference between most money market funds.

While our list of Best Bet funds is by no means complete, we believe these funds are a good starting point for your portfolio. In Appendix II, we present FundLines for most of the largest fund families, as well as the MVA index for those funds with at least a three-year track record. That should help round out your selections and help you assess the diversification of your current mutual fund portfolio.

Appendix III is a list of all the funds that were rated with the MVA index. In this appendix, each fund was sorted by type, by sub-type and, of course, by the MVA index. We also include the index being used as the benchmark.

The Best Bet List (Appendix I)

In the full-page review for the Best Bet funds, we have included selections from the following categories:

- **Equity Assets**
  - Canadian Equity
  - International Equity (excluding Canada and the U.S.)
  - International Equity—Asia Pacific
  - International Equity—Japan
  - International Equity—Europe
  - International Equity—Global
  - U.S. Equity
  - Specialty

- **Income Assets**
  - Dividend Funds
  - Canadian Bond
  - Global Bond

- **Balanced Funds**
  - Canadian Balanced Funds
  - Global Balanced Funds

At the top of each page is the fund name. Beginning on the left under the fund name is the MVA index, the period returns for three months, one year, three years, and five years and the annual returns for 1997, 1996 and 1995 (see Figure 1).

Figure 1

Ivy Foreign Equity

MVA	3 Months*	1 Year*	3 Years*	5 Years*	1997	1996	1995
105.0	-0.4%	16.8%	19.0%	17.1%	23.2%	15.0%	16.4%

* Returns to July 31, 1998

For every Best Bet fund, we identify the sponsor and provide the address and telephone number. The numbers are usually 1-800 numbers, although most fund companies have a direct line if you live in the province in which the fund's head office is located. Your financial planner can help you locate fund companies that might make good investments for your portfolio. We also tell you if a fund is a load or no-load fund. As well, it is important to recognize that most load funds offer negotiated commissions, and investors can purchase a fund with the option of a front or deferred load.

We also tell you whether or not the fund is RRSP-eligible. If the answer is "yes" to the RRSP eligibility question, there are no restrictions on the fund. If the answer is "foreign," that means the fund cannot represent more than 20% of the assets within your RRSP. As well, we have included the minimum initial investment, depending on whether the fund is being purchased inside an RRSP or outside an RRSP.

Next, we acknowledge the fund manager. This year we have added the length of time the manager has been managing the fund (see Figure 2).

Figure 2: Ivy Foreign Equity Fund

Sponsor	Mackenzie Financial Corporation 150 Bloor Street West, Suite M111 Toronto, Ontario, M5S 3B5			**Category** Foreign Equity/Global **Portfolio Manager/Years** Bill Kanko—Bluewater Investment Mngt./24		
Phone	1-800-387-0614			**Minimum Initial Investment**		
Sales Fee	Load	**RRSP Eligibility**	Foreign	**RRSP** $500		**Non-RRSP** $500

Then comes the FundLine, which defines the elements of diversification a specific fund brings to the portfolio (see Figure 3).

Figure 3: Ivy Foreign Equity

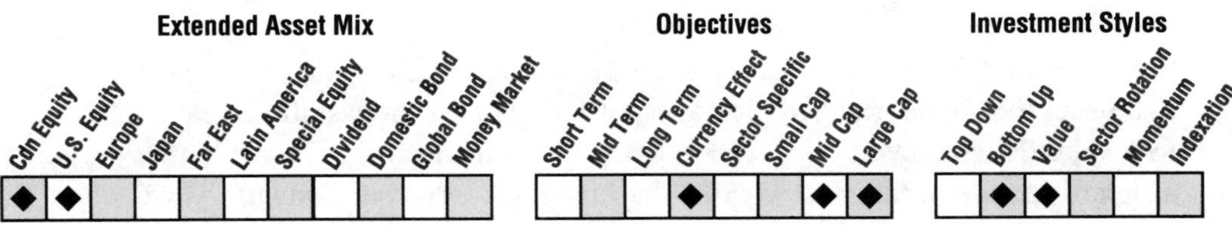

Under the FundLine, we have added some quantitative information about the fund (see Figure 4).

Figure 4

Quantitative		Asset Breakout		Sector Breakout (Equity)
MER	2.39%	Cash	20.9%	Overweighted
Tax Efficiency	93.18%	Cdn Bonds		1 Communication
Std Dev	2.17%	Foreign Bonds		2 Utilities
Beta	0.61	Cdn Equity	5.4%	Underweighted
Alpha	0.66	Foreign Equity	73.6%	1 Consumer
R Squared	0.43	Warrants		2 Financial

- **MER:** The management-expense ratio tells us how much it costs to operate the fund, including transaction costs, management fees and custodial fees. The MER is calculated as a percentage of the fund's assets. For example, a fund with $100 million in assets, and that costs $2 million per year to operate, would have an MER of 2%.

- **Tax Efficiency:** The tax efficiency ratio is a three-year number. According to Pal-Trak, it is an estimate of the fund's return after tax, over the last three years. Tax efficiency is expressed as a percent of the total return. It is a reflection of a fund's returns that could have accrued to unit holders after tax over the previous three years. For example, if the fund's compounded annual return over the past three years was 10%, and it had a tax efficiency of 90%, the unit holders would have received after tax a compounded annual return of 9%.

- **Std Deviation**:Standard deviation is a measure of the fund's risk. We measure risk using the annual standard deviation of returns over the last three years. (Standard deviation was discussed in Chapter 2.) Suffice it to say, the higher the standard deviation, the more volatile the fund is likely to be. Conversely, we would expect that a fund with a low standard deviation will be less volatile.

- **Beta:** Beta measures a fund's performance relative to a market index, such as the TSE 300 Composite Index or the S&P 500 Composite Index. Portfolio Analytics compares Canadian equity funds against the Toronto Stock Exchange 300 Index, over the last 36 to 60 months; bond funds are compared to the ScotiaMcLeod Bond Universe Index, over the last 36 to 60 months. U.S. equity fund betas are calculated relative to the S&P 500 Index, over the last 36 to 60 months. A fund with a beta of 1 means that the fund will likely rise and fall about the same as the comparable benchmark. A beta greater than 1 means that the fund will likely rise or fall at a greater rate than the market. For example, a fund with a beta of, say, 1.5 would expect to rise or fall 1.5 times as fast as the comparable market index.

Similarly, a fund with a beta less than 1 would not be expected to move as dramatically as the comparable index either up or down.

- **Alpha:** According to Portfolio Analytics, alpha defines the incremental or decremental return earned in an average month, given the fund's systematic risk (beta). It is estimated by regressing fund returns against market index returns, over the last 36 to 60 months. In the case of the Ivy Foreign Equity fund, we are saying that the fund would be expected to rise or fall about two-thirds as fast as the comparable index (S&P 500 Composite Index) in an average month.

- **R Squared:** R squared is a statistic calculated by regressing the fund against an appropriate benchmark index. Think of it as a correlation measurement that ranges between 0 (meaning no correlation with the comparable benchmark) and 1 (meaning perfect correlation with the comparable benchmark).

This year we have also included a breakout of the assets within the fund. **This is only a general overview of what the funds are holding. These are broad-based investment assets. Sometimes the assets in the breakout *will not* add up to 100%. On occasion, the value *exceeds* 100% because of the cross-over between asset classes.** As well, we look at what sectors the manager is currently overweighting or underweighting within the equity component of the portfolio. If it is a bond fund, we note what corporate bond sectors the fund is currently holding.

The final chart along the bottom of the page is the trailing returns chart. This chart, which is used with the permission of Portfolio Analytics, is one of the graphic displays available on Pal-Trak mutual fund analysis software (available from Portfolio Analytics in Toronto; phone 416-489-7074, or visit their Web site at *www.pal.com*).

In each trailing return chart we look at every possible two-year performance period since the fund came into existence. This chart measures the annualized returns for each two-year time frame and is a useful visual tool to examine a fund's performance. At the bottom of the chart, we see the worst possible two-year return (both actual return and annualized return), as well as the best possible two-year period return. In Figure 5, for example, we see the trailing two-year returns for the Ivy Foreign Equity Fund. In this case, the worst two-year return was 17.10% (8.21% compounded annually), while the best two-year return was 56.53% (25.11% compounded annually).

Figure 5: TRAILING 24-MONTH ANNUALIZED RETURNS FOR IVY FOREIGN EQUITY FUND

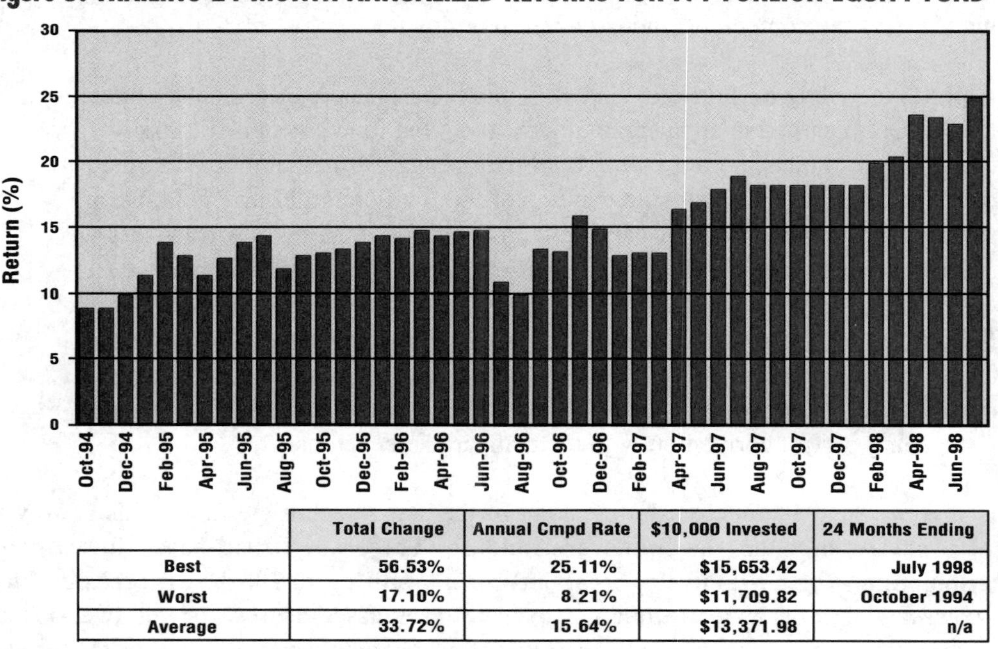

	Total Change	Annual Cmpd Rate	$10,000 Invested	24 Months Ending
Best	56.53%	25.11%	$15,653.42	July 1998
Worst	17.10%	8.21%	$11,709.82	October 1994
Average	33.72%	15.64%	$13,371.98	n/a

Appendix II

In Appendix II, we show the individual FundLines for each of the funds in the largest fund families in Canada. It is quite likely you already hold one or more of these funds in your portfolio. As such, this information provides a tool to help you assess where each fund fits within your overall portfolio of funds and to see how well diversified your portfolio currently is.

One thing you might notice is that we provide no FundLines for Mackenzie's S.T.A.R. asset allocation service, Investors Group Portfolio funds and the Dynamic Managed Portfolio. These fund companies offer a portfolio of their funds in one easy-to-buy package. But since that is the goal of the FundLine, it didn't, in our opinion, add any value to include these services in the appendix.

In future versions of this book, we intend to expand the list of funds covered. In the meantime, if you can't wait, you can e-mail Richard Croft at Croftfin@aol.com or call the R. N. Croft Financial Group at 1-416-751-6267, and we will send you a FundLine for any fund you might be considering.

Appendix III

In Appendix III, we include a list of all the funds for which Portfolio Analytics calculated an MVA index. We have also included the annual returns for the years 1994–1998 (July).

The MVA Index tells us whether the fund manager added value. To do that, we need to look at the fund manager's risk-adjusted returns measured against a risk-adjusted benchmark. A key issue then is defining the appropriate benchmark.

We think it is important to separate the job of assigning a benchmark from the job of calculating the index, which is why we provide the formulas for the number crunching and Portfolio Analytics provides the benchmark comparisons.

Building the Ideal Portfolio

Throughout this book we have emphasized the need to build a long-term portfolio of good quality mutual funds. You now have all the tools necessary to make the best selections for your specific objectives and risk tolerances. We have also tried to point out the most important elements in the construction of a portfolio. The most important element is selecting funds that complement each other using the FundLine. Then, you select the best funds in the categories that will allow you to round out your portfolio.

The ideal portfolio, then, is one where you have filled in all of the boxes to create your personal portfolio line using no more than, say, 10 mutual funds, and within that portfolio your average weighted MVA is in excess of 100.

For example, suppose that 10% of your portfolio was to be invested in a Canadian equity fund, and the fund that fit the criteria had an MVA index of 110.25. That would provide a weighted MVA within the portfolio of 11.02 (i.e. 10% of 110.25). Add the weighted MVA for each fund, and the total—assuming you have filled in as many boxes as possible along the Portfolio Line—should exceed 100.

Summary

Finally, if you don't have a financial advisor, we suggest you consider talking with one. This book provides you with an excellent foundation on which to establish a relationship with a financial advisor. You now have the tools to understand why a financial advisor has recommended specific mutual funds for your portfolio. And conversely, you have the tools to examine whether recommendations made by the financial advisor meet all the elements of diversification you have come to expect. We simply think an educated financial consumer is a better client.

And financial advice does not have to cost very much. Almost all funds—whether load or no-load funds—pay annual trailer fees to financial advisors, to help them offset the cost of managing the day-to-day issues with the client. Those trailer fees are being paid whether or not you use a financial advisor, a discount broker or buy the funds directly. Our view is this: if you are going to pay the fees anyway, get some advice for your money.

Personal Worksheet

Investor Category ______________________________
(from Personality Profile)

	Non-RRSP		RRSP	
Canadian Equity	$______	____%	$______	____%
U.S. Equity	$______	____%	$______	____%
International Equity	$______	____%	$______	____%
Total Equity Assets	$______	____%	$______	____%
Domestic Bond	$______	____%	$______	____%
Global Bond	$______	____%	$______	____%
Total Fixed-Income Assets	$______	____%	$______	____%
Money Market	$______	____%	$______	____%
Total Cash Assets	$______	____%	$______	____%
Total Portfolio	$______	____%	$______	____%

	Extended Asset Mix											Objectives								Investment Styles					
Fund Name	Cdn Equity	U.S. Equity	Europe	Japan	Far East	Latin America	Special Equity	Dividend	Domestic Bond	Global Bond	Money Market	Short Term	Mid Term	Long Term	Currency Effect	Sector Specific	Small Cap	Mid Cap	Large Cap	Top Down	Bottom Up	Value	Sector Rotation	Momentum	Indexation

Ivy Growth & Income Fund

MVA	3 Months*	1 Year*	3 Years*	5 Years*	1997	1996	1995
117.7	-0.6%	10.8%	18.0%	13.5%	18.1%	23.4%	19.7%

* Returns to July 31, 1998

Sponsor Mackenzie Financial Corporation
150 Bloor Street West, Suite M111
Toronto, Ontario, M5S 3B5

Phone 1-800-387-0614

Sales Fee Load **RRSP Eligibility** Yes

Category Balanced/Canadian

Portfolio Manager/Years
Jerry Javasky—Mackenzie Financial/6

Minimum Initial Investment
RRSP $500 **Non-RRSP** $500

Extended Asset Mix

Cdn Equity	U.S. Equity	Europe	Japan	Far East	Latin America	Special Equity	Dividend	Domestic Bond	Global Bond	Money Market
◆								◆		

Objectives

Short Term	Mid Term	Long Term	Currency Effect	Sector Specific	Small Cap	Mid Cap	Large Cap
	◆					◆	◆

Investment Styles

Top Down	Bottom Up	Value	Sector Rotation	Momentum	Indexation
◆				◆	

Quantitative		Asset Breakout		Sector Breakout (Equity)
MER	2.12%	Cash	27.0%	Overweighted
Tax Efficiency	96.51%	Cdn Bonds	36.3%	1 Merchandising
Std Deviation	1.76%	Foreign Bonds		2 Utilities
Beta	0.67	Cdn Equity	32.9%	Underweighted
Alpha	0.51	Foreign Equity	5.7%	1 Oil & Gas
R Squared	0.70	Warrants		2 Pipelines

TRAILING 24-MONTH ANNUALIZED RETURNS FOR IVY GROWTH & INCOME FUND

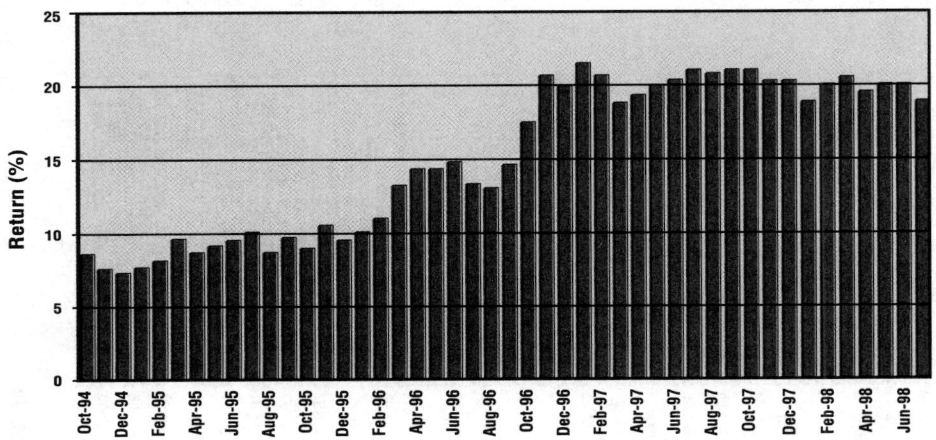

	Total Change	Annual Cmpd Rate	$10,000 Invested	24 Months Ending
Best	50.78%	22.79%	$15,078.10	January 1997
Worst	5.17%	2.55%	$10,516.90	November 1994
Average	31.54%	14.69%	$13,153.62	n/a

Global Strategy Income Plus Fund

MVA	3 Months*	1 Year*	3 Years*	5 Years*	1997	1996	1995
115.3	-4.3%	8.4%	18.2%	14.0%	22.1%	25.8%	13.1%

* Returns to July 31, 1998

Sponsor Global Strategy Financial
33 Bloor Street East, Suite 1600
Toronto, Ontario, M4W 3T8

Phone 1-800-387-1229

Sales Fee Load **RRSP Eligibility** Yes

Category Balanced/Canadian

Portfolio Manager/Years
Tony Massie—Global Strategy Financial/7

Minimum Initial Investment
RRSP $1,000 **Non-RRSP** $1,000

Extended Asset Mix

Cdn Equity	U.S. Equity	Europe	Japan	Far East	Latin America	Special Equity	Dividend	Domestic Bond	Global Bond	Money Market
◆							◆	◆		

Objectives

Short Term	Mid Term	Long Term	Currency Effect	Sector Specific	Small Cap	Mid Cap	Large Cap
	◆						◆

Investment Styles

Top Down	Bottom Up	Value	Sector Rotation	Momentum	Indexation
◆	◆			◆	

Quantitative		Asset Breakout		Sector Breakout (Equity)
MER	2.40%	Cash	21.2%	Overweighted
Tax Efficiency	80.54%	Cdn Bonds	29.4%	1 Financial
Std Deviation	2.05%	Foreign Bonds	0.1%	2 Pipelines
Beta	0.79	Cdn Equity	48.3%	Underweighted
Alpha	0.42	Foreign Equity		1 Conglomerates
R Squared	0.76	Warrants		2 Consumer

TRAILING 24-MONTH ANNUALIZED RETURNS FOR GLOBAL STRATEGY INCOME PLUS FUND

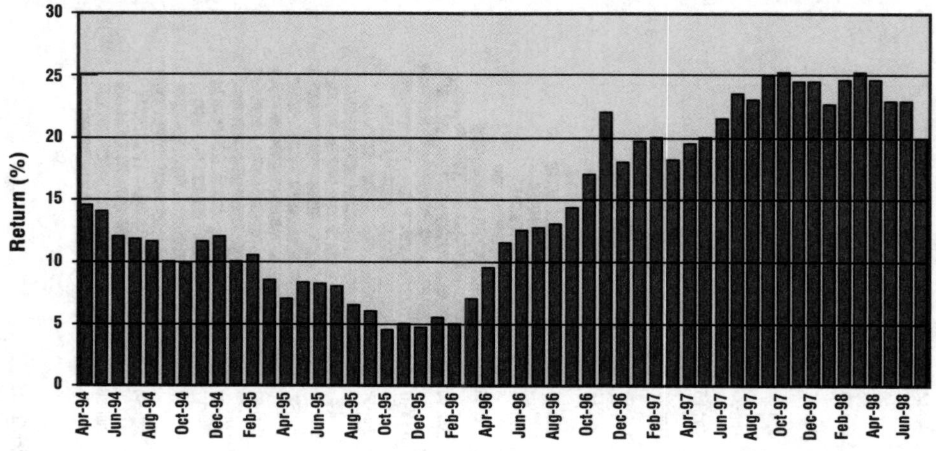

	Total Change	Annual Cmpd Rate	$10,000 Invested	24 Months Ending
Best	52.21%	23.37%	$15,220.63	March 1998
Worst	9.40%	4.59%	$10,939.99	October 1995
Average	32.88%	15.18%	$13,265.34	n/a

Asset Builder I Fund

MVA	3 Months*	1 Year*	3 Years*	5 Years*	1997	1996	1995
110.8	-1.3%	10.1%	17.1%	N/A	21.1%	18.4%	15.4%

* Returns to July 31, 1998

Sponsor Primerica Life Insurance Co. of Canada
350 Burmanthorpe Road, Suite 300
Mississauga, Ontario, L3B 3J1

Phone 1-905-848-7731

Sales Fee Load **RRSP Eligibility** Yes

Category Balanced/Canadian

Portfolio Manager/Years
Jerry Javasky—Mackenzie Financial/2

Minimum Initial Investment
RRSP $500 **Non-RRSP** $500

Extended Asset Mix

Cdn Equity	U.S. Equity	Europe	Japan	Far East	Latin America	Special Equity	Dividend	Domestic Bond	Global Bond	Money Market
◆								◆		

Objectives

Short Term	Mid Term	Long Term	Currency Effect	Sector Specific	Small Cap	Mid Cap	Large Cap
	◆					◆	◆

Investment Styles

Top Down	Bottom Up	Value	Sector Rotation	Momentum	Indexation
◆		◆		◆	

Quantitative		Asset Breakout		Sector Breakout (Equity)
MER	2.25%	Cash	11.5%	Overweighted
Tax Efficiency	N/A	Cdn Bonds	44.9%	1 Oil & Gas
Std Deviation	1.82%	Foreign Bonds		2 Utilities
Beta	0.71	Cdn Equity	30.6%	Underweighted
Alpha	0.47	Foreign Equity	14.2%	1 Industrial
R Squared	0.78	Warrants		2 Pipelines

TRAILING 24-MONTH ANNUALIZED RETURNS FOR ASSET BUILDER I FUND

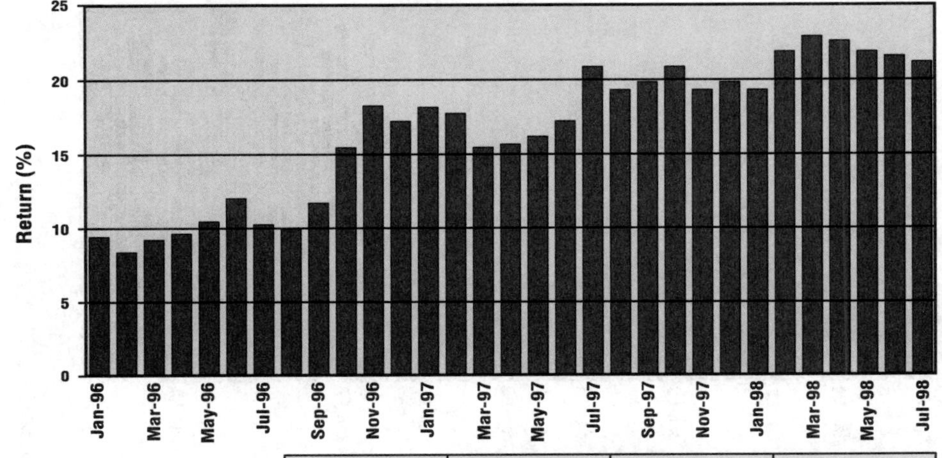

	Total Change	Annual Cmpd Rate	$10,000 Invested	24 Months Ending
Best	50.51%	20.68%	$15,051.49	March 1998
Worst	16.57%	7.97%	$11,657.19	February 1996
Average	35.66%	16.47%	$13,566.08	n/a

Bissett Retirement Fund

MVA	3 Months*	1 Year*	3 Years*	5 Years*	1997	1996	1995
110.5	-2.6%	7.5%	18.1%	14.2%	20.2%	22.2%	19.8%

* Returns to July 31, 1998

Sponsor Bissett & Associates Inv. Mngt.
500 Fourth Street S.W., Suite 1120
Calgary, Alberta,T2P 2V6

Phone 1-800-267-3862

Sales Fee No-Load **RRSP Eligibility** Yes

Category Balanced/Canadian

Portfolio Manager/Years
Michael Quinn—Bissett & Assoc. Inv. Mngt./7

Minimum Initial Investment
RRSP $10,000 **Non-RRSP** $10,000

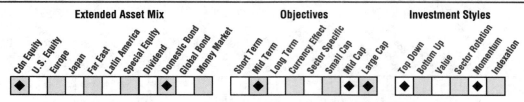

Extended Asset Mix

Cdn Equity	U.S. Equity	Europe	Japan	Far East	Latin America	Special Equity	Dividend	Domestic Bond	Global Bond	Money Market
◆								◆		

Objectives

Short Term	Mid Term	Long Term	Currency Effect	Sector Specific	Small Cap	Mid Cap	Large Cap
	◆					◆	◆

Investment Styles

Top Down	Bottom Up	Value	Sector Rotation	Momentum	Indexation
◆				◆	

Quantitative		Asset Breakout		Sector Breakout (Equity)
MER	1.75%	Cash	3.8%	Overweighted
Tax Efficiency	94.11%	Cdn Bonds	41.8%	1 Industrial
Std Deviation	2.19%	Foreign Bonds		2 Utilities
Beta	0.92	Cdn Equity	35.3%	Underweighted
Alpha	0.31	Foreign Equity	18.8%	1 Oil & Gas
R Squared	0.90	Warrants	0.2%	2 Pipelines

TRAILING 24-MONTH ANNUALIZED RETURNS FOR BISSETT RETIREMENT FUND

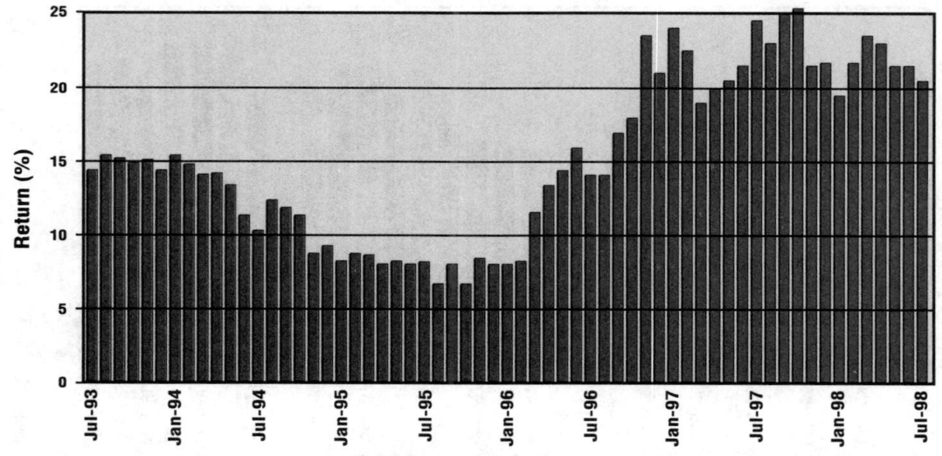

	Total Change	Annual Cmpd Rate	$10,000 Invested	24 Months Ending
Best	55.09%	24.54%	$15,509.34	October 1997
Worst	14.21%	6.87%	$11,421.21	October 1995
Average	32.65%	15.18%	$13,265.33	n/a

Atlas Canadian Balanced Fund

MVA	3 Months*	1 Year*	3 Years*	5 Years*	1997	1996	1995
109.2	-0.1%	10.1%	16.2%	13.1%	18.0%	16.5%	17.8%

* Returns to July 31, 1998

Sponsor Atlas Asset Management
110 Yonge Street, Suite 500
Toronto, Ontario, M5C 1T4
Phone 1-800-463-2857
Sales Fee Load **RRSP Eligibility** Yes

Category Balanced/Canadian
Portfolio Manager/Years
Len Racioppo—Jarislowsky Fraser & Co./9
Minimum Initial Investment
RRSP $500 **Non-RRSP** $500

Extended Asset Mix

Cdn Equity	U.S. Equity	Europe	Japan	Far East	Latin America	Special Equity	Dividend	Domestic Bond	Global Bond	Money Market
◆								◆		

Objectives

Short Term	Mid Term	Long Term	Currency Effect	Sector Specific	Small Cap	Mid Cap	Large Cap
	◆						◆

Investment Styles

Top Down	Bottom Up	Value	Sector Rotation	Momentum	Indexation
◆				◆	

Quantitative		Asset Breakout		Sector Breakout (Equity)
MER	2.20%	Cash	7.5%	Overweighted
Tax Efficiency	93.15%	Cdn Bonds	40.7%	1 Industrial
Std Deviation	1.76%	Foreign Bonds	0.6%	2 Utilities
Beta	0.70	Cdn Equity	30.1%	Underweighted
Alpha	0.37	Foreign Equity	19.5%	1 Oil & Gas
R Squared	0.82	Warrants		2 Pipelines

TRAILING 24-MONTH ANNUALIZED RETURNS FOR ATLAS CANADIAN BALANCED FUND

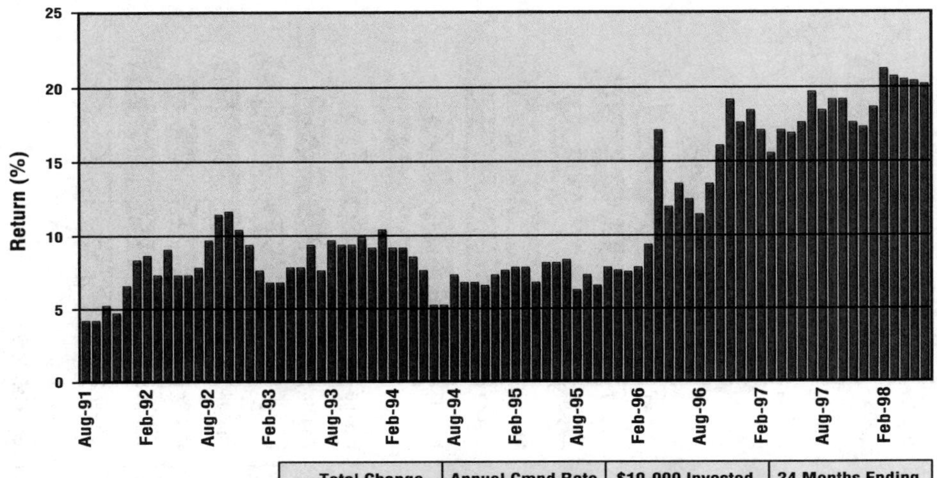

	Total Change	Annual Cmpd Rate	$10,000 Invested	24 Months Ending
Best	45.23%	20.51%	$14,522.64	March 1998
Worst	8.46%	4.14%	$10,845.58	August 1991
Average	22.73%	10.81%	$12,278.81	n/a

Fidelity Canadian Asset Allocation Fund

MVA	3 Months*	1 Year*	3 Years*	5 Years*	1997	1996	1995
106.2	-0.9%	11.3%	20.4%	N/A	23.4%	22.6%	23.4%

* Returns to July 31, 1998

Sponsor Fidelity Investments Canada Ltd.
222 Bay Street, Suite 900
Toronto, Ontario, M5K 1P1
Phone 1-800-387-0074
Sales Fee Load **RRSP Eligibility** Yes

Category Balanced/Canadian
Portfolio Manager/Years
Ford O'Neil—Fidelity Management/4
Minimum Initial Investment
RRSP $500 **Non-RRSP** $500

Extended Asset Mix

Cdn Equity	U.S. Equity	Europe	Japan	Far East	Latin America	Special Equity	Dividend	Domestic Bond	Global Bond	Money Market
◆								◆		

Objectives

Short Term	Mid Term	Long Term	Currency Effect	Sector Specific	Small Cap	Mid Cap	Large Cap
	◆						◆

Investment Styles

Top Down	Bottom Up	Value	Sector Rotation	Momentum	Indexation
◆	◆			◆	

Quantitative		Asset Breakout		Sector Breakout (Equity)
MER	2.48%	Cash	13.5%	Overweighted
Tax Efficiency	94.19%	Cdn Bonds	30.1%	1 Industrial
Std Deviation	2.66%	Foreign Bonds		2 Utilities
Beta	1.08	Cdn Equity	50.6%	Underweighted
Alpha	0.42	Foreign Equity	4.9%	1 Oil & Gas
R Squared	0.81	Warrants	0.2%	2 Pipelines

TRAILING 24-MONTH ANNUALIZED RETURNS FOR FIDELITY CANADIAN ASSET ALLOCATION FUND

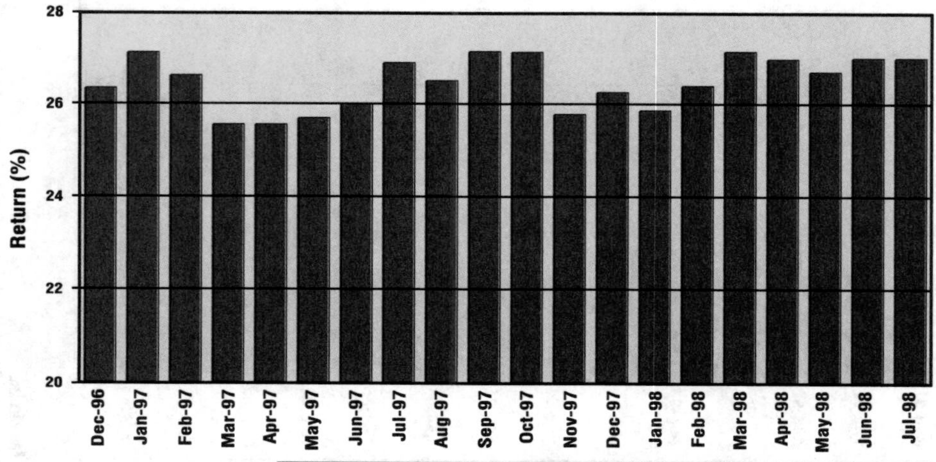

	Total Change	Annual Cmpd Rate	$10,000 Invested	24 Months Ending
Best	59.37%	26.24%	$15,936.97	March 1998
Worst	44.60%	20.25%	$14,460.37	March 1997
Average	53.17%	23.76%	$15,317.28	n/a

Capstone Balanced Fund

MVA	3 Months*	1 Year*	3 Years*	5 Years*	1997	1996	1995
105.8	-1.5%	12.2%	18.0%	12.7%	18.5%	21.4%	13.1%

* Returns to July 31, 1998

Sponsor MMA Investment Managers Ltd.
110 Yonge Street, Suite 1601
Toronto, Ontario, M5C 1T4

Phone 1-800-207-0067

Sales Fee No-Load **RRSP Eligibility** Yes

Category Balanced/Canadian

Portfolio Manager/Years
Michael Smedley—MMA Inv. Managers Ltd./11

Minimum Initial Investment
RRSP $1,000 **Non-RRSP** $1,000

Extended Asset Mix

Cdn Equity	U.S. Equity	Europe	Japan	Far East	Latin America	Special Equity	Dividend	Domestic Bond	Global Bond	Money Market
◆								◆		

Objectives

Short Term	Mid Term	Long Term	Currency Effect	Sector Specific	Small Cap	Mid Cap	Large Cap
		◆					◆

Investment Styles

Top Down	Bottom Up	Value	Sector Rotation	Momentum	Indexation
◆				◆	

Quantitative		Asset Breakout		Sector Breakout (Equity)
MER	2.14%	Cash	0.8%	Overweighted
Tax Efficiency	74.99%	Cdn Bonds	35.2%	1 Merchandising
Std Deviation	2.17%	Foreign Bonds		2 Utilities
Beta	0.83	Cdn Equity	56.9%	Underweighted
Alpha	0.21	Foreign Equity	6.6%	1 Industrial
R Squared	0.79	Warrants		2 Pipelines

TRAILING 24-MONTH ANNUALIZED RETURNS FOR CAPSTONE BALANCED FUND

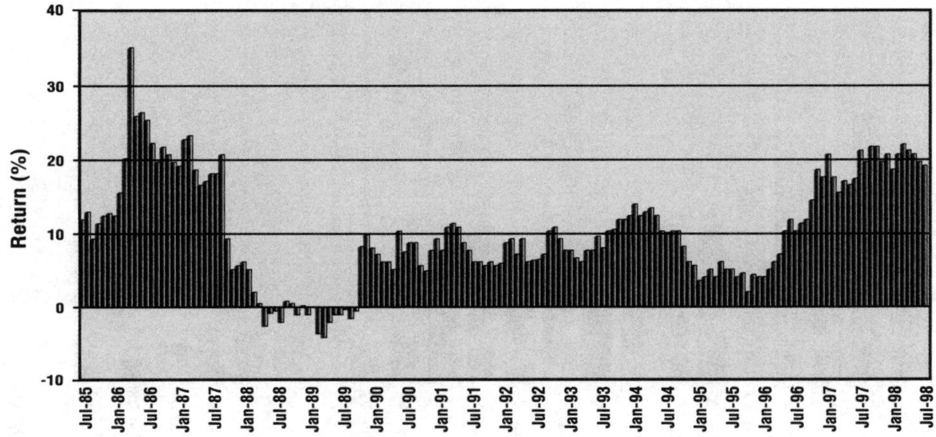

	Total Change	Annual Cmpd Rate	$10,000 Invested	24 Months Ending
Best	78.95%	33.77%	$17,895.31	April 1986
Worst	-8.36%	-4.27%	$9,163.69	March 1989
Average	22.08%	10.49%	$12,208.09	n/a

C.I. Canadian Income Fund

MVA	3 Months*	1 Year*	3 Years*	5 Years*	1997	1996	1995
102.4	-3.7%	2.3%	11.8%	N/A	10.1%	16.2%	20.3%

* Returns to July 31, 1998

Sponsor C.I. Mutual Funds Inc.
151 Yonge Street, 8th Floor
Toronto, Ontario, M5C 2W7

Phone 1-900-563-5181

Sales Fee Load **RRSP Eligibility** Yes

Category Balanced/Canadian

Portfolio Manager/Years
John Zechner—J. Zechner Associates/4

Minimum Initial Investment
RRSP $500 **Non-RRSP** $500

Extended Asset Mix

Cdn Equity	U.S. Equity	Europe	Japan	Far East	Latin America	Special Equity	Dividend	Domestic Bond	Global Bond	Money Market
◆							◆	◆		

Objectives

Short Term	Mid Term	Long Term	Currency Effect	Sector Specific	Small Cap	Mid Cap	Large Cap
	◆						◆

Investment Styles

Top Down	Bottom Up	Value	Sector Rotation	Momentum	Indexation
	◆	◆			

Quantitative		Asset Breakout		Sector Breakout (Equity)
MER	1.82%	Cash	5.5%	Overweighted
Tax Efficiency	60.66%	Cdn Bonds	62.2%	1 Real Estate
Std Deviation	1.76%	Foreign Bonds		2 Utilities
Beta	0.66	Cdn Equity	28.1%	Underweighted
Alpha	0.26	Foreign Equity		1 Industrial
R Squared	0.76	Warrants		2 Pipelines

TRAILING 24-MONTH ANNUALIZED RETURNS FOR C.I. CANADIAN INCOME FUND

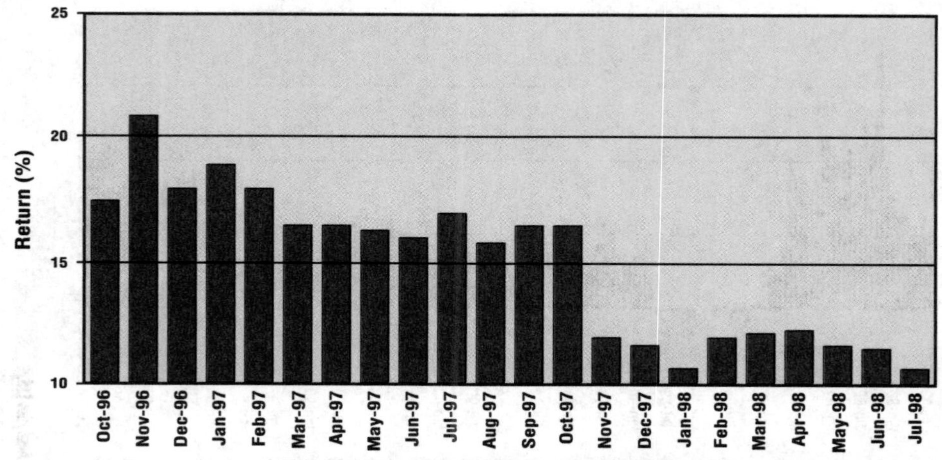

	Total Change	Annual Cmpd Rate	$10,000 Invested	24 Months Ending
Best	47.08%	21.28%	$14,708.35	November 1996
Worst	23.36%	11.07%	$12,335.61	July 1998
Average	33.42%	15.51%	$13,341.87	n/a

Templeton Balanced Fund

MVA	3 Months*	1 Year*	3 Years*	5 Years*	1997	1996	1995
102.2	-4.6%	2.1%	13.3%	12.2%	16.1%	17.9%	13.7%

* Returns to July 31, 1998

Sponsor Templeton Management Ltd
1 Adelaide St. East, Suite 2101
Toronto, Ontario, M5C 3B8
Phone 1-800-387-0830
Sales Fee Load **RRSP Eligibility** Yes

Category Balanced/Canadian
Portfolio Manager/Years
George Moran—Templeton Management/3
Minimum Initial Investment
RRSP $500 **Non-RRSP** $500

Extended Asset Mix

Cdn Equity	U.S. Equity	Europe	Japan	Far East	Latin America	Special Equity	Dividend	Domestic Bond	Global Bond	Money Market
◆								◆		

Objectives

Short Term	Mid Term	Long Term	Currency Effect	Sector Specific	Small Cap	Mid Cap	Large Cap
	◆					◆	◆

Investment Styles

Top Down	Bottom Up	Value	Sector Rotation	Momentum	Indexation
◆	◆	◆			

Quantitative		Asset Breakout		Sector Breakout (Equity)
MER	2.44%	Cash	4.2%	Overweighted
Tax Efficiency	85.87%	Cdn Bonds	31.7%	1 Industrial
Std Deviation	2.19%	Foreign Bonds		2 Utilities
Beta	0.85	Cdn Equity	41.8%	Underweighted
Alpha	0.10	Foreign Equity	20.1%	1 Paper-Forest
R Squared	0.82	Warrants		2 Financial

TRAILING 24-MONTH ANNUALIZED RETURNS FOR TEMPLETON BALANCED FUND

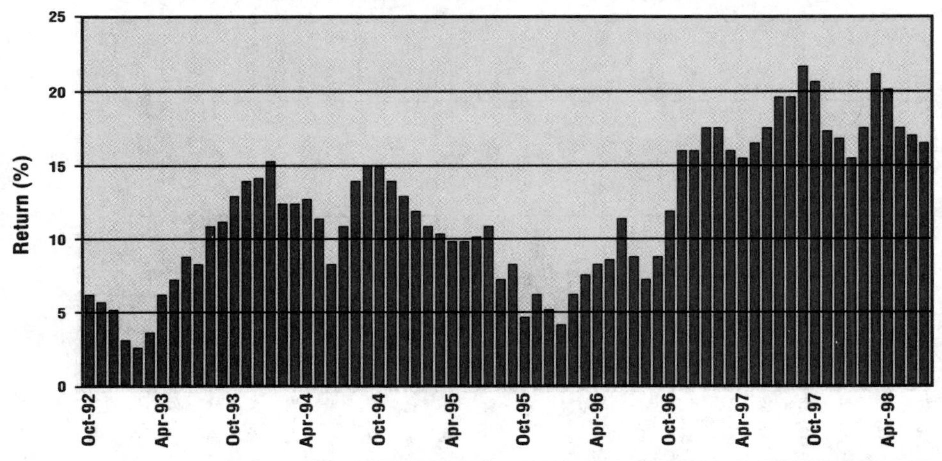

	Total Change	Annual Cmpd Rate	$10,000 Invested	24 Months Ending
Best	46.58%	21.07%	$14,658.45	September 1997
Worst	4.87%	2.40%	$10,486.58	February 1993
Average	25.48%	12.01%	$12,546.43	n/a

Sceptre Balanced Growth Fund

MVA	3 Months*	1 Year*	3 Years*	5 Years*	1997	1996	1995
101.4	-6.4%	1.1%	16.0%	13.3%	14.1%	26.0%	20.4%

* Returns to July 31, 1998

Sponsor	Sceptre Investment Counsel Limited 26 Wellington St. East, Suite 1200 Toronto, Ontario, M5E 1W4	**Category**	Balanced/Canadian
		Portfolio Manager/Years	Lyle Stein—Sceptre Investment Counsel/6
Phone	1-800-265-1888	**Minimum Initial Investment**	
Sales Fee	No-Load **RRSP Eligibility** Yes	**RRSP** $5,000	**Non-RRSP** $5,000

Extended Asset Mix

Cdn Equity	U.S. Equity	Europe	Japan	Far East	Latin America	Special Equity	Dividend	Domestic Bond	Global Bond	Money Market
◆								◆		

Objectives

Short Term	Mid Term	Long Term	Currency Effect	Sector Specific	Small Cap	Mid Cap	Large Cap
	◆						

Investment Styles

Top Down	Bottom Up	Value	Sector Rotation	Momentum	Indexation
◆				◆	

Quantitative		Asset Breakout		Sector Breakout (Equity)
MER	1.44%	Cash	9.6%	Overweighted
Tax Efficiency	77.62%	Cdn Bonds	42.1%	1 Industrial
Std Deviation	2.71%	Foreign Bonds	0.1%	2 Utilities
Beta	1.09	Cdn Equity	33.0%	Underweighted
Alpha	0.12	Foreign Equity	11.7%	1 Oil & Gas
R Squared	0.86	Warrants	0.9%	2 Pipelines

TRAILING 24-MONTH ANNUALIZED RETURNS FOR SCEPTRE BALANCED GROWTH FUND

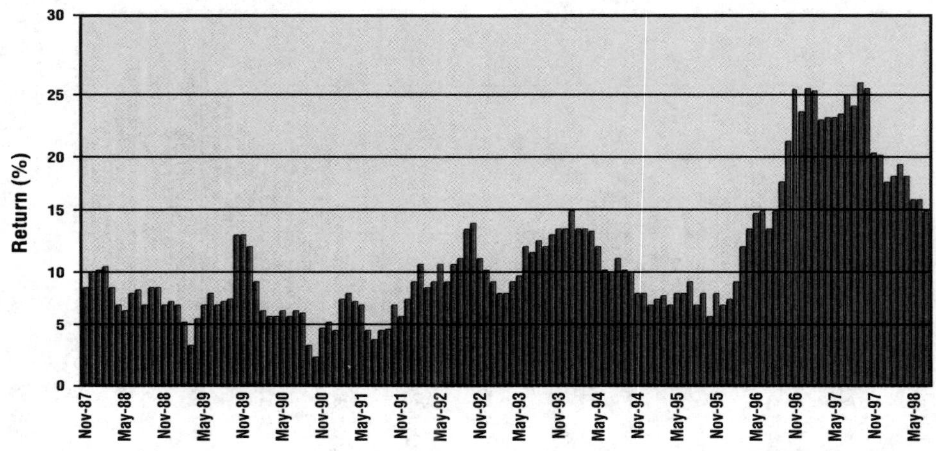

	Total Change	Annual Cmpd Rate	$10,000 Invested	24 Months Ending
Best	59.51%	26.30%	$15,951.35	September 1997
Worst	4.79%	2.37%	$10,478.77	October 1990
Average	24.19%	11.44%	$12,418.71	n/a

Templeton Global Balanced Fund

MVA	3 Months*	1 Year*	3 Years*	5 Years*	1997	1996	1995
97.9	-1.3%	6.2%	12.6%	N/A	10.9%	16.4%	13.4%

* Returns to July 31, 1998

Sponsor Templeton Management Ltd.
1 Adelaide St. East, Suite 2101
Toronto, Ontario, M5C 3B8
Phone 1-800-387-0830
Sales Fee Load **RRSP Eligibility** Foreign

Category Balanced/Global
Portfolio Manager/Years
Thomas Dickson—Templeton Management/4
Minimum Initial Investment
RRSP $500 **Non-RRSP** $500

Extended Asset Mix

Cdn Equity	U.S. Equity	Europe	Japan	Far East	Latin America	Special Equity	Dividend	Domestic Bond	Global Bond	Money Market
◆	◆	◆							◆	

Objectives

Short Term	Mid Term	Long Term	Currency Effect	Sector Specific	Small Cap	Mid Cap	Large Cap
	◆		◆				◆

Investment Styles

Top Down	Bottom Up	Value	Sector Rotation	Momentum	Indexation
◆	◆	◆			

Quantitative		Asset Breakout		Sector Breakout (Equity)
MER	2.55%	Cash	15.1%	Overweighted
Tax Efficiency	94.64%	Cdn Bonds	12.3%	1 Oil & Gas
Std Deviation	1.70%	Foreign Bonds	20.9%	2 Utilities
Beta	0.62	Cdn Equity	0.9%	Underweighted
Alpha	0.29	Foreign Equity	45.3%	1 Financial
R Squared	0.48	Warrants	94.6%	

TRAILING 24-MONTH ANNUALIZED RETURNS FOR TEMPLETON GLOBAL BALANCED FUND

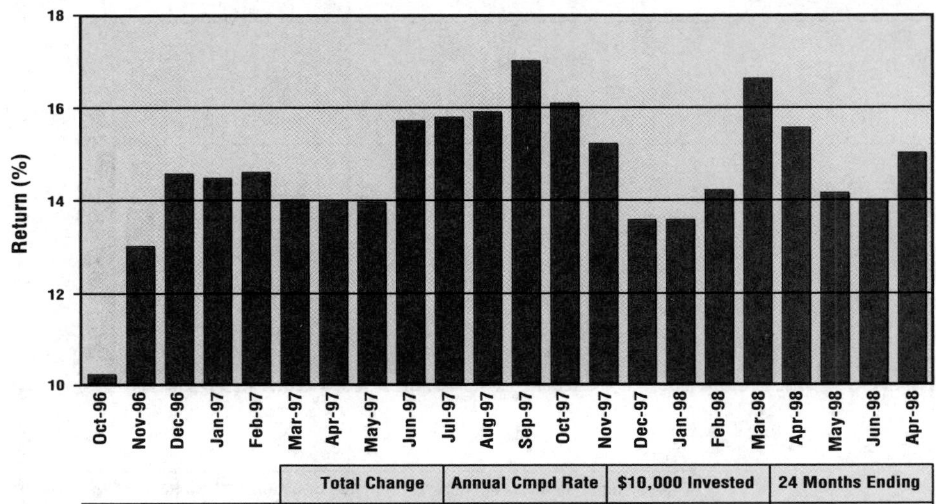

	Total Change	Annual Cmpd Rate	$10,000 Invested	24 Months Ending
Best	37.28%	17.17%	$13,728.31	September 1997
Worst	21.59%	10.27%	$12,158.70	October 1996
Average	31.59%	14.71%	$13,158.74	n/a

C.I. International Balanced Fund

MVA	3 Months*	1 Year*	3 Years*	5 Years*	1997	1996	1995
96.8	3.9%	15.9%	17.2%	N/A	15.7%	13.0%	18.4%

* Returns to July 31, 1998

Sponsor C.I. Mutual Funds Inc.
151 Yonge Street, 8th Floor
Toronto, Ontario, M5C 2W7

Phone 1-900-563-5181

Sales Fee Load **RRSP Eligibility** Foreign

Category Balanced/Global

Portfolio Manager/Years
Gregg Diliberto—BEA Associates/4

Minimum Initial Investment
RRSP $500 **Non-RRSP** $500

Extended Asset Mix

Cdn Equity	U.S. Equity	Europe	Japan	Far East	Latin America	Special Equity	Dividend	Domestic Bond	Global Bond	Money Market
◆	◆	◆							◆	

Objectives

Short Term	Mid Term	Long Term	Currency Effect	Sector Specific	Small Cap	Mid Cap	Large Cap
◆			◆				◆

Investment Styles

Top Down	Bottom Up	Value	Sector Rotation	Momentum	Indexation
◆				◆	

Quantitative		Asset Breakout		Sector Breakout (Equity)
MER	2.41%	Cash	24.4%	Overweighted
Tax Efficiency	91.00%	Cdn Bonds	1.4%	1 Goods & Services
Std Deviation	2.05%	Foreign Bonds	14.2%	2 Financial
Beta	0.70	Cdn Equity	1.5%	Underweighted
Alpha	0.54	Foreign Equity	57.2%	1 Utilities
R Squared	0.41	Warrants		2 Pipelines

TRAILING 24-MONTH ANNUALIZED RETURNS FOR C.I. INTERNATIONAL BALANCED FUND

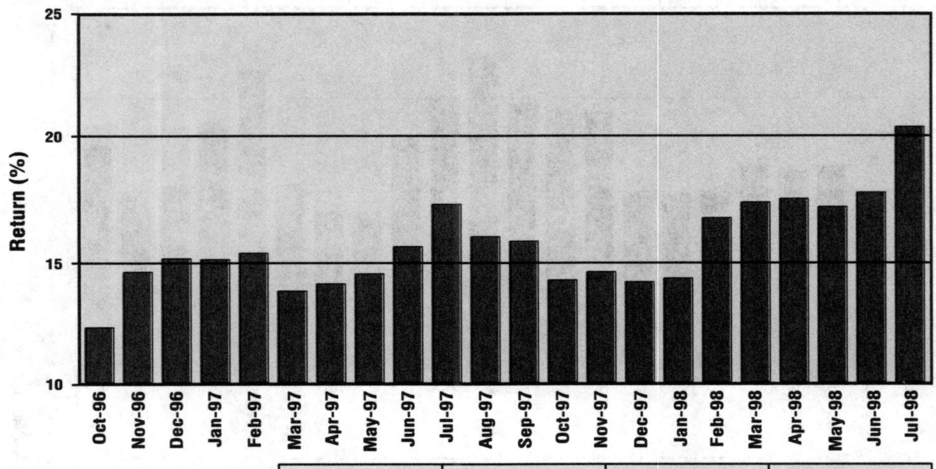

	Total Change	Annual Cmpd Rate	$10,000 Invested	24 Months Ending
Best	45.62%	20.67%	$14,561.53	July 1998
Worst	25.75%	12.14%	$12,574.79	October 1996
Average	34.63%	16.03%	$13,483.78	n/a

FMOQ Fonds de Placement

MVA	3 Months*	1 Year*	3 Years*	5 Years*	1997	1996	1995
94.9	-0.4%	18.4%	22.4%	17.7%	21.2%	20.8%	19.4%

* Returns to July 31, 1998

Sponsor Les Fonds Investissement FMOQ
1440 Ste Catherine Ouest
Montreal, Quebec, H3G 1R8

Phone 1-888-542-8597

Sales Fee No-Load **RRSP Eligibility** Yes

Category Balanced/Global

Portfolio Manager/Years
Guy Normandin—T.A.L. Investment Counsel/15

Minimum Initial Investment
RRSP $5,000 **Non-RRSP** $5,000

Extended Asset Mix

Cdn Equity	U.S. Equity	Europe	Japan	Far East	Latin America	Special Equity	Dividend	Domestic Bond	Global Bond	Money Market
◆		◆	◆	◆					◆	

Objectives

Short Term	Mid Term	Long Term	Currency Effect	Sector Specific	Small Cap	Mid Cap	Large Cap
	◆		◆				◆

Investment Styles

Top Down	Bottom Up	Value	Sector Rotation	Momentum	Indexation
◆				◆	

Quantitative		Asset Breakout		Sector Breakout (Equity)
MER	0.61%	Cash	N/A	Overweighted
Tax Efficiency	80.04%	Cdn Bonds	N/A	N/A
Std Deviation	3.18%	Foreign Bonds	N/A	
Beta	1.36	Cdn Equity	N/A	Underweighted
Alpha	0.12	Foreign Equity	N/A	N/A
R Squared	0.83	Warrants	N/A	

TRAILING 24-MONTH ANNUALIZED RETURNS FOR FMOQ FONDS DE PLACEMENT

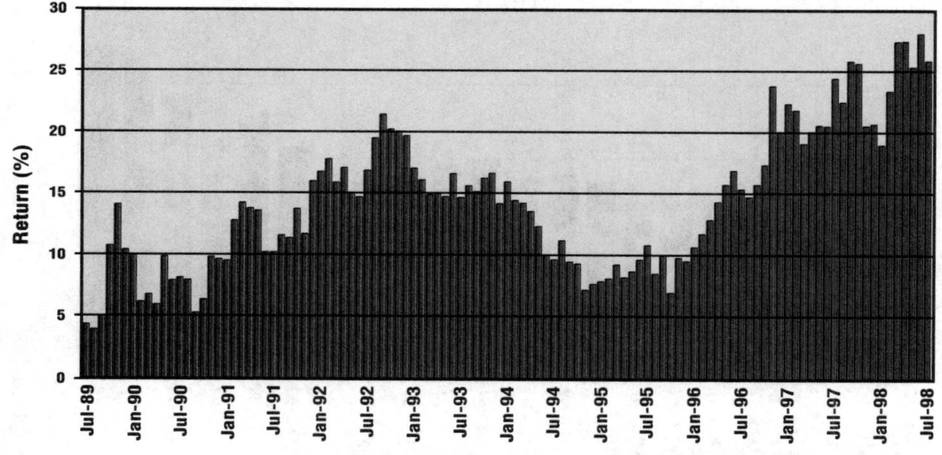

	Total Change	Annual Cmpd Rate	$10,000 Invested	24 Months Ending
Best	64.28%	28.17%	$16,428.32	June 1998
Worst	7.74%	3.80%	$10,773.63	August 1989
Average	31.35%	14.61%	$13,134.75	n/a

AIM GT Global Growth & Income Fund

MVA	3 Months*	1 Year*	3 Years*	5 Years*	1997	1996	1995
94.1	8.1%	26.5%	18.2%	N/A	15.6%	11.9%	12.6%

* Returns to July 31, 1998

Sponsor AIM GT Investments
77 King Street East, Suite 4001
Toronto, Ontario, M5K 1K2
Phone 1-800-588-5684
Sales Fee Load **RRSP Eligibility** Foreign

Category Balanced/Global
Portfolio Manager/Years
Nicholas Train—LGT Asset Management/4
Minimum Initial Investment
RRSP $500 **Non-RRSP** $500

Extended Asset Mix

Cdn Equity	U.S. Equity	Europe	Japan	Far East	Latin America	Special Equity	Dividend	Domestic Bond	Global Bond	Money Market
	◆	◆							◆	

Objectives

Short Term	Mid Term	Long Term	Currency Effect	Sector Specific	Small Cap	Mid Cap	Large Cap
	◆		◆				◆

Investment Styles

Top Down	Bottom Up	Value	Sector Rotation	Momentum	Indexation
◆				◆	

Quantitative		Asset Breakout		Sector Breakout (Equity)
MER	2.95%	Cash	11.5%	Overweighted
Tax Efficiency	97.01%	Cdn Bonds	1.3%	N/A
Std Deviation	1.91%	Foreign Bonds	25.0%	
Beta	0.59	Cdn Equity		Underweighted
Alpha	0.68	Foreign Equity	63.6%	N/A
R Squared	0.25	Warrants		

TRAILING 24-MONTH ANNUALIZED RETURNS FOR AIM GT GLOBAL GROWTH & INCOME FUND

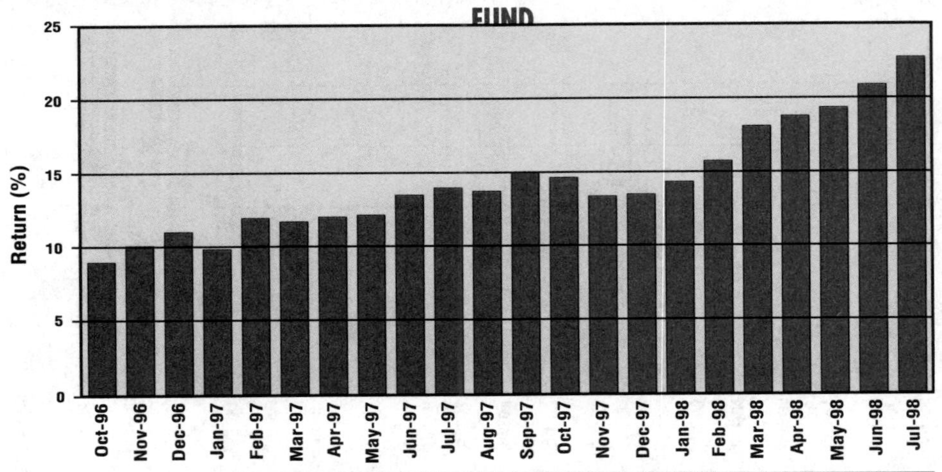

	Total Change	Annual Cmpd Rate	$10,000 Invested	24 Months Ending
Best	51.71%	23.17%	$15,170.95	July 1998
Worst	18.35%	8.79%	$11,834.98	October 1996
Average	31.62%	14.72%	$13,181.80	n/a

Ivy Enterprise Fund

MVA	3 Months*	1 Year*	3 Years*	5 Years*	1997	1996	1995
153.0	-11.4%	4.1%	15.8%	N/A	23.4%	25.0%	14.6%

* Returns to July 31, 1998

Sponsor Mackenzie Financial Corporation
150 Bloor Street West, Suite M111
Toronto, Ontario, M5S 3B5

Phone 1-800-387-0614

Sales Fee Load **RRSP Eligibility** Yes

Category CanadianEquity/Diversified

Portfolio Manager/Years
Chuck Roth—Ultravest Inv. Counsellors/1

Minimum Initial Investment
RRSP $500 **Non-RRSP** $500

Extended Asset Mix

Cdn Equity	U.S. Equity	Europe	Japan	Far East	Latin America	Special Equity	Dividend	Domestic Bond	Global Bond	Money Market
◆										

Objectives

Short Term	Mid Term	Long Term	Currency Effect	Sector Specific	Small Cap	Mid Cap	Large Cap
					◆		

Investment Styles

Top Down	Bottom Up	Value	Sector Rotation	Momentum	Indexation
	◆	◆			

Quantitative		Asset Breakout		Sector Breakout (Equity)
MER	2.39%	Cash	24.5%	Overweighted
Tax Efficiency	100.00%	Cdn Bonds		1 Industrial
Std Deviation	2.19%	Foreign Bonds		2 Utilities
Beta	0.29	Cdn Equity	64.1%	Underweighted
Alpha	0.93	Foreign Equity	11.4%	1 Merchandising
R Squared	0.54	Warrants		2 Pipelines

TRAILING 24-MONTH ANNUALIZED RETURNS FOR IVY ENTERPRISE FUND

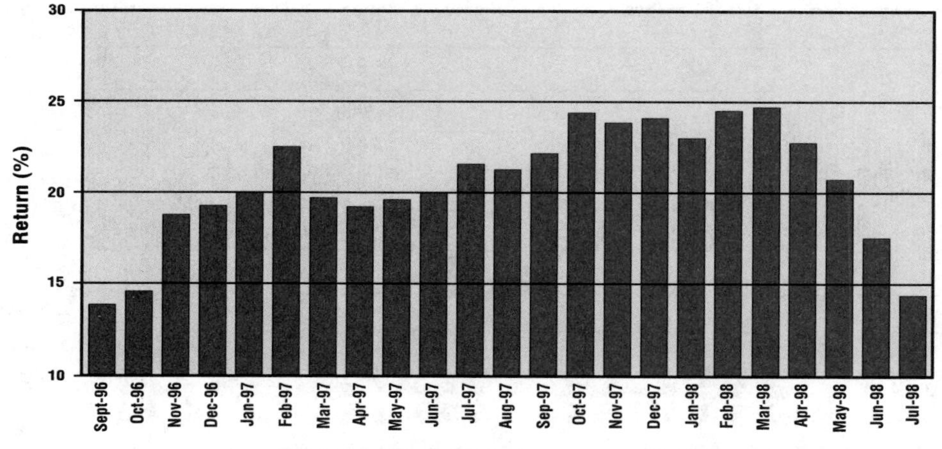

	Total Change	Annual Cmpd Rate	$10,000 Invested	24 Months Ending
Best	58.79%	25.22%	$15,679.26	March 1998
Worst	29.14%	13.64%	$12,914.17	September 1996
Average	46.14%	20.89%	$14,614.13	n/a

Cundill Security Series A Fund

MVA	3 Months*	1 Year*	3 Years*	5 Years*	1997	1996	1995
136.1	-3.3%	17.2%	17.3%	17.4%	18.4%	20.2%	10.4%

* Returns to July 31, 1998

Sponsor Peter Cundill & Associates
1200 Sun Life Plaza, 1100 Melville St.
Vancouver, British Columbia, V6E 4A6
Phone 1-800-663-0156
Sales Fee Load **RRSP Eligibility** Yes

Category Canadian Equity/Value
Portfolio Manager/Years
Peter Cundill—Peter Cundill & Associates/18
Minimum Initial Investment
RRSP $50,000 **Non-RRSP** $50,000

Note: Investors interested in this fund can buy a sister fund, Cundill Securities Series B with a minimum $2,500 investment.

Extended Asset Mix

Cdn Equity	U.S. Equity	Europe	Japan	Far East	Latin America	Special Equity	Dividend	Domestic Bond	Global Bond	Money Market
◆										

Objectives

Short Term	Mid Term	Long Term	Currency Effect	Sector Specific	Small Cap	Mid Cap	Large Cap
					◆		

Investment Styles

Top Down	Bottom Up	Value	Sector Rotation	Momentum	Indexation
	◆	◆			

Quantitative		Asset Breakout		Sector Breakout (Equity)
MER	2.04%	Cash	41.2%	Overweighted
Tax Efficiency	82.54%	Cdn Bonds		1 Merchandising
Std Deviation	2.25%	Foreign Bonds		2 Utilities
Beta	0.24	Cdn Equity	47.4%	Underweighted
Alpha	1.22	Foreign Equity	10.4%	1 Conglomerates
R Squared	0.24	Warrants	0.2%	2 Pipelines

TRAILING 24-MONTH ANNUALIZED RETURNS FOR CUNDILL SECURITIES SERIES A FUND

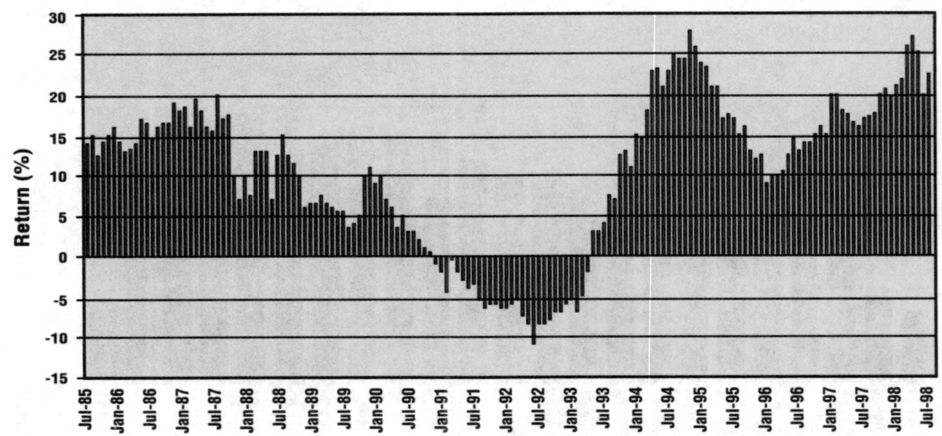

	Total Change	Annual Cmpd Rate	$10,000 Invested	24 Months Ending
Best	62.98%	27.66%	$16,297.56	November 1994
Worst	-19.95%	-10.53%	$8,005.43	May 1992
Average	22.74%	10.79%	$12,274.40	n/a

AIC Diversified Canada Fund

MVA	3 Months*	1 Year*	3 Years*	5 Years*	1997	1996	1995
129.0	-1.8%	21.8%	40.6%	N/A	32.1%	65.1%	26.2%

* Returns to July 31, 1998

Sponsor AIC Limited
1375 Kerns Road
Burlington, Ontario, L7R 4V7

Phone 1-800-263-2144

Sales Fee Load **RRSP Eligibility** Yes

Category Canadian Equity/Growth

Portfolio Manager/Years
Michael Lee-Chin—AIC Limited/12

Minimum Initial Investment
RRSP $500 **Non-RRSP** $500

Extended Asset Mix

Cdn Equity	U.S. Equity	Europe	Japan	Far East	Latin America	Special Equity	Dividend	Domestic Bond	Global Bond	Money Market
◆										

Objectives

Short Term	Mid Term	Long Term	Currency Effect	Sector Specific	Small Cap	Mid Cap	Large Cap
						◆	

Investment Styles

Top Down	Bottom Up	Value	Sector Rotation	Momentum	Indexation
	◆	◆		◆	

Quantitative		Asset Breakout		Sector Breakout (Equity)
MER	2.39%	Cash	12.0%	Overweighted
Tax Efficiency	100.00%	Cdn Bonds	0.3%	1 Financial
Std Deviation	3.81%	Foreign Bonds		2 Utilities
Beta	0.90	Cdn Equity	72.4%	Underweighted
Alpha	1.60	Foreign Equity	14.8%	1 Industrial
R Squared	0.75	Warrants		2 Pipelines

TRAILING 24-MONTH ANNUALIZED RETURNS FOR AIC DIVERSIFIED CANADA FUND

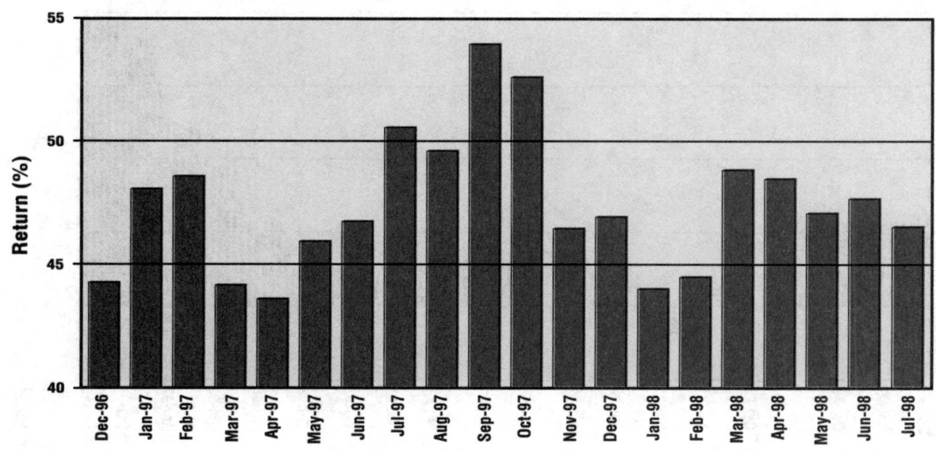

	Total Change	Annual Cmpd Rate	$10,000 Invested	24 Months Ending
Best	137.24%	54.02%	$23,723.50	September 1997
Worst	106.49%	43.70%	$20,649.25	April 1997
Average	118.25%	47.73%	$21,824.88	n/a

Chou RRSP Fund

MVA	3 Months*	1 Year*	3 Years*	5 Years*	1997	1996	1995
128.9	0.4%	38.4%	30.0%	18.5%	50.6%	22.1%	19.0%

* Returns to July 31, 1998

Sponsor Chou Associates Management Inc.
70 Dragoon Cres.
Toronto, Ontario, M1V 1N4
Phone 1-416-288-6749
Sales Fee Load **RRSP Eligibility** Yes

Category Canadian Equity/Value
Portfolio Manager/Years
Francis Chou—Chou Associates/12
Minimum Initial Investment
RRSP $3,500 **Non-RRSP** $3,500

Extended Asset Mix

Cdn Equity	U.S. Equity	Europe	Japan	Far East	Latin America	Special Equity	Dividend	Domestic Bond	Global Bond	Money Market
◆										

Objectives

Short Term	Mid Term	Long Term	Currency Effect	Sector Specific	Small Cap	Mid Cap	Large Cap
					◆		

Investment Styles

Top Down	Bottom Up	Value	Sector Rotation	Momentum	Indexation
	◆	◆			

Quantitative		Asset Breakout		Sector Breakout (Equity)
MER	2.02%	Cash	N/A	Overweighted
Tax Efficiency	93.29%	Cdn Bonds	N/A	N/A
Std Deviation	3.12%	Foreign Bonds	N/A	
Beta	0.34	Cdn Equity	N/A	Underweighted
Alpha	1.26	Foreign Equity	N/A	N/A
R Squared	0.19	Warrants	N/A	

TRAILING 24-MONTH ANNUALIZED RETURNS FOR CHOU RRSP FUND

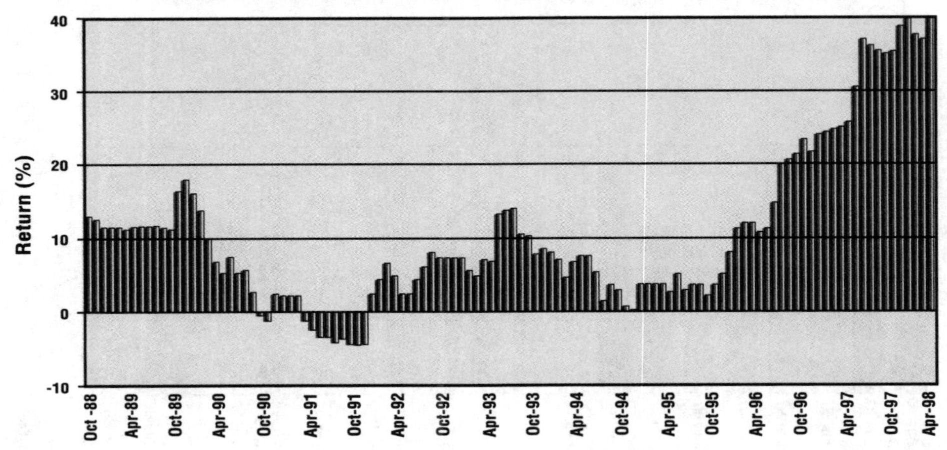

	Total Change	Annual Cmpd Rate	$10,000 Invested	24 Months Ending
Best	95.47%	39.81%	$19,547.20	April 1998
Worst	-7.93%	-4.05%	$9,206.65	November 1991
Average	22.28%	10.58%	$12,227.96	n/a

Fidelity Canadian Growth Company Fund

MVA	3 Months*	1 Year*	3 Years*	5 Years*	1997	1996	1995
126.7	-6.3%	12.6%	22.2%	N/A	28.8%	20.5%	31.1%

* Returns to July 31, 1998

Sponsor Fidelity Investments Canada Ltd.
222 Bay Street, Suite 900
Toronto, Ontario, M5K 1P1
Phone 1-800-387-0074
Sales Fee Load **RRSP Eligibility** Yes

Category Canadian Equity/Growth
Portfolio Manager/Years
Alan Raldo—Fidelity Management/3
Minimum Initial Investment
RRSP $500 **Non-RRSP** $500

Extended Asset Mix

Cdn Equity	U.S. Equity	Europe	Japan	Far East	Latin America	Special Equity	Dividend	Domestic Bond	Global Bond	Money Market
◆										

Objectives

Short Term	Mid Term	Long Term	Currency Effect	Sector Specific	Small Cap	Mid Cap	Large Cap
					◆	◆	

Investment Styles

Top Down	Bottom Up	Value	Sector Rotation	Momentum	Indexation
	◆	◆			

Quantitative		Asset Breakout		Sector Breakout (Equity)
MER	2.46%	Cash	16.0%	Overweighted
Tax Efficiency	97.24%	Cdn Bonds		1 Industrial
Std Deviation	3.38%	Foreign Bonds		2 Utilities
Beta	0.61	Cdn Equity	80.7%	Underweighted
Alpha	1.37	Foreign Equity	2.8%	1 Oil & Gas
R Squared	0.69	Warrants	0.2%	2 Financial

TRAILING 24-MONTH ANNUALIZED RETURNS FOR FIDELITY CANADIAN GROWTH CO. FUND

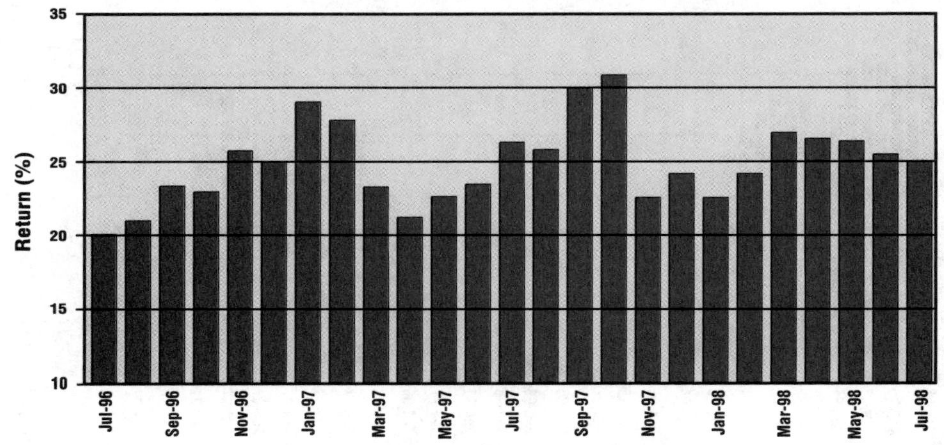

	Total Change	Annual Cmpd Rate	$10,000 Invested	24 Months Ending
Best	72.86%	31.47%	$17,285.62	October 1997
Worst	43.98%	19.99%	$14,397.91	July 1996
Average	57.12%	25.35%	$15,712.21	n/a

Bissett Small Capital Fund

MVA	3 Months*	1 Year*	3 Years*	5 Years*	1997	1996	1995
123.2	-17.0%	-7.7%	20.0%	15.1%	23.8%	51.0%	18.2%

* Returns to July 31, 1998

Sponsor Bissett & Associates Inv. Mngt.
500 Fourth Street S.W., Suite 1120
Calgary, Alberta, T2P 2V6
Phone 1-800-267-3862
Sales Fee No-Load **RRSP Eligibility** Yes

Category Canadian Equity/Diversified
Portfolio Manager/Years
David Bissett—Bissett & Associates/7
Minimum Initial Investment
RRSP $10,000 **Non-RRSP** $10,000

Extended Asset Mix

Cdn Equity	U.S. Equity	Europe	Japan	Far East	Latin America	Special Equity	Dividend	Domestic Bond	Global Bond	Money Market
◆										

Objectives

Short Term	Mid Term	Long Term	Currency Effect	Sector Specific	Small Cap	Mid Cap	Large Cap
					◆		

Investment Styles

Top Down	Bottom Up	Value	Sector Rotation	Momentum	Indexation
	◆			◆	

Quantitative		Asset Breakout		Sector Breakout (Equity)
MER	1.90%	Cash	3.1%	Overweighted
Tax Efficiency	97.35%	Cdn Bonds		1 Industrial
Std Deviation	4.62%	Foreign Bonds		2 Utilities
Beta	0.88	Cdn Equity	93.4%	Underweighted
Alpha	0.76	Foreign Equity	2.8%	1 Oil & Gas
R Squared	0.83	Warrants	1.6%	2 Financial

TRAILING 24-MONTH ANNUALIZED RETURNS FOR BISSETT SMALL CAPITAL FUND

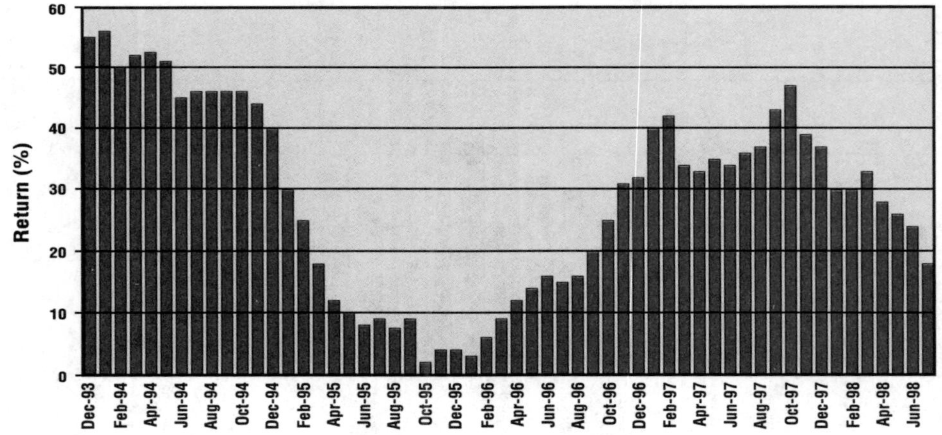

	Total Change	Annual Cmpd Rate	$10,000 Invested	24 Months Ending
Best	142.78%	55.81%	$24,277.61	January 1994
Worst	4.86%	2.40%	$10,485.95	October 1995
Average	69.67%	30.26%	$16,967.44	n/a

Associate Investors Fund

MVA	3 Months*	1 Year*	3 Years*	5 Years*	1997	1996	1995
123.0	-3.4%	19.3%	26.3%	17.0%	35.8%	31.3%	10.8%

* Returns to July 31, 1998

Sponsor Leon Frazer & Associates
8 King Street East, Suite 2001
Toronto, Ontario, M5C 1B6

Phone 1-416-864-1120

Sales Fee No-Load **RRSP Eligibility** Yes

Category Canadian Equity/Value

Portfolio Manager/Years
Lean Frazer—Leon Frazer & Associates/49

Minimum Initial Investment
RRSP $100 **Non-RRSP** $100

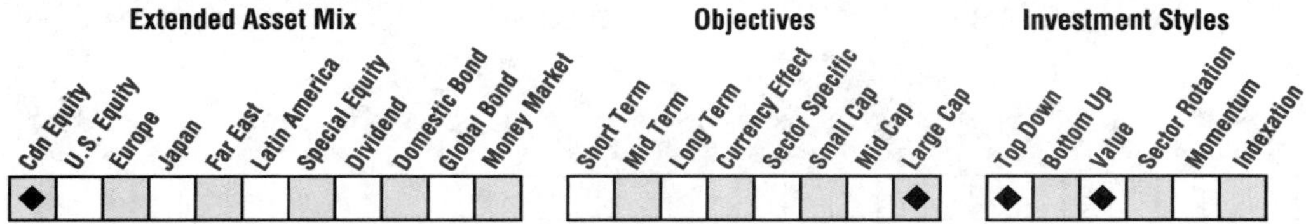

Quantitative		Asset Breakout		Sector Breakout (Equity)
MER	1.83%	Cash	8.3%	Overweighted
Tax Efficiency	92.99%	Cdn Bonds		1 Utilities
Std Deviation	3.03%	Foreign Bonds		2 Consumer
Beta	0.59	Cdn Equity	90.1%	Underweighted
Alpha	0.64	Foreign Equity		1 Industrial
R Squared	0.63	Warrants		2 Financial

TRAILING 24-MONTH ANNUALIZED RETURNS FOR ASSOCIATE INVESTORS FUND

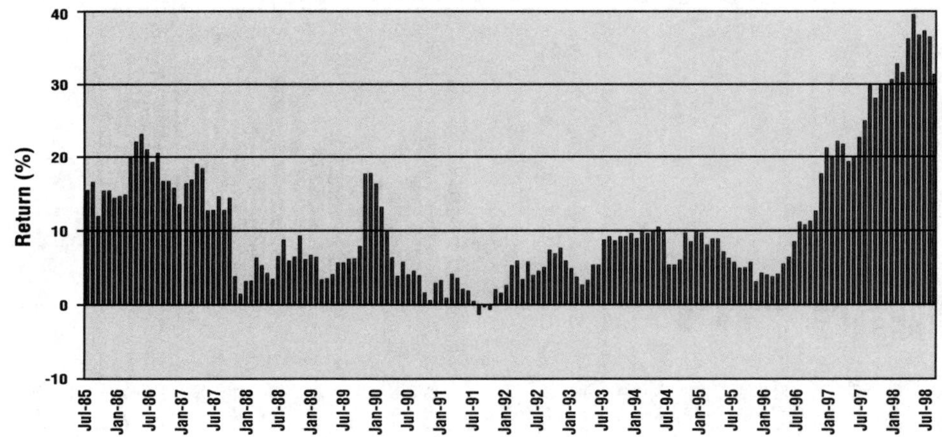

	Total Change	Annual Cmpd Rate	$10,000 Invested	24 Months Ending
Best	94.48%	39.46%	$19,448.16	March 1998
Worst	-2.81%	-1.41%	$9,719.06	Jul 1991
Average	24.10%	11.40%	$12,410.33	n/a

Fonds d'Investissement REA

MVA	3 Months*	1 Year*	3 Years*	5 Years*	1997	1996	1995
119.9	-7.6%	17.4%	20.0%	11.3%	39.2%	10.6%	12.5%

* Returns to July 31, 1998

Sponsor Gentrust Investment Counsellors
1100 University Street, 11th Floor
Montreal, Quebec, H3B 2G7

Phone 1-514-871-7162

Sales Fee Load **RRSP Eligibility** Yes

Category Canadian Equity/Diversified

Portfolio Manager/Years
Josee Legault—Gentrust/6

Minimum Initial Investment
RRSP $2,000 **Non-RRSP** $2,000

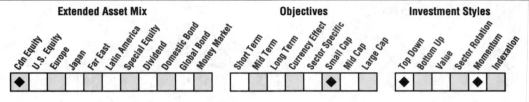

Extended Asset Mix

Cdn Equity	U.S. Equity	Europe	Japan	Far East	Latin America	Special Equity	Dividend	Domestic Bond	Global Bond	Money Market
◆										

Objectives

Short Term	Mid Term	Long Term	Currency Effect	Sector Specific	Small Cap	Mid Cap	Large Cap
					◆		

Investment Styles

Top Down	Bottom Up	Value	Sector Rotation	Momentum	Indexation
◆				◆	

Quantitative		Asset Breakout		Sector Breakout (Equity)
MER	2.69%	Cash	11.4%	Overweighted
Tax Efficiency	97.70%	Cdn Bonds	1.5%	1 Industrial
Std Deviation	3.41%	Foreign Bonds		2 Utilities
Beta	0.47	Cdn Equity	85.4%	Underweighted
Alpha	0.68	Foreign Equity	0.5%	1 Merchandising
R Squared	0.41	Warrants		2 Financial

TRAILING 24-MONTH ANNUALIZED RETURNS FOR FONDS D'INVESTISSEMENT REA

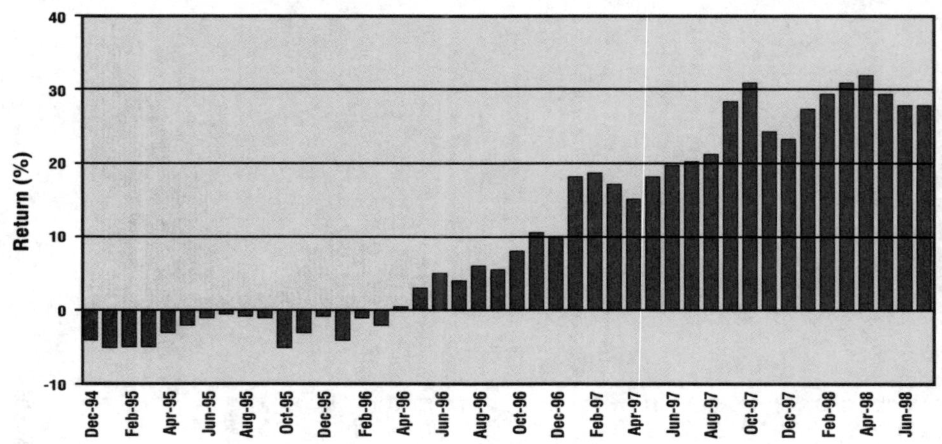

	Total Change	Annual Cmpd Rate	$10,000 Invested	24 Months Ending
Best	77.36%	33.18%	$17,735.71	April 1998
Worst	-9.15%	-4.68%	$9,085.18	January 1995
Average	24.65%	11.65%	$12,465.31	n/a

Saxon Small Cap Fund

MVA	3 Months*	1 Year*	3 Years*	5 Years*	1997	1996	1995
119.6	-4.9%	14.3%	21.5%	15.0%	28.1%	26.2%	9.9%

* Returns to July 31, 1998

Sponsor Saxon-Howson Tattersall Inv. Counsel
20 Queen Street West, Suite 1904
Toronto, Ontario, M5H 3R3

Phone 1-888-287-2966

Sales Fee No-Load **RRSP Eligibility** Yes

Category Canadian Equity/Diversified

Portfolio Manager/Years
Robert Tattersall—Saxon-Howson Tattersall/13

Minimum Initial Investment
RRSP $5,000 **Non-RRSP** $5,000

Extended Asset Mix

Cdn Equity	U.S. Equity	Europe	Japan	Far East	Latin America	Special Equity	Dividend	Domestic Bond	Global Bond	Money Market
◆										

Objectives

Short Term	Mid Term	Long Term	Currency Effect	Sector Specific	Small Cap	Mid Cap	Large Cap
					◆		

Investment Styles

Top Down	Bottom Up	Value	Sector Rotation	Momentum	Indexation
	◆	◆			

Quantitative		Asset Breakout		Sector Breakout (Equity)
MER	1.75%	Cash	3.0%	Overweighted
Tax Efficiency	86.81%	Cdn Bonds		1 Industrial
Std Deviation	3.46%	Foreign Bonds		2 Utilities
Beta	0.68	Cdn Equity	97.5%	Underweighted
Alpha	0.86	Foreign Equity		1 Oil & Gas
R Squared	0.73	Warrants		2 Financial

TRAILING 24-MONTH ANNUALIZED RETURNS FOR SAXON SMALL CAP FUND

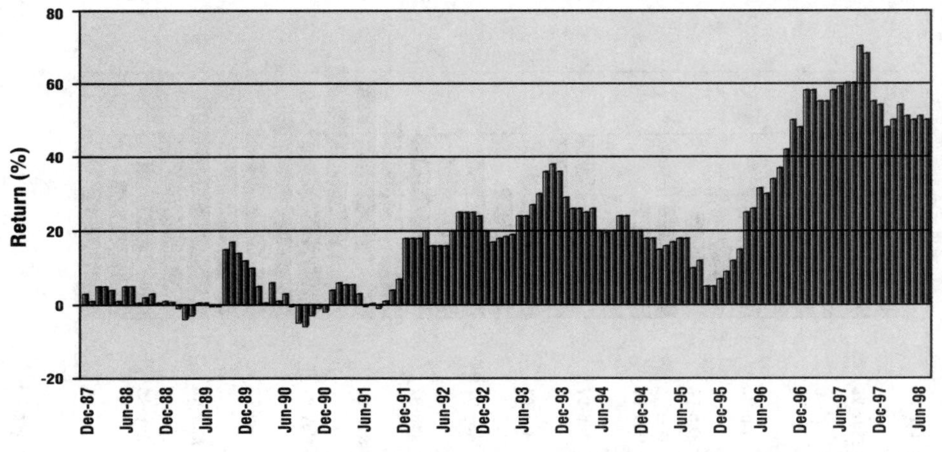

	Total Change	Annual Cmpd Rate	$10,000 Invested	24 Months Ending
Best	190.5%	70.44%	$29,049.82	September 1997
Worst	-12.26%	-6.33%	$8,773.71	October 1990
Average	46.88%	21.20%	$14,688.39	n/a

Talvest/Hyperion Small-Cap Canadian Equity Fund

MVA	3 Months*	1 Year*	3 Years*	5 Years*	1997	1996	1995
118.4	-15.3%	-2.3%	18.6%	N/A	37.6%	31.8%	14.6%

* Returns to July 31, 1998

Sponsor Talvest Fund Management Inc.
1000 de la Gauchetiere West 3200
Montreal, Quebec, H3B 4W5
Phone 1-800-268-8258
Sales Fee Load **RRSP Eligibility** Yes

Category Canadian Equity/Growth
Portfolio Manager/Years
Sabastian Van Berkom—T.A.L. Investment/5
Minimum Initial Investment
RRSP $500 **Non-RRSP** $500

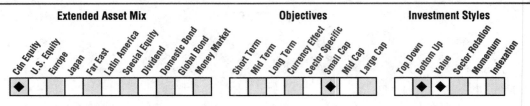

Extended Asset Mix

Cdn Equity	U.S. Equity	Europe	Japan	Far East	Latin America	Special Equity	Dividend	Domestic Bond	Global Bond	Money Market
◆										

Objectives

Short Term	Mid Term	Long Term	Currency Effect	Sector Specific	Small Cap	Mid Cap	Large Cap
					◆		

Investment Styles

Top Down	Bottom Up	Value	Sector Rotation	Momentum	Indexation
	◆	◆			

Quantitative		Asset Breakout		Sector Breakout (Equity)
MER	2.62%	Cash	2.4%	Overweighted
Tax Efficiency	100.00%	Cdn Bonds		1 Utilities
Std Deviation	4.71%	Foreign Bonds		
Beta	0.89	Cdn Equity	96.0%	Underweighted
Alpha	0.66	Foreign Equity	1.6%	1 Consumer
R Squared	0.74	Warrants		2 Pipelines

TRAILING 24-MONTH ANNUALIZED RETURNS FOR TALVEST/HYPERION SMALL-CAP CDN EQUITY

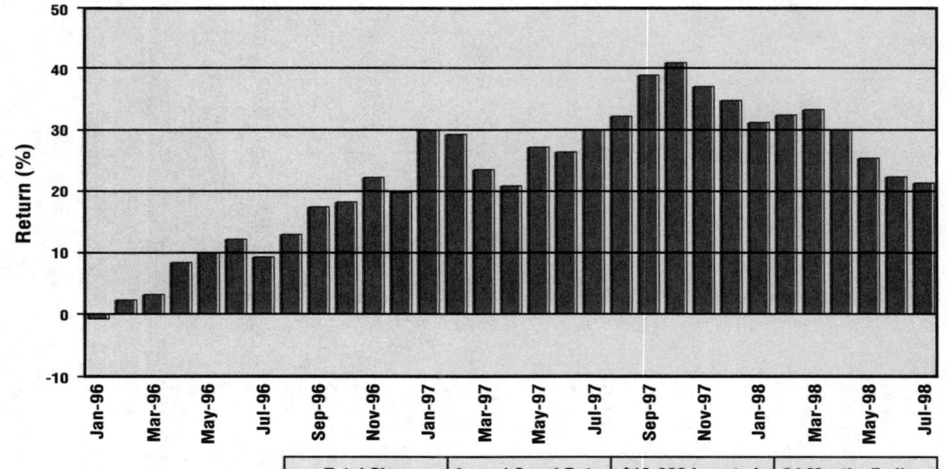

	Total Change	Annual Cmpd Rate	$10,000 Invested	24 Months Ending
Best	103.13%	42.52%	$20,313.24	October 1997
Worst	-1.27%	-0.64%	$9,873.11	January 1996
Average	54.22%	24.18%	$15,421.74	n/a

AIC Advantage Fund

MVA	3 Months*	1 Year*	3 Years*	5 Years*	1997	1996	1995
118.2	-2.8%	16.2%	44.9%	33.0%	43.3%	66.5%	30.7%

* Returns to July 31, 1998

Sponsor AIC Limited Financial Services
1375 Kerns Road
Burlington, Ontario, L7R 4V7

Phone 1-800-263-2144

Sales Fee Load **RRSP Eligibility** Yes

Category Canadian Equity

Portfolio Manager/Years
Michael Lee-Chin—AIC Limited/12

Minimum Initial Investment
RRSP $500 **Non-RRSP** $500

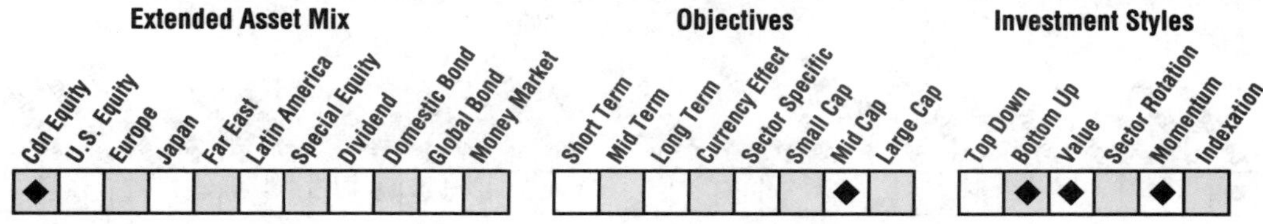

Quantitative		Asset Breakout		Sector Breakout (Equity)
MER	2.31%	Cash	3.5%	Overweighted
Tax Efficiency	100.00%	Cdn Bonds	0.2%	1 Financial
Std Deviation	5.23%	Foreign Bonds		2 Utilities
Beta	0.83	Cdn Equity	81.5%	Underweighted
Alpha	0.63	Foreign Equity	14.5%	1 Communications
R Squared	0.47	Warrants		2 Pipelines

TRAILING 24-MONTH ANNUALIZED RETURNS FOR AIC ADVANTAGE FUND

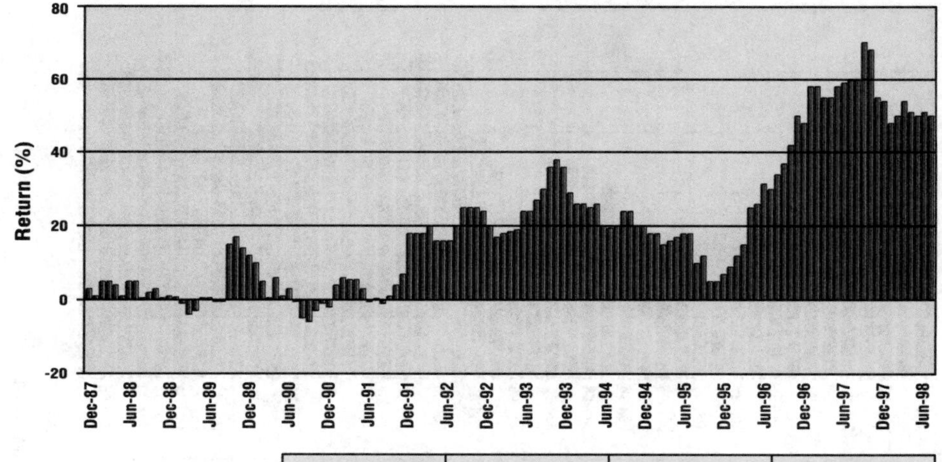

	Total Change	Annual Cmpd Rate	$10,000 Invested	24 Months Ending
Best	190.5%	70.44%	$29,049.82	September 1997
Worst	-12.26%	-6.33%	$8,773.71	October 1990
Average	46.88%	21.20%	$14,688.39	n/a

Ivy Canadian Fund

MVA	3 Months*	1 Year*	3 Years*	5 Years*	1997	1996	1995
117.2	-0.8%	10.9%	17.9%	14.9%	17.6%	25.2%	15.8%

* Returns to July 31, 1998

Sponsor Mackenzie Financial Corporation
150 Bloor Street West, Suite M111
Toronto, Ontario, M5S 3B5

Phone 1-800-387-0614

Sales Fee Load **RRSP Eligibility** Yes

Category Canadian Equity/Value

Portfolio Manager/Years
Jerry Javasky—Mackenzie Financial/6

Minimum Initial Investment
RRSP $500 **Non-RRSP** $500

Extended Asset Mix

Cdn Equity	U.S. Equity	Europe	Japan	Far East	Latin America	Special Equity	Dividend	Domestic Bond	Global Bond	Money Market
◆										

Objectives

Short Term	Mid Term	Long Term	Currency Effect	Sector Specific	Small Cap	Mid Cap	Large Cap
						◆	◆

Investment Styles

Top Down	Bottom Up	Value	Sector Rotation	Momentum	Indexation
	◆	◆			

Quantitative		Asset Breakout		Sector Breakout (Equity)
MER	2.38%	Cash	33.9%	Overweighted
Tax Efficiency	97.23%	Cdn Bonds		1 Oil & Gas
Std Deviation	2.11%	Foreign Bonds		2 Utilities
Beta	0.53	Cdn Equity	54.4%	Underweighted
Alpha	0.61	Foreign Equity	10.8%	1 Merchandising
R Squared	0.85	Warrants		2 Pipelines

TRAILING 24-MONTH ANNUALIZED RETURNS FOR IVY CANADIAN FUND

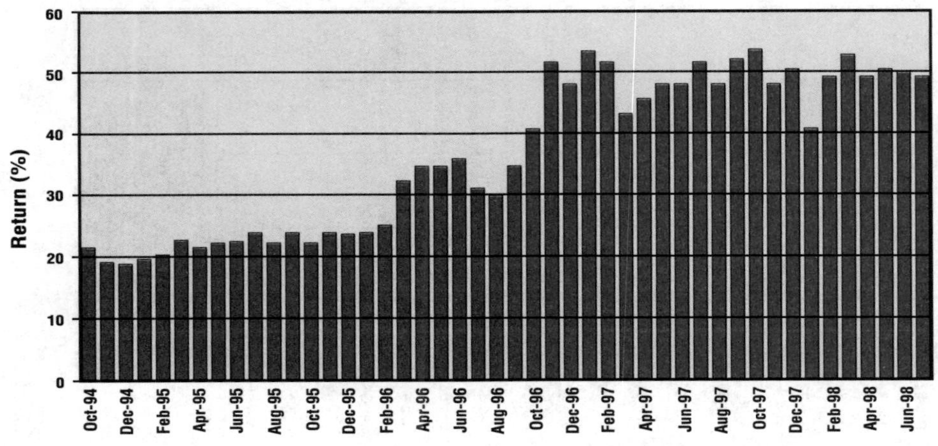

	Total Change	Annual Cmpd Rate	$10,000 Invested	24 Months Ending
Best	49.49%	22.27%	$14,949.49	October 1997
Worst	16.32%	7.85%	$11,632.38	December 1994
Average	33.73%	15.64%	$13,373.40	n/a

Colonia Life Special Growth Fund

MVA	3 Months*	1 Year*	3 Years*	5 Years*	1997	1996	1995
115.4	-10.5%	-6.1%	22.8%	19.4%	23.9%	69.8%	23.7%

* Returns to July 31, 1998

Sponsor Colonia Life Insurance Co
2 St. Clair Ave. East
Toronto, Ontario, M4T 2V6

Phone 1-800-461-1086

Sales Fee Load **RRSP Eligibility** Yes

Category Canadian Equity/Growth

Portfolio Manager/Years
Chuck Roth—Ultravest Inv. Counsellors/4

Minimum Initial Investment
RRSP $500 **Non-RRSP** $500

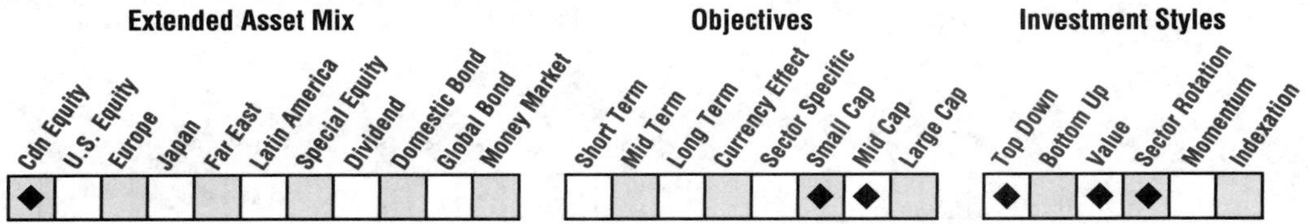

Quantitative		Asset Breakout		Sector Breakout (Equity)
MER	2.27%	Cash	3.3%	Overweighted
Tax Efficiency	N/A	Cdn Bonds		1 Industrial
Std Deviation	5.89%	Foreign Bonds		2 Utilities
Beta	1.03	Cdn Equity	89.2%	Underweighted
Alpha	1.06	Foreign Equity	7.5%	1 Oil & Gas
R Squared	0.65	Warrants		2 Financial

TRAILING 24-MONTH ANNUALIZED RETURNS FOR COLONIA LIFE SPECIAL GROWTH FUND

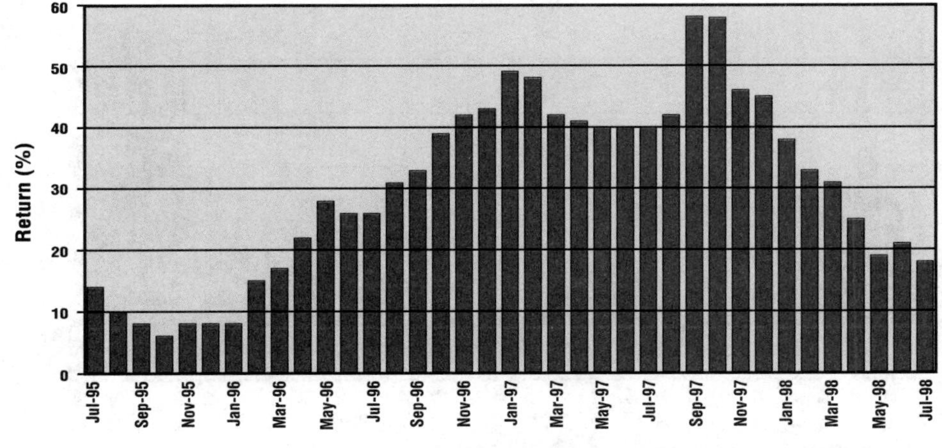

	Total Change	Annual Cmpd Rate	$10,000 Invested	24 Months Ending
Best	151.43%	58.57%	$25,143.48	September 1997
Worst	12.50%	6.07%	$11,250.36	October 1995
Average	73.15%	31.59%	$17,314.97	n/a

Spectrum United Canadian Investment Fund

MVA	3 Months*	1 Year*	3 Years*	5 Years*	1997	1996	1995
115.0	-5.3%	7.8%	20.0%	15.0%	24.0%	27.3%	15.7%

* Returns to July 31, 1998

Sponsor Spectrum United Mutual Funds
145 King St. West, Suite 300
Toronto, Ontario, M5H 1J8

Phone 1-800-404-2227

Sales Fee Load **RRSP Eligibility** Yes

Category Canadian Equity/Value

Portfolio Manager/Years
Kim Shannon—AIM Partners Inc./2

Minimum Initial Investment
RRSP $500 **Non-RRSP** $500

Extended Asset Mix

Cdn Equity	U.S. Equity	Europe	Japan	Far East	Latin America	Special Equity	Dividend	Domestic Bond	Global Bond	Money Market
◆										

Objectives

Short Term	Mid Term	Long Term	Currency Effect	Sector Specific	Small Cap	Mid Cap	Large Cap
							◆

Investment Styles

Top Down	Bottom Up	Value	Sector Rotation	Momentum	Indexation
	◆	◆			

Quantitative		Asset Breakout		Sector Breakout (Equity)
MER	2.33%	Cash	10.4%	Overweighted
Tax Efficiency	93.77%	Cdn Bonds	2.0%	1 Industrial
Std Deviation	2.80%	Foreign Bonds		2 Utilities
Beta	0.71	Cdn Equity	69.5%	Underweighted
Alpha	0.36	Foreign Equity	14.5%	1 Oil & Gas
R Squared	0.91	Warrants		2 Pipelines

TRAILING 24-MONTH ANNUALIZED RETURNS FOR SPECTRUM UNITED CDN INVESTMENT FUND

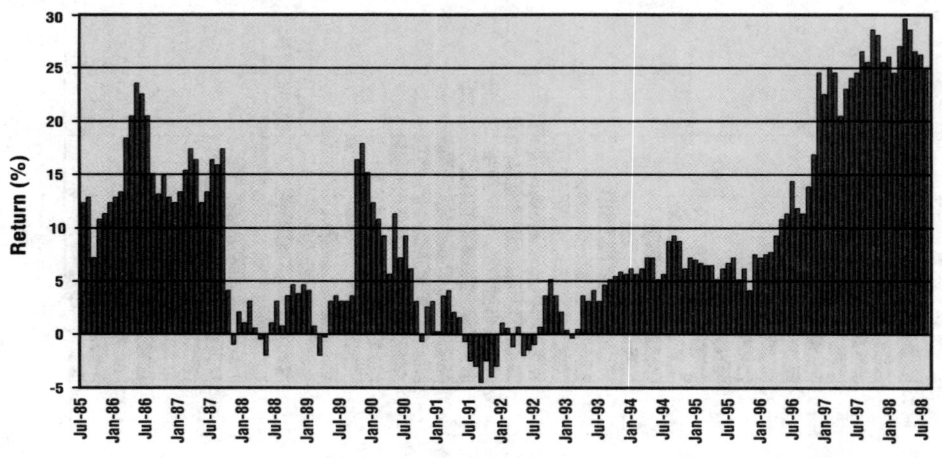

	Total Change	Annual Cmpd Rate	$10,000 Invested	24 Months Ending
Best	67.59%	29.46%	$16,758.73	March 1998
Worst	-8.32%	-4.25%	$9,168.05	September 1991
Average	19.58%	9.35%	$11,958.07	n/a

First Canadian Special Growth Fund

MVA	3 Months*	1 Year*	3 Years*	5 Years*	1997	1996	1995
114.1	-14.0%	-6.7%	15.3%	N/A	23.0%	30.0%	18.4%

* Returns to July 31, 1998

Sponsor First Canadian Funds
302 Bay Street
Toronto, Ontario, M5X 1A1

Phone 1-800-665-7700

Sales Fee No-Load **RRSP Eligibility** Yes

Category Canadian Equity/Growth

Portfolio Manager/Years
James Lawson—Jones Heward/4

Minimum Initial Investment
RRSP $500 **Non-RRSP** $500

Extended Asset Mix

Cdn Equity	U.S. Equity	Europe	Japan	Far East	Latin America	Special Equity	Dividend	Domestic Bond	Global Bond	Money Market
◆										

Objectives

Short Term	Mid Term	Long Term	Currency Effect	Sector Specific	Small Cap	Mid Cap	Large Cap
					◆	◆	

Investment Styles

Top Down	Bottom Up	Value	Sector Rotation	Momentum	Indexation
	◆			◆	

Quantitative		Asset Breakout		Sector Breakout (Equity)
MER	2.23%	Cash	16.8%	Overweighted
Tax Efficiency	99.92%	Cdn Bonds		1 Industrial
Std Deviation	4.24%	Foreign Bonds		2 Utilities
Beta	0.86	Cdn Equity	79.4%	Underweighted
Alpha	0.26	Foreign Equity	0.7%	1 Consumer
R Squared	0.80	Warrants	3.0%	2 Financial

TRAILING 24-MONTH ANNUALIZED RETURNS FOR FIRST CANADIAN SPECIAL GROWTH FUND

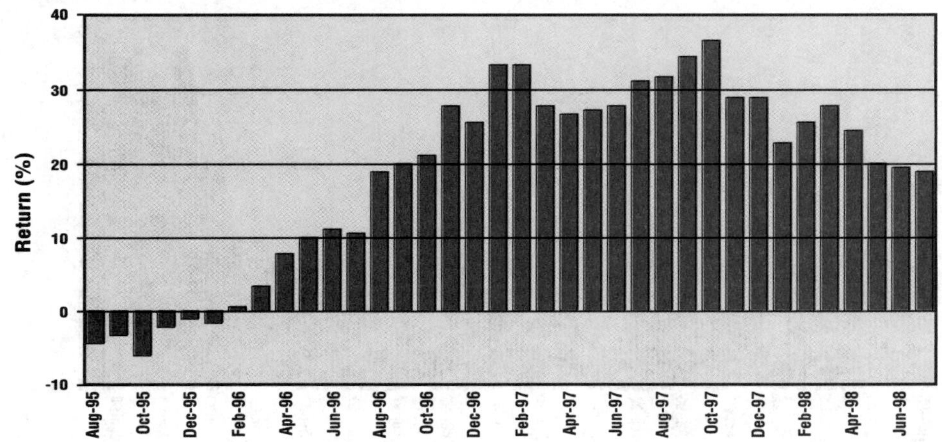

	Total Change	Annual Cmpd Rate	$10,000 Invested	24 Months Ending
Best	82.11%	34.95%	$18,210.83	October 1997
Worst	-10.99%	-5.65%	$8,901.37	October 1995
Average	38.13%	17.53%	$13,813.01	n/a

BPI Dividend Income Fund

MVA	3 Months*	1 Year*	3 Years*	5 Years*	1997	1996	1995
144.1	-0.4%	13.5%	18.5%	14.3%	19.5%	23.3%	19.4%

* Returns to July 31, 1998

Sponsor BPI Mutual Funds
161 Bay Street, Suite 3900
Toronto, Ontario, M5J 2S1

Phone 1-800-263-2427

Sales Fee Load **RRSP Eligibility** Yes

Category Canadian Equity/Dividend

Portfolio Manager/Years
Eric B. Bushell—BPI Investment Mngt./4

Minimum Initial Investment
RRSP $500 **Non-RRSP** $500

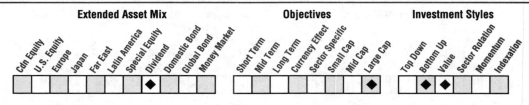

Extended Asset Mix

Cdn Equity	U.S. Equity	Europe	Japan	Far East	Latin America	Special Equity	Dividend	Domestic Bond	Global Bond	Money Market
							◆			

Objectives

Short Term	Mid Term	Long Term	Currency Effect	Sector Specific	Small Cap	Mid Cap	Large Cap
							◆

Investment Styles

Top Down	Bottom Up	Value	Sector Rotation	Momentum	Indexation
	◆	◆			

Quantitative		Asset Breakout		Sector Breakout (Equity)
MER	1.21%	Cash	1.0%	Overweighted
Tax Efficiency	82.54%	Cdn Bonds	0.4%	1 Real Estate
Std Deviation	1.30%	Foreign Bonds		2 Consumer
Beta	0.26	Cdn Equity	69.4%	Underweighted
Alpha	0.72	Foreign Equity	0.5%	1 Communications
R Squared	0.51	Warrants	0.1%	2 Financial

TRAILING 24-MONTH ANNUALIZED RETURNS FOR BPI DIVIDEND INCOME FUND

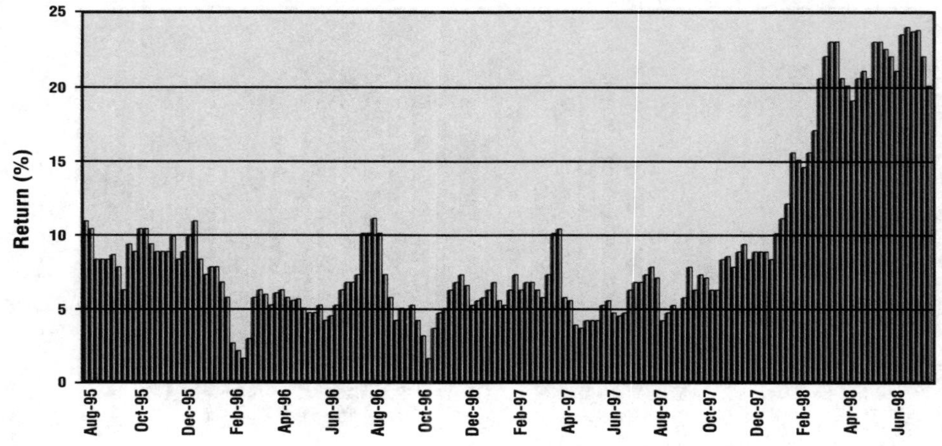

	Total Change	Annual Cmpd Rate	$10,000 Invested	24 Months Ending
Best	52.57%	23.52%	$15,256.69	March 1998
Worst	3.03%	1.50%	$10,302.51	October 1990
Average	19.30%	9.23%	$11,930.49	n/a

NN Dividend Fund

MVA	3 Months*	1 Year*	3 Years*	5 Years*	1997	1996	1995
126.8	-3.7%	3.6%	13.8%	N/A	13.8%	19.2%	17.8%

* Returns to July 31, 1998

Sponsor NN Life Insurance Co. of Canada
1 Concorde Gate
Toronto, Ontario, M3C 3N6
Phone (416) 391-2200
Sales Fee Load **RRSP Eligibility** Yes

Category Canadian Equity/Dividend
Portfolio Manager/Years
Michel Tremblay—Ing Investment Mngt./5
Minimum Initial Investment
RRSP $1,000 **Non-RRSP** $1,000

Extended Asset Mix

Cdn Equity	U.S. Equity	Europe	Japan	Far East	Latin America	Special Equity	Dividend	Domestic Bond	Global Bond	Money Market
							◆			

Objectives

Short Term	Mid Term	Long Term	Currency Effect	Sector Specific	Small Cap	Mid Cap	Large Cap
							◆

Investment Styles

Top Down	Bottom Up	Value	Sector Rotation	Momentum	Indexation
	◆	◆			

Quantitative		Asset Breakout		Sector Breakout (Equity)
MER	2.38%	Cash	4.3%	Overweighted
Tax Efficiency	N/A	Cdn Bonds	9.7%	1 Paper-Forest
Std Deviation	1.53%	Foreign Bonds		2 Utilities
Beta	0.31	Cdn Equity	95.5%	Underweighted
Alpha	0.63	Foreign Equity		1 Industrial
R Squared	0.64	Warrants	0.2%	2 Pipelines

TRAILING 24-MONTH ANNUALIZED RETURNS FOR NN DIVIDEND FUND

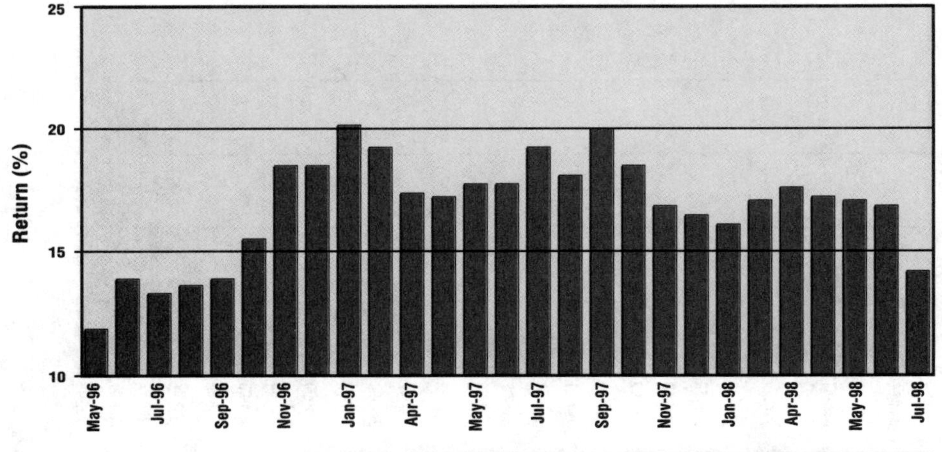

	Total Change	Annual Cmpd Rate	$10,000 Invested	24 Months Ending
Best	44.28%	20.12%	$14,428.04	January 1997
Worst	25.33%	11.95%	$12,532.96	May 1996
Average	36.57%	16.86%	$13,657.20	n/a

PH&N Dividend Income Fund

MVA	3 Months*	1 Year*	3 Years*	5 Years*	1997	1996	1995
126.7	-3.4%	19.7%	29.3%	21.3%	44.5%	33.3%	13.9%

* Returns to July 31, 1998

Sponsor Phillips Hager & North
200 Burrard Street, 21st Floor
Vancouver, British Columbia, V6C 3N5
Phone 1-800-661-6141
Sales Fee No-Load **RRSP Eligibility** Yes

Category Canadian Equity/Dividend
Portfolio Manager/Years
Bill Slatter—PH&N Investment Mngt./21
Minimum Initial Investment
RRSP $25,000 **Non-RRSP** $25,000

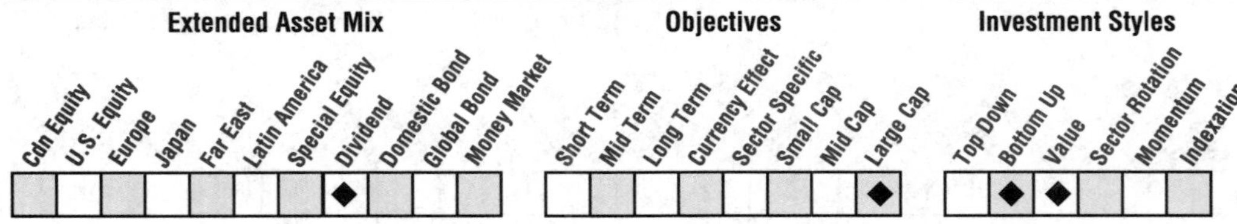

Quantitative		Asset Breakout		Sector Breakout (Equity)
MER	1.21%	Cash	8.4%	Overweighted
Tax Efficiency	95.95%	Cdn Bonds	0.5%	1 Conglomerates
Std Deviation	3.06%	Foreign Bonds		2 Utilities
Beta	0.67	Cdn Equity	90.6%	Underweighted
Alpha	0.75	Foreign Equity		1 Financial
R Squared	0.76	Warrants		2 Consumer

TRAILING 24-MONTH ANNUALIZED RETURNS FOR PH&N DIVIDEND INCOME FUND

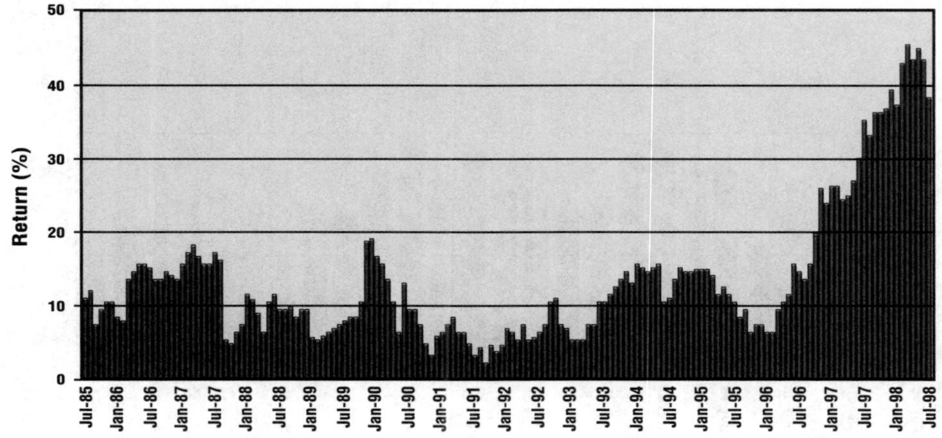

	Total Change	Annual Cmpd Rate	$10,000 Invested	24 Months Ending
Best	107.75%	44.14%	$20,775.24	March 1998
Worst	3.46%	1.72%	$10,346.08	September 1991
Average	29.01%	13.58%	$12,901.07	n/a

Dynamic Dividend Fund

MVA	3 Months*	1 Year*	3 Years*	5 Years*	1997	1996	1995
126.7	-1.2%	5.5%	13.3%	10.4%	13.6%	18.3%	14.6%

* Returns to July 31, 1998

Sponsor Dynamic Mutual Funds
40 King St. West, 55th Floor
Toronto, Ontario, M5H 4A9

Phone 1-800-268-8186

Sales Fee Load **RRSP Eligibility** Yes

Category Canadian Equity/Dividend

Portfolio Manager/Years
Todd Beallor—Dundee Mutual Funds/1

Minimum Initial Investment
RRSP $1,000 **Non-RRSP** $1,000

Extended Asset Mix

Cdn Equity	U.S. Equity	Europe	Japan	Far East	Latin America	Special Equity	Dividend	Domestic Bond	Global Bond	Money Market
							◆			

Objectives

Short Term	Mid Term	Long Term	Currency Effect	Sector Specific	Small Cap	Mid Cap	Large Cap
							◆

Investment Styles

Top Down	Bottom Up	Value	Sector Rotation	Momentum	Indexation
	◆	◆			

Quantitative		Asset Breakout		Sector Breakout (Equity)
MER	1.51%	Cash	9.3%	Overweighted
Tax Efficiency	78.35%	Cdn Bonds	2.9%	1 Paper-Forest
Std Deviation	1.36%	Foreign Bonds		2 Financial
Beta	0.27	Cdn Equity	80.7%	Underweighted
Alpha	0.45	Foreign Equity	7.1%	1 Real Estate
R Squared	0.61	Warrants		2 Utilities

TRAILING 24-MONTH ANNUALIZED RETURNS FOR DYNAMIC DIVIDEND FUND

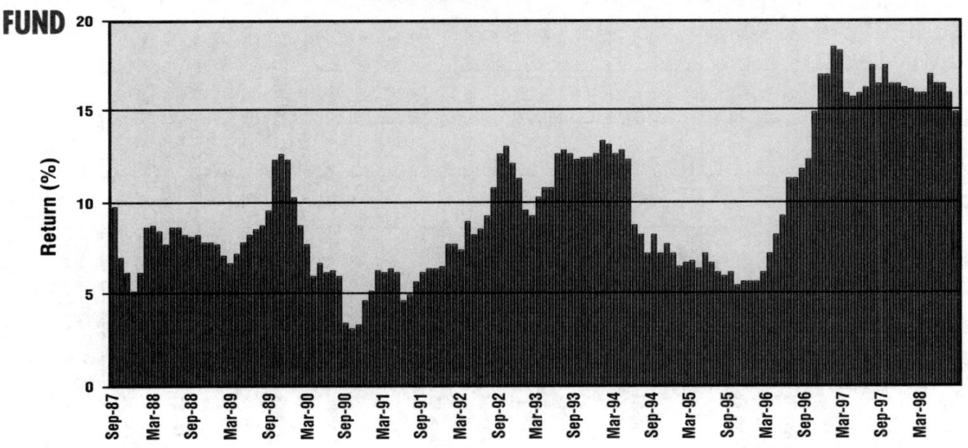

	Total Change	Annual Cmpd Rate	$10,000 Invested	24 Months Ending
Best	39.75%	18.21%	$13,974.68	January 1997
Worst	6.42%	3.16%	$10,641.91	October 1990
Average	20.10%	9.59%	$12,009.78	n/a

Bissett Dividend Income Fund

MVA	3 Months*	1 Year*	3 Years*	5 Years*	1997	1996	1995
125.8	-3.3%	9.2%	21.6%	16.8%	22.5%	28.5%	22.9%

* Returns to July 31, 1998

Sponsor Bissett & Associates Inv. Mngt.
500 Fourth Street S.W., Suite 1120
Calgary, Alberta,T2P 2V6

Phone 1-800-267-3862

Sales Fee No-Load **RRSP Eligibility** Yes

Category Canadian Equity/Dividend

Portfolio Manager/Years
Fred Pynn—Bissett & Associates/7

Minimum Initial Investment
RRSP $10,000 **Non-RRSP** $10,000

Extended Asset Mix

Cdn Equity	U.S. Equity	Europe	Japan	Far East	Latin America	Special Equity	Dividend	Domestic Bond	Global Bond	Money Market
							◆			

Objectives

Short Term	Mid Term	Long Term	Currency Effect	Sector Specific	Small Cap	Mid Cap	Large Cap
							◆

Investment Styles

Top Down	Bottom Up	Value	Sector Rotation	Momentum	Indexation
	◆	◆			

Quantitative		Asset Breakout		Sector Breakout (Equity)
MER	1.50%	Cash	1.1%	Overweighted
Tax Efficiency	90.20%	Cdn Bonds	10.1%	1 Industrial
Std Deviation	2.28%	Foreign Bonds		2 Utilities
Beta	0.54	Cdn Equity	75.4%	Underweighted
Alpha	0.61	Foreign Equity	11.5%	1 Paper-Forest
R Squared	0.81	Warrants	1.9%	2 Consumer

TRAILING 24-MONTH ANNUALIZED RETURNS FOR BISSETT DIVIDEND INCOME FUND

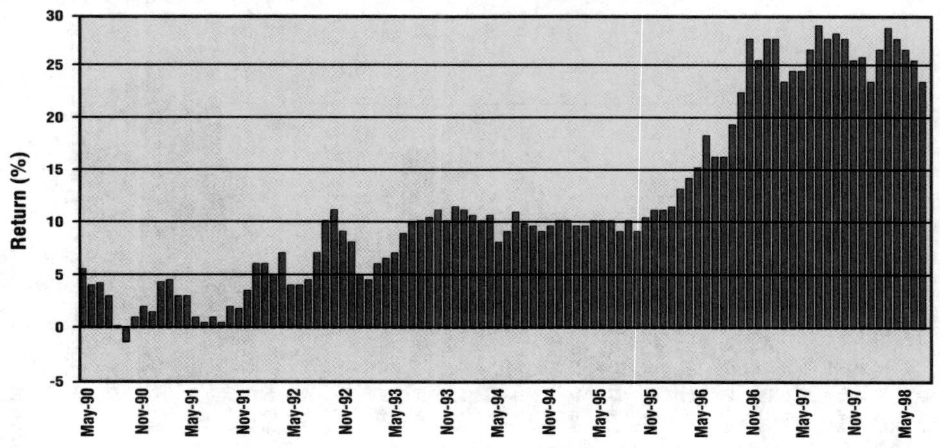

	Total Change	Annual Cmpd Rate	$10,000 Invested	24 Months Ending
Best	64.43%	28.23%	$16,442.71	July 1997
Worst	-2.66%	-1.34%	$9,734.26	October 1990
Average	25.77%	12.15%	$12,577.00	n/a

Pret et Revenu Dividend Fonds

MVA	3 Months*	1 Year*	3 Years*	5 Years*	1997	1996	1995
124.9	-7.6%	1.6%	21.3%	N/A	21.0%	36.2%	17.0%

* Returns to July 31, 1998

Sponsor TPR Investment Management
850 Place du Ville
Quebec City, Quebec, G1R 3P6

Phone 1-800-667-7643

Sales Fee No-Load **RRSP Eligibility** Yes

Category Canadian Equity/Dividend

Portfolio Manager/Years
Ubald Cloutier—TPR Investment Mngt./3

Minimum Initial Investment
RRSP $500 **Non-RRSP** $500

Extended Asset Mix

Cdn Equity	U.S. Equity	Europe	Japan	Far East	Latin America	Special Equity	Dividend	Domestic Bond	Global Bond	Money Market
							◆			

Objectives

Short Term	Mid Term	Long Term	Currency Effect	Sector Specific	Small Cap	Mid Cap	Large Cap
							◆

Investment Styles

Top Down	Bottom Up	Value	Sector Rotation	Momentum	Indexation
	◆	◆			

Quantitative		Asset Breakout		Sector Breakout (Equity)
MER	1.67%	Cash	12.7%	Overweighted
Tax Efficiency	85.56%	Cdn Bonds	12.9%	1 Oil & Gas
Std Deviation	2.63%	Foreign Bonds	0.4%	2 Utilities
Beta	0.51	Cdn Equity	63.9%	Underweighted
Alpha	0.78	Foreign Equity	4.7%	1 Financial
R Squared	0.59	Warrants		2 Consumer

TRAILING 24-MONTH ANNUALIZED RETURNS FOR PRET ET REVENU DIVIDEND FONDS

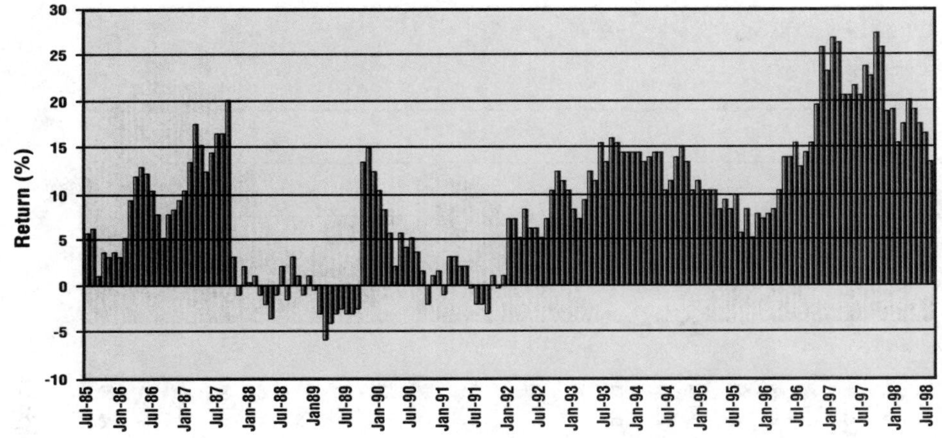

	Total Change	Annual Cmpd Rate	$10,000 Invested	24 Months Ending
Best	59.85%	26.43%	$15,984.52	September 1997
Worst	-11.16%	-5.74%	$8,884.39	March 1989
Average	19.03%	9.10%	$11,903.44	n/a

Dynamic Dividend Growth Fund

MVA	3 Months*	1 Year*	3 Years*	5 Years*	1997	1996	1995
124.1	-3.9%	-0.6%	15.4%	13.0%	15.6%	28.8%	15.2%

* Returns to July 31, 1998

Sponsor Dynamic Mutual Funds
40 King St. West, 55th Floor
Toronto, Ontario, M5H 4A9
Phone 1-800-268-8186
Sales Fee Load **RRSP Eligibility** Yes

Category Canadian Equity/Dividend
Portfolio Manager/Years
Todd Beallor—Dundee Mutual Funds/1
Minimum Initial Investment
RRSP $1,000 **Non-RRSP** $1,000

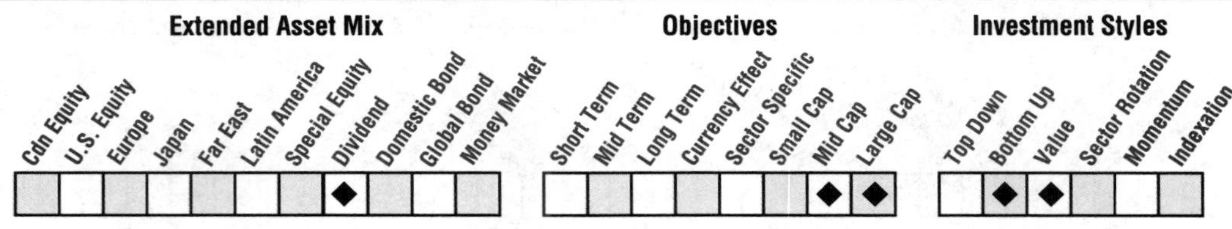

Quantitative		Asset Breakout		Sector Breakout (Equity)
MER	1.57%	Cash	21.5%	Overweighted
Tax Efficiency	87.35%	Cdn Bonds	2.7%	1 Oil & Gas
Std Deviation	1.93%	Foreign Bonds		2 Utilities
Beta	0.39	Cdn Equity	63.1%	Underweighted
Alpha	0.45	Foreign Equity	12.6%	1 Industrial
R Squared	0.69	Warrants	0.1%	2 Financial

TRAILING 24-MONTH ANNUALIZED RETURNS FOR DYNAMIC DIVIDEND GROWTH FUND

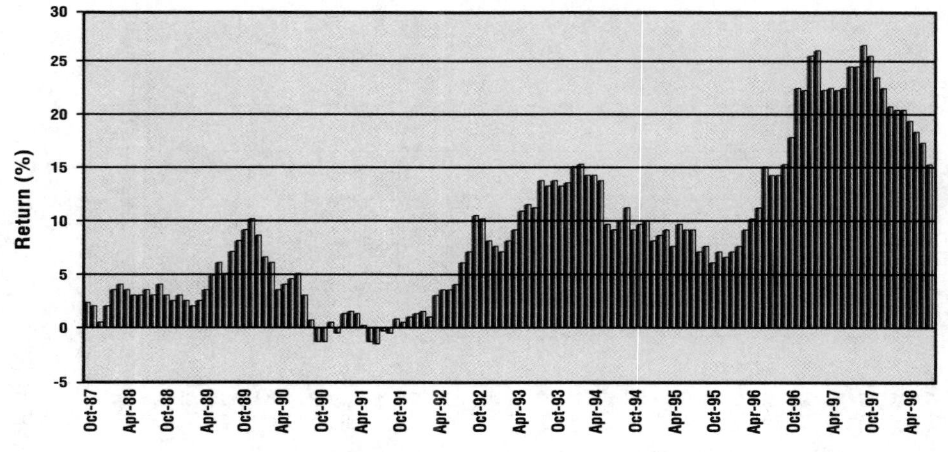

	Total Change	Annual Cmpd Rate	$10,000 Invested	24 Months Ending
Best	58.78%	26.01%	$15,878.44	September 1997
Worst	-2.89%	-1.46%	$9,710.83	July 1991
Average	19.29%	9.22%	$11,929.03	n/a

Standard Life Canadian Dividend Fund

MVA	3 Months*	1 Year*	3 Years*	5 Years*	1997	1996	1995
122.0	-5.9%	21.0%	29.9%	N/A	40.8%	36.3%	14.7%

* Returns to July 31, 1998

Sponsor Standard Life Mutual Funds Ltd.
1245 Sherbrooke St. West
Montreal, Quebec, Canada, H3G 1G3
Phone 1-800-665-6237
Sales Fee Load **RRSP Eligibility** Yes

Category Canadian Equity/Dividend
Portfolio Manager
Peter Hill—Standard Life
Minimum Initial Investment
RRSP $1,000 **Non-RRSP** $1,000

Extended Asset Mix

Cdn Equity	U.S. Equity	Europe	Japan	Far East	Latin America	Special Equity	Dividend	Domestic Bond	Global Bond	Money Market
								◆		

Objectives

Short Term	Mid Term	Long Term	Currency Effect	Sector Specific	Small Cap	Mid Cap	Large Cap
							◆

Investment Styles

Top Down	Bottom Up	Value	Sector Rotation	Momentum	Indexation
	◆	◆			

Quantitative		Asset Breakout		Sector Breakout (Equity)
MER	1.50%	Cash	8.8%	Overweighted
Tax Efficiency	95.93%	Cdn Bonds		1 Financial
Std Deviation	3.44%	Foreign Bonds		2 Utilities
Beta	0.74	Cdn Equity	91.4%	Underweighted
Alpha	0.94	Foreign Equity		1 Merchandising
R Squared	0.74	Warrants		2 Pipelines

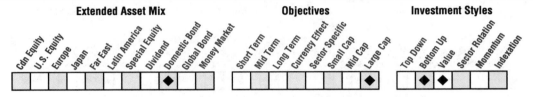

TRAILING 24-MONTH ANNUALIZED RETURNS FOR STANDARD LIFE CANADIAN DIVIDEND FUND

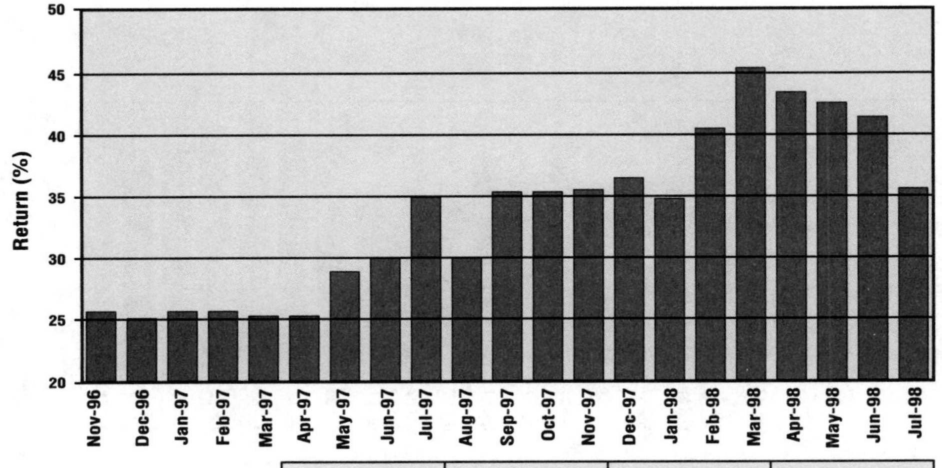

	Total Change	Annual Cmpd Rate	$10,000 Invested	24 Months Ending
Best	111.20%	45.33%	$21,120.40	March 1998
Worst	56.30%	25.02%	$15,629.60	December 1996
Average	79.82%	34.10%	$17,981.59	n/a

CT Dividend Income Fund

MVA	3 Months*	1 Year*	3 Years*	5 Years*	1997	1996	1995
121.4	-4.6%	7.3%	18.0%	N/A	17.2%	26.6%	15.9%

* Returns to July 31, 1998

Sponsor CT Investment Mngt. Group Inc.
110 Yonge Street, 7th Floor
Toronto, Ontario, M5C 1T4

Phone 1-800-668-8888

Sales Fee No-Load **RRSP Eligibility** Yes

Category Canadian Equity/Dividend

Portfolio Manager
Karen Coll—CT Investment Management

Minimum Initial Investment
RRSP $500 **Non-RRSP** $500

Extended Asset Mix

Cdn Equity	U.S. Equity	Europe	Japan	Far East	Latin America	Special Equity	Dividend	Domestic Bond	Global Bond	Money Market
							◆			

Objectives

Short Term	Mid Term	Long Term	Currency Effect	Sector Specific	Small Cap	Mid Cap	Large Cap
							◆

Investment Styles

Top Down	Bottom Up	Value	Sector Rotation	Momentum	Indexation
	◆	◆			

Quantitative		Asset Breakout		Sector Breakout (Equity)
MER	1.85%	Cash	7.6%	Overweighted
Tax Efficiency	93.24%	Cdn Bonds	15.0%	1 Oil & Gas
Std Deviation	2.22%	Foreign Bonds		2 Utilities
Beta	0.52	Cdn Equity	77.4%	Underweighted
Alpha	0.6	Foreign Equity		1 Merchandising
R Squared	0.90	Warrants		2 Consumer

TRAILING 24-MONTH ANNUALIZED RETURNS FOR CT DIVIDEND INCOME FUND

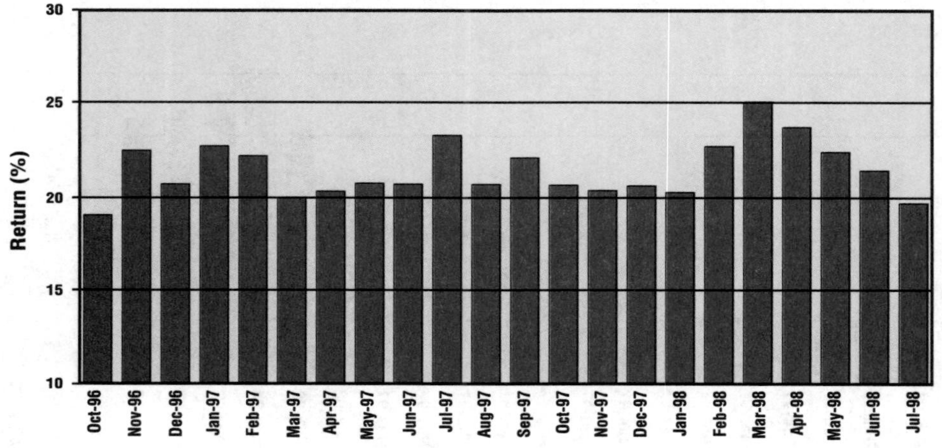

	Total Change	Annual Cmpd Rate	$10,000 Invested	24 Months Ending
Best	56.43%	25.07%	$15,642.78	March 1998
Worst	41.13%	18.80%	$14,112.82	October 1996
Average	48.99%	22.06%	$14,899.18	n/a

Northwest Dividend Fund

MVA	3 Months*	1 Year*	3 Years*	5 Years*	1997	1996	1995
121.1	-6.2%	2.5%	21.2%	N/A	21.0%	36.9%	16.1%

* Returns to July 31, 1998

Sponsor Northwest Mutual Funds Inc.
129 Yorkville Avenue, 3rd Floor
Toronto, Ontario, M5R 1C4

Phone 1-888-809-3333

Sales Fee Load **RRSP Eligibility** Yes

Category Canadian Equity/Dividend

Portfolio Manager/Years
Ubald Cloutier—TPR Investment Mngt./4

Minimum Initial Investment
RRSP $500 **Non-RRSP** $500

Extended Asset Mix

Cdn Equity	U.S. Equity	Europe	Japan	Far East	Latin America	Special Equity	Dividend	Domestic Bond	Global Bond	Money Market
							◆			

Objectives

Short Term	Mid Term	Long Term	Currency Effect	Sector Specific	Small Cap	Mid Cap	Large Cap
							◆

Investment Styles

Top Down	Bottom Up	Value	Sector Rotation	Momentum	Indexation
	◆	◆			

Quantitative		Asset Breakout		Sector Breakout (Equity)
MER	1.75%	Cash	2.1%	Overweighted
Tax Efficiency	82.90%	Cdn Bonds	19.9%	1 Financial
Std Deviation	2.66%	Foreign Bonds	0.8%	2 Utilities
Beta	0.55	Cdn Equity	64.8%	Underweighted
Alpha	0.73	Foreign Equity	2.9%	1 Oil & Gas
R Squared	0.64	Warrants		2 Pipelines

TRAILING 24-MONTH ANNUALIZED RETURNS FOR NORTHWEST DIVIDEND FUND

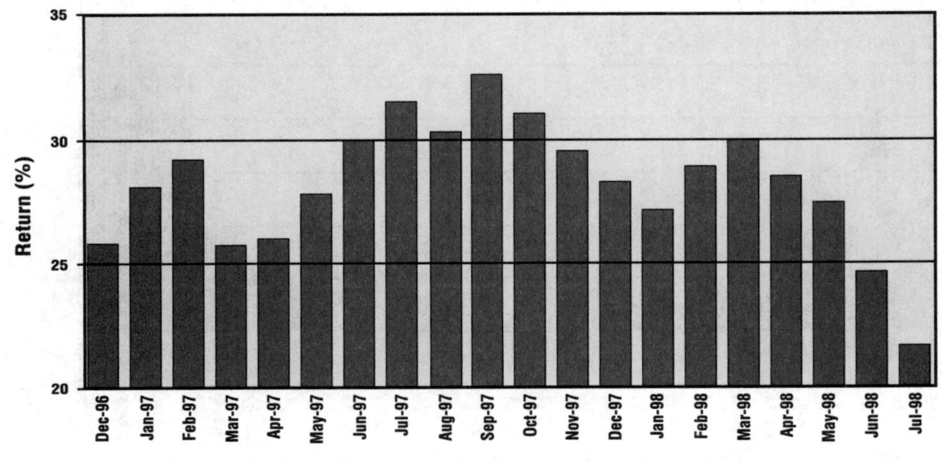

	Total Change	Annual Cmpd Rate	$10,000 Invested	24 Months Ending
Best	76.09%	32.70%	$17,608.56	September 1997
Worst	49.13%	22.12%	$14,913.29	July 1998
Average	65.10%	28.49%	$16,510.47	n/a

Spectrum United Dividend Fund

MVA	3 Months*	1 Year*	3 Years*	5 Years*	1997	1996	1995
121.0	0.3%	10.6%	15.2%	11.4%	18.6%	17.2%	12.2%

* Returns to July 31, 1998

Sponsor Spectrum United Mutual Funds
145 King St. West, Suite 300
Toronto, Ontario, M5H 1J8

Phone 1-800-404-2227

Sales Fee Load **RRSP Eligibility** Yes

Category Canadian Equity/Dividend

Portfolio Manager/Years
Stuart Pomphrey—McLean Budden Ltd./1

Minimum Initial Investment
RRSP $500 **Non-RRSP** $500

Extended Asset Mix

Cdn Equity	U.S. Equity	Europe	Japan	Far East	Latin America	Special Equity	Dividend	Domestic Bond	Global Bond	Money Market
◆										

Objectives

Short Term	Mid Term	Long Term	Currency Effect	Sector Specific	Small Cap	Mid Cap	Large Cap
							◆

Investment Styles

Top Down	Bottom Up	Value	Sector Rotation	Momentum	Indexation
	◆	◆			

Quantitative		Asset Breakout		Sector Breakout (Equity)
MER	1.61%	Cash	2.2%	Overweighted
Tax Efficiency	83.19%	Cdn Bonds	19.1%	1 Utilities
Std Deviation	1.53%	Foreign Bonds		2 Financial
Beta	0.27	Cdn Equity	78.7%	Underweighted
Alpha	0.41	Foreign Equity		1 Pipelines
R Squared	0.58	Warrants		2 Consumer

TRAILING 24-MONTH ANNUALIZED RETURNS FOR SPECTRUM UNITED DIVIDEND FUND

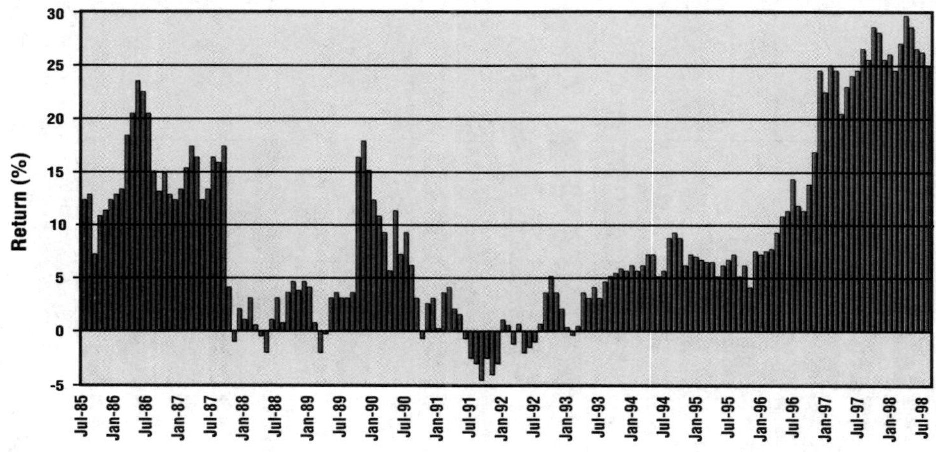

	Total Change	Annual Cmpd Rate	$10,000 Invested	24 Months Ending
Best	67.59%	29.46%	$16,758.73	March 1998
Worst	-8.32%	-4.25%	$9,168.05	September 1991
Average	19.58%	9.35%	$11,958.07	n/a

First Canadian Dividend Income Fund

MVA	3 Months*	1 Year*	3 Years*	5 Years*	1997	1996	1995
121.0	-5.9%	17.1%	25.6%	N/A	35.2%	32.3%	13.2%

* Returns to July 31, 1998

Sponsor First Canadian Funds
302 Bay Street,
Toronto, Ontario, M5X 1A1

Phone 1-800-665-7700

Sales Fee No-Load **RRSP Eligibility** Yes

Category Canadian Equity/Dividend

Portfolio Manager/Years
Michael Stanley—Jones Heward/5

Minimum Initial Investment
RRSP $500 **Non-RRSP** $500

Extended Asset Mix

Cdn Equity	U.S. Equity	Europe	Japan	Far East	Latin America	Special Equity	Dividend	Domestic Bond	Global Bond	Money Market
							◆			

Objectives

Short Term	Mid Term	Long Term	Currency Effect	Sector Specific	Small Cap	Mid Cap	Large Cap
							◆

Investment Styles

Top Down	Bottom Up	Value	Sector Rotation	Momentum	Indexation
	◆	◆			

Quantitative		Asset Breakout		Sector Breakout (Equity)
MER	1.66%	Cash	8.5%	Overweighted
Tax Efficiency	95.83%	Cdn Bonds	1.8%	N/A
Std Deviation	3.06%	Foreign Bonds		
Beta	0.67	Cdn Equity	88.3%	Underweighted
Alpha	0.76	Foreign Equity		N/A
R Squared	0.75	Warrants		

TRAILING 24-MONTH ANNUALIZED RETURNS FOR FIRST CANADIAN DIVIDEND INCOME FUND

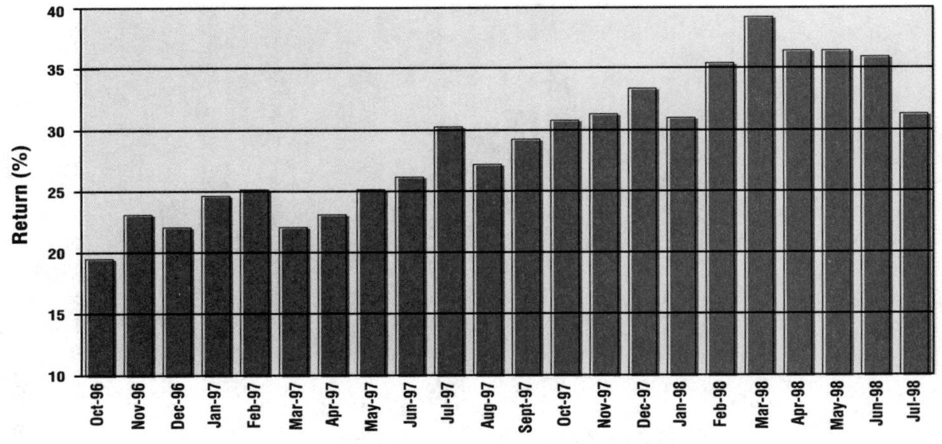

	Total Change	Annual Cmpd Rate	$10,000 Invested	24 Months Ending
Best	93.40%	39.07%	$19,339.51	March 1998
Worst	42.64%	19.43%	$14,263.80	October 1996
Average	67.34%	29.36%	$16,733.78	n/a

Atlas Canadian High-Yield Bond Fund

MVA	3 Months*	1 Year*	3 Years*	5 Years*	1997	1996	1995
111.0	-3.1%	5.0%	11.7%	N/A	10.5%	13.9%	15.1%

* Returns to July 31, 1998

Sponsor Atlas Asset Management
110 Yonge Street, Suite 500
Toronto, Ontario, M5C 1T4

Phone 1-800-463-2857

Sales Fee Load **RRSP Eligibility** Yes

Category Fixed Income/Canadian Bond

Portfolio Manager/Years
Douglas Knight—Deans Knight Capital/4

Minimum Initial Investment
RRSP $500 **Non-RRSP** $500

Extended Asset Mix

Cdn Equity	U.S. Equity	Europe	Japan	Far East	Latin America	Special Equity	Dividend	Domestic Bond	Global Bond	Money Market
								◆		

Objectives

Short Term	Mid Term	Long Term	Currency Effect	Sector Specific	Small Cap	Mid Cap	Large Cap
	◆						

Investment Styles

Top Down	Bottom Up	Value	Sector Rotation	Momentum	Indexation
	◆			◆	

Quantitative		Asset Breakout		Sector Breakout (Equity)
MER	1.87%	Cash	6.9%	Overweighted
Tax Efficiency	74.63%	Cdn Bonds	79.3%	1 Oil & Gas
Std Deviation	1.04%	Foreign Bonds	6.8%	2 Utilities
Beta	0.71	Cdn Equity	3.2%	Underweighted
Alpha	0.25	Foreign Equity		1 Paper–Forest
R Squared	0.74	Warrants		2 Pipelines

TRAILING 24-MONTH ANNUALIZED RETURNS FOR ATLAS CANADIAN HIGH-YIELD BOND FUND

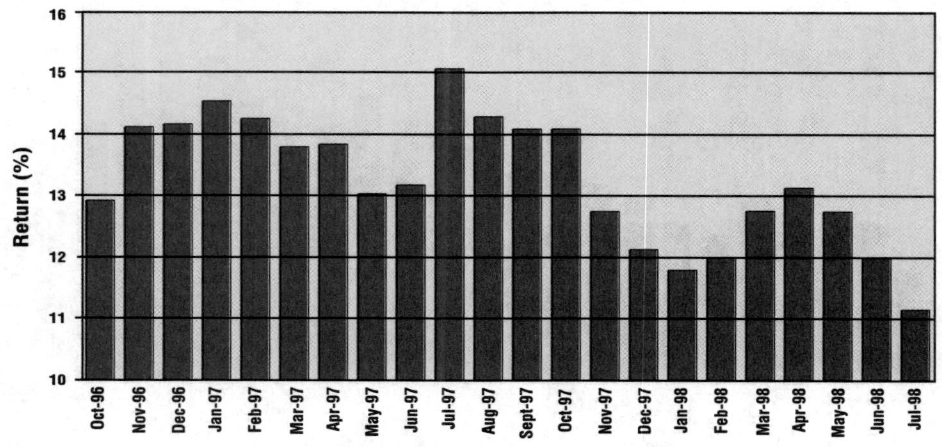

	Total Change	Annual Cmpd Rate	$10,000 Invested	24 Months Ending
Best	32.60%	15.15%	$13,260.23	July 1997
Worst	24.07%	11.39%	$12,406.79	July 1998
Average	28.54%	13.37%	$12,853.81	n/a

Navigator Canadian Income Fund

MVA	3 Months*	1 Year*	3 Years*	5 Years*	1997	1996	1995
110.1	0.6%	5.1%	11.9%	N/A	9.9%	13.3%	15.3%

* Returns to July 31, 1998

Sponsor Navigator Fund Company Ltd.
444 St. Mary Avenue, Suite 1120
Winnipeg, Manitoba, R3C 3T1
Phone 1-800-665-1667
Sales Fee Load **RRSP Eligibility** Yes

Category Fixed Income/Canadian Bond
Portfolio Manager/Years
Wayne Deans—Deans Knight Capital Mngt./4
Minimum Initial Investment
RRSP $1,000 Non-RRSP $1,000

Extended Asset Mix

Cdn Equity	U.S. Equity	Europe	Japan	Far East	Latin America	Special Equity	Dividend	Domestic Bond	Global Bond	Money Market
								◆		

Objectives

Short Term	Mid Term	Long Term	Currency Effect	Sector Specific	Small Cap	Mid Cap	Large Cap
	◆						

Investment Styles

Top Down	Bottom Up	Value	Sector Rotation	Momentum	Indexation
◆				◆	

Quantitative		Asset Breakout		Sector Breakout (Equity)
MER	2.45%	Cash	14.2%	Overweighted
Tax Efficiency	72.61%	Cdn Bonds	76.8%	1 Oil & Gas
Std Deviation	1.07%	Foreign Bonds	4.1%	2 Utilities
Beta	0.68	Cdn Equity	2.6%	Underweighted
Alpha	0.29	Foreign Equity		1 Paper–Forest
R Squared	0.65	Warrants		2 Financial

TRAILING 24-MONTH ANNUALIZED RETURNS FOR NAVIGATOR CANADIAN INCOME FUND

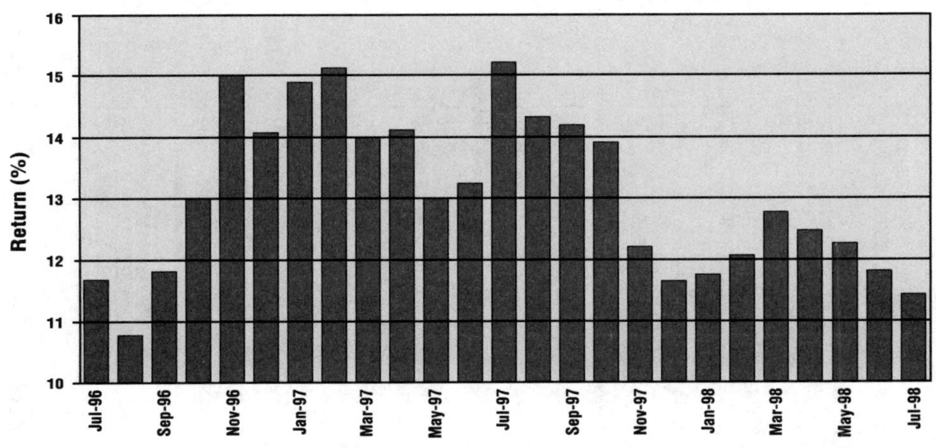

	Total Change	Annual Cmpd Rate	$10,000 Invested	24 Months Ending
Best	33.25%	15.43%	$13,324.57	July 1997
Worst	22.56%	10.71%	$12,256.35	August 1996
Average	27.93%	13.10%	$12,792.59	n/a

C.I. Canadian Bond Fund

MVA	3 Months*	1 Year*	3 Years*	5 Years*	1997	1996	1995
104.6	1.3%	7.1%	12.4%	9.3%	9.5%	14.0%	19.2%

* Returns to July 31, 1998

Sponsor C.I. Mutual Funds Inc.
151 Yonge Street, 8th Floor
Toronto, Ontario, M5C 2W7
Phone 1-800-563-5181
Sales Fee Load **RRSP Eligibility** Yes

Category Fixed Income/Canadian Bond
Portfolio Manager/Years
John Zechner—J. Zechner Associates/6
Minimum Initial Investment
RRSP $500 **Non-RRSP** $500

Extended Asset Mix

Cdn Equity	U.S. Equity	Europe	Japan	Far East	Latin America	Special Equity	Dividend	Domestic Bond	Global Bond	Money Market
								◆		

Objectives

Short Term	Mid Term	Long Term	Currency Effect	Sector Specific	Small Cap	Mid Cap	Large Cap
	◆						

Investment Styles

Top Down	Bottom Up	Value	Sector Rotation	Momentum	Indexation
◆				◆	

Quantitative		Asset Breakout		Sector Breakout (Equity)
MER	1.65%	Cash	18.2%	Overweighted
Tax Efficiency	66.92%	Cdn Bonds	81.8%	N/A
Std Deviation	1.24%	Foreign Bonds		
Beta	0.91	Cdn Equity		Underweighted
Alpha	0.13	Foreign Equity		N/A
R Squared	0.91	Warrants		

TRAILING 24-MONTH ANNUALIZED RETURNS FOR C.I. CANADIAN BOND FUND

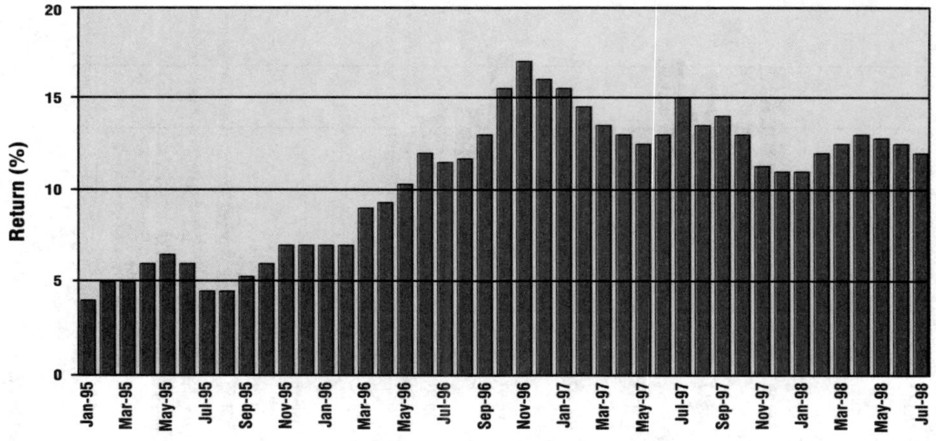

	Total Change	Annual Cmpd Rate	$10,000 Invested	24 Months Ending
Best	38.54%	17.70%	$13,853.87	November 1996
Worst	7.59%	3.73%	$10,758.98	January 1995
Average	22.91%	10.87%	$12,291.22	n/a

Mawer Canadian Income Fund

MVA	3 Months*	1 Year*	3 Years*	5 Years*	1997	1996	1995
104.5	-0.5%	4.4%	11.1%	8.5%	9.6%	13.8%	16.3%

* Returns to July 31, 1998

Sponsor Mawer Investment Management
603-7th Avenue S.W., Suite 900
Calgary, Alberta, T2P 2T5

Phone 1-888-549-6248

Sales Fee No-Load **RRSP Eligibility** Yes

Category Fixed Income/Canadian Bond

Portfolio Manager/Years
Gary Feltham—Mawer Investment Mngt./6

Minimum Initial Investment
RRSP $5,000 **Non-RRSP** $5,000

Extended Asset Mix

Cdn Equity	U.S. Equity	Europe	Japan	Far East	Latin America	Special Equity	Dividend	Domestic Bond	Global Bond	Money Market
								◆		

Objectives

Short Term	Mid Term	Long Term	Currency Effect	Sector Specific	Small Cap	Mid Cap	Large Cap
	◆						

Investment Styles

Top Down	Bottom Up	Value	Sector Rotation	Momentum	Indexation
◆			◆		

Quantitative		Asset Breakout		Sector Breakout (Equity)
MER	0.99%	Cash	10.6%	Overweighted
Tax Efficiency	64.94%	Cdn Bonds	71.7%	1 Financial
Std Deviation	1.24%	Foreign Bonds		2 Utilities
Beta	0.85	Cdn Equity	11.8%	Underweighted
Alpha	0.04	Foreign Equity	1.0%	1 Real Estate
R Squared	0.85	Warrants		2 Financial

TRAILING 24-MONTH ANNUALIZED RETURNS FOR MAWER CANADIAN INCOME FUND

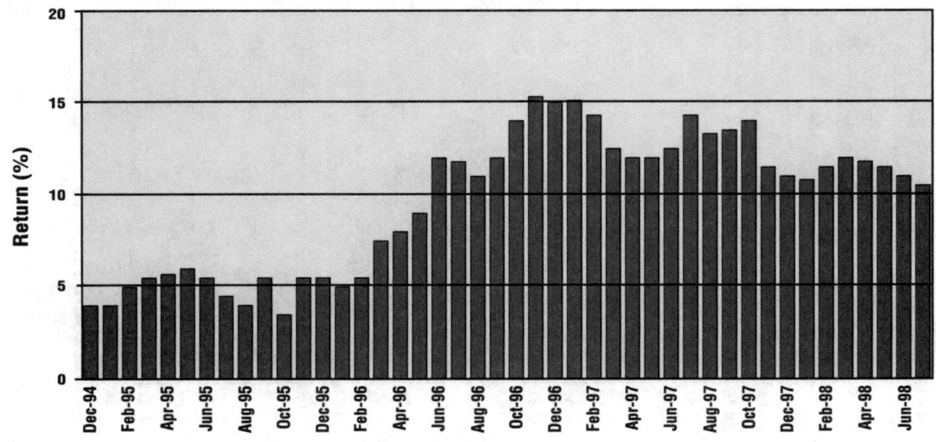

	Total Change	Annual Cmpd Rate	$10,000 Invested	24 Months Ending
Best	33.47%	15.53%	$13,346.70	November 1996
Worst	7.98%	3.91%	$10,797.66	October 1995
Average	21.09%	10.04%	$12,109.28	n/a

London Life Mortgage Fund

MVA	3 Months*	1 Year*	3 Years*	5 Years*	1997	1996	1995
103.9	1.3%	6.5%	7.1%	6.7%	6.2%	7.8%	11.9%

* Returns to July 31, 1998

Sponsor London Life Insurance Co.
255 Dufferin Avenue
London, Ontario, N6A 4K1

Phone 1-519-432-5281

Sales Fee Load **RRSP Eligibility** Yes

Category Fixed Income/Mortgage

Portfolio Manager/Years
Grant McIntosh—London Life Inv. Mngt./1

Minimum Initial Investment
RRSP $300 **Non-RRSP** $300

Extended Asset Mix

Cdn Equity	U.S. Equity	Europe	Japan	Far East	Latin America	Special Equity	Dividend	Domestic Bond	Global Bond	Money Market
								◆		

Objectives

Short Term	Mid Term	Long Term	Currency Effect	Sector Specific	Small Cap	Mid Cap	Large Cap
	◆						

Investment Styles

Top Down	Bottom Up	Value	Sector Rotation	Momentum	Indexation
	◆		◆		

Quantitative		Asset Breakout		Sector Breakout (Equity)
MER	2.00%	Cash	8.3%	Overweighted
Tax Efficiency	N/A	Cdn Bonds	4.0%	N/A
Std Deviation	0.43%	Mortgages	87.7%	
Beta	0.44	Cdn Equity		Underweighted
Alpha	0.26	Foreign Equity		N/A
R Squared	0.52	Warrants		

TRAILING 24-MONTH ANNUALIZED RETURNS FOR LONDON LIFE MORTGAGE FUND

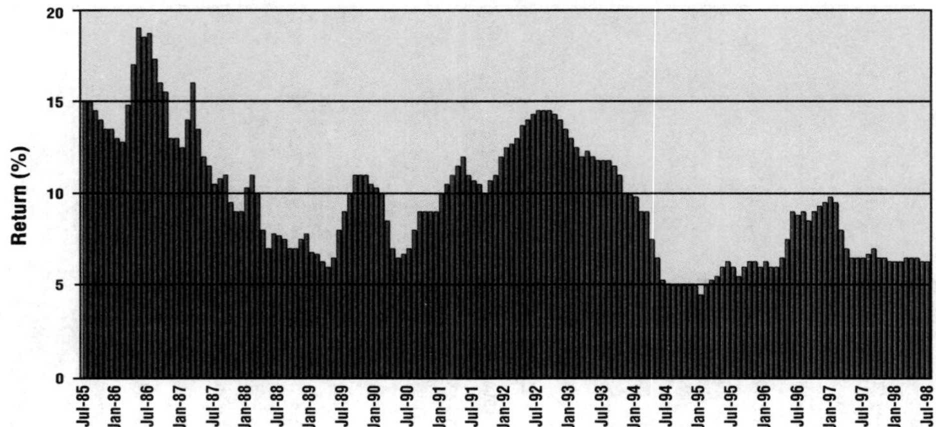

	Total Change	Annual Cmpd Rate	$10,000 Invested	24 Months Ending
Best	41.33%	18.88%	$14,133.23	May 1986
Worst	9.36%	4.58%	$10,936.07	January 1995
Average	21.20%	10.09%	$12,119.88	n/a

Trimark Advantage Bond Fund

MVA	3 Months*	1 Year*	3 Years*	5 Years*	1997	1996	1995
103.5	0.7%	6.6%	13.0%	N/A	10.5%	12.9%	22.7%

* Returns to July 31, 1998

Sponsor Trimark Investment Management Inc.
5140 Yonge St., Suite 900
Toronto, Ontario, M2N 6X7

Phone 1-800-387-9845

Sales Fee Load **RRSP Eligibility** Yes

Category Fixed Income/Canadian Bond

Portfolio Manager/Years
Patrick Farmer—Trimark Investment Mngt./4

Minimum Initial Investment
RRSP $500 **Non-RRSP** $500

Extended Asset Mix

Cdn Equity	U.S. Equity	Europe	Japan	Far East	Latin America	Special Equity	Dividend	Domestic Bond	Global Bond	Money Market
								◆		

Objectives

Short Term	Mid Term	Long Term	Currency Effect	Sector Specific	Small Cap	Mid Cap	Large Cap
	◆						

Investment Styles

Top Down	Bottom Up	Value	Sector Rotation	Momentum	Indexation
	◆		◆		

Quantitative		Asset Breakout		Sector Breakout (Equity)
MER	1.24%	Cash	10.8%	Overweighted
Tax Efficiency	71.50%	Cdn Bonds	73.2%	1 Metals–Minerals
Std Deviation	1.30%	Foreign Bonds	12.7%	2 Utilities
Beta	0.98	Cdn Equity	0.3%	Underweighted
Alpha	0.07	Foreign Equity		1 Oil & Gas
R Squared	0.96	Warrants		2 Financial

TRAILING 24-MONTH ANNUALIZED RETURNS FOR TRIMARK ADVANTAGE BOND FUND

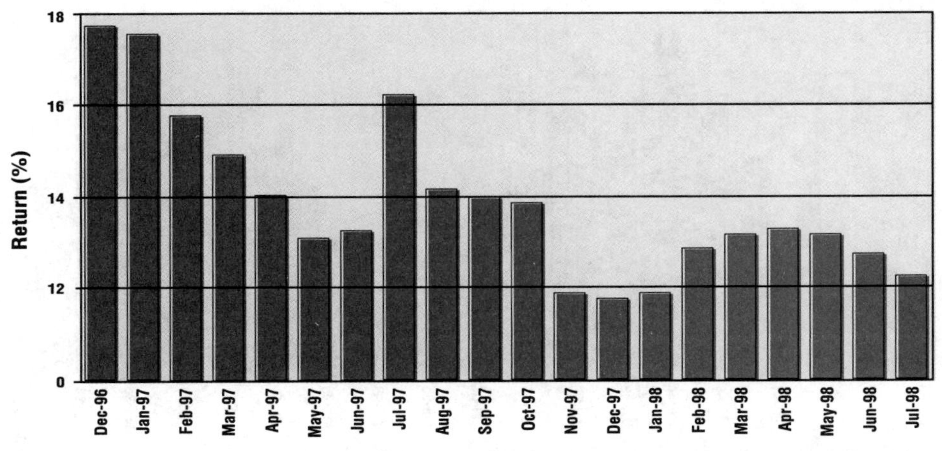

	Total Change	Annual Cmpd Rate	$10,000 Invested	24 Months Ending
Best	38.52%	17.69%	$13,851.95	December 1996
Worst	24.83%	11.73%	$12,482.82	December 1997
Average	29.80%	13.93%	$12,979.56	n/a

Batirente Section Obligations Fonds

MVA	3 Months*	1 Year*	3 Years*	5 Years*	1997	1996	1995
101.1	1.0%	7.2%	13.2%	9.9%	10.9%	13.0%	22.2%

* Returns to July 31, 1998

Sponsor Conseillers Fin du St. Laurent Inc.
425, de Maisonneuve Blvd. Ouest, #1740
Montreal, Quebec, H3A 3G5
Phone 1-514-288-7545
Sales Fee No-Load **RRSP Eligibility** Yes

Category Fixed Income/Canadian Bond
Portfolio Manager/Years
Carmand Normand—Conseillers Fin/11
Minimum Initial Investment
RRSP $500 **Non-RRSP** $500

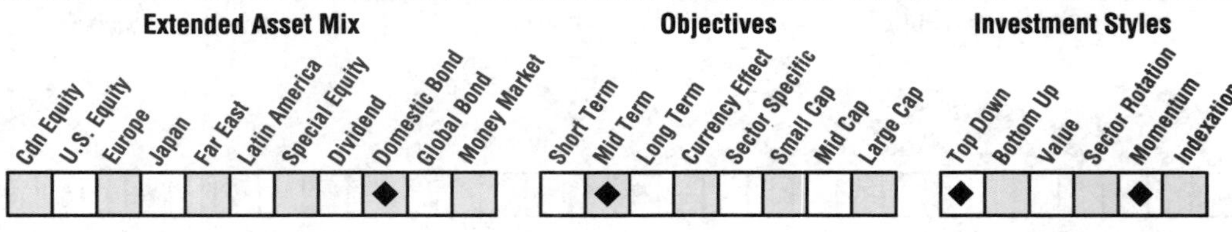

Quantitative		Asset Breakout		Sector Breakout (Equity)
MER	1.50%	Cash	1.3%	Overweighted
Tax Efficiency	100.00%	Cdn Bonds	97.1%	N/A
Std Deviation	1.36%	Foreign Bonds		
Beta	1.02	Cdn Equity		Underweighted
Alpha		Foreign Equity		N/A
R Squared	0.96	Warrants		

TRAILING 24-MONTH ANNUALIZED RETURNS FOR BATIRENTE SECTION OBLIGATIONS FONDS

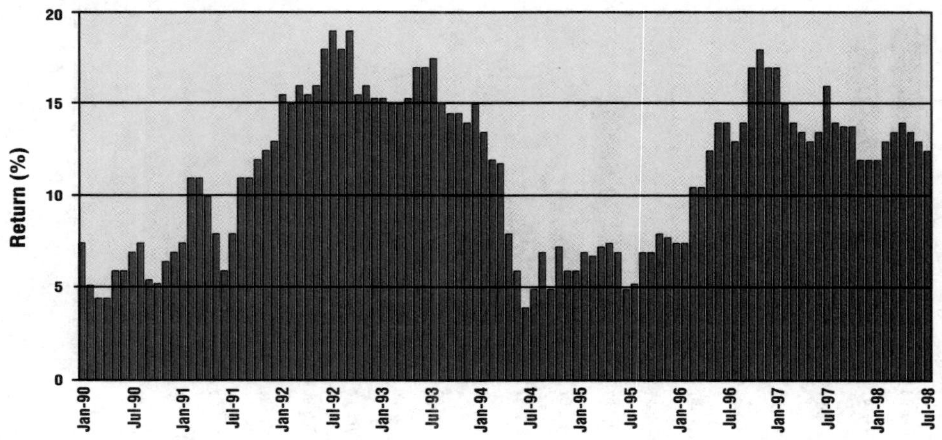

	Total Change	Annual Cmpd Rate	$10,000 Invested	24 Months Ending
Best	43.27%	19.69%	$14,326.55	August 1992
Worst	7.83%	3.84%	$10,783.13	July 1994
Average	24.69%	11.67%	$12,469.27	n/a

Guardian International Income Classic Fund

MVA	3 Months*	1 Year*	3 Years*	5 Years*	1997	1996	1995
96.5	2.8%	8.0%	8.8%	7.5%	7.4%	6.7%	17.8%

* Returns to July 31, 1998

Sponsor Guardian Mutual Funds
Commerce Court West, Suite 3100
Toronto, Ontario, M5L 1E8
Phone 1-800-668-7327
Sales Fee Load **RRSP Eligibility** Yes

Category Fixed Income/Global Bond
Portfolio Manager/Years
Larry Kennedy—Guardian Mutual Funds/5
Minimum Initial Investment
RRSP $500 **Non-RRSP** $500

Extended Asset Mix

Cdn Equity	U.S. Equity	Europe	Japan	Far East	Latin America	Special Equity	Dividend	Domestic Bond	Global Bond	Money Market
									◆	

Objectives

Short Term	Mid Term	Long Term	Currency Effect	Sector Specific	Small Cap	Mid Cap	Large Cap
	◆		◆				

Investment Styles

Top Down	Bottom Up	Value	Sector Rotation	Momentum	Indexation
◆				◆	

Quantitative		Asset Breakout		Sector Breakout (Equity)
MER	2.06%	Cash	34.8%	Overweighted
Tax Efficiency	68.30%	Cdn Bonds	1.2%	N/A
Std Deviation	1.01%	Foreign Bonds	64.6%	
Beta	0.56	Cdn Equity		Underweighted
Alpha	0.33	Foreign Equity		N/A
R Squared	0.23	Warrants		

TRAILING 24-MONTH ANNUALIZED RETURNS FOR GUARDIAN INT. INCOME CLASSIC FUND

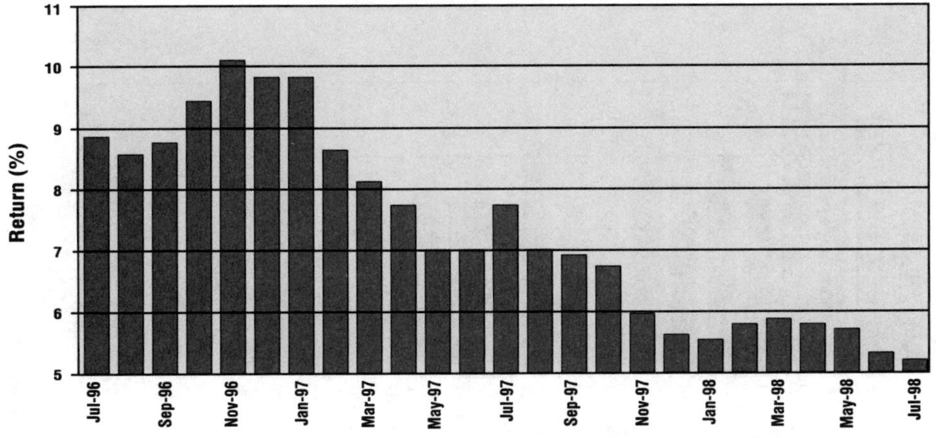

	Total Change	Annual Cmpd Rate	$10,000 Invested	24 Months Ending
Best	21.27%	10.12%	$12,126.86	November 1996
Worst	10.59%	5.16%	$11,059.18	July 1998
Average	15.15%	7.31%	$11,515.43	n/a

Universal World Income RRSP Fund

MVA	3 Months*	1 Year*	3 Years*	5 Years*	1997	1996	1995
96.0	4.5%	12.9%	11.9%	N/A	9.6%	8.8%	14.9%

* Returns to July 31, 1998

Sponsor Mackenzie Financial Corporation
150 Bloor Street West, Suite M111
Toronto, Ontario, M5S 3B5

Phone 1-800-387-0614

Sales Fee Load **RRSP Eligibility** Yes

Category Fixed Income/Global Bond

Portfolio Manager/Years
Brian Barrett—Mackenzie Financial/1

Minimum Initial Investment
RRSP $500 **Non-RRSP** $500

Extended Asset Mix	
Cdn Equity	
U.S. Equity	
Europe	
Japan	
Far East	
Latin America	
Special Equity	
Dividend	
Domestic Bond	
Global Bond	◆
Money Market	

Objectives	
Short Term	
Mid Term	
Long Term	◆
Currency Effect	◆
Sector Specific	
Small Cap	
Mid Cap	
Large Cap	

Investment Styles	
Top Down	◆
Bottom Up	
Value	
Sector Rotation	
Momentum	
Indexation	◆

Quantitative		Asset Breakout*		Sector Breakout (Equity)
MER	2.15%	Cash	0.9%	Overweighted
Tax Efficiency	65.27%	Cdn Bonds	10.6%	N/A
Std Deviation	1.27%	Foreign Bonds	17.8%	
Beta	0.65	Cdn Equity		Underweighted
Alpha	0.36	Foreign Equity	0.5%	N/A
R Squared	0.35	Warrants		

* Seventy percent of assets are held in derivatives.

TRAILING 24-MONTH ANNUALIZED RETURNS FOR UNIVERSAL WORLD INCOME RRSP FUND

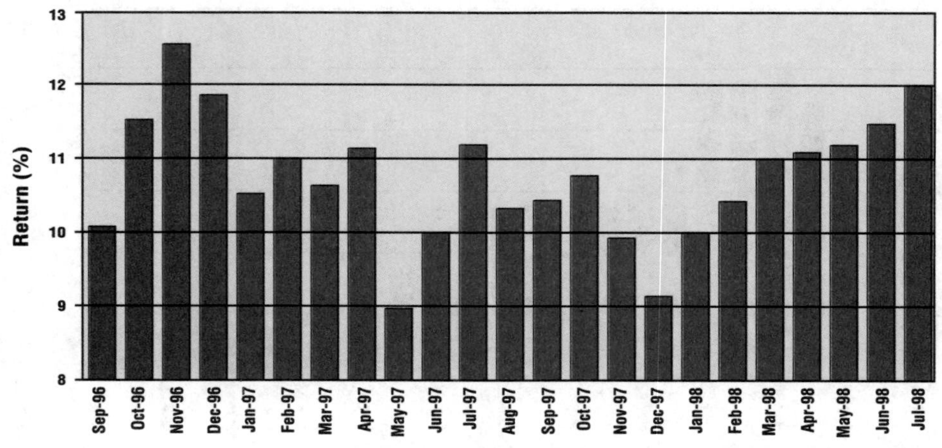

	Total Change	Annual Cmpd Rate	$10,000 Invested	24 Months Ending
Best	26.53%	12.48%	$12,652.79	November 1996
Worst	18.74%	8.97%	$11,874.44	May 1997
Average	22.80%	10.81%	$12,279.56	n/a

Fidelity Emerging Markets Bond Fund

MVA	3 Months*	1 Year*	3 Years*	5 Years*	1997	1996	1995
95.9	-0.8%	4.1%	23.5%	N/A	17.3%	38.1%	12.8%

* Returns to July 31, 1998

Sponsor Fidelity Investments Canada Ltd.
222 Bay Street, Suite 900
Toronto, Ontario, M5K 1P1

Phone 1-800-387-0074

Sales Fee Load **RRSP Eligibility** Yes

Category Fixed Income/Global Bond

Portfolio Manager/Years
John Carlson—Fidelity Management/3

Minimum Initial Investment
RRSP $500 **Non-RRSP** $500

Extended Asset Mix

Cdn Equity	U.S. Equity	Europe	Japan	Far East	Latin America	Special Equity	Dividend	Domestic Bond	Global Bond	Money Market
									◆	

Objectives

Short Term	Mid Term	Long Term	Currency Effect	Sector Specific	Small Cap	Mid Cap	Large Cap
		◆	◆				

Investment Styles

Top Down	Bottom Up	Value	Sector Rotation	Momentum	Indexation
	◆		◆		

Quantitative		Asset Breakout		Sector Breakout (Equity)
MER	2.22%	Cash	4.2%	Overweighted
Tax Efficiency	78.38%	Cdn Bonds	0.6%	N/A
Std Deviation	3.38%	Foreign Bonds	89.8%	
Beta	0.62	Cdn Equity		Underweighted
Alpha	0.68	Foreign Equity	0.9%	N/A
R Squared	0.07	Warrants		

TRAILING 24-MONTH ANNUALIZED RETURNS FOR FIDELITY EMERGING MARKETS BOND FUND

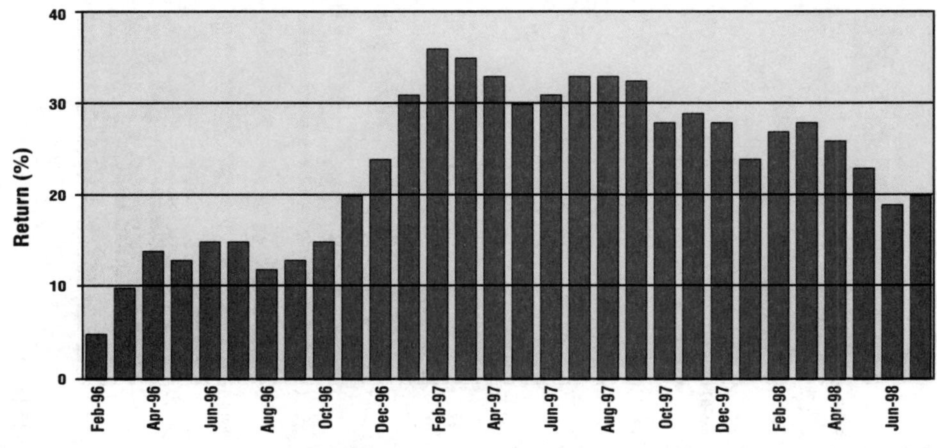

	Total Change	Annual Cmpd Rate	$10,000 Invested	24 Months Ending
Best	85.94%	36.36%	$18,594.21	February 1997
Worst	11.19%	5.45%	$11,119.05	February 1996
Average	54.12%	24.14%	$15,411.93	n/a

Guardian Foreign Income Class A Fund

MVA	3 Months*	1 Year*	3 Years*	5 Years*	1997	1996	1995
94.9	7.5%	17.4%	12.2%	N/A	12.6%	7.4%	14.8%

* Returns to July 31, 1998

Sponsor Guardian Mutual Funds
Commerce Court West, Suite 3100
Toronto, Ontario, M5L 1E8
Phone 1-800-668-7327
Sales Fee Load **RRSP Eligibility** Yes

Category Fixed Income/Global Bond
Portfolio Manager/Years
Lawrence Linklater—Dresdner RCM/4
Minimum Initial Investment
RRSP $500 **Non-RRSP** $500

Extended Asset Mix

Cdn Equity	U.S. Equity	Europe	Japan	Far East	Latin America	Special Equity	Dividend	Domestic Bond	Global Bond	Money Market
									◆	

Objectives

Short Term	Mid Term	Long Term	Currency Effect	Sector Specific	Small Cap	Mid Cap	Large Cap
	◆		◆				

Investment Styles

Top Down	Bottom Up	Value	Sector Rotation	Momentum	Indexation
◆				◆	

Quantitative		Asset Breakout		Sector Breakout (Equity)
MER	1.68%	Cash	36.2%	Overweighted
Tax Efficiency	69.94%	Cdn Bonds		N/A
Std Deviation	1.41%	Foreign Bonds	62.0%	
Beta	0.44	Cdn Equity		Underweighted
Alpha	0.68	Foreign Equity		N/A
R Squared	0.06	Warrants		

TRAILING 24-MONTH ANNUALIZED RETURNS FOR GUARDIAN FOREIGN INCOME CLASS A FUND

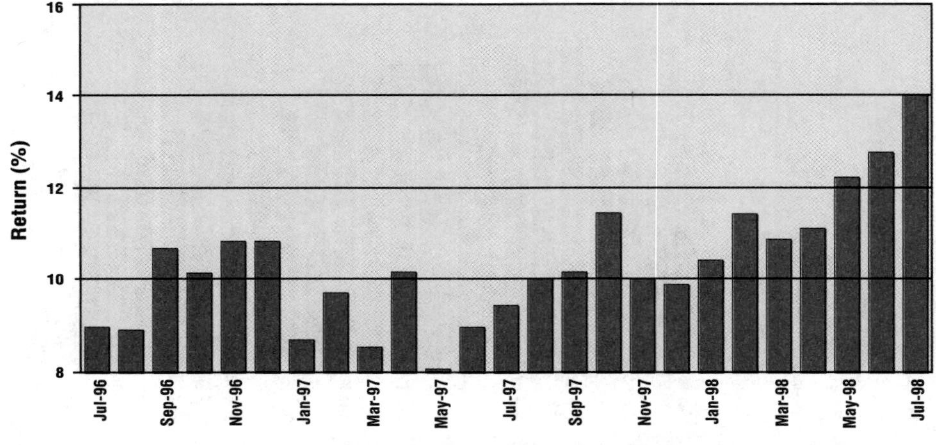

	Total Change	Annual Cmpd Rate	$10,000 Invested	24 Months Ending
Best	30.14%	14.08%	$13,014.22	July 1998
Worst	16.71%	8.03%	$11,671.20	May 1997
Average	22.04%	10.47%	$12,203.61	n/a

Templeton International Stock Fund

MVA	3 Months*	1 Year*	3 Years*	5 Years*	1997	1996	1995
119.6	1.4%	13.4%	18.0%	19.3%	15.9%	21.5%	12.2%

* Returns to July 31, 1998

Sponsor Templeton Management Ltd
1 Adelaide St. East, Suite 2101
Toronto, Ontario, M5C 3B8
Phone 1-800-387-0830
Sales Fee Load **RRSP Eligibility** Foreign

Category Foreign Equity/International
Portfolio Manager/Years
Donald Reed—Templeton Management/10
Minimum Initial Investment
RRSP $500 **Non-RRSP** $500

Extended Asset Mix

Cdn Equity	U.S. Equity	Europe	Japan	Far East	Latin America	Special Equity	Dividend	Domestic Bond	Global Bond	Money Market
◆		◆		◆						

Objectives

Short Term	Mid Term	Long Term	Currency Effect	Sector Specific	Small Cap	Mid Cap	Large Cap
			◆			◆	◆

Investment Styles

Top Down	Bottom Up	Value	Sector Rotation	Momentum	Indexation
	◆	◆			

Quantitative		Asset Breakout		Sector Breakout (Equity)
MER	2.49%	Cash	14.7%	Overweighted
Tax Efficiency	97.77%	Cdn Bonds		N/A
Std Deviation	2.80%	Foreign Bonds		
Beta	0.70	Cdn Equity		Underweighted
Alpha	0.75	Foreign Equity	81.6%	N/A
R Squared	0.57	Warrants		

TRAILING 24-MONTH ANNUALIZED RETURNS FOR TEMPLETON INTERNATIONAL STOCK FUND

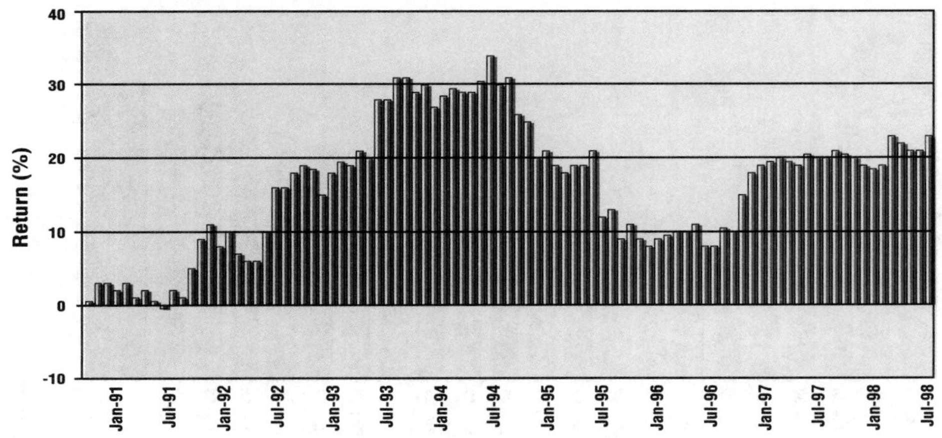

	Total Change	Annual Cmpd Rate	$10,000 Invested	24 Months Ending
Best	79.93%	34.14%	$17,993.14	August 1994
Worst	-0.50%	-0.25%	$9,949.60	June 1991
Average	36.27%	16.74%	$13,627.42	n/a

Optimum International Fund

MVA	3 Months*	1 Year*	3 Years*	5 Years*	1997	1996	1995
110.7	5.6%	23.3%	17.5%	N/A	27.4%	4.0%	14.3%

* Returns to July 31, 1998

Sponsor Optimum Investments Inc.
425, de Maisonneuve Blvd. Ouest, #1720
Montreal, Quebec, H3A 3G5

Phone 1-888-678-4686

Sales Fee No-Load **RRSP Eligibility** Foreign

Category Foreign Equity/International

Portfolio Manager/Years
Not Available

Minimum Initial Investment
RRSP $1,000 **Non-RRSP** $1,000

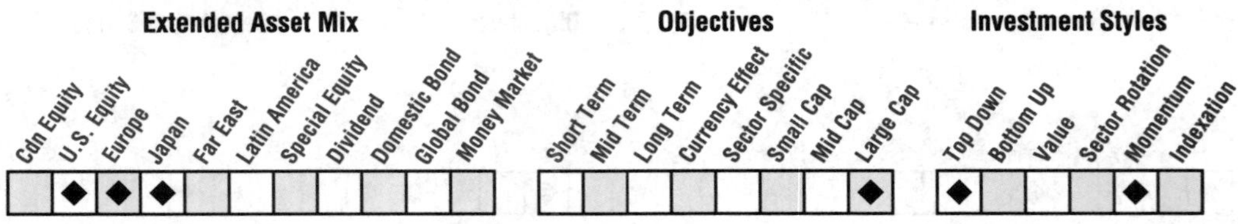

Quantitative		Asset Breakout*		Sector Breakout (Equity)
MER	1.96%	Cash	2.6%	Overweighted
Tax Efficiency	74.33%	Cdn Bonds		N/A
Std Deviation	3.12%	Foreign Bonds		
Beta	0.66	Cdn Equity		Underweighted
Alpha	0.85	Foreign Equity	37.4%	N/A
R Squared	0.37	Warrants		

* Fifty-six percent of assets are held in derivatives.

TRAILING 24-MONTH ANNUALIZED RETURNS FOR OPTIMUM INTERNATIONAL FUND

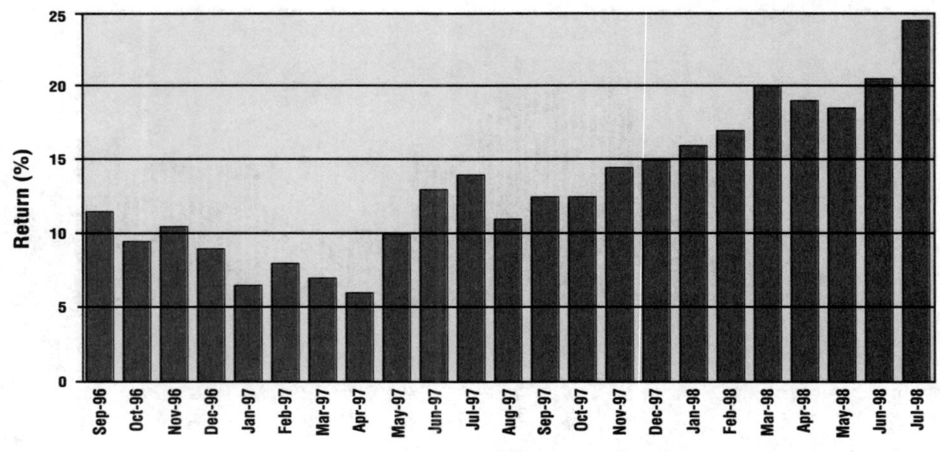

	Total Change	Annual Cmpd Rate	$10,000 Invested	24 Months Ending
Best	55.38%	24.65%	$15,538.19	July 1998
Worst	12.33%	5.99%	$11,233.49	April 1997
Average	29.62%	13.85%	$12,962.04	n/a

Great-West Life International Equity Fund

MVA	3 Months*	1 Year*	3 Years*	5 Years*	1997	1996	1995
108.3	6.7%	18.8%	18.7%	N/A	15.6%	12.1%	8.1%

* Returns to July 31, 1998

Sponsor Great-West Life Assurance Co.
60 Osborne Street North
Winnipeg, Manitoba, R3C 3A5

Phone 1-204-946-1190

Sales Fee Load **RRSP Eligibility** Foreign

Category Foreign Equity/International

Portfolio Manager/Years
Anthony Regan—Putnam Investment Mngt./4

Minimum Initial Investment
RRSP $50 **Non-RRSP** $50

Extended Asset Mix

Cdn Equity	U.S. Equity	Europe	Japan	Far East	Latin America	Special Equity	Dividend	Domestic Bond	Global Bond	Money Market
	◆	◆	◆							

Objectives

Short Term	Mid Term	Long Term	Currency Effect	Sector Specific	Small Cap	Mid Cap	Large Cap
							◆

Investment Styles

Top Down	Bottom Up	Value	Sector Rotation	Momentum	Indexation
◆				◆	

Quantitative		Asset Breakout		Sector Breakout (Equity)
MER	2.69%	Cash	N/A	Overweighted
Tax Efficiency	N/A	Cdn Bonds	N/A	N/A
Std Deviation	3.23%	Foreign Bonds	N/A	
Beta	0.87	Cdn Equity	N/A	Underweighted
Alpha	0.46	Foreign Equity	N/A	N/A
R Squared	0.70	Warrants	N/A	

TRAILING 24-MONTH ANNUALIZED RETURNS FOR GREAT-WEST LIFE INT. EQUITY FUND

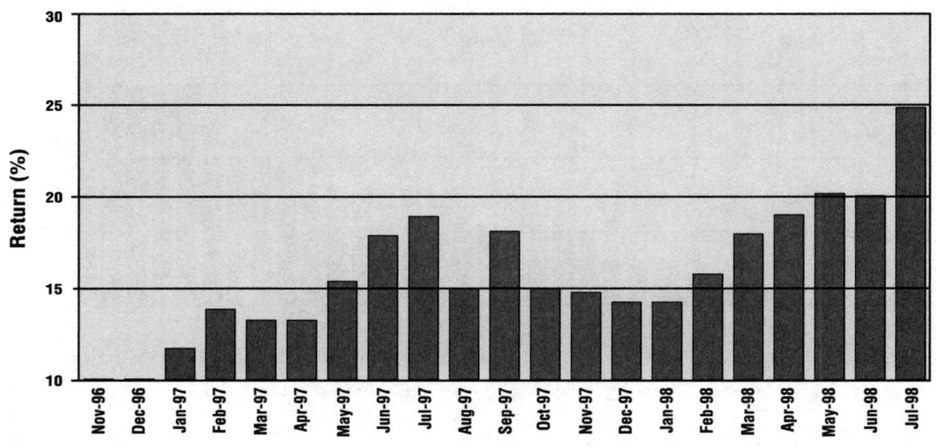

	Total Change	Annual Cmpd Rate	$10,000 Invested	24 Months Ending
Best	56.26%	25.01%	$15,626.30	July 1998
Worst	21.19%	10.09%	$12,119.36	December 1996
Average	34.73%	16.07%	$13,473.34	n/a

AIC World Equity Fund

MVA	3 Months*	1 Year*	3 Years*	5 Years*	1997	1996	1995
107.3	6.7%	35.6%	23.4%	N/A	21.4%	18.9%	2.1%

* Returns to July 31, 1998

Sponsor AIC Limited
1375 Kerns Road
Burlington, Ontario, L7R 4V7

Phone 1-800-263-2144

Sales Fee Load **RRSP Eligibility** Foreign

Category Foreign Equity/International

Portfolio Manager/Years
Michael Lee-Chin—AIC Limited/12

Minimum Initial Investment
RRSP $500 **Non-RRSP** $500

Extended Asset Mix

Cdn Equity	U.S. Equity	Europe	Japan	Far East	Latin America	Special Equity	Dividend	Domestic Bond	Global Bond	Money Market
		◆		◆						

Objectives

Short Term	Mid Term	Long Term	Currency Effect	Sector Specific	Small Cap	Mid Cap	Large Cap
			◆			◆	◆

Investment Styles

Top Down	Bottom Up	Value	Sector Rotation	Momentum	Indexation
	◆	◆		◆	

Quantitative		Asset Breakout		Sector Breakout (Equity)
MER	2.70%	Cash	22.9%	Overweighted
Tax Efficiency	100.00%	Cdn Bonds	0.3%	N/A
Std Deviation	3.26%	Foreign Bonds		
Beta	0.63	Cdn Equity		Underweighted
Alpha	0.61	Foreign Equity	77.3%	N/A
R Squared	0.22	Warrants		

TRAILING 24-MONTH ANNUALIZED RETURNS FOR AIC WORLD EQUITY FUND

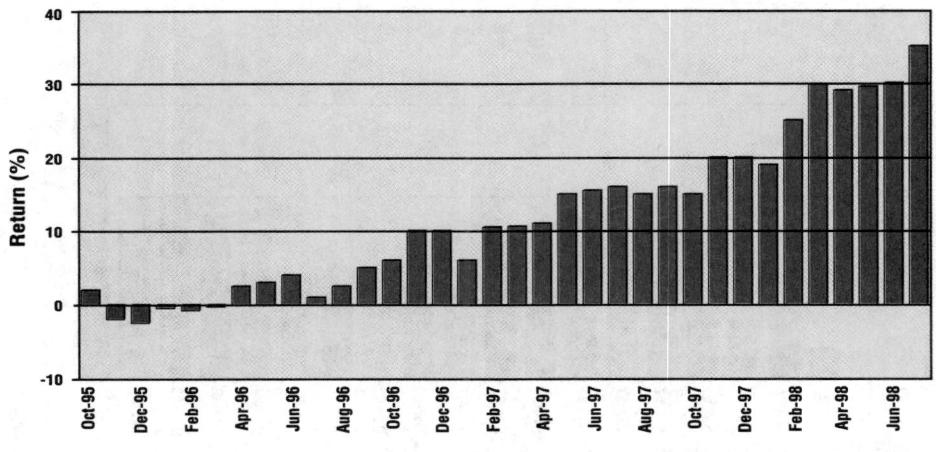

	Total Change	Annual Cmpd Rate	$10,000 Invested	24 Months Ending
Best	81.89%	34.87%	$18,189.32	July 1998
Worst	-4.98%	-2.52%	$9,501.66	December 1995
Average	27.37%	12.86%	$12,736.61	n/a

Universal World Growth RRSP Fund

MVA	3 Months*	1 Year*	3 Years*	5 Years*	1997	1996	1995
107.0	-1.0%	-1.0%	13.9%	N/A	6.3%	19.3%	11.1%

* Returns to July 31, 1998

Sponsor Mackenzie Financial Corporation
150 Bloor Street West, Suite M111
Toronto, Ontario, M5S 3B5

Phone 1-800-387-0614

Sales Fee Load **RRSP Eligibility** Yes

Category Foreign Equity/International

Portfolio Manager/Years
Barbara Trebbi—Mackenzie Financial/4

Minimum Initial Investment
RRSP $500 **Non-RRSP** $500

Extended Asset Mix

Cdn Equity	U.S. Equity	Europe	Japan	Far East	Latin America	Special Equity	Dividend	Domestic Bond	Global Bond	Money Market
	◆	◆		◆						

Objectives

Short Term	Mid Term	Long Term	Currency Effect	Sector Specific	Small Cap	Mid Cap	Large Cap
			◆				◆

Investment Styles

Top Down	Bottom Up	Value	Sector Rotation	Momentum	Indexation
◆					◆

Quantitative		Asset Breakout*		Sector Breakout (Equity)
MER	2.44%	Cash	3.0%	Overweighted
Tax Efficiency	66.59%	Cdn Bonds		N/A
Std Deviation	3.35%	Foreign Bonds	0.1%	
Beta	0.80	Cdn Equity		Underweighted
Alpha	0.26	Foreign Equity	13.1%	N/A
R Squared	0.52	Warrants		

* Eighty-five percent of assets are held in derivatives.

TRAILING 24-MONTH ANNUALIZED RETURNS FOR UNIVERSAL WORLD GROWTH RRSP FUND

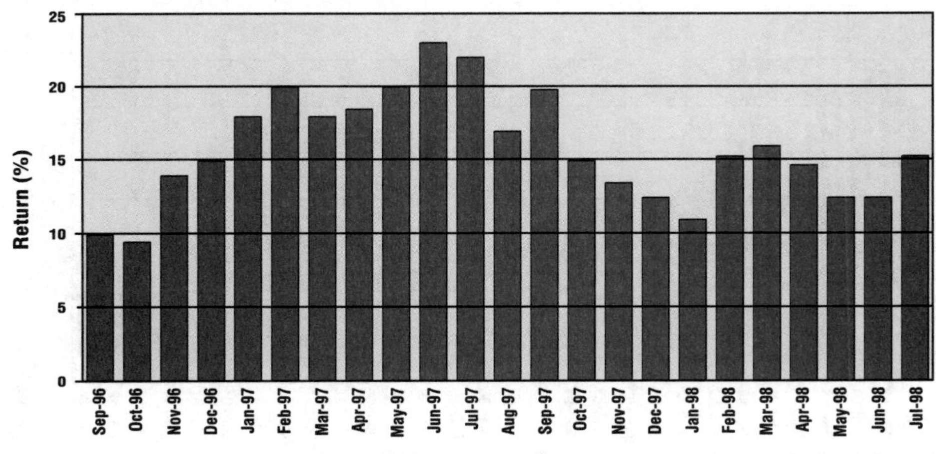

	Total Change	Annual Cmpd Rate	$10,000 Invested	24 Months Ending
Best	50.74%	22.77%	$15,073.56	June 1997
Worst	19.92%	9.51%	$11,991.91	October 1996
Average	34.56%	16.00%	$13,45571	n/a

Fidelity Far East Fund

MVA	3 Months*	1 Year*	3 Years*	5 Years*	1997	1996	1995
116.4	-21.1%	-45.9%	-7.1%	2.3%	-22.6%	21.7%	19.9%

* Returns to July 31, 1998

Sponsor Fidelity Investments Canada Ltd.
222 Bay Street, Suite 900
Toronto, Ontario, M5K 1P1
Phone 1-800-387-0074
Sales Fee Load **RRSP Eligibility** Foreign

Category Foreign Equity/Asia Pacific
Portfolio Manager/Years
K. C. Lee—Fidelity International/7
Minimum Initial Investment
RRSP $500 **Non-RRSP** $500

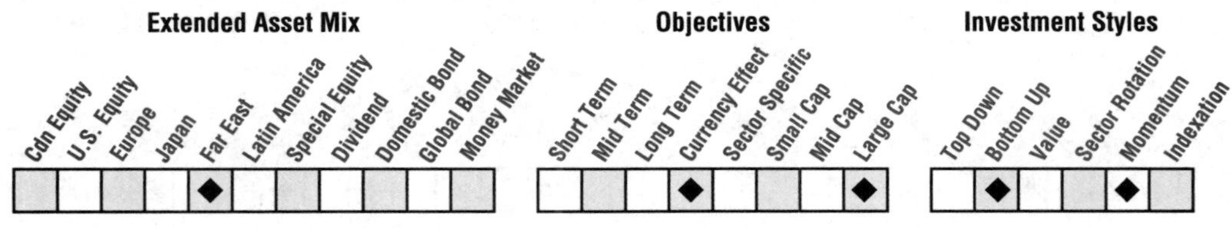

Quantitative		Asset Breakout		Sector Breakout (Equity)
MER	2.84%	Cash	3.5%	Overweighted
Tax Efficiency	100.00%	Cdn Bonds		N/A
Std Deviation	7.42%	Foreign Bonds	0.6%	
Beta	0.79	Cdn Equity		Underweighted
Alpha	0.44	Foreign Equity	94.7%	N/A
R Squared	0.13	Warrants		

TRAILING 24-MONTH ANNUALIZED RETURNS FOR FIDELITY FAR EAST FUND

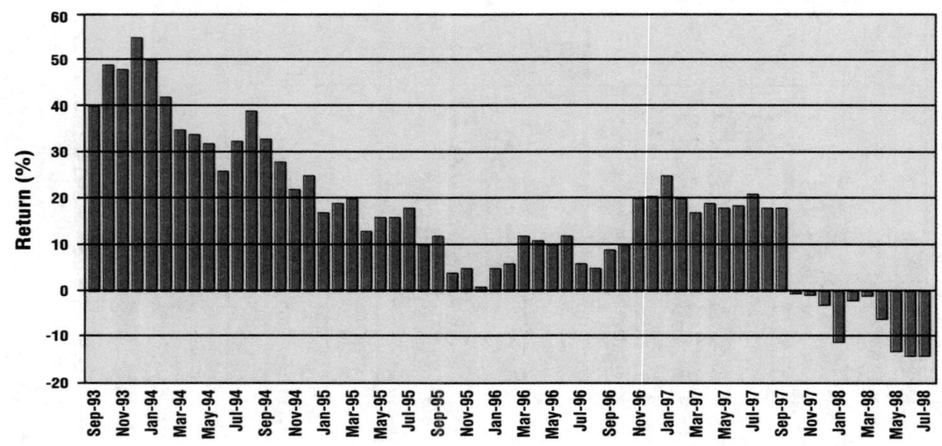

	Total Change	Annual Cmpd Rate	$10,000 Invested	24 Months Ending
Best	139.65%	54.81%	$23,965.35	December 1993
Worst	-26.39%	-14.20%	$7,361.17	July 1998
Average	39.25%	18.00%	$13,925.06	n/a

Scotia Excelsior Pacific Rim Fund

MVA	3 Months*	1 Year*	3 Years*	5 Years*	1997	1996	1995
111.5	-8.4%	-34.8%	-6.6%	N/A	-16.0%	5.5%	10.0%

* Returns to July 31, 1998

Sponsor Bank of Nova Scotia
44 King Street West
Toronto, Ontario, M5H 1H1
Phone 1-800-268-9269
Sales Fee Load **RRSP Eligibility** Foreign

Category Foreign Equity/Asia Pacific
Portfolio Manager/Years
S.I.M.L. Management Team—Scotia/4
Minimum Initial Investment
RRSP $500 **Non-RRSP** $500

Extended Asset Mix

Cdn Equity	U.S. Equity	Europe	Japan	Far East	Latin America	Special Equity	Dividend	Domestic Bond	Global Bond	Money Market
◆			◆	◆						

Objectives

Short Term	Mid Term	Long Term	Currency Effect	Sector Specific	Small Cap	Mid Cap	Large Cap
			◆			◆	◆

Investment Styles

Top Down	Bottom Up	Value	Sector Rotation	Momentum	Indexation
◆				◆	

Quantitative		Asset Breakout		Sector Breakout (Equity)
MER	2.43%	Cash	11.5%	Overweighted
Tax Efficiency	100.00%	Cdn Bonds		N/A
Std Deviation	4.13%	Foreign Bonds		
Beta	0.67	Cdn Equity		Underweighted
Alpha	0.31	Foreign Equity	82.4%	N/A
R Squared	0.59	Warrants		

TRAILING 24-MONTH ANNUALIZED RETURNS FOR SCOTIA EXCELSIOR PACIFIC RIM FUND

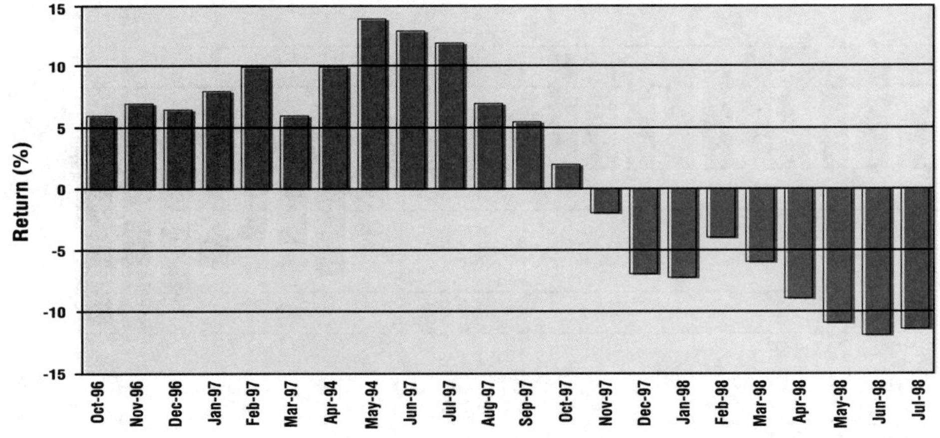

	Total Change	Annual Cmpd Rate	$10,000 Invested	24 Months Ending
Best	30.50%	14.24%	$13,049.82	May 1997
Worst	-22.76%	-12.11%	$7,724.33	June 1998
Average	5.35%	2.64%	$10,534.90	n/a

First Canadian Far East Growth Fund

MVA	3 Months*	1 Year*	3 Years*	5 Years*	1997	1996	1995
111.3	-23.5%	-46.8%	-11.6%	N/A	-26.8%	19.4%	8.8%

* Returns to July 31, 1998

Sponsor First Canadian Funds
302 Bay Street,
Toronto, Ontario, M5X 1A1

Phone 1-800-665-7700

Sales Fee No-Load **RRSP Eligibility** Foreign

Category Foreign Equity/Asia Pacific

Portfolio Manager/Years
Edinburgh Fund Management/5

Minimum Initial Investment
RRSP $500 **Non-RRSP** $500

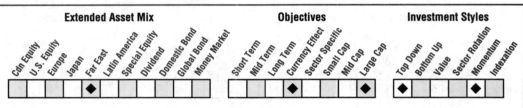

Extended Asset Mix

Cdn Equity	U.S. Equity	Europe	Japan	Far East	Latin America	Special Equity	Dividend	Domestic Bond	Global Bond	Money Market
				◆						

Objectives

Short Term	Mid Term	Long Term	Currency Effect	Sector Specific	Small Cap	Mid Cap	Large Cap
			◆				◆

Investment Styles

Top Down	Bottom Up	Value	Sector Rotation	Momentum	Indexation
◆				◆	

Quantitative		Asset Breakout		Sector Breakout (Equity)
MER	2.36%	Cash	23.4%	Overweighted
Tax Efficiency	100.00%	Cdn Bonds		N/A
Std Deviation	6.26%	Foreign Bonds		
Beta	0.75	Cdn Equity		Underweighted
Alpha	-0.07	Foreign Equity	77.0%	N/A
R Squared	0.25	Warrants		

TRAILING 24-MONTH ANNUALIZED RETURNS FOR FIRST CANADIAN FAR EAST GROWTH FUND

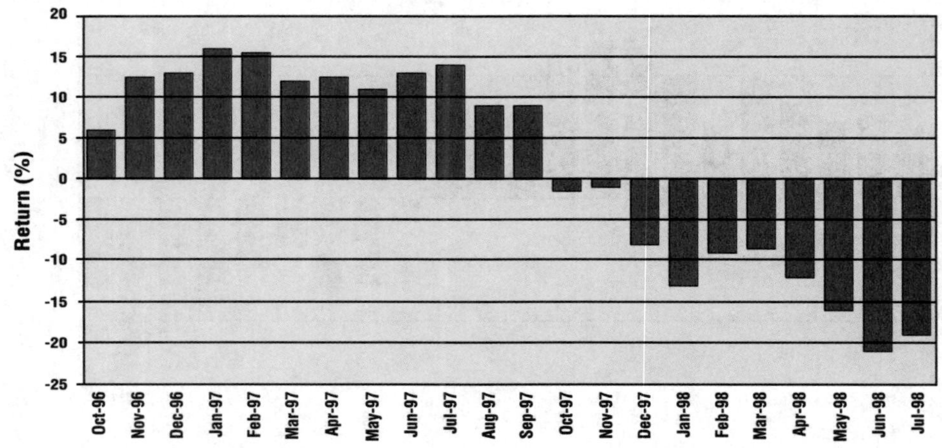

	Total Change	Annual Cmpd Rate	$10,000 Invested	24 Months Ending
Best	38.60%	17.73%	$13,860.40	January 1997
Worst	-36.74%	-20.46%	$6,326.08	June 1998
Average	6.13%	3.02%	$10,613.44	n/a

NN Can-Asian Fund

MVA	3 Months*	1 Year*	3 Years*	5 Years*	1997	1996	1995
111.2	-10.4%	-38.2%	-5.1%	N/A	-23.9%	11.8%	12.1%

* Returns to July 31, 1998

Sponsor NN Life Insurance Co. of Canada
1 Concorde Gate
Toronto, Ontario, M3C 3N6

Phone (416) 391-2200

Sales Fee Load **RRSP Eligibility** Yes

Category Foreign Equity/Asia Pacific

Portfolio Manager/Years
David Patterson—Newcastle Management/5

Minimum Initial Investment
RRSP $1,000 **Non-RRSP** $1,000

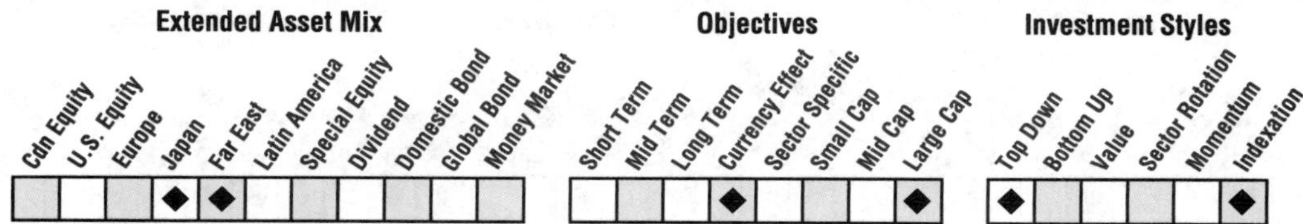

Quantitative		Asset Breakout		Sector Breakout (Equity)
MER	2.71%	Cash	99.3%*	Overweighted
Tax Efficiency	N/A	Cdn Bonds		N/A
Std Deviation	6.00%	Foreign Bonds		
Beta	0.82	Cdn Equity		Underweighted
Alpha	0.16	Foreign Equity		N/A
R Squared	0.36	Warrants		

* Fund uses derivatives for exposure to Japan and Far East, and supports the positions with cash.

TRAILING 24-MONTH ANNUALIZED RETURNS FOR NN CAN-ASIAN FUND

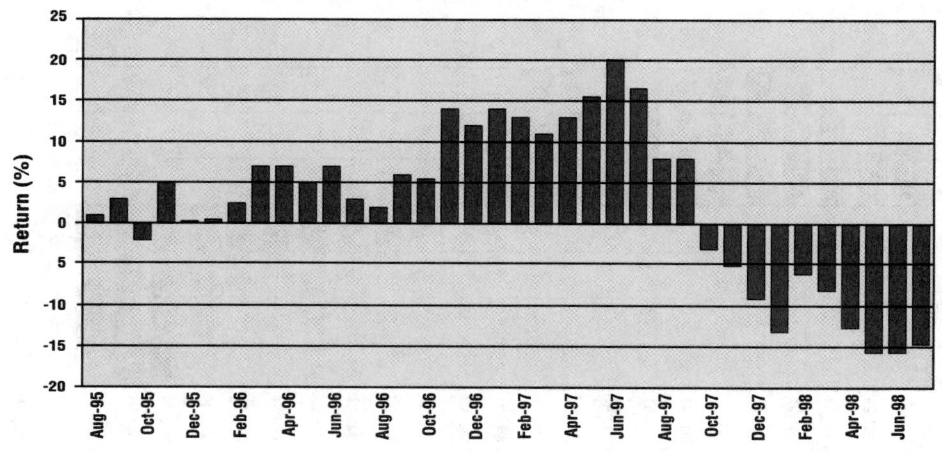

	Total Change	Annual Cmpd Rate	$10,000 Invested	24 Months Ending
Best	44.67%	20.28%	$14,467.46	June 1997
Worst	-28.58%	-15.49%	$7,141.55	June 1998
Average	7.45%	3.66%	$10,744.83	n/a

Trimark Indo-Pacific Fund

MVA	3 Months*	1 Year*	3 Years*	5 Years*	1997	1996	1995
108.8	-12.4%	-46.0%	-10.1%	N/A	-26.7%	18.6%	9.3%

* Returns to July 31, 1998

Sponsor Trimark Investment Management Inc.
5140 Yonge St., Suite 900
Toronto, Ontario, M2N 6X7

Phone 1-800-387-9845

Sales Fee Load **RRSP Eligibility** Foreign

Category Foreign Equity/Asia Pacific

Portfolio Manager/Years
Robert Lloyd George—Lloyd George Mngt./4

Minimum Initial Investment
RRSP $500 **Non-RRSP** $500

Extended Asset Mix

Cdn Equity	U.S. Equity	Europe	Japan	Far East	Latin America	Special Equity	Dividend	Domestic Bond	Global Bond	Money Market
				◆						

Objectives

Short Term	Mid Term	Long Term	Currency Effect	Sector Specific	Small Cap	Mid Cap	Large Cap
			◆			◆	◆

Investment Styles

Top Down	Bottom Up	Value	Sector Rotation	Momentum	Indexation
	◆	◆			

Quantitative		Asset Breakout		Sector Breakout (Equity)
MER	2.95%	Cash	9.3%	Overweighted
Tax Efficiency	100.00%	Cdn Bonds		N/A
Std Deviation	6.58%	Foreign Bonds		
Beta	0.84	Cdn Equity		Underweighted
Alpha	0.11	Foreign Equity	85.1%	N/A
R Squared	0.30	Warrants		

TRAILING 24-MONTH ANNUALIZED RETURNS FOR TRIMARK INDO-PACIFIC FUND

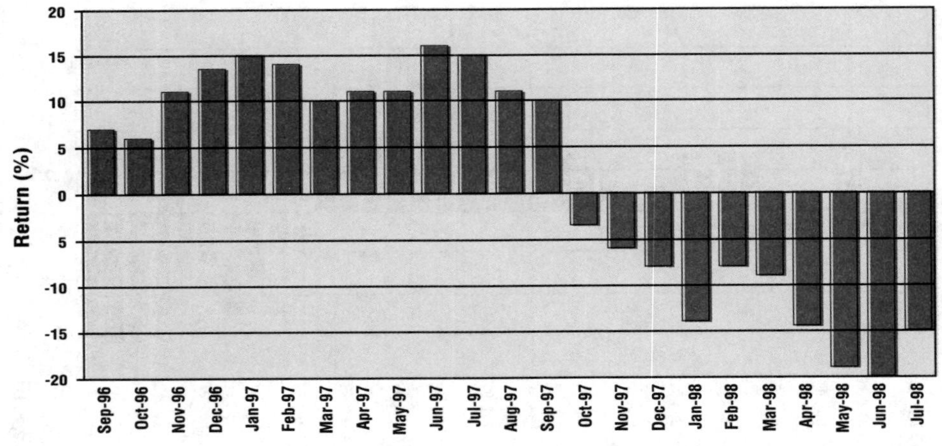

	Total Change	Annual Cmpd Rate	$10,000 Invested	24 Months Ending
Best	36.87%	16.99%	$13,687.33	June 1997
Worst	-35.48%	-19.67%	$6,452.14	June 1998
Average	5.99%	2.95%	$10,599.03	n/a

AGF International Group–Japan Class Fund

MVA	3 Months*	1 Year*	3 Years*	5 Years*	1997	1996	1995
114.7	0.2%	-14.9%	1.1%	-0.2%	8.7%	-6.0%	-9.2%

* Returns to July 31, 1998

Sponsor AGF Funds Inc.
66 Wellington Street West, 31st Floor,
Toronto, Ontario, M5K 1E9

Phone 1-800-268-8583

Sales Fee Load **RRSP Eligibility** Foreign

Category Foreign Equity/Japan

Portfolio Manager/Years
Sumio Sakamoto—Nomura Investment Mngt./2

Minimum Initial Investment
RRSP $1,000 **Non-RRSP** $1,000

Extended Asset Mix

Cdn Equity	U.S. Equity	Europe	Japan	Far East	Latin America	Special Equity	Dividend	Domestic Bond	Global Bond	Money Market
			◆							

Objectives

Short Term	Mid Term	Long Term	Currency Effect	Sector Specific	Small Cap	Mid Cap	Large Cap
			◆				◆

Investment Styles

Top Down	Bottom Up	Value	Sector Rotation	Momentum	Indexation
	◆	◆			

Quantitative		Asset Breakout		Sector Breakout (Equity)
MER	3.07%	Cash	13.5%	Overweighted
Tax Efficiency	100.00%	Cdn Bonds		N/A
Std Deviation	4.47%	Foreign Bonds		
Beta	0.64	Cdn Equity		Underweighted
Alpha	0.46	Foreign Equity	86.9%	N/A
R Squared	0.75	Warrants		

TRAILING 24-MONTH ANNUALIZED RETURNS FOR AGF INT. GROUP–JAPAN CLASS FUND

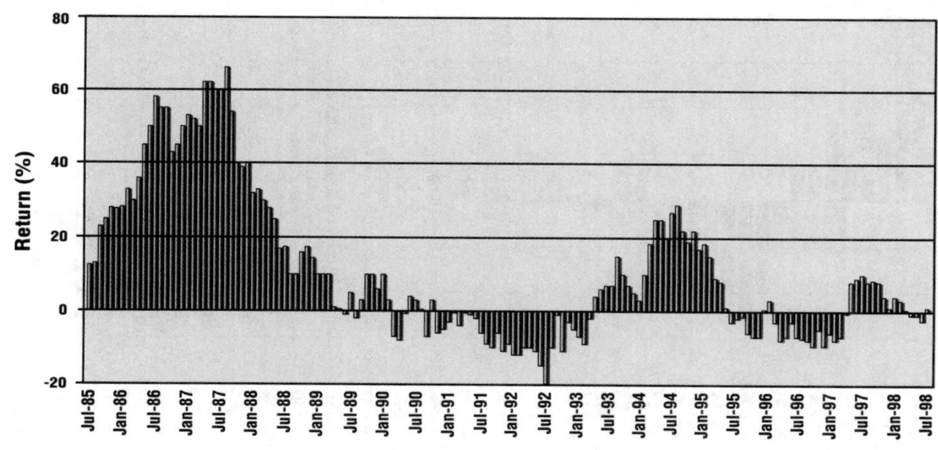

	Total Change	Annual Cmpd Rate	$10,000 Invested	24 Months Ending
Best	173.60%	65.41%	$27,360.28	August 1987
Worst	-34.39%	-19.00%	$6,561.47	July 1992
Average	26.78%	12.60%	$12,677.98	n/a

AIM Nippon Fund

MVA	3 Months*	1 Year*	3 Years*	5 Years*	1997	1996	1995
110.1	2.3%	-24.6%	-3.7%	-5.2%	-21.5%	-3.6%	1.8%

* Returns to July 31, 1998

Sponsor AIM GT Investments
77 King Street East, Suite 4001
Toronto, Ontario, M5K 1K2
Phone 1-800-588-5684
Sales Fee Load **RRSP Eligibility** Foreign

Category Foreign Equity/Japan
Portfolio Manager/Years
Ritsu Matsushita—Invesco/2
Minimum Initial Investment
RRSP $500 **Non-RRSP** $500

Extended Asset Mix

Cdn Equity	U.S. Equity	Europe	Japan	Far East	Latin America	Special Equity	Dividend	Domestic Bond	Global Bond	Money Market
			◆							

Objectives

Short Term	Mid Term	Long Term	Currency Effect	Sector Specific	Small Cap	Mid Cap	Large Cap
			◆				◆

Investment Styles

Top Down	Bottom Up	Value	Sector Rotation	Momentum	Indexation
	◆		◆	◆	

Quantitative		Asset Breakout		Sector Breakout (Equity)
MER	3.26%	Cash	16.6%	Overweighted
Tax Efficiency	100.00%	Cdn Bonds		N/A
Std Deviation	4.85%	Foreign Bonds		
Beta	0.69	Cdn Equity		Underweighted
Alpha	0.03	Foreign Equity	82.6%	N/A
R Squared	0.70	Warrants		

TRAILING 24-MONTH ANNUALIZED RETURNS FOR AIM NIPPON FUND

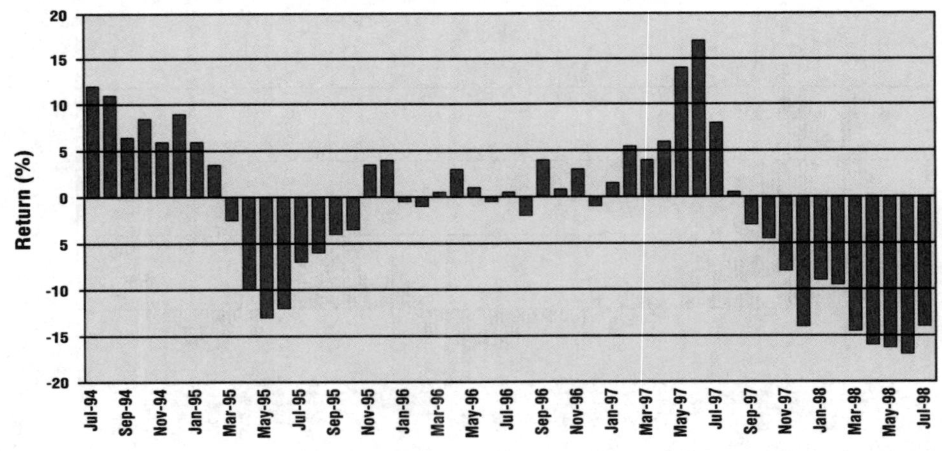

	Total Change	Annual Cmpd Rate	$10,000 Invested	24 Months Ending
Best	37.29%	17.17%	$13,729.16	June 1997
Worst	-31.04%	-16.96%	$6,896.32	June 1998
Average	-0.99%	-0.45%	$9,909.94	n/a

Universal Japan Fund

MVA	3 Months*	1 Year*	3 Years*	5 Years*	1997	1996	1995
108.6	4.2%	-23.1%	-4.8%	N/A	-8.6%	-12.7%	-4.9%

* Returns to July 31, 1998

Sponsor Mackenzie Financial Corporation
150 Bloor Street West, Suite M111
Toronto, Ontario, M5S 3B5
Phone 1-800-387-0614
Sales Fee Load **RRSP Eligibility** Foreign

Category Foreign Equity/Japan
Portfolio Manager/Years
Campbell Gunn—Mackenzie Financial/5
Minimum Initial Investment
RRSP $500 **Non-RRSP** $500

Extended Asset Mix

Cdn Equity	U.S. Equity	Europe	Japan	Far East	Latin America	Special Equity	Dividend	Domestic Bond	Global Bond	Money Market
			◆							

Objectives

Short Term	Mid Term	Long Term	Currency Effect	Sector Specific	Small Cap	Mid Cap	Large Cap
			◆			◆	

Investment Styles

Top Down	Bottom Up	Value	Sector Rotation	Momentum	Indexation
	◆				

Quantitative		Asset Breakout		Sector Breakout (Equity)
MER	2.54%	Cash	12.7%	Overweighted
Tax Efficiency	100.00%	Cdn Bonds		N/A
Std Deviation	5.31%	Foreign Bonds		
Beta	0.8	Cdn Equity		Underweighted
Alpha	0.17	Foreign Equity	86.4%	N/A
R Squared	0.77	Warrants		

TRAILING 24-MONTH ANNUALIZED RETURNS FOR UNIVERSAL JAPAN FUND

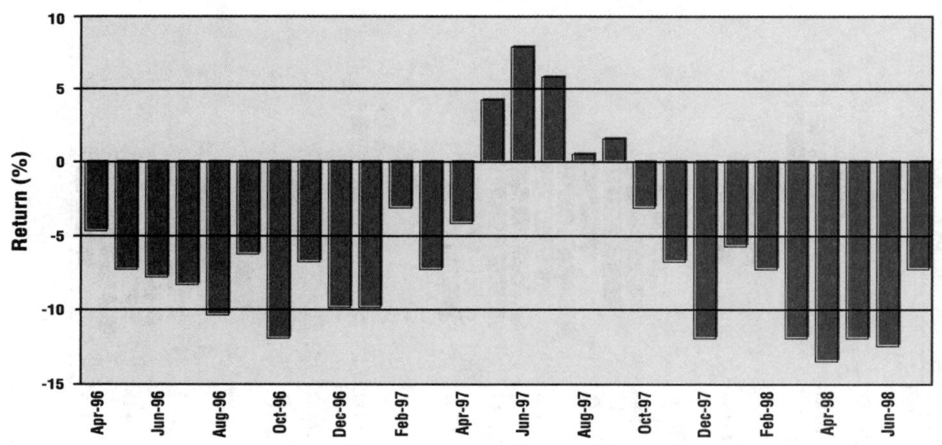

	Total Change	Annual Cmpd Rate	$10,000 Invested	24 Months Ending
Best	15.63%	7.53%	$11,563.23	June 1997
Worst	-24.43%	-13.07%	$7,557.23	April 1998
Average	-10.54%	-5.42%	$8,945.55	n/a

Fidelity Japanese Growth Fund

MVA	3 Months*	1 Year*	3 Years*	5 Years*	1997	1996	1995
106.9	2.3%	-19.6%	-5.4%	-4.0%	-7.4%	-12.1%	-9.3%

* Returns to July 31, 1998

Sponsor Fidelity Investments Canada Ltd.
222 Bay Street, Suite 900
Toronto, Ontario, M5K 1P1

Phone 1-800-387-0074

Sales Fee Load **RRSP Eligibility** Foreign

Category Foreign Equity/Japan

Portfolio Manager/Years
Yoko Tilley—Fidelity Management/5

Minimum Initial Investment
RRSP $500 **Non-RRSP** $500

Extended Asset Mix

Cdn Equity	U.S. Equity	Europe	Japan	Far East	Latin America	Special Equity	Dividend	Domestic Bond	Global Bond	Money Market
			◆							

Objectives

Short Term	Mid Term	Long Term	Currency Effect	Sector Specific	Small Cap	Mid Cap	Large Cap
			◆				◆

Investment Styles

Top Down	Bottom Up	Value	Sector Rotation	Momentum	Indexation
	◆			◆	

Quantitative		Asset Breakout		Sector Breakout (Equity)
MER	3.00%	Cash	1.3%	Overweighted
Tax Efficiency	100.00%	Cdn Bonds		N/A
Std Deviation	5.14%	Foreign Bonds	1.3%	
Beta	0.79	Cdn Equity		Underweighted
Alpha	0.28	Foreign Equity	96.7%	N/A
R Squared	0.82	Warrants		

TRAILING 24-MONTH ANNUALIZED RETURNS FOR FIDELITY JAPANESE GROWTH FUND

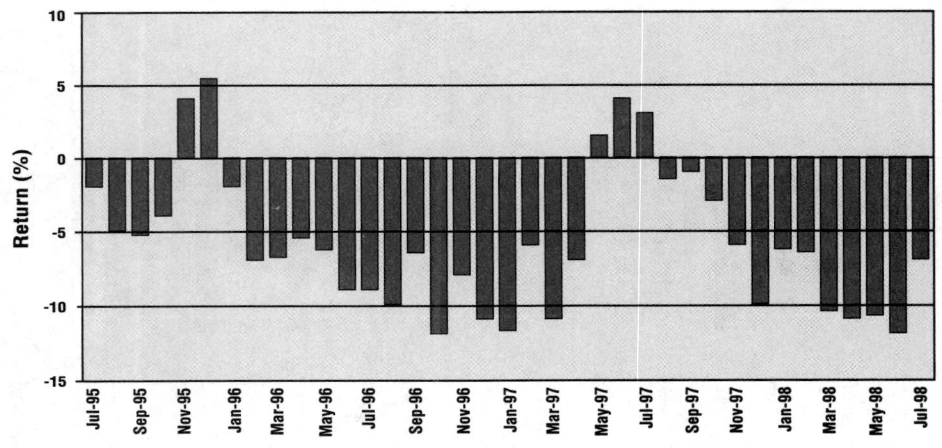

	Total Change	Annual Cmpd Rate	$10,000 Invested	24 Months Ending
Best	11.37%	5.53%	$11,137.11	December 1995
Worst	-22.37%	-11.89%	$7,762.63	June 1998
Average	-10.80%	-5.55%	$8,920.11	n/a

Green Line Japanese Growth Fund

MVA	3 Months*	1 Year*	3 Years*	5 Years*	1997	1996	1995
105.9	-0.4%	-22.6%	-8.2%	N/A	-15.6%	-10.4%	-5.9%

* Returns to July 31, 1998

Sponsor TD Asset Management Inc.
TD Bank Tower, P.O. Box 100
Toronto, Ontario, M5K 1G8
Phone 1-800-268-8166
Sales Fee No-Load **RRSP Eligibility** Foreign

Category Foreign Equity/Japan
Portfolio Manager/Years
Donald Farquharson—Schroder Capital Mngt./4
Minimum Initial Investment
RRSP $2,000 **Non-RRSP** $2,000

Extended Asset Mix: Cdn Equity, U.S. Equity, Europe, Japan ◆, Far East, Latin America, Special Equity, Dividend, Domestic Bond, Global Bond, Money Market

Objectives: Short Term, Mid Term, Long Term, Currency Effect ◆, Sector Specific, Small Cap, Mid Cap ◆, Large Cap ◆

Investment Styles: Top Down, Bottom Up ◆, Value, Sector Rotation, Momentum ◆, Indexation

Quantitative		Asset Breakout		Sector Breakout (Equity)
MER	2.59%	Cash	0.7%	Overweighted
Tax Efficiency	100.00%	Cdn Bonds		N/A
Std Deviation	5.14%	Foreign Bonds		
Beta	0.87	Cdn Equity		Underweighted
Alpha	0.25	Foreign Equity	98.5%	N/A
R Squared	0.93	Warrants		

TRAILING 24-MONTH ANNUALIZED RETURNS FOR GREEN LINE JAPANESE GROWTH FUND

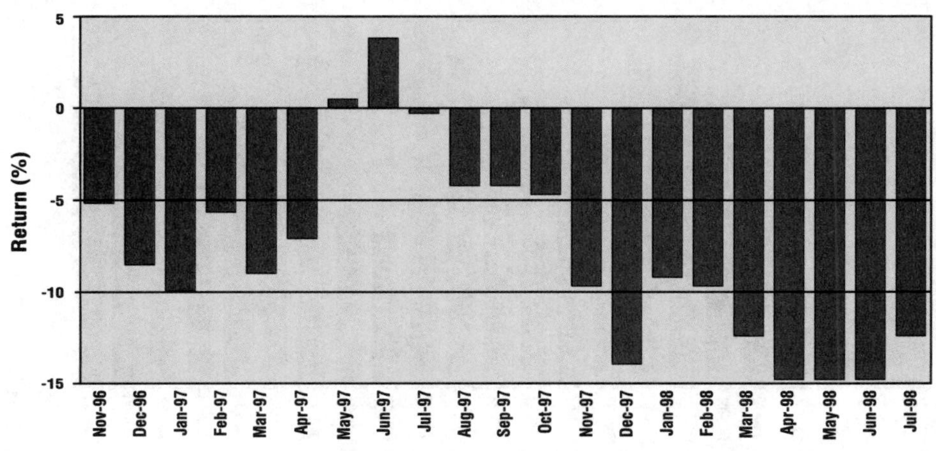

	Total Change	Annual Cmpd Rate	$10,000 Invested	24 Months Ending
Best	7.69%	3.77%	$10,769.22	June 1997
Worst	-27.41%	-14.80%	$7,259.28	May 1998
Average	-14.15%	-7.34%	$8,585.45	n/a

Universal European Opportunities Fund

MVA	3 Months*	1 Year*	3 Years*	5 Years*	1997	1996	1995
111.0	5.5%	44.5%	33.9%	N/A	20.0%	39.2%	28.8%

* Returns to July 31, 1998

Sponsor Mackenzie Financial Corporation
150 Bloor Street West, Suite M111
Toronto, Ontario, M5S 3B5

Phone 1-800-387-0614

Sales Fee Load **RRSP Eligibility** Foreign

Category Foreign Equity/Europe

Portfolio Manager/Years
Stephen Peak—Henderson International/4

Minimum Initial Investment
RRSP $500 **Non-RRSP** $500

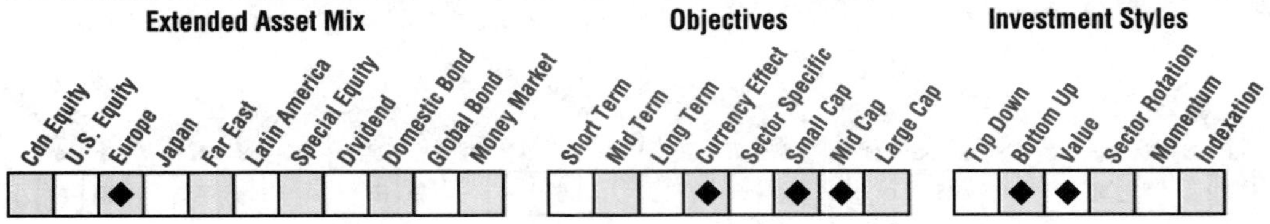

Quantitative		Asset Breakout		Sector Breakout (Equity)
MER	2.48%	Cash	2.6%	Overweighted
Tax Efficiency	97.35%	Cdn Bonds		N/A
Std Deviation	3.00%	Foreign Bonds	0.1%	
Beta	0.70	Cdn Equity		Underweighted
Alpha	1.10	Foreign Equity	94.7%	N/A
R Squared	0.40	Warrants	0.5%	

TRAILING 24-MONTH ANNUALIZED RETURNS FOR UNIVERSAL EUROPEAN OPPORTUNITIES FUND

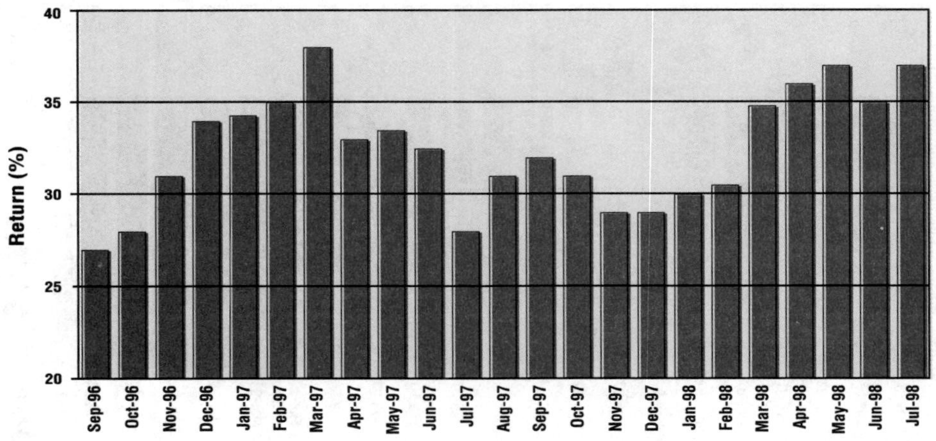

	Total Change	Annual Cmpd Rate	$10,000 Invested	24 Months Ending
Best	90.11%	37.88%	$19,010.91	March 1997
Worst	62.85%	27.61%	$16,285.12	September 1996
Average	76.33%	32.79%	$17,632.95	n/a

Fidelity European Growth Fund

MVA	3 Months*	1 Year*	3 Years*	5 Years*	1997	1996	1995
97.2	12.4%	49.0%	29.0%	26.1%	26.2%	22.9%	13.3%

* Returns to July 31, 1998

Sponsor Fidelity Investments Canada Ltd.
222 Bay Street, Suite 900
Toronto, Ontario, M5K 1P1

Phone 1-800-387-0074

Sales Fee Load **RRSP Eligibility** Foreign

Category Foreign Equity/Europe

Portfolio Manager/Years
Thierry Serero—Fidelity Management/1

Minimum Initial Investment
RRSP $500 **Non-RRSP** $500

Extended Asset Mix

Cdn Equity	U.S. Equity	Europe	Japan	Far East	Latin America	Special Equity	Dividend	Domestic Bond	Global Bond	Money Market
		◆								

Objectives

Short Term	Mid Term	Long Term	Currency Effect	Sector Specific	Small Cap	Mid Cap	Large Cap
			◆			◆	◆

Investment Styles

Top Down	Bottom Up	Value	Sector Rotation	Momentum	Indexation
	◆			◆	

Quantitative		Asset Breakout		Sector Breakout (Equity)
MER	2.70%	Cash	6.1%	Overweighted
Tax Efficiency	97.34%	Cdn Bonds		N/A
Std Deviation	2.86%	Foreign Bonds		
Beta	0.94	Cdn Equity		Underweighted
Alpha	0.07	Foreign Equity	91.4%	N/A
R Squared	0.92	Warrants		

TRAILING 24-MONTH ANNUALIZED RETURNS FOR FIDELITY EUROPEAN GROWTH FUND

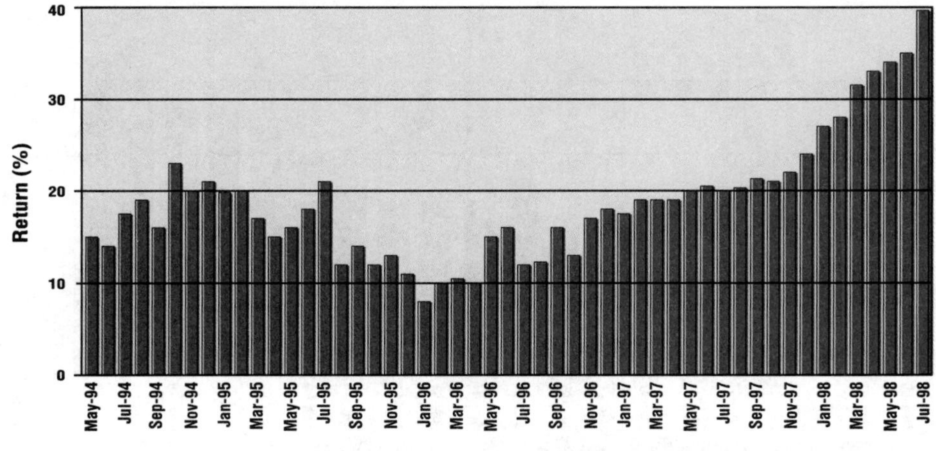

	Total Change	Annual Cmpd Rate	$10,000 Invested	24 Months Ending
Best	95.19%	39.71%	$19,519.08	July 1998
Worst	17.73%	8.51%	$11,773.45	January 1996
Average	42.92%	19.56%	$14,295.33	n/a

Global Strategy Europe Plus Fund

MVA	3 Months*	1 Year*	3 Years*	5 Years*	1997	1996	1995
94.5	6.7%	35.4%	24.5%	N/A	20.8%	24.2%	11.6%

* Returns to July 31, 1998

Sponsor Global Strategy Financial Inc.
33 Bloor Street East, Suite 1600
Toronto, Ontario, M4W 3T8
Phone 1-800-387-1229
Sales Fee Load **RRSP Eligibility** Foreign

Category Foreign Equity/Europe
Portfolio Manager/Years
Roger Guy—Gartmore Capital/4
Minimum Initial Investment
RRSP $1,000 **Non-RRSP** $1,000

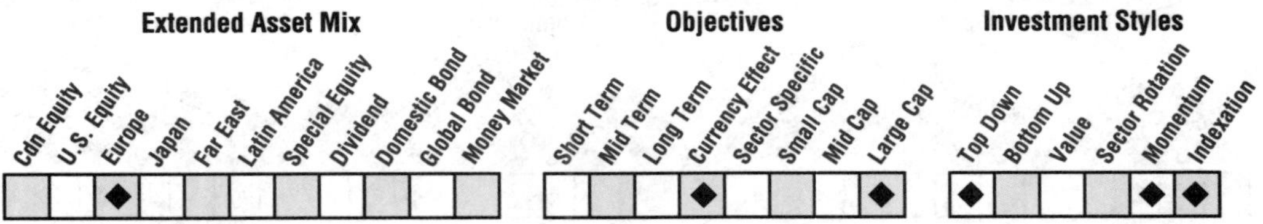

Quantitative		Asset Breakout		Sector Breakout (Equity)
MER	2.80%	Cash		Overweighted
Tax Efficiency	92.87%	Cdn Bonds		1 Financial
Std Deviation	2.71%	Foreign Bonds		2 Utilities
Beta	0.89	Cdn Equity		Underweighted
Alpha	-0.05	Foreign Equity	92.9%	1 Pipelines
R Squared	0.89	Warrants	0.2%	

TRAILING 24-MONTH ANNUALIZED RETURNS FOR GLOBAL STRATEGY EUROPE PLUS FUND

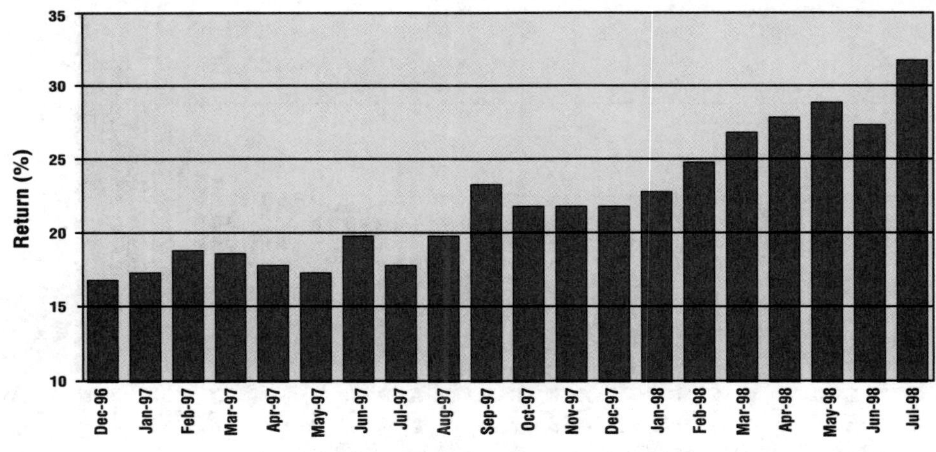

	Total Change	Annual Cmpd Rate	$10,000 Invested	24 Months Ending
Best	75.75%	32.57%	$17,575.30	July 1998
Worst	38.61%	17.73%	$13,860.52	May 1997
Average	51.47%	23.07%	$15,147.03	n/a

Green Line European Growth Fund

MVA	3 Months*	1 Year*	3 Years*	5 Years*	1997	1996	1995
94.5	9.1%	38.5%	28.4%	N/A	21.4%	27.6%	18.7%

* Returns to July 31, 1998

Sponsor TD Asset Management Inc.
TD Bank Tower, P.O. Box 100
Toronto, Ontario, M5K 1G8

Phone 1-800-268-8166

Sales Fee No-Load **RRSP Eligibility** Foreign

Category Foreign Equity/Europe

Portfolio Manager/Years
Patricia Maxwell-Arnot—Credit Suisse/4

Minimum Initial Investment
RRSP $2,000 **Non-RRSP** $2,000

Extended Asset Mix

Cdn Equity	U.S. Equity	Europe	Japan	Far East	Latin America	Special Equity	Dividend	Domestic Bond	Global Bond	Money Market
		◆								

Objectives

Short Term	Mid Term	Long Term	Currency Effect	Sector Specific	Small Cap	Mid Cap	Large Cap
			◆			◆	◆

Investment Styles

Top Down	Bottom Up	Value	Sector Rotation	Momentum	Indexation
	◆	◆		◆	

Quantitative		Asset Breakout		Sector Breakout (Equity)
MER	2.58%	Cash	5.6%	Overweighted
Tax Efficiency	100.00%	Cdn Bonds		N/A
Std Deviation	3.09%	Foreign Bonds	0.1%	
Beta	1.01	Cdn Equity		Underweighted
Alpha	-0.08	Foreign Equity	95.0%	N/A
R Squared	0.88	Warrants		

TRAILING 24-MONTH ANNUALIZED RETURNS FOR GREEN LINE EUROPEAN GROWTH FUND

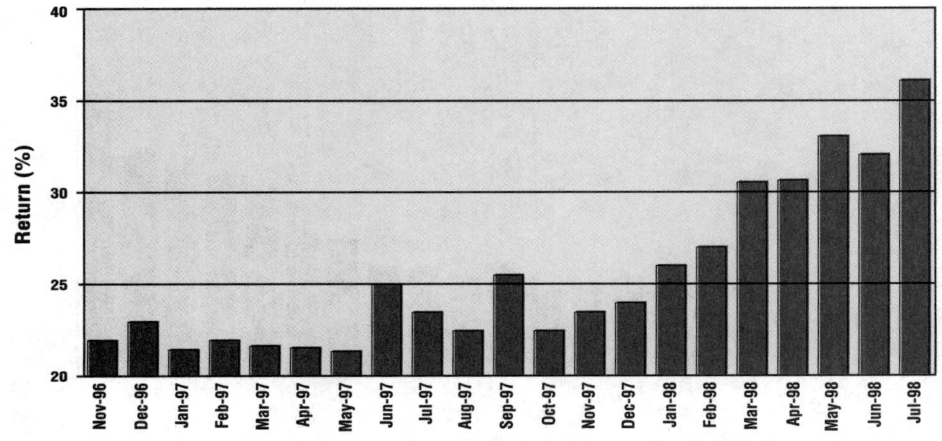

	Total Change	Annual Cmpd Rate	$10,000 Invested	24 Months Ending
Best	85.76%	36.29%	$18,575.66	July 1998
Worst	47.67%	21.52%	$14,767.20	May 1997
Average	58.63%	25.95%	$15,862.66	n/a

Hongkong Bank European Growth Fund

MVA	3 Months*	1 Year*	3 Years*	5 Years*	1997	1996	1995
94.2	14.6%	48.3%	29.5%	N/A	23.7%	22.4%	15.3%

* Returns to July 31, 1998

Sponsor Hongkong Bank Securities Inc.
1066 West Hastings Street, 25th Floor
Vancouver, British Columbia, V6E 3X1

Phone 1-800-830-8888

Sales Fee Load **RRSP Eligibility** Foreign

Category Foreign Equity/Europe

Portfolio Manager/Years
HSBC Canada/4

Minimum Initial Investment
RRSP $500 **Non-RRSP** $500

Extended Asset Mix

Cdn Equity	U.S. Equity	Europe	Japan	Far East	Latin America	Special Equity	Dividend	Domestic Bond	Global Bond	Money Market
		◆								

Objectives

Short Term	Mid Term	Long Term	Currency Effect	Sector Specific	Small Cap	Mid Cap	Large Cap
			◆			◆	◆

Investment Styles

Top Down	Bottom Up	Value	Sector Rotation	Momentum	Indexation
	◆		◆	◆	

Quantitative		Asset Breakout		Sector Breakout (Equity)
MER	2.12%	Cash	0.6%	Overweighted
Tax Efficiency	97.45%	Cdn Bonds		N/A
Std Deviation	3.09%	Foreign Bonds		
Beta	1.00	Cdn Equity		Underweighted
Alpha	-0.08	Foreign Equity	103.4%	N/A
R Squared	0.88	Warrants		

TRAILING 24-MONTH ANNUALIZED RETURNS FOR HONGKONG BANK EUROPEAN GROWTH FUND

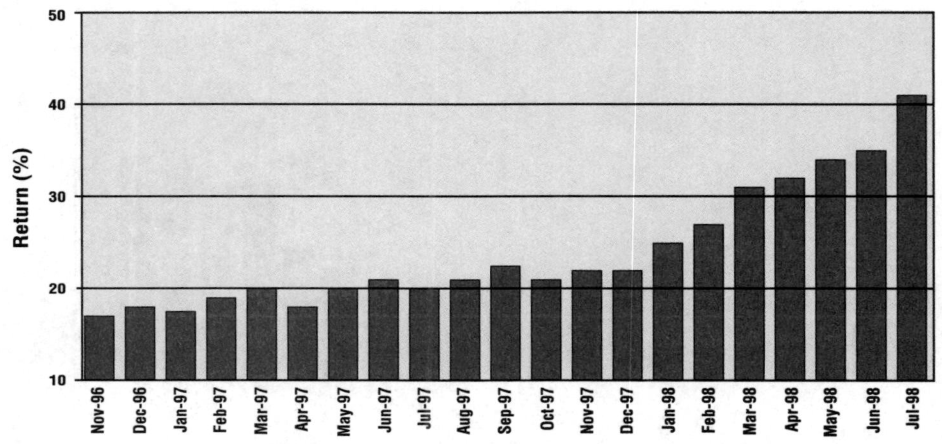

	Total Change	Annual Cmpd Rate	$10,000 Invested	24 Months Ending
Best	98.69%	40.96%	$19,869.46	July 1998
Worst	38.17%	17.55%	$13,817.39	November 1996
Average	55.86%	24.84%	$15,586.10	n/a

Bissett Multinational Growth Fund

MVA	3 Months*	1 Year*	3 Years*	5 Years*	1997	1996	1995
112.1	0.8%	17.7%	27.9%	N/A	33.9%	27.5%	22.0%

* Returns to July 31, 1998

Sponsor Bissett & Associates Inv Mngt
500 Fourth Street S.W., Suite 1120
Calgary, Alberta, T2P 2V6

Phone 1-800-267-3862

Sales Fee No-Load **RRSP Eligibility** Foreign

Category Foreign Equity/Global

Portfolio Manager/Years
David Bissett—Bissett & Assoc. Inv. Mngt./4

Minimum Initial Investment
RRSP $10,000 **Non-RRSP** $10,000

Extended Asset Mix

Cdn Equity	U.S. Equity	Europe	Japan	Far East	Latin America	Special Equity	Dividend	Domestic Bond	Global Bond	Money Market
◆	◆									

Objectives

Short Term	Mid Term	Long Term	Currency Effect	Sector Specific	Small Cap	Mid Cap	Large Cap
			◆			◆	◆

Investment Styles

Top Down	Bottom Up	Value	Sector Rotation	Momentum	Indexation
◆	◆			◆	

Quantitative		Asset Breakout		Sector Breakout (Equity)
MER	1.50%	Cash	5.1%	Overweighted
Tax Efficiency	98.09%	Cdn Bonds		1 Industrial
Std Deviation	3.00%	Foreign Bonds		2 Utilities
Beta	0.93	Cdn Equity	27.2%	Underweighted
Alpha	0.59	Foreign Equity	67.6%	1 Oil & Gas
R Squared	0.73	Warrants		2 Pipelines

TRAILING 24-MONTH ANNUALIZED RETURNS FOR BISSETT MULTINATIONAL GROWTH FUND

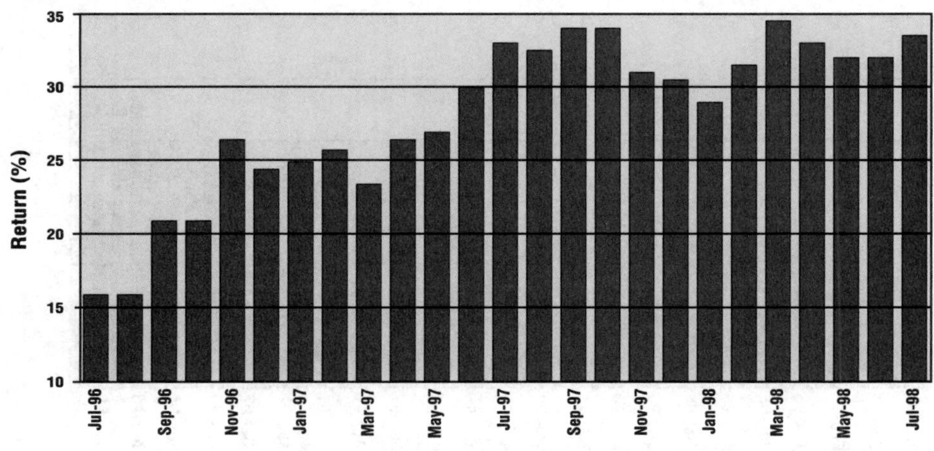

	Total Change	Annual Cmpd Rate	$10,000 Invested	24 Months Ending
Best	81.22%	34.62%	$18,122.00	March 1998
Worst	34.99%	16.18%	$13,498.73	July 1996
Average	65.48%	28.64%	$16,548.27	n/a

Ivy Foreign Equity Fund

MVA	3 Months*	1 Year*	3 Years*	5 Years*	1997	1996	1995
105.0	-0.4%	16.8%	19.0%	17.1%	23.2%	15.0%	16.4%

* Returns to July 31, 1998

Sponsor Mackenzie Financial Corporation
150 Bloor Street West, Suite M111
Toronto, Ontario, M5S 3B5

Phone 1-800-387-0614

Sales Fee Load **RRSP Eligibility** Foreign

Category Foreign Equity/Global

Portfolio Manager/Years
Bill Kanko—Bluewater Investment Mngt./4

Minimum Initial Investment
RRSP $500 **Non-RRSP** $500

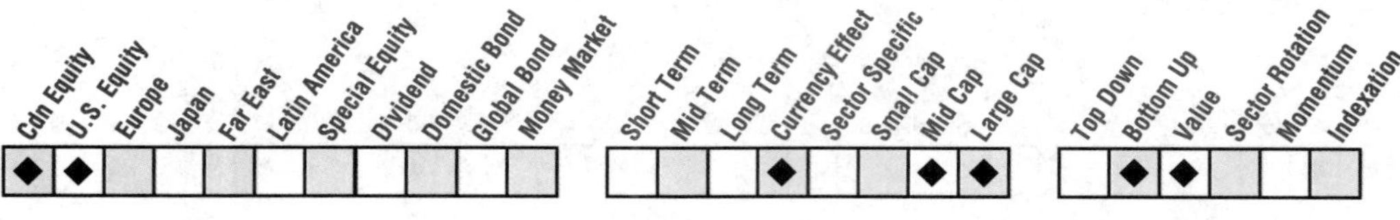

Quantitative		Asset Breakout		Sector Breakout (Equity)
MER	2.39%	Cash	20.9%	Overweighted
Tax Efficiency	93.18%	Cdn Bonds		1 Communication
Std Deviation	2.17%	Foreign Bonds		2 Utilities
Beta	0.61	Cdn Equity	5.4%	Underweighted
Alpha	0.66	Foreign Equity	73.6%	1 Consumer
R Squared	0.43	Warrants		2 Financial

TRAILING 24-MONTH ANNUALIZED RETURNS FOR IVY FOREIGN EQUITY FUND

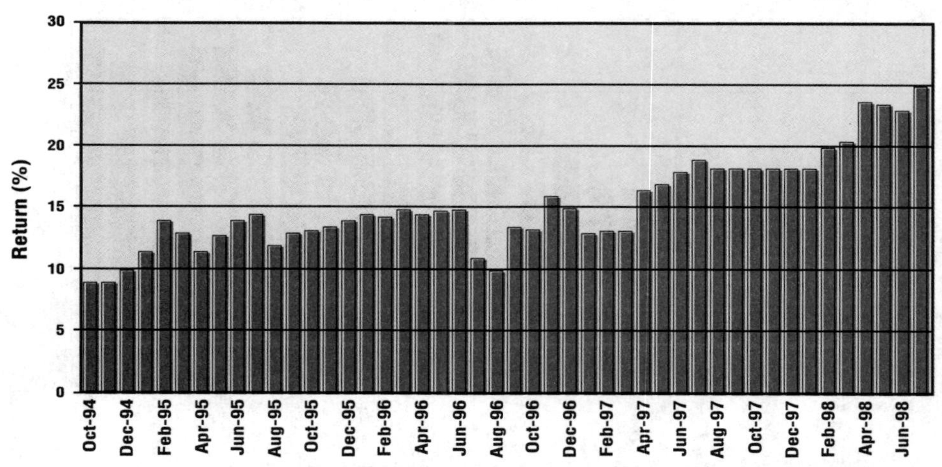

	Total Change	Annual Cmpd Rate	$10,000 Invested	24 Months Ending
Best	56.53%	25.11%	$15,653.42	July 1998
Worst	17.10%	8.21%	$11,709.82	October 1994
Average	33.72%	15.64%	$13,371.98	n/a

Fidelity International Portfolio Fund

MVA	3 Months*	1 Year*	3 Years*	5 Years*	1997	1996	1995
99.7	4.9%	19.2%	21.1%	18.3%	24.1%	16.0%	14.4%

* Returns to July 31, 1998

Sponsor Fidelity Investments Canada Ltd.
222 Bay Street, Suite 900
Toronto, Ontario, M5K 1P1

Phone 1-800-387-0074

Sales Fee Load **RRSP Eligibility** Foreign

Category Foreign Equity/Global

Portfolio Manager/Years
Richard Habermann—Fidelity Management/6

Minimum Initial Investment
RRSP $500 **Non-RRSP** $500

Extended Asset Mix

Cdn Equity	U.S. Equity	Europe	Japan	Far East	Latin America	Special Equity	Dividend	Domestic Bond	Global Bond	Money Market
	◆	◆	◆							

Objectives

Short Term	Mid Term	Long Term	Currency Effect	Sector Specific	Small Cap	Mid Cap	Large Cap
			◆				◆

Investment Styles

Top Down	Bottom Up	Value	Sector Rotation	Momentum	Indexation
	◆			◆	

Quantitative		Asset Breakout		Sector Breakout (Equity)
MER	2.69%	Cash	3.1%	Overweighted
Tax Efficiency	95.27%	Cdn Bonds		1 Industrial
Std Deviation	2.74%	Foreign Bonds	0.1%	2 Utilities
Beta	0.96	Cdn Equity	3.1%	Underweighted
Alpha	-0.03	Foreign Equity	93.0%	1 Oil & Gas
R Squared	0.86	Warrants		2 Pipelines

TRAILING 24-MONTH ANNUALIZED RETURNS FOR FIDELITY INTERNATIONAL PORTFOLIO FUND

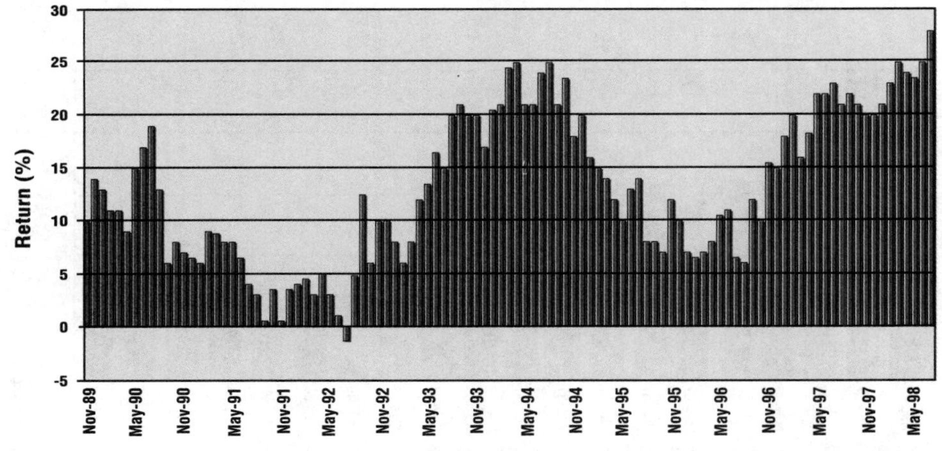

	Total Change	Annual Cmpd Rate	$10,000 Invested	24 Months Ending
Best	65.46%	28.63%	$16,546.04	July 1998
Worst	-2.75%	-1.38%	$9,724.98	July 1992
Average	29.34%	13.73%	$12,933.60	n/a

Global Strategy World Companies Fund

MVA	3 Months*	1 Year*	3 Years*	5 Years*	1997	1996	1995
98.9	4.1%	14.2%	21.0%	N/A	6.7%	19.9%	52.8%

* Returns to July 31, 1998

Sponsor Global Strategy Financial Inc.
33 Bloor Street East, Suite 1600
Toronto, Ontario, M4W 3T8
Phone 1-800-387-1229
Sales Fee Load **RRSP Eligibility** Foreign

Category Foreign Equity/Global
Portfolio Manager
Rupert Robertson—Rothchild Inv. Mngt.
Minimum Initial Investment
RRSP $1,000 **Non-RRSP** $1,000

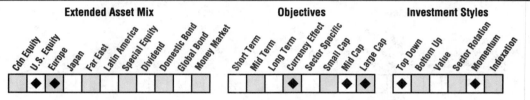

Extended Asset Mix

Cdn Equity	U.S. Equity	Europe	Japan	Far East	Latin America	Special Equity	Dividend	Domestic Bond	Global Bond	Money Market
	◆	◆								

Objectives

Short Term	Mid Term	Long Term	Currency Effect	Sector Specific	Small Cap	Mid Cap	Large Cap
			◆			◆	◆

Investment Styles

Top Down	Bottom Up	Value	Sector Rotation	Momentum	Indexation
◆				◆	

Quantitative		Asset Breakout		Sector Breakout (Equity)
MER	2.89%	Cash	0.1%	Overweighted
Tax Efficiency	95.70%	Cdn Bonds		1 Industrial
Std Deviation	3.06%	Foreign Bonds	0.2%	2 Utilities
Beta	0.82	Cdn Equity	1.9%	Underweighted
Alpha	0.79	Foreign Equity	94.9%	1 Financial
R Squared	0.37	Warrants		

TRAILING 24-MONTH ANNUALIZED RETURNS FOR GLOBAL STRATEGY WORLD COMPANIES FUND

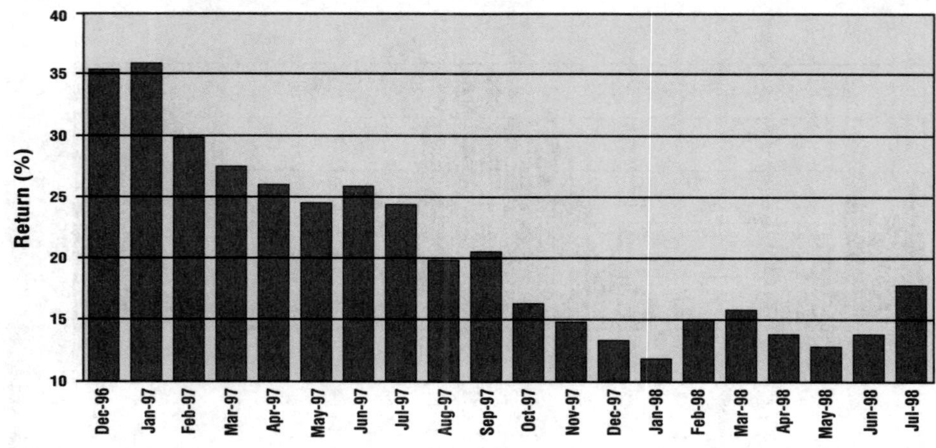

	Total Change	Annual Cmpd Rate	$10,000 Invested	24 Months Ending
Best	85.29%	36.12%	$18,529.24	January 1997
Worst	25.57%	12.06%	$12,556.76	January 1998
Average	46.97%	21.23%	$14,698.63	n/a

AGF International Value Fund

MVA	3 Months*	1 Year*	3 Years*	5 Years*	1997	1996	1995
98.6	2.3%	18.6%	20.1%	17.9%	23.6%	19.0%	15.0%

* Returns to July 31, 1998

Sponsor AGF Funds Inc.
66 Wellington Street West, 31st Floor
Toronto, Ontario, M5K 1E9

Phone 1-800-268-8583

Sales Fee Load **RRSP Eligibility** Foreign

Category Foreign Equity/Global

Portfolio Manager/Years
Charles Brandes—Brandes Investments/4

Minimum Initial Investment
RRSP $500 **Non-RRSP** $500

Extended Asset Mix

Cdn Equity	U.S. Equity	Europe	Japan	Far East	Latin America	Special Equity	Dividend	Domestic Bond	Global Bond	Money Market
	◆	◆								

Objectives

Short Term	Mid Term	Long Term	Currency Effect	Sector Specific	Small Cap	Mid Cap	Large Cap
			◆				◆

Investment Styles

Top Down	Bottom Up	Value	Sector Rotation	Momentum	Indexation
	◆	◆			

Quantitative		Asset Breakout		Sector Breakout (Equity)
MER	2.77%	Cash	2.4%	Overweighted
Tax Efficiency	98.66%	Cdn Bonds		N/A
Std Deviation	3.06%	Foreign Bonds		
Beta	0.85	Cdn Equity		Underweighted
Alpha	0.24	Foreign Equity	98.1%	N/A
R Squared	0.51	Warrants		

TRAILING 24-MONTH ANNUALIZED RETURNS FOR AGF INTERNATIONAL VALUE FUND

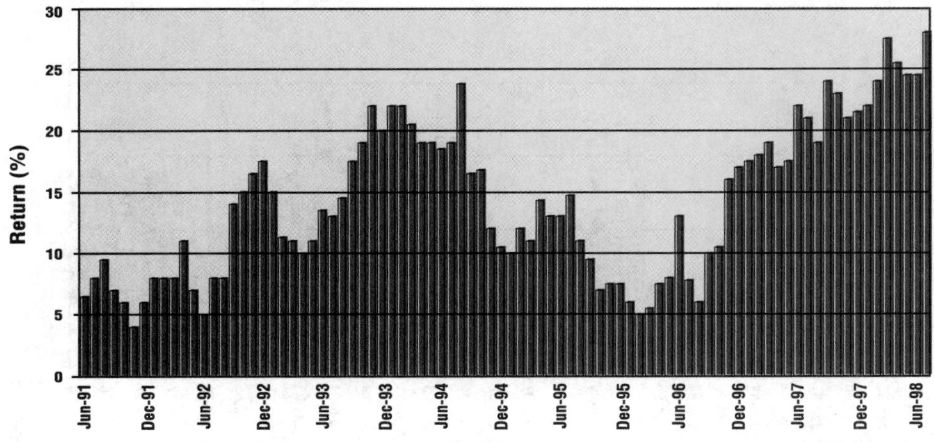

	Total Change	Annual Cmpd Rate	$10,000 Invested	24 Months Ending
Best	65.31%	28.57%	$16,530.76	July 1998
Worst	9.38%	4.58%	$10,937.83	November 1991
Average	31.68%	14.75%	$13,167.51	n/a

Templeton Growth Fund

MVA	3 Months*	1 Year*	3 Years*	5 Years*	1997	1996	1995
97.9	-4.8%	4.5%	13.5%	15.4%	17.1%	18.4%	14.1%

* Returns to July 31, 1998

Sponsor Templeton Management Ltd
1 Adelaide St. East, Suite 2101
Toronto, Ontario, M5C 3B8

Phone 1-800-387-0830

Sales Fee Load **RRSP Eligibility** Foreign

Category Foreign Equity/Global

Portfolio Manager/Years
Mark Holowesko—Templeton Management/12

Minimum Initial Investment
RRSP $500 **Non-RRSP** $500

Extended Asset Mix

Cdn Equity	U.S. Equity	Europe	Japan	Far East	Latin America	Special Equity	Dividend	Domestic Bond	Global Bond	Money Market
	◆	◆								

Objectives

Short Term	Mid Term	Long Term	Currency Effect	Sector Specific	Small Cap	Mid Cap	Large Cap
			◆			◆	◆

Investment Styles

Top Down	Bottom Up	Value	Sector Rotation	Momentum	Indexation
	◆	◆			

Quantitative		Asset Breakout		Sector Breakout (Equity)
MER	2.00%	Cash	22.7%	Overweighted
Tax Efficiency	77.63%	Cdn Bonds		1 Metals–Minerals
Std Deviation	2.57%	Foreign Bonds	2.2%	2 Utilities
Beta	0.78	Cdn Equity	1.0%	Underweighted
Alpha	0.04	Foreign Equity	69.5%	1 Industrial
R Squared	0.68	Warrants		2 Financial

TRAILING 24-MONTH ANNUALIZED RETURNS FOR TEMPLETON GROWTH FUND

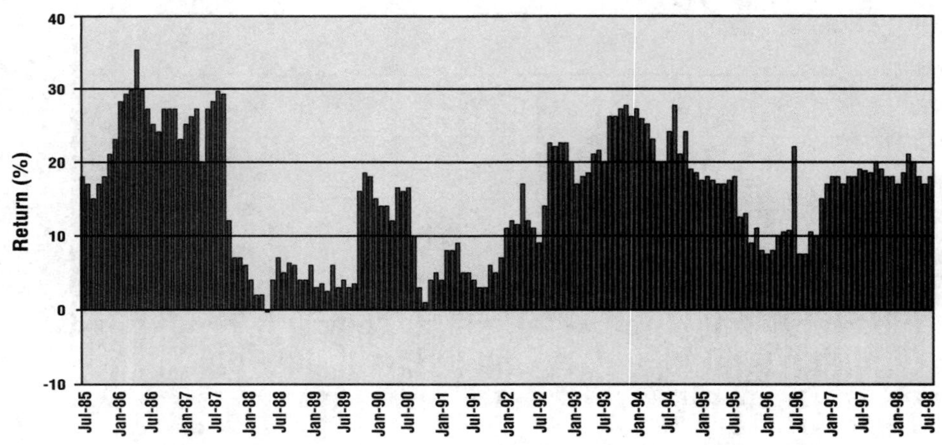

	Total Change	Annual Cmpd Rate	$10,000 Invested	24 Months Ending
Best	83.09%	35.31%	$18,309.17	May 1986
Worst	-0.58%	-0.29%	$9,941.68	May 1988
Average	33.35%	15.48%	$13,334.87	n/a

Investors Real Property Fund

MVA	3 Months*	1 Year*	3 Years*	5 Years*	1997	1996	1995
126.0	1.7%	8.5%	5.7%	3.9%	7.4%	4.2%	4.3%

* Returns to July 31, 1998

Sponsor Investors Group Trust Co., Ltd.
One Canada Centre, 447 Portage Ave.
Winnipeg, Manitoba, R3C 3B6

Phone 1-800-644-7707

Sales Fee Load **RRSP Eligibility** Yes

Category Specialty/Real Estate

Portfolio Manager/Years
Murray Mitchell—Investors Group/4

Minimum Initial Investment
RRSP $1,000 **Non-RRSP** $1,000

Extended Asset Mix

Cdn Equity	U.S. Equity	Europe	Japan	Far East	Latin America	Special Equity	Dividend	Domestic Bond	Global Bond	Money Market
						◆				

Objectives

Short Term	Mid Term	Long Term	Currency Effect	Sector Specific	Small Cap	Mid Cap	Large Cap
				◆			

Investment Styles

Top Down	Bottom Up	Value	Sector Rotation	Momentum	Indexation
	◆	◆			

Quantitative		Asset Breakout*		Sector Breakout (Equity)
MER	2.37%	Cash	39.2%	Overweighted
Tax Efficiency	53.06%	Cdn Bonds	5.1%	1 Real Estate
Std Deviation	0.38%	Foreign Bonds		2 Utilities
Beta	N/A	Cdn Equity	0.4%	Underweighted
Alpha	0.32	Foreign Equity		1 Financial
R Squared	N/A	Warrants		

* Holds physical real estate which is not shown in this asset breakout.

TRAILING 24-MONTH ANNUALIZED RETURNS FOR INVESTORS REAL PROPERTY FUND

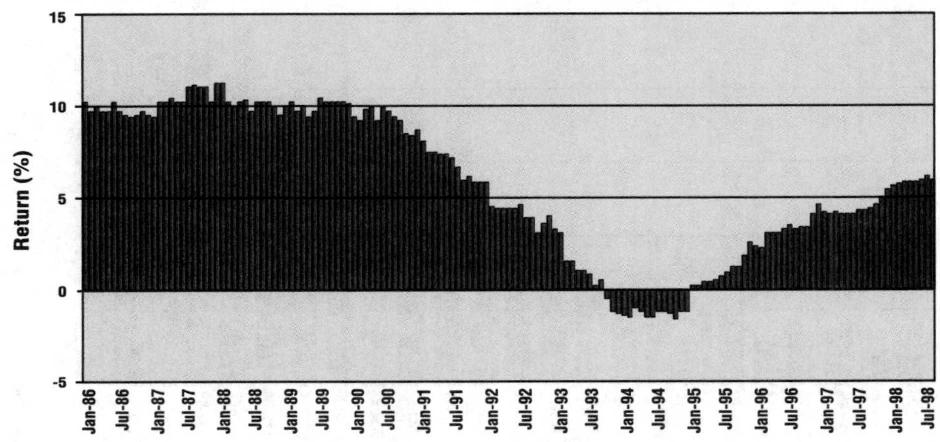

	Total Change	Annual Cmpd Rate	$10,000 Invested	24 Months Ending
Best	23.21%	11.00%	$12,321.08	December 1987
Worst	-3.14%	-1.58%	$9,686.32	September 1994
Average	11.74%	5.71%	$11,174.28	n/a

Great-West Life Canadian Real Estate Fund

MVA	3 Months*	1 Year*	3 Years*	5 Years*	1997	1996	1995
113.3	1.6%	14.4%	7.1%	N/A	13.6%	2.8%	0.1%

* Returns to July 31, 1998

Sponsor Great-West Life Assurance Co.
60 Osborne Street North
Winnipeg, Manitoba, R3C 3A5

Phone 1-204-946-1190

Sales Fee Load **RRSP Eligibility** Yes

Category Specialty/Real Estate

Portfolio Manager/Years
Not Available

Minimum Initial Investment
RRSP $50 **Non-RRSP** $50

Extended Asset Mix

Cdn Equity	U.S. Equity	Europe	Japan	Far East	Latin America	Special Equity	Dividend	Domestic Bond	Global Bond	Money Market
						◆				

Objectives

Short Term	Mid Term	Long Term	Currency Effect	Sector Specific	Small Cap	Mid Cap	Large Cap
				◆			

Investment Styles

Top Down	Bottom Up	Value	Sector Rotation	Momentum	Indexation
	◆	◆			

Quantitative		Asset Breakout*		Sector Breakout (Equity)
MER	2.71%	Cash	20.8%	Overweighted
Tax Efficiency	N/A	Cdn Bonds		N/A
Std Deviation	0.98%	Foreign Bonds		
Beta	0.02	Cdn Equity		Underweighted
Alpha	0.42	Foreign Equity		N/A
R Squared	0.01	Warrants		

* Eighty-eight percent of assets are in physical real estate.

TRAILING 24-MONTH ANNUALIZED RETURNS FOR GREAT-WEST LIFE CDN REAL ESTATE FUND

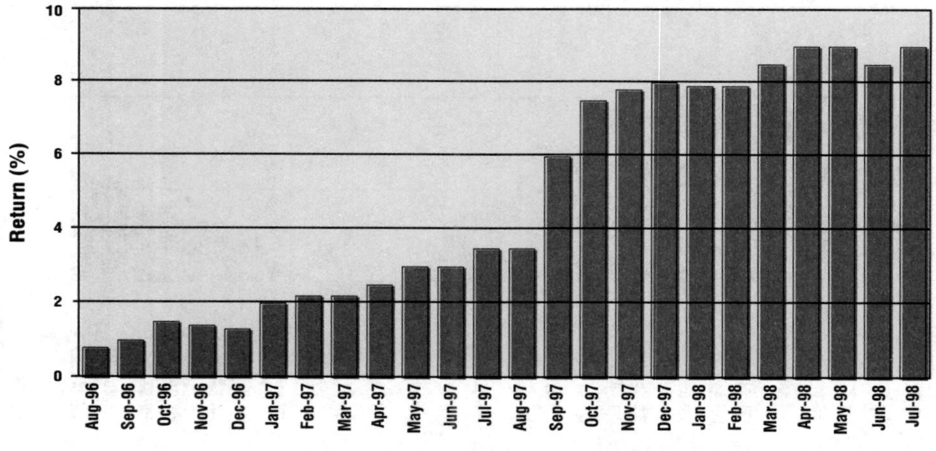

	Total Change	Annual Cmpd Rate	$10,000 Invested	24 Months Ending
Best	19.35%	9.25%	$11,935.11	May 1998
Worst	1.44%	0.72%	$10,143.84	August 1996
Average	10.39%	5.07%	$11,039.40	n/a

Royal Precious Metals Fund

MVA	3 Months*	1 Year*	3 Years*	5 Years*	1997	1996	1995
118.7	-22.0%	-30.2%	-2.8%	4.2%	-33.7%	38.8%	63.8%

* Returns to July 31, 1998

Sponsor Royal Mutual Funds Inc.
Royal Trust Tower, 5th Floor
Toronto, Ontario, M5W 1P9

Phone 1-800-463-3863

Sales Fee No-Load **RRSP Eligibility** Yes

Category Specialty/Precious Metals

Portfolio Manager/Years
John Embry—Royal Bank Investment Mngt./10

Minimum Initial Investment
RRSP $1,000 **Non-RRSP** $1,000

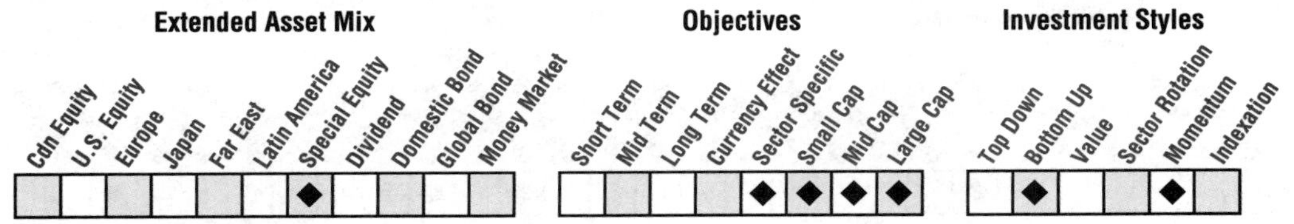

Quantitative		Asset Breakout		Sector Breakout (Equity)
MER	2.41%	Cash	2.3%	Overweighted
Tax Efficiency	100.00%	Cdn Bonds	1.3%	1 Goods & Services
Std Deviation	9.32%	Foreign Bonds	1.0%	2 Utilities
Beta	0.81	Cdn Equity	78.6%	Underweighted
Alpha	1.09	Foreign Equity	13.4%	1 Financial
R Squared	0.75	Warrants	0.8%	

TRAILING 24-MONTH ANNUALIZED RETURNS FOR ROYAL PRECIOUS METALS FUND

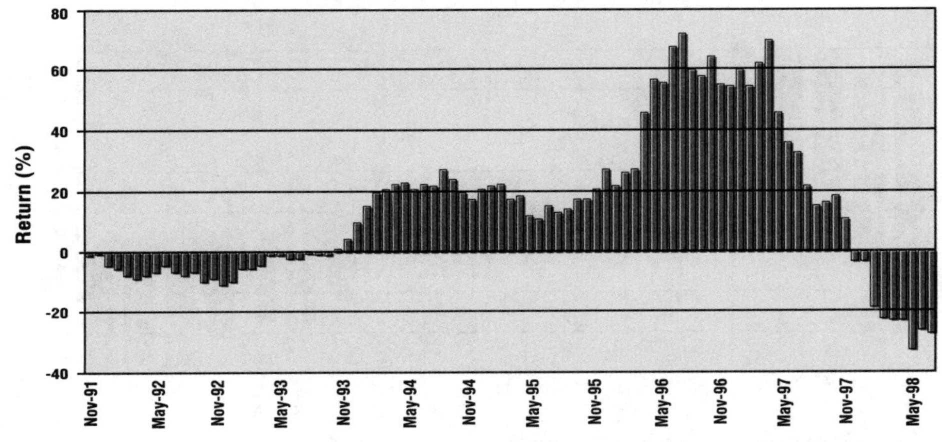

	Total Change	Annual Cmpd Rate	$10,000 Invested	24 Months Ending
Best	175.09%	65.86%	$27,508.83	May 1996
Worst	-50.19%	-29.42%	$4,980.98	May 1998
Average	35.64%	16.46%	$13,563.99	n/a

Green Line Precious Metals Fund

MVA	3 Months*	1 Year*	3 Years*	5 Years*	1997	1996	1995
113.6	-24.8%	-34.4%	-5.8%	N/A	-41.0%	70.1%	23.5%

* Returns to July 31, 1998

Sponsor TD Asset Management Inc.
TD Bank Tower, P.O. Box 100
Toronto, Ontario, M5K 1G8
Phone 1-800-268-8166
Sales Fee No-Load **RRSP Eligibility** Yes

Category Specialty/Precious Metals
Portfolio Manager/Years
John Weatherall—TD Asset Management/4
Minimum Initial Investment
RRSP $2,000 **Non-RRSP** $2,000

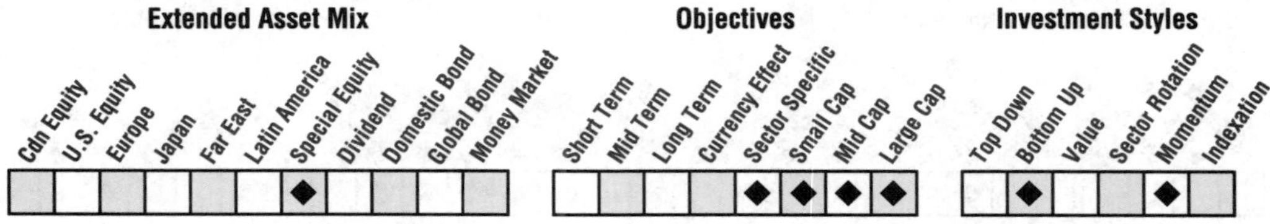

Quantitative		Asset Breakout		Sector Breakout (Equity)
MER	2.12%	Cash	1.8%	Overweighted
Tax Efficiency	100.00%	Cdn Bonds	3.6%	1 Goods & Services
Std Deviation	9.58%	Foreign Bonds		2 Utilities
Beta	0.81	Cdn Equity	70.9%	Underweighted
Alpha	1.04	Foreign Equity	20.4%	1 Metals–Minerals
R Squared	0.69	Warrants	1.5%	2 Financial

TRAILING 24-MONTH ANNUALIZED RETURNS FOR GREEN LINE PRECIOUS METALS FUND

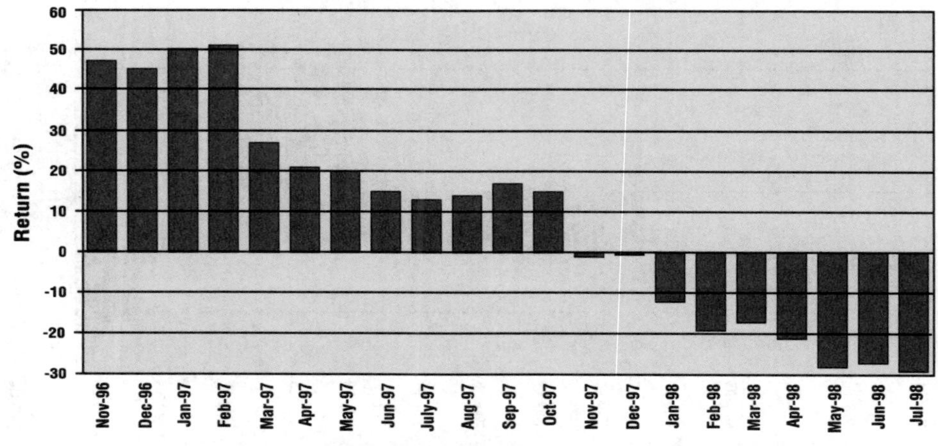

	Total Change	Annual Cmpd Rate	$10,000 Invested	24 Months Ending
Best	127.07%	50.69%	$22,707.39	February 1997
Worst	-50.18%	-29.42%	$4,982.16	July 1998
Average	25.99%	12.25%	$12,599.27	n/a

MAXXUM Precious Metals Fund

MVA	3 Months*	1 Year*	3 Years*	5 Years*	1997	1996	1995
108.9	-29.0%	-37.8%	-11.3%	-3.9%	-44.2%	58.7%	18.5%

* Returns to July 31, 1998

Sponsor London Fund Management Limited
33 Yonge Street, Suite 810
Toronto, Ontario, M5E 1G4

Phone 1-888-462-9986

Sales Fee Load **RRSP Eligibility** Yes

Category Specialty/Precious Metals

Portfolio Manager/Years
Martin Anstee—London Fund Management/3

Minimum Initial Investment
RRSP $500 **Non-RRSP** $500

Extended Asset Mix

Cdn Equity	U.S. Equity	Europe	Japan	Far East	Latin America	Special Equity	Dividend	Domestic Bond	Global Bond	Money Market
						◆				

Objectives

Short Term	Mid Term	Long Term	Currency Effect	Sector Specific	Small Cap	Mid Cap	Large Cap
				◆	◆	◆	◆

Investment Style

Top Down	Bottom Up	Value	Sector Rotation	Momentum	Indexation
	◆			◆	

Quantitative		Asset Breakout		Sector Breakout (Equity)
MER	2.23%	Cash	8.0%	Overweighted
Tax Efficiency	100.00%	Cdn Bonds		1 Goods & Services
Std Deviation	10.36%	Foreign Bonds		2 Utilities
Beta	0.88	Cdn Equity	68.8%	Underweighted
Alpha	0.47	Foreign Equity	20.0%	1 Metals–Minerals
R Squared	0.72	Warrants	0.1%	2 Financial

TRAILING 24-MONTH ANNUALIZED RETURNS FOR MAXXUM PRECIOUS METALS FUND

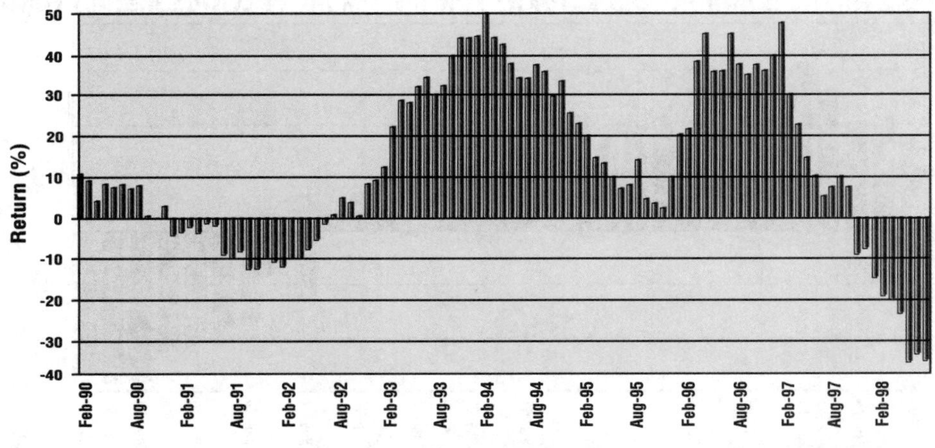

	Total Change	Annual Cmpd Rate	$10,000 Invested	24 Months Ending
Best	124.31%	49.77%	$22,430.74	March 1994
Worst	-57.64%	-34.92%	$4,235.57	May 1998
Average	31.00%	17.16%	$13,099.95	n/a

Universal Precious Metals Fund

MVA	3 Months*	1 Year*	3 Years*	5 Years*	1997	1996	1995
107.1	-24.3%	-28.7%	-11.7%	N/A	-35.2%	34.1%	6.4%

* Returns to July 31, 1998

Sponsor Mackenzie Financial Corporation
150 Bloor Street West, Suite M111
Toronto, Ontario, M5S 3B5

Phone 1-800-387-0614

Sales Fee Load **RRSP Eligibility** Yes

Category Specialty/Precious Metals

Portfolio Manager/Years
Fred Sturn—Mackenzie Financial/5

Minimum Initial Investment
RRSP $500 **Non-RRSP** $500

Extended Asset Mix

Cdn Equity	U.S. Equity	Europe	Japan	Far East	Latin America	Special Equity	Dividend	Domestic Bond	Global Bond	Money Market
						◆				

Objectives

Short Term	Mid Term	Long Term	Currency Effect	Sector Specific	Small Cap	Mid Cap	Large Cap
			◆	◆	◆	◆	

Investment Styles

Top Down	Bottom Up	Value	Sector Rotation	Momentum	Indexation
	◆			◆	

Quantitative		Asset Breakout*		Sector Breakout (Equity)
MER	2.42%	Cash		Overweighted
Tax Efficiency	100.00%	Cdn Bonds	1.2%	1 Goods & Services
Std Deviation	9.79%	Foreign Bonds		2 Utilities
Beta	0.91	Cdn Equity	53.4%	Underweighted
Alpha	0.50	Foreign Equity	21.2%	1 Metals–Minerals
R Squared	0.78	Warrants	0.4%	2 Financial

**This fund holds gold and silver which are not shown in this asset breakout*

TRAILING 24-MONTH ANNUALIZED RETURNS FOR UNIVERSAL PRECIOUS METALS FUND

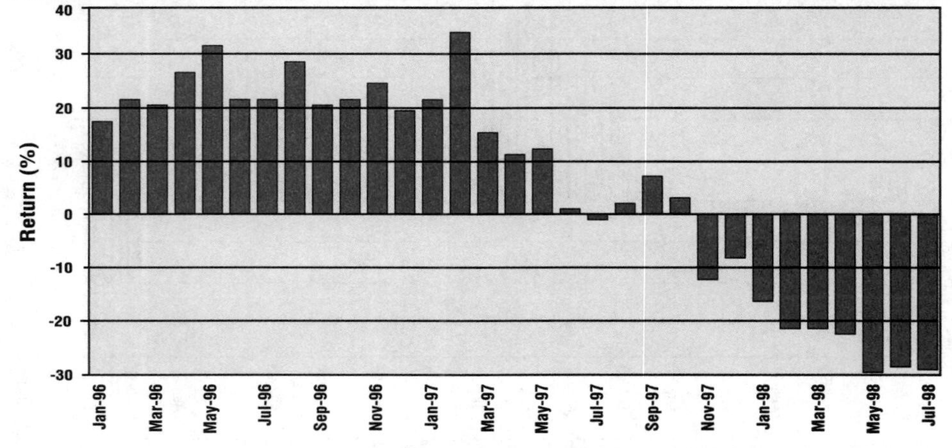

	Total Change	Annual Cmpd Rate	$10,000 Invested	24 Months Ending
Best	78.66%	33.66%	$17,866.33	February 1997
Worst	-50.09%	-29.35%	$4,991.12	May 1998
Average	18.19%	8.72%	$11,818.99	n/a

Royal Energy Fund

MVA	3 Months*	1 Year*	3 Years*	5 Years*	1997	1996	1995
114.3	-18.4%	-24.3%	5.8%	1.4%	3.3%	39.0%	8.1%

* Returns to July 31, 1998

Sponsor Royal Mutual Funds Inc.
Royal Trust Tower, 5th Floor
Toronto, Ontario, M5W 1P9

Phone 1-800-463-3863

Sales Fee No-Load **RRSP Eligibility** Yes

Category Specialty/Resources

Portfolio Manager/Years
Gordon Zive—Royal Bank Investment Mngt./4

Minimum Initial Investment
RRSP $1,000 **Non-RRSP** $1,000

Extended Asset Mix

Cdn Equity	U.S. Equity	Europe	Japan	Far East	Latin America	Special Equity	Dividend	Domestic Bond	Global Bond	Money Market
						◆				

Objectives

Short Term	Mid Term	Long Term	Currency Effect	Sector Specific	Small Cap	Mid Cap	Large Cap
				◆		◆	◆

Investment Styles

Top Down	Bottom Up	Value	Sector Rotation	Momentum	Indexation
	◆			◆	

Quantitative		Asset Breakout		Sector Breakout (Equity)
MER	2.28%	Cash	10.7%	Overweighted
Tax Efficiency	100.00%	Cdn Bonds		1 Oil & Gas
Std Deviation	5.57%	Foreign Bonds		2 Utilities
Beta	0.82	Cdn Equity	89.4%	Underweighted
Alpha	0.13	Foreign Equity		1 Financial
R Squared	0.45	Warrants		

TRAILING 24-MONTH ANNUALIZED RETURNS FOR ROYAL ENERGY FUND

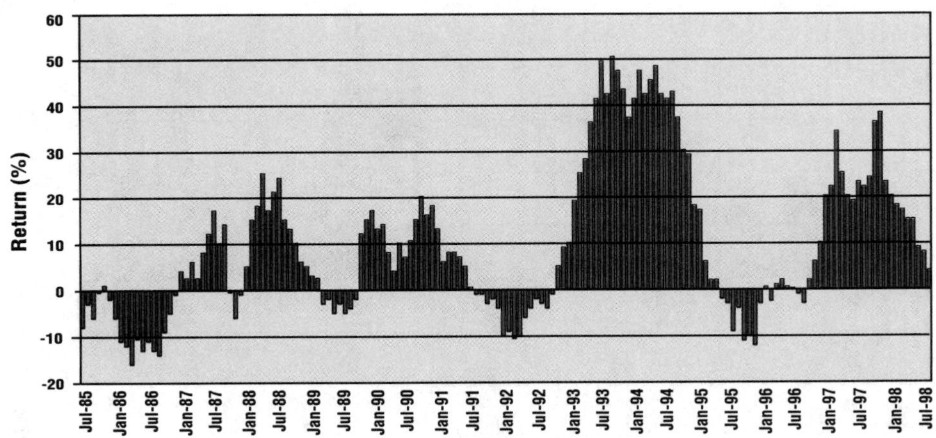

	Total Change	Annual Cmpd Rate	$10,000 Invested	24 Months Ending
Best	126.23%	50.54%	$22,662.92	August 1993
Worst	-29.92%	-16.29%	$7,007.60	April 1986
Average	23.73%	11.24%	$12,373.44	n/a

20/20 Canadian Resources Fund

MVA	3 Months*	1 Year*	3 Years*	5 Years*	1997	1996	1995
111.8	-26.9%	-35.0%	0.1%	-0.9%	-9.4%	50.5%	13.3%

* Returns to July 31, 1998

Sponsor AGF Funds Inc.
66 Wellington Street West, 31st Floor
Toronto, Ontario, M5K 1E9

Phone 1-800-268-8583

Sales Fee Load **RRSP Eligibility** Yes

Category Specialty/Resources

Portfolio Manager/Years
Bob Farquharson—AGF/39

Minimum Initial Investment
RRSP $1,000 **Non-RRSP** $1,000

Extended Asset Mix

Cdn Equity	U.S. Equity	Europe	Japan	Far East	Latin America	Special Equity	Dividend	Domestic Bond	Global Bond	Money Market
◆						◆				

Objectives

Short Term	Mid Term	Long Term	Currency Effect	Sector Specific	Small Cap	Mid Cap	Large Cap
				◆		◆	◆

Investment Styles

Top Down	Bottom Up	Value	Sector Rotation	Momentum	Indexation
◆				◆	

Quantitative		Asset Breakout		Sector Breakout (Equity)
MER	2.88%	Cash	0.4%	Overweighted
Tax Efficiency	100.00%	Cdn Bonds	0.8%	1 Oil & Gas
Std Deviation	6.64%	Foreign Bonds		2 Utilities
Beta	1.10	Cdn Equity	89.7%	Underweighted
Alpha	-0.06	Foreign Equity	6.0%	1 Goods & Services
R Squared	0.71	Warrants	3.5%	2 Financial

TRAILING 24-MONTH ANNUALIZED RETURNS FOR 20/20 CANADIAN RESOURCES FUND

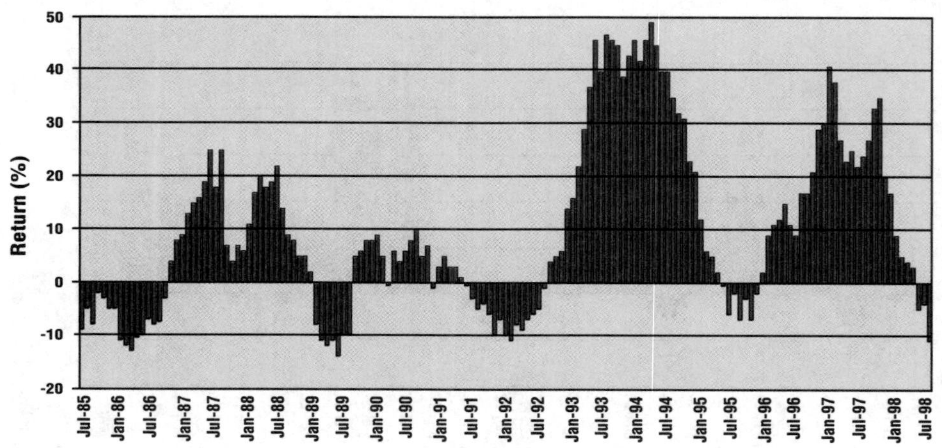

	Total Change	Annual Cmpd Rate	$10,000 Invested	24 Months Ending
Best	123.24%	49.41%	$22,323.88	April 1994
Worst	-25.53%	-13.71%	$7,446.59	July 1989
Average	23.53%	11.15%	$12,353.35	n/a

Green Line Energy Fund

MVA	3 Months*	1 Year*	3 Years*	5 Years*	1997	1996	1995
109.3	-28.5%	-47.2%	-4.4%	N/A	-2.7%	41.3%	7.6%

* Returns to July 31, 1998

Sponsor TD Asset Management Inc.
TD Bank Tower, P.O. Box 100
Toronto, Ontario, M5K 1G8
Phone 1-800-268-8166
Sales Fee No-Load **RRSP Eligibility** Yes

Category Specialty/Resources
Portfolio Manager/Years
Rob Cassels—TD Asset Management/4
Minimum Initial Investment
RRSP $2,000 **Non-RRSP** $2,000

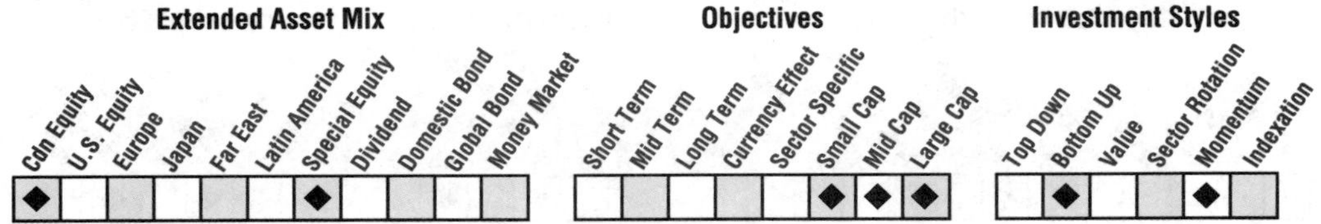

Quantitative		Asset Breakout		Sector Breakout (Equity)
MER	2.10%	Cash	3.9%	Overweighted
Tax Efficiency	100.00%	Cdn Bonds	1.0%	1 Oil & Gas
Std Deviation	6.44%	Foreign Bonds		2 Utilities
Beta	0.77	Cdn Equity	89.0%	Underweighted
Alpha	-0.06	Foreign Equity	3.7%	1 Transportation
R Squared	0.48	Warrants	2.3%	2 Financial

TRAILING 24-MONTH ANNUALIZED RETURNS FOR GREEN LINE ENERGY FUND

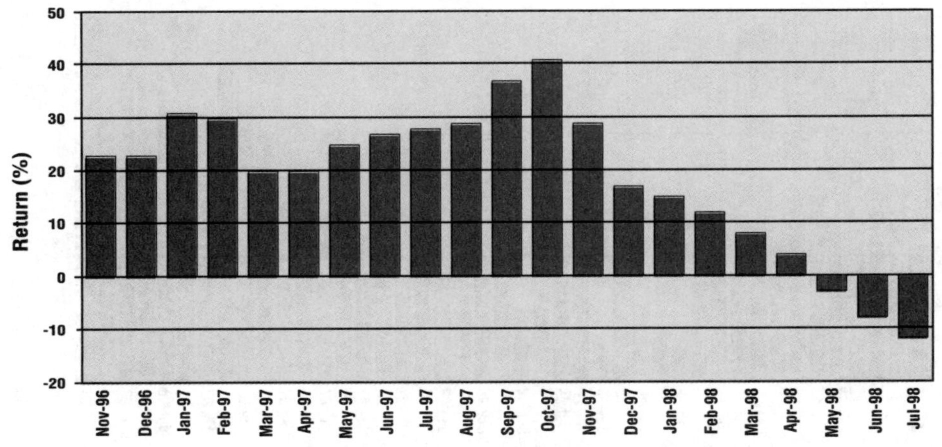

	Total Change	Annual Cmpd Rate	$10,000 Invested	24 Months Ending
Best	98.88%	41.03%	$19,888.17	October 1997
Worst	-22.75%	-12.11%	$7,724.68	July 1998
Average	44.35%	20.14%	$14,434.75	n/a

All-Canadian Consumer Fund Fund

MVA	3 Months*	1 Year*	3 Years*	5 Years*	1997	1996	1995
104.4	-5.1%	2.6%	6.2%	7.3%	19.9%	6.6%	1.0%

* Returns to July 31, 1998

Sponsor All-Canadian Management Inc.
55 Broad Leaf C.r, P.O. Box 7320
Ancaster, Ontario, L9G 3P2

Phone 1-905-648-2025

Sales Fee Load **RRSP Eligibility** Yes

Category Specialty/Consumers

Portfolio Manager/Years
Paul Gratton—All-Canadian Management/7

Minimum Initial Investment
RRSP $1,000 **Non-RRSP** $1,000

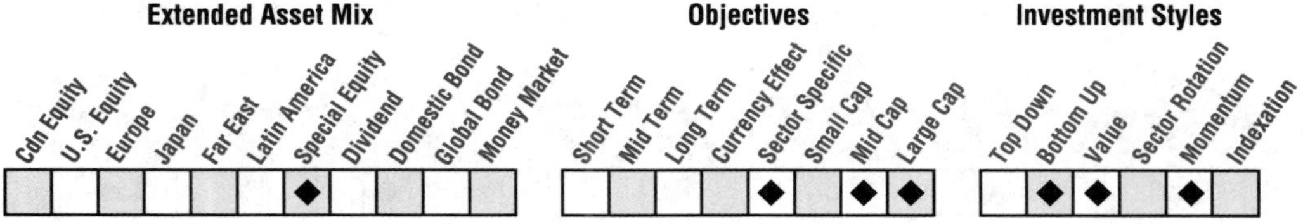

Quantitative		Asset Breakout		Sector Breakout (Equity)
MER	2.00%	Cash	59.3%	Overweighted
Tax Efficiency	54.91%	Cdn Bonds		1 Consumer
Std Deviation	1.70%	Foreign Bonds		2 Utilities
Beta	0.11	Cdn Equity	35.9%	Underweighted
Alpha	0.32	Foreign Equity		1 Merchandising
R Squared	0.17	Warrants		2 Financial

TRAILING 24-MONTH ANNUALIZED RETURNS FOR ALL-CANADIAN CONSUMER FUND FUND

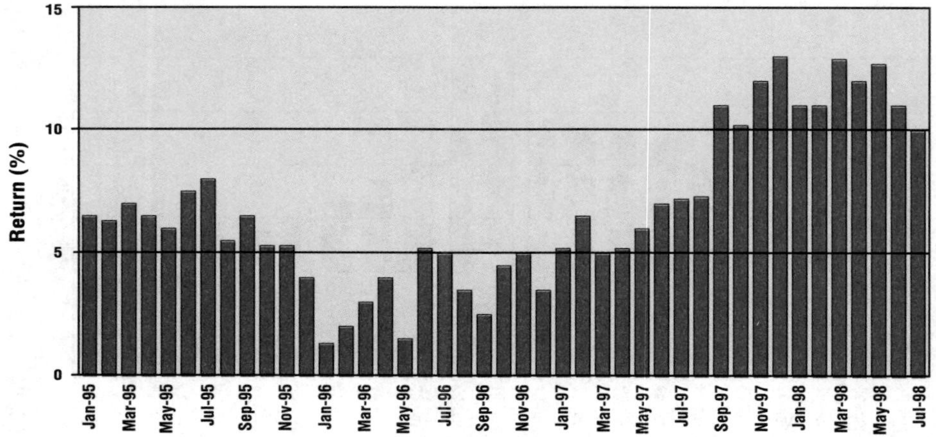

	Total Change	Annual Cmpd Rate	$10,000 Invested	24 Months Ending
Best	27.81%	13.05%	$12,780.75	December 1997
Worst	2.60%	1.29%	$10,260.14	January 1996
Average	14.91%	7.20%	$11,491.37	n/a

Horizons Multi-Asset Fund Inc.

MVA	3 Months*	1 Year*	3 Years*	5 Years*	1997	1996	1995
102.8	-1.1%	-1.6%	6.7%	N/A	9.6%	4.8%	10.0%

* Returns to July 31, 1998

Sponsor Contrarian Strategies Inc.
321 Water Street, Suite 504
Vancouver, British Columbia, V6B 1B8

Phone 1-604-688-7333

Sales Fee Load **RRSP Eligibility** No

Category Specialty/Other

Portfolio Manager/Years
17 Worldwide Independent/4

Minimum Initial Investment
RRSP $25,000 **Non-RRSP** $25,000

Extended Asset Mix

Cdn Equity	U.S. Equity	Europe	Japan	Far East	Latin America	Special Equity	Dividend	Domestic Bond	Global Bond	Money Market
						◆				

Objectives

Short Term	Mid Term	Long Term	Currency Effect	Sector Specific	Small Cap	Mid Cap	Large Cap
			◆	◆		◆	◆

Investment Styles

Top Down	Bottom Up	Value	Sector Rotation	Momentum	Indexation
◆			◆	◆	

Quantitative		Asset Breakout		Sector Breakout (Equity)
MER	2.00%	Cash	N/A	Overweighted
Tax Efficiency	46.05%	Cdn Bonds	N/A	N/A
Std Deviation	1.93%	Foreign Bonds	N/A	
Beta	0.06	Cdn Equity	N/A	Underweighted
Alpha	0.52	Foreign Equity	N/A	N/A
R Squared	0.02	Warrants	N/A	

TRAILING 24-MONTH ANNUALIZED RETURNS FOR HORIZONS MULTI-ASSET FUND INC.

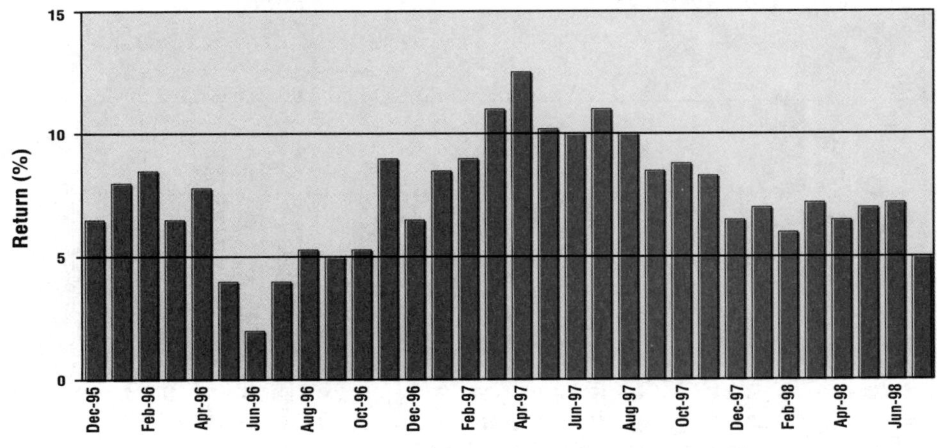

	Total Change	Annual Cmpd Rate	$10,000 Invested	24 Months Ending
Best	26.38%	12.42%	$12,637.67	April 1997
Worst	3.15%	1.56%	$10,315.43	June 1996
Average	16.31%	7.85%	$11,631.30	n/a

Atlas American Advantage Value Fund

MVA	3 Months*	1 Year*	3 Years*	5 Years*	1997	1996	1995
100.1	-0.5%	12.5%	21.2%	N/A	25.2%	21.4%	30.8%

* Returns to July 31, 1998

Sponsor Atlas Asset Management
110 Yonge Street, Suite 500
Toronto, Ontario, M5C 1T4

Phone 1-800-463-2857

Sales Fee Load **RRSP Eligibility** Foreign

Category U.S. Equity/Large Cap

Portfolio Manager/Years
Richard Glasebrook—Oppenheimer/4

Minimum Initial Investment
RRSP $500 **Non-RRSP** $500

Extended Asset Mix

Cdn Equity	U.S. Equity	Europe	Japan	Far East	Latin America	Special Equity	Dividend	Domestic Bond	Global Bond	Money Market
	◆									

Objectives

Short Term	Mid Term	Long Term	Currency Effect	Sector Specific	Small Cap	Mid Cap	Large Cap
			◆				◆

Investment Styles

Top Down	Bottom Up	Value	Sector Rotation	Momentum	Indexation
◆			◆		

Quantitative		Asset Breakout		Sector Breakout (Equity)
MER	2.52%	Cash	8.0%	Overweighted
Tax Efficiency	99.90%	Cdn Bonds		N/A
Std Deviation	2.42%	Foreign Bonds		
Beta	0.66	Cdn Equity		Underweighted
Alpha	0.15	Foreign Equity	91.8%	N/A
R Squared	0.73	Warrants		

TRAILING 24-MONTH ANNUALIZED RETURNS FOR ATLAS AMERICAN ADVANTAGE VALUE FUND

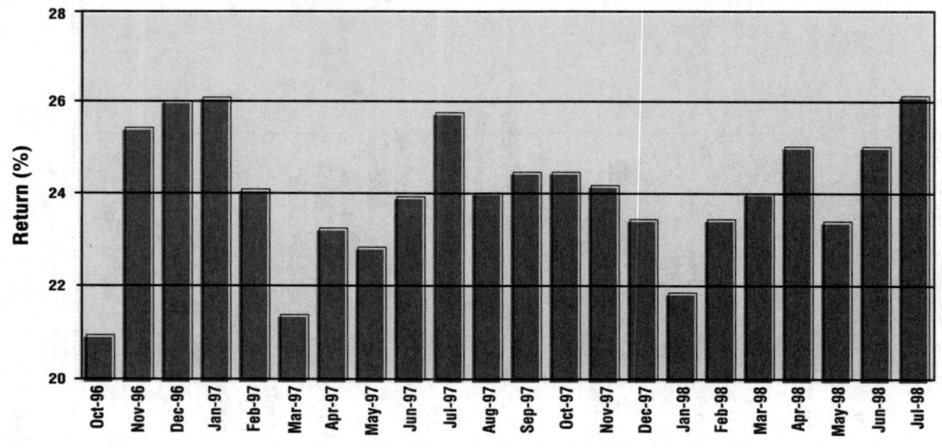

	Total Change	Annual Cmpd Rate	$10,000 Invested	24 Months Ending
Best	59.64%	26.35%	$15,964.30	July 1998
Worst	46.28%	20.95%	$14,627.95	October 1996
Average	54.12%	24.14%	$15,411.75	n/a

AIC Value Fund

MVA	3 Months*	1 Year*	3 Years*	5 Years*	1997	1996	1995
98.8	2.9%	22.5%	35.7%	27.4%	37.3%	35.4%	31.6%

* Returns to July 31, 1998

Sponsor AIC Limited
1375 Kerns Road
Burlington, Ontario, L7R 4V7

Phone 1-800-263-2144

Sales Fee Load **RRSP Eligibility** Foreign

Category U.S. Equity/Large Cap

Portfolio Manager/Years
Michael Lee-Chin—AIC Limited/12

Minimum Initial Investment
RRSP $500 **Non-RRSP** $500

Extended Asset Mix

Cdn Equity	U.S. Equity	Europe	Japan	Far East	Latin America	Special Equity	Dividend	Domestic Bond	Global Bond	Money Market
◆	◆									

Objectives

Short Term	Mid Term	Long Term	Currency Effect	Sector Specific	Small Cap	Mid Cap	Large Cap
			◆			◆	◆

Investment Styles

Top Down	Bottom Up	Value	Sector Rotation	Momentum	Indexation
	◆	◆		◆	

Quantitative		Asset Breakout		Sector Breakout (Equity)
MER	2.44%	Cash	20.1%	Overweighted
Tax Efficiency	100.00%	Cdn Bonds	0.3%	1 Financial
Std Deviation	3.46%	Foreign Bonds		2 Utilities
Beta	0.90	Cdn Equity	15.3%	Underweighted
Alpha	0.05	Foreign Equity	63.8%	1 Goods & Services
R Squared	0.62	Warrants		2 Pipelines

TRAILING 24-MONTH ANNUALIZED RETURNS FOR AIC VALUE FUND

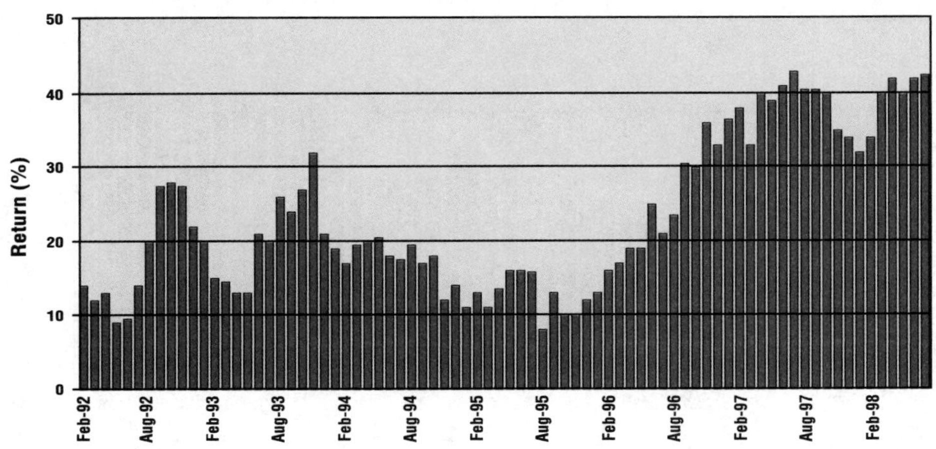

	Total Change	Annual Cmpd Rate	$10,000 Invested	24 Months Ending
Best	104.21%	42.90%	$20,421.25	July 1997
Worst	16.72%	8.04%	$11,671.91	August 1995
Average	54.16%	24.16%	$15,416.23	n/a

Mawer U.S. Equity Fund

MVA	3 Months*	1 Year*	3 Years*	5 Years*	1997	1996	1995
95.3	0.3%	23.0%	26.0%	20.4%	29.3%	23.9%	24.4%

* Returns to July 31, 1998

Sponsor Mawer Investment Management
603-7th Avenue S.W., Suite 900
Calgary, Alberta, T2P 2T5
Phone 1-888-549-6248
Sales Fee No-Load **RRSP Eligibility** Foreign

Category U.S. Equity/Large Cap
Portfolio Manager/Years
Darrell Anderson—Mawer Invesment Mngt./4
Minimum Initial Investment
RRSP $5,000 **Non-RRSP** $5,000

Extended Asset Mix

Cdn Equity	U.S. Equity	Europe	Japan	Far East	Latin America	Special Equity	Dividend	Domestic Bond	Global Bond	Money Market
	◆									

Objectives

Short Term	Mid Term	Long Term	Currency Effect	Sector Specific	Small Cap	Mid Cap	Large Cap
			◆				◆

Investment Styles

Top Down	Bottom Up	Value	Sector Rotation	Momentum	Indexation
	◆	◆			

Quantitative		Asset Breakout		Sector Breakout (Equity)
MER	1.27%	Cash	3.1%	Overweighted
Tax Efficiency	90.41%	Cdn Bonds		N/A
Std Deviation	3.03%	Foreign Bonds		
Beta	0.81	Cdn Equity		Underweighted
Alpha	0.07	Foreign Equity	97.0%	N/A
R Squared	0.71	Warrants		

TRAILING 24-MONTH ANNUALIZED RETURNS FOR MAWER U.S. EQUITY FUND

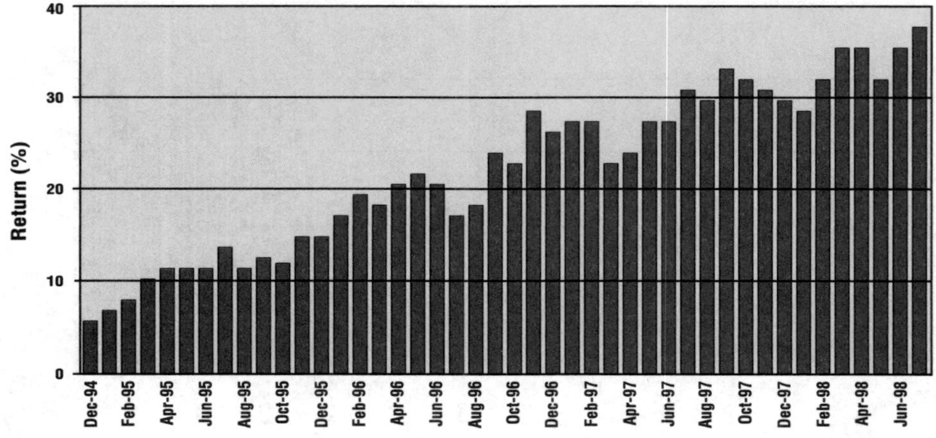

	Total Change	Annual Cmpd Rate	$10,000 Invested	24 Months Ending
Best	77.16%	33.10%	$17,716.00	July 1998
Worst	11.43%	5.56%	$11,142.92	December 1994
Average	44.53%	20.22%	$14,453.11	n/a

PH&N U.S. Equity Fund

MVA	3 Months*	1 Year*	3 Years*	5 Years*	1997	1996	1995
94.3	0.6%	18.3%	26.2%	21.3%	29.4%	25.6%	25.9%

* Returns to July 31, 1998

Sponsor Phillips Hager & North
200 Burrard Street, 21st floor
Vancouver, British Columbia, V6C 3N5

Phone 1-800-661-6141

Sales Fee No-Load **RRSP Eligibility** Foreign

Category U.S. Equity/Large Cap

Portfolio Manager/Years
John Montalhano—PH&N Management/5

Minimum Initial Investment
RRSP $25,000 **Non-RRSP** $25,000

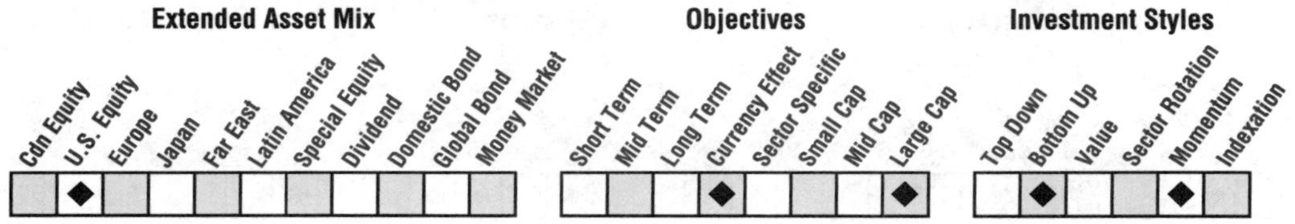

Quantitative		Asset Breakout		Sector Breakout (Equity)
MER	1.10%	Cash	4.9%	Overweighted
Tax Efficiency	80.84%	Cdn Bonds		N/A
Std Deviation	2.92%	Foreign Bonds		
Beta	0.82	Cdn Equity		Underweighted
Alpha	-0.06	Foreign Equity	95.1%	N/A
R Squared	0.81	Warrants		

TRAILING 24-MONTH ANNUALIZED RETURNS FOR PH&N U.S. EQUITY FUND

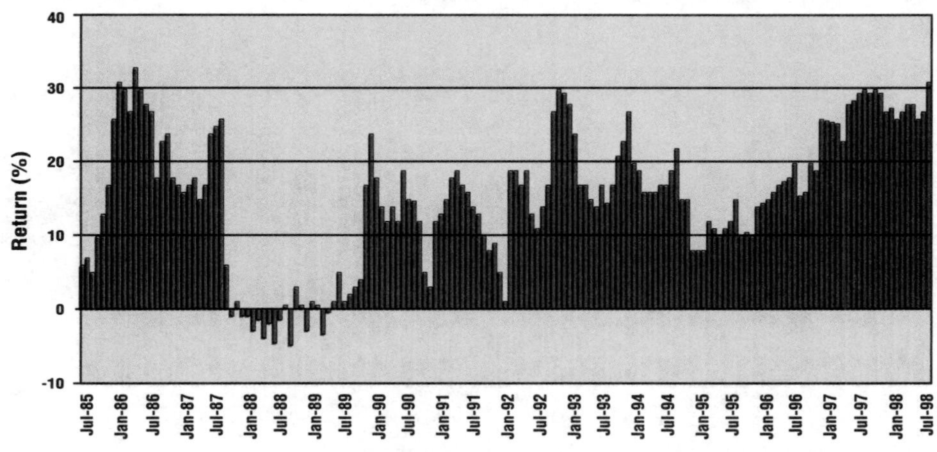

	Total Change	Annual Cmpd Rate	$10,000 Invested	24 Months Ending
Best	77.58%	33.26%	$17,758.30	May 1986
Worst	-9.17%	-4.70%	$9,082.72	August 1988
Average	34.98%	16.18%	$13,497.90	n/a

Zweig Strategic Growth Fund

MVA	3 Months*	1 Year*	3 Years*	5 Years*	1997	1996	1995
93.4	-3.9%	17.3%	17.7%	15.9%	26.8%	14.6%	21.2%

* Returns to July 31, 1998

Sponsor Royal Mutual Funds Inc.
Royal Trust Tower, P.O. Box 7500, Stn. A
Toronto, Ontario, M5W 1P9

Phone 1-800-463-3863

Sales Fee No-Load **RRSP Eligibility** Foreign

Category U.S. Equity/Diversified

Portfolio Manager/Years
Dr. Martin Zweig—Zweig/Glaser Advisors/7

Minimum Initial Investment
RRSP $500 **Non-RRSP** $500

Extended Asset Mix

Cdn Equity	U.S. Equity	Europe	Japan	Far East	Latin America	Special Equity	Dividend	Domestic Bond	Global Bond	Money Market
	◆									

Objectives

Short Term	Mid Term	Long Term	Currency Effect	Sector Specific	Small Cap	Mid Cap	Large Cap
			◆		◆	◆	

Investment Styles

Top Down	Bottom Up	Value	Sector Rotation	Momentum	Indexation
◆				◆	

Quantitative		Asset Breakout		Sector Breakout (Equity)
MER	2.49%	Cash	5.4%	Overweighted
Tax Efficiency	95.57%	Cdn Bonds		1 Conglomerates
Std Deviation	2.40%	Foreign Bonds		2 Utilities
Beta	0.45	Cdn Equity	3.2%	Underweighted
Alpha	0.25	Foreign Equity	92.3%	1 Oil & Gas
R Squared	0.41	Warrants		2 Financial

TRAILING 24-MONTH ANNUALIZED RETURNS FOR ZWEIG STRATEGIC GROWTH FUND

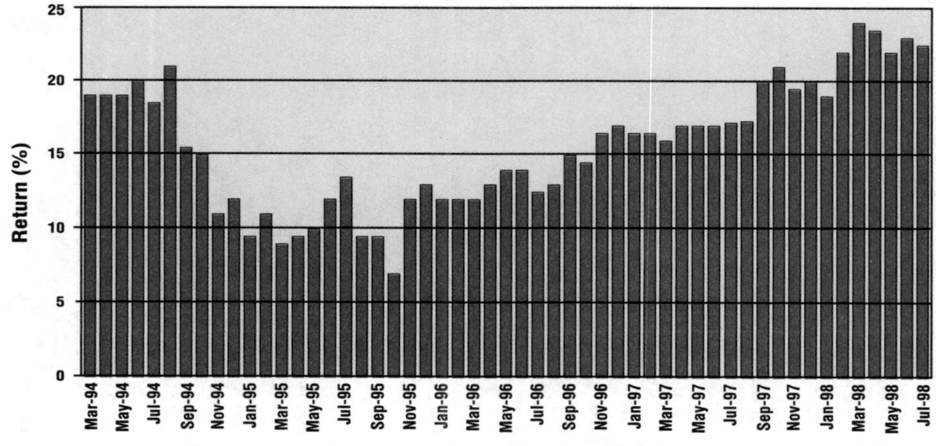

	Total Change	Annual Cmpd Rate	$10,000 Invested	24 Months Ending
Best	53.27%	23.80%	$15,326.79	March 1998
Worst	17.52%	8.41%	$11,751.70	October 1995
Average	34.36%	15.91%	$13,436.16	n/a

Green Line U.S. Index Fund

MVA	3 Months*	1 Year*	3 Years*	5 Years*	1997	1996	1995
93.2	1.0%	18.5%	27.2%	21.7%	32.3%	21.8%	35.3%

* Returns to July 31, 1998

Sponsor TD Asset Management Inc.
TD Bank Tower, P.O. Box 100
Toronto, Ontario, M5K 1G8

Phone 1-800-268-8166

Sales Fee No-Load **RRSP Eligibility** Foreign

Category U.S. Equity/Diversified

Portfolio Manager/Years
Tim Thompson—TD Asset Management/7

Minimum Initial Investment
RRSP $2,000 **Non-RRSP** $2,000

Extended Asset Mix

Cdn Equity	U.S. Equity	Europe	Japan	Far East	Latin America	Special Equity	Dividend	Domestic Bond	Global Bond	Money Market
	◆									

Objectives

Short Term	Mid Term	Long Term	Currency Effect	Sector Specific	Small Cap	Mid Cap	Large Cap
			◆				◆

Investment Styles

Top Down	Bottom Up	Value	Sector Rotation	Momentum	Indexation
					◆

Quantitative		Asset Breakout		Sector Breakout (Equity)
MER	0.66%	Cash	0.1%	Overweighted
Tax Efficiency	97.68%	Cdn Bonds		1 Industrial
Std Deviation	3.49%	Foreign Bonds		2 Utilities
Beta	1.03	Cdn Equity	0.7%	Underweighted
Alpha	-0.32	Foreign Equity	99.2%	1 Consumer
R Squared	0.85	Warrants		2 Financial

TRAILING 24-MONTH ANNUALIZED RETURNS FOR GREEN LINE U.S. INDEX FUND

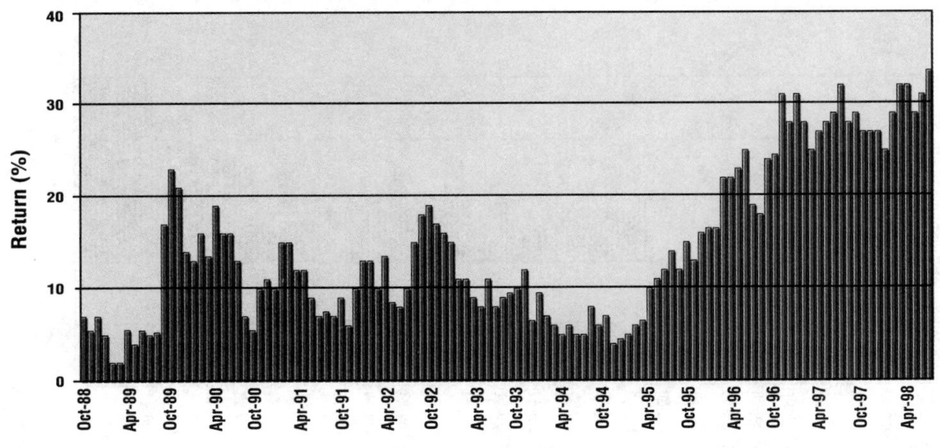

	Total Change	Annual Cmpd Rate	$10,000 Invested	24 Months Ending
Best	78.44%	33.58%	$17,844.01	July 1998
Worst	3.76%	1.86%	$10,375.56	March 1989
Average	32.00%	14.89%	$13,200.29	n/a

Cornerstone U.S. Fund

MVA	3 Months*	1 Year*	3 Years*	5 Years*	1997	1996	1995
92.6	5.8%	27.4%	28.7%	22.7%	36.1%	19.0%	24.9%

* Returns to July 31, 1998

Sponsor Cornerstone Group of Funds
1981 McGill College Ave., Suite 1550
Montreal, Quebec, H3A 3K3

Phone 1-514-284-3971

Sales Fee Load **RRSP Eligibility** Foreign

Category U.S. Equity/Large Cap

Portfolio Manager
Matthew Megarel—Wellington Management

Minimum Initial Investment
RRSP $500 **Non-RRSP** $500

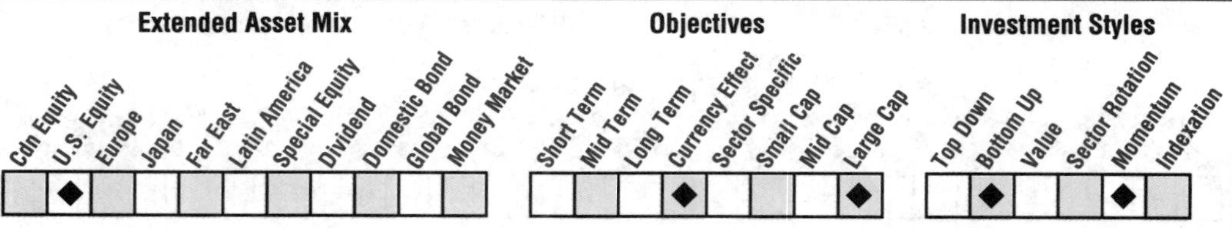

Quantitative		Asset Breakout		Sector Breakout (Equity)
MER	2.23%	Cash	0.8%	Overweighted
Tax Efficiency	94.21%	Cdn Bonds		N/A
Std Deviation	3.23%	Foreign Bonds		
Beta	1	Cdn Equity		Underweighted
Alpha	-0.19	Foreign Equity	99.2%	N/A
R Squared	0.95	Warrants		

TRAILING 24-MONTH ANNUALIZED RETURNS FOR CORNERSTONE U.S. FUND

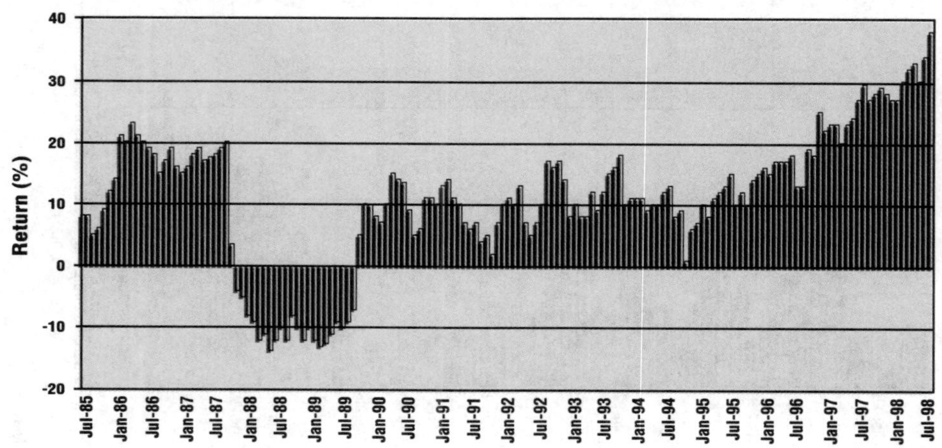

	Total Change	Annual Cmpd Rate	$10,000 Invested	24 Months Ending
Best	90.02%	37.85%	$19,002.46	July 1998
Worst	-25.46%	-13.66%	$7,454.38	May 1988
Average	24.34%	11.51%	$12,433.60	n/a

Atlas American Large-Cap Growth Fund

MVA	3 Months*	1 Year*	3 Years*	5 Years*	1997	1996	1995
92.3	1.2%	17.6%	25.5%	21.0%	33.4%	19.6%	29.6%

* Returns to July 31, 1998

Sponsor Atlas Asset Management
110 Yonge Street, Suite 500
Totonto, Ontario, M5C 1T4

Phone 1-800-463-2857

Sales Fee Load **RRSP Eligibility** Foreign

Category U.S. Equity/Large Cap

Portfolio Manager/Years
Len Racioppo—Jarislowsky, Fraser & Co./13

Minimum Initial Investment
RRSP $500 **Non-RRSP** $500

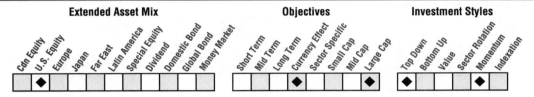

Extended Asset Mix

Cdn Equity	U.S. Equity	Europe	Japan	Far East	Latin America	Special Equity	Dividend	Domestic Bond	Global Bond	Money Market
	◆									

Objectives

Short Term	Mid Term	Long Term	Currency Effect	Sector Specific	Small Cap	Mid Cap	Large Cap
			◆				◆

Investment Styles

Top Down	Bottom Up	Value	Sector Rotation	Momentum	Indexation
◆				◆	

Quantitative		Asset Breakout		Sector Breakout (Equity)
MER	2.54%	Cash	4.0%	Overweighted
Tax Efficiency	100.00%	Cdn Bonds		1 Consumer
Std Deviation	3.12%	Foreign Bonds		2 Utilities
Beta	0.91	Cdn Equity	3.1%	Underweighted
Alpha	-0.24	Foreign Equity	92.7%	1 Financial
R Squared	0.86	Warrants		

TRAILING 24-MONTH ANNUALIZED RETURNS FOR ATLAS AMERICAN LARGE-CAP GROWTH FUND

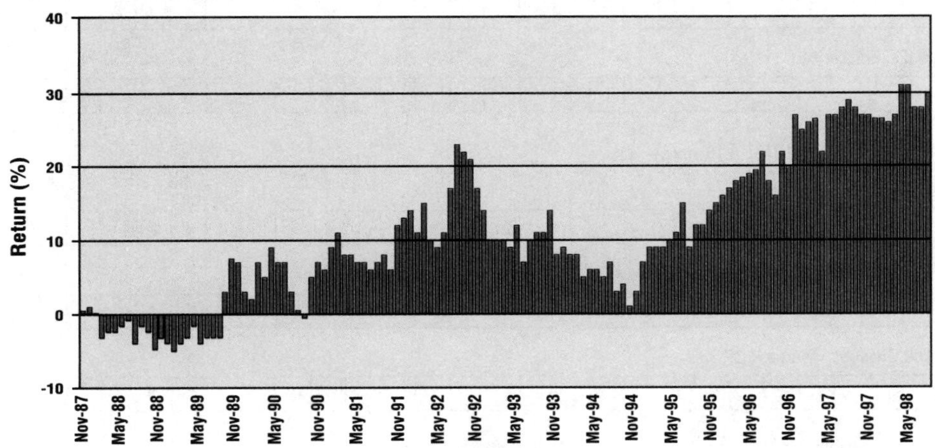

	Total Change	Annual Cmpd Rate	$10,000 Invested	24 Months Ending
Best	72.10%	31.19%	$17,210.25	March 1998
Worst	-11.00%	-5.66%	$8,899.57	February 1989
Average	23.57%	11.16%	$12,357.38	n/a

Canadian Equity Funds (MVA Index)

Fund	Extended Asset Mix											Objectives								Management Style					
	Canadian Equity	U.S. Equity	Europe	Japan	Far East	Latin America	Special Equity	Dividend	Domestic Bond	Global Bond	Money Market	Short Term	Mid Term	Long Term	Currency Effect	Sector Specific	Small Cap	Mid Cap	Large Cap	Top Down	Bottom Up	Value	Sector Rotation	Momentum	Indexation
Ivy Enterprise (153.0)	◆																◆				◆	◆			
AIC Diversified Canada (129.0)	◆																	◆			◆	◆		◆	
Fidelity Canadian Growth (126.7)	◆																◆	◆			◆	◆			
Bissett Small Capital (123.2)	◆																◆				◆			◆	
Talvest/Hyperion Small-Cap Canadian Equity (118.4)	◆																◆				◆	◆			
AIC Advantage (118.2)	◆																	◆			◆	◆		◆	
Ivy Canadian (117.2)	◆																	◆	◆		◆	◆			
Spectrum United Canadian Investments (115.0)	◆																		◆		◆	◆			
Bissett Canadian Equity (113.9)	◆																	◆	◆		◆		◆		
Guardian Enterprise C (113.0)	◆																	◆			◆			◆	

Canadian Dividend Funds (MVA Index)

Fund	Canadian Equity	U.S. Equity	Europe	Japan	Far East	Latin America	Special Equity	Dividend	Domestic Bond	Global Bond	Money Market	Short Term	Mid Term	Long Term	Currency Effect	Sector Specific	Small Cap	Mid Cap	Large Cap	Top Down	Bottom Up	Value	Sector Rotation	Momentum	Indexation
BPI Dividend Income (144.1)								◆											◆		◆	◆			
Dynamic Dividend (126.7)								◆											◆		◆	◆			
Bissett Dividend Income (125.8)								◆											◆		◆	◆			
Dynamic Dividend Growth (124.0)								◆										◆	◆		◆	◆			
Spectrum United Dividend (121.0)								◆											◆		◆	◆			

Canadian Fixed-Income Funds (MVA Index)

Fund	Extended Asset Mix: Canadian Equity	U.S. Equity	Europe	Japan	Far East	Latin America	Special Equity	Dividend	Domestic Bond	Global Bond	Money Market	Objectives: Short Term	Mid Term	Long Term	Currency Effect	Sector Specific	Small Cap	Mid Cap	Large Cap	Management Style: Top Down	Bottom Up	Value	Sector Rotation	Momentum	Indexation
Atlas Canadian High-Yield Bond (111.0)									◆				◆								◆			◆	
C.I. Canadian Bond (104.6)									◆				◆							◆				◆	
Trimark Canadian Bond (96.5)									◆				◆							◆			◆	◆	
Altamira Bond (96.3)									◆					◆						◆				◆	
Bissett Bond (96.2)									◆				◆							◆				◆	
Ivy Mortgage (94.9)									◆				◆												◆
Fidelity Canadian Bond (94.3)									◆				◆								◆		◆		

Global Fixed-Income Funds (MVA Index)

Fund	Extended Asset Mix: Canadian Equity	U.S. Equity	Europe	Japan	Far East	Latin America	Special Equity	Dividend	Domestic Bond	Global Bond	Money Market	Objectives: Short Term	Mid Term	Long Term	Currency Effect	Sector Specific	Small Cap	Mid Cap	Large Cap	Management Style: Top Down	Bottom Up	Value	Sector Rotation	Momentum	Indexation
Guardian International Income C (96.5)										◆			◆		◆					◆				◆	
Universal World Income RRSP (96.0)										◆				◆	◆					◆					◆
Fidelity Emerging Markets Bond (95.9)										◆				◆	◆						◆		◆		

Global Equity Funds (MVA Index)

Fund	Extended Asset Mix: Canadian Equity	U.S. Equity	Europe	Japan	Far East	Latin America	Special Equity	Dividend	Domestic Bond	Global Bond	Money Market	Objectives: Short Term	Mid Term	Long Term	Currency Effect	Sector Specific	Small Cap	Mid Cap	Large Cap	Management Style: Top Down	Bottom Up	Value	Sector Rotation	Momentum	Indexation
Bissett Multinational Growth (112.1)	◆	◆													◆			◆	◆	◆	◆			◆	
Ivy Foreign Equity (105.0)	◆	◆													◆			◆	◆		◆	◆			
Fidelity International Portfolio (99.7)		◆	◆	◆											◆				◆		◆			◆	

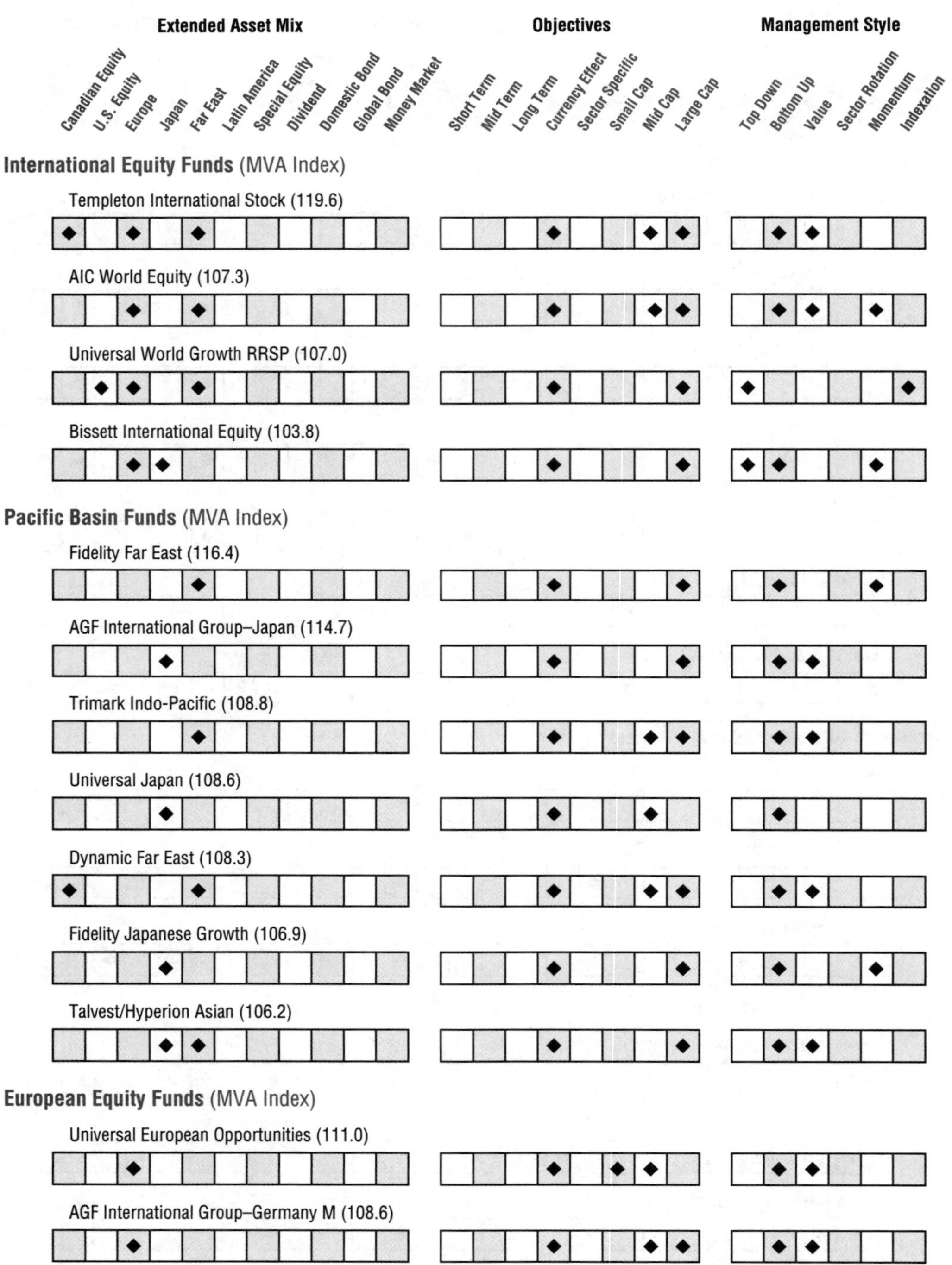

	Extended Asset Mix											Objectives								Management Style					
Fund (MVA Index)	Canadian Equity	U.S. Equity	Europe	Japan	Far East	Latin America	Special Equity	Dividend	Domestic Bond	Global Bond	Money Market	Short Term	Mid Term	Long Term	Currency Effect	Sector Specific	Small Cap	Mid Cap	Large Cap	Top Down	Bottom Up	Value	Sector Rotation	Momentum	Indexation
International Equity Funds (MVA Index)																									
Templeton International Stock (119.6)	◆		◆		◆										◆			◆	◆		◆	◆			
AIC World Equity (107.3)			◆		◆										◆			◆	◆		◆	◆		◆	
Universal World Growth RRSP (107.0)		◆	◆		◆										◆				◆	◆					◆
Bissett International Equity (103.8)			◆	◆											◆				◆	◆	◆			◆	
Pacific Basin Funds (MVA Index)																									
Fidelity Far East (116.4)					◆										◆				◆		◆			◆	
AGF International Group–Japan (114.7)				◆											◆				◆		◆	◆			
Trimark Indo-Pacific (108.8)					◆										◆			◆	◆		◆	◆			
Universal Japan (108.6)				◆											◆			◆			◆				
Dynamic Far East (108.3)	◆				◆										◆			◆	◆		◆	◆			
Fidelity Japanese Growth (106.9)				◆											◆				◆		◆			◆	
Talvest/Hyperion Asian (106.2)				◆	◆										◆				◆		◆	◆			
European Equity Funds (MVA Index)																									
Universal European Opportunities (111.0)			◆												◆		◆	◆			◆	◆			
AGF International Group–Germany M (108.6)			◆												◆			◆	◆		◆	◆			

Extended Asset Mix

Fund (MVA Index)	Canadian Equity	U.S. Equity	Europe	Japan	Far East	Latin America	Special Equity	Dividend	Domestic Bond	Global Bond	Money Market
U.S. Equity Funds (MVA Index)											
Atlas American Advantage Value (100.1)		◆									
AIC Value (98.8)	◆	◆									
Green Line U.S. Index (93.2)		◆									
Specialty Funds (MVA Index)											
Green Line Precious Metals (113.6)							◆				
20/20 Canadian Resources (111.8)	◆						◆				
Green Line Energy (109.3)	◆						◆				
Universal Canadian Resources (107.6)	◆						◆				
Universal Precious Metals (107.1)							◆				
Altamira Precious & Strategic Metals (106.1)							◆				
Global Strategy Gold Plus (104.2)							◆				
AIM Global Health Sciences (99.3)							◆				
Green Line Science & Technology* (82.3)							◆				
Latin America Funds (MVA Index)											
GT Global Latin America Growth (80.8)						◆					
Money Market Funds—Generic											◆

Objectives

Fund (MVA Index)	Short Term	Mid Term	Long Term	Currency Effect	Sector Specific	Small Cap	Mid Cap	Large Cap
U.S. Equity Funds (MVA Index)								
Atlas American Advantage Value (100.1)				◆				◆
AIC Value (98.8)				◆			◆	◆
Green Line U.S. Index (93.2)				◆				◆
Specialty Funds (MVA Index)								
Green Line Precious Metals (113.6)					◆	◆	◆	◆
20/20 Canadian Resources (111.8)					◆		◆	◆
Green Line Energy (109.3)						◆	◆	◆
Universal Canadian Resources (107.6)					◆	◆		
Universal Precious Metals (107.1)				◆	◆	◆	◆	
Altamira Precious & Strategic Metals (106.1)					◆	◆	◆	◆
Global Strategy Gold Plus (104.2)				◆	◆		◆	
AIM Global Health Sciences (99.3)				◆	◆			◆
Green Line Science & Technology* (82.3)				◆		◆	◆	◆
Latin America Funds (MVA Index)								
GT Global Latin America Growth (80.8)				◆			◆	
Money Market Funds—Generic	◆							

Management Style

Fund (MVA Index)	Top Down	Bottom Up	Value	Sector Rotation	Momentum	Indexation
U.S. Equity Funds (MVA Index)						
Atlas American Advantage Value (100.1)	◆				◆	
AIC Value (98.8)		◆	◆		◆	
Green Line U.S. Index (93.2)						◆
Specialty Funds (MVA Index)						
Green Line Precious Metals (113.6)		◆			◆	
20/20 Canadian Resources (111.8)	◆				◆	
Green Line Energy (109.3)		◆			◆	
Universal Canadian Resources (107.6)		◆			◆	
Universal Precious Metals (107.1)		◆			◆	
Altamira Precious & Strategic Metals (106.1)		◆			◆	
Global Strategy Gold Plus (104.2)		◆	◆		◆	
AIM Global Health Sciences (99.3)		◆			◆	
Green Line Science & Technology* (82.3)	◆				◆	
Latin America Funds (MVA Index)						
GT Global Latin America Growth (80.8)	◆	◆			◆	
Money Market Funds—Generic						◆

* This was the best technology-specific fund with at least a three-year track-record.

20/20 FAMILY OF FUNDS

Fund Name	Extended Asset Mix											Objectives								Management Style					
	Canadian Equity	U.S. Equity	Europe	Japan	Far East	Latin America	Special Equity	Dividend	Domestic Bond	Global Bond	Money Market	Short Term	Mid Term	Long Term	Currency Effect	Sector Specific	Small Cap	Mid Cap	Large Cap	Top Down	Bottom Up	Value	Sector Rotation	Momentum	Indexation
20/20 Aggressive Global Stock		◆	◆		◆										◆			◆			◆			◆	
20/20 Aggressive Growth		◆													◆			◆			◆			◆	
20/20 Canadian Resources	◆						◆									◆		◆	◆	◆				◆	
20/20 Emerging Markets Value						◆									◆			◆	◆		◆	◆			
20/20 India					◆										◆			◆	◆		◆	◆		◆	
20/20 Latin America						◆									◆			◆	◆		◆	◆		◆	
20/20 Managed Futures Value (capped)							◆								◆					◆					◆
20/20 RSP Aggressive Equity (capped)	◆																◆	◆			◆			◆	
20/20 RSP Aggressive Smaller Companies	◆																◆				◆			◆	

AGF FAMILY OF FUNDS

Extended Asset Mix

Fund Name	Canadian Equity	U.S. Equity	Europe	Japan	Far East	Latin America	Special Equity	Dividend	Domestic Bond	Global Bond	Money Market
AGF American T.A. Allocation		◆								◆	
AGF Canadian Bond									◆		
AGF Canadian Equity	◆										
AGF Canadian Growth	◆										
AGF Canadian Tactical Asset Allocation	◆								◆		
AGF Dividend	◆							◆			
AGF European Asset Allocation			◆							◆	
AGF Global Government Bond										◆	
AGF Growth & Income	◆								◆		
AGF Growth Equity	◆										
AGF High Income	◆							◆	◆		
AGF Intl Group–American Growth		◆									
AGF Intl Group–Asian Growth					◆						
AGF Intl Group–Canada Class	◆										
AGF Intl Group–China Focus				◆	◆						
AGF Intl Group–European Growth			◆								
AGF Intl Group–Germany [1]			◆								
AGF Intl Group–Japan				◆							

Objectives

Fund Name	Short Term	Mid Term	Long Term	Currency Effect	Sector Specific	Small Cap	Mid Cap	Large Cap
AGF American T.A. Allocation		◆		◆				◆
AGF Canadian Bond		◆						
AGF Canadian Equity							◆	◆
AGF Canadian Growth							◆	
AGF Canadian Tactical Asset Allocation								◆
AGF Dividend								◆
AGF European Asset Allocation		◆		◆				◆
AGF Global Government Bond		◆		◆				
AGF Growth & Income		◆						◆
AGF Growth Equity						◆	◆	
AGF High Income		◆						◆
AGF Intl Group–American Growth				◆				◆
AGF Intl Group–Asian Growth				◆			◆	◆
AGF Intl Group–Canada Class								◆
AGF Intl Group–China Focus				◆				◆
AGF Intl Group–European Growth				◆		◆	◆	
AGF Intl Group–Germany [1]				◆			◆	◆
AGF Intl Group–Japan				◆				◆

Management Style

Fund Name	Top Down	Bottom Up	Value	Sector Rotation	Momentum	Indexation
AGF American T.A. Allocation	◆				◆	◆
AGF Canadian Bond	◆				◆	
AGF Canadian Equity		◆			◆	
AGF Canadian Growth		◆			◆	
AGF Canadian Tactical Asset Allocation	◆				◆	
AGF Dividend		◆	◆			
AGF European Asset Allocation	◆				◆	
AGF Global Government Bond	◆				◆	
AGF Growth & Income	◆				◆	
AGF Growth Equity		◆			◆	
AGF High Income	◆				◆	
AGF Intl Group–American Growth		◆			◆	
AGF Intl Group–Asian Growth		◆			◆	
AGF Intl Group–Canada Class		◆	◆			
AGF Intl Group–China Focus		◆			◆	
AGF Intl Group–European Growth		◆	◆			
AGF Intl Group–Germany [1]		◆	◆			
AGF Intl Group–Japan		◆	◆			

* Also applies to AGF International Group–Germany M Fund.

AGF FAMILY OF FUNDS

Fund Name	Extended Asset Mix: Canadian Equity	U.S. Equity	Europe	Japan	Far East	Latin America	Special Equity	Dividend	Domestic Bond	Global Bond	Money Market	Objectives: Short Term	Mid Term	Long Term	Currency Effect	Sector Specific	Small Cap	Mid Cap	Large Cap	Management Style: Top Down	Bottom Up	Value	Sector Rotation	Momentum	Indexation
AGF Intl Group–Short-Term Income										◆		◆													◆
AGF Intl Group–Special U.S.		◆													◆		◆	◆			◆			◆	
AGF Intl Group–World Equity		◆	◆												◆				◆		◆	◆			
AGF International Value		◆	◆												◆				◆		◆	◆			
AGF Money Market Account											◆	◆													◆
AGF RSP Global Bond										◆			◆		◆					◆				◆	
AGF RSP Inernational Equity Allocation		◆	◆	◆											◆				◆	◆				◆	◆
AGF U.S. Income										◆		◆			◆					◆				◆	
AGF U.S.$ Money Market Account											◆	◆			◆										◆
AGF U.S. Short-Term High Yield										◆		◆			◆						◆		◆		
AGF World Balanced		◆	◆							◆			◆		◆				◆	◆				◆	

AIC FAMILY OF FUNDS

Extended Asset Mix

Fund Name	Canadian Equity	U.S. Equity	Europe	Japan	Far East	Latin America	Special Equity	Dividend	Domestic Bond	Global Bond	Money Market
AIC Advantage Fund I*	◆										
AIC Advantage Fund II	◆										
AIC Diversified Canada	◆										
AIC Emerging Markets					◆						
AIC Money Market											◆
AIC Value	◆	◆									
AIC World Equity			◆		◆						

Objectives

Fund Name	Short Term	Mid Term	Long Term	Currency Effect	Sector Specific	Small Cap	Mid Cap	Large Cap
AIC Advantage Fund I*							◆	
AIC Advantage Fund II							◆	
AIC Diversified Canada							◆	
AIC Emerging Markets				◆			◆	
AIC Money Market	◆							
AIC Value				◆			◆	◆
AIC World Equity				◆			◆	◆

Management Style

Fund Name	Top Down	Bottom Up	Value	Sector Rotation	Momentum	Indexation
AIC Advantage Fund I*		◆	◆		◆	
AIC Advantage Fund II		◆	◆		◆	
AIC Diversified Canada		◆	◆		◆	
AIC Emerging Markets		◆	◆		◆	
AIC Money Market						◆
AIC Value		◆	◆		◆	
AIC World Equity		◆	◆		◆	

*AIC Advantage Fund was re-opened but re-closed by on June 30, 1998

AIM FAMILY OF FUNDS

Fund Name	Extended Asset Mix											Objectives								Management Style					
	Canadian Equity	U.S. Equity	Europe	Japan	Far East	Latin America	Special Equity	Dividend	Domestic Bond	Global Bond	Money Market	Short Term	Mid Term	Long Term	Currency Effect	Sector Specific	Small Cap	Mid Cap	Large Cap	Top Down	Bottom Up	Value	Sector Rotation	Momentum	Indexati
AIM American Premier		◆													◆				◆	◆			◆	◆	
AIM Canadian Balanced	◆								◆				◆						◆	◆				◆	
AIM Canadian Premier	◆																		◆	◆			◆	◆	
AIM Canadian Select Growth (capped)	◆																		◆	◆				◆	
AIM Cash Performance											◆	◆													◆
AIM Dragon 888 (capped)					◆										◆				◆	◆				◆	
AIM Europa Performance			◆												◆				◆	◆				◆	
AIM Global Health Sciences							◆								◆	◆			◆		◆			◆	
AIM Global RSP Income										◆			◆		◆	◆					◆			◆	
AIM Global RSP Index (capped)	◆	◆	◆				◆								◆	◆			◆	◆					◆
AIM Global Technology							◆								◆	◆			◆		◆			◆	
AIM International		◆	◆												◆				◆	◆				◆	
AIM Korea					◆										◆				◆		◆		◆	◆	
AIM Nippon				◆											◆				◆		◆		◆	◆	
AIM Tiger					◆										◆				◆		◆		◆	◆	

ALTAMIRA FAMILY OF FUNDS

	Extended Asset Mix											Objectives								Management Style					
Fund Name	Canadian Equity	U.S. Equity	Europe	Japan	Far East	Latin America	Special Equity	Dividend	Domestic Bond	Global Bond	Money Market	Short Term	Mid Term	Long Term	Currency Effect	Sector Specific	Small Cap	Mid Cap	Large Cap	Top Down	Bottom Up	Value	Sector Rotation	Momentum	Indexation
Altafund Investment Corporation	◆																	◆		◆			◆	◆	
Altamira Asia Pacific				◆	◆										◆					◆				◆	
Altamira Balanced	◆								◆				◆						◆	◆			◆		
Altamira Bond									◆					◆						◆				◆	
Altamira Capital Growth	◆																		◆	◆			◆		
Altamira Dividend Fund Inc.								◆					◆						◆		◆	◆			
Altamira Equity	◆																	◆	◆	◆			◆	◆	
Altamira European Equity			◆												◆			◆	◆	◆				◆	
Altamira Global Bond										◆			◆		◆					◆			◆	◆	
Altamira Global Discovery					◆	◆									◆		◆	◆		◆				◆	
Altamira Global Diversified		◆	◆	◆														◆	◆	◆				◆	
Altamira Global Small Company		◆	◆												◆		◆				◆			◆	
Altamira Growth & Income	◆								◆				◆					◆	◆	◆			◆	◆	
Altamira Income									◆				◆							◆				◆	
Altamira Japanese Opportunity				◆													◆				◆			◆	
Altamira North American Recovery	◆	◆																◆	◆		◆			◆	
Altamira Precious & Strategic Metals							◆									◆	◆	◆	◆		◆			◆	
Altamira Resource	◆						◆									◆	◆	◆	◆		◆		◆	◆	

ALTAMIRA FAMILY OF FUNDS

Fund Name	Extended Asset Mix											Objectives								Management Style					
	Canadian Equity	U.S. Equity	Europe	Japan	Far East	Latin America	Special Equity	Dividend	Domestic Bond	Global Bond	Money Market	Short Term	Mid Term	Long Term	Currency Effect	Sector Specific	Small Cap	Mid Cap	Large Cap	Top Down	Bottom Up	Value	Sector Rotation	Momentum	Indexation
Altamira Science & Technology		◆					◆								◆	◆	◆	◆	◆		◆			◆	
Altamira Select American		◆													◆		◆	◆			◆			◆	
Altamira Short-Term Canadian Income											◆	◆													◆
Altamira Short-Term Global Income										◆		◆			◆										◆
Altamira Short-Term Government Bond									◆			◆													◆
Altamira Special Growth	◆																◆				◆			◆	
Altamira Special High-Yield Bond										◆			◆								◆	◆			
Altamira T-Bill											◆	◆													◆
Altamira U.S. Larger Company		◆													◆				◆	◆			◆	◆	

ATLAS ASSET MANAGEMENT FAMILY OF FUNDS

	Extended Asset Mix											Objectives								Management Style					
Fund Name	Canadian Equity	U.S. Equity	Europe	Japan	Far East	Latin America	Special Equity	Dividend	Domestic Bond	Global Bond	Money Market	Short Term	Mid Term	Long Term	Currency Effect	Sector Specific	Small Cap	Mid Cap	Large Cap	Top Down	Bottom Up	Value	Sector Rotation	Momentum	Indexation
Atlas American Advantage Value		◆													◆				◆	◆			◆		
Atlas American Large-Cap Growth		◆													◆				◆	◆				◆	
Atlas American Money Market											◆	◆			◆										◆
Atlas American RSP Index		◆													◆		◆	◆	◆						◆
Atlas Canadian Balanced	◆								◆				◆						◆	◆				◆	
Atlas Canadian Bond									◆				◆							◆				◆	
Atlas Canadian Dividend Growth								◆	◆				◆						◆		◆	◆			
Atlas Canadian Emerging Growth	◆																◆	◆			◆			◆	
Atlas Canadian High-Yield Bond									◆				◆								◆			◆	
Atlas Canadian Income Trust	◆							◆									◆				◆				
Atlas Canadian Large-Cap Growth	◆																		◆		◆			◆	
Atlas Canadian Large-Cap Value	◆																		◆		◆	◆			
Atlas Canadian Money Market											◆	◆													◆
Atlas Canadian Small-Cap Growth	◆																◆				◆			◆	
Atlas Canadian Small-Cap Value	◆																◆				◆	◆			
Atlas Canadian T-Bill											◆	◆													◆
Atlas European Value			◆												◆				◆		◆			◆	
Atlas Global Value		◆	◆												◆				◆	◆				◆	

ATLAS ASSET MANAGEMENT FAMILY OF FUNDS

	Extended Asset Mix											Objectives								Management Style					
Fund Name	Canadian Equity	U.S. Equity	Europe	Japan	Far East	Latin America	Special Equity	Dividend	Domestic Bond	Global Bond	Money Market	Short Term	Mid Term	Long Term	Currency Effect	Sector Specific	Small Cap	Mid Cap	Large Cap	Top Down	Bottom Up	Value	Sector Rotation	Momentum	Indexation
Atlas International Emerging Markets Growth	◆		◆			◆									◆		◆				◆			◆	
Atlas International Large-Cap Growth	◆		◆												◆				◆		◆		◆		
Atlas International RRSP Index			◆	◆											◆				◆	◆					◆
Atlas Latin American Value						◆									◆			◆	◆	◆			◆		
Atlas Pacific Basin Value				◆	◆										◆				◆	◆		◆			
Atlas World Bond										◆			◆		◆					◆				◆	

AZURA FAMILY OF FUNDS*

	Extended Asset Mix											Objectives								Management Style					
Fund Name	Canadian Equity	U.S. Equity	Europe	Japan	Far East	Latin America	Special Equity	Dividend	Domestic Bond	Global Bond	Money Market	Short Term	Mid Term	Long Term	Currency Effect	Sector Specific	Small Cap	Mid Cap	Large Cap	Top Down	Bottom Up	Value	Sector Rotation	Momentum	Indexation
Azura Balanced Pooled	◆	◆							◆						◆			◆	◆	◆				◆	
Azura Balanced RSP Pooled	◆								◆									◆	◆	◆				◆	
Azura Conservative Pooled	◆								◆		◆	◆	◆						◆	◆				◆	
Azura Growth Pooled		◆	◆	◆	◆					◆			◆		◆				◆	◆				◆	
Azura Growth RRSP Pooled	◆	◆																◆	◆	◆				◆	

This is an asset-allocation service that invests in mutual funds from other fund families, and is available only in Quebec.

BPI FAMILY OF FUNDS

Fund Name	Extended Asset Mix											Objectives								Management Style					
	Canadian Equity	U.S. Equity	Europe	Japan	Far East	Latin America	Special Equity	Dividend	Domestic Bond	Global Bond	Money Market	Short Term	Mid Term	Long Term	Currency Effect	Sector Specific	Small Cap	Mid Cap	Large Cap	Top Down	Bottom Up	Value	Sector Rotation	Momentum	Indexation
BPI American Equity Value		◆													◆			◆	◆		◆	◆			
BPI American Small Companies		◆													◆		◆				◆	◆			
BPI Asia Pacific					◆										◆					◆				◆	
BPI Canadian Balanced	◆								◆				◆						◆		◆	◆			
BPI Canadian Bond									◆				◆							◆			◆	◆	
BPI Canadian Equity Value	◆																		◆		◆	◆			
BPI Canadian Mid-Cap	◆																	◆			◆			◆	
BPI Canadian Opportunities RSP (capped)	◆																	◆	◆		◆	◆			
BPI Canadian Resource Fund Inc.	◆						◆											◆	◆		◆	◆			
BPI Canadian Small Companies	◆																◆				◆	◆			
BPI Canadian Small Companies (capped)	◆																◆				◆			◆	
BPI Corporate Bond									◆								◆				◆	◆			
BPI Dividend Income	◆							◆											◆		◆	◆			
BPI Emerging Markets					◆	◆									◆			◆	◆		◆	◆			
BPI Global Balanced RSP	◆	◆								◆			◆		◆				◆		◆	◆			
BPI Global Equity		◆	◆	◆											◆				◆		◆	◆			
BPI Global Opportunities*		◆	◆												◆		◆	◆			◆	◆			

*This fund is ineligible for Manulife Securities account representatives.

BPI FAMILY OF FUNDS

Fund Name	Extended Asset Mix: Canadian Equity	U.S. Equity	Europe	Japan	Far East	Latin America	Special Equity	Dividend	Domestic Bond	Global Bond	Money Market	Objectives: Short Term	Mid Term	Long Term	Currency Effect	Sector Specific	Small Cap	Mid Cap	Large Cap	Management Style: Top Down	Bottom Up	Value	Sector Rotation	Momentum	Indexation
BPI Global RSP Bond									◆				◆		◆					◆				◆	
BPI Global Small Companies		◆	◆		◆										◆		◆				◆			◆	
BPI High Income								◆	◆				◆				◆				◆				
BPI Income & Growth	◆								◆				◆						◆	◆				◆	
BPI International Equity Value			◆												◆				◆		◆			◆	
BPI T-Bill											◆	◆													◆
BPI US Money Market											◆	◆			◆										◆

BANK OF MONTREAL FAMILY OF FUNDS

Fund Name	Extended Asset Mix											Objectives								Management Style					
	Canadian Equity	U.S. Equity	Europe	Japan	Far East	Latin America	Special Equity	Dividend	Domestic Bond	Global Bond	Money Market	Short Term	Mid Term	Long Term	Currency Effect	Sector Specific	Small Cap	Mid Cap	Large Cap	Top Down	Bottom Up	Value	Sector Rotation	Momentum	Indexation
First Canadian Asset Allocation	◆								◆				◆						◆	◆				◆	
First Canadian Bond									◆				◆								◆		◆		
First Canadian Dividend Income	◆							◆											◆		◆	◆			
First Canadian Emerging Markets					◆	◆									◆			◆	◆	◆				◆	
First Canadian Equity Index	◆																		◆						◆
First Canadian European Growth			◆												◆				◆	◆			◆		
First Canadian Far East Growth					◆										◆				◆	◆				◆	
First Canadian Global Science & Technology							◆								◆	◆		◆	◆		◆			◆	
First Canadian Growth	◆																	◆	◆		◆		◆	◆	
First Canadian International Bond										◆			◆		◆					◆				◆	
First Canadian International Growth			◆	◆											◆			◆	◆	◆		◆			
First Canadian Japanese Growth				◆											◆				◆	◆			◆		
First Canadian Latin America						◆									◆				◆	◆				◆	
First Canadian Money Market											◆	◆													◆
First Canadian Mortage									◆				◆								◆	◆			
First Canadian NAFTA Advantage	◆	◆				◆									◆			◆	◆		◆			◆	
First Canadian Precious Metals							◆								◆	◆	◆	◆	◆		◆			◆	
First Canadian Premium Money Market											◆	◆													◆

BANK OF MONTREAL FAMILY OF FUNDS

Fund Name	Extended Asset Mix											Objectives								Management Style					
	Canadian Equity	U.S. Equity	Europe	Japan	Far East	Latin America	Special Equity	Dividend	Domestic Bond	Global Bond	Money Market	Short Term	Mid Term	Long Term	Currency Effect	Sector Specific	Small Cap	Mid Cap	Large Cap	Top Down	Bottom Up	Value	Sector Rotation	Momentum	Indexation
First Canadian Resource							◆									◆		◆	◆		◆			◆	
First Canadian Special Growth	◆																◆	◆			◆			◆	
First Canadian T-Bill											◆	◆													◆
First Canadian U.S. Equity Index		◆													◆				◆						◆
First Canadian U.S. Growth		◆													◆				◆	◆			◆		
First Canadian U.S. Special Growth		◆													◆		◆	◆			◆			◆	
First Canadian U.S. Value		◆													◆				◆		◆	◆			

BISSETT FAMILY OF FUNDS

Fund Name	Extended Asset Mix											Objectives								Management Style					
	Canadian Equity	U.S. Equity	Europe	Japan	Far East	Latin America	Special Equity	Dividend	Domestic Bond	Global Bond	Money Market	Short Term	Mid Term	Long Term	Currency Effect	Sector Specific	Small Cap	Mid Cap	Large Cap	Top Down	Bottom Up	Value	Sector Rotation	Momentum	Indexation
Bissett American Equity		◆													◆			◆	◆		◆			◆	
Bissett Bond									◆				◆							◆				◆	
Bissett Canadian Equity	◆																	◆	◆		◆		◆		
Bissett Dividend Income	◆							◆											◆		◆	◆			
Bissett Income Trust	◆							◆									◆	◆			◆	◆			
Bissett International Equity			◆	◆											◆				◆	◆	◆			◆	
Bissett Money Market											◆	◆													◆
Bissett Multinational Growth	◆	◆													◆			◆	◆	◆	◆			◆	
Bissett Retirement*	◆								◆				◆					◆	◆	◆				◆	
Bissett Small Capital	◆																◆				◆			◆	

* This is an asset allocation service that invests in other Bissett funds.

BANK OF NOVA SCOTIA FAMILY OF FUNDS

	Extended Asset Mix											Objectives								Management Style					
Fund Name	Canadian Equity	U.S. Equity	Europe	Japan	Far East	Latin America	Special Equity	Dividend	Domestic Bond	Global Bond	Money Market	Short Term	Mid Term	Long Term	Currency Effect	Sector Specific	Small Cap	Mid Cap	Large Cap	Top Down	Bottom Up	Value	Sector Rotation	Momentum	Indexation
Scotia CanAm Growth		◆													◆				◆						◆
Scotia CanAm Income										◆			◆		◆					◆				◆	
Scotia CanAm Money Market											◆	◆			◆										◆
Scotia Excelsior American Equity Growth		◆													◆			◆	◆		◆			◆	
Scotia Excelsior Balanced	◆								◆				◆						◆	◆				◆	
Scotia Excelsior Canadian Blue Chip	◆																	◆	◆	◆			◆		
Scotia Excelsior Canadian Growth	◆																	◆	◆		◆	◆		◆	
Scotia Excelsior Defensive Income									◆			◆									◆	◆			
Scotia Excelsior Dividend	◆							◆											◆		◆	◆			
Scotia Excelsior European Growth			◆												◆				◆		◆	◆			
Scotia Excelsior Global Bond										◆			◆		◆					◆				◆	
Scotia Excelsior Income									◆				◆							◆				◆	
Scotia Excelsior International Equity		◆	◆	◆											◆				◆	◆		◆			
Scotia Excelsior Latin America	◆					◆									◆			◆	◆	◆				◆	
Scotia Excelsior Money Market											◆	◆													◆
Scotia Excelsior Mortgage									◆				◆								◆	◆			
Scotia Excelsior Pacific Rim	◆			◆	◆										◆			◆	◆	◆				◆	
Scotia Excelsior Precious Metals	◆						◆									◆		◆	◆		◆			◆	
Scotia Excelsior Premium T-Bill											◆	◆													◆
Scotia Excelsior T-Bill											◆	◆													◆
Scotia Excelsior Total Return	◆								◆				◆					◆	◆	◆				◆	

BEUTEL GOODMAN MANAGED FUNDS

Fund Name	Extended Asset Mix											Objectives								Management Style					
	Canadian Equity	U.S. Equity	Europe	Japan	Far East	Latin America	Special Equity	Dividend	Domestic Bond	Global Bond	Money Market	Short Term	Mid Term	Long Term	Currency Effect	Sector Specific	Small Cap	Mid Cap	Large Cap	Top Down	Bottom Up	Value	Sector Rotation	Momentum	Indexation
Beutel Goodman American		◆													◆				◆		◆	◆			
Beutel Goodman Balanced	◆								◆				◆						◆	◆				◆	
Beutel Goodman Canadian Equity	◆																		◆	◆		◆			
Beutel Goodman Income									◆				◆							◆				◆	
Beutel Goodman International Equity		◆	◆												◆				◆	◆				◆	
Beutel Goodman Money Market											◆	◆													◆
Beutel Goodman Private Balanced	◆								◆				◆						◆	◆				◆	
Beutel Goodman Private Bond									◆				◆							◆				◆	
Beutel Goodman Small Cap	◆																◆				◆	◆			

CIBC FAMILY OF FUNDS

Fund Name	Extended Asset Mix: Canadian Equity	U.S. Equity	Europe	Japan	Far East	Latin America	Special Equity	Dividend	Domestic Bond	Global Bond	Money Market	Objectives: Short Term	Mid Term	Long Term	Currency Effect	Sector Specific	Small Cap	Mid Cap	Large Cap	Management Style: Top Down	Bottom Up	Value	Sector Rotation	Momentum	Indexation
CIBC Balanced	◆								◆				◆						◆	◆		◆		◆	
CIBC Canadian Bond									◆				◆							◆				◆	
CIBC Canadian Equity	◆																	◆	◆		◆	◆			
CIBC Canadian Index	◆																		◆						◆
CIBC Canadian Real Estate							◆									◆		◆			◆			◆	
CIBC Canadian Resources	◆						◆									◆		◆			◆			◆	
CIBC Canadian Short Term									◆			◆									◆			◆	
CIBC Canadian T-Bill											◆	◆													◆
CIBC Capital Appreciation	◆																◆				◆			◆	
CIBC Dividend	◆							◆											◆		◆	◆			
CIBC Emerging Economies			◆			◆									◆			◆	◆	◆				◆	
CIBC Energy	◆						◆									◆		◆			◆			◆	
CIBC European Equity			◆												◆				◆		◆	◆			
CIBC Far East Prosperity				◆	◆										◆			◆	◆	◆				◆	
CIBC Financial Services							◆									◆		◆			◆			◆	
CIBC Global Bond										◆			◆		◆					◆				◆	
CIBC Global Equity	◆		◆												◆				◆	◆				◆	
CIBC Global Technology		◆					◆								◆	◆		◆			◆			◆	

CIBC FAMILY OF FUNDS

Fund Name	Extended Asset Mix											Objectives								Management Style					
	Canadian Equity	U.S. Equity	Europe	Japan	Far East	Latin America	Special Equity	Dividend	Domestic Bond	Global Bond	Money Market	Short Term	Mid Term	Long Term	Currency Effect	Sector Specific	Small Cap	Mid Cap	Large Cap	Top Down	Bottom Up	Value	Sector Rotation	Momentum	Indexation
CIBC International Index Fund RSP			◆												◆				◆	◆					◆
CIBC International Small Companies			◆												◆		◆				◆			◆	
CIBC Japanese Equity				◆											◆				◆		◆	◆		◆	
CIBC Latin America						◆									◆			◆	◆		◆	◆		◆	
CIBC Money Market											◆	◆													◆
CIBC Mortgage									◆				◆								◆	◆			
CIBC North American Demographics	◆	◆					◆								◆	◆			◆	◆				◆	
CIBC Precious Metals	◆						◆									◆		◆			◆			◆	
CIBC Premium T-Bill											◆	◆													◆
CIBC U.S. Dollar Money Market											◆	◆			◆										◆
CIBC U.S. Equity		◆													◆			◆	◆		◆			◆	
CIBC U.S. Index RRSP		◆													◆				◆						◆
CIBC U.S. Opportunities		◆													◆		◆	◆			◆			◆	

C.I. MUTUAL FUNDS FAMILY OF FUNDS

Fund Name	Extended Asset Mix											Objectives								Management Style					
	Canadian Equity	U.S. Equity	Europe	Japan	Far East	Latin America	Special Equity	Dividend	Domestic Bond	Global Bond	Money Market	Short Term	Mid Term	Long Term	Currency Effect	Sector Specific	Small Cap	Mid Cap	Large Cap	Top Down	Bottom Up	Value	Sector Rotation	Momentum	Indexation
C.I. American		◆													◆			◆	◆		◆	◆		◆	
C.I. American RRSP		◆													◆			◆	◆		◆			◆	
C.I. Canadian Balanced	◆								◆				◆						◆	◆				◆	
C.I. Canadian Bond									◆				◆							◆				◆	
C.I. Canadian Growth	◆																	◆	◆	◆			◆		
C.I. Canadian Income	◆							◆	◆				◆						◆		◆	◆			
C.I. Convington (Labor-Sponsored Inv. Fund)	◆																◆				◆				
C.I. Emerging Markets					◆	◆									◆			◆	◆	◆				◆	
C.I. Global Bond (RRSP)										◆			◆		◆					◆					◆
C.I. Global Equity (RRSP)		◆	◆												◆			◆	◆	◆					◆
C.I. Global Fund		◆	◆												◆			◆	◆	◆				◆	
C.I. Global High Yield										◆			◆		◆					◆		◆			
C.I. International Balanced	◆	◆	◆							◆		◆			◆				◆	◆				◆	
C.I. International Balanced (RRSP)	◆	◆	◆							◆		◆			◆				◆	◆					◆
C.I. Latin America						◆									◆			◆	◆	◆				◆	
C.I. Money Market											◆	◆													◆
C.I. Pacific	◆				◆										◆			◆	◆	◆				◆	
C.I. U.S. Money Market											◆	◆			◆										◆
C.I. World Bond										◆			◆		◆					◆				◆	

C.I. MUTUAL FUNDS FAMILY OF FUNDS

Fund Name	Extended Asset Mix											Objectives								Management Style					
	Canadian Equity	U.S. Equity	Europe	Japan	Far East	Latin America	Special Equity	Dividend	Domestic Bond	Global Bond	Money Market	Short Term	Mid Term	Long Term	Currency Effect	Sector Specific	Small Cap	Mid Cap	Large Cap	Top Down	Bottom Up	Value	Sector Rotation	Momentum	Indexation
SECTOR SHARES																									
C.I. American Sector		◆													◆			◆	◆		◆	◆		◆	
C.I. Canadian Sector	◆																	◆	◆	◆			◆		
C.I. Canadian Short-Term Sector											◆	◆													◆
C.I. Emerging Markets Sector					◆	◆									◆			◆	◆	◆				◆	
C.I. Global Consumer Products Sector		◆	◆			◆									◆	◆		◆	◆		◆			◆	
C.I. Global Financial Services Sector		◆	◆	◆			◆								◆	◆		◆	◆		◆			◆	
C.I. Global Health Sciences Sector		◆	◆				◆								◆	◆		◆	◆		◆			◆	
C.I. Global Resources Sector	◆	◆					◆								◆	◆		◆	◆		◆			◆	
C.I. Global Sector		◆	◆												◆			◆	◆	◆				◆	
C.I. Global Technology Sector		◆	◆			◆									◆	◆		◆	◆		◆			◆	
C.I. Global Telecommunications Sector		◆	◆			◆									◆	◆		◆	◆		◆			◆	
C.I. Latin America Sector						◆									◆			◆	◆	◆				◆	
C.I. Pacific Sector	◆				◆										◆			◆	◆	◆				◆	

C.I. MUTUAL FUNDS FAMILY OF FUNDS

Extended Asset Mix

Fund Name	Canadian Equity	U.S. Equity	Europe	Japan	Far East	Latin America	Special Equity	Dividend	Domestic Bond	Global Bond	Money Market
Hansberger Asian Fund					◆						
Hansberger Developing Markets					◆	◆					
Hansberger European			◆								
Hansberger Global Small Cap		◆	◆								
Hansberger International			◆		◆						
Hansberger Value			◆		◆						
SECTOR SHARES											
Hansberger Asian Sector Shares					◆						
Hansberger Developing Markets Sector					◆	◆					
Hansberger European Sector Shares			◆								
Hansberger Global Small-Cap Sector		◆	◆								
Hansberger International Sector			◆		◆						
Hansberger Value Sector Shares			◆		◆						

Objectives

Fund Name	Short Term	Mid Term	Long Term	Currency Effect	Sector Specific	Small Cap	Mid Cap	Large Cap
Hansberger Asian Fund				◆			◆	◆
Hansberger Developing Markets				◆			◆	◆
Hansberger European				◆			◆	◆
Hansberger Global Small Cap				◆		◆		
Hansberger International				◆			◆	◆
Hansberger Value				◆			◆	◆
SECTOR SHARES								
Hansberger Asian Sector Shares				◆			◆	◆
Hansberger Developing Markets Sector				◆			◆	◆
Hansberger European Sector Shares				◆			◆	◆
Hansberger Global Small-Cap Sector				◆		◆		
Hansberger International Sector				◆			◆	◆
Hansberger Value Sector Shares				◆			◆	◆

Management Style

Fund Name	Top Down	Bottom Up	Value	Sector Rotation	Momentum	Indexation
Hansberger Asian Fund		◆	◆			
Hansberger Developing Markets	◆		◆			
Hansberger European		◆	◆			
Hansberger Global Small Cap	◆		◆			
Hansberger International	◆		◆			
Hansberger Value	◆		◆			
SECTOR SHARES						
Hansberger Asian Sector Shares		◆	◆			
Hansberger Developing Markets Sector	◆		◆			
Hansberger European Sector Shares		◆	◆			
Hansberger Global Small-Cap Sector	◆		◆			
Hansberger International Sector	◆		◆			
Hansberger Value Sector Shares	◆		◆			

C.I. MUTUAL FUNDS FAMILY OF FUNDS

Fund Name	Extended Asset Mix											Objectives								Management Style					
	Canadian Equity	U.S. Equity	Europe	Japan	Far East	Latin America	Special Equity	Dividend	Domestic Bond	Global Bond	Money Market	Short Term	Mid Term	Long Term	Currency Effect	Sector Specific	Small Cap	Mid Cap	Large Cap	Top Down	Bottom Up	Value	Sector Rotation	Momentum	Indexation
C.I. Harbour Explorer	◆																◆				◆	◆			
C.I. Harbour Fund	◆																	◆	◆		◆	◆			
C.I. Harbour Growth & Income	◆								◆				◆						◆	◆				◆	
SECTOR SHARES																									
C.I. Harbour Explorer	◆																◆				◆	◆			
C.I. Harbour Fund	◆																	◆	◆		◆	◆			
C.I. Harbour Growth & Income	◆								◆										◆	◆				◆	

C.I. MUTUAL FUNDS FAMILY OF FUNDS

Fund Name	Extended Asset Mix											Objectives								Management Style					
	Canadian Equity	U.S. Equity	Europe	Japan	Far East	Latin America	Special Equity	Dividend	Domestic Bond	Global Bond	Money Market	Short Term	Mid Term	Long Term	Currency Effect	Sector Specific	Small Cap	Mid Cap	Large Cap	Top Down	Bottom Up	Value	Sector Rotation	Momentum	Indexation
C.I. American Segregated		◆													◆			◆	◆		◆	◆		◆	
C.I. Global Segregated		◆	◆												◆			◆	◆	◆				◆	
C.I. Hansberger Value Segregated			◆		◆										◆			◆	◆	◆		◆			
C.I. Harbour Segregated	◆																	◆	◆		◆	◆			
C.I. Money Market Segregated											◆	◆													◆

CAMBRIDGE (SAGIT) FAMILY OF FUNDS

	Extended Asset Mix											Objectives								Management Style					
Fund Name	Canadian Equity	U.S. Equity	Europe	Japan	Far East	Latin America	Special Equity	Dividend	Domestic Bond	Global Bond	Money Market	Short Term	Mid Term	Long Term	Currency Effect	Sector Specific	Small Cap	Mid Cap	Large Cap	Top Down	Bottom Up	Value	Sector Rotation	Momentum	Indexation
Cambridge American Growth		◆													◆				◆		◆			◆	
Cambridge Americas	◆	◆													◆				◆		◆			◆	
Cambridge Balanced	◆								◆					◆			◆	◆		◆				◆	
Cambridge China	◆		◆		◆										◆		◆	◆			◆				
Cambridge Global	◆														◆		◆	◆		◆				◆	
Cambridge Growth	◆																◆	◆		◆			◆		
Cambridge Pacific	◆				◆										◆			◆	◆	◆				◆	
Cambridge Precious Metals							◆									◆	◆	◆	◆		◆			◆	
Cambridge Resource							◆									◆	◆	◆	◆		◆			◆	
Cambridge Special Equity	◆																◆				◆			◆	

CANADA TRUST FAMILY OF FUNDS

Fund Name	Extended Asset Mix											Objectives								Management Style					
	Canadian Equity	U.S. Equity	Europe	Japan	Far East	Latin America	Special Equity	Dividend	Domestic Bond	Global Bond	Money Market	Short Term	Mid Term	Long Term	Currency Effect	Sector Specific	Small Cap	Mid Cap	Large Cap	Top Down	Bottom Up	Value	Sector Rotation	Momentum	Indexation
C T Amerigrowth		◆													◆				◆						◆
C T Asia Growth				◆	◆										◆				◆						◆
C T Balanced	◆								◆				◆						◆	◆				◆	
C T Bond									◆					◆						◆				◆	
C T Canadian Equity	◆																		◆						◆
C T Dividend Income								◆											◆		◆	◆			
C T Emerging Markets					◆	◆									◆			◆	◆	◆			◆	◆	
C T Euro Growth			◆												◆				◆						◆
C T Global Growth		◆	◆	◆											◆				◆	◆					◆
C T International Bond										◆			◆							◆				◆	
C T International Equity		◆	◆												◆			◆	◆	◆	◆			◆	
C T International Equity Index		◆	◆												◆				◆	◆					◆
C T Money Market											◆	◆													◆
C T Mortgage									◆				◆								◆	◆			
C T North American	◆	◆													◆			◆	◆		◆			◆	
C T Premium Money Market											◆	◆													◆
C T Retirement Balanced	◆								◆				◆							◆				◆	◆
C T Short-Term Bond									◆			◆									◆	◆			

CANADA TRUST FAMILY OF FUNDS

Fund Name	Extended Asset Mix											Objectives								Management Style					
	Canadian Equity	U.S. Equity	Europe	Japan	Far East	Latin America	Special Equity	Dividend	Domestic Bond	Global Bond	Money Market	Short Term	Mid Term	Long Term	Currency Effect	Sector Specific	Small Cap	Mid Cap	Large Cap	Top Down	Bottom Up	Value	Sector Rotation	Momentum	Indexation
C T Special Equity	◆																◆	◆			◆			◆	
C T Stock	◆																	◆	◆		◆			◆	
C T U.S. Equity		◆													◆				◆		◆			◆	
C T U.S. Equity Index		◆													◆				◆						◆

CLARINGTON FAMILY OF FUNDS

Fund Name	Extended Asset Mix											Objectives								Management Style					
	Canadian Equity	U.S. Equity	Europe	Japan	Far East	Latin America	Special Equity	Dividend	Domestic Bond	Global Bond	Money Market	Short Term	Mid Term	Long Term	Currency Effect	Sector Specific	Small Cap	Mid Cap	Large Cap	Top Down	Bottom Up	Value	Sector Rotation	Momentum	Indexation
Clarington Asia Pacific					◆										◆				◆	◆				◆	
Clarington Canadian Balanced	◆								◆				◆						◆	◆				◆	
Clarington Canadian Equity	◆																		◆		◆	◆			
Clarington Canadian Income	◆							◆	◆				◆						◆	◆	◆			◆	
Clarington Canadian Small Cap	◆																◆				◆			◆	
Clarington Global Communications							◆								◆	◆	◆	◆	◆		◆			◆	
Clarington Global Opportunities		◆	◆												◆		◆	◆			◆	◆			
Clarington Money Market											◆	◆													◆
Clarington U.S. Equity		◆													◆			◆	◆		◆			◆	
Clarington U.S. Small Companies Growth		◆													◆		◆				◆	◆			

CLEAN ENVIRONMENT FAMILY OF FUNDS

Extended Asset Mix

Fund Name	Canadian Equity	U.S. Equity	Europe	Japan	Far East	Latin America	Special Equity	Dividend	Domestic Bond	Global Bond	Money Market
Clean Environment Balanced	◆								◆		
Clean Environment Equity	◆										
Clean Environment Income								◆			
Clean Environment International Equity	◆	◆									

Objectives

Fund Name	Short Term	Mid Term	Long Term	Currency Effect	Sector Specific	Small Cap	Mid Cap	Large Cap
Clean Environment Balanced		◆						◆
Clean Environment Equity							◆	◆
Clean Environment Income							◆	◆
Clean Environment International Equity				◆			◆	◆

Management Style

Fund Name	Top Down	Bottom Up	Value	Sector Rotation	Momentum	Indexation
Clean Environment Balanced	◆				◆	
Clean Environment Equity		◆			◆	
Clean Environment Income		◆	◆			
Clean Environment International Equity		◆			◆	

DYNAMIC FAMILY OF FUNDS

Extended Asset Mix

Fund Name	Canadian Equity	U.S. Equity	Europe	Japan	Far East	Latin America	Special Equity	Dividend	Domestic Bond	Global Bond	Money Market
Dynamic Americas	◆	◆									
Dynamic Canadian Growth	◆										
Dynamic Canadian Real Estate							◆				
Dynamic Dividend								◆			
Dynamic Dividend Growth								◆			
Dynamic Dollar Cost Averaging									◆		
Dynamic Europe			◆								
Dynamic Far East	◆				◆						
Dynamic Fund of Canada	◆										
Dynamic Global Bond										◆	

Objectives

Fund Name	Short Term	Mid Term	Long Term	Currency Effect	Sector Specific	Small Cap	Mid Cap	Large Cap
Dynamic Americas				◆			◆	◆
Dynamic Canadian Growth						◆	◆	
Dynamic Canadian Real Estate					◆	◆	◆	
Dynamic Dividend								◆
Dynamic Dividend Growth							◆	◆
Dynamic Dollar Cost Averaging	◆							
Dynamic Europe				◆				◆
Dynamic Far East				◆			◆	◆
Dynamic Fund of Canada								◆
Dynamic Global Bond		◆		◆				

Management Style

Fund Name	Top Down	Bottom Up	Value	Sector Rotation	Momentum	Indexation
Dynamic Americas		◆	◆			
Dynamic Canadian Growth		◆	◆			
Dynamic Canadian Real Estate		◆	◆			
Dynamic Dividend		◆	◆			
Dynamic Dividend Growth		◆	◆			
Dynamic Dollar Cost Averaging						◆
Dynamic Europe		◆	◆			
Dynamic Far East		◆	◆			
Dynamic Fund of Canada		◆	◆			
Dynamic Global Bond	◆				◆	

DYNAMIC FAMILY OF FUNDS

Fund Name	Extended Asset Mix											Objectives								Management Style					
	Canadian Equity	U.S. Equity	Europe	Japan	Far East	Latin America	Special Equity	Dividend	Domestic Bond	Global Bond	Money Market	Short Term	Mid Term	Long Term	Currency Effect	Sector Specific	Small Cap	Mid Cap	Large Cap	Top Down	Bottom Up	Value	Sector Rotation	Momentum	Indexation
Dynamic Global Income & Growth	◆								◆				◆						◆	◆				◆	
Dynamic Global Millennia	◆						◆								◆	◆		◆	◆		◆	◆			
Dynamic Global Partners	◆	◆	◆		◆					◆			◆		◆				◆	◆				◆	
Dynamic Global Precious Metals							◆								◆	◆	◆	◆	◆		◆	◆			
Dynamic Global Resource	◆		◆				◆								◆	◆		◆	◆		◆	◆			
Dynamic Government Income									◆			◆								◆		◆			
Dynamic Income									◆				◆		◆					◆				◆	
Dynamic International	◆	◆	◆												◆				◆	◆		◆			
Dynamic Latin America						◆									◆				◆		◆	◆			
Dynamic Money Market											◆	◆													◆
Dynamic Partners	◆								◆				◆					◆	◆	◆				◆	
Dynamic Precious Metals							◆									◆	◆	◆	◆		◆	◆			
Dynamic Quebec							◆										◆	◆	◆		◆	◆			
Dynamic Real Estate Equity							◆									◆		◆	◆		◆	◆			
Dynamic Small Cap	◆																◆				◆	◆			
Dynamic Team*	◆																	◆	◆	◆					

*The Dynamic Team fund holds a portfolio of other Dynamic funds.

ELLIOTT & PAGE FAMILY OF FUNDS

Fund Name	Extended Asset Mix											Objectives								Management Style					
	Canadian Equity	U.S. Equity	Europe	Japan	Far East	Latin America	Special Equity	Dividend	Domestic Bond	Global Bond	Money Market	Short Term	Mid Term	Long Term	Currency Effect	Sector Specific	Small Cap	Mid Cap	Large Cap	Top Down	Bottom Up	Value	Sector Rotation	Momentum	Indexation
Elliott & Page American Growth		◆													◆			◆	◆		◆	◆			
Elliott & Page Asian Growth				◆	◆										◆			◆		◆				◆	
Elliott & Page Balanced	◆								◆				◆						◆	◆			◆	◆	
Elliott & Page Bond									◆				◆							◆				◆	
Elliott & Page Emerging Markets					◆	◆									◆			◆		◆				◆	
Elliott & Page Equity	◆																		◆	◆			◆		
Elliott & Page Global Balanced		◆	◆						◆	◆			◆		◆				◆	◆				◆	
Elliott & Page Global Bond									◆	◆			◆		◆					◆				◆	
Elliott & Page Global Equity		◆	◆												◆				◆	◆				◆	
Elliott & Page Money Market											◆	◆													◆
Elliott & Page Monthly High Income	◆							◆	◆				◆				◆				◆	◆			
Elliott & Page T-Bill											◆	◆													◆
Elliott & Page U.S. Mid Cap		◆																◆			◆	◆			
Elliott & Page Value Equity	◆																		◆		◆	◆			

ETHICAL FAMILY OF FUNDS

Fund Name	Canadian Equity	U.S. Equity	Europe	Japan	Far East	Latin America	Special Equity	Dividend	Domestic Bond	Global Bond	Money Market	Short Term	Mid Term	Long Term	Currency Effect	Sector Specific	Small Cap	Mid Cap	Large Cap	Top Down	Bottom Up	Value	Sector Rotation	Momentum	Indexation
	Extended Asset Mix											**Objectives**								**Management Style**					
Ethical Balanced	◆	◆							◆				◆						◆	◆				◆	
Ethical Global Bond										◆			◆							◆				◆	
Ethical Growth	◆																		◆	◆				◆	
Ethical Income									◆				◆								◆		◆		
Ethical Money Market											◆	◆													◆
Ethical North American Equity	◆	◆													◆				◆	◆				◆	
Ethical Pacific Rim	◆				◆										◆				◆	◆				◆	
Ethical Special Equity	◆																◆	◆			◆			◆	

FIDELITY FAMILY OF FUNDS

Fund Name	Extended Asset Mix: Canadian Equity	U.S. Equity	Europe	Japan	Far East	Latin America	Special Equity	Dividend	Domestic Bond	Global Bond	Money Market	Objectives: Short Term	Mid Term	Long Term	Currency Effect	Sector Specific	Small Cap	Mid Cap	Large Cap	Management Style: Top Down	Bottom Up	Value	Sector Rotation	Momentum	Indexation
Fidelity Asset Manager		◆								◆			◆						◆		◆			◆	
Fidelity Canadian Asset Allocation	◆								◆				◆						◆	◆	◆			◆	
Fidelity Canadian Bond									◆				◆								◆		◆		
Fidelity Canadian Growth	◆																◆	◆			◆	◆			
Fidelity Canadian Income									◆				◆								◆		◆		
Fidelity Canadian Short Term											◆	◆													◆
Fidelity Capital Builder	◆	◆																	◆		◆			◆	
Fidelity Emerging Markets Bond										◆				◆	◆						◆		◆		
Fidelity Emerging Markets Portfolio					◆	◆									◆			◆	◆		◆			◆	
Fidelity European Growth			◆												◆			◆	◆		◆			◆	
Fidelity Far East					◆										◆				◆		◆			◆	
Fidelity Focus Consumer Industries		◆					◆								◆	◆			◆		◆			◆	
Fidelity Focus Financial Services		◆					◆								◆	◆			◆		◆			◆	
Fidelity Focus Health Care		◆					◆								◆	◆			◆		◆			◆	
Fidelity Focus Natural Resources		◆					◆								◆	◆			◆		◆			◆	
Fidelity Focus Technology		◆					◆								◆	◆			◆		◆			◆	
Fidelity Global Asset Allocation		◆								◆			◆		◆				◆	◆				◆	
Fidelity Growth America		◆													◆				◆		◆			◆	

FIDELITY FAMILY OF FUNDS

Fund Name	Extended Asset Mix: Canadian Equity	U.S. Equity	Europe	Japan	Far East	Latin America	Special Equity	Dividend	Domestic Bond	Global Bond	Money Market	Objectives: Short Term	Mid Term	Long Term	Currency Effect	Sector Specific	Small Cap	Mid Cap	Large Cap	Management Style: Top Down	Bottom Up	Value	Sector Rotation	Momentum	Indexation
Fidelity International Portfolio		◆	◆	◆											◆				◆		◆			◆	
Fidelity Japanese Growth				◆											◆				◆		◆			◆	
Fidelity Latin America Growth	◆					◆									◆			◆	◆		◆			◆	
Fidelity North America Income									◆			◆			◆						◆		◆		
Fidelity RRSP Global Bond									◆				◆		◆						◆		◆		
Fidelity Small-Cap America		◆													◆		◆				◆			◆	
Fidelity True North	◆																◆	◆			◆	◆			
Fidelity U.S. Money Market											◆	◆			◆										◆

G.T. GLOBAL FAMILY OF FUNDS

Fund Name	Extended Asset Mix: Canadian Equity	U.S. Equity	Europe	Japan	Far East	Latin America	Special Equity	Dividend	Domestic Bond	Global Bond	Money Market	Objectives: Short Term	Mid Term	Long Term	Currency Effect	Sector Specific	Small Cap	Mid Cap	Large Cap	Management Style: Top Down	Bottom Up	Value	Sector Rotation	Momentum	Indexation
G.T. American Growth Class		◆															◆	◆			◆			◆	
G.T. Canada Income Class	◆							◆											◆		◆	◆			
G.T. Canada Growth Class	◆																	◆			◆			◆	
G.T. Global Canada Money Market											◆	◆													◆
G.T. Global Growth & Income		◆	◆							◆			◆		◆				◆	◆				◆	
G.T. Global Health Care Class							◆								◆	◆		◆	◆		◆			◆	
G.T. Global Infrastructure Class	◆	◆					◆								◆	◆		◆	◆		◆			◆	
G.T. Global Natural Resources Class					◆										◆	◆		◆	◆		◆			◆	
G.T. Global Pacific Growth Class					◆										◆				◆		◆			◆	
G.T. Global Theme Class							◆								◆	◆	◆	◆			◆			◆	
G.T. Global World Bond Fund Class										◆		◆			◆					◆				◆	
G.T. Latin America Growth Class						◆									◆			◆		◆	◆			◆	
G.T. Short-Term Income Class A or B											◆	◆													◆
G.T. Telecommunications Class							◆								◆				◆		◆			◆	

GLOBAL STRATEGY FAMILY OF FUNDS

	Extended Asset Mix											Objectives								Management Style					
Fund Name	Canadian Equity	U.S. Equity	Europe	Japan	Far East	Latin America	Special Equity	Dividend	Domestic Bond	Global Bond	Money Market	Short Term	Mid Term	Long Term	Currency Effect	Sector Specific	Small Cap	Mid Cap	Large Cap	Top Down	Bottom Up	Value	Sector Rotation	Momentum	Indexation
Global Strategy Asia					◆										◆			◆	◆	◆			◆	◆	
Global Strategy Bond									◆				◆							◆				◆	
Global Strategy Canada Growth	◆																	◆	◆		◆	◆		◆	
Global Strategy Canada Small Cap	◆																◆				◆	◆			
Global Strategy Canadian Opportunities	◆																	◆			◆	◆			
Global Strategy Europe Plus			◆												◆				◆	◆				◆	◆
Global Strategy Gold Plus							◆								◆	◆		◆			◆	◆		◆	
Global Strategy Income Plus	◆							◆	◆				◆						◆	◆	◆			◆	
Global Strategy Japan				◆											◆			◆	◆		◆	◆		◆	
Global Strategy Latin America						◆									◆				◆	◆				◆	
Global Strategy Money Market											◆	◆													◆
Global Strategy U.S. Equity		◆													◆			◆	◆		◆	◆		◆	
Global Strategy World Balanced	◆	◆	◆							◆			◆		◆				◆	◆				◆	
Global Strategy World Bond										◆			◆		◆					◆			◆		
Global Strategy World Emerging Companies		◆	◆		◆										◆		◆		◆		◆	◆		◆	
Global Strategy World Equity		◆	◆	◆											◆			◆	◆	◆			◆	◆	

GLOBAL STRATEGY FAMILY OF FUNDS

Fund Name	Extended Asset Mix											Objectives								Management Style					
	Canadian Equity	U.S. Equity	Europe	Japan	Far East	Latin America	Special Equity	Dividend	Domestic Bond	Global Bond	Money Market	Short Term	Mid Term	Long Term	Currency Effect	Sector Specific	Small Cap	Mid Cap	Large Cap	Top Down	Bottom Up	Value	Sector Rotation	Momentum	Indexation
Global Strategy Diversified Funds																									
Global Strategy Diversified Asia					◆										◆				◆	◆		◆		◆	
Global Strategy Diversified Bond										◆			◆		◆					◆				◆	
Global Strategy Diversified Europe			◆												◆				◆	◆		◆		◆	
Global Strategy Diversified Foreign Bond										◆			◆		◆					◆				◆	
Global Strategy Diversified Japan Plus				◆											◆				◆	◆				◆	◆
Global Strategy Diversified Latin America						◆									◆			◆	◆	◆		◆		◆	
Global Strategy Diversified World Equity		◆	◆	◆											◆				◆	◆				◆	◆

GREAT-WEST LIFE FUNDS (MANAGED BY AGF)

Fund Name	Extended Asset Mix: Canadian Equity	U.S. Equity	Europe	Japan	Far East	Latin America	Special Equity	Dividend	Domestic Bond	Global Bond	Money Market	Objectives: Short Term	Mid Term	Long Term	Currency Effect	Sector Specific	Small Cap	Mid Cap	Large Cap	Management Style: Top Down	Bottom Up	Value	Sector Rotation	Momentum	Indexation
Great-West Life American Growth		◆													◆				◆		◆			◆	
Great-West Life Asian Growth					◆										◆				◆	◆				◆	
Great-West Life Canadian Bond[1]									◆				◆								◆			◆	
Great-West Life Canadian Equity [2]	◆																		◆		◆			◆	
Great-West Life Canadian Resource	◆						◆									◆		◆	◆	◆				◆	
Great-West Life Equity Index	◆																		◆						◆
Great-West Life Global Income										◆			◆		◆					◆				◆	
Great-West Life Growth & Income[3]	◆								◆				◆						◆	◆				◆	
Great-West Life Money Market											◆	◆													◆
Great-West Life Mortgage									◆					◆							◆	◆			
Great-West Life North American	◆	◆																	◆		◆			◆	
Great-West Life Canadian Real Estate							◆									◆					◆	◆			
Great-West Life Small Companies	◆																◆				◆			◆	
Great-West Life U.S. Equity		◆													◆				◆		◆	◆			

1:This also applies to Great-West Life Bond and GWL Government Bond.
2:This also applies to Great-West Life Aggressive and GWL Larger Companies.
3:This also applies to Great-West Life Advanced, GWL Balanced, GWL Conservative, GWL Diversified, GWL Equity Bond and GWL Moderate.

GUARDIAN FAMILY OF FUNDS

Fund Name	Extended Asset Mix: Canadian Equity	U.S. Equity	Europe	Japan	Far East	Latin America	Special Equity	Dividend	Domestic Bond	Global Bond	Money Market	Objectives: Short Term	Mid Term	Long Term	Currency Effect	Sector Specific	Small Cap	Mid Cap	Large Cap	Management Style: Top Down	Bottom Up	Value	Sector Rotation	Momentum	Indexation
Guardian American Equity		◆													◆				◆		◆			◆	
Guardian Asia Pacific				◆	◆										◆			◆	◆	◆				◆	
Guardian Canadian Balanced	◆								◆				◆						◆	◆				◆	
Guardian Canadian Income									◆			◆									◆	◆			
Guardian Canadian Money Market											◆	◆													◆
Guardian Emerging Markets			◆		◆	◆									◆				◆	◆				◆	
Guardian Enterprise	◆																	◆			◆			◆	
Guardian Foreign Income										◆			◆		◆					◆				◆	
Guardian Global Equity		◆	◆												◆				◆	◆				◆	
Guardian Growth & Income	◆								◆				◆						◆	◆				◆	
Guardian Growth Equity	◆																		◆		◆			◆	
Guardian International Balanced	◆	◆								◆			◆		◆				◆	◆					◆
Guardian International Income										◆			◆		◆					◆				◆	
Guardian Monthly High Income	◆							◆									◆	◆			◆	◆			
Guardian Monthly Dividend (capped)	◆							◆											◆		◆	◆			
Guardian U.S. Money Market											◆	◆			◆										◆

INVESTORS GROUP FUND FAMILY

Fund Name	Extended Asset Mix											Objectives								Management Style					
	Canadian Equity	U.S. Equity	Europe	Japan	Far East	Latin America	Special Equity	Dividend	Domestic Bond	Global Bond	Money Market	Short Term	Mid Term	Long Term	Currency Effect	Sector Specific	Small Cap	Mid Cap	Large Cap	Top Down	Bottom Up	Value	Sector Rotation	Momentum	Indexation
Investors Asset Allocation	◆								◆				◆						◆	◆				◆	
Investors Canadian Equity	◆																	◆	◆	◆			◆		
Investors Canadian Natural Resources	◆						◆									◆		◆			◆			◆	
Investors Canadian Small Cap	◆																◆				◆			◆	
Investors Corporate Bond									◆				◆								◆	◆			
Investors Dividend	◆							◆											◆		◆	◆			
Investors European Growth			◆												◆				◆	◆			◆	◆	
Investors Global Bond										◆			◆		◆					◆				◆	
Investors Global		◆	◆	◆											◆				◆		◆	◆			
Investors Government Bond									◆					◆						◆				◆	
Investors Japanese Growth				◆											◆			◆			◆	◆			
Investors Latin America Growth						◆									◆				◆	◆				◆	
Investors Money Market											◆	◆													◆
Investors Mortgage									◆				◆							◆		◆			
Investors Mutual of Canada	◆								◆				◆						◆	◆				◆	
Investors North American Growth	◆	◆													◆				◆		◆			◆	
Investors North American High Yield									◆				◆								◆	◆			
Investors Pacific International Fund					◆										◆				◆		◆	◆			

INVESTORS GROUP FUND FAMILY

Fund Name	Extended Asset Mix											Objectives								Management Style					
	Canadian Equity	U.S. Equity	Europe	Japan	Far East	Latin America	Special Equity	Dividend	Domestic Bond	Global Bond	Money Market	Short Term	Mid Term	Long Term	Currency Effect	Sector Specific	Small Cap	Mid Cap	Large Cap	Top Down	Bottom Up	Value	Sector Rotation	Momentum	Indexation
Investors Real Property							◆									◆					◆	◆			
Investors Retirement Mutual	◆																		◆	◆		◆			
Investors Special	◆	◆													◆			◆			◆			◆	
Investors Summa	◆																◆	◆			◆			◆	
Investors U.S. Growth		◆													◆				◆		◆	◆			
Investors U.S. Money Market											◆	◆			◆										◆
Investors U.S. Opportunities		◆													◆			◆			◆	◆			

Note: We did not include any Investors Group Portfolio funds, because the portfolio funds for the most part simply buy other Investors Group funds.

JONES HEWARD FUNDS FAMILY

Fund Name	Extended Asset Mix											Objectives								Management Style					
	Canadian Equity	U.S. Equity	Europe	Japan	Far East	Latin America	Special Equity	Dividend	Domestic Bond	Global Bond	Money Market	Short Term	Mid Term	Long Term	Currency Effect	Sector Specific	Small Cap	Mid Cap	Large Cap	Top Down	Bottom Up	Value	Sector Rotation	Momentum	Indexation
Jones Heward	◆																		◆	◆			◆		
Jones Heward American		◆													◆				◆	◆				◆	
Jones Heward Bond									◆				◆							◆				◆	
Jones Heward Canadian Balanced	◆								◆				◆						◆	◆				◆	
Jones Heward Money Market											◆	◆													◆

MACKENZIE FAMILY OF FUNDS

Fund Name	Extended Asset Mix: Canadian Equity	U.S. Equity	Europe	Japan	Far East	Latin America	Special Equity	Dividend	Domestic Bond	Global Bond	Money Market
Industrial American		◆									
Industrial Balanced	◆								◆		
Industrial Bond									◆		
Industrial Cash Management											◆
Industrial Dividend Growth	◆							◆			
Industrial Equity	◆										
Industrial Future	◆										
Industrial Growth	◆										
Industrial Horizon	◆										
Industrial Income	◆								◆		
Industrial Mortgage Securities									◆		
Industrial Pension	◆								◆		
Industrial Short Term											◆
Ivy Canadian	◆										
Ivy Enterprise	◆										
Ivy Foreign Equity	◆	◆									
Ivy Growth & Income	◆								◆		

Fund Name	Objectives: Short Term	Mid Term	Long Term	Currency Effect	Sector Specific	Small Cap	Mid Cap	Large Cap	Management Style: Top Down	Bottom Up	Value	Sector Rotation	Momentum	Indexation
Industrial American				◆			◆	◆	◆		◆			
Industrial Balanced			◆				◆	◆	◆			◆		
Industrial Bond			◆						◆				◆	
Industrial Cash Management	◆													◆
Industrial Dividend Growth								◆		◆	◆			
Industrial Equity						◆			◆			◆		
Industrial Future								◆		◆			◆	
Industrial Growth							◆		◆			◆		
Industrial Horizon								◆	◆			◆		
Industrial Income			◆					◆	◆				◆	
Industrial Mortgage Securities		◆							◆		◆		◆	
Industrial Pension		◆					◆	◆	◆	◆				
Industrial Short Term	◆													◆
Ivy Canadian							◆	◆		◆	◆			
Ivy Enterprise						◆				◆	◆			
Ivy Foreign Equity				◆			◆	◆		◆	◆			
Ivy Growth & Income		◆					◆	◆	◆				◆	

MACKENZIE FAMILY OF FUNDS

Fund Name	Extended Asset Mix											Objectives								Management Style					
	Canadian Equity	U.S. Equity	Europe	Japan	Far East	Latin America	Special Equity	Dividend	Domestic Bond	Global Bond	Money Market	Short Term	Mid Term	Long Term	Currency Effect	Sector Specific	Small Cap	Mid Cap	Large Cap	Top Down	Bottom Up	Value	Sector Rotation	Momentum	Indexation
Ivy Mortgage									◆				◆												◆
Mackenzie Sentinel Canadian Equity	◆																	◆	◆		◆			◆	
Mackenzie Sentinel Global			◆	◆															◆	◆				◆	◆
Universal Americas		◆				◆									◆			◆	◆	◆	◆		◆		
Universal Canadian Balanced	◆								◆				◆						◆	◆				◆	
Universal Canadian Growth	◆																	◆			◆	◆			
Universal Canadian Resources	◆						◆									◆	◆				◆			◆	
Universal European Opportunities			◆												◆		◆	◆			◆	◆			
Universal Far East	◆				◆										◆				◆	◆			◆		
Universal Growth		◆													◆			◆			◆	◆			
Universal Japan				◆											◆			◆			◆				
Universal Precious Metals							◆								◆	◆	◆	◆			◆			◆	
Universal Tactical Bond										◆				◆	◆					◆				◆	
Universal U.S. Emerging Growth		◆													◆		◆				◆	◆			
Universal U.S. Money Market											◆	◆			◆										◆
Universal World Asset Allocation		◆	◆							◆			◆		◆				◆	◆				◆	
Universal World Balanced RRSP		◆	◆		◆					◆			◆		◆				◆	◆					◆
Universal World Emerging Growth	◆		◆			◆									◆			◆		◆	◆	◆			

MACKENZIE FAMILY OF FUNDS

Fund Name	Extended Asset Mix: Canadian Equity	U.S. Equity	Europe	Japan	Far East	Latin America	Special Equity	Dividend	Domestic Bond	Global Bond	Money Market	Objectives: Short Term	Mid Term	Long Term	Currency Effect	Sector Specific	Small Cap	Mid Cap	Large Cap	Management Style: Top Down	Bottom Up	Value	Sector Rotation	Momentum	Indexation
Universal World Equity			◆	◆											◆				◆	◆				◆	
Universal World Growth RRSP		◆	◆		◆										◆				◆	◆					◆
Universal World High Yield										◆			◆		◆						◆		◆		
Universal World Income RRSP										◆				◆	◆					◆					◆
Universal World International Stock			◆	◆											◆				◆		◆			◆	
Universal World Real Estate							◆								◆	◆		◆	◆	◆					◆
Universal World Science & Technology							◆								◆	◆		◆	◆		◆			◆	
Universal World Value	◆	◆	◆	◆											◆				◆	◆		◆			

MANULIFE GUARANTEED INVESTMENT FUNDS

Fund Name	Extended Asset Mix											Objectives								Management Style					
	Canadian Equity	U.S. Equity	Europe	Japan	Far East	Latin America	Special Equity	Dividend	Domestic Bond	Global Bond	Money Market	Short Term	Mid Term	Long Term	Currency Effect	Sector Specific	Small Cap	Mid Cap	Large Cap	Top Down	Bottom Up	Value	Sector Rotation	Momentum	Indexation
Money Market Funds																									
Elliott & Page Money Market GIF											◆	◆													◆
Fixed-Income Canadian Funds																									
AGF Canadian Bond									◆				◆							◆				◆	
AGF High-Income GIF	◆							◆	◆				◆						◆	◆				◆	
Fidelity Canadian Bond GIF									◆				◆								◆		◆		
Talvest Income GIF									◆			◆									◆		◆		
Canadian Dividend Funds																									
AGF Dividend GIF	◆							◆											◆		◆	◆			
Dynamic Dividend Growth GIF	◆							◆										◆	◆		◆	◆			
Balanced Funds																									
AGF Growth and Income GIF	◆								◆				◆						◆	◆				◆	
C.I. Harbour Growth & Income GIF	◆								◆				◆						◆	◆				◆	
Dynamic Partners GIF	◆								◆				◆					◆	◆	◆				◆	
Elliott & Page Balanced GIF	◆								◆				◆						◆	◆			◆	◆	
Fidelity Canadian Asset Allocation GIF	◆								◆				◆						◆	◆	◆			◆	
Talvest Canadian Asset Allocation GIF	◆								◆				◆						◆	◆		◆		◆	
Trimark Select Balanced GIF	◆								◆				◆						◆	◆				◆	

MANULIFE GUARANTEED INVESTMENT FUNDS

Fund Name	Extended Asset Mix											Objectives								Management Style					
	Canadian Equity	U.S. Equity	Europe	Japan	Far East	Latin America	Special Equity	Dividend	Domestic Bond	Global Bond	Money Market	Short Term	Mid Term	Long Term	Currency Effect	Sector Specific	Small Cap	Mid Cap	Large Cap	Top Down	Bottom Up	Value	Sector Rotation	Momentum	Indexation
Canadian Equity Funds																									
AGF Canadian Equity GIF	◆																	◆	◆		◆			◆	
C.I. Harbour GIF	◆																	◆	◆		◆	◆			
Elliott & Page Equity GIF	◆																		◆	◆			◆		
Elliott & Page Value Equity GIF	◆																		◆		◆	◆			
Fidelity Capital Builder GIF	◆	◆																	◆		◆			◆	
Fidelity True North GIF	◆																◆	◆			◆	◆			
G.T. Global Canada Growth Class GIF	◆																	◆			◆			◆	
O'Donnell Canadian GIF	◆																		◆		◆			◆	
O'Donnell Select GIF	◆																		◆		◆	◆			
Trimark Select Canadian Growth GIF	◆																		◆		◆	◆			
Global Fixed-Income Funds																									
AGF Global Government Bond GIF										◆			◆		◆					◆				◆	
Dynamic Global Bond GIF										◆			◆		◆					◆				◆	

MANULIFE GUARANTEED INVESTMENT FUNDS

Extended Asset Mix

Fund Name	Canadian Equity	U.S. Equity	Europe	Japan	Far East	Latin America	Special Equity	Dividend	Domestic Bond	Global Bond	Money Market
U.S. Equity Funds											
AGF Intl Group American Growth Class GIF		◆									
Elliott & Page American Growth GIF		◆									
Fidelity Growth America GIF		◆									
G.T. American Growth Class GIF		◆									
Talvest/Hyperion Value Line U.S. Equity GIF		◆									
Global Equity Funds											
Fidelity International Portfolio GIF		◆	◆	◆							
Trimark Select Growth GIF	◆	◆		◆							
Index Funds											
Canadian Equity Index GIF	◆										
U.S. Equity Index GIF		◆									

Objectives

Fund Name	Short Term	Mid Term	Long Term	Currency Effect	Sector Specific	Small Cap	Mid Cap	Large Cap
U.S. Equity Funds								
AGF Intl Group American Growth Class GIF				◆				◆
Elliott & Page American Growth GIF				◆			◆	◆
Fidelity Growth America GIF				◆				◆
G.T. American Growth Class GIF						◆	◆	
Talvest/Hyperion Value Line U.S. Equity GIF				◆			◆	◆
Global Equity Funds								
Fidelity International Portfolio GIF				◆				◆
Trimark Select Growth GIF				◆				◆
Index Funds								
Canadian Equity Index GIF								◆
U.S. Equity Index GIF				◆				◆

Management Style

Fund Name	Top Down	Bottom Up	Value	Sector Rotation	Momentum	Indexation
U.S. Equity Funds						
AGF Intl Group American Growth Class GIF		◆			◆	
Elliott & Page American Growth GIF		◆	◆			
Fidelity Growth America GIF		◆			◆	
G.T. American Growth Class GIF		◆			◆	
Talvest/Hyperion Value Line U.S. Equity GIF		◆			◆	
Global Equity Funds						
Fidelity International Portfolio GIF		◆			◆	
Trimark Select Growth GIF		◆	◆			
Index Funds						
Canadian Equity Index GIF						◆
U.S. Equity Index GIF						◆

MANULIFE CABOT FAMILY OF FUNDS

Fund Name	Extended Asset Mix											Objectives								Management Style					
	Canadian Equity	U.S. Equity	Europe	Japan	Far East	Latin America	Special Equity	Dividend	Domestic Bond	Global Bond	Money Market	Short Term	Mid Term	Long Term	Currency Effect	Sector Specific	Small Cap	Mid Cap	Large Cap	Top Down	Bottom Up	Value	Sector Rotation	Momentum	Indexation
Cabot Blue Chip Fund	◆																		◆	◆			◆	◆	
Cabot Canadian Equity Fund	◆																		◆	◆			◆	◆	
Cabot Canadian Growth	◆																◆	◆			◆			◆	
Cabot Diversified Bond									◆				◆							◆				◆	
Cabot Emerging Growth	◆																◆	◆			◆			◆	
Cabot Global Equity		◆	◆	◆														◆	◆	◆	◆			◆	
Cabot Money Market											◆	◆													◆

MANULIFE NAL-INVESTOR FAMILY OF FUNDS

Fund Name	Extended Asset Mix											Objectives								Management Style					
	Canadian Equity	U.S. Equity	Europe	Japan	Far East	Latin America	Special Equity	Dividend	Domestic Bond	Global Bond	Money Market	Short Term	Mid Term	Long Term	Currency Effect	Sector Specific	Small Cap	Mid Cap	Large Cap	Top Down	Bottom Up	Value	Sector Rotation	Momentum	Indexation
NAL-Investor Balanced Growth	◆								◆				◆						◆	◆		◆		◆	
NAL-Investor Canadian Bond									◆				◆							◆				◆	
NAL-Investor Canadian Diversified	◆								◆				◆						◆	◆			◆	◆	
NAL-Investor Canadian Equity	◆																		◆	◆			◆		
NAL-Investor Equity Growth	◆																		◆		◆			◆	
NAL-Investor Money Market											◆	◆													◆
NAL-Investor Global Equity		◆	◆	◆											◆				◆		◆	◆			
NAL-Investor U.S. Equity		◆													◆			◆	◆		◆	◆			

MANULIFE VISTA FAMILY OF FUNDS

	Extended Asset Mix											Objectives								Management Style					
Fund Name	Canadian Equity	U.S. Equity	Europe	Japan	Far East	Latin America	Special Equity	Dividend	Domestic Bond	Global Bond	Money Market	Short Term	Mid Term	Long Term	Currency Effect	Sector Specific	Small Cap	Mid Cap	Large Cap	Top Down	Bottom Up	Value	Sector Rotation	Momentum	Indexation
Vista Fund American Stock*		◆													◆				◆	◆			◆	◆	
Vista Fund Bond*									◆					◆						◆				◆	
Vista Fund Capital Gains Growth*	◆																◆	◆			◆		◆	◆	
Vista Fund Diversified*	◆								◆				◆						◆	◆			◆		
Vista Fund Equity*	◆																		◆	◆			◆		
Vista Fund Global Bond*										◆			◆		◆					◆		◆			
Vista Fund Global Equity*			◆	◆											◆				◆		◆			◆	
Vista Fund Short Term*											◆	◆													◆

* These funds were closed to new investors as of December 31, 1997.

MARATHON FAMILY OF FUNDS

	Extended Asset Mix											Objectives								Management Style					
Fund Name	Canadian Equity	U.S. Equity	Europe	Japan	Far East	Latin America	Special Equity	Dividend	Domestic Bond	Global Bond	Money Market	Short Term	Mid Term	Long Term	Currency Effect	Sector Specific	Small Cap	Mid Cap	Large Cap	Top Down	Bottom Up	Value	Sector Rotation	Momentum	Indexation
Marathon Equity Fund	◆								◆				◆						◆		◆			◆	
Marathon Performance Balanced	◆								◆				◆						◆	◆				◆	
Marathon Performance Cdn Large Cap	◆																		◆		◆	◆			
Marathon Performance Cdn Money Market											◆	◆													◆
Marathon Performance U.S. Large Cap		◆													◆				◆		◆	◆			
Marathon Resource Fund									◆				◆								◆			◆	

MAWER FAMILY OF FUNDS

Fund Name	Extended Asset Mix											Objectives								Management Style					
	Canadian Equity	U.S. Equity	Europe	Japan	Far East	Latin America	Special Equity	Dividend	Domestic Bond	Global Bond	Money Market	Short Term	Mid Term	Long Term	Currency Effect	Sector Specific	Small Cap	Mid Cap	Large Cap	Top Down	Bottom Up	Value	Sector Rotation	Momentum	Indexation
Mawer Canadian Balanced RRSP	◆								◆				◆						◆	◆				◆	
Mawer Canadian Bond									◆				◆							◆				◆	
Mawer Canadian Diversified	◆								◆				◆						◆	◆				◆	
Mawer Canadian Equity	◆																		◆		◆	◆			
Mawer Canadian High-Yield Bond									◆				◆								◆		◆		
Mawer Canadian Income									◆				◆							◆			◆		
Mawer Canadian Money Market											◆	◆													◆
Mawer New Canada	◆																◆				◆	◆			
Mawer U.S. Equity		◆													◆				◆		◆	◆			
Mawer World Investment			◆												◆				◆	◆		◆			

NN FINANCIAL FAMILY OF FUNDS

Fund Name	Extended Asset Mix											Objectives								Management Style					
	Canadian Equity	U.S. Equity	Europe	Japan	Far East	Latin America	Special Equity	Dividend	Domestic Bond	Global Bond	Money Market	Short Term	Mid Term	Long Term	Currency Effect	Sector Specific	Small Cap	Mid Cap	Large Cap	Top Down	Bottom Up	Value	Sector Rotation	Momentum	Indexation
NN Asset Allocation	◆								◆				◆						◆	◆				◆	
NN Bond									◆					◆						◆				◆	
NN Canadian 35 Index	◆																		◆						◆
NN Canadian Growth	◆																		◆	◆				◆	
NN Can-Am		◆													◆				◆						◆
NN Can-Asian				◆	◆										◆				◆	◆					◆
NN Can-Daq 100		◆													◆		◆	◆							◆
NN Can-Emerging (Latin America)						◆									◆			◆	◆	◆					◆
NN Can-Emerging (Europe)			◆												◆			◆	◆	◆					◆
NN Can-Global Bond										◆			◆		◆					◆				◆	
NN Dividend								◆											◆		◆	◆			
NN Elite	◆									◆		◆			◆				◆	◆				◆	
NN Money Market											◆	◆													◆
NN T-Bill											◆	◆													◆

NATIONAL TRUST FAMILY OF FUNDS

Fund Name	Extended Asset Mix											Objectives								Management Style					
	Canadian Equity	U.S. Equity	Europe	Japan	Far East	Latin America	Special Equity	Dividend	Domestic Bond	Global Bond	Money Market	Short Term	Mid Term	Long Term	Currency Effect	Sector Specific	Small Cap	Mid Cap	Large Cap	Top Down	Bottom Up	Value	Sector Rotation	Momentum	Indexation
National Trust American Equity		◆													◆				◆	◆				◆	
National Trust Balanced	◆								◆				◆						◆	◆				◆	
National Trust Canadian Bond									◆				◆							◆				◆	
National Trust Canadian Equity	◆																		◆	◆				◆	
National Trust Dividend								◆											◆		◆	◆			
National Trust Emerging Markets			◆		◆	◆									◆			◆	◆	◆				◆	
National Trust International Equity			◆												◆				◆	◆				◆	
National Trust International RSP Bond										◆			◆		◆					◆				◆	
National Trust Money Market											◆	◆													◆

NAVIGATOR FAMILY OF FUNDS

Fund Name	Extended Asset Mix											Objectives								Management Style					
	Canadian Equity	U.S. Equity	Europe	Japan	Far East	Latin America	Special Equity	Dividend	Domestic Bond	Global Bond	Money Market	Short Term	Mid Term	Long Term	Currency Effect	Sector Specific	Small Cap	Mid Cap	Large Cap	Top Down	Bottom Up	Value	Sector Rotation	Momentum	Indexation
Navigator American Growth		◆													◆			◆	◆	◆				◆	
Navigator American Value		◆													◆			◆	◆		◆	◆			
Navigator Asia Pacific	◆				◆										◆				◆	◆				◆	
Navigator Canadian Growth	◆																	◆	◆	◆				◆	
Navigator Canadian Growth & Income	◆								◆				◆						◆	◆				◆	
Navigator Canadian Income									◆				◆							◆				◆	
Navigator Canadian Technology							◆									◆	◆	◆	◆		◆			◆	
Navigator Investment Retirement	◆																	◆	◆		◆			◆	

O'DONNELL FAMILY OF FUNDS

Fund Name	Canadian Equity	U.S. Equity	Europe	Japan	Far East	Latin America	Special Equity	Dividend	Domestic Bond	Global Bond	Money Market	Short Term	Mid Term	Long Term	Currency Effect	Sector Specific	Small Cap	Mid Cap	Large Cap	Top Down	Bottom Up	Value	Sector Rotation	Momentum	Indexation
	Extended Asset Mix											**Objectives**								**Management Style**					
O'Donnell American Sector Growth		◆													◆				◆	◆			◆	◆	
O'Donnell Balanced	◆								◆				◆				◆	◆		◆				◆	
O'Donnell Canadian	◆																		◆		◆			◆	
O'Donnell Canadian Emerging Growth	◆																◆	◆			◆	◆		◆	
O'Donnell Growth	◆																	◆	◆	◆			◆	◆	
O'Donnell High Income									◆				◆								◆		◆		
O'Donnell Money Market											◆	◆													◆
O'Donnell Select	◆																		◆		◆	◆			
O'Donnell Short Term Fund											◆	◆													◆
O'Donnell U.S. Mid-Cap Fund		◆													◆			◆			◆	◆			
O'Donnell World Equity	◆	◆																	◆		◆	◆			
O'Donnell World Precious Metals							◆								◆	◆		◆	◆		◆			◆	

PHILLIPS HAGER & NORTH FAMILY OF FUNDS

Fund Name	Extended Asset Mix: Canadian Equity	U.S. Equity	Europe	Japan	Far East	Latin America	Special Equity	Dividend	Domestic Bond	Global Bond	Money Market	Objectives: Short Term	Mid Term	Long Term	Currency Effect	Sector Specific	Small Cap	Mid Cap	Large Cap	Management Style: Top Down	Bottom Up	Value	Sector Rotation	Momentum	Indexation
PH&N Balanced	◆								◆				◆						◆	◆				◆	
PH&N Bond									◆				◆							◆				◆	
PH&N Canadian Equity	◆																	◆	◆	◆				◆	
PH&N Canadian Equity Plus	◆																		◆	◆				◆	
PH&N Canadian Money Market											◆	◆													◆
PH&N Dividend Income								◆											◆		◆	◆			
PH&N International Equity			◆												◆				◆	◆					◆
PH&N North American Equity	◆	◆													◆			◆	◆		◆			◆	
PH&N Short-Term Bond & Mortgage									◆			◆													◆
PH&N U.S. Equity		◆													◆				◆		◆			◆	
PH&N U.S.$ Money Market											◆	◆			◆										◆
PH&N Vintage	◆																	◆	◆		◆	◆		◆	

PRIMERICA INSURANCE CO. OF CANADA FAMILY OF FUNDS

	Extended Asset Mix											Objectives								Management Style					
Fund Name	Canadian Equity	U.S. Equity	Europe	Japan	Far East	Latin America	Special Equity	Dividend	Domestic Bond	Global Bond	Money Market	Short Term	Mid Term	Long Term	Currency Effect	Sector Specific	Small Cap	Mid Cap	Large Cap	Top Down	Bottom Up	Value	Sector Rotation	Momentum	Indexation
Asset Builder I	◆								◆				◆					◆	◆	◆		◆		◆	
Asset Builder II	◆								◆				◆					◆	◆	◆		◆		◆	
Asset Builder III	◆								◆				◆					◆	◆	◆		◆		◆	
Asset Builder IV	◆								◆				◆					◆	◆	◆		◆		◆	
Asset Builder V	◆								◆				◆					◆	◆	◆		◆		◆	

ROYAL BANK FAMILY OF FUNDS

	Extended Asset Mix											Objectives								Management Style					
Fund Name	Canadian Equity	U.S. Equity	Europe	Japan	Far East	Latin America	Special Equity	Dividend	Domestic Bond	Global Bond	Money Market	Short Term	Mid Term	Long Term	Currency Effect	Sector Specific	Small Cap	Mid Cap	Large Cap	Top Down	Bottom Up	Value	Sector Rotation	Momentum	Indexation
Royal Asian Growth					◆										◆			◆	◆	◆				◆	
Royal Balanced	◆								◆				◆						◆	◆				◆	
Royal Bond									◆					◆							◆			◆	
Royal Canadian Equity	◆																		◆		◆			◆	
Royal Canadian Growth	◆																◆	◆			◆			◆	
Royal Canadian Money Market											◆	◆													◆
Royal Canadian Small-Cap	◆																◆				◆			◆	
Royal Canadian T-Bill											◆	◆													◆
Royal Dividend	◆							◆											◆		◆	◆			

ROYAL BANK FAMILY OF FUNDS

	Extended Asset Mix											Objectives								Management Style					
Fund Name	Canadian Equity	U.S. Equity	Europe	Japan	Far East	Latin America	Special Equity	Dividend	Domestic Bond	Global Bond	Money Market	Short Term	Mid Term	Long Term	Currency Effect	Sector Specific	Small Cap	Mid Cap	Large Cap	Top Down	Bottom Up	Value	Sector Rotation	Momentum	Indexation
Royal Energy							◆									◆		◆	◆		◆			◆	
Royal European Growth			◆												◆			◆	◆		◆			◆	
Royal Global Bond										◆			◆		◆						◆			◆	
Royal International Equity			◆		◆										◆			◆	◆	◆	◆			◆	
Royal Japanese Stock				◆											◆			◆	◆		◆			◆	
Royal Latin America						◆									◆			◆	◆		◆	◆		◆	
Royal Monthly Income								◆										◆	◆		◆				
Royal Mortgage									◆				◆								◆	◆			
Royal Precious Metals							◆									◆	◆	◆	◆		◆			◆	
Royal Premium Money Market											◆	◆													◆
Royal Strategic Index Canadian	◆																	◆		◆				◆	
Royal Strategic Index U.S. Growth		◆														◆		◆		◆				◆	
Royal Strategic Index U.S. Value		◆														◆		◆		◆		◆			
Royal Trust Life Science & Technology							◆								◆	◆		◆	◆		◆			◆	
Royal U.S.$ Money Market											◆	◆			◆										◆
Royal U.S. Equity		◆													◆			◆	◆	◆			◆	◆	
Zweig Global Managed Assets		◆	◆												◆			◆	◆	◆				◆	
Zweig Strategic Growth Fund		◆									◆				◆		◆	◆		◆				◆	◆

Note: We did not include any Royal Trust Advantaged funds, as these funds, for the most part, simply buy other Royal Trust mutual funds.

SCEPTRE FAMILY OF FUNDS

	Extended Asset Mix											Objectives								Management Style					
Fund Name	Canadian Equity	U.S. Equity	Europe	Japan	Far East	Latin America	Special Equity	Dividend	Domestic Bond	Global Bond	Money Market	Short Term	Mid Term	Long Term	Currency Effect	Sector Specific	Small Cap	Mid Cap	Large Cap	Top Down	Bottom Up	Value	Sector Rotation	Momentum	Indexation
Sceptre Asian Growth				◆	◆										◆			◆	◆	◆				◆	
Sceptre Balanced Growth	◆								◆				◆							◆				◆	
Sceptre Bond									◆				◆							◆				◆	
Sceptre Equity Growth	◆																◆	◆			◆	◆		◆	
Sceptre International		◆	◆	◆	◆														◆	◆				◆	
Sceptre Money Market											◆	◆													◆

SCUDDER FAMILY OF FUNDS

	Extended Asset Mix											Objectives								Management Style					
Fund Name	Canadian Equity	U.S. Equity	Europe	Japan	Far East	Latin America	Special Equity	Dividend	Domestic Bond	Global Bond	Money Market	Short Term	Mid Term	Long Term	Currency Effect	Sector Specific	Small Cap	Mid Cap	Large Cap	Top Down	Bottom Up	Value	Sector Rotation	Momentum	Indexation
Scudder Canadian Bond									◆				◆							◆				◆	
Scudder Canadian Equity	◆																	◆	◆	◆			◆	◆	
Scudder Canadian Money Market											◆	◆													◆
Scudder Canadian Short-Term Bond											◆	◆													◆
Scudder Emerging Markets			◆			◆									◆			◆	◆	◆				◆	
Scudder Global		◆	◆												◆			◆	◆	◆				◆	
Scudder Greater Europe			◆												◆			◆	◆	◆				◆	
Scudder Pacific				◆	◆										◆			◆	◆	◆				◆	
Scudder U.S. Growth & Income		◆													◆			◆	◆	◆				◆	

SPECTRUM UNITED MUTUAL FUNDS

	Extended Asset Mix											Objectives								Management Style					
Fund Name	Canadian Equity	U.S. Equity	Europe	Japan	Far East	Latin America	Special Equity	Dividend	Domestic Bond	Global Bond	Money Market	Short Term	Mid Term	Long Term	Currency Effect	Sector Specific	Small Cap	Mid Cap	Large Cap	Top Down	Bottom Up	Value	Sector Rotation	Momentum	Indexation
Spectrum United American Equity		◆													◆				◆		◆			◆	
Spectrum United American Growth		◆													◆			◆			◆			◆	
Spectrum United Asian Dynasty				◆	◆										◆			◆	◆		◆			◆	
Spectrum United Asset Allocation	◆								◆				◆						◆	◆				◆	
Spectrum United Canadian Equity	◆																		◆		◆		◆	◆	
Spectrum United Canadian Growth (capped)	◆																◆	◆			◆		◆	◆	
Spectrum United Canadian Investment	◆																		◆		◆	◆			
Spectrum United Canadian Money Market											◆	◆													◆
Spectrum United Canadian Resources							◆										◆	◆	◆		◆			◆	
Spectrum United Canadian Stock	◆																		◆		◆	◆			
Spectrum United Canadian T-Bill											◆	◆													◆
Spectrum United Diversified	◆								◆				◆						◆	◆				◆	
Spectrum United Dividend								◆											◆		◆	◆			
Spectrum United Emerging Markets						◆									◆			◆	◆		◆			◆	
Spectrum United European Growth			◆												◆		◆				◆			◆	

SPECTRUM UNITED MUTUAL FUNDS

	Extended Asset Mix											Objectives								Management Style					
Fund Name	Canadian Equity	U.S. Equity	Europe	Japan	Far East	Latin America	Special Equity	Dividend	Domestic Bond	Global Bond	Money Market	Short Term	Mid Term	Long Term	Currency Effect	Sector Specific	Small Cap	Mid Cap	Large Cap	Top Down	Bottom Up	Value	Sector Rotation	Momentum	Indexation
Spectrum United Global Bond										◆					◆					◆				◆	
Spectrum United Global Diversified	◆	◆	◆							◆			◆		◆				◆	◆				◆	
Spectrum United Global Equity		◆	◆												◆				◆	◆			◆	◆	
Spectrum United Global Growth	◆	◆	◆												◆		◆				◆		◆	◆	
Spectrum United Global Telecom							◆								◆	◆	◆	◆	◆		◆			◆	
Spectrum United Long-Term Bond									◆					◆						◆			◆		
Spectrum United Mid-Term Bond									◆				◆							◆			◆		
Spectrum United Optimax USA		◆													◆			◆	◆		◆			◆	
Spectrum United RRSP International Bond										◆			◆		◆					◆				◆	
Spectrum United Savings											◆	◆													◆
Spectrum United Short-Term Bond											◆	◆													◆
Spectrum United U.S.$ Money Market											◆	◆			◆										◆

T.D. GREEN LINE FAMILY OF FUNDS

	Extended Asset Mix											Objectives								Management Style					
Fund Name	Canadian Equity	U.S. Equity	Europe	Japan	Far East	Latin America	Special Equity	Dividend	Domestic Bond	Global Bond	Money Market	Short Term	Mid Term	Long Term	Currency Effect	Sector Specific	Small Cap	Mid Cap	Large Cap	Top Down	Bottom Up	Value	Sector Rotation	Momentum	Indexation
Green Line Asian Growth					◆										◆			◆	◆	◆				◆	
Green Line Balanced Growth	◆								◆				◆						◆	◆				◆	
Green Line Balanced Income	◆								◆				◆						◆		◆	◆			
Green Line Blue Chip Equity	◆																		◆		◆		◆	◆	
Green Line Canadian Bond									◆					◆						◆			◆	◆	
Green Line Canadian Equity	◆																		◆	◆			◆	◆	
Green Line Canadian Government Bond									◆				◆							◆			◆	◆	
Green Line Canadian Index Fund	◆																		◆						◆
Green Line Canadian Money Market											◆	◆													◆
Green Line Canadian Small Cap	◆																◆				◆			◆	
Green Line Canadian T-Bill											◆	◆													◆
Green Line Dividend	◆							◆											◆		◆	◆			
Green Line Emerging Markets					◆	◆									◆			◆	◆	◆		◆		◆	
Green Line Energy	◆						◆										◆	◆	◆		◆			◆	
Green Line Entertainment & Communications							◆								◆		◆	◆	◆	◆				◆	

T.D. GREEN LINE FAMILY OF FUNDS

Fund Name	Canadian Equity	U.S. Equity	Europe	Japan	Far East	Latin America	Special Equity	Dividend	Domestic Bond	Global Bond	Money Market	Short Term	Mid Term	Long Term	Currency Effect	Sector Specific	Small Cap	Mid Cap	Large Cap	Top Down	Bottom Up	Value	Sector Rotation	Momentum	Indexation
	Extended Asset Mix											**Objectives**								**Management Style**					
Green Line European Growth			◆												◆			◆	◆		◆	◆		◆	
Green Line Global Government Bond										◆			◆		◆					◆				◆	
Green Line Global RRSP Bond										◆			◆		◆					◆				◆	
Green Line Global Select		◆	◆												◆			◆	◆	◆		◆		◆	
Green Line Health Sciences							◆								◆		◆	◆	◆		◆			◆	
Green Line International Equity			◆	◆											◆			◆	◆	◆		◆		◆	
Green Line International RRSP Index			◆	◆											◆				◆	◆					◆
Green Line Japanese Growth				◆											◆			◆	◆		◆			◆	
Green Line Latin America Growth						◆									◆			◆	◆	◆			◆	◆	
Green Line Mortgage Back									◆				◆								◆	◆			
Green Line Mortgage									◆				◆								◆	◆			
Green Line Precious Metals							◆				◆				◆	◆	◆	◆	◆		◆			◆	◆
Green Line Premium Money Market											◆					◆	◆	◆	◆		◆			◆	
Green Line Real Return Bond									◆			◆													◆
Green Line Resource							◆										◆	◆	◆		◆			◆	
Green Line Science & Technology							◆								◆		◆	◆	◆	◆				◆	
Green Line Short-Term Income											◆	◆													◆

T.D. GREEN LINE FAMILY OF FUNDS

Fund Name	Extended Asset Mix: Canadian Equity	U.S. Equity	Europe	Japan	Far East	Latin America	Special Equity	Dividend	Domestic Bond	Global Bond	Money Market	Objectives: Short Term	Mid Term	Long Term	Currency Effect	Sector Specific	Small Cap	Mid Cap	Large Cap	Management Style: Top Down	Bottom Up	Value	Sector Rotation	Momentum	Indexation
Green Line U.S. Blue Chip Equity		◆													◆				◆		◆			◆	
Green Line U.S. Index		◆													◆				◆						◆
Green Line U.S. Mid-Cap Growth		◆													◆			◆			◆			◆	
Green Line U.S. Money Market Fund											◆	◆			◆										◆
Green Line U.S. RSP Index		◆													◆				◆						◆
Green Line U.S. Small Cap		◆													◆		◆				◆			◆	
Green Line Value Fund	◆														◆			◆	◆		◆	◆			

TALVEST FAMILY OF FUNDS

Fund Name	Extended Asset Mix: Canadian Equity	U.S. Equity	Europe	Japan	Far East	Latin America	Special Equity	Dividend	Domestic Bond	Global Bond	Money Market	Objectives: Short Term	Mid Term	Long Term	Currency Effect	Sector Specific	Small Cap	Mid Cap	Large Cap	Management Style: Top Down	Bottom Up	Value	Sector Rotation	Momentum	Indexation
Talvest Bond									◆				◆							◆			◆		
Talvest Canadian Asset Allocation	◆								◆				◆						◆	◆		◆		◆	
Talvest Canadian Equity Value	◆																		◆		◆	◆			
Talvest Dividend	◆							◆											◆		◆	◆			
Talvest Foreign Pay Canadian Bond										◆			◆		◆					◆				◆	
Talvest Global Asset Allocation		◆	◆		◆					◆			◆		◆				◆	◆			◆	◆	
Talvest Global RRSP Fund			◆		◆										◆			◆	◆	◆				◆	◆
Talvest Income Fund									◆			◆									◆		◆		
Talvest Money Fund											◆	◆													◆
Talvest New Economy Fund	◆																	◆			◆			◆	
Talvest Hyperion Funds																									
Hyperion Asian				◆	◆										◆				◆		◆	◆			
Hyperion Canadian Equity Growth	◆																		◆		◆			◆	
Hyperion European			◆												◆				◆		◆	◆		◆	
Hyperion Global Health Care							◆								◆	◆			◆		◆			◆	
Hyperion Global Science & Technology							◆								◆	◆			◆		◆			◆	
Hyperion High-Yield Bond									◆				◆							◆			◆		
Hyperion Small-Cap Equity	◆																◆				◆	◆			
Hyperion Value Line U.S. Equity		◆													◆			◆	◆		◆			◆	

TEMPLETON FAMILY OF FUNDS

Fund Name	Extended Asset Mix											Objectives								Management Style					
	Canadian Equity	U.S. Equity	Europe	Japan	Far East	Latin America	Special Equity	Dividend	Domestic Bond	Global Bond	Money Market	Short Term	Mid Term	Long Term	Currency Effect	Sector Specific	Small Cap	Mid Cap	Large Cap	Top Down	Bottom Up	Value	Sector Rotation	Momentum	Indexation
Templeton Balanced	◆								◆				◆					◆	◆	◆	◆	◆			
Templeton Canadian Asset Allocation	◆								◆				◆					◆	◆	◆	◆	◆			
Templeton Canadian Bond									◆				◆							◆				◆	
Templeton Canadian Stock	◆																		◆		◆	◆			
Templeton Emerging Markets			◆		◆	◆									◆			◆	◆		◆	◆			
Templeton Global Balanced	◆	◆	◆							◆			◆		◆				◆	◆	◆	◆			
Templeton Global Bond										◆			◆		◆					◆		◆			
Templeton Global Smaller Companies		◆	◆												◆		◆				◆	◆			
Templeton Growth		◆	◆												◆			◆	◆		◆	◆			
Templeton International Balanced	◆		◆		◆								◆		◆			◆	◆	◆	◆	◆			
Templeton International Stock	◆		◆		◆										◆			◆	◆		◆	◆			
Templeton Mutual Beacon		◆													◆			◆	◆		◆	◆			
Templeton Treasury Bill											◆	◆													◆

TRIMARK FAMILY OF FUNDS

		Extended Asset Mix											Objectives								Management Style					
Fund Name	**MVA Index**	Canadian Equity	U.S. Equity	Europe	Japan	Far East	Latin America	Special Equity	Dividend	Domestic Bond	Global Bond	Money Market	Short Term	Mid Term	Long Term	Currency Effect	Sector Specific	Small Cap	Mid Cap	Large Cap	Top Down	Bottom Up	Value	Sector Rotation	Momentum	Indexation
Trimark Advantage Bond	103.5									◆				◆								◆		◆		
Trimark Americas	79.5		◆				◆									◆		◆				◆			◆	
Trimark Canadian		◆																		◆		◆	◆			
Trimark Canadian Bond	96.5									◆				◆							◆			◆	◆	
Trimark Discovery		◆	◆															◆	◆			◆			◆	
Trimark Europlus	95.6			◆												◆				◆		◆	◆			
Trimark Fund	92.4	◆	◆													◆				◆		◆	◆			
Trimark Government Income										◆			◆								◆		◆	◆		
Trimark Income/Growth		◆								◆				◆					◆	◆	◆		◆		◆	
Trimark Indo-Pacific	94.7					◆										◆			◆	◆		◆	◆			
Trimark Interest	92.4											◆	◆													◆
Trimark RRSP Equity	95.4	◆																		◆		◆	◆			
Trimark Select Balanced	97.2	◆								◆				◆						◆	◆				◆	
Trimark Select Canadian Growth		◆																		◆		◆	◆			
Trimark Select Growth		◆	◆		◆											◆				◆		◆	◆			

UNIVERSITY AVENUE FAMILY OF FUNDS

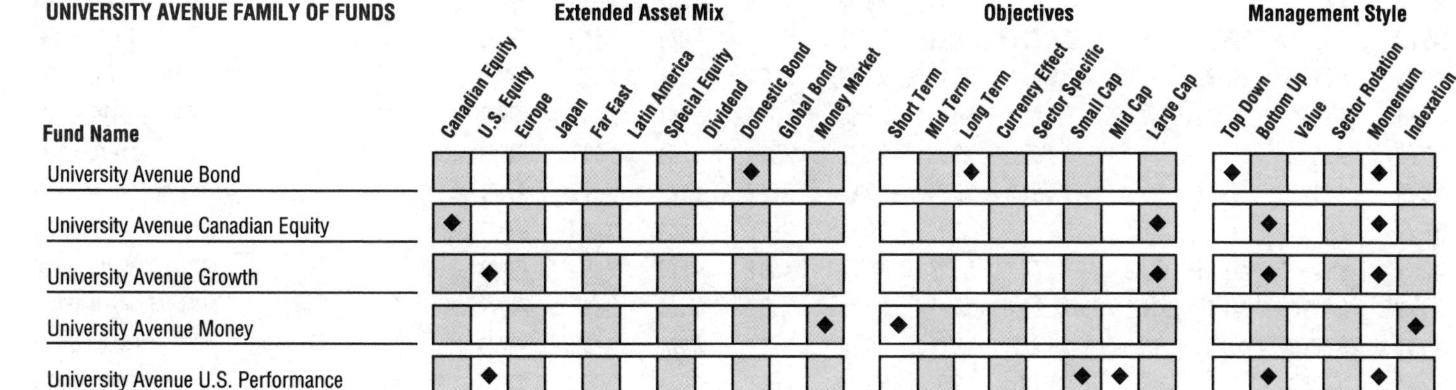

Fund Name	Extended Asset Mix: Canadian Equity	U.S. Equity	Europe	Japan	Far East	Latin America	Special Equity	Dividend	Domestic Bond	Global Bond	Money Market
University Avenue Bond									◆		
University Avenue Canadian Equity	◆										
University Avenue Growth		◆									
University Avenue Money											◆
University Avenue U.S. Performance		◆									

Fund Name	Objectives: Short Term	Mid Term	Long Term	Currency Effect	Sector Specific	Small Cap	Mid Cap	Large Cap
University Avenue Bond			◆					
University Avenue Canadian Equity								◆
University Avenue Growth								◆
University Avenue Money	◆							
University Avenue U.S. Performance						◆	◆	

Fund Name	Management Style: Top Down	Bottom Up	Value	Sector Rotation	Momentum	Indexation
University Avenue Bond	◆				◆	
University Avenue Canadian Equity		◆			◆	
University Avenue Growth		◆			◆	
University Avenue Money						◆
University Avenue U.S. Performance		◆			◆	

APPENDIX III
MVA Index Ranking

Fund Name	Fund Type	MER	MVA	3-Year Std Dev (Monthly)	Percent Return 1997	Percent Return 1996	Percent Return 1995	Percent Return 1994	Percent Return 1993	Assets $ Mill	Tax Efficiency (3 Years)
Ivy Enterprise	CdnEq	2.33%	153.0	3.44%	23.4%	25.0%	14.6%	—	—	328.5	100.0%
BPI Dividend Income	CdnEq	1.22%	144.1	2.28%	19.5%	23.3%	19.4%	-0.6%	15.0%	572.7	76.2%
Cundill Security Series A	CdnEq	2.04%	136.1	3.03%	18.4%	20.2%	10.4%	14.1%	39.9%	27.6	75.5%
AIC Diversified Canada	CdnEq	2.39%	129.0	4.99%	32.1%	65.1%	26.2%	—	—	1,866.3	100.0%
Chou RRSP	CdnEq	2.02%	128.9	3.32%	50.6%	22.1%	19.0%	-10.6%	15.4%	2.2	92.6%
NN Dividend	CdnEq	2.38%	126.8	2.45%	13.8%	19.2%	17.8%	—	—	241.1	—
Dynamic Dividend	CdnEq	1.51%	126.7	1.96%	13.6%	18.3%	14.6%	-2.5%	18.1%	373.5	70.6%
Fidelity Canadian Growth Company	CdnEq	2.46%	126.7	4.39%	28.8%	20.5%	31.1%	—	—	1,329.4	95.8%
PH&N Dividend Income	CdnEq	1.21%	126.7	4.33%	44.5%	33.3%	13.9%	1.3%	28.0%	539.6	94.2%
Investors Real Property	Spclty	2.37%	126.0	0.38%	7.4%	4.2%	4.3%	1.4%	-1.1%	566.8	53.6%
Bissett Dividend Income	CdnEq	1.50%	125.8	3.09%	22.5%	28.5%	22.9%	0.7%	18.7%	44.5	86.8%
IRIS Dividend	CdnEq	1.67%	124.9	3.75%	21.0%	36.2%	17.0%	—	—	45.7	77.9%
Dynamic Dividend Growth	CdnEq	1.57%	124.1	2.71%	15.6%	28.8%	15.2%	-1.4%	22.3%	417.7	82.2%
Cote 100 EXP	CdnEq	2.60%	123.9	4.68%	13.3%	39.3%	26.0%	—	—	37.8	100.0%
Bissett Small Capital	CdnEq	1.90%	123.2	5.60%	23.8%	51.0%	18.2%	-8.6%	112.5%	93.1	95.5%
Associate Investors	CdnEq	1.83%	123.0	4.30%	35.8%	31.3%	10.8%	-3.0%	23.7%	12.3	89.6%
MD Dividend	CdnEq	1.29%	122.1	2.22%	16.7%	15.8%	12.9%	-0.3%	15.6%	153.6	80.5%
Standard Life Canadian Dividend	CdnEq	1.50%	122.0	5.05%	40.8%	36.3%	14.7%	—	—	34.4	93.5%
CT Dividend Income	CdnEq	1.85%	121.4	3.18%	17.2%	26.6%	15.9%	—	—	393.9	90.3%
Northwest Dividend	CdnEq	1.75%	121.1	4.04%	21.0%	36.9%	16.1%	—	—	15.6	71.8%
First Canadian Dividend Income	CdnEq	1.67%	121.0	4.33%	35.2%	32.3%	13.2%	—	—	1,023.6	93.8%
Spectrum United Dividend	CdnEq	1.61%	121.0	1.93%	18.6%	17.2%	12.2%	-3.2%	20.6%	288.4	79.5%
Hongkong Bank Dividend Income	CdnEq	1.84%	120.9	3.35%	23.2%	29.8%	—	—	—	190.2	89.4%
National Trust Dividend	CdnEq	1.76%	120.8	3.81%	37.6%	26.8%	9.9%	-4.4%	19.9%	134.4	92.7%
Scotia Excelsior Dividend	CdnEq	1.09%	120.8	3.46%	25.4%	24.6%	15.4%	-2.9%	14.4%	818.7	86.3%

Fund Name	Fund Type	MER	MVA	3-Year Std Dev (Monthly)	Percent Return 1997	Percent Return 1996	Percent Return 1995	Percent Return 1994	Percent Return 1993	Assets $ Mill	Tax Efficiency (3 Years)
CDA Pacific Basin (KBSH)	FgnEq	1.45%	120.5	4.88%	-8.2%	4.2%	—	—	—	1.0	—
Desjardins Dividend	CdnEq	1.85%	120.3	3.44%	24.6%	21.7%	14.2%	—	—	430.3	87.8%
Fonds d'Investissement REA	CdnEq	2.26%	119.9	4.10%	39.2%	10.6%	12.5%	-12.8%	6.7%	56.7	96.7%
Saxon Small Cap	CdnEq	1.75%	119.6	4.76%	28.1%	26.2%	9.9%	-8.7%	44.6%	18.0	77.8%
Templeton International Stock	FgnEq	2.49%	119.6	3.38%	15.9%	21.5%	12.2%	5.2%	48.2%	5,398.1	97.2%
Royal Precious Metals	CdnEq	2.41%	118.7	9.87%	-33.7%	38.8%	63.8%	-3.9%	44.0%	160.9	100.0%
Talvest/Hyperion Small-Cap Canadian Equity	CdnEq	2.62%	118.4	5.80%	37.6%	31.8%	14.6%	—	—	201.1	100.0%
AIC Advantage	CdnEq	2.31%	118.2	6.55%	43.3%	66.5%	30.7%	-12.9%	65.9%	2,323.3	100.0%
InvesNat Dividend	CdnEq	1.64%	118.0	1.70%	7.1%	15.5%	13.9%	-0.5%	13.0%	103.2	76.3%
Ivy Growth & Income	Balan	2.07%	117.7	2.25%	18.1%	23.4%	19.7%	-0.7%	6.9%	2,410.0	95.8%
Royal Dividend	CdnEq	1.77%	117.7	4.27%	35.4%	33.1%	13.1%	-0.7%	—	1,826.5	89.8%
GBC Canadian Growth	CdnEq	1.90%	117.4	5.51%	27.0%	35.3%	16.1%	-5.8%	33.0%	179.1	98.7%
Ivy Canadian	CdnEq	2.32%	117.2	2.94%	17.6%	25.2%	15.8%	4.9%	10.8%	4,978.9	96.2%
Investors Dividend	CdnEq	2.37%	116.8	3.00%	23.2%	20.3%	10.3%	-1.5%	16.8%	4,397.6	86.0%
Altamira Dividend	CdnEq	1.55%	116.6	3.81%	23.9%	23.8%	16.1%	—	—	220.7	80.0%
Fidelity Far East	FgnEq	2.87%	116.4	7.82%	-22.6%	21.7%	19.9%	-16.7%	86.4%	567.7	100.0%
MetLife Mvp Growth	CdnEq	2.19%	116.1	5.17%	26.3%	29.3%	16.8%	-5.9%	—	109.0	—
Millennium Next Generation	CdnEq	2.50%	116.0	6.15%	29.2%	39.2%	37.6%	-5.9%	—	26.8	77.4%
Colonia Life Special Growth	CdnEq	2.27%	115.4	6.67%	23.9%	69.8%	23.7%	-5.0%	—	22.7	—
Global Strategy Income Plus	Balan	2.40%	115.3	2.80%	22.1%	25.8%	13.1%	-3.0%	28.7%	1,974.3	73.8%
Spectrum United Canadian Investment	CdnEq	2.33%	115.0	3.84%	24.0%	27.3%	15.7%	-1.4%	17.4%	264.7	90.8%
MAXXUM Dividend	CdnEq	1.73%	114.9	4.19%	25.8%	27.7%	16.6%	2.9%	35.1%	210.5	90.8%
AGF International Group—Japan Class	FgnEq	3.07%	114.7	4.56%	8.7%	-6.0%	-9.2%	16.9%	20.6%	83.5	100.0%
Strategic Value Dividend	CdnEq	2.70%	114.7	2.71%	18.9%	20.5%	11.2%	-3.1%	17.6%	451.2	78.9%
Royal Energy	CdnEq	2.28%	114.3	6.52%	3.3%	39.0%	8.1%	-7.1%	45.6%	175.0	100.0%

Fund Name	Fund Type	MER	MVA	3-Year Std Dev (Monthly)	Percent Return 1997	Percent Return 1996	Percent Return 1995	Percent Return 1994	Percent Return 1993	Assets $ Mill	Tax Efficiency (3 Years)
First Canadian Special Growth	CdnEq	2.24%	114.1	5.54%	23.0%	30.0%	18.4%	-17.9%	—	329.1	99.8%
Bissett Canadian Equity	CdnEq	1.33%	113.9	4.91%	31.5%	36.0%	16.4%	-2.3%	33.5%	392.2	99.1%
Clean Environment Equity	CdnEq	2.60%	113.8	4.94%	34.3%	31.5%	21.6%	-13.6%	40.3%	249.3	96.9%
Green Line Precious Metals	CdnEq	2.12%	113.6	10.25%	-41.0%	70.1%	23.5%	—	—	65.3	100.0%
Quebec Growth Fund Inc.	CdnEq	2.00%	113.6	4.97%	40.5%	34.9%	6.8%	-14.6%	27.9%	22.9	100.0%
Great-West Life Canadian Real Estate (G) B	Spclty	2.71%	113.3	0.98%	13.6%	2.8%	0.1%	—	—	58.2	—
Guardian Enterprise Classic	CdnEq	2.10%	113.0	6.03%	13.6%	44.6%	31.4%	-9.9%	28.7%	40.8	100.0%
CIBC Dividend	CdnEq	1.88%	112.5	3.44%	16.1%	21.2%	10.8%	-6.8%	26.9%	533.2	81.7%
Great-West Life Canadian Real Estate (G) A	Spclty	2.95%	112.4	0.98%	13.4%	2.6%	—	-4.5%	-9.9%	133.3	—
Manulife Cabot Canadian Growth	CdnEq	2.50%	112.2	5.74%	16.3%	45.9%	8.5%	—	—	11.8	84.5%
Bissett Multinational Growth	FgnEq	1.50%	112.1	3.64%	33.9%	27.5%	22.0%	—	—	76.1	97.6%
Industrial Dividend Growth	CdnEq	2.33%	111.9	4.01%	25.9%	30.5%	10.5%	0.8%	58.4%	808.5	81.4%
20/20 Canadian Resources	CdnEq	2.88%	111.8	7.68%	-9.4%	50.5%	13.3%	-12.1%	67.7%	147.1	100.0%
Optima Strategy—Canadian Equity	CdnEq	0.39%	111.8	5.14%	31.1%	32.4%	17.0%	—	3.3%	639.7	100.0%
Maritime Life Dividend Income Series A	CdnEq	2.10%	111.7	3.67%*	24.5%	18.4%	—	—	—	131.6	—
Scotia Excelsior Pacific Rim	FgnEq	2.43%	111.5	4.30%	-16.0%	5.5%	10.0%	—	—	26.6	100.0%
Middlefield Growth	CdnEq	2.59%	111.4	4.39%	3.6%	21.5%	11.6%	-10.7%	22.4%	26.1	66.6%
First Canadian Far East Growth	FgnEq	2.33%	111.3	6.55%	-26.8%	19.4%	8.8%	—	—	10.2	100.0%
NN Can-Asian	FgnEq	2.71%	111.2	6.35%	-23.9%	11.8%	12.1%	-11.1%	—	58.9	—
Atlas Canadian High-Yield Bond	FixInc	1.87%	111.0	1.53%	10.5%	13.9%	15.1%	—	—	434.7	65.8%
Universal European Opportunities	FgnEq	2.43%	111.0	3.67%	20.0%	39.2%	28.8%	—	—	873.3	96.8%
Asset Builder I	Balan	2.25%	110.8	2.31%	21.1%	18.4%	15.4%	—	—	53.1	—
Optimum International	FgnEq	1.96%	110.7	3.46%	27.4%	4.0%	14.3%	—	—	6.3	67.3%
Asset Builder III	Balan	2.25%	110.6	3.18%	29.2%	23.6%	13.1%	—	—	70.1	—
Bissett Retirement	Balan	0.44%	110.5	2.86%	20.2%	22.2%	19.8%	-1.8%	22.2%	191.1	92.1%

* 2-year standard deviation.

Fund Name	Fund Type	MER	MVA	3-Year Std Dev (Monthly)	Percent Return 1997	Percent Return 1996	Percent Return 1995	Percent Return 1994	Percent Return 1993	Assets $ Mill	Tax Efficiency (3 Years)
Cote 100 REER	CdnEq	1.38%	110.5	4.94%	18.4%	34.3%	25.4%	-14.9%	34.8%	35.4	100.0%
Investors Summa	CdnEq	2.50%	110.5	4.62%	23.0%	29.7%	13.3%	-3.9%	21.5%	442.7	80.3%
Asset Builder II	Balan	2.26%	110.4	2.92%	26.7%	21.6%	14.8%	—	—	79.1	—
Asset Builder V	Balan	2.26%	110.4	3.32%	28.9%	23.7%	12.8%	—	—	13.8	—
Green Line Dividend	CdnEq	2.00%	110.4	4.24%	33.2%	28.5%	3.1%	-0.7%	18.2%	395.9	96.4%
AIM Nippon	FgnEq	3.26%	110.1	4.73%	-21.5%	-3.6%	1.8%	6.0%	13.7%	4.9	100.0%
Asset Builder IV	Balan	2.25%	110.1	3.29%	28.6%	24.0%	11.9%	—	—	34.6	—
Navigator Canadian Income	FixInc	2.45%	110.1	1.41%	9.9%	13.3%	15.3%	—	—	21.0	65.2%
AGF High Income	CdnEq	1.68%	109.9	1.13%	6.2%	12.5%	14.0%	-1.3%	15.4%	578.5	54.8%
General Trust of Canada Growth	CdnEq	2.14%	109.8	5.17%	23.4%	29.3%	4.3%	-13.2%	35.3%	13.1	77.4%
Quebec Professionals Bond	FixInc	0.95%	109.8	0.87%	9.8%	9.4%	15.5%	-2.6%	12.0%	62.8	52.8%
Beutel Goodman Private Balanced	Balan	1.10%	109.3	2.86%	23.1%	19.3%	18.1%	-0.1%	17.8%	55.4	66.2%
Green Line Energy	CdnEq	2.10%	109.3	7.22%	-2.7%	41.3%	7.6%	—	—	58.2	100.0%
AGF Dividend	CdnEq	1.87%	109.2	4.30%	24.1%	29.1%	16.3%	0.4%	26.3%	1,966.1	97.2%
Atlas Canadian Balanced	Balan	2.20%	109.2	2.25%	18.0%	16.5%	17.8%	-0.9%	15.0%	329.7	91.6%
Global Strategy Canadian Small Cap	CdnEq	2.73%	109.0	5.72%	19.8%	42.7%	14.9%	—	—	280.4	96.8%
Leith Wheeler Balanced	Balan	1.10%	108.9	2.57%	19.1%	17.6%	12.5%	-1.7%	23.5%	164.6	77.4%
MAXXUM Precious Metals	CdnEq	2.23%	108.9	11.11%	-44.2%	58.7%	18.5%	-10.6%	97.7%	7.0	100.0%
Trimark Indo-Pacific	FgnEq	2.95%	108.8	6.61%	-26.7%	18.6%	9.3%	—	—	129.8	100.0%
Greystone Managed Global	FgnEq	2.46%	108.7	3.15%	23.9%	17.6%	17.4%	—	—	45.4	87.1%
AGF International Group–Germany M	FgnEq	1.60%	108.6	4.39%	26.7%	29.5%	12.0%	—	—	39.3	100.0%
Mawer New Canada	CdnEq	1.46%	108.6	5.43%	16.4%	44.4%	5.5%	-2.9%	63.4%	35.3	9.1%
Spectrum United Canadian Growth	CdnEq	2.35%	108.6	6.00%	10.7%	21.7%	33.2%	-1.5%	54.8%	567.5	100.0%
Universal Japan	FgnEq	2.50%	108.6	5.34%	-8.6%	-12.7%	-4.9%	—	—	16.3	100.0%
Beutel Goodman Small Cap	CdnEq	2.39%	108.5	5.66%	6.1%	52.8%	—	—	—	11.5	83.2%

Fund Name	Fund Type	MER	MVA	3-Year Std Dev (Monthly)	Percent Return 1997	Percent Return 1996	Percent Return 1995	Percent Return 1994	Percent Return 1993	Assets $ Mill	Tax Efficiency (3 Years)
Dynamic Far East	FgnEq	2.78%	108.3	4.91%	-12.0%	12.5%	2.1%	—	—	7.9	100.0%
Great-West Life International Equity (P) B	FgnEq	2.69%	108.3	3.93%	15.6%	12.1%	8.1%	—	—	78.7	—
Ideal Equity	CdnEq	2.00%	108.3	4.47%	19.5%	27.0%	18.1%	2.7%	20.8%	183.1	—
InvesNat Far East Equity	FgnEq	2.52%	108.0	5.95%	-31.2%	20.8%	10.6%	—	—	10.8	100.0%
Great-West Life International Equity (P) A	FgnEq	2.92%	107.8	3.93%	15.3%	11.8%	8.0%	—	—	90.4	—
Universal Canadian Resource	CdnEq	2.35%	107.6	8.03%	-10.2%	41.1%	2.7%	-8.4%	89.2%	115.2	100.0%
AIC World Equity	FgnEq	2.70%	107.3	3.93%	21.4%	18.9%	2.1%	-7.0%	—	352.1	100.0%
Atlas Canadian Large Cap Growth	CdnEq	2.44%	107.2	4.76%	26.7%	29.7%	12.5%	—	16.6%	503.5	100.0%
Universal Precious Metals	CdnEq	2.40%	107.1	10.45%	-35.2%	34.1%	6.4%	—	—	41.8	100.0%
Manulife Cabot Emerging Growth	CdnEq	2.50%	107.0	4.97%	6.4%	39.6%	8.7%	—	—	7.8	87.2%
Mutual Premier Growth	CdnEq	2.27%	107.0	5.51%	14.0%	26.2%	22.3%	-0.9%	33.3%	781.6	69.5%
PH&N U.S.$ Money Market	FixInc	0.52%	107.0	0.03%	5.1%	4.9%	5.5%	3.8%	2.7%	76.2	50.0%
Quebec Professionals Balanced	Balan	0.95%	107.0	1.53%	8.7%	12.4%	14.3%	-1.3%	13.0%	461.3	55.3%
Universal World Growth RRSP	FgnEq	2.38%	107.0	4.07%	6.3%	19.3%	11.1%	—	—	360.8	46.9%
Fidelity Japanese Growth	FgnEq	3.01%	106.9	5.23%	-7.4%	-12.1%	-9.3%	22.7%	—	95.9	100.0%
Mawer World Investment	FgnEq	1.42%	106.9	4.04%	13.3%	16.7%	7.8%	3.9%	36.7%	45.1	94.3%
CDA Aggressive Equity (Altamira)	CdnEq	1.00%	106.7	5.80%	19.6%	28.9%	7.1%	—	—	5.3	—
Templeton Canadian Stock	CdnEq	2.44%	106.7	3.44%	17.5%	23.8%	7.2%	0.2%	36.5%	432.3	93.9%
Dominion Equity Resource	CdnEq	2.40%	106.2	7.07%	-11.6%	38.6%	5.1%	-15.6%	79.7%	10.7	100.0%
Fidelity Canadian Asset Allocation	Balan	2.47%	106.2	3.26%	23.4%	22.6%	23.4%	—	—	2,997.1	92.6%
Optima Strategy—U.S. Equity	USEq	0.40%	106.2	3.72%	40.0%	27.0%	38.7%	—	—	278.5	100.0%
Standard Life Equity	CdnEq	2.00%	106.2	4.39%	21.1%	23.9%	14.8%	0.6%	23.8%	16.5	77.3%
Talvest/Hyperion Asian	FgnEq	3.25%	106.2	5.72%	-23.5%	10.3%	-2.5%	-20.1%	117.0%	46.8	100.0%
Altamira Precious & Strategy Metal	CdnEq	2.30%	106.1	9.50%	-41.3%	23.7%	26.6%	—	—	30.4	100.0%
Green Line Value	CdnEq	2.09%	106.1	5.02%	17.2%	48.3%	11.3%	-6.1%	—	413.0	93.6%

Fund Name	Fund Type	MER	MVA	3-Year Std Dev (Monthly)	Percent Return 1997	Percent Return 1996	Percent Return 1995	Percent Return 1994	Percent Return 1993	Assets $ Mill	Tax Efficiency (3 Years)
Saxon Stock	CdnEq	1.75%	106.1	4.33%	10.6%	29.9%	22.9%	-4.4%	43.8%	17.8	90.5%
Sunfund	CdnEq	1.53%	106.1	4.76%	22.6%	26.2%	12.9%	1.4%	22.9%	34.6	—
AGF International Group—Germany Class	FgnEq	2.99%	106.0	4.36%	24.2%	28.4%	10.5%	—	—	58.4	100.0%
National Equities	CdnEq	2.40%	106.0	4.88%	19.9%	29.9%	12.3%	-0.4%	30.9%	163.2	—
Elliott & Page Asian Growth	FgnEq	3.76%	105.9	4.45%	-21.5%	1.5%	8.7%	—	—	4.4	100.0%
Green Line Japanese Growth	FgnEq	2.59%	105.9	5.17%	-15.6%	-10.4%	-5.9%	—	—	31.2	100.0%
Altamira Special Growth	CdnEq	1.80%	105.8	5.77%	15.1%	28.8%	13.1%	-19.6%	46.5%	177.5	45.3%
Capstone Balanced	Balan	2.14%	105.8	3.20%	18.5%	21.4%	13.1%	-4.8%	17.9%	6.5	62.5%
Investors Income Plus Portfolio	Balan	2.29%	105.8	1.65%	11.4%	12.9%	13.0%	-2.5%	12.8%	1,493.8	71.4%
ABC Fundamental-Value	CdnEq	2.00%	105.6	4.99%	20.3%	31.7%	11.1%	3.0%	121.7%	222.3	21.1%
STAR Inv Conservative Income & Growth	Alloc	—	105.6	1.79%*	8.0%	17.4%	—	—	—	—	—
Marathon Equity	CdnEq	2.51%	105.5	6.73%	-9.4%	49.9%	46.9%	-6.7%	102.9%	83.7	100.0%
Royal & SunAlliance Canadian Growth	CdnEq	2.35%	105.5	5.60%	14.9%	24.1%	20.9%	—	—	45.0	—
Chou Associates	FgnEq	1.86%	105.4	2.66%	40.3%	22.7%	31.0%	-2.6%	16.2%	10.6	80.1%
OTGIF Mortgage Income	FixInc	0.75%	105.4	0.75%	7.5%	9.3%	13.1%	2.2%	11.2%	112.5	54.8%
Scotia Excelsior Precious Metals	CdnEq	2.19%	105.3	9.81%	-39.4%	45.8%	4.5%	-11.7%	—	34.4	100.0%
CIBC Far East Prosperity	FgnEq	2.69%	105.1	5.89%	-24.9%	7.6%	-3.4%	-15.2%	—	80.9	100.0%
CT International Equity	FgnEq	2.42%	105.1	3.72%	10.5%	13.4%	-0.5%	2.1%	34.0%	459.4	100.0%
Ivy Foreign Equity	FgnEq	2.33%	105.0	2.66%	23.2%	15.0%	16.4%	11.3%	9.9%	1,095.8	91.6%
Leith Wheeler Canadian Equity	CdnEq	1.40%	105.0	4.94%	27.1%	29.8%	6.7%	—	—	9.1	90.3%
MB Balanced Growth Pension	Balan	—	105.0	2.83%	14.9%	22.4%	18.6%	-2.7%	21.7%	269.1	63.6%
Ethical Special Equity	CdnEq	2.71%	104.9	4.68%*	16.3%	22.1%	—	—	—	70.5	52.4%
Sceptre Equity Growth	CdnEq	1.42%	104.9	5.89%	15.0%	37.9%	37.2%	5.9%	41.0%	308.4	91.9%
ICM International	FgnEq	0.40%	104.8	3.38%	6.5%	11.9%	9.1%	11.0%	—	44.8	71.9%
C.I. Canadian Bond	FixInc	1.65%	104.6	1.30%	9.5%	14.0%	19.2%	-4.3%	—	170.0	62.9%

* 2-year standard deviation.

Fund Name	Fund Type	MER	MVA	3-Year Std Dev (Monthly)	Percent Return 1997	Percent Return 1996	Percent Return 1995	Percent Return 1994	Percent Return 1993	Assets $ Mill	Tax Efficiency (3 Years)
C.I. Pacific	FgnEq	2.55%	104.5	6.58%	-29.5%	16.2%	-4.1%	-12.3%	91.7%	306.1	100.0%
Mawer Canadian Income	FixInc	0.99%	104.5	1.39%	9.6%	13.8%	16.3%	-4.4%	13.6%	27.0	59.3%
OTGIF Growth	CdnEq	1.00%	104.5	4.94%	8.5%	23.5%	12.3%	-4.6%	22.0%	16.7	49.3%
All-Canadian Consumer Fund	CdnEq	2.00%	104.4	2.05%	19.9%	6.6%	1.0%	6.9%	—	0.8	31.9%
Navigator Value Inv Retirement	CdnEq	2.99%	104.4	6.15%	-4.1%	42.5%	32.8%	-3.5%	70.5%	26.2	100.0%
Industrial Pension	Balan	2.33%	104.3	3.41%	20.7%	27.6%	11.4%	1.0%	50.5%	288.7	99.2%
AIM GT Pacific Growth	FgnEq	3.02%	104.2	7.07%	-37.3%	25.4%	8.9%	—	—	13.5	100.0%
Global Strategy Gold Plus	CdnEq	2.82%	104.2	11.37%	-48.2%	57.5%	8.3%	2.8%	—	35.5	100.0%
Maritime Life Pacific Basin Equities A	FgnEq	2.75%	104.1	5.66%	-24.8%	7.3%	-1.0%	—	—	7.4	—
O.I.Q. Ferique International	FgnEq	0.63%	104.0	3.35%	17.6%	8.1%	1.0%	3.2%	—	22.2	74.1%
Royal International Equity	FgnEq	2.68%	104.0	3.29%	5.5%	15.6%	6.3%	5.8%	—	206.5	96.5%
London Life Mortgage	FixInc	2.00%	103.9	0.49%	6.2%	7.8%	11.9%	0.6%	9.4%	466.6	—
Standard Life Natural Resources	CdnEq	2.00%	103.9	5.92%	-15.8%	24.0%	11.3%	—	—	4.2	100.0%
Bissett International Equity	FgnEq	2.50%	103.8	3.20%	12.6%	7.6%	8.9%	—	—	34.7	80.9%
C.I. Pacific Sector	FgnEq	2.60%	103.8	6.55%	-29.8%	15.4%	-4.6%	-12.2%	90.4%	52.9	100.0%
PH&N Vintage	CdnEq	1.76%	103.6	5.40%	17.3%	39.2%	20.0%	1.4%	27.1%	109.7	61.8%
Trimark Advantage Bond	FixInc	1.24%	103.5	1.41%	10.5%	12.9%	22.7%	—	—	722.5	65.4%
Guardian U.S. Money Market Classic	FixInc	0.89%	103.4	0.03%	4.8%	4.4%	5.1%	3.4%	2.5%	14.5	50.0%
Hongkong Bank Small-Cap Growth	CdnEq	2.16%	103.4	5.98%*	15.5%	40.3%	—	—	—	42.8	92.5%
Perigee North American Equity Trust	CdnEq	—	103.4	5.14%	26.8%	22.9%	16.6%	-2.7%	24.4%	123.2	—
Royal Japanese Stock	FgnEq	2.82%	103.2	4.45%	-7.8%	-15.8%	-10.4%	19.1%	26.8%	33.8	100.0%
Hongkong Bank Asian Growth	FgnEq	2.29%	103.1	6.18%	-37.3%	9.8%	7.9%	-6.5%	—	23.5	100.0%
Tradex Equity	CdnEq	1.35%	103.1	5.17%	19.0%	36.0%	17.1%	1.7%	26.4%	78.7	76.1%
Altamira Japanese Opportunity	FgnEq	2.36%	103.0	4.85%	-17.9%	-10.3%	-7.7%	—	—	12.2	100.0%
CT Special Equity	CdnEq	2.13%	103.0	5.63%	22.8%	19.2%	7.7%	-18.5%	47.1%	260.5	100.0%

* 2-year standard deviation.

Fund Name	Fund Type	MER	MVA	3-Year Std Dev (Monthly)	Percent Return 1997	Percent Return 1996	Percent Return 1995	Percent Return 1994	Percent Return 1993	Assets $ Mill	Tax Efficiency (3 Years)
Perigee Equity Fund B	CdnEq	—	103.0	5.23%	26.8%	22.8%	17.1%	-3.2%	24.0%	12.3	—
Empire Equity Growth #3	CdnEq	1.24%	102.9	4.56%	13.5%	31.5%	14.8%	-5.1%	34.0%	11.8	—
Horizons Multi-Asset Fund Inc.	Spclty	2.00%	102.8	2.08%	9.6%	4.8%	10.0%	4.6%	—	19.6	59.1%
Atlas Canadian Small-Cap Value	CdnEq	2.57%	102.6	6.18%	20.7%	33.3%	4.4%	—	—	27.7	100.0%
Green Line Asian Growth	FgnEq	2.60%	102.6	7.13%	-28.0%	9.7%	0.9%	-7.8%	—	36.4	100.0%
AGF U.S. $ Money Market Account	FixInc	0.84%	102.5	0.03%	4.6%	4.5%	4.9%	3.4%	2.7%	19.3	50.0%
Global Mgr—Japan Bear	FgnEq	1.82%	102.5	5.63%	11.2%	-14.9%	-11.7%	—	—	0.2	12.1%
MB Canadian Equity Growth	CdnEq	—	102.5	5.46%	18.6%	41.9%	15.6%	-3.1%	30.5%	450.1	67.3%
C.I. Canadian Income	Balan	1.82%	102.4	2.34%	10.1%	16.2%	20.3%	—	—	205.2	40.6%
ICM Short-Term Investment	FixInc	0.07%	102.4	0.12%	3.3%	5.3%	7.4%	5.5%	6.1%	178.4	50.0%
OTGIF Diversified	CdnEq	1.00%	102.4	4.36%	20.5%	25.0%	14.3%	-1.4%	21.8%	48.3	71.8%
Mutual Premier International	FgnEq	2.32%	102.3	3.32%	3.9%	15.5%	6.3%	—	3.0%	75.5	99.3%
Royal & SunAlliance Equity	CdnEq	2.37%	102.3	4.50%	21.3%	24.9%	12.5%	-0.1%	22.3%	164.6	—
Atlas American Money Market	FixInc	1.13%	102.2	0.03%	4.5%	4.4%	5.0%	3.1%	2.1%	87.9	50.0%
Templeton Balanced	Balan	2.44%	102.2	2.80%	16.1%	17.9%	13.7%	-3.0%	31.0%	57.1	80.5%
First Canadian Growth	CdnEq	2.21%	102.1	4.88%	19.3%	30.7%	12.0%	-5.4%	—	956.0	98.2%
National Balanced	Balan	2.40%	102.1	2.97%	14.3%	19.8%	15.0%	-3.7%	23.2%	199.9	—
Working Opportunity (EVCC)	Labour	2.70%	102.1	1.30%	7.0%	9.9%	4.8%	1.6%	2.0%	188.8	100.0%
Guardian Monthly Dividend Fund Ltd. C	CdnEq	1.25%	102.0	1.93%	3.1%	15.9%	13.0%	-3.2%	15.0%	71.7	32.2%
Co-Operators Balanced	Balan	2.06%	101.9	3.55%	18.7%	18.5%	19.7%	-2.4%	22.9%	68.4	—
Empire Premier Equity	CdnEq	1.44%	101.9	4.53%	12.3%	30.9%	14.2%	-3.3%	26.7%	177.2	—
CT AsiaGrowth	FgnEq	2.44%	101.8	5.46%	-28.8%	0.1%	9.4%	—	—	78.7	100.0%
Quebec Professionals Short-Term	FixInc	0.30%	101.8	0.14%	3.0%	5.2%	8.0%	4.4%	6.6%	26.5	37.5%
SSQ/Marche Monetaire	FixInc	—	101.8	0.14%	3.2%	5.3%	7.7%	—	—	7.6	—
Royal U.S. Dollar Money Market	FixInc	1.12%	101.7	0.03%	4.5%	4.3%	4.8%	3.1%	2.0%	236.3	50.0%

Fund Name	Fund Type	MER	MVA	3-Year Std Dev (Monthly)	Percent Return 1997	Percent Return 1996	Percent Return 1995	Percent Return 1994	Percent Return 1993	Assets $ Mill	Tax Efficiency (3 Years)
SSQ/Hypotheques	FixInc	—	101.7	0.64%	4.8%	9.5%	12.2%	3.2%	11.5%	1.9	—
APEX Asian Pacific	FgnEq	2.81%	101.6	4.97%	-30.4%	1.7%	6.5%	—	—	7.1	—
CIBC U.S. $Money Market	FixInc	1.08%	101.6	0.03%	4.6%	4.3%	4.7%	3.3%	2.1%	139.7	50.0%
Ethical Balanced	Balan	2.08%	101.4	3.55%	20.8%	16.6%	19.2%	-4.1%	17.1%	614.4	88.0%
Green Line U.S. Money Market	FixInc	1.24%	101.4	0.03%	4.5%	4.3%	4.9%	3.0%	2.2%	352.2	50.0%
NAL-Balanced Growth	Balan	2.00%	101.4	2.83%*	14.4%	20.2%	—	—	—	115.8	—
Pursuit Money Market	FixInc	0.50%	101.4	0.09%	3.4%	4.9%	6.8%	4.5%	5.9%	1.2	50.0%
Sceptre Balanced Growth	Balan	1.44%	101.4	3.12%	14.1%	26.0%	20.4%	-4.2%	23.9%	219.8	71.1%
Ethical Pacific Rim	FgnEq	3.15%	101.3	7.56%*	-38.1%	17.8%	—	—	—	23.2	100.0%
Ideal Money Market	FixInc	1.00%	101.3	0.14%	3.0%	5.3%	7.7%	4.6%	—	68.9	—
McLean Budden Pooled Fixed Income	FixInc	—	101.3	1.44%	11.3%	12.6%	22.0%	-5.1%	18.5%	647.6	58.9%
Royal Canadian Growth	CdnEq	2.23%	101.3	5.17%	7.4%	19.3%	14.3%	-10.1%	—	513.3	-13.7%
Standard Life Balanced	Balan	2.00%	101.3	2.83%	14.7%	19.3%	17.1%	-3.6%	17.6%	20.2	76.9%
McLean Budden Balanced	Balan	1.25%	101.2	2.92%	14.9%	21.6%	18.0%	-4.2%	19.3%	19.7	77.3%
O.I.Q. Ferique Revenu	FixInc	0.35%	101.2	0.12%	3.3%	5.0%	7.1%	5.1%	5.6%	37.3	53.8%
BNP (Canada) Equity	CdnEq	2.38%	101.1	4.85%	20.5%	26.0%	14.1%	-2.1%	19.2%	6.0	54.3%
Batirente Section Obligations	FixInc	1.50%	101.1	1.36%	10.9%	13.0%	22.2%	-4.6%	18.2%	41.0	100.0%
Atlas Pacific Basin Value	FgnEq	2.90%	101.0	4.85%	-13.5%	-13.1%	-3.9%	1.2%	—	6.4	100.0%
Great-West Life Income (G) B	FixInc	1.93%	101.0	1.70%	11.2%	15.6%	15.4%	—	—	28.6	—
InvesNat U.S. Money Market	FixInc	1.12%	101.0	0.03%	4.5%	4.4%	4.6%	3.0%	1.9%	11.5	50.0%
MD Growth Investments	FgnEq	1.28%	101.0	3.38%	21.1%	20.4%	15.3%	-1.1%	44.9%	3,200.4	84.1%
Optimum Actions	CdnEq	1.62%	101.0	4.56%	19.6%	26.8%	12.7%	—	—	4.2	76.1%
STAR Reg Conservative Income & Growth	Alloc	—	101.0	1.73%*	7.8%	14.7%	—	—	—	—	—
Empire Elite Equity	CdnEq	2.42%	100.9	4.30%	9.9%	28.4%	14.5%	-4.8%	23.5%	523.8	—
Ethical Growth	CdnEq	2.10%	100.9	4.71%	17.4%	28.2%	17.5%	-1.7%	27.4%	656.7	95.0%

* 2-year standard deviation.

Fund Name	Fund Type	MER	MVA	3-Year Std Dev (Monthly)	Percent Return 1997	Percent Return 1996	Percent Return 1995	Percent Return 1994	Percent Return 1993	Assets $ Mill	Tax Efficiency (3 Years)
Montrusco Select Balanced Plus	Balan	—	100.9	2.86%	15.2%	22.9%	17.8%	-1.7%	—	324.4	64.8%
Montrusco Select Income	FixInc	—	100.9	1.33%	8.7%	11.1%	20.3%	-4.4%	18.1%	116.6	52.4%
OTGIF Balanced	Balan	1.00%	100.9	2.66%	14.8%	17.6%	16.6%	-2.9%	18.1%	63.6	67.5%
PH&N Canadian Equity Plus Pension	CdnEq	0.54%	100.9	4.99%	17.4%	30.3%	14.6%	3.8%	23.4%	1,065.8	85.1%
Standard Life International Equity	FgnEq	2.00%	100.9	3.49%	9.5%	6.4%	10.2%	—	—	8.0	93.3%
Beutel Goodman International Equity	FgnEq	2.60%	100.8	3.23%	5.7%	14.0%	1.1%	0.9%	60.8%	12.8	66.0%
Bissett Money Market	FixInc	0.50%	100.8	0.12%	3.2%	5.1%	7.0%	4.9%	5.3%	73.0	50.0%
Desjardins Environment	CdnEq	2.07%	100.8	4.94%	17.8%	26.4%	12.6%	-2.0%	19.9%	107.1	86.7%
Equitable Life Canada Accum. Income	FixInc	0.36%	100.8	1.30%	9.6%	11.9%	19.6%	-4.7%	15.3%	13.6	—
Mawer Canadian Diversified Investment	Balan	1.08%	100.8	2.68%	14.2%	17.2%	14.9%	-2.6%	19.4%	27.3	70.8%
Montrusco Select Growth	CdnEq	—	100.8	6.90%	24.5%	47.5%	29.6%	-7.0%	18.9%	205.4	79.0%
NAL-Equity Growth	CdnEq	2.00%	100.8	4.73%*	15.9%	30.3%	—	—	—	86.2	—
PH&N Balance Pension Trust	Balan	—	100.8	2.83%	12.9%	19.7%	17.1%	0.4%	19.4%	2,164.0	73.4%
Fidelity U.S. Money Market	FixInc	1.25%	100.7	0.03%	4.4%	4.2%	4.7%	—	—	43.0	50.0%
Saxon Balanced	Balan	1.75%	100.7	3.03%	9.5%	23.3%	21.5%	-3.2%	34.4%	9.8	78.9%
Batirente Section Actions	CdnEq	1.54%	100.6	4.97%	19.6%	25.3%	13.3%	—	—	3.6	100.0%
MAXXUM Natural Resource	CdnEq	2.23%	100.6	7.97%	-39.2%	42.5%	36.2%	-2.5%	78.3%	30.9	100.0%
Green Line Balanced Growth	Balan	1.95%	100.5	2.94%	14.0%	21.9%	17.0%	-4.1%	11.9%	562.6	92.7%
O.I.Q. Ferique Obligations	FixInc	0.53%	100.5	1.30%	8.5%	10.4%	19.5%	-4.0%	16.1%	54.5	59.8%
SSQ-Obligations	FixInc	—	100.4	1.39%	9.3%	13.0%	20.5%	-3.9%	16.8%	58.4	—
Great-West Life Income (G) A	FixInc	2.17%	100.2	1.70%	11.0%	15.3%	15.2%	—	—	31.5	—
Manulife Vistafund 1 Global Equity	FgnEq	1.63%	100.2	3.55%*	5.6%	7.4%	—	—	—	6.3	—
Mawer Canadian Balanced RSP	Balan	0.99%	100.2	2.77%	15.4%	17.4%	15.0%	-2.2%	19.8%	71.8	67.1%
Royal & SunAlliance Money Market	FixInc	1.00%	100.2	0.14%	2.9%	5.3%	7.0%	5.2%	—	36.7	—
Atlas American Advantage Value	USEq	2.52%	100.1	3.38%	25.2%	21.4%	30.8%	—	—	39.7	99.9%

* 2-year standard deviation.

Fund Name	Fund Type	MER	MVA	3-Year Std Dev (Monthly)	Percent Return 1997	Percent Return 1996	Percent Return 1995	Percent Return 1994	Percent Return 1993	Assets $ Mill	Tax Efficiency (3 Years)
Cassels Blaikie Canadian	Balan	1.04%	100.1	2.77%	18.3%	19.8%	14.9%	-1.0%	16.7%	12.5	56.3%
Investors Growth Plus Portfolio	Balan	2.45%	100.1	2.37%	15.5%	14.2%	15.3%	3.4%	18.5%	374.1	90.0%
Global Mgr–Japan Geared	FgnEq	1.82%	100.0	11.17%	-49.5%	-17.9%	-10.5%	—	—	0.3	100.0%
Guardian Asia Pacific Classic	FgnEq	1.72%	100.0	5.17%	-30.0%	3.8%	4.6%	—	—	1.5	100.0%
Westbury Canadian Life A	CdnEq	1.05%	100.0	5.40%	20.3%	28.3%	14.1%	-3.2%	28.9%	2.0	—
First Canadian Resource	CdnEq	2.30%	99.9	6.78%	-18.2%	28.7%	7.3%	-11.7%	—	31.0	100.0%
Green Line Resource	CdnEq	2.12%	99.9	6.81%	-24.1%	38.6%	7.9%	-3.2%	—	76.2	100.0%
Quebec Professionals Canadian Equity	CdnEq	0.95%	99.9	4.62%	14.3%	22.6%	15.9%	-4.8%	21.3%	88.9	64.7%
Mawer Canadian Bond	FixInc	1.00%	99.8	1.30%	8.4%	11.0%	18.9%	-5.5%	15.7%	38.6	62.7%
Spectrum United Canadian Stock	CdnEq	2.33%	99.8	4.56%	18.4%	22.2%	10.9%	1.0%	21.3%	141.2	67.1%
Fidelity International Portfolio	FgnEq	2.68%	99.7	3.52%	24.1%	16.0%	14.4%	6.3%	35.1%	3,478.1	93.8%
Green Line Canadian Equity	CdnEq	2.10%	99.7	4.99%	24.4%	25.6%	9.5%	-4.6%	40.0%	720.7	95.5%
MD Select	CdnEq	1.29%	99.7	4.50%	9.2%	36.3%	10.1%	-4.6%	—	215.5	87.6%
McLean Budden Equity Growth	CdnEq	1.75%	99.7	5.43%	16.1%	37.9%	13.8%	-3.9%	24.9%	12.9	93.9%
Spectrum United U.S. Dollar Money Market	FixInc	1.20%	99.7	0.03%	4.2%	4.0%	5.1%	3.8%	2.7%	4.9	50.0%
Clean Environment Balanced	Balan	2.60%	99.6	3.84%	20.2%	30.7%	10.1%	-8.0%	38.4%	100.2	97.3%
Guardian Growth Equity Classic	CdnEq	2.15%	99.6	4.99%	9.6%	39.9%	7.9%	-4.5%	35.6%	51.8	81.6%
NN Asset Allocation	Balan	2.69%	99.6	2.77%	12.4%	19.7%	15.4%	-3.4%	20.8%	127.6	—
Desjardins Distinct–Bond	FixInc	1.66%	99.5	1.24%	8.8%	11.4%	21.0%	-4.9%	16.3%	28.8	—
Optimum Equilibre	Balan	1.46%	99.5	1.99%	11.1%	12.0%	20.0%	-4.1%	19.5%	28.9	63.6%
Universal Far East	FgnEq	2.57%	99.5	6.81%	-34.6%	9.9%	-1.2%	-11.5%	—	29.5	100.0%
AIM Global Health Sciences	Spclty	2.94%	99.3	4.71%	21.9%	15.3%	66.3%	4.2%	15.7%	307.4	99.4%
ICM Balanced	Balan	0.17%	99.3	2.31%	7.1%	17.2%	17.3%	-0.5%	24.7%	168.4	56.7%
Green Line Canadian Bond	FixInc	0.94%	99.2	1.47%	10.6%	12.4%	21.5%	-5.6%	16.2%	933.5	68.1%
National Trust Special Equity	CdnEq	2.54%	99.2	6.44%	12.0%	27.1%	10.1%	-14.9%	44.3%	35.7	100.0%

Fund Name	Fund Type	MER	MVA	3-Year Std Dev (Monthly)	Percent Return 1997	Percent Return 1996	Percent Return 1995	Percent Return 1994	Percent Return 1993	Assets $ Mill	Tax Efficiency (3 Years)
Trans-Canada Money Market	FixInc	0.65%	99.2	0.09%	3.2%	4.8%	6.4%	5.3%	4.6%	10.2	50.0%
Global Mgr—Japan Index	FgnEq	1.82%	99.1	6.41%	-27.9%	-14.3%	-4.7%	—	—	2.2	100.0%
Ideal Balanced	Balan	2.00%	99.1	2.71%	13.4%	15.1%	18.3%	-1.2%	16.1%	453.6	—
PH&N International Equity	FgnEq	1.49%	99.1	3.55%	3.1%	10.4%	8.9%	—	—	493.0	84.0%
Canada Life S-2	CdnEq	1.50%	99.0	4.45%	11.7%	26.1%	14.2%	-2.8%	26.7%	149.8	—
National Trust Balanced	Balan	1.74%	99.0	2.89%	15.6%	17.9%	16.8%	-4.5%	18.0%	296.6	81.4%
FMOQ Money Market	FixInc	0.79%	98.9	0.12%	3.0%	4.8%	6.8%	5.0%	5.4%	4.5	50.0%
Global Strategy World Companies	FgnEq	2.89%	98.9	4.01%	6.7%	19.9%	52.8%	—	—	132.7	93.3%
Royal Trust Advantage Income	Balan	1.63%	98.9	1.96%	10.6%	13.6%	14.7%	-2.7%	15.5%	147.9	78.7%
Westbury Canadian Life B	FixInc	1.06%	98.9	1.39%	9.3%	11.7%	18.9%	-5.0%	17.0%	1.3	—
AIC Value	USEq	2.44%	98.8	4.59%	37.3%	35.4%	31.6%	-4.2%	35.9%	1,303.3	100.0%
Global Strategy Asia	FgnEq	2.80%	98.8	7.45%	-39.5%	10.5%	1.4%	-16.5%	—	9.0	100.0%
Pursuit Canadian Equity	CdnEq	1.50%	98.8	4.97%	19.1%	29.5%	17.7%	-4.8%	31.7%	9.5	85.9%
Trimark Canadian	CdnEq	1.52%	98.8	3.64%	3.2%	26.0%	11.1%	2.4%	37.9%	1,729.2	44.4%
Global Mgr—German Geared	FgnEq	1.82%	98.7	10.25%	79.4%	35.6%	8.0%	—	—	2.5	95.9%
OTGIF Fixed Value	FixInc	0.50%	98.7	0.09%	3.0%	4.9%	6.6%	5.1%	6.3%	24.0	50.0%
Strategic Value Canadian Small Companies	CdnEq	2.70%	98.7	5.20%	14.9%	19.4%	8.1%	-1.8%	35.9%	138.0	71.1%
AGF International Value	FgnEq	2.77%	98.6	3.98%	23.6%	19.0%	15.0%	1.0%	21.6%	2,016.1	98.1%
Equitable Life Canada Common Stock	CdnEq	1.04%	98.6	5.05%	13.2%	32.7%	14.9%	4.9%	22.7%	17.0	—
InvesNat Corporate Cash Management	FixInc	0.50%	98.6	0.09%*	3.1%	4.7%	—	—	—	265.8	50.0%
Manulife Cabot Blue Chip	CdnEq	2.50%	98.6	4.45%	13.6%	19.1%	18.4%	—	—	20.6	72.2%
Manulife Vistafund 2 Global Equity	FgnEq	2.38%	98.6	3.55%*	4.8%	6.6%	—	—	—	40.2	—
PH&N Balanced	Balan	0.91%	98.6	2.80%	11.8%	18.8%	16.4%	0.4%	20.2%	501.6	73.4%
General Trust of Canada Bond	FixInc	1.56%	98.5	1.36%	7.3%	11.0%	18.8%	-7.1%	15.8%	39.6	60.6%
MD Bond	FixInc	1.03%	98.5	1.44%	8.6%	11.4%	20.1%	-5.4%	17.9%	508.8	70.1%

* 2-year standard deviation.

Fund Name	Fund Type	MER	MVA	3-Year Std Dev (Monthly)	Percent Return 1997	Percent Return 1996	Percent Return 1995	Percent Return 1994	Percent Return 1993	Assets $ Mill	Tax Efficiency (3 Years)
PH&N Bond	FixInc	0.57%	98.4	1.30%	8.7%	11.2%	20.4%	-4.1%	17.8%	2,000.4	59.2%
Royal & SunAlliance International Equity	FgnEq	2.60%	98.3	3.41%	4.1%	8.5%	7.3%	—	—	18.7	—
Investors Growth Portfolio	FgnEq	2.61%	98.2	3.67%	19.5%	18.4%	15.5%	7.1%	26.1%	749.4	98.8%
Investors Pacific International	FgnEq	2.62%	98.2	6.78%	-36.4%	8.7%	1.4%	-6.7%	88.1%	465.2	100.0%
Multiple Opportunities	CdnEq	2.50%	98.2	6.52%	-13.7%	52.3%	58.7%	-15.3%	159.3%	8.9	-206.1%
Desjardins Distinct–Equity	CdnEq	1.99%	98.1	5.31%	18.6%	23.0%	14.3%	-1.1%	28.3%	26.9	—
ICM Bond	FixInc	0.16%	98.1	0.92%	6.5%	9.8%	18.4%	-3.5%	17.7%	70.2	65.4%
Maritime Life Growth Series A&C	CdnEq	2.55%	98.1	5.11%	15.8%	28.7%	13.4%	-7.0%	31.6%	227.3	—
NN Money Market	FixInc	0.77%	98.1	0.09%	3.0%	4.6%	6.8%	4.6%	4.8%	10.9	—
Desjardins Distinct–Diversified	Balan	1.80%	98.0	2.97%	13.8%	16.9%	16.1%	-2.5%	21.6%	36.8	—
Mutual Diversifund 40	Balan	1.77%	98.0	2.57%	11.7%	17.5%	17.4%	-2.7%	16.7%	282.2	62.5%
Investors Japanese Growth	FgnEq	2.46%	97.9	4.53%	-20.6%	-15.6%	-6.7%	21.2%	35.3%	404.1	100.0%
Mawer Canadian Equity	CdnEq	1.30%	97.9	4.91%	22.4%	18.1%	11.8%	-2.6%	27.1%	16.4	82.2%
McLean Budden Money Market	FixInc	0.60%	97.9	0.09%	2.9%	4.7%	6.6%	4.5%	4.3%	8.5	50.0%
Templeton Global Balanced	Balan	2.55%	97.9	2.22%	10.9%	16.4%	13.4%	—	—	72.8	93.1%
Templeton Growth	FgnEq	2.00%	97.9	3.46%	17.1%	18.4%	14.1%	3.8%	36.3%	9,221.0	64.9%
Beutel Goodman Money Market	FixInc	0.59%	97.8	0.09%	3.0%	4.6%	6.8%	4.8%	5.2%	66.1	50.0%
CDA Money Market (Canagex)	FixInc	0.66%	97.8	0.14%	2.7%	4.5%	7.2%	4.7%	5.3%	23.2	—
Green Line Blue Chip Equity	CdnEq	2.25%	97.8	4.97%	15.1%	26.5%	12.3%	-5.2%	18.4%	333.1	96.4%
Green Line Canadian Index	CdnEq	0.80%	97.8	5.23%	13.7%	26.6%	13.2%	-1.2%	31.0%	317.6	97.7%
Hongkong Bank Equity	CdnEq	1.87%	97.8	4.91%	13.8%	31.3%	6.8%	-6.7%	49.9%	149.6	97.7%
MAXXUM Money Market	FixInc	0.84%	97.8	0.09%	3.0%	4.7%	6.5%	4.9%	5.0%	53.0	50.0%
Royal Asian Growth	FgnEq	2.97%	97.8	6.67%	-38.1%	8.5%	3.1%	-17.4%	—	52.7	100.0%
STAR Registered Balanced Growth & Income	Alloc	—	97.8	2.02%*	10.5%	15.2%	—	—	—	—	—
Strategic Value Asia Pacific	FgnEq	2.70%	97.8	4.62%	-26.7%	-1.1%	5.4%	—	—	5.3	100.0%

* 2-year standard deviation.

Fund Name	Fund Type	MER	MVA	3-Year Std Dev (Monthly)	Percent Return 1997	Percent Return 1996	Percent Return 1995	Percent Return 1994	Percent Return 1993	Assets $ Mill	Tax Efficiency (3 Years)
Atlas Canadian Emerging Growth	CdnEq	2.48%	97.7	6.38%	-8.0%	38.4%	26.5%	—	—	37.0	100.0%
Crocus Investment Fund	Labor	3.78%	97.7	1.10%	12.9%	4.9%	3.8%	9.9%	—	86.4	100.0%
Maritime Life Balanced A&C	Balan	2.45%	97.7	2.57%	9.7%	16.4%	16.9%	-1.5%	16.7%	380.9	—
Universal International Stock	FgnEq	2.37%	97.7	3.87%	3.8%	4.9%	7.2%	7.8%	43.8%	227.7	96.1%
BPI T-Bill	FixInc	0.65%	97.6	0.09%	2.9%	4.7%	6.6%	4.4%	4.7%	204.2	50.0%
Friedberg Currency	Spclty	4.24%	97.6	8.86%*	-1.5%	72.0%	—	—	—	67.4	100.0%
YMG Money Market	FixInc	0.62%	97.6	0.09%	2.9%	4.6%	6.8%	4.6%	4.8%	8.5	50.0%
First Canadian Equity Index	CdnEq	1.21%	97.5	5.20%	13.5%	26.5%	12.5%	-2.0%	29.0%	301.4	96.0%
Global Mgr–Hong Kong Index	FgnEq	1.82%	97.5	7.94%	-15.6%	30.3%	17.2%	—	—	0.4	53.2%
MD Money	FixInc	0.52%	97.5	0.12%	2.9%	4.6%	6.7%	4.7%	5.0%	386.2	68.5%
Optima Strategy–Short-Term	FixInc	0.27%	97.5	0.49%	4.1%	8.1%	10.5%	0.2%	—	193.7	100.0%
CDA International Equity (KBSH)	FgnEq	1.45%	97.4	4.07%*	-0.1%	9.5%	—	—	—	3.7	—
McLean Budden Fixed Income	FixInc	1.00%	97.4	1.44%	10.1%	11.6%	20.2%	-6.2%	17.4%	19.0	68.3%
AGF International Group-Asian Growth	FgnEq	3.03%	97.3	6.73%	-41.5%	6.2%	7.8%	-6.5%	87.0%	147.7	100.0%
First Heritage	CdnEq	4.01%	97.3	6.75%	-19.4%	19.2%	7.3%	-5.1%	55.2%	2.4	100.0%
InvesNat Japanese Equity	FgnEq	2.52%	97.3	5.60%	-28.9%	-17.0%	-7.2%	—	—	9.8	100.0%
PH&N Canadian Equity	CdnEq	1.09%	97.3	5.14%	14.2%	30.0%	13.1%	3.9%	27.6%	607.0	95.6%
Perigee Income Fund 2	FixInc	—	97.3	0.89%	4.7%	11.3%	17.8%	-2.5%	17.0%	4.1	—
Royal Canadian Equity	CdnEq	1.95%	97.3	4.50%	12.9%	21.9%	13.2%	-0.4%	31.8%	2,607.9	90.0%
Sceptre Money Market	FixInc	0.75%	97.3	0.09%	2.9%	4.6%	6.5%	4.6%	5.2%	41.3	50.0%
Spectrum United Asian Dynasty	FgnEq	2.58%	97.3	6.09%	-36.3%	4.2%	2.2%	-8.4%	—	9.9	100.0%
Standard Life Money Market	FixInc	0.90%	97.3	0.14%	2.5%	5.4%	6.6%	4.1%	4.4%	9.8	49.2%
Beutel Goodman Balanced	Balan	2.11%	97.2	2.54%	12.5%	15.9%	12.8%	-0.3%	23.1%	176.7	69.7%
CT Balanced	Balan	2.09%	97.2	2.68%	10.9%	15.3%	16.5%	-6.8%	22.6%	1,556.8	78.9%
Fidelity European Growth	FgnEq	2.69%	97.2	3.81%	26.2%	22.9%	13.3%	10.1%	33.0%	2,170.9	96.6%

* 2-year standard deviation.

Fund Name	Fund Type	MER	MVA	3-Year Std Dev (Monthly)	Percent Return 1997	Percent Return 1996	Percent Return 1995	Percent Return 1994	Percent Return 1993	Assets $ Mill	Tax Efficiency (3 Years)
PH&N Pooled U.S. Pension	USEq	0.05%	97.2	3.90%	30.8%	27.5%	27.1%	3.8%	17.3%	510.8	100.0%
Talvest Money	FixInc	0.77%	97.2	0.12%	2.8%	4.8%	6.6%	4.8%	5.1%	129.5	50.0%
Trimark Select Canadian Growth	CdnEq	2.30%	97.2	3.58%	3.4%	23.3%	11.7%	3.8%	29.8%	3,947.0	48.7%
YMG International	FgnEq	1.78%	97.2	3.78%	6.6%	9.0%	3.1%	5.8%	—	70.0	89.7%
Canada Life Canadian Equity	CdnEq	2.25%	97.1	4.50%	10.6%	25.8%	13.6%	-3.3%	24.5%	549.5	—
Sceptre Bond	FixInc	0.95%	97.1	1.50%	10.2%	10.5%	18.6%	-4.4%	14.4%	53.8	72.6%
Scotia Excelsior Canadian Growth	CdnEq	2.09%	97.1	5.23%	6.8%	34.6%	19.8%	-1.2%	31.6%	744.1	80.0%
YMG Growth	CdnEq	2.02%	97.1	6.21%	26.4%	24.9%	8.1%	-14.9%	37.1%	5.3	43.9%
BPI Canadian Equity Value	CdnEq	2.55%	97.0	4.97%	14.9%	25.1%	14.4%	-9.4%	23.9%	375.9	78.7%
Canada Life Managed	Balan	2.25%	97.0	2.71%	9.6%	17.8%	16.1%	-4.0%	20.3%	1,163.7	—
Global Strategy Canada Growth	CdnEq	2.60%	97.0	4.47%	15.0%	23.7%	9.9%	-8.5%	34.0%	456.5	37.1%
Green Line Canadian Govt Bond Index	FixInc	0.80%	97.0	1.30%	8.4%	11.0%	19.7%	-5.2%	14.9%	211.9	65.2%
PH&N Canadian Equity Plus	CdnEq	1.18%	97.0	5.02%	12.9%	28.7%	13.0%	3.5%	27.4%	178.6	88.9%
Colonia Life Equity	CdnEq	2.27%	96.9	5.05%	20.2%	27.5%	11.3%	-10.5%	18.5%	26.2	—
O.I.Q. Ferique Equilibre	Balan	0.44%	96.9	3.23%	16.5%	17.7%	15.8%	-0.3%	19.9%	332.0	67.8%
Royal & SunAlliance Balanced	Balan	2.34%	96.9	2.74%	14.1%	17.2%	15.3%	-4.6%	18.3%	236.3	—
SSQ–Actions Canadiennes	CdnEq	—	96.9	5.66%	13.9%	24.5%	16.9%	-6.1%	23.6%	35.2	—
C.I. International Balanced	Balan	2.41%	96.8	2.31%	15.7%	13.0%	18.4%	—	—	175.5	89.7%
Capstone Cash Management	FixInc	0.60%	96.8	0.14%	2.4%	4.3%	7.3%	4.7%	5.7%	2.2	50.0%
Lotus Group–Income	FixInc	0.75%	96.8	0.09%	2.9%	4.5%	6.5%	4.3%	4.8%	2.6	50.0%
Montrusco Select E.A.F.E.	FgnEq	—	96.8	3.81%	5.8%	7.5%	9.2%	18.7%	31.6%	408.8	78.9%
Spectrum United Canadian Equity	CdnEq	2.35%	96.8	4.85%	13.8%	26.1%	11.8%	-0.7%	42.9%	1,266.2	81.7%
Templeton Canadian Asset Allocation	Balan	2.15%	96.8	2.40%	10.3%	16.2%	11.5%	—	—	121.9	88.0%
Cormel Equilibre	Balan	0.96%	96.7	2.71%	15.2%	15.4%	15.6%	-2.7%	20.8%	22.2	68.7%
Green Line Balanced Income	Balan	1.95%	96.7	2.83%	13.6%	18.1%	14.0%	-5.4%	15.4%	267.8	86.1%

Fund Name	Fund Type	MER	MVA	3-Year Std Dev (Monthly)	Percent Return 1997	Percent Return 1996	Percent Return 1995	Percent Return 1994	Percent Return 1993	Assets $ Mill	Tax Efficiency (3 Years)
Leith Wheeler Fixed Income	FixInc	0.75%	96.7	1.04%	7.0%	10.8%	17.4%	—	—	10.1	57.9%
Lotus Group—Bond	FixInc	0.75%	96.7	1.36%	8.6%	11.6%	18.5%	—	—	1.3	57.1%
Manulife Cabot Canadian Equity	CdnEq	2.50%	96.7	5.28%	12.6%	22.0%	18.8%	—	—	35.2	61.9%
SSQ—Equilibre	Balan	—	96.7	3.18%	10.7%	18.2%	17.9%	-3.6%	17.4%	31.1	—
First Canadian Japanese Growth	FgnEq	2.16%	96.6	4.85%	-25.5%	-14.2%	-7.3%	—	—	18.1	100.0%
Investors U.S. Growth	USEq	2.41%	96.6	3.64%	43.2%	20.4%	24.8%	7.0%	13.7%	1,686.7	99.8%
Mackenzie Sentinel Global	FgnEq	0.47%	96.6	3.81%	3.1%	4.0%	6.8%	6.8%	41.5%	6.2	100.0%
Spectrum United Diversified	Balan	2.08%	96.6	2.86%	14.3%	16.5%	14.6%	-4.8%	18.5%	205.8	66.4%
Green Line Canadian Money Market	FixInc	0.84%	96.5	0.09%	2.9%	4.4%	6.3%	4.6%	4.8%	3,832.0	50.0%
Guardian International Income Classic	FixInc	2.06%	96.5	1.10%	7.4%	6.7%	17.8%	-6.3%	16.7%	35.8	71.9%
Hongkong Bank Balanced	Balan	1.81%	96.5	3.00%	10.6%	20.5%	14.5%	-5.4%	23.1%	325.5	85.8%
PH&N Canadian Money Market	FixInc	0.48%	96.5	0.09%	2.9%	4.2%	6.7%	4.7%	5.0%	872.5	50.0%
Trimark Canadian Bond	FixInc	1.24%	96.5	1.27%	8.7%	10.9%	21.6%	158.6	57.3%		
Beutel Goodman Canadian Equity	CdnEq	2.08%	96.4	4.30%	13.3%	21.6%	8.3%	6.4%	24.7%	48.6	76.7%
Beutel Goodman Income	FixInc	0.66%	96.4	1.41%	8.8%	11.7%	20.6%	-7.2%	17.2%	56.0	60.8%
C.I. Money Market	FixInc	0.77%	96.4	0.09%	2.8%	4.3%	6.7%	4.7%	4.7%	344.1	50.0%
Dynamic Precious Metals	CdnEq	2.47%	96.4	8.92%	-45.9%	24.8%	—	3.4%	96.2%	146.0	100.0%
National Trust Canadian Bond	FixInc	1.22%	96.4	1.41%	8.3%	11.6%	21.2%	-5.9%	14.3%	215.1	66.0%
National Trust International Equity	FgnEq	3.05%	96.4	4.01%	1.3%	7.1%	7.1%	—	—	15.3	96.6%
Optimum Obligations	FixInc	1.39%	96.4	1.41%	8.8%	12.3%	22.4%	-5.5%	18.2%	5.3	50.2%
Resolute Growth	CdnEq	2.00%	96.4	7.25%	-5.4%	49.1%	8.5%	-5.1%	—	3.9	100.0%
Altamira Bond	FixInc	1.29%	96.3	2.02%	19.6%	9.0%	27.4%	-8.9%	21.6%	427.2	82.0%
Equitable Life Canada Canadian Stock	CdnEq	2.25%	96.3	4.71%	11.6%	27.1%	11.1%	2.7%	20.1%	62.6	—
Investors Corporate Bond	FixInc	1.89%	96.3	1.30%	8.6%	10.5%	17.9%	—	—	944.5	60.2%
Bissett Bond	FixInc	0.75%	96.2	1.47%	9.6%	11.8%	20.6%	-3.8%	15.6%	186.6	66.7%

Fund Name	Fund Type	MER	MVA	3-Year Std Dev (Monthly)	Percent Return 1997	Percent Return 1996	Percent Return 1995	Percent Return 1994	Percent Return 1993	Assets $ Mill	Tax Efficiency (3 Years)
CDA Bond & Mortgage (Canagex)	FixInc	0.95%	96.2	1.13%	5.9%	10.0%	18.6%	-3.5%	15.3%	35.1	—
Empire Balanced	Balan	2.44%	96.2	2.54%	8.0%	18.8%	15.7%	-3.3%	19.9%	245.2	—
Sceptre Asian Growth	FgnEq	2.45%	96.2	8.66%	-37.7%	7.2%	-4.6%	-14.7%	—	7.0	100.0%
CDA Balanced (KBSH)	Balan	0.96%	96.1	2.80%	11.4%	17.4%	14.8%	-1.6%	17.6%	41.8	—
ICM Equity	CdnEq	0.09%	96.1	4.07%	6.5%	20.0%	12.8%	3.5%	31.8%	193.6	24.4%
Investors Income Portfolio	FixInc	2.06%	96.1	1.04%	6.0%	9.9%	16.1%	-3.6%	12.6%	789.8	60.1%
FMOQ Canadian Equity	CdnEq	0.82%	96.0	5.20%	18.8%	20.0%	12.1%	—	—	3.9	76.8%
InvesNat T-Bill Plus	FixInc	0.78%	96.0	0.09%	2.8%	4.4%	6.4%	4.4%	4.6%	218.1	50.0%
NN Bond	FixInc	2.21%	96.0	1.62%	10.7%	10.8%	20.7%	-4.7%	16.4%	43.4	—
Scotia Excelsior Premium T-Bill	FixInc	0.52%	96.0	0.09%	2.7%	4.3%	6.6%	4.5%	4.7%	860.6	50.0%
Universal World Income RRSP	FixInc	2.10%	96.0	1.27%	9.6%	8.8%	14.9%	—	—	631.7	65.9%
Fidelity Emerging Markets Bond	FixInc	2.24%	95.9	6.03%	17.3%	38.1%	12.8%	—	—	37.6	46.0%
Westbury Canadian Life C	FixInc	0.09%	95.9	0.20%	3.1%	4.6%	6.8%	4.5%	5.4%	0.1	—
ABC Fully-Managed	Balan	2.00%	95.8	3.93%	10.6%	32.0%	17.3%	2.8%	64.4%	67.8	42.4%
CIBC Premium Canadian T-Bill	FixInc	0.55%	95.8	0.09%	2.8%	4.3%	6.5%	4.6%	4.3%	1,956.9	50.0%
Investors Retirement Growth Portfolio	CdnEq	2.62%	95.8	4.65%	10.8%	21.9%	11.6%	1.9%	24.5%	2,017.0	72.8%
NN Canadian 35 Index	CdnEq	2.36%	95.8	5.37%	13.2%	26.2%	10.8%	4.9%	19.4%	60.6	—
O.I.Q. Ferique Actions	CdnEq	0.52%	95.8	4.56%	12.6%	24.9%	13.7%	1.5%	23.2%	95.1	63.6%
Global Strategy Japan	FgnEq	2.82%	95.7	5.48%	-28.4%	-17.0%	-10.2%	—	—	9.4	100.0%
Hongkong Bank Money Market	FixInc	0.91%	95.7	0.09%	2.8%	4.3%	6.4%	3.9%	4.3%	403.0	50.0%
Spectrum United Canadian Balanced Pfl	Balan	2.16%	95.7	2.97%	10.1%	16.0%	19.2%	-4.0%	27.1%	477.7	74.1%
Co-Operators Canadian Equity	CdnEq	2.06%	95.6	5.14%	18.7%	22.4%	9.3%	-0.1%	28.3%	19.6	—
Mutual Equifund	CdnEq	1.78%	95.6	5.08%	10.7%	26.4%	17.3%	-0.1%	20.2%	91.8	42.5%
Trimark Fund	FgnEq	1.52%	95.6	3.38%	16.0%	14.7%	16.7%	14.9%	31.6%	2,621.2	56.6%
Beutel Goodman Private Bond	FixInc	0.70%	95.5	1.44%	8.1%	11.8%	20.7%	-6.1%	15.4%	5.7	65.7%

Fund Name	Fund Type	MER	MVA	3-Year Std Dev (Monthly)	Percent Return 1997	Percent Return 1996	Percent Return 1995	Percent Return 1994	Percent Return 1993	Assets $ Mill	Tax Efficiency (3 Years)
Canada Life U.S. & International Equity	FgnEq	2.40%	95.5	4.10%	18.0%	20.3%	17.6%	2.0%	27.3%	682.2	—
Desjardins Divers Moderate	Balan	1.76%	95.5	1.47%*	6.2%	10.5%	—	—	—	533.0	67.9%
Global Mgr—German Index	FgnEq	1.82%	95.5	4.94%	31.6%	14.9%	10.0%	—	—	12.9	91.3%
Strategic Value Income	FixInc	2.20%	95.5	1.47%	11.5%	8.7%	17.9%	-5.1%	14.7%	170.4	61.8%
Great-West Life Equity Index (G) B	CdnEq	2.28%	95.4	5.20%	12.3%	25.2%	11.6%	—	—	20.8	—
PH&N S-T Bond & Mortgage	FixInc	0.64%	95.4	0.75%	4.5%	10.1%	15.4%	-1.3%	174.5	53.1%	—
Trimark Select Balanced	Balan	2.23%	95.4	2.77%	7.4%	18.9%	15.0%	1.5%	27.4%	4,069.4	60.5%
Universal U.S. Money Market	FixInc	1.25%	95.4	0.03%	3.8%	3.7%	4.1%	—	—	7.9	50.0%
Allstar AIG Canadian Equity	CdnEq	2.68%	95.3	4.79%	13.0%	24.8%	9.0%	-5.8%	19.2%	3.1	58.0%
Mawer U.S. Equity	USEq	1.27%	95.3	4.07%	29.3%	23.9%	24.4%	3.8%	7.4%	28.3	86.8%
STAR Investment Balanced Growth & Income	Alloc	—	95.3	1.93%*	10.9%	10.8%	—	—	—	—	—
Goldtrust	CdnEq	1.81%	95.2	7.19%	-33.8%	21.6%	-17.1%	-2.1%	81.1%	5.6	100.0%
Green Line Canadian T-Bill	FixInc	0.86%	95.2	0.09%	2.7%	4.3%	6.2%	4.5%	4.2%	343.4	50.0%
Mutual Premier Blue Chip	CdnEq	2.27%	95.2	4.82%	10.1%	26.4%	13.8%	-0.1%	16.3%	660.1	86.0%
NN Canadian Growth	CdnEq	2.69%	95.2	4.62%	12.1%	26.2%	9.9%	-4.3%	25.0%	31.9	—
Altamira Short-Term Government Bond	FixInc	1.26%	95.1	0.58%	4.1%	8.1%	15.0%	—	—	67.5	54.3%
First Canadian International Growth	FgnEq	2.02%	95.1	3.35%	5.5%	5.2%	2.7%	11.1%	35.9%	361.7	92.7%
Great-West Life Mortgage (G) B	FixInc	2.16%	95.1	0.95%	7.2%	9.2%	14.3%	—	—	65.3	—
CCPE Diversified	Balan	1.35%	95.0	2.97%	13.2%	18.1%	14.4%	-0.6%	15.7%	31.3	—
Colonia Life Money Market	FixInc	1.00%	95.0	0.12%	2.4%	4.0%	6.9%	3.8%	4.4%	3.4	—
Industrial Cash Management	FixInc	0.50%	95.0	0.09%	2.6%	4.2%	6.6%	4.8%	4.9%	462.9	50.0%
Lotus Group—Balanced	Balan	2.00%	95.0	3.09%	11.2%	18.9%	13.2%	-8.1%	26.8%	30.9	59.7%
Mawer Canadian Money Market	FixInc	0.67%	95.0	0.09%	2.7%	4.2%	6.4%	4.4%	4.5%	46.6	50.0%
Co-Operators Fixed Income	FixInc	2.06%	94.9	1.59%	10.6%	10.6%	21.7%	-6.1%	17.4%	11.8	—
FMOQ Fonds de Placement	Balan	0.61%	94.9	4.13%	21.2%	20.8%	19.4%	0.6%	15.5%	26.5	71.1%

* 2-year standard deviation.

Fund Name	Fund Type	MER	MVA	3-Year Std Dev (Monthly)	Percent Return 1997	Percent Return 1996	Percent Return 1995	Percent Return 1994	Percent Return 1993	Assets $ Mill	Tax Efficiency (3 Years)
Great-West Life Equity Index (G) A	CdnEq	2.52%	94.9	5.20%	12.0%	24.9%	11.5%	-2.7%	29.7%	51.3	—
Guardian Foreign Income Class A	FixInc	1.68%	94.9	1.59%	12.6%	7.4%	14.8%	—	—	15.0	75.5%
IRIS Canadian Equity	CdnEq	2.19%	94.9	5.37%	10.2%	28.5%	16.7%	-2.6%	27.2%	92.2	26.0%
Ivy Mortgage	FixInc	1.84%	94.9	0.61%	3.3%	9.1%	12.3%	—	—	287.8	56.6%
Royal Trust Advantage Balanced	Balan	1.75%	94.9	2.66%	11.3%	15.1%	14.6%	-2.4%	17.4%	433.7	87.1%
AGF Growth Equity	CdnEq	2.80%	94.8	5.86%	17.1%	29.3%	14.3%	-13.6%	65.3%	641.9	100.0%
Global Strategy Diversified Japan Plus	FgnEq	2.54%	94.8	5.28%	-26.9%	-16.4%	-6.7%	—	—	7.2	100.0%
Industrial Alliance Bonds	FixInc	1.50%	94.8	1.15%	7.0%	9.5%	18.2%	-5.7%	14.6%	37.4	—
London Life Diversified	Balan	2.35%	94.8	2.86%	13.4%	18.7%	13.7%	-3.6%	19.1%	2,422.4	—
Millennium Diversified	Balan	2.50%	94.8	3.23%	20.7%	16.5%	19.1%	-6.4%	—	9.3	79.7%
Elliott & Page Money	FixInc	0.24%	94.7	0.12%	2.6%	4.2%	6.7%	4.7%	5.2%	457.6	50.0%
Fidelity Canadian Income	FixInc	1.25%	94.7	0.87%*	4.5%	9.4%	—	—	—	70.4	52.9%
Hongkong Bank Canadian Bond	FixInc	1.11%	94.7	1.39%*	8.6%	10.6%	—	—	—	73.3	68.0%
Investors Retirement Mutual	CdnEq	2.42%	94.7	5.14%	10.0%	23.6%	11.9%	1.7%	26.5%	2,328.6	100.0%
MAXXUM Income	FixInc	1.73%	94.7	1.91%	14.0%	10.2%	21.9%	-6.6%	18.7%	124.7	78.2%
Trimark Interest	FixInc	0.75%	94.7	0.09%	2.7%	4.0%	6.5%	4.5%	4.5%	933.5	50.0%
CentrePost Balanced	Balan	1.00%	94.6	2.71%	4.5%	21.2%	15.2%	-2.2%	13.4%	2.3	33.2%
Desjardins Divers Secure	Balan	1.67%	94.6	0.78%*	4.3%	6.9%	—	—	—	273.3	64.9%
London Life Canadian Equity	CdnEq	2.35%	94.6	5.37%	17.2%	30.4%	11.1%	-3.7%	29.2%	1,210.8	—
Spectrum United Asset Allocation	Balan	2.22%	94.6	2.83%	14.1%	13.9%	13.1%	-3.6%	19.8%	477.2	79.5%
AIM Global RSP Income	FixInc	2.39%	94.5	1.24%	8.2%	12.9%	9.7%	3.1%	11.7%	29.5	60.5%
Global Strategy Europe Plus	FgnEq	2.80%	94.5	3.29%	20.8%	24.2%	11.6%	—	—	117.3	91.3%
Great-West Life Diversified Rs (G) B	Balan	2.40%	94.5	2.94%	14.2%	14.5%	13.1%	—	—	101.8	—
Green Line European Growth	FgnEq	2.58%	94.5	3.44%	21.4%	27.6%	18.7%	—	—	205.8	100.0%
Industrial Income Class A	Balan	1.82%	94.5	2.08%	8.0%	12.8%	18.8%	-5.5%	18.0%	2,311.5	27.2%

* 2-year standard deviation.

Fund Name	Fund Type	MER	MVA	3-Year Std Dev (Monthly)	Percent Return 1997	Percent Return 1996	Percent Return 1995	Percent Return 1994	Percent Return 1993	Assets $ Mill	Tax Efficiency (3 Years)
STAR Investment Long-Term Growth	Alloc	—	94.5	2.60%*	11.6%	13.2%	—	—	—	—	—
Atlas World Bond	FixInc	2.07%	94.4	0.81%	4.6%	6.9%	18.1%	-4.3%	—	22.8	50.6%
CCPE Fixed Income	FixInc	1.35%	94.4	1.18%	7.0%	9.6%	18.4%	-4.0%	16.1%	17.3	—
Leith Wheeler Money Market	FixInc	0.60%	94.4	0.09%	2.6%	4.1%	6.2%	—	—	10.3	50.0%
C.I. Covington	Labour	4.68%	94.3	1.39%	7.5%	10.7%	1.2%	—	—	138.4	100.0%
Desjardins Bond	FixInc	1.58%	94.3	1.21%	7.0%	9.5%	19.3%	-6.4%	17.0%	151.3	63.6%
Fidelity Canadian Bond	FixInc	1.34%	94.3	1.33%	8.3%	10.5%	16.6%	-9.4%	20.9%	188.8	65.8%
First Canadian Asset Allocation	Balan	1.95%	94.3	2.66%	10.1%	16.1%	15.8%	-6.1%	18.7%	369.3	75.7%
Global Mgr–UK Index	FgnEq	1.82%	94.3	2.94%	31.0%	25.3%	15.6%	—	—	5.5	91.2%
PH&N U.S. Equity	USEq	1.10%	94.3	3.87%	29.4%	25.6%	25.9%	2.4%	15.4%	610.3	74.3%
Royal & SunAlliance Income	FixInc	1.88%	94.3	1.41%	8.5%	10.5%	18.9%	-7.1%	14.7%	44.5	—
AGF International Group–European Growth	FgnEq	3.03%	94.2	3.81%	27.3%	17.7%	10.1%	—	—	262.3	100.0%
CentrePost Short-Term	FixInc	0.75%	94.2	0.12%	2.6%	4.0%	6.4%	4.4%	5.3%	63.5	50.0%
Clean Environment Income	FixInc	1.98%	94.2	1.18%	8.0%	10.3%	5.6%	5.7%	—	20.5	80.7%
First Canadian Bond	FixInc	1.51%	94.2	1.24%	6.8%	10.0%	20.2%	-6.1%	15.8%	1,536.7	71.1%
GBC International Growth	FgnEq	1.91%	94.2	3.20%	5.5%	7.7%	-3.0%	-1.2%	30.9%	20.1	100.0%
Green Line Short-Term Income	FixInc	1.10%	94.2	0.43%	2.9%	7.7%	11.9%	-0.7%	6.8%	167.7	43.2%
Hongkong Bank European Growth	FgnEq	2.11%	94.2	3.49%	23.7%	22.4%	15.3%	—	—	101.8	97.0%
IRIS Canadian Money Market	FixInc	1.34%	94.2	0.09%	2.6%	4.1%	6.1%	4.4%	4.6%	93.8	50.0%
Industrial Horizon	CdnEq	2.33%	94.2	4.24%	14.7%	20.5%	7.0%	2.8%	38.1%	812.3	73.9%
AIM GT Global Growth & Income	Balan	2.78%	94.1	1.93%	15.6%	11.9%	12.6%	—	—	54.3	96.9%
Canadian Anaesthetists Mutual Accumulating	CdnEq	1.70%	94.1	5.11%	12.1%	26.1%	13.1%	-4.0%	25.1%	30.6	67.1%
Dynamic Fund of Canada	CdnEq	2.24%	94.1	4.68%	10.9%	21.3%	5.1%	-11.6%	53.4%	184.9	1.4%
Ethical Income	FixInc	1.63%	94.1	1.50%	9.2%	10.1%	21.7%	-6.2%	16.9%	196.9	71.3%
STAR Registered Long-Term Growth	Alloc	—	94.1	2.40%*	9.3%	16.1%	—	—	—	—	—

* 2-year standard deviation.

Fund Name	Fund Type	MER	MVA	3-Year Std Dev (Monthly)	Percent Return 1997	Percent Return 1996	Percent Return 1995	Percent Return 1994	Percent Return 1993	Assets $ Mill	Tax Efficiency (3 Years)
Universal Future	CdnEq	2.33%	94.1	4.62%	14.4%	16.3%	18.2%	3.1%	53.4%	573.6	95.8%
AGF Canadian Bond	FixInc	1.93%	94.0	1.50%	8.7%	11.1%	20.6%	-8.5%	19.6%	759.1	64.0%
BPI Canadian Small Companies	CdnEq	2.98%	94.0	6.64%	-18.6%	50.5%	24.2%	-6.3%	38.1%	246.3	100.0%
CIBC Canadian Bond	FixInc	1.55%	94.0	1.36%	7.9%	10.2%	20.0%	-9.2%	16.0%	821.9	69.7%
Cambridge Resource	CdnEq	3.42%	94.0	12.99%	-42.3%	36.3%	13.0%	-13.4%	85.3%	4.3	100.0%
Global Strategy Diversified Asia	FgnEq	2.70%	94.0	7.01%	-39.6%	5.7%	-2.8%	—	—	6.0	100.0%
Great-West Life Mortgage (G) A	FixInc	2.40%	94.0	0.95%	6.9%	8.9%	14.1%	-2.8%	11.9%	100.4	—
Guardian Canadian Income Classic	FixInc	1.13%	94.0	0.58%	3.6%	7.5%	12.2%	—	—	10.0	50.3%
MetLife Mvp Equity	CdnEq	2.19%	94.0	4.94%	18.8%	20.0%	9.3%	-2.9%	21.4%	61.2	—
Montrusco Select Canadian Equity	CdnEq	0.08%	94.0	5.17%	9.9%	26.3%	18.4%	1.8%	26.7%	109.2	7.9%
BPI Canadian Resource Fund Inc.	CdnEq	2.99%	93.9	8.14%	-30.3%	26.3%	3.7%	-13.5%	51.5%	20.8	100.0%
GBC Canadian Bond	FixInc	1.09%	93.9	1.41%	8.3%	11.3%	20.2%	-5.6%	17.3%	50.8	64.4%
Acadia Bond	FixInc	2.16%	93.8	1.01%	6.0%	10.2%	10.5%	—	—	3.2	76.0%
Great-West Life Diversified Rs (G) A	Balan	2.64%	93.8	2.94%	13.9%	14.2%	13.0%	-4.3%	18.1%	324.0	—
Montrusco Select Balanced	Balan	0.14%	93.8	2.80%	9.6%	18.1%	17.7%	-0.3%	23.2%	62.2	40.7%
BPI Global Equity Value	FgnEq	2.47%	93.7	3.72%	18.0%	16.6%	14.3%	4.5%	27.4%	458.4	89.0%
Ficadre Actions	CdnEq	2.14%	93.7	5.37%	7.6%	28.6%	17.1%	-6.3%	27.6%	12.1	64.3%
General Trust of Canada Money Market	FixInc	1.14%	93.7	0.12%	2.5%	4.0%	6.4%	4.1%	4.9%	15.7	50.2%
Investors Government Bond	FixInc	1.89%	93.7	1.41%	8.1%	10.5%	19.4%	-5.2%	15.0%	1,637.3	59.1%
Northwest Money Market	FixInc	1.00%	93.7	0.09%	2.5%	4.0%	6.2%	4.5%	4.6%	7.0	50.0%
Fonds de Croissance Select	USEq	1.00%	93.6	3.98%	29.9%	24.6%	16.0%	10.8%	—	18.7	84.5%
Green Line International Equity	FgnEq	2.32%	93.6	3.49%	4.4%	8.4%	0.6%	7.7%	31.6%	116.4	98.1%
InvesNat Money Market	FixInc	1.04%	93.6	0.09%	2.5%	4.1%	6.1%	4.2%	4.5%	413.5	50.0%
Optimum Epargne	FixInc	0.71%	93.6	0.09%	2.7%	3.6%	6.8%	4.1%	5.1%	1.4	48.2%
Talvest Bond	FixInc	2.01%	93.6	1.36%	7.6%	10.1%	19.3%	-6.1%	17.2%	99.1	67.9%

Fund Name	Fund Type	MER	MVA	3-Year Std Dev (Monthly)	Percent Return 1997	Percent Return 1996	Percent Return 1995	Percent Return 1994	Percent Return 1993	Assets $ Mill	Tax Efficiency (3 Years)
Dynamic Government Income	FixInc	0.85%	93.5	0.89%	3.5%	10.9%	15.3%	—	—	12.1	58.9%
InvesNat Short-Term Government Bond	FixInc	1.33%	93.5	0.78%	3.4%	9.2%	13.7%	-2.3%	10.4%	149.2	50.1%
London Life Bond	FixInc	1.75%	93.5	1.30%	7.4%	9.4%	19.6%	-6.9%	15.5%	1,382.9	—
Optima Strategy—Canadian Fixed Income	FixInc	0.36%	93.5	1.91%	12.2%	11.5%	22.5%	-5.8%	—	483.0	100.0%
FMOQ Omnibus	Balan	0.59%	93.4	3.20%	16.1%	16.4%	17.3%	—	19.1%	207.9	100.0%
Ficadre Monetaire	FixInc	1.00%	93.4	0.09%	2.7%	4.2%	6.0%	4.1%	4.9%	4.0	50.0%
National Trust Money Market	FixInc	1.15%	93.4	0.09%	2.5%	4.1%	5.9%	3.9%	4.5%	116.6	50.0%
Scotia Excelsior Mortgage	FixInc	1.56%	93.4	0.64%	3.0%	9.5%	13.0%	-0.3%	11.3%	407.1	49.6%
Zweig Strategic Growth	USEq	2.49%	93.4	3.35%	26.8%	14.6%	21.2%	3.7%	20.1%	203.1	93.4%
CIBC Core Canadian Equity	CdnEq	2.20%	93.3	5.46%	16.5%	20.5%	7.7%	-7.3%	25.8%	888.2	86.4%
Fidelity Global Asset Allocation	Balan	2.67%	93.3	2.83%	22.1%	16.0%	10.0%	-4.1%	—	443.4	85.0%
Global Mgr—Hong Kong Geard	FgnEq	1.82%	93.3	14.72%	-40.1%	50.4%	21.6%	—	—	0.2	100.0%
InvesNat Mortgage	FixInc	1.56%	93.3	0.61%	3.1%	8.6%	11.3%	1.7%	10.7%	220.8	50.2%
Lasalle Balanced	Balan	2.32%	93.3	2.89%	13.9%	15.2%	13.9%	-4.2%	19.9%	3.7	54.0%
Royal Bond	FixInc	1.39%	93.3	1.67%	10.5%	10.6%	20.2%	-6.5%	16.7%	2,591.0	65.6%
Transamerica Growsafe Canadian Equity	CdnEq	2.45%	93.3	4.53%	6.5%	24.7%	11.7%	—	—	74.5	—
Altamira Resource	CdnEq	2.36%	93.2	6.06%	-27.0%	22.5%	5.8%	-14.8%	65.2%	98.1	100.0%
Green Line U.S. Index	USEq	0.66%	93.2	3.87%	38.0%	22.2%	31.7%	6.5%	12.9%	199.6	97.6%
Greystone Managed Wealth	Balan	2.50%	93.2	2.86%	17.0%	14.3%	11.5%	—	—	3.0	59.4%
IRIS Global Equity	FgnEq	2.37%	93.2	2.89%	14.2%	13.6%	17.9%	3.9%	16.3%	39.9	89.2%
Investors Canadian Equity	CdnEq	2.46%	93.2	5.23%	9.0%	24.9%	10.6%	0.2%	31.2%	2,811.3	65.3%
Investors Retirement Plus Portfolio	Balan	2.41%	93.2	2.42%	8.4%	14.4%	11.9%	0.2%	19.1%	1,699.7	66.9%
London Life Money Market	FixInc	1.20%	93.2	0.12%	2.2%	4.1%	6.9%	4.2%	4.3%	89.6	—
National Trust Canadian Equity	CdnEq	1.56%	93.2	5.14%	17.5%	24.6%	7.1%	-6.3%	28.2%	174.1	86.0%
BNP (Canada) Canadian Money Markets	FixInc	1.31%	93.1	0.09%	2.4%	4.2%	5.9%	4.2%	4.3%	5.4	50.2%

Fund Name	Fund Type	MER	MVA	3-Year Std Dev (Monthly)	Percent Return 1997	Percent Return 1996	Percent Return 1995	Percent Return 1994	Percent Return 1993	Assets $ Mill	Tax Efficiency (3 Years)
CT Bond	FixInc	1.33%	93.1	1.36%	7.8%	9.3%	19.8%	-6.8%	15.6%	729.0	66.2%
CentrePost Bond	FixInc	1.00%	93.1	1.18%	6.2%	10.0%	19.1%	-6.0%	15.1%	37.3	56.8%
Desjardins Equity	CdnEq	1.89%	93.1	5.34%	15.1%	21.2%	11.8%	-1.8%	25.5%	145.0	86.8%
Investors Mutual	Balan	2.37%	93.1	3.41%	12.6%	17.3%	12.5%	-0.8%	27.8%	1,017.3	61.5%
National Trust Mortgage	FixInc	1.61%	93.1	0.61%	2.9%	9.7%	12.1%	-0.6%	8.8%	66.2	47.7%
Talvest Income	FixInc	1.69%	93.1	0.84%	3.1%	9.9%	14.5%	-2.9%	13.8%	95.0	52.0%
Westbury Canadian Life Equity Growth	CdnEq	2.40%	93.1	5.20%	17.3%	26.6%	8.9%	-4.7%	31.9%	55.0	—
CT Stock	CdnEq	1.82%	93.0	5.14%	18.4%	22.5%	9.1%	-6.6%	32.3%	787.9	73.5%
Industrial Alliance Ecoflex B	FixInc	1.86%	93.0	1.15%	6.7%	8.9%	17.6%	-6.2%	—	69.5	—
Royal Canadian T-Bill	FixInc	0.92%	93.0	0.09%	2.4%	4.0%	6.1%	4.3%	4.3%	2,897.7	50.0%
Empire Asset Allocation	Balan	2.46%	92.9	2.83%	8.2%	18.4%	11.6%	—	—	157.5	—
Goldfund Limited	Spclty	2.18%	92.9	7.74%	-36.8%	14.0%	-17.5%	-2.8%	115.9%	2.3	100.0%
Jones Heward Bond	FixInc	1.75%	92.9	1.18%	6.7%	10.0%	18.5%	-7.6%	15.6%	4.5	63.9%
Spectrum United Savings	FixInc	1.00%	92.9	0.12%	2.2%	3.9%	6.3%	4.3%	4.4%	9.8	50.0%
Tradex Bond	FixInc	1.00%	92.9	1.47%	7.4%	10.5%	17.6%	-8.0%	13.2%	12.3	64.6%
CCPE Growth Fund R	CdnEq	1.35%	92.8	4.76%	9.2%	26.4%	12.6%	2.1%	17.9%	30.2	—
Ficadre Equilibre	Balan	2.01%	92.8	2.94%	8.1%	19.1%	17.3%	-4.0%	17.6%	63.2	74.3%
Global Strategy Money Market	FixInc	0.80%	92.8	0.09%	2.5%	3.7%	6.2%	4.4%	4.7%	138.3	50.0%
Jones Heward Money Market	FixInc	0.50%	92.8	0.12%	2.2%	4.2%	6.3%	—	—	3.1	50.0%
Transamerica Growsafe Canadian Bond	FixInc	2.25%	92.8	0.95%	7.4%	5.9%	12.3%	—	—	28.1	—
Empire International Growth	FgnEq	2.45%	92.7	3.61%	11.8%	21.2%	11.1%	-1.5%	31.8%	115.9	—
IRIS Balanced	Balan	2.25%	92.7	3.29%	8.3%	20.7%	18.2%	-3.2%	18.7%	121.6	51.0%
Industrial Alliance Mortgages	FixInc	1.50%	92.7	0.49%	4.1%	6.8%	11.4%	0.1%	9.9%	5.9	—
MD Balanced	Balan	1.28%	92.7	3.23%	12.8%	18.6%	16.5%	-2.4%	21.9%	795.3	87.8%
Royal Balanced	Balan	2.20%	92.7	2.80%	11.0%	15.7%	14.3%	-2.4%	22.5%	6,828.8	86.9%

Fund Name	Fund Type	MER	MVA	3-Year Std Dev (Monthly)	Percent Return 1997	Percent Return 1996	Percent Return 1995	Percent Return 1994	Percent Return 1993	Assets $ Mill	Tax Efficiency (3 Years)
Spectrum United Canadian Money Market	FixInc	0.92%	92.7	0.09%	2.4%	3.8%	6.1%	4.2%	4.4%	214.7	50.0%
CIBC Canadian Short-Term Bond Index	FixInc	0.90%	92.6	0.89%	3.3%	9.0%	17.0%	-3.4%	—	143.2	57.0%
Canada Life Fixed Income	FixInc	2.00%	92.6	1.33%	7.4%	9.4%	18.5%	-7.0%	15.7%	393.2	—
Guardian Canadian Money Market Classic	FixInc	0.86%	92.6	0.09%	2.5%	3.7%	6.3%	4.4%	4.5%	55.3	50.0%
IRIS U.S. Equity	USEq	2.23%	92.6	3.78%	36.1%	19.0%	24.9%	5.6%	6.3%	51.1	93.0%
Maritime Life Bond Series A	FixInc	1.80%	92.6	1.21%	6.6%	9.3%	17.4%	-6.1%	16.4%	56.3	—
C.I. International Balanced RSP	Balan	2.40%	92.5	2.40%	13.2%	10.5%	19.6%	—	—	252.5	75.1%
CIBC Money Market	FixInc	0.99%	92.5	0.09%	2.4%	3.9%	6.0%	3.9%	3.6%	1,871.3	50.0%
Global Mgr—U.S. Index	USEq	1.82%	92.5	3.09%	31.8%	23.0%	28.1%	—	—	15.4	92.4%
MetLife Mvp Balanced	Balan	2.20%	92.5	2.80%	12.6%	14.3%	12.9%	-5.0%	16.0%	95.1	—
VenGrowth Fund	Labor	3.90%	92.5	1.39%	11.7%	7.1%	0.8%	—	—	197.6	100.0%
AIM Cash Performance	FixInc	1.03%	92.4	0.06%	2.5%	3.9%	5.6%	3.7%	4.0%	19.5	50.0%
Atlas Canadian Money Market	FixInc	1.09%	92.4	0.09%	2.4%	3.8%	6.2%	4.4%	4.3%	328.0	50.0%
C.I. Global Bond RSP	FixInc	2.06%	92.4	1.10%	5.1%	8.2%	18.2%	-2.9%	91.6	54.3%	—
Ethical Money Market	FixInc	1.25%	92.4	0.09%	2.4%	4.0%	6.0%	4.1%	4.4%	116.9	50.0%
Guardian Canadian Balanced Classic	Balan	1.66%	92.4	1.99%	3.7%	13.5%	12.4%	1.7%	15.5%	81.0	56.2%
Investors Global	FgnEq	2.44%	92.4	3.20%	16.6%	13.5%	13.6%	6.2%	22.3%	1,588.4	93.7%
Templeton Global Smaller Companies	FgnEq	2.61%	92.4	3.18%	7.8%	17.6%	17.9%	0.4%	29.7%	303.4	72.5%
Trimark Government Income	FixInc	1.24%	92.4	0.66%	3.0%	8.6%	14.2%	—	—	253.5	47.6%
Trimark RSP Equity	CdnEq	2.00%	92.4	4.07%	0.6%	23.3%	9.9%	3.3%	31.5%	2,038.8	-69.0%
Atlas American Large Cap Growth	USEq	2.54%	92.3	3.58%	33.4%	19.6%	29.6%	2.8%	4.1%	47.4	100.0%
First Canadian Money Market	FixInc	1.10%	92.3	0.09%	2.3%	4.0%	6.0%	4.2%	4.4%	1,072.0	50.0%
Lotus Group—Canadian Equity	CdnEq	2.00%	92.3	6.52%	18.5%	45.2%	8.3%	-16.1%	—	6.0	62.8%
Scotia Excelsior Money Market	FixInc	1.00%	92.3	0.09%	2.3%	3.9%	6.2%	4.2%	4.1%	531.6	50.0%
BNP (Canada) Bond	FixInc	1.67%	92.2	1.56%	8.1%	10.0%	19.2%	-5.8%	16.0%	5.5	61.8%

Fund Name	Fund Type	MER	MVA	3-Year Std Dev (Monthly)	Percent Return 1997	Percent Return 1996	Percent Return 1995	Percent Return 1994	Percent Return 1993	Assets $ Mill	Tax Efficiency (3 Years)
CCPE Money Market	FixInc	0.75%	92.2	0.43%*	2.2%	4.4%	—	—	—	13.9	—
Imperial Growth Canadian Equity	CdnEq	1.96%	92.2	5.31%	16.1%	19.4%	11.2%	-0.9%	24.0%	51.8	—
Empire Bond	FixInc	2.05%	92.1	1.33%	7.8%	8.8%	17.8%	-5.7%	14.7%	71.1	—
Hansberger Asian	FgnEq	2.79%	92.1	7.71%	-46.9%	8.7%	-8.5%	-18.5%	—	19.7	100.0%
Royal Canadian Money Market	FixInc	0.95%	92.1	0.09%	2.5%	3.7%	5.9%	3.9%	4.1%	1,931.9	50.0%
Scotia Excelsior Total Return	Balan	2.27%	92.1	2.97%	12.0%	17.5%	13.2%	-4.8%	31.1%	821.8	74.1%
Atlas Canadian Bond	FixInc	1.97%	92.0	1.39%	7.4%	10.2%	18.9%	-5.1%	14.1%	55.0	66.8%
Batirente Section Marche Monetair	FixInc	0.75%	92.0	0.09%	2.4%	3.6%	6.7%	3.8%	4.8%	1.6	—
CIBC Canadian T-Bill	FixInc	0.99%	92.0	0.09%	2.4%	3.8%	5.9%	3.9%	3.7%	482.7	50.0%
CT Mortgage	FixInc	1.58%	92.0	0.52%	3.2%	7.1%	11.8%	1.2%	10.9%	483.2	45.6%
Desjardins Balanced	Balan	1.89%	92.0	3.18%	11.8%	14.3%	14.5%	-2.3%	20.5%	783.8	81.8%
MD Equity	CdnEq	1.27%	92.0	4.91%	16.7%	21.5%	7.0%	-1.6%	43.6%	1,518.2	79.1%
Manulife Vistafund 1 Short-Term Securities	FixInc	1.63%	92.0	0.17%	1.8%	4.2%	7.3%	3.9%	5.0%	3.8	—
BPI American Equity Value	USEq	2.44%	91.9	4.07%	29.7%	17.4%	26.4%	3.5%	12.5%	97.6	78.6%
Desjardins Mortgage	FixInc	1.61%	91.9	0.49%	3.4%	6.9%	11.4%	0.5%	10.5%	161.2	45.9%
Mutual Money Market	FixInc	1.02%	91.9	0.09%	2.3%	3.8%	6.4%	4.3%	4.5%	281.4	50.0%
Ficadre Obligations	FixInc	1.45%	91.8	1.47%	7.7%	9.3%	18.6%	-5.7%	13.4%	19.4	58.9%
InvesNat Canadian Equity	CdnEq	2.11%	91.8	5.17%	1.8%	25.7%	15.7%	-1.0%	24.5%	198.6	8.9%
MAXXUM Canadian Equity Growth	CdnEq	2.13%	91.8	4.91%	—	23.9%	26.1%	-7.6%	45.2%	107.5	44.6%
Scotia Excelsior Balanced	Balan	1.90%	91.8	2.68%	7.3%	15.8%	14.9%	-2.2%	21.8%	644.3	71.9%
Templeton Treasury Bill	FixInc	0.75%	91.8	0.09%	2.2%	3.9%	6.2%	4.2%	4.6%	383.5	50.0%
Atlas European Value	FgnEq	2.62%	91.7	3.38%	22.1%	25.6%	10.9%	6.8%	—	67.3	94.6%
CentrePost Canadian Equity	CdnEq	1.00%	91.7	5.20%	1.2%	31.5%	10.5%	-8.2%	38.8%	16.1	-77.9%
Dynamic Money Market	FixInc	0.80%	91.7	0.09%	2.2%	3.8%	6.6%	4.4%	4.2%	191.0	50.0%
First Canadian T-Bill	FixInc	1.14%	91.7	0.09%	2.2%	3.9%	6.0%	4.2%	—	749.3	50.0%

* 2-year standard deviation.

Fund Name	Fund Type	MER	MVA	3-Year Std Dev (Monthly)	Percent Return 1997	Percent Return 1996	Percent Return 1995	Percent Return 1994	Percent Return 1993	Assets $ Mill	Tax Efficiency (3 Years)
MB American Equity	USEq	—	91.7	4.62%	39.0%	25.4%	29.2%	6.7%	5.0%	153.4	100.0%
Quebec Professionals Growth & Income	Balan	0.95%	91.7	2.48%	8.3%	13.5%	13.7%	—	—	57.0	49.7%
Desjardins Divers Audacious	Balan	1.87%	91.6	2.31%*	8.4%	12.5%	—	—	—	265.1	78.0%
Equitable Life Canada Canadian Bond	FixInc	2.00%	91.6	1.41%	7.7%	10.1%	17.5%	-5.8%	13.8%	38.2	—
GBC Money Market	FixInc	0.75%	91.6	0.09%	2.3%	3.8%	6.3%	4.7%	4.8%	15.8	50.0%
Lion Knowledge Industries	CdnEq	2.90%	91.6	6.58%	-23.6%	35.1%	45.2%	-11.9%	—	—	100.0%
Scotia Excelsior T-Bill	FixInc	1.00%	91.6	0.09%	2.2%	3.8%	6.2%	4.3%	4.2%	328.6	50.0%
AIC Money Market	FixInc	1.00%	91.5	0.09%	2.3%	3.7%	6.0%	—	—	315.0	50.0%
Elliott & Page American Growth	USEq	1.41%	91.5	3.98%	36.1%	19.3%	22.1%	3.5%	4.8%	139.9	80.8%
Global Mgr–UK Geared	FgnEq	1.82%	91.5	6.06%	55.5%	33.1%	31.4%	—	—	1.0	94.3%
Hansberger Asian Sector	FgnEq	2.84%	91.5	7.62%	-46.9%	8.1%	-8.8%	—	—	3.8	100.0%
Investors Money Market	FixInc	1.07%	91.5	0.09%	2.2%	3.8%	6.1%	4.5%	4.3%	658.2	50.0%
National Fixed Income	FixInc	2.00%	91.5	1.47%	8.2%	10.1%	18.7%	-6.1%	17.0%	67.0	—
Talvest/Hyperion European	FgnEq	3.00%	91.5	3.20%	29.3%	19.4%	10.7%	3.0%	25.3%	84.7	84.2%
CT Money Market	FixInc	1.08%	91.4	0.09%	2.3%	3.7%	5.9%	4.1%	3.9%	907.2	50.0%
CentrePost Foreign Equity	FgnEq	1.75%	91.2	4.07%	23.1%	15.5%	13.5%	12.3%	17.8%	2.5	70.6%
Desjardins Distinct–Mortgage	FixInc	1.66%	91.2	0.64%	3.0%	8.4%	12.0%	2.7%	10.1%	13.7	—
IRIS Canadian Bond	FixInc	1.82%	91.2	1.47%	8.3%	9.3%	18.7%	-5.6%	16.1%	91.2	60.3%
Industrial Alliance Diversified	Balan	1.57%	91.2	3.15%	7.8%	16.3%	15.5%	-0.7%	23.9%	238.4	—
Royal Canadian Small-Cap	CdnEq	2.23%	91.2	5.77%	-1.9%	17.0%	14.4%	-11.9%	31.8%	140.9	100.0%
AGF Canadian Asset Allocation Service	Alloc	—	91.1	1.56%	3.5%	13.0%	12.2%	-5.2%	26.1%	421.0	100.0%
Canada Life Money Market	FixInc	1.25%	91.1	0.12%	2.1%	4.0%	6.1%	3.9%	4.4%	180.9	—
Investors Mortgage	FixInc	1.89%	91.1	0.55%	2.5%	8.9%	11.5%	-1.7%	10.6%	2,204.5	46.7%
Strategic Value Canadian Equity	CdnEq	2.70%	91.1	4.97%	14.0%	18.7%	10.4%	-2.8%	22.3%	214.2	75.5%
Great-West Life Canadian Equity (G) B	CdnEq	2.40%	91.0	5.69%	13.5%	23.3%	10.9%	—	—	105.2	—

* 2-year standard deviation.

Fund Name	Fund Type	MER	MVA	3-Year Std Dev (Monthly)	Percent Return 1997	Percent Return 1996	Percent Return 1995	Percent Return 1994	Percent Return 1993	Assets $ Mill	Tax Efficiency (3 Years)
MAXXUM Canadian Balanced	Balan	2.13%	91.0	3.29%	5.9%	21.9%	18.3%	-8.6%	29.5%	96.5	83.5%
Spectrum United American Equity	USEq	2.30%	91.0	4.30%	24.2%	23.2%	33.1%	-2.8%	4.0%	330.2	80.6%
General Trust of Canada Canadian Equity	CdnEq	2.14%	90.9	5.34%	1.1%	26.4%	16.8%	-3.3%	21.7%	24.7	-80.1%
Industrial Alliance Stocks	CdnEq	1.57%	90.9	5.02%	5.5%	22.7%	14.4%	2.2%	34.0%	30.4	—
Scotia Excelsior Income	FixInc	1.38%	90.9	1.15%	5.7%	7.6%	21.5%	-5.0%	14.9%	366.0	60.4%
Transamerica Growsafe Canadian Money Market	FixInc	0.96%	90.9	0.09%	2.5%	4.0%	4.1%	—	—	33.2	—
APEX Fixed Income	FixInc	2.30%	90.8	1.36%	6.7%	9.7%	16.9%	-5.2%	20.8%	51.3	—
CIBC Balanced	Balan	2.24%	90.8	3.41%	13.2%	16.0%	13.2%	-5.6%	20.4%	1,113.1	82.7%
Industrial Bond	FixInc	1.83%	90.8	1.79%	8.9%	12.1%	21.7%	-8.7%	17.1%	601.4	63.4%
MAXXUM American Equity	USEq	2.48%	90.8	4.59%*	19.1%	23.9%	—	—	—	30.7	72.5%
Mutual Bond	FixInc	1.85%	90.8	1.24%	6.7%	8.1%	17.5%	-6.2%	15.2%	18.1	67.2%
Mutual Premier Diversified	Balan	2.28%	90.8	3.26%	10.0%	20.1%	16.3%	—	—	602.8	91.7%
Trimark Income Growth	Balan	1.56%	90.8	2.86%	3.0%	17.8%	17.0%	0.9%	32.0%	768.4	50.4%
Altamira European Equity	FgnEq	2.35%	90.7	3.52%	21.8%	23.7%	12.1%	8.5%	—	272.7	92.4%
Dynamic Americas	USEq	2.37%	90.7	3.95%	40.5%	26.9%	19.0%	-4.0%	17.8%	130.2	82.5%
Fidelity North American Income	FixInc	1.75%	90.7	0.46%	3.8%	6.0%	6.0%	-12.2%	—	65.5	53.5%
Green Line Mortgage	FixInc	1.59%	90.7	0.55%	2.1%	8.5%	11.7%	-0.7%	11.5%	620.5	44.4%
Mutual Premier Bond	FixInc	1.88%	90.7	1.39%	7.5%	9.1%	18.0%	-6.0%	14.6%	255.5	69.6%
Mutual Premier Mortgage	FixInc	1.58%	90.7	0.58%	2.8%	8.2%	11.7%	0.5%	—	149.6	49.8%
Spectrum United Mid-Term Bond	FixInc	1.59%	90.7	1.39%	6.8%	9.9%	18.9%	-7.6%	16.6%	411.0	59.6%
Standard Life Bond	FixInc	1.50%	90.7	1.41%	7.2%	10.0%	20.3%	-5.8%	15.5%	8.6	63.8%
Fidelity Growth America	USEq	2.33%	90.6	3.84%	33.6%	18.9%	29.3%	6.2%	17.2%	1,551.5	75.7%
General Trust of Canada Mortgage	FixInc	1.57%	90.6	0.58%	4.1%	6.5%	7.9%	3.0%	10.4%	39.4	46.0%
Great-West Life Canadian Equity (G) A	CdnEq	2.64%	90.6	5.69%	13.2%	23.0%	10.8%	-6.3%	31.5%	169.4	—
Green Line Mortgage-Backed	FixInc	1.55%	90.6	0.55%	3.0%	8.1%	11.7%	-1.1%	9.6%	74.3	53.8%

* 2-year standard deviation.

Fund Name	Fund Type	MER	MVA	3-Year Std Dev (Monthly)	Percent Return 1997	Percent Return 1996	Percent Return 1995	Percent Return 1994	Percent Return 1993	Assets $ Mill	Tax Efficiency (3 Years)
Trimark Select Growth	FgnEq	2.32%	90.6	3.41%	12.6%	14.0%	14.2%	13.5%	27.3%	5,039.6	62.3%
Westbury Canadian Life Balanced	Balan	2.41%	90.6	3.75%	9.5%	19.0%	15.8%	-1.3%	16.4%	28.7	—
AIM GT Canada Growth	CdnEq	2.42%	90.5	5.77%*	12.4%	38.1%	—	—	—	674.7	94.6%
C.I. World Bond	FixInc	2.06%	90.5	1.07%	3.7%	8.4%	17.0%	-4.9%	17.5%	75.6	59.2%
Global Strategy World Equity	FgnEq	2.78%	90.5	3.35%	14.7%	13.2%	10.6%	—	—	127.6	76.3%
Great-West Life Canadian Bond (G) B	FixInc	1.74%	90.5	1.39%	7.9%	9.7%	17.7%	—	—	31.2	—
Hongkong Bank Mortgage	FixInc	1.46%	90.5	0.87%	2.6%	11.0%	13.1%	3.6%	12.4%	198.6	55.9%
Vision Europe	FgnEq	3.16%	90.5	3.64%	22.5%	22.8%	16.8%	3.1%	20.8%	41.2	87.7%
Co-Operators U.S. Equity	USEq	2.12%	90.4	6.61%	48.6%	27.8%	53.1%	—	—	10.1	—
Colonia Life Bond	FixInc	1.63%	90.4	1.33%	6.9%	6.6%	19.8%	-4.1%	12.4%	14.4	—
MAXXUM Global Equity	FgnEq	2.48%	90.4	3.64%*	14.2%	11.5%	—	—	—	20.8	85.3%
C.I. Short-term Sector	FixInc	0.05%	90.3	0.14%	3.7%	2.4%	3.2%	2.7%	3.6%	91.8	—
CIBC Mortgage	FixInc	1.69%	90.3	0.75%	2.6%	10.3%	12.0%	0.0%	10.7%	1,380.2	49.4%
Royal Mortgage	FixInc	1.56%	90.3	0.72%	3.0%	9.2%	11.4%	1.0%	12.3%	1,265.7	47.5%
Industrial Balanced	Balan	2.32%	90.2	3.18%	9.8%	16.5%	14.1%	-3.5%	25.4%	282.6	47.5%
Maritime Life American Growth & Inc A&C	USEq	2.55%	90.2	3.15%	33.5%	15.9%	22.6%	—	—	249.3	—
STAR Registered Maximum Long-Term Growth	Alloc	—	90.2	2.92%*	7.9%	14.8%	—	—	—	—	—
Talvest Canadian Equity Value	CdnEq	2.42%	90.2	4.94%	13.0%	17.1%	12.3%	0.9%	19.7%	93.2	24.9%
20/20 RSP Aggressive Equity	CdnEq	2.47%	90.1	8.17%	-2.1%	46.7%	41.9%	-14.1%	—	248.1	69.3%
Desjardins Money Market	FixInc	1.10%	90.1	0.09%	2.2%	3.5%	5.9%	3.9%	4.5%	80.3	50.0%
Elliott & Page Equity	CdnEq	1.94%	90.1	5.25%	-1.9%	24.5%	22.4%	-1.5%	31.1%	604.2	12.3%
Equitable Life Canada Money Market	FixInc	1.75%	90.1	0.12%	2.6%	3.0%	5.4%	—	—	6.3	—
Northwest Income	FixInc	1.75%	90.1	1.44%	8.1%	8.9%	17.2%	-5.8%	14.1%	6.3	57.5%
Strategic Value Money Market	FixInc	0.88%	90.1	0.09%	2.0%	3.7%	6.1%	4.0%	4.3%	31.2	50.0%
C.I. Global	FgnEq	2.46%	90.0	3.52%	21.1%	15.4%	4.0%	-2.1%	35.7%	987.1	82.6%

* 2-year standard deviation.

Fund Name	Fund Type	MER	MVA	3-Year Std Dev (Monthly)	Percent Return 1997	Percent Return 1996	Percent Return 1995	Percent Return 1994	Percent Return 1993	Assets $ Mill	Tax Efficiency (3 Years)
Manulife Cabot Money Market	FixInc	1.25%	90.0	0.09%	2.1%	3.5%	6.3%	—	—	4.0	50.0%
MetLife Mvp Bond	FixInc	2.21%	90.0	1.21%	6.5%	5.3%	16.8%	-7.0%	13.5%	35.8	—
Royal Trust Advantage Growth	Balan	1.90%	90.0	3.15%	9.7%	16.1%	13.6%	-2.2%	18.7%	157.3	89.9%
Strategic Value Government Bond	FixInc	2.20%	90.0	0.72%	3.7%	7.2%	13.0%	-1.8%	10.0%	55.8	50.8%
Industrial Alliance Ecoflex H	FixInc	1.86%	89.9	0.49%	3.7%	6.2%	10.8%	-0.4%	—	15.4	—
NN T-Bill	FixInc	1.26%	89.9	0.09%	2.1%	3.7%	5.4%	3.5%	4.0%	35.9	—
Transamerica Growsafe Canadian Balanced	Balan	2.46%	89.9	2.51%	6.8%	14.3%	11.0%	—	—	125.7	—
CT AmeriGrowth	USEq	1.35%	89.8	4.45%	27.8%	19.5%	36.6%	0.1%	—	677.8	41.9%
Global Strategy Diversified Bond	FixInc	2.20%	89.8	1.10%	5.0%	7.3%	11.6%	-7.9%	12.8%	266.3	64.3%
InvesNat Retirement Balanced	Balan	2.10%	89.8	2.97%	5.1%	16.5%	15.4%	-2.3%	14.8%	694.0	70.6%
Northwest Growth	CdnEq	2.00%	89.8	4.97%	4.3%	28.4%	17.1%	-1.0%	20.7%	40.4	52.8%
Spectrum United Short-Term Bond	FixInc	1.45%	89.8	0.55%	2.7%	8.2%	13.0%	-2.6%	9.8%	28.9	52.2%
Westbury Canadian Life Bond	FixInc	2.07%	89.8	1.44%	7.1%	8.4%	16.6%	-6.0%	13.7%	10.8	—
Altamira Income	FixInc	1.00%	89.7	1.41%	7.8%	8.6%	22.7%	-6.6%	20.2%	511.1	56.0%
CIBC Global Equity	FgnEq	2.50%	89.7	3.46%	22.6%	12.4%	7.4%	-1.8%	24.2%	300.8	87.2%
Desjardins Growth	CdnEq	1.87%	89.7	5.77%	18.5%	20.3%	10.5%	—	—	92.4	100.0%
Elliott & Page Global Equity	FgnEq	2.00%	89.7	3.70%	11.8%	14.5%	12.9%	—	—	34.7	99.3%
Fidelity Canadian Short-Term Asset	FixInc	1.25%	89.7	0.09%	2.1%	3.4%	5.9%	3.9%	3.9%	511.4	50.0%
Great-West Life Canadian Bond (G) A	FixInc	1.98%	89.7	1.39%	7.6%	9.4%	17.6%	-6.7%	14.3%	49.4	—
Hongkong Bank U.S. Equity	USEq	2.11%	89.7	3.95%	33.0%	23.4%	13.5%	—	—	50.3	99.8%
Investors Asset Allocation	Balan	2.73%	89.7	4.39%	8.8%	18.2%	16.7%	—	—	1,531.5	62.7%
London Life U.S. Equity	USEq	2.55%	89.7	4.19%	38.1%	26.8%	17.0%	-2.4%	9.4%	360.4	—
OTGIF Global	FgnEq	1.00%	89.7	3.20%	17.1%	13.1%	16.5%	-3.1%	16.1%	11.0	67.5%
Scotia Excelsior Defensive Income	FixInc	1.37%	89.7	0.64%	3.0%	6.9%	14.9%	-2.6%	13.1%	115.7	55.7%
All-Canadian Resources Corporation	CdnEq	2.00%	89.6	5.54%	-18.3%	-1.0%	4.7%	7.5%	82.7%	2.5	100.0%

Fund Name	Fund Type	MER	MVA	3-Year Std Dev (Monthly)	Percent Return 1997	Percent Return 1996	Percent Return 1995	Percent Return 1994	Percent Return 1993	Assets $ Mill	Tax Efficiency (3 Years)
Global Mgr—U.S. Geared	USEq	1.82%	89.6	6.55%	56.0%	36.7%	56.7%	—	—	6.6	95.9%
Global Strategy Diversified Europe	FgnEq	2.52%	89.6	3.44%	23.9%	22.0%	11.5%	-4.6%	18.2%	165.0	69.0%
Industrial Alliance Ecoflex A	CdnEq	2.48%	89.6	5.02%	4.6%	22.1%	13.8%	1.6%	—	151.6	—
NAL-Canadian Equity	CdnEq	1.75%	89.6	5.05%	-2.0%	24.9%	22.4%	-2.2%	23.7%	51.0	—
AGF Canadian Growth	CdnEq	2.46%	89.4	5.20%	15.6%	16.1%	9.2%	-0.1%	29.3%	302.5	70.1%
Global Strategy Bond	FixInc	1.50%	89.4	0.72%	3.2%	8.6%	12.5%	—	—	17.3	40.8%
Industrial Alliance Ecoflex D	Balan	2.48%	89.4	3.15%	6.8%	15.7%	14.9%	-1.3%	—	673.7	—
NAL-Canadian Bond	FixInc	1.75%	89.4	1.50%	8.1%	8.7%	19.6%	-4.6%	14.9%	21.4	—
General Trust of Canada Balanced	Balan	2.10%	89.3	3.03%	4.9%	16.2%	15.5%	-3.4%	16.2%	77.2	65.3%
Ideal Bond	FixInc	2.00%	89.3	1.41%	6.3%	9.6%	19.1%	-6.4%	15.8%	42.5	—
Scotia CanAm Growth	USEq	1.34%	89.3	4.47%	27.9%	19.5%	35.8%	0.5%	—	276.2	45.8%
Strategic Value Canadian Balanced	Balan	2.70%	89.3	3.06%	11.3%	14.8%	13.8%	-2.7%	14.1%	154.8	59.7%
Jones Heward Fund Limited	CdnEq	2.50%	89.2	5.34%	14.0%	27.6%	4.7%	-10.2%	37.7%	53.7	59.9%
Montrusco Select Non-Taxable U.S. Equities	USEq	—	89.2	3.84%	39.7%	23.1%	22.3%	-0.4%	23.2%	157.7	84.5%
Talvest Global RRSP	FgnEq	2.52%	89.2	3.09%	17.9%	13.9%	7.4%	-2.7%	26.2%	42.9	60.0%
Transamerica Balanced Investment Growth	Balan	1.80%	89.2	2.74%	5.5%	14.3%	13.5%	1.6%	16.2%	60.0	—
APEX Money Market	FixInc	1.56%	89.1	0.12%	1.7%	3.8%	6.3%	—	—	7.7	—
Global Strategy U.S. Equity	USEq	2.60%	89.1	3.55%	32.2%	17.7%	26.9%	—	—	13.7	94.9%
Maritime Life S&P 500 Series A&C	USEq	2.20%	89.1	4.47%*	26.6%	18.8%	—	—	—	272.2	—
AGF Money Market Account	FixInc	1.42%	89.0	0.12%	1.7%	3.8%	6.2%	4.2%	4.4%	693.4	50.0%
Atlas Canadian T-Bill	FixInc	1.29%	89.0	0.09%	1.9%	3.7%	5.8%	4.1%	4.1%	285.2	50.0%
Spectrum United Long-Term Bond	FixInc	1.66%	89.0	2.14%	11.8%	11.3%	21.3%	-9.1%	17.7%	165.2	72.3%
Great-West Life Government Bond (G) B	FixInc	1.76%	88.9	0.92%	4.0%	8.7%	15.3%	—	—	7.2	—
Imperial Growth Diversified	Balan	2.00%	88.9	3.44%	12.5%	15.8%	14.9%	-1.7%	15.4%	10.7	—
AGF American Tactical Allocation	Balan	2.56%	88.8	2.60%	24.9%	10.0%	22.9%	0.6%	17.3%	423.5	87.3%

* 2-year standard deviation.

Fund Name	Fund Type	MER	MVA	3-Year Std Dev (Monthly)	Percent Return 1997	Percent Return 1996	Percent Return 1995	Percent Return 1994	Percent Return 1993	Assets $ Mill	Tax Efficiency (3 Years)
Industrial Alliance Ecoflex M	FixInc	1.36%	88.8	0.12%	2.0%	3.5%	5.7%	—	—	16.7	—
NAL-Canadian Money Market	FixInc	1.25%	88.8	0.43%	1.8%	3.6%	6.1%	3.6%	4.3%	13.9	—
Dynamic International	FgnEq	2.57%	88.7	4.01%	22.0%	20.7%	8.2%	-2.8%	34.1%	120.4	94.9%
Global Strategy World Bond	FixInc	2.14%	88.7	1.10%	4.7%	7.3%	11.7%	-8.8%	14.6%	192.0	74.6%
Strategic Value Europe	FgnEq	2.70%	88.7	3.38%	20.2%	19.2%	10.3%	—	—	54.3	96.3%
Caldwell Associate	Balan	2.37%	88.6	4.30%	12.8%	20.5%	13.3%	10.6%	27.0%	87.7	32.5%
First Canadian Mortgage	FixInc	1.39%	88.6	0.87%	2.5%	9.7%	12.9%	-0.5%	11.6%	1,246.5	48.0%
Scotia Excelsior Canadian Blue Chip	CdnEq	1.93%	88.6	5.02%	6.3%	23.3%	8.0%	-7.0%	22.6%	307.7	57.0%
Acadia Money Market	FixInc	1.56%	88.5	0.12%	1.8%	3.6%	6.1%	—	—	0.4	50.0%
First Ontario	Labor	4.75%	88.5	0.35%*	3.0%	2.9%	—	—	—	31.1	100.0%
Hemisphere Value	Balan	1.80%	88.5	2.54%	7.2%	14.5%	11.8%	—	—	1.6	71.4%
Royal U.S. Equity	USEq	2.11%	88.5	3.70%	31.7%	16.0%	28.0%	2.6%	9.1%	533.1	86.6%
Fidelity Capital Builder	CdnEq	2.44%	88.3	5.02%	3.0%	18.0%	15.1%	-7.5%	26.8%	269.6	-2399.0%
C.I. Global Sector	FgnEq	2.51%	88.2	3.52%	21.2%	13.6%	3.5%	-2.0%	35.4%	212.7	90.7%
Great-West Life Money Market (G) B	FixInc	1.26%	88.2	0.09%	1.9%	3.3%	5.6%	—	—	29.3	—
STAR Foreign Balanced Growth & Income	Alloc	—	88.1	2.05%*	8.6%	8.4%	—	—	—	—	—
Templeton Canadian Bond	FixInc	1.65%	88.1	0.89%	3.6%	8.3%	10.3%	-3.6%	13.0%	46.4	52.1%
C.I. Global High Yield	FixInc	2.16%	88.0	4.13%	8.5%	23.2%	11.8%	—	—	12.0	19.3%
Great-West Life Equity/Bond (G) B	Balan	2.40%	88.0	3.72%	11.9%	17.9%	14.0%	—	—	93.4	—
Mutual Premier American	USEq	2.30%	88.0	4.19%	32.6%	21.7%	21.0%	0.3%	—	107.0	98.8%
Great-West Life Government Bond (G) A	FixInc	2.00%	87.9	0.95%	3.7%	8.4%	15.2%	—	—	12.9	—
Industrial Short-Term	FixInc	1.25%	87.9	0.09%	1.8%	3.5%	5.8%	3.9%	3.7%	396.0	50.0%
Manulife Cabot Global Equity	FgnEq	2.50%	87.9	2.83%	12.2%	9.1%	12.0%	—	—	55.0	91.3%
Cundill Value Series A	FgnEq	2.01%	87.8	2.42%	3.5%	10.8%	8.2%	15.4%	43.1%	295.1	-66.5%
McLean Budden American Growth	USEq	1.75%	87.8	4.68%	36.5%	22.9%	26.6%	4.5%	2.8%	20.1	93.9%

* 2-year standard deviation.

Fund Name	Fund Type	MER	MVA	3-Year Std Dev (Monthly)	Percent Return 1997	Percent Return 1996	Percent Return 1995	Percent Return 1994	Percent Return 1993	Assets $ Mill	Tax Efficiency (3 Years)
National Trust American Equity	USEq	2.24%	87.8	3.98%	39.3%	14.9%	20.8%	-2.1%	8.0%	43.9	99.7%
AIM Tiger	FgnEq	3.36%	87.7	7.79%	-33.7%	-1.4%	-19.0%	4.8%	62.2%	11.6	100.0%
Empire Money Market	FixInc	1.43%	87.7	0.09%	1.9%	3.4%	5.7%	3.6%	4.3%	23.8	—
Industrial Alliance Money Market	FixInc	1.50%	87.7	0.12%	1.7%	3.5%	5.7%	3.1%	4.5%	6.9	—
MetLife Mvp Money Market	FixInc	1.71%	87.6	0.12%	1.6%	3.6%	5.7%	3.8%	3.6%	13.0	—
Dynamic Partners	Balan	2.30%	87.5	2.25%	6.4%	13.1%	10.7%	-1.1%	42.2%	1,686.8	65.0%
Great-West Life Equity/Bond (G) A	Balan	2.64%	87.5	3.72%	11.6%	17.6%	13.8%	-5.8%	22.0%	212.0	—
NN Can-Am	USEq	2.69%	87.4	4.47%	26.2%	18.2%	34.9%	0.2%	7.6%	210.5	—
AGF Canadian Tactical Asset Allocation	Balan	2.42%	87.3	3.67%	12.6%	17.3%	12.5%	-4.1%	22.7%	938.2	—
First Canadian European Growth	FgnEq	2.12%	87.3	3.49%	22.6%	19.2%	8.6%	—	—	98.6	99.0%
Green Line Global Select	FgnEq	2.34%	87.2	3.70%	14.0%	13.2%	14.0%	14.0%	—	221.4	93.0%
IRIS Mortgage	FixInc	1.79%	87.2	0.61%	1.8%	8.0%	11.4%	-1.6%	11.2%	57.8	40.7%
Maritime Life Money Market Series A	FixInc	1.00%	87.2	0.09%	2.0%	3.2%	5.0%	3.1%	4.6%	65.0	—
NAL-Canadian Diversified	Balan	1.75%	87.2	3.20%	2.5%	18.2%	21.5%	-3.0%	19.4%	65.4	—
Standard Life U.S. Equity	USEq	2.00%	87.2	4.07%	30.0%	17.3%	22.6%	—	—	5.4	77.3%
CCPE U.S. Equity	USEq	1.75%	87.1	4.30%	34.8%	19.9%	22.7%	—	—	37.1	—
Green Line U.S. Mid-Cap Growth	USEq	2.33%	87.1	4.73%	21.7%	23.6%	30.1%	4.4%	—	189.6	99.1%
Spectrum United Global Diversified	Balan	2.30%	87.1	2.19%	8.6%	8.6%	17.5%	-4.5%	20.5%	31.2	74.2%
Colonia Life Mortgage	FixInc	1.88%	87.0	0.64%	2.6%	7.5%	13.2%	-0.1%	9.6%	2.2	—
AGF European Asset Allocation	Balan	2.56%	86.9	4.01%	24.1%	21.9%	5.4%	1.7%	—	106.8	89.6%
Atlas Canadian Large Cap Value	CdnEq	2.55%	86.9	4.91%	12.9%	16.4%	8.9%	—	—	42.6	98.7%
Mutual Amerifund	USEq	1.98%	86.9	4.39%	33.3%	22.6%	21.9%	0.4%	9.8%	7.3	96.9%
National Money Market	FixInc	1.60%	86.9	0.09%	1.7%	3.2%	5.7%	3.6%	3.8%	12.0	—
AIM Europa	FgnEq	2.91%	86.8	3.90%	25.2%	18.6%	6.7%	2.3%	0.1%	28.6	98.8%
National Trust International RSP Bond	FixInc	2.35%	86.7	1.82%	2.0%	11.4%	17.1%	—	—	17.4	68.6%

Fund Name	Fund Type	MER	MVA	3-Year Std Dev (Monthly)	Percent Return 1997	Percent Return 1996	Percent Return 1995	Percent Return 1994	Percent Return 1993	Assets $ Mill	Tax Efficiency (3 Years)
Northwest Mortgage	FixInc	1.75%	86.7	0.64%	3.2%	7.8%	9.2%	-1.2%	12.2%	3.4	42.1%
AIM GT Global Bond	FixInc	2.60%	86.6	1.36%	4.6%	11.3%	10.7%	—	—	8.0	75.8%
Equitable Life Canada Asset Allocation	Balan	2.25%	86.6	3.09%	8.8%	16.3%	13.8%	—	—	65.1	—
MetLife Mvp U.S. Equity	USEq	2.21%	86.6	4.56%	33.7%	20.2%	25.5%	-1.0%	—	30.0	—
Green Line Global RSP Bond	FixInc	2.00%	86.5	1.59%	7.5%	10.6%	12.8%	2.2%	—	290.7	78.4%
Ethical Global Bond	FixInc	2.56%	86.4	1.30%*	6.6%	6.7%	—	—	—	19.3	76.7%
Imperial Growth Money Market	FixInc	1.50%	86.4	0.09%	1.7%	3.1%	5.6%	3.6%	3.9%	2.2	—
Investors European Growth	FgnEq	2.45%	86.3	3.29%	17.1%	19.6%	15.2%	5.2%	22.7%	1,650.5	96.6%
InvesNat European Equity	FgnEq	2.30%	86.2	3.52%	19.9%	21.7%	8.8%	7.2%	24.3%	43.9	96.0%
Trans-Canada Dividend	CdnEq	3.51%	86.2	4.91%	12.0%	21.8%	10.9%	-1.6%	16.8%	4.5	-70.4%
Great-West Life Money Market (G) A	FixInc	1.50%	86.1	0.09%	1.7%	3.1%	5.5%	3.5%	4.0%	81.9	—
Great-West Life U.S. Equity (G) B	USEq	2.53%	86.1	3.72%	34.7%	14.1%	17.2%	—	—	30.8	—
NAL-U.S. Equity	USEq	2.25%	86.0	4.30%	34.5%	19.4%	22.0%	1.5%	—	37.1	—
SSQ–Actions Americaines	USEq	—	86.0	4.79%	25.9%	25.8%	30.1%	5.4%	-2.3%	6.6	—
C.I. American	USEq	2.38%	85.9	3.64%	27.0%	15.7%	27.4%	8.1%	33.1%	237.3	100.0%
CIBC Capital Appreciation	CdnEq	2.40%	85.9	5.31%	8.6%	20.6%	7.3%	-13.1%	28.3%	421.9	87.7%
Templeton International Balanced	Balan	2.55%	85.9	2.51%	8.3%	17.1%	10.3%	—	—	45.4	92.9%
Dynamic Canadian Growth	CdnEq	2.31%	85.8	5.37%	0.8%	29.7%	4.2%	-8.3%	100.1%	468.7	100.0%
Leith Wheeler U.S. Equity	USEq	1.25%	85.8	3.20%	32.0%	14.3%	17.0%	—	—	4.0	81.1%
Sportfund	Labor	4.85%	85.8	2.86%	10.3%	15.3%	2.2%	—	—	12.0	100.0%
Dynamic Team	Balan	0.52%	85.7	3.03%	2.0%	19.3%	9.8%	-5.0%	40.6%	174.0	35.7%
Great-West Life U.S. Equity (G) A	USEq	2.77%	85.6	3.72%	34.4%	13.8%	17.0%	—	—	38.5	—
Manulife Vistafund 2 Short-Term Securities	FixInc	2.38%	85.6	0.17%	1.1%	3.5%	6.5%	3.2%	4.2%	35.3	—
Universal World Balance RRSP	Balan	2.36%	85.6	3.09%	8.4%	17.3%	11.6%	—	—	248.3	48.7%
AIM Canadian Premier	CdnEq	2.80%	85.5	5.48%	8.5%	18.2%	12.0%	-5.2%	26.8%	44.4	82.2%

* 2-year standard deviation.

Fund Name	Fund Type	MER	MVA	3-Year Std Dev (Monthly)	Percent Return 1997	Percent Return 1996	Percent Return 1995	Percent Return 1994	Percent Return 1993	Assets $ Mill	Tax Efficiency (3 Years)
AIM Korea	FgnEq	3.25%	85.5	11.58%	-61.9%	-33.1%	-24.0%	31.3%	26.1%	14.2	100.0%
Manulife VistaFund 1 Bond	FixInc	1.63%	85.5	1.53%	7.0%	7.5%	18.7%	-9.4%	15.9%	9.3	—
Manulife Vistafund 1 Equity	CdnEq	1.63%	85.5	4.71%	6.8%	11.0%	13.8%	1.6%	23.0%	22.0	—
Jones Heward Canadian Balanced	Balan	2.40%	85.4	2.89%	9.6%	13.2%	15.0%	-6.4%	20.8%	47.6	65.8%
Ethical North American Equity	USEq	2.47%	85.3	5.28%	41.8%	21.2%	29.8%	-4.2%	26.5%	199.1	90.7%
Cambridge Pacific	FgnEq	3.68%	85.1	9.41%	-44.7%	3.9%	-13.1%	-25.6%	61.6%	0.4	100.0%
MD U.S. Equity	USEq	1.29%	85.1	5.43%	42.4%	20.5%	31.6%	2.0%	21.7%	331.6	93.9%
Manulife Cabot Diversified Bond	FixInc	2.00%	85.1	1.21%	5.8%	5.4%	13.8%	—	—	14.2	62.2%
Talvest Canadian Asset Allocation	Balan	2.44%	85.1	3.46%	13.1%	14.6%	12.6%	-0.5%	18.8%	319.6	67.9%
Elliott & Page Bond	FixInc	1.94%	85.0	1.62%	7.4%	8.0%	16.2%	-8.3%	13.3%	22.1	66.3%
Beutel Goodman American Equity	USEq	2.46%	84.9	3.87%	30.8%	17.1%	18.9%	0.5%	24.3%	7.2	64.3%
Saxon World Growth	FgnEq	1.75%	84.9	3.52%	12.6%	14.8%	12.0%	16.8%	44.5%	43.7	62.0%
Altamira Asia Pacific	FgnEq	2.37%	84.7	4.76%	-20.6%	-18.5%	-17.4%	7.6%	48.8%	64.9	100.0%
CIBC U.S. Equity Index	USEq	0.90%	84.7	4.01%	30.1%	16.9%	22.5%	3.4%	2.6%	338.3	92.1%
Scotia Excelsior International	FgnEq	2.23%	84.7	3.35%	13.9%	9.5%	7.2%	2.0%	29.6%	205.7	82.4%
C.I. Canadian Growth	CdnEq	2.35%	84.4	5.20%	5.9%	15.7%	11.5%	0.4%	—	616.6	-123.7%
APEX Balanced (AGF)	Balan	3.00%	84.3	2.22%	2.4%	11.7%	11.6%	-1.6%	25.4%	80.1	—
Manulife Vistafund 1 Diversified	Balan	1.63%	84.3	3.03%	8.3%	9.6%	16.5%	-2.9%	19.8%	27.5	—
Universal Americas	FgnEq	2.47%	84.3	5.14%	18.8%	19.1%	2.3%	-3.1%	32.1%	70.3	66.5%
Altamira Equity	CdnEq	2.28%	84.2	5.48%	4.1%	17.0%	14.8%	1.7%	46.6%	1,082.5	100.0%
Elliott & Page Balanced	Balan	1.80%	84.2	3.03%	2.0%	17.0%	18.2%	-3.0%	32.4%	264.1	58.5%
C.I. Canadian Balanced	Balan	2.30%	84.1	3.15%	6.3%	11.8%	15.1%	1.1%	—	295.0	18.0%
Manulife Vistafund 2 Equity	CdnEq	2.38%	84.1	4.68%	6.0%	10.2%	13.0%	0.8%	22.1%	127.1	—
Montrusco Select Taxable U.S. Equity	USEq	—	84.1	4.10%	36.4%	19.0%	23.0%	1.6%	22.2%	18.4	66.5%
National Global Equities	FgnEq	2.75%	84.1	3.32%	12.2%	13.3%	11.0%	2.1%	37.8%	68.0	—

Fund Name	Fund Type	MER	MVA	3-Year Std Dev (Monthly)	Percent Return 1997	Percent Return 1996	Percent Return 1995	Percent Return 1994	Percent Return 1993	Assets $ Mill	Tax Efficiency (3 Years)
Scotia Canam Income $U.S.	FixInc	1.60%	84.0	1.65%	11.0%	0.9%	14.1%	1.1%	12.7%	30.6	78.2%
C.I. American Sector	USEq	2.43%	83.8	3.61%	25.6%	14.9%	26.5%	8.3%	32.1%	61.6	90.2%
CDA European (KBSH)	FgnEq	1.45%	83.8	3.67%*	13.5%	24.7%	—	—	—	4.1	—
Elliott & Page T-Bill	FixInc	1.72%	83.8	0.12%	1.4%	2.8%	5.2%	—	—	27.6	50.0%
Cote 100 Amerique	FgnEq	1.38%	83.7	5.23%	12.9%	31.1%	33.1%	-14.7%	23.8%	21.3	100.0%
Industrial Mortgage Securities	FixInc	1.81%	83.7	1.59%	1.1%	11.5%	15.7%	-6.2%	20.4%	388.2	33.8%
AGF U.S. Short-Term High Yield	FixInc	2.48%	83.6	1.65%	9.4%	13.6%	-1.1%	—	—	25.4	45.9%
Guardian Global Equity Classic	FgnEq	1.35%	83.6	3.55%	4.0%	14.1%	10.9%	3.6%	31.8%	2.9	100.0%
Bissett American Equity	USEq	1.50%	83.4	3.67%*	24.9%	12.8%	26.8%	4.9%	7.2%	26.4	99.4%
C.I. Global Equity RSP	FgnEq	2.44%	83.4	3.70%	13.7%	13.6%	5.5%	-4.6%	288.2	67.2%	—
Dynamic Europe	FgnEq	2.50%	83.4	5.17%	21.3%	34.7%	6.8%	2.2%	31.1%	330.5	94.5%
Optima Strategy—International Equity	FgnEq	0.46%	83.3	3.78%	7.5%	20.6%	9.4%	—	—	211.9	100.0%
YMG Income	FixInc	1.67%	83.1	3.26%	0.4%	10.5%	18.9%	-6.0%	15.4%	5.1	100.0%
Altamira Balanced	Balan	2.00%	83.0	3.20%	8.4%	9.3%	14.3%	-6.2%	31.1%	64.8	70.0%
Century DJ	USEq	0.80%	83.0	0.12%	4.5%	5.2%	4.4%	4.1%	4.2%	0.4	100.0%
Manulife VistaFund 2 Bond	FixInc	2.38%	83.0	1.53%	6.1%	6.7%	17.8%	-10.1%	15.1%	69.2	—
NN Elite	Balan	2.12%	83.0	1.82%	9.3%	10.6%	4.3%	—	—	70.5	—
Talvest Foreign Pay Canadian Bond	FixInc	2.17%	83.0	1.39%	7.7%	5.6%	13.6%	-0.1%	15.1%	77.9	69.6%
AGF Global Government Bond	FixInc	1.86%	82.9	1.56%	5.8%	6.8%	13.9%	1.1%	12.0%	180.7	76.0%
Equitable Life Canada International	FgnEq	2.75%	82.9	3.72%	13.6%	11.7%	7.2%	—	—	27.9	—
Champion Growth	FgnEq	2.50%	82.8	3.81%	21.5%	22.6%	14.4%	—	—	4.0	—
Altafund Investment Corporation	CdnEq	2.30%	82.7	5.31%	-12.6%	44.9%	11.4%	-2.9%	41.1%	107.5	100.0%
FMOQ International Equity	FgnEq	0.83%	82.7	3.06%	22.5%	6.7%	1.5%	—	—	9.1	83.2%
AGF RSP International Equity Allocation	FgnEq	2.45%	82.6	4.42%	12.6%	11.6%	13.4%	-1.2%	290.4	47.6%	
AIM GT Global Infrastructure	Spclty	2.78%	82.6	3.90%	9.8%	20.1%	10.8%	—	—	57.6	98.0%

* 2-year standard deviation.

Fund Name	Fund Type	MER	MVA	3-Year Std Dev (Monthly)	Percent Return 1997	Percent Return 1996	Percent Return 1995	Percent Return 1994	Percent Return 1993	Assets $ Mill	Tax Efficiency (3 Years)
C.I. Canadian Sector	CdnEq	2.40%	82.6	5.08%	5.2%	14.8%	10.9%	0.4%	51.7%	26.0	-140.0%
Dynamic Global Millennia	Spclty	2.41%	82.5	6.81%	10.7%	33.0%	8.6%	-18.6%	38.7%	12.2	29.2%
AGF International Group–American Growth	USEq	2.78%	82.4	5.25%	29.7%	22.2%	28.8%	3.5%	16.6%	610.1	100.0%
Altamira Capital Growth	CdnEq	2.00%	82.4	5.05%	7.8%	10.4%	9.1%	3.3%	30.9%	110.6	54.7%
Guardian International Balanced Classic	Balan	2.12%	82.4	2.42%	7.8%	10.2%	11.2%	-6.8%	—	5.5	39.9%
Talvest New Economy	CdnEq	2.52%	82.4	5.98%	9.4%	13.9%	17.4%	-8.2%	—	71.8	100.0%
Canada Life International Bond	FixInc	2.00%	82.3	1.73%	6.8%	5.2%	13.1%	—	—	54.7	—
Green Line Science & Technology	Spclty	2.58%	82.3	6.75%	5.9%	12.7%	51.2%	28.3%	—	161.2	71.1%
Hansberger European	FgnEq	2.45%	82.3	3.67%	21.1%	24.7%	1.8%	-2.2%	19.9%	129.4	100.0%
Manulife Vistafund 2 Diversified	Balan	2.38%	82.3	3.03%	7.5%	8.8%	15.7%	-3.6%	18.9%	243.4	—
Templeton Global Bond	FixInc	2.25%	82.2	1.47%	-0.9%	10.2%	11.9%	-0.7%	11.3%	46.7	40.7%
Imperial Growth North American Equity	FgnEq	1.59%	82.1	4.24%	27.7%	11.1%	22.1%	7.7%	13.4%	3.3	—
Industrial Growth	CdnEq	2.35%	82.1	5.66%	-1.5%	20.5%	5.8%	-1.4%	46.9%	502.7	100.0%
Transamerica Growsafe Intl Balanced	Balan	2.79%	82.1	2.14%	11.8%	9.0%	8.1%	—	—	50.4	—
FMOQ Bond Fund	FixInc	0.99%	82.0	1.44%	5.3%	7.2%	15.5%	-1.0%	16.2%	4.1	64.4%
AGF Growth & Income	Balan	2.50%	81.8	4.27%	7.7%	27.4%	13.8%	-2.2%	27.2%	528.0	77.9%
AGF World Balanced	Balan	2.46%	81.8	2.92%	11.6%	11.1%	0.9%	-4.8%	44.4%	113.0	71.5%
BPI Global Balanced RSP	Balan	2.27%	81.8	3.93%	21.8%	7.7%	9.2%	5.1%	33.2%	183.7	22.8%
CT EuroGrowth	FgnEq	2.02%	81.6	4.39%	25.9%	19.3%	10.4%	—	—	233.4	67.9%
Global Strategy Diversified World Equity	FgnEq	2.40%	81.5	3.46%	14.4%	11.2%	4.8%	—	—	45.8	61.8%
AGF International Group–China Focus	FgnEq	3.49%	81.3	6.61%	-20.5%	12.1%	-8.5%	—	—	9.5	100.0%
STAR Investment Maximum Long-Term Growth	Alloc	—	81.3	2.77%*	2.7%	12.1%	—	—	—	—	—
AGF Canadian Equity	CdnEq	2.95%	81.2	6.12%	0.5%	21.7%	12.1%	-8.4%	30.4%	484.1	100.0%
Hansberger European Sector	FgnEq	2.50%	81.1	3.67%	19.8%	23.9%	1.2%	-1.9%	18.6%	56.5	96.3%
Spectrum United Optimax U.S.A.	USEq	2.35%	81.1	3.64%	24.9%	12.8%	21.2%	1.7%	—	19.9	90.2%

* 2-year standard deviation.

Fund Name	Fund Type	MER	MVA	3-Year Std Dev (Monthly)	Percent Return 1997	Percent Return 1996	Percent Return 1995	Percent Return 1994	Percent Return 1993	Assets $ Mill	Tax Efficiency (3 Years)
Cassels Blaikie American	USEq	1.13%	81.0	4.50%	22.0%	17.9%	37.3%	-5.1%	-1.4%	5.8	60.0%
AIM Canadian Balanced	Balan	2.71%	80.9	3.12%	5.5%	16.4%	5.2%	0.3%	19.7%	5.9	72.7%
AGF RSP Global Bond	FixInc	1.97%	80.8	1.53%	5.1%	4.1%	14.1%	-5.7%	—	103.3	74.9%
AIM GT Latin America Growth	FgnEq	2.94%	80.8	8.92%	28.5%	35.2%	4.0%	—	—	13.2	100.0%
Spectrum United Global Equity	FgnEq	2.30%	80.8	3.81%	11.1%	10.9%	8.4%	-0.7%	25.6%	56.5	93.2%
Pursuit Canadian Bond	FixInc	0.80%	80.7	2.05%	11.0%	5.4%	12.4%	-2.9%	14.7%	24.8	66.5%
AGF U.S. Income	FixInc	2.46%	80.6	1.65%	8.9%	2.7%	7.8%	-2.1%	11.4%	20.8	84.4%
CDA Common Stock (Altamira)	CdnEq	0.96%	80.6	5.05%	3.7%	9.9%	11.2%	-2.6%	30.8%	28.1	—
Formula Growth	USEq	0.95%	80.6	5.89%	26.2%	25.8%	33.6%	4.2%	32.9%	304.0	100.0%
Quebec Professionals International Equity	FgnEq	1.25%	80.5	2.94%	2.0%	16.5%	10.6%	4.2%	17.9%	22.4	73.0%
AIM GT Global Telecom	Spclty	2.78%	80.4	6.87%	17.2%	3.2%	34.4%	—	—	383.7	97.2%
Orbit World	FgnEq	2.65%	80.4	3.44%	30.0%	6.9%	-11.6%	10.2%	24.0%	7.1	100.0%
APEX Canadian Growth (AGF)	CdnEq	3.01%	80.3	5.77%	0.2%	22.6%	13.0%	-2.9%	21.4%	37.3	—
Atlas Global Value	FgnEq	2.75%	80.3	3.32%	6.8%	12.1%	7.9%	1.6%	34.5%	14.7	76.3%
BPI American Small Companies	USEq	2.59%	80.3	4.85%	29.9%	26.1%	19.5%	7.5%	45.1%	129.1	66.2%
Royal European Growth	FgnEq	2.51%	80.3	4.07%	21.5%	19.5%	8.9%	9.4%	36.2%	568.7	95.2%
Strategic Value Global Balanced	Balan	2.70%	80.2	2.17%	8.1%	5.8%	12.6%	1.9%	19.9%	24.1	86.7%
20/20 India	FgnEq	3.74%	80.1	6.70%	4.2%	-27.4%	-46.2%	—	—	32.9	100.0%
Altamira U.S. Larger Company	USEq	2.30%	80.1	4.50%	24.2%	12.8%	37.9%	3.3%	—	120.0	88.3%
All-Canadian CapitalFund	CdnEq	2.00%	80.0	2.89%	6.2%	7.9%	3.3%	10.1%	35.0%	11.6	100.0%
Scotia Excelsior Latin American	FgnEq	2.39%	80.0	7.36%	26.2%	29.3%	3.7%	—	—	35.2	64.6%
Spectrum United American Growth	USEq	2.35%	80.0	5.34%	23.9%	18.1%	37.2%	6.7%	20.0%	545.0	87.5%
Desjardins International	FgnEq	2.29%	79.7	3.49%	6.6%	6.4%	11.0%	7.3%	26.8%	55.1	95.0%
Global Mgr—Hong Kong Bear	FgnEq	1.82%	79.7	9.44%	21.1%	-25.5%	-21.8%	—	—	0.8	61.9%
APEX Mortgage	FixInc	2.00%	79.6	0.55%	2.2%	6.2%	7.0%	—	—	5.2	—

Fund Name	Fund Type	MER	MVA	3-Year Std Dev (Monthly)	Percent Return 1997	Percent Return 1996	Percent Return 1995	Percent Return 1994	Percent Return 1993	Assets $ Mill	Tax Efficiency (3 Years)
CIBC Global Bond	FixInc	1.95%	79.6	1.21%	4.6%	5.2%	12.5%	—	—	94.9	69.1%
Trimark Americas	FgnEq	2.65%	79.5	5.31%	20.5%	20.6%	-0.6%	4.0%	—	254.5	86.1%
All-Canadian Compound	CdnEq	—	79.4	2.83%	6.3%	7.2%	3.0%	10.0%	33.8%	10.3	100.0%
Clean Environment International Equity	FgnEq	2.62%	79.4	5.28%	35.1%	24.7%	9.2%	-6.6%	—	36.2	98.4%
First Canadian U.S. Growth	USEq	2.20%	79.3	4.24%	36.6%	13.0%	14.8%	3.4%	—	185.3	93.1%
Talvest/Hyperion Value Line U.S. Equity	USEq	3.00%	79.3	4.82%	23.1%	19.2%	37.4%	0.6%	13.6%	108.0	88.8%
MacKenzie Sentinel Canada Equity	CdnEq	1.91%	79.1	4.27%	0.9%	26.5%	-1.8%	10.3%	51.0%	8.1	100.0%
CT U.S. Equity	USEq	2.21%	79.0	3.87%*	25.4%	13.2%	22.1%	-1.0%	10.4%	245.7	86.6%
Global Strategy World Balanced	Balan	2.30%	79.0	2.02%	6.3%	6.7%	11.1%	—	—	12.0	92.0%
CCPE Global Equity	FgnEq	1.75%	78.9	3.87%*	10.9%	8.5%	—	—	—	56.9	—
Dynamic Income	FixInc	1.55%	78.9	1.30%	-1.1%	6.3%	14.5%	6.7%	8.2%	305.6	25.5%
Global Strategy Diversified Foreign Bond	FixInc	2.40%	78.9	1.70%	4.8%	6.9%	8.2%	—	—	6.2	70.0%
Capital Alliance Ventures	Labor	4.00%	78.8	2.08%	4.9%	7.9%	4.0%	—	—	41.9	100.0%
Guardian American Equity Classic	USEq	2.19%	78.7	4.10%	23.4%	12.4%	26.1%	5.0%	18.2%	34.6	52.6%
Spectrum United Global Telecommunications	Spclty	2.55%	78.7	5.43%	9.9%	6.1%	17.7%	—	—	86.0	96.6%
Investors North American Growth	FgnEq	2.38%	78.6	4.13%	13.9%	19.4%	16.7%	4.8%	18.0%	1,412.1	79.0%
YMG Balanced	Balan	1.78%	78.5	4.01%	5.4%	15.0%	11.7%	-5.0%	21.8%	14.5	-174.7%
Industrial American	USEq	2.34%	78.3	3.72%	23.3%	14.0%	16.3%	2.6%	23.4%	216.6	71.4%
Capstone International Investment	FgnEq	2.14%	78.2	4.91%	7.8%	17.5%	10.6%	-2.0%	21.4%	2.0	32.1%
AIM International	FgnEq	2.97%	78.1	3.90%	20.1%	5.5%	-2.1%	5.8%	56.8%	27.3	98.7%
NAL-Global Equity	FgnEq	2.50%	78.1	3.84%	10.2%	7.5%	6.0%	14.3%	33.2%	56.9	—
Trans-Canada Bond	FixInc	2.92%	78.1	1.30%	2.7%	6.4%	13.5%	-2.4%	8.3%	0.8	42.4%
Standard Life Growth Equity	FgnEq	2.00%	78.0	5.34%	16.5%	25.7%	11.3%	—	—	7.4	50.9%
Strategic Value Commonwealth	FgnEq	2.70%	78.0	3.03%	6.8%	5.0%	9.3%	4.3%	23.0%	262.3	83.4%
Altamira Global Bond	FixInc	1.84%	77.8	1.96%	5.1%	5.4%	13.6%	-1.1%	—	40.2	78.0%

* 2-year standard deviation.

Fund Name	Fund Type	MER	MVA	3-Year Std Dev (Monthly)	Percent Return 1997	Percent Return 1996	Percent Return 1995	Percent Return 1994	Percent Return 1993	Assets $ Mill	Tax Efficiency (3 Years)
Maritime Life Global Equities Series A&C	FgnEq	2.75%	77.7	3.90%*	12.5%	8.5%	—	—	—	18.1	—
Standard Life Intl Bond	FixInc	2.00%	77.4	1.99%	8.0%	-0.2%	16.6%	—	—	7.2	73.1%
Strategic Value American Equity	USEq	2.70%	77.4	4.04%	26.1%	9.1%	22.6%	6.4%	11.8%	134.0	83.4%
Optima Strategy-Global Fix Income	FixInc	0.45%	77.3	1.76%	5.1%	5.7%	12.9%	—	—	137.1	100.0%
AGF International Group-Short-Term Income	FixInc	2.69%	77.2	0.87%	1.3%	1.5%	5.3%	—	—	40.5	—
Dynamic Global Partners	Balan	2.47%	77.2	2.68%	6.8%	12.7%	10.1%	—	—	59.7	79.2%
Hongkong Bank Global Bond	FixInc	2.07%	76.9	1.53%	4.0%	4.8%	11.7%	—	—	14.5	74.0%
Acadia Mortgage	FixInc	2.00%	76.8	0.52%	3.3%	3.1%	5.2%	—	—	6.7	47.3%
Dynamic Global Resource	FgnEq	2.63%	76.8	8.75%	-12.1%	68.5%	5.7%	—	—	36.4	100.0%
Global Mgr—U.S. Bond Index	FixInc	1.82%	76.8	2.74%	14.6%	-2.6%	22.8%	—	—	0.3	86.0%
Elliott & Page Global Balanced	Balan	2.74%	76.5	2.40%	6.9%	7.6%	11.1%	—	—	11.1	96.0%
First Canadian NAFTA Advantage	FgnEq	2.10%	76.5	5.43%	31.4%	21.3%	12.1%	—	—	38.2	95.3%
DGC Entertainment Ventures	Labor	5.60%	76.3	2.17%	-0.9%	11.4%	3.1%	1.0%	—	7.1	100.0%
Jones Heward American	USEq	2.50%	76.1	4.73%	37.4%	13.8%	8.4%	-12.9%	19.5%	22.1	95.7%
CT North American	FgnEq	2.29%	76.0	4.19%	16.4%	17.5%	11.3%	-9.2%	26.4%	35.1	87.2%
Investors Special	FgnEq	2.39%	76.0	4.73%	16.5%	21.5%	14.9%	-1.2%	22.3%	427.7	76.7%
Scotia Excelsior American Growth	USEq	2.19%	76.0	4.07%	28.1%	11.4%	21.4%	4.6%	14.2%	115.7	70.7%
Industrial Equity	CdnEq	2.43%	75.9	5.98%	-26.6%	19.7%	0.1%	-10.3%	72.6%	44.6	100.0%
Working Ventures Canadian	Labor	2.96%	75.9	0.92%	0.4%	1.9%	7.2%	0.3%	5.3%	716.3	100.0%
Altamira North American Recovery	FgnEq	2.30%	75.6	4.76%	25.9%	29.6%	1.3%	-1.7%	—	74.2	78.3%
Trans-Canada Pension	Balan	3.48%	75.6	4.91%	18.5%	33.2%	-3.4%	-4.8%	62.6%	1.6	85.0%
Royal Global Bond	FixInc	1.87%	75.5	1.79%	3.2%	3.8%	15.9%	1.1%	18.2%	273.4	76.7%
Cambridge Special Equity	CdnEq	3.46%	75.4	10.45%	-43.9%	5.0%	22.1%	-20.3%	146.9%	2.6	100.0%
Strategic Value International	FgnEq	2.70%	75.3	3.52%	7.1%	4.5%	9.0%	7.3%	25.1%	158.5	84.8%
Fidelity Small-Cap America	USEq	2.50%	75.2	4.82%	31.9%	17.0%	18.6%	—	—	87.6	86.3%

* 2-year standard deviation.

Fund Name	Fund Type	MER	MVA	3-Year Std Dev (Monthly)	Percent Return 1997	Percent Return 1996	Percent Return 1995	Percent Return 1994	Percent Return 1993	Assets $ Mill	Tax Efficiency (3 Years)
Universal World Tactical Bond	FixInc	2.19%	75.1	2.19%	4.9%	-0.4%	16.7%	—	—	65.3	82.4%
AIM GT Global Natural Resources	FgnEq	2.96%	74.9	6.32%	1.6%	46.5%	10.8%	—	—	15.1	78.7%
Cambridge China	FgnEq	3.51%	74.8	8.63%	-14.3%	-2.8%	-9.6%	—	—	0.3	100.0%
Trans-Canada Value	CdnEq	3.52%	74.7	6.06%	1.0%	16.8%	8.1%	-12.4%	54.2%	1.8	100.0%
University Avenue Canadian	CdnEq	2.40%	74.7	5.40%	-5.0%	19.4%	2.9%	-9.5%	41.5%	6.9	100.0%
Manulife Vistafund 1 Capital Gains	CdnEq	1.63%	74.5	5.31%	-4.8%	12.4%	13.2%	-3.6%	31.7%	19.9	—
BPI Canadian Bond	FixInc	1.50%	74.4	1.82%	9.1%	1.0%	15.1%	-6.8%	14.9%	31.7	48.6%
Manulife Vistafund 1 American Stock	USEq	1.63%	74.4	4.27%*	22.9%	11.1%	—	—	—	8.2	—
Investors World Growth Portfolio	FgnEq	2.62%	74.3	3.38%	-0.4%	10.6%	8.8%	5.5%	—	720.7	68.3%
PH&N North American Equity	FgnEq	1.18%	74.3	5.43%	24.5%	31.6%	5.3%	-10.3%	23.6%	63.3	74.1%
STAR Foreign Maximum Long-Term Growth	Alloc	—	73.9	3.41%*	3.1%	12.0%	—	—	—	—	—
Green Line Real Return Bond	FixInc	1.53%	73.8	2.51%	4.7%	10.3%	13.9%	—	—	20.8	68.4%
Altamira Global Diversified	Balan	2.00%	73.6	3.18%	1.9%	12.3%	9.4%	3.8%	22.8%	46.9	100.0%
Canadian Protected	CdnEq	2.40%	73.6	2.02%	2.9%	4.1%	3.9%	-1.5%	20.8%	1.4	78.6%
Royal LePage Commercial	Spclty	3.40%	73.6	4.62%	-19.3%	-0.9%	4.2%	8.5%	-5.7%	10.3	100.0%
BPI Global Small Companies	FgnEq	2.55%	73.3	4.07%	10.2%	21.5%	-4.5%	13.3%	—	82.7	77.3%
McDonald Canada Plus	Balan	2.88%	73.3	4.91%	8.9%	11.0%	8.4%	-7.4%	—	1.2	61.2%
Sceptre International	FgnEq	2.07%	73.3	4.16%	4.7%	12.3%	4.6%	-5.6%	63.6%	136.2	86.1%
Green Line Global Government Bond	FixInc	2.07%	73.2	1.79%	3.8%	3.8%	13.6%	-0.1%	16.0%	110.6	76.7%
Manulife Vistafund 2 Capital Gains	CdnEq	2.38%	73.2	5.28%	-5.5%	11.6%	12.3%	-4.4%	30.7%	90.1	—
Manulife Vistafund 2 American Stock	USEq	2.38%	73.1	4.24%*	21.9%	10.2%	—	—	—	48.8	—
InvesNat International RSP Bond	FixInc	1.99%	72.6	1.65%*	3.9%	7.2%	—	—	—	8.5	77.6%
Spectrum United Emerging Markets	FgnEq	2.66%	72.0	7.25%	10.4%	23.6%	-0.1%	-14.0%	—	29.5	100.0%
MD Global Bond	FixInc	1.20%	71.8	1.62%	5.1%	3.0%	13.7%	—	—	47.8	83.0%
Fidelity Latin American Growth	FgnEq	3.09%	71.7	9.41%	35.7%	28.9%	-22.3%	—	—	66.5	100.0%

* 2-year standard deviation.

Fund Name	Fund Type	MER	MVA	3-Year Std Dev (Monthly)	Percent Return 1997	Percent Return 1996	Percent Return 1995	Percent Return 1994	Percent Return 1993	Assets $ Mill	Tax Efficiency (3 Years)
GBC North American Growth	FgnEq	1.95%	71.7	5.54%	24.5%	10.8%	27.2%	-4.0%	27.0%	84.4	100.0%
Acadia Balanced	Balan	2.42%	71.6	3.75%	4.3%	16.8%	8.8%	—	—	15.2	-21.4%
Spectrum United Global Bond	FixInc	2.03%	71.6	1.44%	1.6%	3.4%	16.0%	-1.0%	—	14.2	70.6%
Scotia Excelsior Global Bond	FixInc	1.99%	71.4	1.50%	3.9%	2.6%	12.4%	—	—	13.2	74.4%
Atlas Latin American Value	FgnEq	2.95%	70.8	8.37%	32.9%	28.3%	-24.3%	-15.4%	—	7.9	100.0%
Caldwell International	Balan	2.64%	70.6	3.12%	4.1%	9.0%	11.1%	0.3%	26.1%	3.5	53.4%
Global Strategy Latin America	FgnEq	3.00%	70.6	6.99%	27.1%	23.0%	-14.8%	—	—	4.6	100.0%
Great-West Life International Bond (P) B	FixInc	2.52%	70.6	1.65%	4.9%	1.1%	11.9%	—	—	6.3	—
CT International Bond	FixInc	1.98%	70.1	1.65%	0.6%	2.7%	13.5%	—	—	188.2	66.7%
Great-West Life International Bond (P) A	FixInc	2.76%	70.0	1.65%	4.6%	0.8%	11.7%	—	—	7.3	—
Dynamic Global Bond	FixInc	1.78%	69.9	1.65%	-4.3%	3.9%	19.8%	4.9%	14.8%	211.2	-4.1%
First Canadian International Bond	FixInc	2.01%	69.7	1.93%	-0.8%	4.7%	17.6%	5.7%	—	269.0	74.2%
Altamira Short-Term Global Income	Spclty	1.21%	69.5	1.59%	-1.3%	6.4%	-1.4%	10.1%	9.3%	25.8	92.2%
Green Line Latin American Growth	FgnEq	2.66%	69.4	9.09%	34.6%	19.4%	-16.7%	—	—	28.2	100.0%
Cambridge Americas	FgnEq	3.50%	69.1	8.52%	0.7%	26.0%	7.0%	-5.9%	9.9%	1.3	80.7%
Global Strategy Diversified Latin America	FgnEq	2.95%	69.0	8.78%	36.7%	21.6%	-20.4%	—	—	9.2	100.0%
Investors Global Bond	FixInc	2.19%	69.0	1.36%	2.8%	2.6%	11.4%	1.0%	15.8%	256.2	72.9%
Elliott & Page Global Bond	FixInc	1.97%	68.7	1.24%	3.3%	3.0%	12.0%	—	—	13.0	73.0%
University Avenue Growth	USEq	2.40%	68.7	4.71%	27.1%	2.7%	22.0%	-3.2%	-4.9%	0.9	100.0%
Talvest Global Asset Allocation	Balan	2.75%	68.4	2.89%	6.3%	6.2%	4.3%	4.0%	31.9%	51.4	81.6%
Altamira Select American	USEq	2.28%	68.1	5.31%	23.3%	12.7%	22.3%	2.1%	28.3%	162.4	81.2%
C.I. Emerging Markets	FgnEq	2.73%	67.1	4.82%	19.7%	7.8%	-15.6%	-12.1%	65.0%	198.0	100.0%
Cambridge Growth	CdnEq	3.46%	67.1	8.26%	-31.5%	6.7%	2.7%	-21.3%	61.7%	7.6	100.0%
20/20 Latin America	FgnEq	3.24%	66.9	9.30%	26.4%	42.8%	-29.5%	—	—	116.7	100.0%
C.I. Emerging Markets Sector	FgnEq	2.78%	66.5	4.79%	19.4%	7.2%	-16.0%	-11.6%	63.2%	32.3	100.0%

Fund Name	Fund Type	MER	MVA	3-Year Std Dev (Monthly)	Percent Return 1997	Percent Return 1996	Percent Return 1995	Percent Return 1994	Percent Return 1993	Assets $ Mill	Tax Efficiency (3 Years)
Spectrum United RSP International Bond	FixInc	1.98%	65.7	1.76%	-1.2%	0.3%	15.6%	2.6%	—	53.8	63.1%
AIM American Premier	USEq	2.78%	65.5	3.95%	30.0%	13.7%	1.3%	6.6%	4.5%	4.2	90.7%
20/20 Aggressive Growth	USEq	2.55%	65.3	6.21%	20.6%	1.2%	37.5%	-0.6%	—	241.1	60.4%
IRIS North American High Yield Bond	FixInc	2.63%	65.2	1.56%	0.1%	3.4%	4.3%	—	—	2.1	44.1%
Universal World Asset Allocation	Balan	2.41%	65.2	3.49%	11.4%	-7.5%	8.3%	9.8%	—	100.2	81.5%
AIM GT America Growth	USEq	2.92%	64.4	5.72%	11.2%	18.1%	22.0%	—	—	29.1	85.7%
Manulife Vistafund 1 Global Bond	FixInc	1.63%	64.1	1.99%*	-4.8%	7.6%	—	—	—	1.2	—
Empire Foreign Currency Canadian Bond	FixInc	2.11%	64.0	1.10%	6.3%	-1.2%	5.1%	—	—	2.9	—
Templeton Emerging Markets	FgnEq	3.24%	64.0	6.90%	-1.5%	22.5%	-4.4%	-4.4%	82.8%	611.8	100.0%
Universal World Emerging Growth	FgnEq	2.50%	63.8	6.24%	5.0%	12.6%	-7.5%	-7.1%	—	74.9	100.0%
C.I. Latin American	FgnEq	2.81%	63.4	8.00%	14.7%	18.6%	-20.9%	-8.1%	—	118.7	100.0%
C.I. Latin American Sector	FgnEq	2.86%	63.0	8.00%	14.1%	18.0%	-20.8%	—	—	12.0	100.0%
Special Opportunities	FgnEq	2.14%	62.0	8.17%	22.0%	24.9%	18.8%	-13.7%	33.2%	3.1	100.0%
Tradex Emerging Markets Country	FgnEq	2.50%	62.0	5.51%*	-1.7%	4.3%	—	—	—	2.2	100.0%
Manulife Vistafund 2 Global Bond	FixInc	2.38%	61.6	1.99%*	-5.5%	6.8%	—	—	—	6.5	—
Spectrum United Global Growth	FgnEq	2.30%	61.4	3.93%	6.7%	-5.3%	-3.3%	-0.7%	37.2%	13.2	100.0%
Universal U.S. Emerging Growth	USEq	2.50%	61.4	7.77%	4.7%	16.1%	40.8%	7.2%	20.2%	241.0	71.3%
Altamira Growth & Income	Balan	1.40%	61.1	5.28%	-6.2%	12.1%	3.6%	2.1%	35.3%	95.7	100.0%
Altamira Global Discovery	FgnEq	2.98%	60.8	7.13%	-2.1%	14.2%	-12.6%	—	—	11.5	100.0%
First Canadian Emerging Markets	FgnEq	2.21%	60.7	7.01%	2.0%	5.4%	-9.0%	—	—	75.3	100.0%
Protected American	Balan	2.30%	58.9	2.54%	1.3%	-2.3%	3.3%	-0.3%	25.3%	3.1	90.5%
Guardian Emerging Markets Classic	FgnEq	0.80%	58.6	7.04%	-6.7%	12.9%	0.7%	—	—	0.4	100.0%
Elliott & Page Emerging Markets	FgnEq	4.69%	58.5	7.88%	6.1%	4.3%	-15.1%	—	—	4.4	100.0%
Enterprise Fund	Labor	6.60%	58.5	2.71%	-4.3%	8.9%	-8.0%	—	—	6.9	100.0%
Green Line Emerging Markets	FgnEq	2.69%	57.8	7.13%	-1.8%	7.0%	-15.1%	-5.0%	70.0%	73.1	100.0%

* 2-year standard deviation.

Fund Name	Fund Type	MER	MVA	3-Year Std Dev (Monthly)	Percent Return 1997	Percent Return 1996	Percent Return 1995	Percent Return 1994	Percent Return 1993	Assets $ Mill	Tax Efficiency (3 Years)
CT Emerging Markets	FgnEq	3.11%	56.8	7.27%*	-1.4%	11.5%	—	—	—	55.5	100.0%
Strategic Value Emerging Markets	FgnEq	2.95%	55.2	6.99%	-6.5%	3.7%	0.9%	—	—	2.5	100.0%
AGF International Group-Special U.S.	USEq	2.86%	55.1	6.78%	1.7%	10.5%	19.9%	-0.7%	9.5%	95.9	100.0%
Hongkong Bank Emerging Markets	FgnEq	2.70%	53.5	7.13%	-9.4%	6.9%	-10.3%	—	—	5.3	100.0%
National Trust Emerging Markets	FgnEq	3.75%	52.5	7.59%	-9.0%	10.1%	-16.1%	—	—	6.4	100.0%
MD Emerging Markets	FgnEq	2.84%	51.7	7.25%	-17.4%	15.1%	-3.6%	—	—	32.3	100.0%
20/20 Emerging Markets Value	FgnEq	3.57%	51.0	7.42%	-15.7%	5.6%	-15.4%	—	—	19.1	100.0%
Cambridge American Growth	USEq	3.56%	51.0	6.61%	44.0%	-14.4%	1.3%	-16.9%	17.6%	0.6	95.0%
Fidelity Emerging Markets Portfolio	FgnEq	3.61%	49.8	8.83%	-44.9%	26.5%	19.6%	—	—	27.8	100.0%
Cambridge Balanced	Balan	3.48%	48.3	7.19%	-27.5%	12.8%	2.3%	-15.2%	43.7%	3.6	100.0%
Canadian Venture Opportunities	Labor	6.30%	47.2	5.92%	6.4%	-10.2%	-18.8%	—	—	11.7	100.0%
First American	FgnEq	2.80%	44.8	2.08%	-0.9%	-1.6%	4.8%	-3.4%	19.6%	11.4	91.0%
Cambridge Global	FgnEq	3.54%	42.4	20.96%	-52.0%	-7.6%	-7.7%	-16.9%	43.7%	0.6	100.0%
CDA Emerging Markets (KBSH)	FgnEq	1.45%	38.5	7.45%*	-24.6%	-6.4%	—	—	—	0.3	—

* 2-year standard deviation.